UNITED STATES

ECONOMIC HISTORY

Selected Readings

UNITED STATES
Economic History

SELECTED READINGS

HARRY · N · SCHEIBER

Dartmouth College

NEW YORK

Alfred · A · Knopf   1964

L.C. catalog card number: 64-17759

THIS IS A BORZOI BOOK
PUBLISHED BY ALFRED A. KNOPF, INC.

FIRST EDITION

PREFACE

THIS COLLECTION is designed to make readily accessible a group of significant scholarly writings in American economic history. It is intended primarily for use as supplementary reading in courses in economic or business history, or in United States history survey courses that give some emphasis to economic development. Of the twenty-six selections here, three are excerpts from longer monographs; and the rest were published originally as articles in scholarly journals or as essays in collections. The footnotes are reprinted in the belief that to delete documentation would handicap the student in his effort to read critically, to consult the sources, and to assess the historical method and its limitations. Of course, it has not been possible to include articles on all subjects that ideally ought to be represented, for limitations of space make comprehensiveness unattainable.

Some of the essays are classics in the field. The earliest was published in 1936, and most have appeared since 1950; but new and old alike represent fresh approaches, explore neglected subjects, or suggest important new interpretations. In the introductions, the editor attempts to indicate the place of each reading within the scholarly literature on the subject and to explain, where necessary, the significance of the particular subject treated. Bibliographies are appended and will serve as guides to further reading, especially when the selections are used as the basis of interpretative essays or as starting-points for research papers. For convenience, the readings are arranged according to topics within broad time periods; but it should be noted that some articles go beyond the chronological limits of the section in which they appear.

The reader will find several different approaches to economic history represented here, for the discipline has undergone profound change in the last four decades.* Early in this century, at least in the United States, economic history was largely a specialized branch of political history. Most scholars in the field were concerned with the relationship of political, constitutional, and legal development to economic change. By the 1930's, however, many American historians were being influenced by the work of a German school of economists who, in the tradition of Marx, had developed a theory of the stages of capitalist development. At the same time, in the United States and England, economists were prompted by the Great Depression to turn to business-cycle theory, and they produced a large volume of historical business-cycle studies that were read with interest by historians. Meanwhile, the scope of economic history as a discipline was being widened by a new interest in history of businessmen and the administration of business firms, so that "entrepreneurial history" became an important common meeting-ground for historians and economists. The rapid advancement of research in sociology, political science, geography, and history of science and technology further enriched the writing of economic history; from these fields, historians derived both data and theory that permitted re-evaluation of crucial problems in historical interpretation. The cumulative impact of all these developments was to arouse among historians a greater interest in application of theory and a sharpened awareness of the potential contribution that their discipline might make to related fields.

In the last decade, two important new approaches have further reshaped and diversified the study of economic history: first, the recognition of economic growth as an urgent contemporary problem, and, second, a renewed interest in quantification. Economists concerned with growth theory, like the earlier school of business-cycle analysts, have used historical data (and have written historical studies) in order to test hypotheses and to develop new theory. In the process, they have inspired historians to apply and test theory relating to growth and stagnation. The surge of interest in quantification is perhaps best described as a product of modern social scientists' healthy skepticism of anything less reliable than "hard data." Given the nature of much of the data with which they work,

---

* Important studies of the writing of economic history and its historical development include T. S. Ashton's evocative essay on "The Relation of Economic History to Theory," *Economica*, new series, XIII (1946), pp. 81–96; Carter Goodrich: "Economic History, One Field or Two?" *Journal of Economic History*, XX (1960), pp. 531–38; and Herbert Heaton: "Clio's New Overalls," *Canadian Journal of Economics and Political Science*, XX (1954), pp. 467–77.

economic historians have of course been prone to quantify; but their penchant for precise measurement has been given additional strength by developments in statistical theory and by availability of electronic machines that permit analysis of enormous bodies of statistics.

Historians of the more traditional cast (and, for that matter, the best of sociologists, growth theorists, and statisticians working with historical subjects) maintain a vigorous interest in topics that defy precise quantification: governmental policy and its impact, the nature of socio-economic institutions and mores, the relationship of social and political factors to development or stagnation, and so on. In this volume, both the more traditional types of economic history and some of the newer approaches are represented—though the editor hardly expects the space accorded each to please every reader. While the editor's introductions give considerable attention to shifting interpretations and new techniques, it is not the intention here to focus on the historian rather than on history. Nor is the volume meant to be a showcase of contemporary social science. Rather, it seeks primarily to reprint in convenient form a group of excellent studies that pose provocative questions and identify key issues in American economic history from colonial times to the present.

*   *   *

I am indebted to authors and publishers who have granted permission to reprint the materials in this volume. I wish to thank also the staff of the Baker Library of Dartmouth College; Professors Harold F. Williamson of Northwestern University and Morton Rothstein of the University of Wisconsin, who provided advice and criticism when this work was in its early stages of preparation; and my wife, Jane Lang Scheiber, who gave invaluable aid throughout the period of editing and preparation of the manuscript. Students in my economic history courses at Dartmouth College have been willing experimenters and trenchant critics, and I acknowledge with thanks their important role in this undertaking.

CONTENTS

Part I: THE EARLY ECONOMY, 1607–1790

Part II: TRANSFORMATION OF THE ECONOMY, 1790–1870

Part III: EMERGENCE OF THE MODERN ECONOMY, 1870–1920

Part I

THE
EARLY ECONOMY
1607 - 1790

I

Farmers on the Land

AN OHIO FARMER, writing in 1852 on land-management practices in his locality, summarized two centuries of agricultural development in America when he said that "among old-school or anti-book farmers" the standard rotation of crops was "corn, corn, corn, forty years in succession, and then move to the Far West." * In the colonial South, the land was planted in tobacco as long as it would sustain production, and in the Middle Colonies and New England, farming practices were much the same wherever the soil would produce a profitable cash crop. Endowed with what seemed boundless opportunity to remove to new lands, the early American farmer characteristically paid little attention to scientific rotation, use of fertilizer, or even livestock improvement.

In regions such as the tobacco country of colonial Maryland and Virginia, monoculture and soil-mining were legendary. But even in the Old South, the farming techniques of one ethnic group, the Germans, deviated sharply from the practices of their English neighbors.† The Germans carried with them to America a tradition of farming born of the Old World experience. Accustomed to cultivating small plots, the resources of which had to be replenished constantly to provide for future generations, the German farmer set a high standard of diversified, conservationist agriculture.

Eastern Pennsylvania was the great seat of German settlement in the American colonies. In the following essay, John G. Gagliardo

* U. S. Patent Office Report: Agrciulture, 1852 (Washington, 1853), p. 244.
† See Richard Shryock: "British versus German Traditions in Colonial Agriculture," Mississippi Valley Historical Review, XXVI (1939).

portrays in rich detail the life of the eighteenth-century Pennsylvania German on the land. Gagliardo does not neglect the effects of soil, climate or market conditions on German agriculture. Nor does he idealize the soil-management practices of the Germans; he suggests, in fact, that this group's traditionalism may well have retarded its adoption of valuable innovations late in the century. Nevertheless, he argues that the key role in shaping the prosperous course of German agriculture in colonial Pennsylvania must be ascribed to cultural factors.

GERMANS AND AGRICULTURE IN
COLONIAL PENNSYLVANIA

John G. Gagliardo

Throughout most of the eighteenth century, Germans formed the largest national minority group within the British colonies. The first group immigration of Germans occurred in 1683, and the first major settlement, that of Germantown, was associated with Francis Daniel Pastorius, who, as agent for the Frankfurt Land Company of Germany, purchased 15,000 acres from William Penn. German immigration, spurred on by political, economic, and religious dissatisfactions in the homeland, steadily increased until in 1790 first-generation Germans and descendants of earlier settlers made up about one third of the total population of Pennsylvania.[1]

The agricultural contributions of the colonial German farmers form a significant part of the history of Pennsylvania. Although the importance of specifically German farming methods and practices was to be attenuated somewhat by the introduction of a scientific agriculture after 1800, and by the gradual lessening of German cultural individualism, the Germans were in large part responsible for the reputation of Pennsylvania in the eighteenth century as one of the best farming provinces in North America.

*   *   *

Reprinted by permission from *The Pennsylvania Magazine of History and Biography*, LXXXIII (1959).

The size of the German farm varied considerably from family to family. General abundance and relative cheapness of land enabled virtually every free settler to purchase some land within a comparatively short time after his arrival; on the other hand, farms of more than four hundred acres were rare. As a general rule, land prices rose throughout the eighteenth century as the number of settlers increased. A traveler of the 1750's remarked that rich Englishmen had already bought a great deal of land, even into the farthest backcountry, in order to sell it again to the European immigrants who were coming to the country in increasing numbers. "Our German people who emigrate there," he commented, "do not get land enough for nothing upon which to build a cottage." [2]

Land prices decreased, however, as one moved away from eastern Pennsylvania, and particularly from Philadelphia, which was the distributing point for nearly all immigrants. As a result, the average size of farms in western areas of the settled portion of the state was larger, on the whole, than in the eastern sections.[3] A visitor to Pennsylvania of the 1790's had the impression that farms around Kutztown were of an average size of one hundred fifty acres, and were larger than farms around Nazareth and Bethlehem to the east; correspondingly, he noted, farms in Cumberland County, west of Kutztown, averaged between 200 and 400 acres. Farms in York County, south of both Cumberland County and Kutztown, but between them on a east-west line, averaged 200–300 acres, with the average in the immediate neigborhood of Abbottstown about 200 acres.[4] Doubtless this observer was concerned primarily with larger farms when he made these averages, for land warranties of the second quarter of the eighteenth century indicate that the average German farm in Cumberland County comprised about 150–175 acres, and farms in most other areas about one hundred acres.[5] The difference between the average size of German farms in eastern and western areas of Pennsylvania tended to become smaller as the century wore on. By 1780, the average Cumberland County farm, for example, was only slightly larger than farms in other areas.[6]

In the neighborhood of Kutztown, a 150-acre farm normally had fifty to sixty acres of woods and ninety to a hundred acres under cultivation. Cumberland County farms of 200–400 acres were normally half cleared, while the other half contained woods, with space for the house and barn. "Half or a large third" of farms of 200 acres around Abbottstown in York County remained in forest, while 300-acre farms in the county averaged 140 acres of plowland, 20 of meadow, and 140 of woods.[7] Some acreage was allotted to orchards on every farm; observers' estimates ranged anywhere from two to twenty acres per farm.[8] The exact amount of land given over to particular crops varied considerably, but wheat, recognized in the eighteenth century as Pennsylvania's main export crop, certainly was given a preferred position.

The German farmer in Pennsylvania was characteristically independent of sources of farm labor outside his own family. Centuries of peasant tradition in Germany encouraged an attitude of thrift, which one contemporary observer regarded as approaching the point of avarice, and the Germans depended upon members of the family for all types of work.[9] The women as well as the men were included in the labor force: especially at harvest, the women "forsake the dairy and spinning wheel to share with [the farmer] in the toils of harvest." [10] The practice of employing women in field work was not wholly approved by Thomas Hill, who, while traveling through German country near Easton in 1799, commented that "The women, all at work in the fields, seem very active, but are masculine in the extreme." [11]

While field work was thus seldom hired, house servants were not uncommon among the Germans, especially as the farmers' wealth increased. House servants were frequently redemptioners: a German will of 1775 stated that the wife of the decedent "shall have the Services of my Servant Girl Polly during all the Residue of her Term of Servitude agreeable to her Indentures." [12] Other similar evidence confirms this use of indentured help. In the middle colonies in general throughout the eighteenth century, redemptioners were more commonly employed than slaves; Pennsylvania Germans rarely possessed slaves, for whom they apparently had little use and still less desire.[13]

Farm animals of the Pennsylvania Germans included horses, oxen, sheep, cattle, swine, goats and chickens. With the exception of oxen, all were to be found in numbers on farms during the eighteenth century. Not until late in the century, apparently, did the use of oxen make a serious bid to replace horses in such draft work as plowing and hauling. A traveler of the 1790's remarked that oxen were just beginning to be used in the neighborhood of Ealer's Tavern, near Allentown; farther west, in Maxatawny Township, around Kutztown, the custom of plowing with oxen was increasing, but in Cumberland County, still farther west, the use of oxen for any sort of farm work was little known.[14] The lower price of oxen might have been respon-

sible for their increasingly widespread employment: prices quoted in
1794 were £20 to £25 for a good plow horse, whereas a pair of oxen
sold for from £18 to £20.[15] On the other hand, an account of 1698
stated that oxen were usually used for plowing, although there was
no lack of good horses.[16] It seems clear, however, that for some time
horses were preferred by the immigrant farmers who entered the
province after 1700.

The horses of the German farmers, known generally as "Conestoga horses," enjoyed a wide reputation throughout Pennsylvania.
Benjamin Rush, writing in 1789, attributed the remarkable size and
strength of German horses to particularly good feeding and to the
prevalence of large stoves, rather than fireplaces, in German farmhouses. Since less wood for the same amount of heat was required in
a stove than in a fireplace, the horses were spared much hauling of
wood in the winter, "which frequently unfits the horses of their
(*Scotch*) neighbors for the toils of the ensuing spring." [17] A German
observer who had an opportunity to compare Pennsylvania with
other regions in the young United States remarked that Pennsylvanians regarded size and strength of breed in horses more than their
beauty.[18] Perhaps, for the practical Germans, beauty lay in size and
strength.

The concern of Pennsylvanians with ensuring a continuing supply
of large and powerful draft horses was manifested in at least two acts
of the Pennsylvania Assembly during the eighteenth century. An
act of 1724 stipulated that horses under thirteen **hands** (fifty-two
inches) were to be prevented from running free and from breeding
indiscriminately.[19] In 1749 horse dealers were prohibited from introducing into the province horses shorter than fourteen hands (fifty-
six inches), or more than eight years old, or unhealthy.[20]

Animals on the German farm were raised chiefly to fill the needs
of the household, or the needs of a rather restricted group of consumers in the immediate neighborhood. Horses and oxen were, of
course, used for labor. Goats were raised for milk and cheese, chickens for eggs and meat, and swine and cattle for meat. Sheep were
raised largely to supply the family with clothing.[21] Apiaries, too, had
a place on many farms by the end of the century.[22] Since the main
sale product of Pennsylvania farms was wheat, and other important
exports were almost exclusively products of the soil, farm animals
were not considered export commodities. The number of animals on
a farm varied as the wealth of the farmer; tax lists of 1779 would indicate that the average German farmer possessed two or three horses

(two were virtually a necessity, to form a team), and four or five cattle.[23]

The Germans differed from practically all other Pennsylvania farmers, with the exception of the few Dutch, in providing shelter for their animals in winter. A traveler of the mid-eighteenth century noted shortly after his arrival in Pennsylvania that cattle around Philadelphia were neither housed in winter nor tended in the fields; after having been in the country for some time, however, he remarked that while the English and Swedes had no stables, the Germans and Dutch had "preserved the custom of their country, and generally kept their cattle in barns during the winter." [24] In settling a tract of land, the Germans normally provided good quarters for their horses and cattle before they built any but the crudest accommodations for themselves. They kept their animals as warm as possible in winter, and thereby effected considerable savings in hay and grain, for they found that cold animals eat more than warm ones.[25] It was usually only in the hardest part of winter, from December to April, that stock was kept in the stables.[26]

Except in winter, animals were apparently pastured on the farm proper, or were allowed to run about the countryside, where they found their own food by forage.[27] Those farmers who did not winter their stock in stables placed haystacks on a field for winter feeding.[28] The pasturing of horses and cattle on stubble fields was also a widely used practice: whatever grew on hay fields after the second cutting in August was used as forage, as were wheat sowed in September and early rye.[29] Land lying temporarily fallow was often turned into pasture on farms which had sufficient acreage.[30] Since pasture in the forest consisted mainly of leaves, orchards were in many cases used before the stubble fields and meadows were ready.[31] Sheep and goats were treated in much the same way as horses and cattle, but hogs were often fattened on the peaches which fell from the trees in the orchard.[32] Since swine were not allowed to run at large,[33] some farmers maintained peach orchards exclusively to feed the swine.[34]

Hay was certainly the chief element in the diet of most farm animals, but, as has been noted, wheat and rye straw was also used. Other types of feed included oats, used exclusively for horses, buckwheat, blades from cornstalks cut at the moment of greatest growth, and wheat bran, normally fed only to milch cows.[35] Good farmers recognized clearly that hay alone was not sufficient to maintain weight and strength in stock, and they therefore added considerable amounts of grain to the diet.[36]

"In the productions commonly cultivated," wrote the author of *American Husbandry*, "wheat is the grand article of the province." [37] Wheat was more consistently grown in Pennsylvania in the eighteenth century than any other export crop. Pennsylvania's position as the leader in wheat exports was due not only to the south's concentration on tobacco, but also to the poor quality of land in New England, and, of course, to the good land and favorable climate of Pennsylvania itself. Indeed, Israel Acrelius in the 1750's was convinced that climate was more responsible for Pennsylvania's high position in the cultivation of grains than was the fertility of the soil. [38]

But there was a market demand for products other than wheat, and the self-sufficiency of the Pennsylvania farm, especially the German farm, required that attention be given to raising a wide diversity of crops. Field crops besides wheat included buckwheat, rye, barley, oats, speltz, clover, corn, hay, flax, hemp and grass. Buckwheat, along with rye and barley, became especially popular when farmers found that it was particularly resistant to attacks of the Hessian fly, an insect which plagued Pennsylvania wheat farms in the last two decades of the eighteenth century on into the nineteenth. Germans raised flax and hemp partially as marketable commodities, but largely to supply their own clothing needs: Cazenove remarked that in 1794 every farm in the neighborhood of Kutztown was self-sufficient in this respect. [39] Grass, especially timothy, was deliberately cultivated on many of the best farms as fodder for stock. [40] Especially characteristic of Pennsylvania was this attention to grass, which was grown in meadows which often were irrigated.

One of the earmarks of the German farmer in Pennsylvania was his assiduous cultivation of large vegetable gardens. [41] Among the vegetables most frequently to be found were turnips, white and sweet potatoes, carrots, cabbage, peas, beans, cucumbers, beets, onions, lettuce and German lettuce. Both turnips and potatoes were often grown in large quantities as field crops. Less frequently seen, but still generally cultivated, were parsnips, red peppers, artichokes, and parsley. [42] Kohlrabi, broccoli, and black radishes began to appear in gardens late in the eighteenth century, and were probably first introduced by German troops during the Revolutionary War. [43] Tobacco, too, had its place in the garden, but only in a quantity sufficient for the use of the farmer and his family. Some herbs for home remedies were also grown, including wormwood, rue, sage, thyme and camomile.[44]

Plums, peaches, apples and cherries were the chief products of orchards on Pennsylvania farms.[45] Apples were used principally for apple juice, from which cider was made; virtually every farm possessed an apple mill and a cider press.[46] Peaches, as noted above, were frequently fed to the hogs, while cherries were converted into brandy. All of these, including plums, were used fresh on the table, and were also dried for winter use.

Wine making, one of the traditional occupations of many Germans, especially in the Palatinate, was not a major industry on German farms in eighteenth-century Pennsylvania. Gottlieb Mittelberger at mid-century wrote that although vines grew plentifully, not much wine was made because of the large amounts of sugar required. Grapes in the area would be better, he said, if the vines were cut, as in Europe, but since the population was too dispersed to care for vines properly, animals and birds would soon put an end to any cultivation which might be undertaken.[47]

The yields of different crops varied with the fertility of the soil, the amount of seed sowed, the amount and frequency of fertilization, and, of course, the weather. Gabriel Thomas wrote in 1698 that between twenty and thirty bushels of wheat were reaped from every bushel sowed.[48] This was certainly an excellent yield, and must have been due to the newness of the ground, for the author of *American Husbandry* some seventy-five years later noted that on good land between twenty-five and thirty-two bushels were harvested from two or three bushels of seed per acre, and that on inferior ground only fifteen to twenty-five bushels were reaped from the same amount of seed.[49] Schoepf remarked that old seed was sowed at the rate of one bushel to the acre, and new seed at half that proportion.[50] Other wheat yields, taken in 1794, were fifteen bushels around both Bethlehem and Kutztown; fifteen to twenty bushels, sowed with one bushel, in Cumberland County; twelve to fifteen bushels in York County; and twelve to sixteen bushels near Abbottstown.[51] Thomas Hill, traveling in east-central Pennsylvania in 1799, found average yields around Easton to be about twelve bushels per acre, except on land on which red clover had been grown, where the yield was twenty-five bushels.[52]

Buckwheat gave much higher yields than wheat, although as a food product it was not regarded as highly as wheat. In 1775, buckwheat sowed with one and a half bushels of seed sometimes yielded more than forty bushels per acre, but more commonly from thirty to thirty-six bushels.[53] Theophile Cazenove somewhat later listed buckwheat yields around Kutztown at twenty-five bushels, in York County at fifteen to forty bushels, and in the immediate vicinity of Abbottstown at ten to forty bushels.[54] Oats gave a crop in Cumberland County reported at thirty to fifty bushels an acre [55]; another statement indicated that thirty-five bushels were regarded as a good crop.[56] Hay, reckoned in tons per acre, yielded one to one and a half tons in Cumberland and York counties, and one and a half tons in the neighborhood of Easton in the 1790's.[57] Yields from "common meadows" around Philadelphia in 1797 were given at three tons, and as high as eight tons on meadows "in good situation." [58] Yields for other crops in 1794 were: fifteen bushels of rye in the area of Kutztown; twenty to thirty bushels of corn in Cumberland County, and twenty in York County; one to one and a half tons of clover in Berks and Cumberland counties; and fifteen bushels of barley in Berks County.[59] The land around Kutztown, in Berks County, must have been highly inferior or exhausted in 1794 to produce only fifteen bushels of barley, for the author of *American Husbandry* noted in 1775 that the barley yield on good land was from thirty to forty bushels, and on bad land from twenty to twenty-five bushels.[60] This example serves to indicate how irregular yields were, and how dependent upon soil care and other factors.

The abundance of good land in Pennsylvania unquestionably acted as a deterrent to the development of enlightened practices of soil conservation in the eighteenth century. German farmers were, in general, less given to thoughtless exploitation of the soil than other farmers of colonial Pennsylvania, largely by reason of attitudes stemming from their German traditions. But even they, to some extent, must have inclined toward the careless methods of cultivation fostered by the great amounts of land available to them in the new country.

It was apparent to all farmers, of course, that soil did become exhausted, and that its strength had to be renewed periodically. The easiest method of restoring the land, and doubtless the one of most ancient institution, was simply to let the ground lie fallow. In Pennsylvania, farmers apparently observed no real system or definite time interval in this practice, the criterion generally being the capacity of a tract to produce a reasonably good crop. One contemporary observer in the 1750's commented that when a farmer had exhausted one piece of land, he moved to another, which he treated in the same manner, and so on, until he had exhausted all his lands; he then moved back to the first, which by that time had recovered its fertility.[61] Similar practices were noted in 1775. The opinion was expressed that most farmers had bought too much land in their original purchase, and had insufficient means to care for the land properly through the use of artificial or other fertilizers.[62] Those conversant with the problems and techniques of agriculture heartily condemned the policy of unthinking exploitation of the land. To the Swede Peter Kalm, who was aware of the problems in his own land caused by the scarcity of good soil, the system in use in Pennsylvania must have seemed a travesty, and he expressed his heartfelt disapproval of easy methods which had "induced [Pennsylvania farmers] to adopt the same method of agriculture as the Indians." [63]

Combined with the custom of letting land lie fallow was the use of crop rotation. Depending, of course, on the individual farmer, these two practices could form a reasonably intelligent system of cultivation. Schoepf found that "usual practice" in Bucks County in 1783 was to plant maize the first year, wheat and English grass the second year, then to pasture for four or five years. Sometimes, he added, buckwheat or turnips were planted after wheat before the ground was allowed to lie fallow.[64] Cazenove in his *Journal* gives a very complete picture of crop rotation in various parts of Pennsylvania in 1794. Around Bethlehem, wheat was sowed the first year, followed by oats, corn, or buckwheat in the second year, clover in the third year, and clover and plowing to sow in the fourth.[65] The cycle was then repeated. Around Kutztown, on the other hand, a fairly regular system of allowing the land to rest fallow every three years, with the addition of artificial fertilizer at the same interval, was in use.[66]

In the rotation of crops, a distinction was usually made between new land—*i.e.*, land being put under cultivation for the first time—and lands in use for some time. On new land around Lebanon, wheat was sowed the first two years, followed in the third by oats, fallow the fourth, wheat the fifth, fallow the sixth, and so on. On older lands, wheat in the first year was followed by barley in the second, corn or oats in the third, fallow or buckwheat the fourth year, and buckwheat the fifth year unless it had been sowed in the fourth year, in which case the land lay fallow.[67] In Cumberland County, no "consistent [or] very well thought-out" crop rotation was practiced, and the farmers "followed too much their humor," but good farmers, on good land, sowed wheat the first year, after thrice plowing the land, oats or corn the second year, and clover and fallow the third and fourth years. An alternative rotation, practiced by those who apparently were not such good farmers, was wheat the first year, barley the second, corn the third, oats the fourth, fallow the fifth, and fallow and wheat the sixth, whereupon the cycle was repeated. On new ground in the same area, fields were planted with turnips and sweet potatoes in equal proportions the first year, followed by flax in the second.[68] Orchards, too, were in a sense rotated: Schoepf remarked that when trees in an orchard began to show age, a new orchard was set up on fresh land, since it was not regarded as good practice to put young trees where old ones had stood.[69] A travel account of 1794, which indicated that Lancaster County was the best cultivated of any part of Pennsylvania, gave the following account of rotation there: the first crop, Indian corn, was planted in late May or early June, and was harvested in the fall in time to sow the second crop, wheat. In the spring of the second year, before the wheat sowed the previous fall had been harvested, clover was sowed among the wheat. After the wheat was reaped in late summer, a few cattle were turned into the now ripe clover for a short time. In the third and fourth years, clover was sowed, and was mowed twice in each year. After the last mowing in autumn of the fourth year, the ground was plowed and harrowed, and in May of the fifth year the cycle was begun again with Indian corn. Occasionally, rye or winter barley was substituted for wheat, and oats for Indian corn, in which case the oats were sowed in April. Frequently, buckwheat was sowed in June on a field containing wheat to be harvested in late summer, the buckwheat being reaped just before the November frosts.[70]

Some rotation practices showed an almost criminal forcing of the land. For example, on a farm some fifty miles north of Philadelphia, on new land, wheat was grown the first two years, maize the third, wheat again the fourth and fifth, barley the sixth, seventh, and eighth, oats the ninth, barley the tenth, buckwheat the eleventh, barley the twelfth, oats the thirteenth, and peas the fourteenth. The ground then lay fallow for seven years. To the observer who noted the system, nothing could have provided better proof of the excellence of land in Pennsylvania! [71] One reason for forcing the land may be found in the customs of land inheritance. Particularly among the Germans, a father often willed his farm to his eldest son, requiring him to pay a certain amount of money to younger brothers and sisters. In order to pay off the debts, which sometimes might even exceed the value of the farm itself, crops were forced beyond the normal ability of the land to produce.[72]

Within the systems of rotation sketched above, the use of clover appears toward the end of the rotation cycle. In the last quarter of the eighteenth century, clover began to be generally recognized in Pennsylvania as an excellent crop for enriching and restoring the soil. It also provided good pasture for farm animals. Cazenove noted the use of clover around Kutztown in Berks County, and remarked that in Cumberland County and in the area of Bethlehem clover was just beginning to be sowed in considerable amounts in 1794.[73] Thomas Hill in 1799 commented that whereas seven years before he had been able to find no clover sowed except near cities, he now noticed its cultivation "wherever you find a mill, or a store." [74] Cultivation of turnips was also thought to be of some importance in restoring the vigor of the soil, and the product itself was used partly for table and partly for cattle.[75]

The use of soil-restoring crops such as clover and the rotation of crops which went along with it were not, however, the only means of maintaining the fertility of the soil. Farm manure was one of the earliest fertilizers known to man, and its use in Pennsylvania in the eighteenth century was not neglected. But because of the large amount of land under cultivation and the relatively small number of farm animals, manure was not used as extensively as it was in Europe. The German farmers of Pennsylvania, in following traditional practice, were able to make wider use of manure than many other farmers, for they kept their cattle enclosed in their famous "Swisser" barns for a large part of the winter. This, of course, immensely facilitated the collection of dung.[76] Observers saw clearly that the common practice of allowing stock to run free through the countryside all year long was the chief reason for the lack of dung on many farms.[77] Those who did not have stables obtained their manure as best they could by picking up after their animals on pastures and fields; sometimes, too, they developed schemes to prevent too wide a scattering of dung. On the field in which the animals were fed in winter, for example, some farmers scattered haystacks about, which, trampled by the cattle feeding on them and becoming mixed with their manure, formed a compost which could then be gathered for distribution on fields. This mixture was reported to be both unequal and insufficient, but it did provide more natural fertilizer than many farmers would otherwise have had.[78]

There were two soil amendments used in the eighteenth century: lime, used throughout the century, and gypsum, or plaster of Paris, which was introduced for that purpose apparently only after the

American Revolution. Gabriel Thomas in 1698 remarked on the abundance of limestone in Pennsylvania, which he indicated was of great utility not only in building, but also in "Manuring land." At the same time, however, he suggested that there was little use for any fertilizer, because nature itself had made the land sufficiently fruitful.[79] At the latter end of the next century, however, farmers were using lime in great quantities: Cazenove remarked that German farmers around Bethlehem in 1794 were using forty bushels of lime per acre, along with farm manure.[80] Another traveler reported that fifteen to twenty bushels of lime per acre were spread on ordinary uplands, but more than twice that much on "clayey lowground." [81] On the other hand, an observer of the 1790's reported seeing no lime used as manure around Easton, fifteen miles northeast of Bethlehem, and yet another traveler indicated that farmers in Cumberland County were loath to employ lime, claiming that it impaired their land.[82] The use of lime depended to a certain extent upon its availability in different parts of Pennsylvania. The first settled areas of southeastern Pennsylvania had scattered deposits of limestone, from which lime was made.[83] German farmers were among the first to use it, and often had lime kilns on their own farms: Governor Pownall remarked in 1754 that every farm in Lancaster County possessed one.[84]

An argument still exists as to who first introduced gypsum (plaster of Paris) into Pennsylvania as a fertilizer. Some claim the honor for the Germans, who supposedly had used it for years in Germany prior to its debut in America; others maintain that the English were responsible. Whoever deserves the credit, it seems clear that gypsum was not used for agricultural purposes in Pennsylvania until after the American Revolution. Travel accounts do not mention it prior to the Revolution, whereas in the 1780's and 1790's narratives are filled with references to it. Schoepf in 1783–1784 commented that the use of gypsum around Philadelphia and Germantown had recently become a favorite practice, "because there is less trouble involved than in the collecting, lading, hauling, and spreading of the common dung of cattle—trouble which the farmer here does not willingly submit to." [85] Gypsum found its greatest application on clover, where its salutary effects were first noted. The amount used for clover was reported in one area at four bushels per acre.[86] Around Kutztown, farmers found that gypsum was beneficial on clover for the first two years, but that after that it "used up" the land; just west of Kutztown, it was applied every three years only:

put on more often, it ruined the ground.[87] As the use of gypsum increased, so did its price: Cazenove noted that the price of plaster of Paris before the war was a half-dollar per bushel, whereas in 1794 the same amount was a dollar.[88]

Gypsum acted as a soil stimulant, but added none of the organic elements needed by the soil to retain its fertility. Naturally, any reliance on gypsum alone to improve land, without further fertilization, would end in disappointment. In the eighteenth century, before artificial fertilizers had been developed, manure remained the best fertilizer in every way. And because of their consistent concern for the collection of dung, German farmers for a long time maintained an important advantage over their English and Scotch-Irish neighbors.

Before land could be plowed or sowed, it naturally had to be cleared. Not only the original settlers, but virtually all other farmers who came after them were forced to reclaim from the forest much of the land they intended to cultivate. Even in areas that had been settled for many years, the clearing of land for crops was a steady occupation. But farmers did not indiscriminately rid themselves of their forest holdings; indeed, if we are to believe the testimony of one traveler, the exact opposite was the case: "The farmers keep too much woods, they are always afraid of not having enough, either for their fires, field-fences, or buildings." [89] German farmers distinguished themselves from other farmers by their method of clearing land. English and Scotch-Irish farmers usually cleared by "girdling" trees—by removing a ring of bark, three or four inches wide, from the trunk of the tree, thus causing it to die and eventually fall. The Germans cut down their trees immediately and burned them. The German farmer, while able to clear less land initially because of the great amount of labor required by this method, nevertheless had the advantage of possessing a completely clear field right away, which made the tasks of plowing, harrowing, and reaping much easier.[90] Girdled trees did not fall for several years, but eventually they were chopped up, and the logs rolled together and burned; until this time, however, fields were plowed, sowed, and reaped around the fallen trees: ". . . one may often see fields filled with dry trees, and a heavy crop of grain growing under them." [91] Underbrush and bushes, which English and Scottish farmers frequently cut off just at ground level, were entirely grubbed out by the Germans; the expense of repairing a plow broken on roots was greater than the expense of complete grubbing.[92] Two men might clear twenty or thirty acres a year, and have them ready for plowing.[93]

Once cleared, the land was plowed in preparation for harrowing and planting. The plowman, guiding the plow drawn by a pair of oxen or horses, turned the field up into high ridges and, plowing first on one and then on the other side of these ridges, turned up the whole field.[94] By this method, "the plow turns the stubs down and the earth up, and so the turf is sooner rotted, and the field kept free from weeds." [95] Deep plowing had not yet come into common use: the colonial plow was unfit for it, and there was a general prejudice against turning up the soil too deeply. Four or five inches was the normal maximum depth.[96] Harrowing was done immediately after plowing with a team of oxen or horses; sometimes two harrows were fastened together after the same team.[97] Twice over the field with a harrow was usually sufficient to prepare it for sowing.[98]

Where the seed drill or seeding plow was not in use,[99] both sowing and planting were done entirely by hand, the sowing mostly by the broadcast method. Wheat was sowed at the beginning of September, after three plowings (assuming that no crop was on the field immediately before the wheat was to be sowed) in May, July, and just before planting.[100] It was normally harvested before the end of June, but sometimes not until the middle of July.[101] The wheat stalk was cut at about half its length, so that the stubble was quite high, and the wheat was gathered into short and small sheaves, with a dozen sheaves reckoned to one bushel.[102]

Rye was sowed in November, mostly upon sandy ground or upon land which had borne wheat or some other crop the previous summer.[103] One plowing was normally regarded as sufficient, and rye was cut at the same time and in the same manner as wheat.[104] Oats were sowed at the beginning of March, usually on good ground which had been plowed some days before, and cut in July. If plowing was done the previous November or December, then again just before sowing, a better crop was produced.[105] Flax required new or especially fertile ground, and was sowed after the ground had been plowed some days before; it was pulled in July.[106] Hay was usually mowed twice—once in the second half of June, and once early in August. Hay was not kept under cover in most cases, but was left on the field in large stacks.[107] Buckwheat, sowed at the end of July, was harvested in October, poor ground and one plowing being sufficient.[108]

Procedures involved in planting corn are known in some detail. After a plowing in March, corn was planted at the end of April or the beginning of May. Planting was done with a broad hoe, which opened up the ground in holes three or four inches deep and approximately four feet apart. In each hole the farmer put from three to five grains of corn, occasionally adding a few Turkish beans which ran up the corn stalks. As soon as the young plants came up, they were plowed and even harrowed to rid them of weeds. At a height of about two feet, and again at four feet, ground was hoed up around the stalks. In September, the farmer sometimes plowed or hoed crisscross between the rows of corn, sowed wheat, and harrowed it in; the wheat then produced a full crop the next year. The ears of corn were removed from the stalks in late October, and the stalks and roots were grubbed from the field during the winter.[109]

Potatoes, which were cultivated in increasingly larger quantities as the century wore on, were planted in different ways according to type. Irish potatoes were generally planted by putting whole potatoes on a smooth, hard ground already prepared with a bed of dung; portions of dung were then thrown on the potatoes, and they were covered with any kind of soil. When stalks came up to a height of four inches, they were hilled up with earth. By another method, the potato was planted on manure in a long ditch dug to the depth of a spade. Maryland potatoes (sweet potatoes) were planted from sprouts in hills or round heaps of good earth.[110]

Apples and peaches were planted more or less formally in orchards. Peach trees stood in enclosures by themselves, and grew in even the poorest and most rock-ridden ground without special care. Apple trees were planted in rows, at intervals of from twelve to fifteen paces. Their cultivation consisted in grafting, if seedlings, and pruning in the spring, and every five or six years in plowing the ground. While the trees were young, either corn was planted or rye or oats sowed.[111] Cherry trees, whose fruit was normally ripe by the end of June, were planted "here and there" around houses and along roads.[112]

Agricultural methods in eighteenth-century Pennsylvania were in many ways not as primitive or backward as might be supposed. Among the techniques at which many farmers excelled was that of irrigating meadows. It was found that properly irrigated lands would produce much more grass than those left entirely to nature's whim. Peter Kalm in 1750 observed methods of irrigation then in use. Because a meadow usually lay in a dale between hills, farmers looked for streams on higher ground and channeled them to flow through the meadow in ditches dug for the purpose. Wooden irrigation flumes, or gutters, were used to bridge low areas between hill and meadow. Where necessary, high dikes were built near springs to raise the water level. Kalm went on to say that "Industry and ingenuity" went further: when a brook flowed away from a meadow, and it was found by leveling and surveying that the brook could be diverted, a dam was built. The water was then led around the hillside, "sometimes for the space of an English mile and further, partly across valleys in wooden pipes," until at last it was conducted into the meadow to be irrigated.[113] The author of *American Husbandry* also commented on this practice, "the husbandry of watering meadow lands." [114]

Legislation in 1760 and later was passed by the Pennsylvania Assembly to tax farmers and others in the immediate vicinity of Philadelphia for the maintenance of banks, dams, and sluices for the irrigation of meadows—not, as might be supposed, for the benefit of the farmers primarily (although that, of course, was one of the effects), but for the protection of the health of Philadelphians: stagnant water was thought to give rise to disease, and by providing for the introduction of fresh water into the meadows around the city, the city insured itself against the dangers of foul water.[115]

Fences were another object of major concern on good farms in Pennsylvania. Frequent trespassing by both domestic and wild animals on lands under cultivation, and the quarrels and litigation arising from such trespassing, moved the Pennsylvania Assembly in 1700 to pass a law, elaborating on earlier laws of 1676, 1682, and 1685, which provided that all corn fields and grounds kept for enclosures must have fences, which had to be at least five feet high and be constructed of rails or logs.[116] A law of 1729 specified that a fence was to be regarded as "sufficient" if it was four and a half feet high, with the bottom rails not more than nine inches from the ground.[117] Later acts passed against trespassing would indicate that the fence requirement was by no means universally observed. The most common fence in Pennsylvania in the eighteenth century, and by no accident the one which required the least amount of effort to build, was the worm fence, made of logs or rails of cedar, oak, and chestnut.[118] The logs, ten to twelve feet in length, were laid upon the ground, without any further support, and were crisscrossed at the ends as they were built up. Not only did this type of fence require a certain width of ground, but it also demanded a tremendous supply of wood. It is understandable why the average farmer prized his forest possessions so highly. According to Dr. Rush, German fences were high, well built and well kept,[119] but other evidence indicates that Pennsylvanians in general were quite careless about erecting and maintaining fences.[120]

The eighteenth century, although a century of agricultural revolution in England and much of Europe, produced few changes in the farm implements used in Pennsylvania. What changes were made affected the Germans probably less than their English-speaking neighbors, both because there were few German-language publications through which they could learn of new methods and machines, and because the Germans as a group appear to have been less prone to experiment and to accept new ideas than the English and Scotch-Irish. Probably much of their stubborn adherence to old practices was tied up with superstitions and time-honored proverbs to which they seem to have been highly susceptible, and to which they assigned great importance.

The farm implement which was to see perhaps the greatest modification and improvement around the turn of the century was the plow. For the mass of farmers in Pennsylvania, however, the plow most used in the eighteenth century was in no essentials different from that used when the colony was first settled. The colonial plow was so made that two pieces with a handle on each ascended from the rear of the moldboard, about three feet apart at the handles. Put together with screws, it was light (when the moldboard was made of wood) and easy to handle.[121] In most cases, the moldboard was wooden, sometimes reinforced with strips of iron. The coulter was frequently of iron, but in the early part of the century almost always of wood. Iron moldboards and shares did not come into general use until the nineteenth century, in part because of the prohibitive cost of iron, but to some extent because of the mistrust of many farmers, among them the Germans, who believed that iron poisoned the soil.[122] A double moldboard was extremely uncommon in the eighteenth century, and the single board was frequently not curved. Even where an iron share and a curved moldboard were to be found, however, as in Reading in the 1790's, the entire plow was characterized as ill-contrived, and the observer commented that the plow "turns up the ground very imperfectly." Two horses, in this case, were able to draw the plow "in a strong soil." [123] The so-called "seeding-plow," or seed drill, introduced into America after its invention by Jethro Tull in England about 1750, and improved by Tull and others in subsequent years, was not properly a plow at all; rather, it was a horse-drawn device which "drilled," or sowed, seed more efficiently than by hand. The use of a seed drill was observed in Pennsylvania in the latter part of the century,[124] but its use appears to have been quite restricted.[125]

The harrow, designed to smooth and break clods of earth after plowing, was of relatively simple construction. To a heavy wooden frame, often made of logs, spikes or teeth were attached by various means, and the contrivance was then dragged by horses across the ground. In 1698, the teeth on the harrows were universally made of wood [126]; as time went on, wood was often replaced with iron, although the frame itself remained wood. Harrows of two shapes could be found, one square or rectangular, the other triangular. The harrow was fastened to the traces with a link, which in the case of the triangular model made turning at the end of a field easy; the square harrow, on the other hand, was extremely difficult to turn, and was usually provided with two links, on opposite sides, so that the draft could be changed at the end of a field.[127]

"Horse gear" included all the harness, which was made of rope, chain, and leather, or, in some cases, strips of raw deer hide dried and twisted together.[128] An arrangement of singletrees and doubletrees was used to attach the draft animals to the plow, for the beam of the plow did not come forward between the animals.[129] This type of harness obviated the necessity of putting wheels under the beam, a method sometimes employed to make plowing less erratic. The addition of wheels rendered the whole apparatus so heavy and clumsy, however, that the animals had difficulty in pulling the plow. Kalm, who observed wheeled plows in Canada, remarked that one horse was required merely to drag the contrivance along the surface of the ground.[130]

There were many other everyday tools of farm life. According to a Pennsylvania German's will of 1760, his son was to inherit, among other things, a "Crobin How" (grubbing hoe) and an axe [131]; another German will of 1792 bequeathed to the son "two waggons Two ploughs 1 harrow all the Horse Geers Fan and Hand Screw one shovel spade Grubbing Hoe Pitch fork Dung fork." [132] A will probated in 1736 listed weeding hoes, dung hooks, scythes, and sickles.[133] Apple mills and cider presses were frequently mentioned in wills, and Thomas Cooper confirmed the existence of at least one still on virtually every farm in Pennsylvania.[134]

Perhaps the greatest single German contribution to farm equipment, and one for which the Germans were justly honored in their own day, was the Conestoga wagon.[135] Every German farm possessed one of these vehicles, which were uncommonly stout and had a large carrying capacity. An observer of the 1780's remarked that these wagons were the strongest and best in America, and were covered with sailcloth stretched over hoops to protect their cargoes in any weather.[136] Drawn by four or five Conestoga horses, they were employed chiefly to take produce to the market centers of Pennsylvania, especially Philadelphia. Since the Germans often came from considerable distances, the wagons carried provisions and bedding as well as produce.[137] As one contemporary remarked, "The Waggon is their Bed, their Inn, their every thing, many of them will come one hundred & fifty miles without spending one Shilling." [138] It is interesting to speculate on the possible effects of the Conestoga wagon on the course of inland settlement and on the production of such crops as wheat, the extensive cultivation of which in an area without close urban or export markets would have been unprofitable. As professional wagoners developed in the later years of the eighteenth century, great amounts of grain and flour could be transported in these wagons, whose load capacity was greater than that of any other vehicle then on the road.

If one word could be used to describe the manner in which the German inhabitants of colonial Pennsylvania lived, that word would be "thrift." Luxury was a stranger to the Pennsylvania German. His life was dedicated to the development of the land and livestock of his farm, and the money he saved by denying himself an easy life contributed to make the farm more valuable to succeeding generations of his own family and to the community as a whole.

Examples of thrift among the Germans are manifold. They used large stoves, which enabled them to heat the farmhouse with a fraction of the amount of wood required in a fireplace [139]; they sold their best products, such as wheat, and consumed the less profitable ones, such as rye, corn, potatoes, and buckwheat [140]; they hired few farm laborers, relying almost exclusively on the members of their own families, wives and daughters as well as sons [141]; they bought few good clothes, and wore these only on Sundays.[142] Especially noteworthy was their refusal to build nice houses for themselves before they had provided sufficiently, sometimes almost luxuriantly, for their animals, and had otherwise set the economy of their farms on a firm basis. The first house they built was usually of logs, and lasted their lifetime; it was left to the second generation to construct larger quarters.[143] Cazenove described the dwellings in which the new farmers lived as "wretched log houses without windows, and with chimneys of sticks and clay"; even when their land yielded good wheat and they came into better circumstances, the Germans began to build large barns rather than houses.[144] The attention paid by Germans to the construction of barns, which became the envy of the non-German countryside, was brought out by one observer of 1753, who commented that "It is pretty to behold our back-Settlements, where the barns are large as pallaces, while the Owners live in log hutts; a sign tho' of thriving farmers." [145]

Those aspects of the farm which related strictly to the household, and did not touch the fields, crops, fences, barns, or livestock, were frequently neglected by the austere Germans. Cazenove disapprovingly noted that often no care was taken to keep the entrance to the farmhouse free and clear of stones and mud, and that neither trees nor flowers were to be seen in the farmhouse yard. The vegetable gardens were filled with weeds, intermingled with cabbages, turnips, and other plants. He commented further that although numbers of rich German farmers in Berks, Dauphin, and Lancaster counties possessed fine stone houses of two stories, with English windows and other improvements, inside they were almost totally unfurnished. He found dishes still standing on the immense stove, potatoes and turnips on the floor, beds without curtains (a fastidious criticism, indeed!), no mirrors, and no good tables, chairs, or wardrobes. Cazenove apparently made inquiry into this state of affairs, and was given to understand that the lack of neatness and improvements stemmed from the inheritance customs of the Germans. The eldest son usually received his father's farm mortgaged or in debt to the other children for their shares: "Then the new owner exerts himself, and employs all his savings in the payment of the debt; so being used to think only of making money, he keeps on after he has paid out." Sometimes a father might buy farms "part cash and part time-payment" and give these to his sons, indebted; the result, however, was still the same.[146] Wills of Pennsylvania Germans tend to confirm this explanation, at least as far as farmers' bequests are concerned.[147]

Traveling through German country in the neighborhood of Germantown in the late 1790's, the Duke de la Rochefoucauld-Liancourt was led to remark that the farmers whom he met were by no means intelligent, that they were unusually stubborn in clinging to old customs, and loath to adopt new methods.[148] Rochefoucauld-Liancourt's use of the word "intelligent" might be disputed, but that the Germans were slower than their neighbors to adopt many of the more efficient tools and methods of the late eighteenth- and early nineteenth-century agricultural revolution in America is probably quite true. During the eighteenth century, however, the Germans were highly respected as farmers, and this reputation has survived to the present day largely, as Rochefoucauld-Liancourt himself admitted, because of their industrious nature: "their assiduity to labour counteracts, in some measure, their repugnance to all improvement." [149] Lewis Evans expressed what was perhaps the prevailing attitude of eighteenth-century Pennsylvanians: "it may be observed how much we are indebted to the Germans for the Oeconomy they have introduced amongst us & how serviceable these People are in an infant Colony." [150]

In the final analysis, it was the personal traits of the Germans, their thrift, their unswerving loyalty to the land, and their sheer hard work, as well as their inherited and acquired knowledge of good farming, which were responsible for their outstanding success as colonial farmers. While it is true that certain agricultural practices of the Germans gave them some advantages over their neighbors, their inability (and, in some cases, unwillingness) to read English and their suspicion of things new deprived them for a long time of the beneficial effects of the agricultural revolution. The new methods and practices which arose from that revolution equalled, then surpassed, the particular achievements of the Germans, and after 1800 they fell somewhat behind in the march of agricultural progress. By that time, however, Pennsylvania's farm economy was already set on a permanently solid foundation, in the attainment of which the colonial German farmer had played a remarkably significant role.

NOTES

1. Jesse L. Rosenberger, *The Pennsylvania Germans* (Chicago, 1923), 9. There has been some argument about the number of Germans in Pennsylvania. A higher estimate than the one above has been given by William Beidelman, *The Story of the Pennsylvania Germans* (Easton, Pa., 1898), 54; a lower one will be found in Oscar Kuhns, *The German and Swiss Settlements of Colonial Pennsylvania* (New York, 1901), 59.

2. Gottlieb Mittelberger, *Gottlieb Mittelberger's Journey to Pennsylvania in the Year 1750 and Return to Germany in the Year 1754,* trans. by Carl T. Eben (Philadelphia, 1898), 119.

3. Land Warranties of Bucks, Cumberland, Lancaster, and Philadelphia Counties, *Pennsylvania Archives, Third Series,* XXIV.

4. Theophile Cazenove, *Cazenove Journal 1794: A Record of the Journey of Theophile Cazenove through New Jersey and Pennsylvania*, trans. by Rayner W. Kelsey (Haverford, Pa., 1922), 35, 58, 67, 69.

5. Land Warranties of Bucks, Cumberland, Lancaster, and Philadelphia Counties, *Pennsylvania Archives, Third Series*, XXIV.

6. Tax Lists of Berks, Bucks, Cumberland, Lancaster, and York Counties, 1779, *ibid.*, XIII, XVII, XVIII.

7. Cazenove, 35, 58, 67, 69.

8. Israel Acrelius, *A History of New Sweden; or, The Settlements of the River Delaware*, trans. by W. M. Reynolds (Philadelphia, 1876), 152; Mittelberger, 67.

9. Cazenove, 34; Benjamin Rush, *An Account of the Manners of the German Inhabitants of Pennsylvania*, ed. by I. Daniel Rupp (Philadelphia, 1875 [originally printed in Philadelphia, 1789]), 24–25.

10. Benjamin Rush, *Letters of Benjamin Rush*, ed. by L. H. Butterfield (Princeton, N.J., 1951), I, 403.

11. Thomas Hill, "A Journey on Horseback from New Brunswick, New Jersey, to Lycoming County, Pennsylvania, in 1799," *The Pennsylvania Magazine of History and Biography*, XIV (1890), 191, hereinafter cited as Hill.

12. Russell W. Gilbert, "Pennsylvania German Wills," *Yearbook of the Pennsylvania German Folklore Society*, XV (1950), 97.

13. *Ibid.*, 96.

14. Cazenove, 29, 33, 59.

15. *Ibid.*, 29.

16. Gabriel Thomas, *An Account of Pennsylvania and West New Jersey* (Cleveland, Ohio, 1903 [originally published in London, 1698]), 27–28.

17. Rush, *An Account*, 17.

18. Johann David Schoepf, *Travels in the Confederation, 1783–1784*, trans. and ed. by A. J. Morrison (Philadelphia, 1911), I, 204.

19. *Statutes-at-Large of Pennsylvania from 1682 to 1801* (Harrisburg, 1896–1908), III, 422 ff.

20. *Ibid.*, V, 65–68.

21. Cazenove, 34.

22. *Ibid.*

23. Tax Lists of Berks, Bucks, Cumberland, Lancaster, and York Counties, *Pennsylvania Archives, Third Series*, XIII, XVII, XVIII.

24. Peter Kalm, *The America of 1750: Peter Kalm's Travels in North America*, trans. and ed. by Adolph B. Benson (New York, 1937), I, 55, 236.

25. Rush, *An Account*, 19–20.

26. Cazenove, 49.

27. Mittelberger, 68; *American Husbandry*, ed. by Harry J. Carman (New York, 1939 [originally published in two volumes, London, 1775]), 119.

28. Acrelius, 146–147.

29. Schoepf, I, 128; Acrelius, 149.

30. Schoepf, I, 130; Kalm, I, 308.

31. Acrelius, 154.

32. *American Husbandry*, 112.

33. An act of the Pennsylvania Assembly of 1706 prohibited swine from running at large without a yoke to prevent them from going under or through fences, and a nose ring to prevent them from rooting up the ground. *Statutes-at-Large*, II, 261–263.

34. Acrelius, 152.

35. *Ibid.*, 148, 150, 156.
36. *Ibid.*, 156.
37. *American Husbandry*, 113.
38. Acrelius, 147.
39. Cazenove, 34.
40. Cazenove, 67; Rush, *An Account*, 13–14.
41. *Ibid.*, 23–24.
42. These vegetables are mentioned in Acrelius, 150–151; *American Husbandry*, 118; Rush, *Letters*, I, 403; and Schoepf, I, 130. Many are mentioned as early as 1698, in Thomas, 35.
43. Schoepf, I, 94.
44. Acrelius, 151.
45. Schoepf, I, 158; Cazenove, 24; Acrelius, 151; Mittelberger, 67.
46. Gilbert, 43.
47. Mittelberger, 70.
48. Thomas, 27–28.
49. *American Husbandry*, 113.
50. Schoepf, I, 130.
51. Cazenove, 24, 35, 58, 67, 69.
52. Hill, 190.
53. *American Husbandry*, 119.
54. Cazenove, 35, 67, 69.
55. *Ibid.*, 58.
56. *American Husbandry*, 115.
57. Cazenove, 58, 67, 69; Hill, 190.
58. Duke de la Rochefoucauld-Liancourt, *Travels through the United States of North America, 1795, 1796, 1797* (London, 1799), I, 11–12.
59. Cazenove, 35, 58, 67, 69.
60. *American Husbandry*, 115.
61. Kalm, I, 97.
62. *American Husbandry*, 113, 123.
63. Kalm, I, 308.
64. Schoepf, I, 130.
65. Cazenove, 29.
66. *Ibid.*, 35.
67. *Ibid.*, 48.
68. *Ibid.*, 58–59.
69. Schoepf, I, 131.
70. Thomas Cooper, *Some Information Concerning America* (Dublin, 1794), 137–138.
71. *American Husbandry*, 122–123.
72. Cazenove, 33.
73. *Ibid.*, 24, 59.
74. Hill, 190.
75. *American Husbandry*, 118.
76. Cazenove, 29; Kalm, I, 236.
77. *Ibid.*, 55; *American Husbandry*, 125.
78. Acrelius, 146–147.
79. Thomas, 30.
80. Cazenove, 29.
81. Schoepf, II, 2–3.
82. Hill, 190; Cazenove, 58.

83. Stevenson W. Fletcher, *Pennsylvania Agriculture and Country Life,*
1640–1840 (Harrisburg, 1950), 133.
84. Thomas Pownall, "Address on the Early Settlement of the Valley of
the Pequea," 1754, quoted in Fletcher, 133.
85. Schoepf, I, 196 (note).
86. Cazenove, 29.
87. *Ibid.,* 33, 35–36.
88. *Ibid.,* 29.
89. *Ibid.,* 58.
90. Rush, *An Account,* 14–15. There is evidence, however, that this practice was not universal among the Germans. Acrelius nowhere mentioned that
cutting and burning was done, but did mention girdling, and Schoepf, while
traveling from Christiansbrunn to Allentown, an essentially German region,
mentioned seeing girdling done, but did not refer to the other method. Acrelius, 147; Schoepf, I, 192.
91. Acrelius, 147.
92. Rush, *An Account,* 15.
93. Thomas, 27–28.
94. Acrelius, 147.
95. *Ibid.,* 147 (note).
96. Rochefoucauld-Liancourt, I, 31.
97. Acrelius, 148.
98. Thomas, 27–28.
99. See p. 20, above.
100. Acrelius, 149.
101. *American Husbandry,* 112; Thomas, 27–28; Acrelius, 149.
102. Acrelius, 149.
103. *American Husbandry,* 115; Acrelius, 149.
104. *Ibid.,* 149.
105. *Ibid.,* 148.
106. *Ibid.*
107. Schoepf, I, 128.
108. Acrelius, 149.
109. *Ibid.,* 149–150; Cooper, 137.
110. Acrelius, 150.
111. *Ibid.,* 151–152.
112. *American Husbandry,* 112; Acrelius, 151.
113. Kalm, I, 162.
114. *American Husbandry,* 119.
115. *Statutes-at-Large,* VI, 22–33, 33–46, 54–65 (all 1760) and others following.
116. *Ibid.,* II, 70–71. The earlier ordinances may be found in *Charter to
William Penn and Laws of the Province of Pennsylvania Passed between 1682
and 1700, Preceded by Duke of Yorke's Book of Laws,* ed. by Staughton
George et al. (Harrisburg, 1879), 15, 136, 179.
117. *Statutes-at-Large,* IV, 119.
118. Kalm, I, 238.
119. Rush, *An Account,* 17.
120. *American Husbandry,* 120.
121. Acrelius, 147.
122. Fletcher, 93.
123. Rochefoucauld-Liancourt, I, 31.

124. *American Husbandry*, 114; Schoepf, I, 130, noted that the seed drill was called the "Bucks County plough."

125. Cooper, 126.

126. Thomas, 27–28.

127. Acrelius, 148 and note.

128. *Ibid.*, 148.

129. *Ibid.*

130. Kalm, II, 383.

131. Gilbert, 64

132. *Ibid.*, 66.

133. Edward Welles, "Falkner-Swamp: Early Wills and Inventories of the Hollenbach Family," *The Pennsylvania German*, XII (1911), 679.

134. Gilbert, 43; Cooper, 121–122.

135. The name "Conestoga" was apparently first applied to the wagon by James Logan, who bought one of the vehicles to transport goods to and from his trading post on Conestoga Creek. Frederick B. Tolles, *James Logan and the Culture of Provincial America* (Boston, 1957), 90–91.

136. Schoepf, I, 204.

137. Rush, *An Account*, 26; Schoepf, I, 112.

138. Lewis Evans, "A Brief Account of Pennsylvania," in Lawrence Henry Gipson, *Lewis Evans: To Which is Added Evans' "A Brief Account of Pennsylvania"* (Philadelphia, 1939), 100–101.

139. Rush, *An Account*, 17.

140. Cazenove, 34; Rush, *An Account*, 20.

141. *Ibid.*, 24–25.

142. Cazenove, 34.

143. Rush, *An Account*, 12–13.

144. Cazenove, 61–62.

145. Evans, 100–101.

146. Cazenove, 82–84.

147. Gilbert, 67; Welles, 677–678.

148. Rochefoucauld-Liancourt, II, 392.

149. *Ibid.*

150. Evans, 100–101.

2

Commerce and
Urban Growth

THE FOUNDING of the British colonies in America was fostered by
Crown officials who thought of colonies as "plantations" and the
trade of colonies as complementary to the economy of the home
islands. Militating against the officially ordained role of the colonies,
however, were geography and the aspirations of the men who settled
America. Much of the colonial surplus production could not be
sold profitably within the Empire. Moreover, American merchants
sought new markets aggressively, and hesitated neither to compete
with English merchants nor to seek trade (legal or illicit) outside
the Empire. While building up their trade with Britain and other
nations, the American merchants also expanded their functions as
middlemen within the developing colonial economy itself. The
wealth they accumulated inevitably sought new investment outlets;
hence the movement of mercantile capital into agricultural loans,
banking, industrial enterprises, warehouses, shipping and shipbuilding.

The increasingly diversified urban economies of the American
seaboard gave new impetus to the merchants' continuing competition with their English commercial rivals, creating deep tensions
between the colonies and the mother country. Most historians have
given considerable emphasis to these tensions in tracing the origins
of the American Revolution. As middleman in domestic trade and
lender to farmers in the hinterland, moreover, the American merchant often found himself at odds with the agricultural interests in

local or provincial politics. Those students who view the Revolution as being, in part, the result of a struggle between social classes in the colonies have given a central place in their interpretations to this mercantile-agrarian conflict.

The following essay by Bernard Bailyn casts new light on urban growth in seventeenth-century America. It also questions the usual interpretations of colonial class division and of conflict between American and English merchants. Even before enforcement of the British navigation acts became effective, Bailyn argues, kinship among merchants was a potent force holding together imperial commerce. In the last third of the seventeenth century, however, the need for tighter imperial administration brought to the major Atlantic trading towns a new class of men, the colonial officials. Their appearance enhanced the importance of these commercial centers, but also created "a great divide" in town society. The presence of officialdom, Bailyn asserts, undermined much of the established urban economic and social structure. In addition, it created new distinctions among colonial merchants—distinctions which belie the notion, central to older interpretations, of a monolithic American merchant class whose interests opposed the English. The resultant tensions, the author argues, may well have become "a major determinant of the movement that led to Revolution."

COMMUNICATIONS AND TRADE:
THE ATLANTIC IN
THE SEVENTEENTH CENTURY

Bernard Bailyn

In the first half of the seventeenth century the northern mercantile nations of Europe followed Spain and Portugal in flinging their commercial frontiers westward to the New World. By the end of the century they had surpassed the Iberian nations in western trade and made of the Atlantic basin a single great trading area. Their

Reprinted by permission from *The Journal of Economic History*, XIII, No. 4 (Fall, 1953), 378–87.

economic enterprises created not only a crisscrossing web of trans-
oceanic traffic but also a cultural community that came to form the
western periphery of European civilization. The members of this
community were widely separated, scattered across three thousand
miles of ocean and up and down the coasts of two continents. But
the structure of commerce furnished a communication system that
brought these far-flung settlements together. The same structure
proved to be a framework upon which certain important elements
in colonial society took form. My purpose is to sketch certain characteristics of the Atlantic colonies in the seventeenth century which
relate to these social consequences of commercial growth.

The formative period of northern Atlantic trade was the second
third of the seventeenth century. In those years there were important commercial developments on the American continent by the
English, the Dutch, and the French; but the swiftest advance took
place in the Caribbean. "After 1625," A. P. Newton writes, "swarms
of English and French colonists poured like flies upon the rotting
carcase of Spain's empire in the Caribbean, and within ten years
the West Indian scene was changed forever." [1] The Lesser Antilles
became a battleground of the expanding European empires. The
island of St. Christopher in the Leewards was jointly possessed by
the French and English; Barbados, Nevis, Antigua, and Montserrat
were indisputably English; Guadeloupe and Martinique were
French; and Curaçao, St. Eustatius, and Tobago were in the hands
of the Dutch.

The feverish activity that lay behind these developments resulted
from the belief of numerous Europeans that wealth could be readily
extracted from the places in the New World with which they were
acquainted. But for every success there were a dozen failures. Hopes
were held for commercial designs that strike us now as ill-conceived,
even stupid. Yet to contemporary merchants, cautious men who
built fortunes on their ability to judge investments shrewdly, they
were at least as promising as the schemes that succeeded.

Remarkable only for its subsequent fame but typical in its results
was the Plymouth Company's colony at the mouth of the Sagadahoc
River in New Hampshire. Behind the failure of this venture lay the
belief that exploiters of North America, like those of Asia, had only
to build coastal trading factories, to which throngs of natives would
haul precious piles of goods to exchange for tinkling bells and snip-
pets of bright cloth. English merchants invested approximately
£15,000 in the Lynn Ironworks, which collapsed within two decades

of its promising start in the early 1640's. At least three major fur companies foundered on the belief that the heartland of American pelts lay in the swampy margins of a mythical "Great Lake of the Iroquois," from which were supposed to flow all the main rivers emptying into the Atlantic. The Virginia settlements after the mid-twenties gradually gained a solid economic base, but only after a decade and a half of continuous failure. In the Caribbean islands, experimentation in all sorts of commodities preceded and accompanied the development of sugar as a staple crop.

Patterns of trade were established, of course, around the poles of successful economic ventures, and it was, therefore, only after the broad wave of failures had receded, leaving behind clear indications of natural possibilities, that the commercial system in its familiar form became evident.

The result was a network of trading routes woven by the enterprises of merchants, shipmasters, and colonists representing all the leading mercantile nations of western Europe. The character of each nation's involvement in the web of traffic was determined largely by the resources it controlled and its place in European affairs. Holland's concentration on the carriage of other nations' goods shaped its position; the commerce of France came to rest upon Canadian furs and West Indian sugar; England's position was determined by the very variety of her colonial products and of the interests of her merchants.

The form of England's commercial system was an interlocked group of irregular circles linking the fixed points of port towns in the British Isles, Newfoundland, the American mainland, the West Indies, the Wine Islands, and the continent of Europe. Outward from the larger ports in the British Isles flowed shipping, manufactures, and investments in colonial property, the enhanced value of which returned as colonial products to be sold at home or abroad. No important part of this flow was self-sufficient. Merchants in the colonies, who profited by injecting into the flow goods of their ownership which would be carried one or more stages closer to the ultimate resolution, became important agents in maintaining the efficiency of this mechanism. Their commerce was not independent, and if it appeared to be so to some of them that was because the efficiency of the system permitted them to operate successfully within a limited area. A breakdown in any major part of the mechanism affected all other parts. When, at the outbreak of the American Revolution, the link between England and her colonies was broken, the whole system, in so far as it affected the colonial merchants, was destroyed.

To contemporaries, the commercial system, which we may describe in abstract, geometrical terms, was not something impersonal existing above men's heads, outside their lives, to which they attached themselves for purpose of trade. Unconcerned with abstract economic forces, they knew that their trade was the creation of men and that the bonds that kept its parts together were the personal relationships existing among them.

Overseas commerce in the seventeenth century was capricious. Arrangements were interminably delayed by the accidents of sailing. Demand fluctuated almost incalculably, as one unforeseen crop failure could create a market which the arrival of a few ships could eliminate overnight. Reliable factors and correspondents were, therefore, of paramount importance, for the success of large enterprises rested on their judgment. In such a situation the initiation and continuance of commerce demanded deep personal commitments between people separated by hundreds of miles of ocean. How could such commitments be made? Not, in these early years, by impersonal correspondences between men brought into temporary contact by complementary business needs. The logic of the situation demanded that they follow pre-existent ties of blood or long acquaintance.

To a striking degree first commercial contacts were secured by the cement of kinship. Very frequently brothers, sons, and "in-laws" became the colonial agents of their European relatives. In the middle years of the seventeenth century a number of European—especially English and French—trading families spread out over the Atlantic world. Sons of Londoners seeking their fortunes entered trade in the West Indies and drew on their London connections who were themselves anxious to profit from the importation of colonial goods. Thus Richard Povey, brother of the famous London merchant-politician Thomas Povey, looked after the family interests in Jamaica, while another brother, William, attended to affairs in Barbados. Not infrequently the same family had other relatives on the American mainland who joined in the growing enterprise. The Winthrop family, starting with representatives in England and Massachusetts, ended with ties to Rhode Island, New London and Hartford, Connecticut, Teneriffe in the Canaries, and Antigua in the West Indies. Typical of the reports by young Samuel Winthrop of his progress in securing the last-named contacts are these sentences from a letter of 1648 to his father:

Captain Clement everet a Justice of peace [in St. Christopher], who being our country man and hearing our name vsed me verry Courtiously, and assisted me much in my law suites which were there verry many. Justice Froth, who was of your acquantance in England (as he informes me), was his Granfather. I haue left in his handes my busines in St. Christpors.[2]

Jean Bailly of La Rochelle conducted his West Indian trade through two relatives in the Caribbean islands, especially Clerbaut Bergier in Martinique. But the most complete family commercial system of which we have any knowledge is that of the Hutchinsons; it is an almost ideal type of this sort of arrangement.

The Hutchinson family trading unit was based upon the continuous flow of manufactures exported from London by the affluent Richard Hutchinson to his brothers Samuel and Edward and his nephews Elisha and Eliakim in Boston, Massachusetts. They, together with Thomas Savage, who had married Richard's sister, retailed the goods in the Bay area and, through middlemen, sold also to the inland settlers. They conducted a large trade with the West Indies, sending provisions and cattle in exchange for cotton and sugar which they sold for credit on London. This West Indian trade of the Hutchinsons was largely handled for them by Peleg Sanford of Portsmouth, Rhode Island, whose mother was another sister of Richard and who was, hence, cousin and nephew of the Boston merchants of the family. Peleg, who had started his career as a commercial agent in the West Indies, exported their horses and provisions to Barbados where they were sold by his brothers, the Barbadian merchants William and Elisha Sanford.

The Hutchinsons with their Rhode Island and West Indian relations formed a self-conscious family group which considered it unfortunate but not unnatural that Edward Hutchinson should go to jail, as he did in 1667, as a consequence of his support of his nephew Peleg in a law suit.

Since commerce was so dependent upon personal relationships, the weaving of a network of correspondences was greatly facilitated by the migrations within the colonial area. Many mainland settlers transplanted themselves to the Caribbean islands and became factors in the West Indies for the merchant friends they had left behind. On the other hand, several merchants were involved in the movement of people among and out of the West Indies, and some of them became residents of the continental colonies. Thus, John Parris, a relative of the New Englander John Hull, moved from the West Indies to Boston where he engaged in large operations in an attempt to stock his Barbados plantation with slaves. Men who moved south to the Indies or north to the continent carried with them friendships and a knowledge of affairs in their old home towns which were used in broadening the foreign contacts of the colonial merchants.

A further consequence of the personal nature of commercial ties in this early period was the consistency, long before mercantilist legislation became effective, with which Frenchmen and Britishers dealt with their fellow nationals in trade. Correspondences with foreigners were difficult to establish and maintain. To British colonials in this period, it seemed that little reliance could be placed on the bonds of Frenchmen who desired nothing more than the collapse of the British settlements in the New World. In long-distance transactions Englishmen preferred to deal with their relatives and friends who, if necessary, could be brought to law in the British courts far more easily than could Frenchmen. Richard Wharton, one of the most enterprising colonial merchants of the seventeenth century, failed to extend his contacts into the French West Indies because of his inability to secure reliable French correspondents. The later enforcement of mercantilist legislation was greatly facilitated by this early tendency of overseas merchants to favor connections with, if not relatives or old friends, at least fellow countrymen.

Through channels of trade created by personal ties among Europeans scattered about the Atlantic world flowed not only physical commodities but the human communications that related the settlers to European life. The orbits of commerce formed by lines drawn between the fixed points of correspondents helped shape the character of urban development and the structure of society in the colonial settlements.

On the American continent, as certain trading centers became poles in the primary cycles of trade, others slipped back toward ruralism. In the passage of generations the communities involved in the major orbits came into closer cultural relations with Europe than they did with some of the neighboring backwoods villages. The Boston merchants' meeting place in their Townhouse Exchange was in every way, except geographically, closer to the "New-England walke" on the London Exchange than to the market places of most inland towns. Study of any of the continental trading regions reveals the varying degrees of provincialism that followed the solidification of the routes of commerce.

In New England, the most important commercial center in North America during the seventeenth century, Boston, with its excellent harbor and access to the provincial government and to flourishing agricultural markets, became the major terminus of traffic originating in Europe. With the exception of Salem and Charlestown, the other promising mercantile centers of the 1630's and 1640's fell back into secondary economic roles and relative seclusion from the cultural life of the Atlantic community. Plymouth, which had been the first trading center east of Manhattan, was described in 1660 as "a poor small Towne now, The People being removed into Farmes in the Country," and New Haven, whose optimistic merchant leaders had laid out "stately and costly houses," was "not so glorious as once it was," with its "Merchants either dead or come away, the rest gotten to their Farmes." [3] This is not to say that these essentially rural districts had no trade. On the contrary, there were men in the Connecticut River towns and along Long Island Sound who managed a considerable exchange of goods; but their dealings were different from those of the Bostonians. Engaged in secondary orbits of trade, they sent small but steady flows of local produce only to other American colonies or occasionally to the West Indies. The Connecticut River grandees were, like the younger Pynchon, primarily landed squires and only secondarily merchants. The few men in the small coastal villages who did devote themselves primarily to trade operated within a commercial sphere subordinate to that of the Bostonians and the Dutchmen.

Life in the inland areas and in the minor ports came to differ significantly from that in the commercial centers in direct contact with Europe. While Boston and New York assumed characteristics of British provincial outports and while their leading residents groped for an understanding of their place as colonials in British society, towns like Scarborough, Maine, and Wethersfield, Connecticut, became models of new types of communities; and their inhabitants, restricted in experience to the colonial world, came to lack the standards by which to measure or even to perceive their provincialism. Fashion, patterns for styles of living, and the emulative spirit of provincialism followed the routes of trade, which, throughout the colonial world, became important social boundaries.

This fact became particularly evident in the last third of the century when national rivalries, both military and economic, required the presence of official representatives in the colonies from the home countries. These officers, civil and military, settled for the most part in the large trading centers, close to the main objects of their supervision. Their presence in what might be called the focuses of the primary trading orbits had a most important social consequence. These home country representatives were quickly surrounded by a number of Europeans new to the colonies: men seeking careers in the quickly expanding colonial administrations. Customs functionaries, lesser bureaucrats, fortune hunters in official positions—these newcomers, grouped around the chief European representatives, came to constitute colonial officialdom, which in all the main colonial ports became a major social magnet for the residents. For not only did it represent cosmopolitan fashion and political influence, but, in its access to those who controlled government contracts and who wielded the weapon of customs regulations, it offered great economic opportunities.

Toward these groups, therefore, moved every colonial with ambition and the slightest hope of success. The threshold of officialdom became a great divide in the society of the commercial towns. Next to this principle of association, "class," in the traditional European sense, was meaningless. In Europe the word "merchant" meant not only an occupation but a status and a way of life. In America, where, as Madam Knight discovered in her famous journey of 1704, they gave the title of merchant to every backwoods huckster,[4] trade was not so much a way of life as a way of making money, not a social condition but an economic activity. Similarly, how could the well-known American mariner, Captain Cyprian Southack, be prevented from describing himself, as he did on occasion, as "gent."?[5]

The limits of officialdom, however, were palpable. No merchant would confuse failure with success in obtaining favors from customs officials or in gaining contracts for provisions and naval stores. It was well worth a merchant's noting, as Samuel Sewall did in his *Diary,* that he was not invited to the governor's dinner parties or to the extravagant funerals staged by the members of his group.[6]

It was as true in the seventeenth century as it is now that the introduction of an important new social barrier necessarily intrudes upon a variety of interests. The advent of officialdom was attended by upheavals throughout the Atlantic world. Wherever we turn in this period we find evidence of social dislocation as successful resident entrepreneurs came to terms with this important new force in the colonial world.

One of the first successful agricultural districts in Carolina was Albemarle County. Behind the barrier of shifting sand bars that blocked Albemarle Sound to all but the most shallow-draft ocean-going vessels lived, in the 1670's, approximately 3,000 settlers—farmers, coastal backwoodsmen, many of them tough, stubborn refugees from better-organized communities. Their one cash crop was tobacco, of which they prepared nearly one million pounds a year. This they disposed of to northerners on peddling voyages in exchange for the commodities they needed. The Navigation Law of 1673 levied duties on tobacco at the port of lading, and Albemarle, like all other commercial centers, was soon visited by a customs collector. The settlers resisted, fearing an increase in the price of their goods if their tobacco was taxed, and they forced the governor to remit to the traders three farthings in every penny taken. In 1677 the appointment of an imperious collector of customs determined to enforce the law led to a rebellion of the settlers headed by one John Culpeper. Until the legal authorities could regain control, Culpeper acted as collector, formed a temporary government, and barred the royal comptroller and surveyor of customs at Albemarle from the exercise of his office.

Culpeper's rebellion, though it was soon quelled and finds little mention in American history, was a significant event. It is a simplified example of what was taking place throughout the colonies. We do not yet have a full account of Leisler's rebellion which kept New York in turmoil for two years. But when we do, it will be found that it was in great part the culmination of resentments that accompanied the introduction of English officialdom into that province. Leisler's career, in fact, can only be understood against the background of family rivalries that grew up around this pre-eminent principle of association.[7] Edmund Andros, famous for his difficulties as the governor of the Dominion of New England, had a less notorious but equally important reign as the Duke of York's governor in New York. In this position he precipitated social differences among the merchants who resisted when they could not take advantage of his influence. He was finally recalled on charges of excessive fee-taking and profiteering.

The rebellion of 1689, which overthrew his administration of the Dominion of New England, divided the northern merchants on lines not of ideology but of interests defined by the degree of proximity to officialdom. No ideology, no religious belief, no abstract political principle or party loyalty separated the Boston merchants Richard Wharton and Charles Lidget, but in 1689 they were on opposite sides of the political fence. Lidget ended up in the Boston jail with Andros because his connections, inherited from his father who had built the family fortune on the timber he sold to the Navy mast contractors, linked him to the leaders of the official group. Wharton died in the midst of his fight for the removal of Andros whose favor he had been denied. The fact that Lidget was one of the founders of the first Anglican Church in New England does not indicate a religious or ideological orientation different from Wharton's. The latter, if he was not an active Anglican, certainly was not a dissenter. Both men married heiress daughters of nonconformist New Englanders.

In the West Indies the same principle was at work during most of the seventeenth century. But toward the end of the century controversies touched off by the intrusion of officialdom diminished in the islands as a consequence of the consolidation of large plantations and the growth of absenteeism. The resident nonofficial population became less active politically as the large planters returned to the home country, leaving their estates in the hands of managers and agents. But battles over the economic benefits of political and social advantage were not ended; they were merely transferred to London where they punctuated the history of the West India interest.

By the end of the century this principle of association in the commercial centers was deeply woven into the fabric of American society. Its importance did not diminish thereafter. Recently, Oliver Dickerson in his book *The Navigation Acts and the American Revolution* [8] destroyed a number of myths by pointing out the importance of what he called "customs racketeering." From his researches it appears that the merchant group was as deeply divided on the eve of the Revolution as it was in 1689. Both John Hancock and Thomas Hutchinson were leading Boston merchants, but the former was clearly victimized by the strategy of the Hutchinson-Bernard clique which controlled the channels of prerogative. And in South Carolina, Henry Laurens, probably the richest merchant in the southern colonies, whose mercantile connections were with the opponents of the King's Friends, suffered equally from the rapacity of the official group.

Further study of the merchants as a social group may reveal that this principle of association, which emerged as an important social force when the nations of Europe undertook to draw together the threads of trade spun by seventeenth-century entrepreneurs, was a major determinant of the movement that led to Revolution.

NOTES

1. Arthur P. Newton, *The European Nations in the West Indies, 1493–1688* (London: A. and C. Black, 1933), p. 149.

2. Samuel Winthrop, Fayal, to John Winthrop, January 10, 1648, *Winthrop Papers* (Boston: Massachusetts Historical Society, 1929–47), V, 196.

3. Samuel Maverick, *A Briefe Discription of New England and the Severall Townes therein, together with the Present Government thereof* ([ca. 1660]; reprinted in *Proceedings of the Massachusetts Historical Society*, Ser. 2, I), pp. 243, 245.

4. *The Journal of Madam Knight* (New York: Peter Smith, 1935), p. 40.

5. *Calendar of State Papers, Colonial Series, America and West Indies, 1712–1714*, ¶ 520.

6. *Diary of Samuel Sewall*, April 13, 1686; June 15, 19, and October 3, 1688; December 8, 1690 (*Collections of the Massachusetts Historical Society*, Ser. 5, V, 132, 217, 228, 338).

7. Jerome R. Reich's *Leisler's Rebellion: A Study of Democracy in New York, 1664–1720* (Chicago: University of Chicago Press, 1953) came to my attention after the writing of this paper. The information it contains bears out the above interpretation. See especially pp. 37–40, 44, 50–51, 58–59, 70, 71–73, 87, 98, 126, 138–41, 143, 160–66.

8. Philadelphia: University of Pennsylvania Press, 1951.

3

British Mercantilism and
the American Economy

In THEORY, and certainly in practice, British mercantilism conferred certain advantages upon the American colonies and, at the same time, imposed important constraints. Mercantilism was designed to maximize the self-sufficiency of the empire, to assure the profits of trade and shipping to British subjects, and to foster the development of all parts of the empire in such a way as to enhance the wealth and power of the mother country. From an early period, however, the British government found it difficult to harmonize conflicting economic interests within a diverse, expanding empire. In some cases—notably, that of the Molasses Act of 1733—such conflicts of interest were resolved only by permitting almost universal evasion of key mercantilist statutes. Yet until 1763 restrictive mercantilist legislation created no very serious political crises for the British in America, and the colonies prospered under English rule.

After 1763, a new objective entered into British policy formulation: the need to support, through increased American revenues, a standing army in the colonies. There followed a series of Parliamentary acts and administrative adjustments, all perfectly consistent with traditional mercantilist objectives but involving abandonment of the policy of benevolent non-enforcement. These new acts and administrative reforms provoked the conflict over political liberties and the final separation of the colonies from England in 1776.

During the political crisis of the 1770's, both in the colonies and in England some argued that mercantilism had become so disadvantageous to the Americans as to make revolution almost inevitable. One school of historians has accepted this argument, asserting that British policies imposed intolerable limits upon the growth of a rapidly maturing, vigorous economy. They conclude from this that the Revolution was indeed an inevitable response to post-1763 British acts, and they portray the economic situation of the colonies as basic to an understanding of the movement for American independence. According to another view, however, mercantilism was on balance beneficial to the colonies; and students subscribing to this thesis either conclude that Revolutionary leaders who emphasized the economic disadvantages of mercantilist policy rested their case on spurious assumptions, or else argue that economic issues could not have been important, however much the colonists debated them.

In the article which follows, the colonial historian Lawrence A. Harper attempts to measure the impact of mercantilist policy. Relevant as his theme is to interpreting the Revolution, it is also valuable for the broader question with which it is concerned: to what extent did the imperial tie influence the pace and character of American economic development in the colonial era?

THE EFFECT OF THE NAVIGATION ACTS
ON THE THIRTEEN COLONIES

Lawrence A. Harper

The English Navigation Acts have long been a topic of great interest to both British and American historians, but there has been no agreement as to their effect upon the colonies. The opposite extremes are represented by George Bancroft, who viewed the Acts as horrible instruments of English tyranny against which the colonies nobly arose to throw off the oppressive yoke, and George Louis

Reprinted by permission of the publishers from *The Era of the American Revolution*, edited by Richard B. Morris (New York: The Columbia University Press, 1939), pp. 3–39.

Beer, who veered to the other extreme in pointing out that the measures were not unfair and who maintained that the old colonial system was so nicely balanced that both the colonies and the mother country bore burdens for the good of the Empire and shared in the general advantages.

The ultimate answer to the question must be deferred until more detailed knowledge of colonial trade and commerce is available. Work which has been done and research now in progress make it possible at this time to outline the factors involved in the problems and to formulate tentative hypotheses.[1] The difficulties are many, but most critics of attempts to solve the problem emphasize two points: that the existence of smuggling renders it impossible for us to determine what happened when the laws were in force and that any conclusions which we may reach will be mere conjecture, since we cannot reorder the past to determine what would have happened if the laws had never been enacted. Neither objection, however, should prove insuperable.

Although the exact extent of smuggling cannot be determined with accuracy because of the nature of the smugglers' activities, we can establish its limits. We know that great quantities of European goods, of tobacco, and of rice, the three most important items regulated, passed through England as the law required. In comparison with the volume of such trade, the amount of goods smuggled was necessarily small because by far the greater percentage of colonial shipping is known to have been engaged in legal trades, and, however illicit their intentions, the smugglers could not find sufficient cargo capacity to present formidable competition. Moreover, the very existence of so great a legal commerce discloses that the community was not a unit in violating the laws. There were "fair traders" whose own financial interests led them to oppose smuggling, which if unchecked might have driven them out of business. Most important of all, the continued existence of legal trade implies either that smuggling was negligible or that it encountered sufficient hazards to equalize the burdens that the laws placed upon legal commerce. As a consequence we can concentrate our attention upon legal trade in the belief that indirectly the English commercial system exercised a similar influence over illicit trade.[2]

Although we cannot state with absolute certainly "what might have been" if there had been no Navigation Acts, we can attain a degree of probability far beyond mere conjecture by comparing what actually happened when the laws were in force with conditions which existed when their restraints were removed. Lack of data for the seventeenth century prevents much comparison of conditions before and after the enactment of the laws, but we do have adequate figures which permit us to compare the course of trade before and after the Revolution freed the thirteen colonies from British commercial regulations.[3] The fact that in the nineteenth century the former thirteen colonies were economically much more developed than in the seventeenth century, when they did not even number thirteen, is not fatal to our proposed analysis. The Britain of 1776 also had far outstripped the England of 1660 in commercial importance. At the earlier date Holland was the acknowledged commercial, industrial, and financial center of Europe. It was the Dutch who paid most, sold cheapest, carried goods most economically, and extended the most liberal terms of credit.[4] Under a system of free economy American trade would naturally have gravitated to the Netherlands. Dutch capital would have sought investment in the colonies. In fact both developments occurred and were the principal reasons for legislative restraints.[5] By 1776 Britain had taken Holland's place as the predominant trading center. The commercial ties which would thus naturally develop between Britain and the United States were strengthened after cotton became the South's chief crop and the Industrial Revolution made Britain the chief cotton manufacturer. Thus conclusions based upon evidence that America's trade turned to countries other than Britain after 1776 should underestimate rather than overstate the tendency which existed in 1660.

The general history of the acts is too well known to require a chronological account of their development or any extended introduction concerning their provisions. We will do best to pass directly to an analysis of the regulations, proceeding from the simplest to the most complex, from those dealing with manufacturing and shipbuilding to those concerning shipping and trade.

The rule forbidding shipment of colonial wool or woolen manufactures outside the border of a colony appears to have been passed primarily as a precautionary measure [6] and to have had no material restraint upon colonial activity. Although there are few records of shipping for the seventeenth century, those which we do have for Massachusetts from 1686 to 1688 disclose no shipments of such products when they would still have been legal, and the statistics of American exports following the Revolution fail to disclose any potential foreign market from which the colonists were excluded.

Regardless of legislation the colonial woolen industry would probably have been confined primarily to the production of homespun garments. The exigencies of frontier life did not provide the labor to establish the industry on a broader scale.[7]

The restraints on the colonial manufacture of hats, however, present another story. The labor problem here did not offer so great an obstacle, and the local supply of furs acted as a stimulus. By 1732, when the company of felt makers in London prevailed upon Parliament to forbid any colonial exportations of hats, to require a seven-year apprenticeship, to exclude Negroes from the industry, and to limit each manufacturer to two apprentices,[8] a flourishing industry had developed, especially in New England and New York, which were exporting hats to neighboring colonies, the West Indies, and southern Europe. The law doubtless was not perfectly enforced, but there is reason to suspect that it hindered colonial activity. Before its passage England exported only 2,650 dozen beaver hats to all her colonies in 1698 out of a total of 5,761 dozen, while in 1773 her total exports were 13,000 dozen, of which 9,562 dozen went to the colonies. Moreover, the importation of hats from Britain declined sharply after the Revolution, and the United States once again began to export them to southern Europe, the West Indies, and South America.[9]

The regulations governing iron represented a clash between conflicting English interests, the natural result of which was legislation that on the one hand granted colonial pig and bar iron preferential treatment when entering England and on the other forbade the erection of any additional slitting mills in the colonies or the exportation of colonial iron outside the Empire.[10] Studies of the subject by Bining suggest that the preferential duties had little effect upon the colonial development, since the American market was much the greater factor in its growth, and that the prohibition of the erection of new mills was openly defied—the most flagrant instance being that of the Pennsylvania colonial assembly which gave financial aid to Whitehead Humphries in developing his steel mill.[11] But it seems unwise to dismiss the law as immaterial. Although some investors undoubtedly were willing to assume the risk, capital is notoriously timid, and many investors probably directed their funds into other channels where there was not added to the customary hazards of starting a new industry the danger that their competitors in England might ruin it merely by persuading colonial officials to enforce the law. In this connection it is interesting to note that during the twenty-five years from 1750 to 1775 only thirty-eight iron-producing establishments were founded in Pennsylvania and Delaware, whereas the number was almost doubled in the ten years from 1790 to 1800.[12] The multiplicity of other factors which intervened forbid any dogmatic conclusions, but the statistics tend to support rather than to confute the theory that the Iron Act had some restraining influence.

In the field of colonial shipbuilding, we find that the industry benefited from the English legislation, but the gain was probably not great. Although the Navigation Acts discouraged use of foreign-built vessels in the English merchant marine, they did not forbid it until 1786, except in the colonial trade, and in the seventeenth century, when protection afforded by the laws would have been of the greatest aid to the colonial industry, the frequent grant of dispensations lessened their effect.[13] Moreover, the colonists apparently could hold their own in free competition with foreign builders, such as the Dutch, because colonial shipbuilding had attained respectable proportions before 1660, and American ships found a market abroad without the benefit of protection after the Revolution.[14] Certainly as far as the English builders were concerned the colonists proved formidable rivals. In 1724, the Thames shipbuilders sought unsuccessfully to procure protection against their competition,[15] and in 1739, when permission was granted to ship West Indian sugar to ports south of Cape Finisterre without going to England, the privilege was at first confined to English-built vessels although later amended to include the cheaper, colonial-built vessels.[16] It has been said that by the time of the American Revolution one-third of the British merchant marine was colonial-built, and the thirteen colonies were building 28,747 tons per year.[17] Yet American shipbuilding was not dependent upon sales to Britain, because after independence closed that outlet the tonnage built in the United States was at least 29,606 tons by 1790 and 154,624 tons in 1815.[18] Apparently the benefits conferred by opening the English market for the sale of ships were offset by the limitation of the American market which resulted from the restrictions placed upon colonial shipping.

For most practical purposes, colonial-owned ships were entitled to the same privileges as British-owned vessels, in contradistinction to foreign vessels, which were excluded from the plantation trade. Yet the protection thereby afforded does not appear to be very important. In the early stages of American maritime development navigation would naturally be limited to the coasting trade, in which small colonial vessels would actually have an advantage over their greatest potential rivals, the larger, ocean-going Dutch fly-boats. Later, when the colonies had developed to such an extent that one might expect their shipping to branch out into broader fields, we find it mostly confined to the coasting and West Indian trade, four-fifths of the traffic crossing the Atlantic in 1769–71 being carried in British bottoms.[19] Although we cannot conclusively demonstrate the connection between this phenomenon and the laws, it probably resulted from the natural tendency of the British merchant, who controlled the disposal of the goods, to use his own or his friend's shipping. Certainly there seems to be significance in the fact that after control over colonial trade passed from British hands the situation was reversed, and four-fifths of the trans-Atlantic trade in 1821 was carried by American rather than British vessels.[20]

The rules governing shipping were simple as compared with the complex maze of restrictions, duties, preferential rates, drawbacks, penalties, and charter monopolies which governed trade. Any one desiring to make order out of the confusion must proceed warily, step by step.

Trade with Africa and in America was subjected to few regulations of importance. Until 1698 colonists who wished to go to Africa ran afoul of the Royal African Company's privileges,[21] but thereafter they met no important hindrances in trading with that continent. Except for the assessment in 1673 of the so-called "plantation duties" upon the transshipment between colonies of the enumerated commodities,[22] trade in nonenumerated American products was free until the Molasses Act of 1733.[23] It can be disregarded as not being enforced, but the acts of 1764 and 1765 cannot.[24] The resentment aroused by the attempts to collect duties upon foreign molasses and sugar demonstrates beyond question the importance placed upon trade with the foreign West Indies; but there is room for argument as to whether this trade would have been deemed so important if England had not restrained American commerce with Europe.

The legislation governing colonial importations from Europe and Asia required that with a few exceptions, such as Madeira wine, salt for the fisheries, and provisions and servants from Scotland and Ireland, all goods be procured in England or, after 1707, in Britain. Bounties were granted on the export of certain commodities, including gunpowder, linen, sailcloth, silk, and refined sugar,[25] but these bounties were not special favors to the colonies, being granted on exportations to all countries and designed to develop British manufactures. Merchants reëxporting goods during the greater part of the colonial period were repaid all the duties on most commodities which had been paid upon importation to England, except one-half of the Old Subsidy. Yet the fact that drawbacks were usually allowed must not cause us to forget that the duties had been assessed and that when England wished extra revenue she could decrease the drawback as she did in 1764,[26] or that she could withhold it entirely when she wished to protect her industries, as she did in the case of unwrought iron or steel, cordage, sailcloth, unwrought hemp, paper, and oysters.[27]

The artificiality of the indirect routing of European goods is revealed clearly by the sharp decline of goods shipped in that manner after the Revolution. During the colonial period such goods averaged almost one-quarter of the value of the thirteen colonies' imports of British, European, and Asian goods (excepting such imports as Madeira wine and salt, which were not covered by the laws), but they represented less than two percent in the nineteenth century.[28] The effect of these burdens upon the colonists' purchases of European goods was to increase the proportion of British manufactures which they acquired, a tendency which was reversed after independence. Despite the influence of established consumer habits, commercial connections, and long-time credits, Britain, which had produced almost 73 percent of the goods imported by the thirteen colonies from elsewhere than Africa or America in 1773, supplied only 54 percent in 1799, 55 percent in 1821, and 45 percent in 1840.[29]

In turning to the legislation governing exportations from the colonies, we find that only the enumerated commodities were regulated, but they constituted one-half of the total shipments from the continental colonies in 1770 and much more of those from the British West Indies.[30] Since such goods had to be marketed through Britain, we must endeavor to understand the British customs system. As Parliament confessed when reconstructing it in 1787, the manner of charging and computing the duties was "in many instances intricate and complicated, and productive of much embarrassment to the persons who are to pay the same, as well of great perplexity on the accounts of the public revenue," [31] an acknowledgment which historians will agree to be a masterpiece of understatement. It will only add to the confusion if we attempt to trace the evolution of the various provisions, which frequently

ARTICLE AND UNIT OF MEASUREMENT	BOUNTY AND PREFERENCE	IMPORT DUTY	DUTY RETAINED, EXPORT TAX, AND BOUNTY REPAID	QUANTITY IMPORTED AND TOTAL ESTIMATED VALUE	PERCENTAGE REËXPORTED
ACT OF 1660					
Cotton wool (lb.)	$\frac{15\%(P)}{20}$	free	5% (E)	2,386,509 £78,576	1.11
Ginger (cwt.)	£2 0s. 8d. $\frac{7\frac{1}{2}(P)}{20}$	9s. 6d. $\frac{4}{20}$	5d. $\frac{14}{20}$ (D)	8,280 £7,153	69.87
Sugar (white) (cwt.)	14s. 5d. $\frac{16}{20}$(P)	£1 1s. 1d.		none	none
Sugar (brown) (cwt.)	13s. 0d. $\frac{18}{20}$(P)	6s. 3d. $\frac{18}{20}$ (P)		1,784,499 £2,025,983	10.46
Fustic (ton)		free		761 £6,838	64.13
Logwood (cwt.)		free		44,790 £26,583	117·75 [a]
Other dyewoods (ton)		free		780 £7,665	46.03
ACT OF 1705					
Molasses (ton)	£7 10s.(P)	£2 11s. 4d.	6s. 4d.(D)	61 £797	12.05
ACT OF 1764					
Pimento (lb.)		1d. $\frac{14\frac{2}{40}}{20}$	$\frac{2\frac{17}{40}(D)}{20}$	2,282,071 £57,434	103·42 [a]
Coffee (cwt.) [b]	£5 12s.(P)	£1 13s. 6d. $\frac{3}{20}$		44,741 £311,980	109.14 [a]
Cocoa nuts (cwt.)		11s. 11d. $\frac{12\frac{1}{2}}{20}$		7,305 £18,265	94.94

The statutes of enumeration are as follows: 1660—12 Car. II, c. 18; 1705—3 and 4 Anne, c. 3; 1764—4 Geo. III, c. 15. In calculating preferences granted for plantation commodities, comparisons were made with foreign goods carried in British ships and the discriminatory duties on French goods were disregarded. The percentages of goods exported are based upon quantity rather than value.

[a] Presumably the excess of exportations is accounted for by importations held over from previous years.

[b] The preference resulted from the assessment by 5 Geo. III, c. 45, of an "inland duty" on coffee used for domestic consumption.

TABLE 2. GOODS PRODUCED CHIEFLY IN THE THIRTEEN COLONIES, ENUMERATED BEFORE THE REIGN OF GEORGE III

ARTICLE AND UNIT OF MEASUREMENT	BOUNTY AND PREFERENCE	IMPORT DUTY	DUTY RETAINED, EXPORT TAX, AND BOUNTY REPAID	QUANTITY IMPORTED AND TOTAL ESTIMATED VALUE	PERCENTAGE REËXPORTED
ACT OF 1660					
Indigo (lb.)	4d.(B)	free		1,385,139 £87,156	40.12
Tobacco (lb.)[a]	$\dfrac{\text{1s. 10d. }15\frac{19}{20}\text{(P)}}{20}$	$\dfrac{\text{6d. }19\frac{9}{20}}{20}$		100,482,007 £1,006,530	96.27
ACT OF 1705					
Rice (cwt.)	6s. 4d. $1\frac{2}{20}$(P)	free	8d.(E)	468,915 £347,245	79.30
Naval stores[b]					
Tar (last)	$\dfrac{\text{1s. 2d. }1\frac14\text{(P)}}{20}$	9s. 7d. $1\frac{10}{20}$	1s. 2d. $\frac{5}{20}$(D) £3 6s.(B)	7,691 68,847	4.79
Pitch (last)	£3 6s.(B) $\dfrac{\text{1s. 2d. }1\frac14\text{(P)}}{20}$ £1 10s.(B)	9s. 7d. $1\frac{10}{20}$	1s. 2d. $\frac{5}{20}$(D) £1 10s.(B)	2,324 £20,893	.57
Rosin (cwt.)	7d. $\frac{10}{20}$(P)	1s. 3d. $\frac{8}{20}$	1d. $\frac{18}{20}$(D)	none	none[c]
Turpentine (cwt.)	1s. 6d. (ton)(B)	1s. 11d. $\frac{5}{20}$	2d. $\frac{17}{20}$(D) 1s. 6d.(B)	28,652 £13,716	none[c]
Hemp (cwt.)	3s. 2d. $\frac{9}{20}$(P) 6s.(B)	free	6s.(B)	none	none[c]
Masts, yards, and bowsprits (ton)[a]	11d. $\frac{5}{20}$(P) £1 (B)	1s. 11d. $\frac{2}{20}$	2d. $\frac{17}{20}$(D) £1 (B)	4,442 £13,866	none[c]

ACT OF 1722				
Beaver skins (ea.)	1d.	1d.(D) 7d.(E)	6,170 pieces £509	57.81
Other furs (ea.)^e	1d. $8^{29}/40$ doz. $\overline{20}$ to £2 7s. 10d. $1^9/20$ ea. 7d. $3^1/8$ $\overline{20}$	$2^3/5$ doz.(D) $\overline{20}$ to 4s. 9d. ea.(D) $1^3/8$(D) $\overline{20}$	133,153 pieces £7,447	95.56
Copper ore (cwt.)			382 £48	none

The statutes of enumeration are as follows: 1660—12 Car. II, c. 18; 1705—3 and 4 Anne, c. 3, c. 9; 1722—8 Geo. I, c. 15, c. 18. In calculating preferences granted for plantation commodities, comparisons were made with foreign goods carried in British ships and the discriminatory duties on French goods were disregarded. Although the import figures are for the thirteen colonies and West Indies only, the reëxport percentage has been computed from the total quantity imported from America and the total quantity reëxported from Britain, except in the case of beaver skins and other furs when imports from all areas were included.

^{a} The duties listed are those for bonded tobacco, since 91.06 percent of the tobacco imported into England was this type.

^{b} The figures given for tar are for common tar. Green tar, which received a bounty of £4 a ton in 1773, was seldom imported from the colonies. For ease in comparison, bounties have been converted from tons to units used in assessing duties. The enumeration of rosin lapsed in 1725, of hemp in 1741.

^{c} Here (as elsewhere "none" is listed) most exports are shown not to be colonial products, the remainder being disregarded as negligible or obviously European.

^{d} The duty given is that for middle masts. The duty varied for small and great masts. Yards and bowsprits are included as masts (Albion, Forests and Sea Power, p. xi).

^{e} A duty of $8/20d.$ each was charged on the exportation of black fox skins. Import duties on furs ranged from a low for mole to a high for black fox.

TABLE 3. GOODS PRODUCED CHIEFLY IN THE THIRTEEN COLONIES, FIRST ENUMERATED IN THE REIGN OF GEORGE III

ARTICLE AND UNIT OF MEASUREMENT	BOUNTY AND PREFERENCE	IMPORT DUTY	DUTY RETAINED, EXPORT TAX, AND BOUNTY REPAID	QUANTITY IMPORTED AND TOTAL ESTIMATED VALUE	PERCENTAGE REËXPORTED
ACT OF 1764					
Whale fins (ton)	£81 14s. 6d. to £84 2s. (P)[a]	free to £2 7s. 6d.	none to £1 3s. 9d. (D)	10 / £1,641	1.20
Raw silk (lb.)	1s. 3d. (P) 25% ad valorem (B)	free		1,317 / £1,119	none[b]
Hides and skins (ea.)[c]		$14\frac{2\%}{40}$ ea. to 2s. 4d. $14\frac{1}{2}$ ea. $/20$	$1\frac{7}{80}d.$ to 2d. $\frac{17}{20}$ (D)[d] $/20$	387,472 / £45,129	25.75
Pot and pearl ashes (bbl.)	12s. 3d. $\frac{15}{20}$ (P)	free		27,407 / £68,576	12.84
Iron to Europe (ton)					
Bar	£2 8s. 6d. $\frac{3}{20}$ (P)	free		847 / £8,567	2.36
Pig	4s. 9d. $\frac{9}{20}$ (P)	free		3,153 / £4,595	none[b]
Lumber to Europe					
Staves (per 120)	6d. $17\frac{3}{4}$ to £1 2s. 10d. $\frac{9}{20}$ (P) $/20$ from £6 per 2,400 to £6 per 1,200 (B)[e]	free		52,080 / £34,010	14.61

Headings (per 120)	1s. 10d. $\frac{18}{20}$(P) £6 per 1,200(B)	free	392 £184	none
Deals, planks, and boards (per 120)	1s. 5d. 3¼ to £4 5s. 10d. $\frac{10}{20}$(P) 20	free	varied quantities £29,606	none
All other	10s. per 120(B) various	free	varied quantities f £25,404	none
ACT OF 1766				
All nonenumerated goods to Europe north of Cape Finisterre	various		various g £425,778	small

The statutes of enumeration are as follows: 1764—4 Geo. III, c. 15; 1766—6 Geo. III, c. 52.

In calculating preferences granted for plantation commodities, comparisons were made with foreign goods carried in British ships and the discriminatory duties on French goods were disregarded. Although the import figures are for articles from the thirteen colonies and the West Indies only, the reëxport percentage has been computed from the total quantity imported and the total quantity reëxported from Britain.

a In addition a bounty was allowed upon certain ships in the whaling trade, effective Dec. 25, 1771 (11 Geo. III, c. 38).

b The negligible reëxportations which occurred were attributed to European rather than to colonial importations because of the comparative unimportance of the latter.

c The range in duty is from that for sheep to that for moose. In distinguishing between hides, skins, and furs, deer, moose, elk, sheep, cow, ox, calf, and horsehide are listed as hides and skins; other skins, such as fox, bear, etc., are listed with beaver skins and furs. The statistics for deer skins have been reduced to a common denominator on the assumption that the average skin weighed 1½ lbs. Infra, note 42.

d There was also an export tax of 3s. 4d. per 100 on sheep pelts.

e The bounty was granted only to white-oak staves and headings. Entry figures do not give the composition of the staves and headings listed and all have been assumed to be of white oak.

f The value given here does not include that of foreign reëxports, such as mahogany, of which £14,434 was reëxported from the thirteen colonies and £40,130 shipped direct from the West Indies.

g Computed by subtracting enumerated goods from the total British imports from the thirteen colonies and West Indies.

changed in matters of detail. Our best chance to obtain a working knowledge of the rules is to analyze them at the eve of the Revolution when British mercantilism had attained its maturity. In the case of the British West Indies an analysis discloses that the benefits they received outweighed the burdens incurred (see Table 1, page 49).

The great bulk of the shipments to Britain in both quantity and value consisted of sugar. All except 10.46 percent was consumed in England, and 98.7 percent of the small portion reëxported was shipped to Ireland, which cannot really be classed as a foreign country for the purposes of this discussion. Originally, the enumeration of sugar had inconvenienced the West Indian planters, but by 1773 the greater fertility of the foreign islands enabled their rivals to undersell them by at least five shillings per hundredweight.[32] Thus, the preferential duty of 13s. 0d.$1\frac{8}{20}$ per hundredweight was a real boon since it virtually excluded foreign competition from the English market. Calculated on the conservative basis of five shillings a hundred, it appears that the West Indies benefited to the extent of £446,125 a year and were assessed very little in duties retained on reëxported West Indian products, the £1,382 collected on Jamaican pimento being the largest item, except for the discriminating duties against Dominican products, which were charged the same rate as French goods.

When we turn to the regulations governing the products of the continental colonies, we find a very different picture. Although there were bounties and preferential duties provided for by law, neither gave, in fact, the same advantage that the preferential rate on sugar accorded the West Indies. Moreover, as can readily be seen from the following chart, the price of many commodities was obviously determined by a world market, and great quantities passed through England merely en route to the Continent.

The requirement beginning in 1767 that all nonenumerated commodities shipped north of Cape Finisterre pass through England made surprisingly little difference to commerce. Such commodities exported from the continental colonies in 1770 amounted to only £117,771, which was 6.7 percent of their shipments to Britain that year, and only 3.4 percent of their entire exports. Moreover, since most of the newly restricted commodities consisted of wheat, flaxseed, or foreign lumber destined for consumption in Britain or Ireland, the regulation had little economic significance.[33] The purpose of the act was probably administrative—to minimize fraudulent shipments. It was easier to detect illicit cargoes by requiring all goods for northern Europe to be unladen in Britain than by an examination upon the high seas. Also the new method prevented the making of claims that shipments of indigo, dyewoods, sugar, and other commodities grown in both the British and foreign plantations were foreign products and therefore not covered by the enumeration when in fact they were of British growth and subject to the law.

Most of the continental products enumerated in 1764 do not appear to have been particularly affected by the new legislation. Despite the bounty, raw silk showed no greater tendency then than now to commercial cultivation in America.[34] The colonies themselves provided a growing market for American iron, and, except for that drawn to England by the preferential duties, there is no reason to expect that any quantity would have made its way to Europe.[35] Certainly little or none did after the Revolution. In the case of lumber, bounties drew a quantity of deals, planks, boards, and white-oak staves to Britain, a few of which were reëxported. Other shipments went to southern Europe and to Ireland, since exportation there had again been made legal only one year after the enumeration.[36] In northern Europe the Baltic forests were too close for American products to attain much success, although they did surprisingly well after the Revolution. Their chief markets had been and were destined to be in the West Indies, with which trade was not restricted.[37] At all events, the enumeration does not seem to have adversely affected the price of staves in the Philadelphia market, which in general was higher after it than before, if we disregard the abnormally high prices during the closing years of the French and Indian War.[38] Although whale fins (whale bones) were enumerated and whale oil was not, both were drawn to Britain by the preferential treatment offered there. After the Revolution the American whaling industry was to find a market for its products in northern Europe. When it recovered from the losses incurred during wartime, it eventually attained much greater success than in the colonial period, but the reasons therefor are another story.[39]

The statistics for pot and pearl ashes and for hides and skins do not answer the question of how they were affected by the acts except to suggest that other factors were more potent. Although no preference was granted upon the importation of pot and pearl ashes, the duty granted upon reëxportation was not great. The quantity shipped from the thirteen colonies increased from 2,447 tons in

1773 to 8,599 tons in 1790, and was 7,164 tons in 1799, 8,553 tons in 1821, and 5,572 tons in 1840. The destinations varied markedly. In 1773 all, of course, was exported to Britain and comparatively little was reëxported. Britain took 89 percent or more in 1790 and in 1799 either directly or through Ireland and British North America. In 1821, 37.2 percent went to the British Isles and 43 percent to British North America, but in 1840 none went directly to Britain and only 7.2 percent to British North America.[40]

Hides and skins likewise were not materially affected by the customs duties. The chief difference between pre-Revolutionary and post-Revolutionary trade was the decrease in the quantity exported, which naturally resulted from the ruthless slaughter of deer in the colonial period.[41] Apparently England was the best market for about three-quarters of the United States' exports because, except for 1799 (when shipments to Britain dropped to 55.1 percent), she took approximately that percentage. Also it would seem to follow that it was cheaper to ship the remainder directly to its destination.[42]

Similarly, other factors appear to have played a greater part than the Navigation Acts in the production of copper ore and in the fur trade's development. The mine in New Jersey, news of which led to copper ore's enumeration in 1722,[43] produced 338 casks of ore for shipment to Britain and 110 casks for Holland in 1721, but production of that ore was not destined to be of great economic importance. Shipments from New York from 1720 to 1734 averaged slightly more than 400 casks and 200 barrels,[44] while the total quantity exported was only 19 tons in 1773, and none is listed in the post-Revolutionary years studied.

As for furs, their enumeration in 1722 does not appear to have had an immediately detrimental effect upon the volume of exports at New York, although 30 to 40 percent had been sent to Holland during the seven years preceding.[45] The fur trade of the thirteen colonies was destined to decline in comparative importance,[46] but the causes were other than legislative. Most of the furs from the thirteen colonies were of the cheaper sort, muskrat, martin, and raccoon, and the acquisition of Canada in 1763 provided a new source of supply for the more valuable otter, beaver, mink, fox, wolf, bear, and wolverine. Only 4.8 percent of the beaver skins shipped to Britain in 1773 came from the thirteen colonies, while their shipments formed 41.8 percent of the total of other furs. Most of the furs imported were reëxported, to the dismay of the

London hatters, who had been losing their export trade to the French despite the fact that after 1763 the latter had to obtain their raw materials from Britain. Parliament attempted to help the hatters in 1764 when it repealed the old duty of 7d. on each beaver skin imported, all but 3d. of which had been repaid upon reëxportation, and substituted an import duty of 1d. without benefit of drawback, together with an export tax of 7d. per skin.[47] Except for beaver skins, however, the taxes not drawn back probably did not seriously affect trade. Unfortunately, statistics of post-Revolutionary trade show no consistent trend and consequently throw little light upon the rout s that it might have followed if it had been unrestrained.[48]

The bounties granted for colonial naval stores had a greater effect than the restrictions placed upon their exportation.[49] By 1716, they at least permitted England to obtain most of her tar, pitch, rosin, and turpentine from her colonies rather than from the Baltic. When the bounties were discontinued from 1725 to 1729, shipments of turpentine continued to cross the Atlantic, but those of pitch and tar fell off markedly.[50] Exportations of tar and pitch diminished similarly after the Revolution, but those of rosin and turpentine increased.[51] If the Philadelphia quotations can be trusted, however, and if other circumstances were not exceptional, the prices of pitch and tar were determined by colonial conditions rather than by the bounty because from 1725 to 1729, contrary to what one would expect, they were higher rather than lower both before and after the five-year lapse in the bounty.[52] Hemp was offered a bounty also, but only 86 tons made its way to England in 1770, and none in 1773. The course of trade ran in the other direction, more than 1,000 tons being shipped from Britain to New England alone in 1773. Judging from the lack of any large shipments after the Revolution,[53] the transportation of masts across the Atlantic, which totaled 3,043 tons valued at £16,616 in 1770, was the result of artificial stimulation. In all, the various bounties cost the British government £1,471,719, but whatever may have been the appreciation of the chief beneficiary, North Carolina, gratitude in New England was overwhelmed by hostility to the restrictions of the "Broad Arrow" policy which reserved the best trees for His Majesty's Navy.[54]

The extent of the burden placed upon rice does not appear at first glance. Permission was granted in 1730 to export rice south of Cape Finisterre and in 1764 to ship it to any part of America south of Georgia,[55] but other shipments, which formed about one-half of the total in 1770, were limited to the Empire. Until the British desire to develop a starch industry caused colonial rice to be made free, it normally paid the same duty on entering Britain as foreign rice, 6s. $4\frac{12}{20}d$. a hundredweight, all of which could be drawn back upon reëxportation except 7d. and $1\frac{2}{20}$ per hundredweight. Although removal of import duties did not become a definite policy until 1773, a series of annual exemptions date it back to 1767. The gain, however, was primarily to the British consumer, because an export tax of 8d. per hundredweight was added when the import duty was removed.[56] The colonial producer was more interested in the world price, since 79 percent of the rice shipped to Britain was reëxported. After the Revolution, shipments to Britain dropped from 457,072 hundredweight in 1773 to 197,849 hundredweight in 1790 and even less thereafter.[57] The United States lost the southern European market but generally improved its position by gains in the West Indies and South America and by taking over the northern European market, especially in Germany, Holland, and France, which had previously been supplied by English merchants.[58]

The cultivation of indigo in Carolina and Georgia was undoubtedly stimulated by the bounty granted in Britain, which totaled £145,032 for the years 1749–73.[59] Strange to relate, indigo benefited most when the bounty was lowered in 1770 from 6d. to 4d. a pound, the explanation of the apparent paradox being that the 6d. had to be repaid upon reëxportation and the 4d. did not.[60] Consequently the reëxports, which had equaled 15.1 percent of the 647,960 pounds imported into Britain in 1767, rose to 40.12 percent of the 1,385,139 pounds imported in 1773.[61] Although large crops continued to be produced for a few years after the Revolution, the encouragement given by the British government to indigo's production in the British East Indies, together with the increased profitableness of cotton crops, caused the cultivation of indigo to be virtually abandoned.[62]

Tobacco ranked with sugar as the most important of the enumerated commodities but, unlike sugar, it proved a source of profit rather than an expense of mercantilism. Much emphasis has been laid upon the preferential duties granted American tobacco as against the products of Spain's and Portugal's colonies. They unquestionably were high, but there is reason to doubt whether colonial tobacco gained much from the preference. During the most difficult years of its early growth, in the first quarter of the seventeenth century, tobacco received more opposition than encouragement in England and turned to foreign markets, where it appeared able to hold its own in free competition.[63] Similarly, the prohibition of tobacco planting in England would appear to have had little effect upon American production. Although tobacco can be grown successfully in Great Britain, the colonial product had greater natural advantages. The reason for the English farmer's desire to grow tobacco and for the government's determination to stamp out its cultivation is to be found in the taxes assessed on it. They could be collected more easily at the waterside, and the difficulty which administrators had even there shows how impossible it would have been under seventeenth-century conditions to have assessed crops scattered throughout the English countryside.

The ultimate destination of most American tobacco was the continent of Europe. In 1773, Britain officially consumed only 3,747,979 pounds of the 100,482,007 pounds imported, the remainder being reëxported, mostly to Holland and Germany.[64] After the Revolution, the British government made a strenuous effort to retain her control of the trade, greatly simplifying the customs regulations governing tobacco passing through England, but without success. British importations of American tobacco steadily declined from 99.8 percent in 1773 to 62.2 percent in 1790, 45.5 percent in 1799, 31.7 percent in 1821, and 22.7 percent in 1840. Tobacco went direct to its destination in Germany, Holland, France, and elsewhere.[65] It is true that the wars with France tended to disturb previous conditions, but if Britain had been a natural entrepôt, trade would once again have returned to the most favorable channel. It was not, and Bremen became the center for hogshead tobacco.[66]

The indirect routing required by the law had many detrimental effects on American economic interests. The import duty on tobacco was raised from time to time until it totaled $6d. \frac{19\frac{2}{3}}{20}$ per pound at the Revolution.[67] Although only $\frac{1}{2}d.$ a pound was retained upon exportation until 1723 and nothing thereafter,[68] the necessity of paying the entire amount or giving bond therefor upon entry placed control of the trade in the hands of the British. Few if any colonists had enough cash or sufficient security in England to meet the requirements.

So much of the pre-Revolutionary agitation centered around the taxes assessed in America that comparatively little attention is paid to the duties upon colonial trade which were actually collected in Britain. When examining the English Book of Rates and confronting charges of 5d. $\frac{13\frac{5}{8}}{20}$ per skin for deerskins "in the hair" and 2d. $16\frac{13/_{16}}{20}$ a pound for the same article "Indian half-dressed" there is reason for hesitation, but fortunately the Inspector General's accounts give us contemporary figures which permit easy computations of the tax burden at the end of the seventeenth century.[69] They show that in 1698 the duties collected upon goods imported into England from the thirteen colonies amounted to £471,214 and upon those from the West Indies, £96,994. Of these duties, more than one-half were repaid when the commodities were reëxported to Europe. Ordinarily one would expect the duties on the goods sold in England to be paid by the English consumer, but the retail prices which we have are so fragmentary that we can draw no definite conclusion other than that the spread between the cost to the consumer and the price received by the producer was so great that the duties might well have been taken out of the wholesaler's profits.[70] Certainly all of the increases could not have been taken from the colonial planter's portion of the selling price because his entire share would have been insufficient. The duties, however, undoubtedly tended to hold down the amount which he might otherwise have received. But we cannot attempt to measure the extent at this point and shall have to pass on to those duties about which we can form more exact judgments. They fall into the following groups:

Taxes Levied in 1698 on Colonial Trade in England

	THIRTEEN COLONIES	WEST INDIES
Duties retained on enumerated goods reëxported from England	£36,047	£12,425
Duties retained on foreign goods reëxported in time	2,493	2,786
Duties on foreign goods reëxported out of time	4,653	3,552
Duties on English manufactures exported to the colonies	5,394	3,032
TOTAL	£48,587	£21,795

The duties retained on the enumerated goods reëxported from England, on foreign goods reëxported "in time," and on English exports to the colonies were undoubtedly passed on to the colonists, but it is more difficult to determine the incidence of taxation in the case of foreign goods shipped to the colonies "out of time," after the period allowed to receive the drawback had expired. Unlike their northern cousins who lived up to their Scottish traditions by collecting all but one-tenth of one percent of the drawback which the law allowed,[71] the English merchants were careless. The colonial planters were so far away and usually so deeply in debt that the English factors, instead of paying for their own carelessness, may have added the extra duty to their accounts—and collected a commission on it.

Unfortunately the customs system became too complex for the Inspector General's accounts to continue listing items about duties, and we must make our own estimate for 1773. Many changes had occurred between 1698 and the later date. In addition to allowing drawback of all the duties on tobacco beginning in 1723 and the change in the method of collecting the rice duties, which we have already noted, the most important were the removal of export duties on all British commodities, with a few exceptions like coal, and the abandonment in 1764 of the usual practice of repaying one-half of the Old Subsidy in so far as reëxports to the colonies in America were concerned. It would be a hopeless task to determine the exact amount of the duties, but we can come reasonably close by concentrating our efforts upon the most important. If, because of the impossibility of ascertaining what proportion was borne by the colonists, we again disregard the duties collected upon plantation goods imported into Britain, the amounts collected in 1773 can be divided into four groups:

TAXES LEVIED IN 1773 ON COLONIAL TRADE IN BRITAIN

Export duties paid on rice	£12,397
Duties retained on foreign goods reëxported to the colonies in time	19,625
Duties on foreign goods reëxported out of time	333
Duties on coal exported to the colonies	675
Total of duties borne by the thirteen colonies	£33,030

The elimination of the ½d. per pound on tobacco reëxported and of export duties on British manufactures accounts for the great decrease in these items. Scottish competition, which was absent in 1698, probably explains the decline in carelessness about exporting goods "out of time," while the natural growth of trade and the denial of drawback on one-half the Old Subsidy accounts for the increase in the amount retained on foreign goods reëxported to the colonies. Some adjustments in the figures should be made for the minor items necessarily omitted from our calculations, but even after making a liberal allowance for error, two points stand out clearly. The indirect taxes collected in Britain from the thirteen colonies each year exceeded the £31,000 raised annually in the colonies by measures such as the Sugar Acts, the Stamp Tax, and the Townshend Revenue Act [72] which caused so much excitement. Moreover, the burden of British mercantilism bore much more heavily upon the thirteen colonies in 1698 than in 1773, the per capita charge at the end of the seventeenth century being more than five times that of both the direct and indirect taxation of the Revolutionary era.[73]

The taxes collected by the government were, however, only a minor element in the burden which was placed upon the colonies. The normal uncertainties which attend trade and commerce were considerably increased by confusion in the laws. As Governor Glen of South Carolina said, "far from being so clear as he that runs may read them," the laws were "dark and difficult." [74] Even the authorities in England sometimes could not agree, as in the case of Canary wines, which could be legally imported if the Canary Islands were in Africa and could not if they formed part of Europe.[75] Also the rules and regulations necessary to keep the potential smuggler in line were a considerable nuisance burden which was borne by the fair trader as well as by the wrongdoer. In a frontier community of settlements scattered over a long coast line, the requirement that ships enter and clear at designated ports was a serious inconvenience to settlers. However well intentioned a merchant might have been, the complexities of commerce sometimes rendered it impossible to conform to regulations which administrative necessities required. Innocent mistakes might also occur. Such cases are ordinarily excused upon application or payment of a nominal fine. Yet under the Navigation Acts they led to forfeiture of the goods unless expensive petitions were sent across three thousand miles of ocean—and even then it was usually impossible to recover the third of the forfeiture which went to the officer who seized the goods. Honest and discreet officials might do much to mitigate administrative inconveniences, but on the other hand, as Laurens discovered in South Carolina, dishonest or malicious officials had many opportunities to harass those who had incurred their displeasure.[76]

Most important of all, the control of policy was in the hands of British mercantilists. It is difficult to support the concept of an impartial administrator carefully balancing the equities between the economic interests of colonies and those of mother country. All Englishmen did not state their views as bluntly as did Lord Cornbury, who declared in the early eighteenth century that "all these Colloneys which are but twigs belonging to the main Tree (England) ought to be kept entirely dependent upon and subservient to England, and that can never be, if they are suffered to goe on in the notions they have," or William Pitt, who recommended in 1766 that the sovereign authority of Britain over the colonies should be "made to extend to every part of legislation whatever, that we may bind their trade, confine their manufactures, and exercise every power whatsoever, except that of taking their money out of their pockets without their consent." [77] But all thought of the colonies in the terms of what England could gain from them. The statutes made it clear that England desired the colonies to be subservient to her. Sometimes Parliament clearly expressed its intention that the colonies be kept "in a firmer dependance" upon England and rendered "yet more beneficiall and advantagious unto it," as in the Act of 1663,[78] and sometimes the preferences accorded British interests were so subtly provided that the Acts appear to be examples of British generosity. In mentioning the permission to ship sugar and rice south of Cape Finisterre, for example, notice is seldom taken of the administrative requirements which permitted the privilege to be enjoyed only by vessels which had sailed from Britain and eventually were to return there; thus control of the trade was retained for British merchants.[79]

The grant of bounties helped some of the colonies, but Parliament's purpose was not altruistic. It was to prevent the drain of coin from England and to provide the colonies with funds for the purchase of British manufactures.[80] Parliament declined to restrain colonial shipbuilding as the Thames shipbuilders wished, because by doing so it would increase freight costs and injure an even more important British group, the merchants. But it did try to restrain the manufacture of woolens, of hats, and of iron.

Certainly on fundamental issues there is no evidence of British self-sacrifice. In the enumeration clauses of 1660 and the Staple Act of 1663 the colonial producer and consumer gave way to the English merchant. In the Molasses Act of 1733 and the Sugar Act of 1764, the interests of the continental colonies which could only present arguments yielded to those of the absentee sugar planters who controlled votes in Parliament, but even the favored sugar colonies lost out after the American Revolution when the clash became one between the West Indian interest in cheap provisions and the British interest in more cargoes for British ships. These results were merely natural—not immoral—and we only blind ourselves to the nature of social processes if we endow imperialism with an altruism that it does not possess. Even assuming that those who determined policies were completely unbiased and were anxious to treat all parts of the Empire with perfect fairness, the colonies were at a disadvantage. It is human nature to yield to constant pressure, and the colonists resided across the Atlantic while their English competitors were always at hand to press their claims.

Although the full effect of economic dependence upon the colonies cannot be measured in dollars and cents, an estimate of its monetary cost should be of value. The requirement that goods pass through England imposed many obligations upon colonial trade in the guise of taxes, fees, cooperage, porterage, brokerage, warehouse rent, commissions, extra merchants' profits, and the like, which would never have been incurred in a direct trade with the ultimate markets. A Revolutionary pamphleteer claimed that the English mercantile system cost Virginia alone £5,987,500 currency, and William Pitt declared that colonial trade produced an annual profit of £2,000,000 sterling for British merchants.[81] Since it is probable that these claims, made in the heat of political controversy, are exaggerated and include costs of manufacture which the colonists would have had to pay wherever the goods were purchased, we must attempt to form our own estimate. Scattered bits of interesting information are readily available, such as that it cost £100,000 each year in commissions to send Chesapeake tobacco by way of England,[82] but they will not suffice. Our task is to determine how much less the colonists received for their products and how much more they had to pay for their purchases because of the Navigation Acts than would have been the case if their commerce had been unfettered.

Ideally, we should have lists of wholesale prices in America, Britain, and the principal markets of Europe. Some day the data may be more nearly complete, but meanwhile we must exercise our ingenuity in dealing with the data available and in devising methods to minimize the danger of error.

We can simplify our task by directing attention toward the principal drains upon the colonial economy: the restrictions placed upon the marketing of colonial tobacco and rice and the requirement that European manufactures be obtained in Britain. Some help can be had from the testimony of contemporaries about the elements of cost involved, but such testimony is often missing and usually fragmentary. Fortunately, recent studies of prices in the United States offer another point of departure.[83] They permit us to ascertain the average price of tobacco at Philadelphia and of rice at both Philadelphia and Charleston before and after the Revolution together with the prices of a few imported products. The chief objection to proceeding in this fashion is the chance that prices were influenced by other factors than freedom from English restraints. This objection can be met in part by increasing the prices for the colonial period by 78 percent to correspond with the increase in the general price level thereafter,[84] although there is always the danger that the commodities in which we are interested did not even approximately conform to the average.

Another method of procedure which avoids comparisons between different periods is the work from the Inspector General's accounts after making such corrections in the official values as seem necessary. A comparison of the value given tobacco, rice, and European products with the valuation set upon the same goods as they were exported to their ultimate destinations in Europe or America should represent the cost of their passing through Britain. The difficulty lies in the failure of subsequent officials to keep the estimates of 1696 up to date.[85] This unsatisfactory condition may be offset in part by the fact that our interest lies only in the difference between the import and reëxport values. Any tendency to overstatement may be guarded against by adjusting the official values on the basis of Moreau's "real values" for the twelve years 1763–74, which value imports as sold to the consumer, including the importer's profits and freight but excluding duties, and reëxports according to "the average price current" exclusive of the freight outwards.[86]

There is a surprising unanimity of result in the various analyses of the effect of enumeration upon tobacco. The estimates of contemporary merchants placed the cost of sending tobacco through Britain at 2d. or 4 cents per pound.[87] A comparison of the prices at Philadelphia of unspecified qualities of tobacco during the years

1720–75 with those for James River tobacco from 1784 to 1861, adjusted to allow for a 78 percent rise in the general price level, indicates that the planters received 3.50 cents more per pound after they were freed from the restraints of the British legislation than before. Since the quality of pre-Revolutionary tobacco was unspecified, the comparison might involve an element of error for which allowance can be made by discounting the James River tobacco by 13.4 percent, which was the difference in price in 1770 betwen Virginia and Maryland tobacco.[88] On this basis the loss is 2.51 cents per pound instead of 3.50 cents. A comparison of the official valuations of imported and reëxported tobacco shows a spread of $2\frac{1}{4}d.$ a pound. Deducting an allowance of £7 a ton or $\frac{3}{4}d.$ a pound for freight from America to England, the estimated loss to the colonists is $1\frac{1}{2}d.$ or 3 cents a pound. Corrected to correspond with Moreau's tables, the loss is further reduced to only $1.14d.$ or $2\frac{1}{4}$ cents a pound.

In ascertaining the total cost of the enumeration, a question arises as to whether to calculate it against the total quantity shipped from the colonies or only against the amount reëxported from England. There should be no question as far as the Philadelphia prices are concerned, and in all probability the extra costs of shipping tobacco to Europe helped to beat down its price in Britain. Yet for conservatism's sake it may be well to assume that it was borne only by reëxported tobacco. Calculating on that basis, the lowest estimate of the burden laid upon the thirteen colonies in 1773 by the enumeration of tobacco is $2,176,516 and the highest is $3,400,714.

The greater freedom which apparently was allowed in the exportation of rice might cause one to believe that unlike tobacco it did not feel the weight of the Navigation Acts, but such figures as we have do not support the assumption. Using the same procedure as followed in comparing the prices of tobacco, we find that an analysis of rice prices at Philadelphia assesses the cost of British mercantilism at $.62 per hundredweight of rice and of those at Charleston, $1.39 per hundredweight. The official British valuations did not provide as great a write-up in the value of reëxported rice as in the case of tobacco: 33 percent for rice as compared with 100 percent for tobacco, making the spread between import and reëxport values 5s. per hundredweight, from which we should probably deduct the freight rate, which ought not to have averaged more than £3 a ton or 3s. a hundredweight.[89] Calculations based upon Moreau make the import value higher than the reëxport value and obviously must be disregarded. Thus the burden arising from the enumeration of rice is between $185,925 and $516,871.

The variety of European commodities imported by the colonies complicates the problem of ascertaining the extra expense involved in making shipments by way of England. A weighted average compiled from the official import and reëxport values in England for more than 75 percent of the foreign products sent to the thirteen colonies in 1773 shows that the average mark-up in prices was 53.1 percent of the import value or 34.8 percent of the reëxport value.[90] Recalculated to correspond with Moreau's ratio between official and real values, the percentages are lowered to 22.2 percent and 18.2 percent respectively. Although no sufficiently continuous series of prices for imported goods in the colonies is available to corroborate the English figures, those which exist tend to confirm rather than to confute the theory that transshipment was costly. At Philadelphia the price of gunpowder fell markedly; that of pepper declined from an average of 41 cents a pound for the years 1766–75 to an average of 29 cents from 1784 to 1823; and at Boston the price of Russian duck, which had averaged 77.1 shillings per piece from 1753 to 1775, fell to 68.2 shillings from 1784 to 1795, all contrary to the trend of the general price level. Moreover, ample support is found in contemporary comments about the greater cheapness of Dutch products, especially in the seventeenth century when the English themselves acknowledged that the Dutch could undersell them by a third or a half.[91] Since the extra expense of importing competitive European products from England acted as a protective wall which permitted increases in English prices, the question arises as to whether in computing the cost of the Staple Act of 1663 to the colonies we should base our calculations only upon the value of the goods reëxported or upon the total value of both British and foreign goods sent to the colonies.[92] Depending upon the method employed, our estimates will range from $521,-290 to $3,444,185.

Obviously, all the estimates cannot be correct, but the chances appear excellent that the truth lies somewhere between the extremes. Whenever two of the methods produce substantially the same result the probabilities would appear to be definitely in favor of its accuracy, and any estimate that is supported by three should be as certain as one can hope to obtain. There appears to be little likelihood that any except the highest estimate overstates the colonial losses, because our calculations omit so many items which might well be included in a list of charges against British mercantilism. We have excluded the expense to which smugglers were put in their efforts to evade the laws, which were none the less real because their activities were illicit. No allowance has been made for various legal trades forced to pass through Britain which, however minor in themselves, were not inconsiderable in the aggregate. Most important of all, no mention has been made of the fact that, thanks to the hold which the Navigation Acts gave it on trade, British shipping managed to carry four-fifths of the trans-Atlantic commerce in the colonial period as contrasted with one-fifth in 1821 when competitive conditions were equal.[93] According to Champion, the carriage of tobacco and rice alone employed 80,000 tons of shipping,[94] which, at an average freightage of £4 a ton, represented no inconsiderable sum. Although many elements other than the Navigation Acts doubtless hindered participation of the colonial merchant marine in the trans-Atlantic trade until after independence, it would seem probable that some part of the $1,600,-000 annual freight bill represents a profit which the colonists would have enjoyed except for their economic subservience under the Act.

Using only the estimates we have calculated and leaving the more intangible items as a margin of error, we can prepare a balance sheet of the cash burdens and advantages of British mercantilism in 1773. In arranging the figures it is interesting to note that the much-criticized values of the Inspector General's accounts appear to be the medium which is most probably in accord with the facts:

COST TO THE THIRTEEN COLONIES	LOWEST ESTIMATE	INTERMEDIATE ESTIMATE	HIGHEST ESTIMATE
On tobacco	$2,177,000	$2,428,000	$3,401,000
On rice	186,000	231,000	517,000
On European goods	521,000	997,000	3,444,000
	$2,884,000	$3,656,000	$7,362,000

CREDIT TO BOUNTIES PAID ON COLONIAL PRODUCTS			
On indigo [95]	£23,086		
On naval stores [96]	35,203		
On lumber [97]	6,557		
£64,846 or	324,000	324,000	324,000
	$2,560,000	$3,332,000	$7,038,000

At first glance the amounts do not appear particularly impressive, but the lowest estimate, which is made up of the figures from Moreau, is undoubtedly an understatement because the import values, which are necessarily used as a basis for ascertaining the price received by the colonial planter, include the British importer's profit which certainly never made its way to America. Yet, even so, the annual per capita burden it represented came within sixteen cents a person of meeting all the expenses of operating the national government during the last six years of Washington's administration, including the amortization costs of the Revolutionary War debt, the expenses of the Indian War of 1790 in the Northwest, the Whiskey Insurrection of 1794, and the tribute paid to Algiers in 1795. An annual per capita tax based upon the highest estimate would have raised an amount sufficient to pay all the costs of government and would have produced at the end of the ten-year period, 1791–1800, a fund sufficient to pay both the foreign and domestic Revolutionary War debt and still have left $7,000,000 with which to help meet the obligations incurred in assuming the state debts.[98]

Worst of all, the burdens under mercantilism were paid in Brittain. The tax burden after independence could have been much higher than before with much less detrimental effect because the money would have been spent for the most part within the United States. Conceding that frontier communities are usually in debt and that the colonies would probably have incurred obligations in any case, it seems reasonable to believe that the adverse balance of trade would have been smaller if the Navigation Acts had not been in force. The basic elements of the system—which did not originate with George III but date back to the reign of Charles II—tended to drain specie from America to Britain.[99] There is no need to quote colonial witnesses concerning the distress which results from a lack of ready cash. More than a century before the Revolution occurred, when England herself was pinched by lack of bullion, William Hodges called attention to "The Groans of the Poor, the Misery of Traders, and the Calamity of the Publick for the Spoiling of our Money, for the Want of our Money . . . ," and William Potter in his *Tradesman's Jewel* summarized the whole subject by quoting Ecclesiastes 10:19:

> They prepare bread for laughter
> and wine comforteth the living
> but money answereth to all.

Emphasis upon the burdens which were placed upon the thirteen colonies does not necessarily lead to a condemnation of British mercantilism nor to the conclusion that the Navigation Acts caused the Revolution. Other factors enter into the determination of those problems. Man can adjust himself to much, and the colonists had lived under the Acts for many years. During the Revolutionary period, public resentment was most actively directed against the taxes upon the West Indian trade, in which the colonists had sought a means of meeting their trans-Atlantic obligations. Moreover, the colonies received many advantages from the imperial tie, apart from the bounties and preferences of mercantilism, of which military and naval protection are merely the most conspicuous examples. Judged by contemporary standards, the colonies might have fared much worse. But the evaluation of all such considerations is another problem. The task undertaken here was merely to determine what price the colonists paid for what they received.

NOTES

1. For many years George Louis Beer's excellent volumes *The Old Colonial System* (2 vols., New York, 1912) and *British Colonial Policy, 1754–1765* (New York, 1907) have supplied our best account of the Acts. No modern work has been devoted to the laws themselves except the fourth volume of C. M. Andrews's *The Colonial Period of American History* (New Haven, 1938), which only recently appeared, and L. A. Harper's *The English Navigation Laws* (New York, 1939). Neither, however, treats at length the effect of the laws upon the colonies, each examining the legislation primarily from the point of view of English administration and policies. The present study has been facilitated by the use of basic data now being compiled by WPA Project No. 10482-A-10, which has been supplemented for present purposes by student help supplied by the National Youth Administration. Thanks are also due to the Social Science Research Council of the University of California for financial assistance and to Miss Frances Burke and Dr. Gerald White for help in collecting and analyzing statistics and laws.

2. The extent of colonial smuggling is discussed more fully in L. A. Harper, *The English Navigation Laws*, pp. 247–71. It should be noted that the argument presented applies only to the trans-Atlantic trade, not to violations of the Molasses Act of 1733. There it was possible for the continental colonists, in part at least, to force the British West Indies to accept competitive prices; and as the provisions shipped to the Caribbean were more bulky than sugar, there was always plenty of room for returning cargoes, whether licit or illicit.

3. Unless otherwise noted, in the statistics cited hereafter the figures for 1770 for the continental colonies are those prepared by Thomas Irving, Inspector General of Imports and Exports of North America, and printed in Timothy Pitkin, *A Statistical View of the Commerce of the United States*

(Hartford, 1816), and in Lord Sheffield, *Observations on the Commerce of the American States* (London, 1784); those for 1773 for England are from Customs 3/73, for Scotland from Customs 14/1B; those for the United States in 1790, 1799, and 1821 are from American State Papers, Class IV, *Commerce and Navigation,* and in 1840 are in U.S. 26th Congress, second session, *Senate Documents,* No. 238. Statements as to duties and bounties are based upon material set forth in Henry Crouch, *A Complete View of the British Customs* (London, 1730), S. Baldwin, *Survey of the British Customs* (London, 1770), and William Sims and Richard Frewin, *Rates of Merchandize* (London, 1782), so corrected by the references therein cited as to apply to the dates under discussion. For statutes prior to 1714 the citations are those given in the *Statutes of the Realm* (London, 1810–28).

4. Violet Barbour, "Dutch and English Merchant Shipping in the Seventeenth Century," *Econ. Hist. Rev.,* II, 261–90 (1929–30); G. L. Beer, *Origins of the British Colonial System, 1578–1660* (New York, 1908), pp. 209, 389, 392; *The Advocate* (London, 1651), p. 4; Sir Josiah Child, *A Short Reply to a Treatise, Entitled Interest of Money Mistaken,* p. 22.

5. *The Advocate,* p. 6; *Calendar of State Papers, Venetian* (1647–52), pp. 230–231, 234; (1653–54), p. 103; Edmund Ludlow, *Memoirs, 1625–1672* (Oxford, 1894), I, 266–67; John Thurloe, *A Collection of the State Papers* (London, 1742), III, 494; *Maryland Archives,* XLIX, 299, 323–24, 341–42, 388, 391–93; *Documents Relative to the Colonial History of the State of New York,* XIV, 126–28; Andrews, *Colonial Period,* II, 263–64; V. T. Harlow, *A History of Barbados, 1628–1685* (Oxford, 1926), pp. 37–43, 65–68, 85–93; C. S. S. Higham, *Development of the Leeward Islands under the Restoration* (Cambridge, 1921), pp. 37, 143; A. P. Newton, *Colonizing Activities of the English Puritans* (New Haven, 1914), pp. 221, 261–62.

6. 10 Gul. III, c. 16, sec. 19 (effective Dec. 1, 1699).

7. C.O. 5/848; J. L. Bishop, *History of American Manufactures* (Philadelphia, 1861), I, 326–30, 344–45; V. S. Clark, *History of Manufactures in the United States* (New York, 1929), I, 22, 81–82, 204–9.

8. 5 Geo. II, c. 22 (1732).

9. C.O. 5/1224 and 1225. The value of fur and felt hats imported from Britain declined from £44,769 in 1773 to $11,027 in 1821 and $4,246 in 1840. Exports rose from nothing in 1773 to $63,363 in 1821 and $103,398 in 1840. There were 68 hatters in Philadelphia City and County in 1791 (Tench Coxe, *A View of the United States* [London, 1794], p. 158; J. T. Scharf and Thompson Westcott, *History of Philadelphia* [Philadelphia, 1884], III, 2336). Earlier figures from the tax lists are not altogether satisfactory because of gaps in the record and failures to list occupations in some years. Correcting the figures as best we can by interpolation, it appears that there were 24 hatters in 1769 and 43 in 1774 and 1780 (*Pennsylvania Archives,* 3d ser., Vols. XIV, XV).

10. 23 Geo. II, c. 29 (1750); 30 Geo. II, c. 16 (1757).

11. A. C. Bining, *British Regulation of the Colonial Iron Industry* (Philadelphia, 1933), pp. 82–83, and *Pennsylvania Iron Manufacture in the Eighteenth Century* (Harrisburg, 1938), pp. 154–59.

12. Bining, *Pennsylvania Iron Manufacture,* pp. 188–92. It is not clear how many of the furnaces, forges, etc., established between 1750 and 1775 were legal under the provisions of the Iron Act. It also should be noted that there may have been illegal mills set up of which we now have no record.

13. 12 Car. II, c. 18 (1660); 15 Car. II, c. 7 (1663); 7 and 8 Gul. III,

c. 22 (1696); 26 Geo. III, c. 60 (1786); Barbour, "Dutch and English Merchant Shipping," *Econ. Hist. Rev.*, II, 289. The provision in the Act of 1662 (14 Car. II, c. 11) that thereafter foreign-built ships should be deemed to be foreign vessels was held merely to require that they pay certain alien duties charged on goods imported in foreign vessels.

14. In the 34 years between 1815 and 1848 the United States sold an average of 10,584 tons of sailing vessels each year (Hans Keiler, *American Shipping* [Jena, 1913], p. 62). It should be remembered that the two principal markets for ships, Great Britain and France, were closed to the American shipbuilders (Coxe, *A View of the United States*, p. 184). The tonnage built for sale abroad jumped to 60,033 when the British shippers were allowed to purchase American-built bottoms in 1854 (Keiler, *loc. cit.*).

15. W. B. Weeden, *Economic and Social History of New England, 1620–1789* (Boston, 1891), II, 573.

16. 12 Geo. II, c. 30 (1739); 15 Geo. II, c. 33 (1742); F. W. Pitman, *The Development of the British West Indies* (New Haven, 1917), p. 184.

17. Richard Champion, *Considerations on the Present Situation of Great Britain and the United States* (London, 1784), p. 13; R. G. Albion, *Forests and Sea Power* (Cambridge, 1926), p. 246. The figure represents an average of the three years 1769 to 1771 (Pitkin, *Statistical View*, p. 17) to which has been added one-third for understatements of tonnage; see Sheffield, *Observations*, p. 96.

18. Coxe, *A View of the United States*, pp. 217–18; Keiler, *American Shipping*, p. 62.

19. Champion, *Considerations*, pp. 27–28, 65, 66.

20. Immediately after the Revolution the carriage was still in British hands, for their Navigation Acts were still in force and the United States had not yet built up her own shipping. The year 1821 was chosen as offering a sounder basis of comparison, since it was typical of conditions following the Reciprocity Treaty with Great Britain.

21. 9 Gul. III, c. 26 (1697–98).

22. 25 Car. II, c. 7 (1673).

23. 6 Geo. II, c. 13.

24. 4 Geo. III, c. 15; 6 Geo. III, c. 52.

25. Champion, *Considerations*, p. 40.

26. 4 Geo. III, c. 15.

27. 2 & 3 Anne, c. 18, xii (1703, iron and steel); 6 Anne, c. 73, xiii (1707, cordage); 4 Geo. II, c. 27 (1731, sailcloth and cordage); 10 Geo. II, c. 27, iv (1737, paper); 10 Geo. II, c. 30, iv (1737, oysters). The denial of drawback was general except in the case of unwrought iron, steel, and hemp, when it was denied only in the case of reëxportation to the British colonies in America.

28. Reëxported goods constituted only 2.8 percent of the goods shipped to the United States from Great Britain from 1806 to 1808 (Pitkin, *Statistical View*, p. 223); 1.5 percent in 1821 (Great Britain, House of Commons Sessional Papers [1822], XXI, No. 274); and 4.4 percent in 1828 (*ibid.* [1830], XXVII, No. 292). At that time Britain supplied only slightly more than one-half of the total of British, European, and Asian goods imported into the United States.

29. Statistics in César Moreau (*Chronological Records of the British Royal and Commercial Navy* [London, 1827], pp. 13, 15, 17–18) show that British goods had constituted 75 percent of such colonial imports in 1698–

1701; 73 percent in 1713–17; 64 percent in 1722–38; 86 percent in 1749–55; and 83 percent in 1763–74.

30. In this calculation shipments of enumerated products to the other colonies have been disregarded as negligible.

31. 27 Geo. III, c. 13.

32. Beer, *The Old Colonial System,* II, 1–30; Pitman, *Development of the British West Indies,* pp. 160–67; Sheffield, *Observations,* p. 121.

33. The nonenumerated commodities were allowed to go to Ireland, despite 6 Geo. III, c. 52 (1765), by 7 Geo. III, c. 2 (1766).

34. In 1773 Georgia shipped 1,091 pounds of silk to England, Pennsylvania 216 pounds, and Carolina 10 pounds. The total exports in 1790 were 93 pounds to Britain and 84 pounds to France.

35. *Supra,* p. 45.

36. 5 Geo. III, c. 45 (1765); 11 Geo. III, c. 50 (1770).

37. In 1770 about 70 percent of all lumber exports, valued at £167,412, went to the West Indies; in 1790, 64.6 percent of total exports of $1,263,534; and in 1821, 84.4 percent out of $1,627,896. In 1790 Britain was the second largest purchaser of lumber, receiving 19 percent, valued at $240,174, and northern Europe was third with 9.3 percent or $117,127. In 1821, however, exports to Britain had fallen to $32,230 or 2.9 percent and those to northern Europe to $13,553 or only 1.2 percent.

38. Anne Bezanson, R. D. Gray, and Miriam Hussey, *Prices in Colonial Pennsylvania* (Philadelphia, 1935), pp. 122–23.

39. 91.7 percent of the 5,667 tons of whale oil exported from the continental colonies in 1770 went to Great Britain. Following the Revolution between 80 and 90 percent of both whale oil and whale fins went to north Europe, but the quantity declined to 1,971 tons of whale oil, 679 tons of sperm oil, and 54 tons of whale fins. These quantities rose markedly by 1840 to 17,940 tons of whale oil, 1,725 tons of sperm oil, and 845 tons of whale fins.

40. In each of the years mentioned practically all of the remainder of the exports went to northern Europe.

41. V. W. Crane, *The Southern Frontier,* 1670–1732 (Philadelphia, 1929), pp. 111–12.

42. In 1773, 25.75 percent of the skins Britain imported were reëxported; in 1790, she took 76.6 percent of the United States exports, in 1821 70.2 percent; and in 1840, although she received only 3.4 percent directly, 66.4 percent went to British North America, the remainder usually going to North Europe. Exact comparisons are rendered difficult because of changes in the base of compiling statistics, and consequently it is useful to know that the average skin weighed about one or two pounds (Leila Sellers, *Charleston Business on the Eve of the American Revolution* [Chapel Hill, 1934], p. 173; Crane, *The Southern Frontier,* p. 111). In 1773 the total imported to Britain from the thirteen colonies was given as 243,213 pieces and 208,576 pounds and was valued at £41,448. The total exports from the United States were valued at $33,494 in 1790 and amounted to 72,650 skins in 1799, 13,558 in 1821, and 112,500 in 1840. No segregation was made between domestic and foreign products in 1790 and 1799, but in 1821 and 1840 the value of foreign reëxports totaled $61,921 and $406,234 respectively, most of which went to northern Europe, less than 15 percent going to Britain directly or by way of her colonies.

43. Andrews, *Colonial Period,* IV, 104–5.

44. L. A. Harper and J. H. Cox, *A Commodity Analysis of the Imports*

and Exports of the Port of New York, 1716–1764 (a film book produced as a part of WPA Project No. 465–03–3–264 [Berkeley, 1938]).

45. *Idem.*

46. It is difficult to give comparative figures because the exportation of furs was not restricted in 1698, but an idea of the relative decline in the fur trade of the thirteen colonies can be gained by comparing the 104,755 skins valued at £7,605 which were exported by them to England in 1698 and the 140,319 skins valued at £7,912 which they sent to Britain in 1773. England's total importations in 1698 were 143,066 skins, valued at £14,933; in 1773, Britain imported 451,450 skins valued at £101,623.

47. 4 Geo. III, c. 9. An export tax of 1s. 6d. was also placed upon every pound avoirdupois of beaver wool or wombs exported from Great Britain.

48. In 1790, 59.3 percent of a total exportation valued at $60,515 went to Britain; in 1799, 68.1 percent of $493,724; in 1821, 43.1 percent of $766,205; in 1840, 90.3 percent of $1,237,789. It should also be remembered that by virtue of the Louisiana Purchase and the opening of the West conditions differed greatly from those in colonial days.

49. Naval stores, including hemp and rosin, first received bounties but at different rates in 1705 (3 & 4 Anne, c. 9). Both enumeration and bounties except for hemp lapsed from 1725 to 1729 when they were renewed by 2 Geo. II, c. 35, which omitted rosin and added a bounty for turpentine. The bounty and enumeration on hemp lapsed in 1741 (8 Geo. I, c. 12). The bounty was renewed in 1764 but not the enumeration (4 Geo. III, c. 26). Flax, which was never enumerated, was placed on the free list in 1731 (4 Geo. II, c. 27) and its importation encouraged by a bounty of £8 per ton, which was lowered to £6 in 1771 (4 Geo. III, c. 26). But the colonists continued to prefer to export flaxseed rather than flax.

50. E. L. Lord, *Industrial Experiments in the British Colonies of North America* (Baltimore, 1896), Appendix. The export from South Carolina of tar and pitch averaged 2,625 last per year from 1721 through 1724; there was no immediate drop following the lapse of the bounties, as the years 1725 and 1726 showed an exportation of 4,329 last and 3,153 last respectively, but the export for the years following fell sharply, being only 223 last in 1728 and 643 in 1729. There was a gradual rise from then on, from 1,025 last in 1730 to 2,760 in 1733, yet the quantities exported did not attain the pre-1725 average again until 1732 (Customs 3/23–3/33).

51. Exports of rosin and turpentine were 17,237 barrels to Britain alone in 1773 and 2,063 more to the British West Indies. The total exports of such goods were 28,642 barrels in 1790, 56,778 barrels in 1799, 79,213 barrels in 1821, and 215,121 barrels in 1840. Exports of pitch and tar were 99,592 barrels in 1773, 93,942 barrels in 1790, 60,846 barrels in 1799, 71,196 barrels in 1821, and 44,655 in 1840. The percentage going to Great Britain was 95.4 percent in 1770, 83.1 percent in 1790, 50.3 percent in 1799, 59.8 percent in 1821, and 30.9 percent in 1840. In addition, sizeable shipments went to the British West Indies; others to British North America which probably eventually found their way to England constituted 6.4 percent of the total in 1799, 8.5 percent in 1821, and 27 percent in 1840.

52. Bezanson, Gray, and Hussey, *Prices in Colonial Pennsylvania*, p. 424.

53. The exports of masts were not listed separately in 1790 or in 1799. They were valued at only $54,627 in 1821 when none went to Britain and 43.6 percent went to British North America. The value of the exports declined further to $29,049 in 1840, most of which went to the West Indies and

South America, the figures for northern Europe being only $901, for British North America $1,260, and for the British Isles nothing at all.

54. Albion, *Forests and Sea Power*, pp. 251–54, 418.

55. 3 Geo. II, c. 28 (1730); 8 Geo. II, c. 19 (1735); 4 Geo. III, c. 27 (1764).

56. 7 Geo. III, c. 47 (1767); 13 Geo. III, c. 7 (1773).

57. Tierces were converted to hundredweight in accordance with the ration of 600 pounds per tierce, following G. K. Holmes, *Rice Crop of the United States* (U.S. Dept. of Agriculture; Bureau of Statistics, Circular 34 [Washington, 1912]).

58. The following chart shows the distribution of rice exports before and after the Revolution:

Year	1770	1790	1799	1821	1840
Total quantity (in 1,000 lbs.)	76,511	74,136	67,234	52,253	60,970
Percent of total quantity to: Great Britain					
and Ireland	49.21	36.62	12.83	20.25	17.44
Northern Europe	none	34.75	19.94	37.20	40.43
Southern Europe	24.11	4.75	12.54	1.78	1.96
West Indies and South America	26.60	23.63	52.59	34.86	38.38
Other ports	.08	.43	2.10	5.91	1.79

The fact that the shipments in 1770 were exceptionally high causes the other figures to suggest that rice exports suffered after the Revolution. But figures in L. C. Gray (*History of Agriculture in the Southern United States* [Washington, 1933], II, 1030), which were used in the foregoing table to give the quantities exported but not the percentages to the several countries, show that the annual average of exports for the 25 years between 1744 and 1773 inclusive for which we have records was 45,606,000 lbs. and that it was 59,967,500 lbs. for the years 1790–1814, if one does not exclude 1807 and 1813, which were abnormally low because of the Embargo and the War of 1812, and 64,642,000 lbs. if one does. During the next quarter-century (1815–39) exports maintained an even higher average, 68,669,000 lbs.

59. Edward Channing, *History of the United States* (New York, 1912), III, 35.

60. The bounty was originally granted by 21 Geo. II, c. 30 (1748), and the rate was lowered by 3 Geo. III, c. 25 (1763).

61. Customs 3/67, 3/73, 14/1B. For other statistics concerning indigo see Sellers, *Charleston Business on the Eve of the American Revolution*, p. 166; Gray, *History of Agriculture*, II, 1024. It is interesting to note that not only did the quantity exported increase but wholesale prices at Charleston rose. From 1765 to 1769 the average price was 22.84 shillings per pound; it rose to a peak of 41.2 shillings in 1772 and settled to an average of 31.93 shillings for 1773–75 (A. H. Cole, *Wholesale Commodity Prices in the United States, 1700–1861*, Statistical Supplement, Cambridge, 1938, pp. 54–70).

62. Gray, *op. cit.*, II, 610–11. In 1821 only $714 worth of the $417,682 of indigo exported had been produced in the United States, and in 1840 only $209 out of $179,419.

63. Beer, *Origins*, pp. 78–94, 188–94.

64. The actual consumption may have been greater because part of the exportations in 1773 may have been made from the previous year's crop. Also part of the tobacco exported may have been fraudulently relanded.

65. The following chart shows distribution of tobacco exports before and after the Revolution:

TOBACCO EXPORTS FROM THE UNITED STATES

Year	1770	1790	1799	1821	1840
Total quantity (hogsheads)		118,460	95,980	66,858	89,949
Total value	£906,637	$4,349,567		$5,648,962	$9,883,957
Percent of total quantity to:					
Great Britain and Ireland	99.8 [a]	61.41	45.56	30.8	30.17
North Europe					
Holland		19.79	1.79	19.76	28.52
France		9.18		4.76	14.91
Prussia		4.74	33.97	15.66	
Other countries		.68	3.76	2.68	4.45
South Europe		.47	5.79	7.26	9.47
West Indies	.17 [a]	3.16	6.85	6.65	4.89
Other ports	.03 [a]	.58	2.28	12.43	7.59

[a] Only percent of total value (not quantity) figures are given for 1770.

66. J. R. Smith, "The World Entrepôt," *Jour. Pol. Econ.* XVIII (1910), 697–713, at p. 709.

67. If paid in cash at entry the duty was only 6d.%20.

68. 9 Geo. I, c. 21.

69. Customs 3/1 (1698).

70. J. E. T. Rogers, *A History of Agricultural Prices in England* (Oxford, 1866–1902), V, 467–68; VII, pt. i, 372–78.

71. Customs 14/1B (1773).

72. Channing, *op. cit.*, III, 90.

73. The population appears to have been between 200,000 and 250,000 in 1698 and between 2,000,000 and 2,500,000 in 1773 (E. B. Greene and V. D. Harrington, *American Population before the Federal Census of 1790* [New York, 1932], pp. 3–4, 6–7).

74. Cited in L. W. Labaree, *Royal Instructions to British Colonial Governors, 1670–1776* (New York, 1935), II, 885–86.

75. Andrews, *Colonial Period*, IV, 110–13.

76. Harper, *The English Navigation Laws*, pp. 161–227; Sellers, *Charleston Business on the Eve of the American Revolution*, pp. 192–201.

77. Bishop, *American Manufactures*, pp. 329, 370.

78. 15 Car. II, c. 7.

79. 3 Geo. II, c. 28 (1730); 12 Geo. II, c. 30 (1739).

80. See, for example, 3 and 4 Anne, c. 9.

81. A. M. Schlesinger, *The Colonial Merchants and the American Revolution, 1763–1776* (New York, 1918), p. 602; Channing, *op. cit.*, III, 34–35.

82. Channing, *op. cit.*, III, 34.

83. The colonial price quotations cited hereafter for Philadelphia are based upon the tables of Anne Bezanson, R. D. Gray, and Miriam Hussey, *Whole-*

sale Prices in Philadelphia, 1784–1861 (2 vols., Philadelphia, 1936) and those in the volume by the same authors on *Prices in Colonial Pennsylvania*. The prices for Charleston and Boston are based upon the Statistical Supplement to Cole, *Wholesale Commodity Prices*. Percentages have been computed upon annual averages except in the case of Russian sail duck where they are based upon the average of separate monthly quotations. Colonial prices have been converted to dollars at the rates given in Cole, *op. cit.*, p. ix, but for the sake of convenience the pound sterling has been considered to be worth $5.

84. Bezanson, Gray, and Hussey, *Wholesale Prices in Philadelphia*, 1784–1861, I, 301.

85. G. N. Clark, *Guide to English Commercial Statistics* (London, 1938), pp. 33–42.

86. Moreau, *Chronological Records of the British Navy*, pp. 17, 23, gives only the total value of England's trade with different countries, but such figures should be sufficient for our purposes because the commodities we are considering bulk so large in the trades which we have to study. The average error in the official valuation given upon importation of reëxports should correspond to the undervaluation of imports from northern Europe and Asia, since almost all of the goods reëxported to the thirteen colonies came from those regions. Similarly the undervaluation in the reëxport price of tobacco and rice can be considered to be the same as that given for foreign or plantation goods reëxported to northern Europe, which was the great market for such products. On this basis a comparison of the official values with the "real values" given by Moreau shows an undervaluation in the official values for imports (of tobacco and rice) from the thirteen colonies of 58.14 percent; in the reëxport price (of tobacco and rice) of 4.32 percent; in the imported value of goods later reëxported to the thirteen colonies of 40.34 percent; in the value given on reëxportation of 11.60 percent.

87. Gray, *op. cit.*, I, 223; C. P. Nettels, *The Roots of American Civilization* (New York, 1938), pp. 254–55.

88. Gray, *op. cit.*, I, 274. The allowance probably was excessive because at least some of the tobacco in Philadelphia should have been Virginia tobacco. On the other hand, earlier differences in price between Maryland and Virginia tobacco may have been greater (*ibid.*, I, 270). A comparison of the post-Revolutionary prices for Kentucky tobacco instead of James River tobacco gives a figure of 2.76 cents per pound.

89. Sellers, *op. cit.*, pp. 154–55.

90. The total value of the reëxports from Britain to the thirteen colonies in 1773 was £572,845. The following are the most important examples of the mark-up between the import and reëxport prices: 37.5% on £17,711 of Russian broad linen; 100% on £148,316 of tea; 70% on £31,191 of Port; 47% on £38,775 of rough hemp; 37.5% on £38,154 of calico; 22.2% on £75,651 of German narrow linen; and 20% on £63,219 of Irish linen.

91. *Supra*, note 5.

92. In 1773 the total official value of British exports to the colonies, including reëxports, was £1,980,412.

93. *Supra*, p. 47.

94. Champion, *Considerations*, p. 66.

95. Calculated at 4*d.* per pound on total imports to Great Britain, see chart, *supra*, note 58.

96. Albion, *Forests and Sea Power*, p. 418.

97. In 1769, the highest figure given in Beer, *British Colonial Policy*, p. 224.

98. The figures for United States expenditures beginning in 1791 are given in D. R. Dewey, *Financial History of the United States* (New York, 1934), pp. 89, 90, 93, 111. The annual average expenditure was $5,434,666 from 1791–96 and $6,633,100 from 1791–1800. Statistics for population growth furnish more difficulty but the population in 1775 was taken to be 2,507,180, as stated in S. H. Sutherland, *Population Distribution in Colonial America* (New York, 1936), p. 271, and the population during Washington's administration was assumed to be the mean between the 3,929,625 of the 1790 census and the 5,308,483 of the 1800 census (W. J. Rossiter, *A Century of Population Growth, 1790–1900*, Dept. of Commerce and Labor, Bur. of the Census [Washington, 1909], p. 56). The calculations are not altogether accurate but should be sufficient for all practical purposes.

99. For a good discussion of the early problems of the colonial money supply, see Nettels, *op. cit.*, pp. 266–75.

4

The Revolutionary Era

In two of his early historical works—*An Economic Interpretation of the Constitution* (1913) and *Economic Origins of Jeffersonian Democracy* (1915)—Charles Beard portrayed the period 1763–1800 as an integrated historical epoch, the major theme of which was a continuing struggle between American social classes. From 1763 to the outbreak of the Revolution, Beard argued, there was a conflict in the colonies between the entrenched aristocracy and the popular interests, between "men of substance" and "mechanics and yeomen farmers." The Revolutionary War itself gave a new configuration to this struggle, but did not end it. Whereas the Declaration of Independence and the Articles of Confederation were radical in purpose, as were many of the first state constitutions, the federal Constitution of 1787 was a reactionary document; and the centralized government erected by the Founders in 1787 and defended in *The Federalist Papers* was a breakwater built to stem the tide of social revolution. It was not until the 1800 election, Beard asserted, that conservative dominance, established by the Constitution, was finally ended.

For several decades, the substance of the Beard thesis was incorporated in almost all the histories of the period. In our own generation too, a number of the most important studies of the Revolutionary era have been much influenced by Beard. Merrill Jensen, for example, emphasizes social conflict as basic to the changes of the Revolutionary epoch. "It is this continuity of conflict," Jensen writes, "that gives coherence to the age of the American Revolution. Otherwise many men and events must be ignored, or their significance distorted, if they are fitted into a pattern that assumes a sharp break in political history in 1776. The roots of this struggle lay deep in colonial history." *

In recent years, the Beard-Jensen thesis has been subjected to searching criticism. Several historians, notably Edmund S. Morgan, Forrest McDonald and Robert E. Brown, have attacked the logic of Beard's argument. Thus Morgan asserts that exceptional unity, and not intense social conflict, marked domestic life in the Revolutionary period; for while Americans employed force to win independence from Britain, no comparable resort to violence was necessary to settle domestic differences.† Both Brown and McDonald have criticized Beard sharply on grounds of misuse of evidence; and some scholars regard McDonald's *We, the People* (Chicago, 1958) as a decisive refutation of the class-conflict interpretation of the Constitution.

The work of Staughton Lynd, however, suggests that it is not time to reject the Beard thesis altogether. In the following article, Lynd examines one local community, Dutchess County of New York, and defines the economic basis of social classes there, the impact of war on social structure, and manifestations of class conflict in local politics. Referring to the phrase of Carl Becker (who anticipated the Beard thesis by a few years in his study of Revolutionary politics in New York), Lynd finds that the question "Who should rule at home?" was indeed a vital one in Dutchess County.

* Merrill Jensen: *The New Nation, A History of the United States During the Confederation, 1781–1789* (New York, 1950), p. 19.
† Edmund S. Morgan: *The Birth of the Republic* (Chicago, 1957).

WHO SHOULD RULE AT HOME?
DUTCHESS COUNTY, NEW YORK,
IN THE AMERICAN REVOLUTION

Staughton Lynd

I

In the summer of 1831, one of the numerous New York Livingstons told the inquiring Alexis de Tocqueville: "All classes joined together in the Revolution. Afterwards the strength of Democracy was so paramount that no one attempted to struggle against it." [1] The two sentences point to a paradox in the American Revolution which historians have never fully resolved. All classes did join together in the War for Independence. Thus in Dutchess County the aristocratic landlord Robert R. Livingston,[2] who would lead off for the Federalists at the New York ratifying convention in 1788, and the plebeian entrepreneur Melancton Smith, the principal anti-Federalist spokesman, were both good Whigs in 1776. But it is equally true that in Dutchess, as in New York state as a whole, the Revolution challenged "the aristocratic flavor which everywhere permeated society" before 1775.[3] "If one may judge anything by the number and the nature of the cases in Dutchess County courts," writes the county's most recent historian, "the period of the Revolution witnessed a conflict in society beginning twenty years earlier and lasting ten years longer than the actual hostilities of war." [4]

Contemporaries had no doubt that the War for Independence was accompanied by a struggle over who should rule at home. Fear of just such an internal revolution made Robert R. Livingston hesitate long on the brink of independence.[5] By the winter of 1777–78,

Reprinted by permission from *The William and Mary Quarterly*, 3d Series, XVIII (1961), 330–359. This article is part of a larger study which has appeared as *Anti-Federalism in Dutchess County, New York* (Chicago: Loyola University Press, 1962).

the historian William Smith observed that the New York Whigs were splitting into "the Popular & the landed Interest" and wrote with some smugness of the latter: "These People have had no Foresight of the natural Consequences of a republican Spirit in a poor Country, where Gentlemen of Fortune are but few. . . . They are losing their Significance every Day. They will be happy if they can save their Estates." [6] The financial crisis of 1779–80, with its attendant clashes over price regulation and the confiscation of Loyalist lands, drew from Robert R. Livingston's mother a prayer for "Peace and Independence and deliverance from the persecutions of the Lower Class who I forsee will be as dispotic as any Prince (if not more so) in Europe." [7] As the war drew to a close, Thomas Tillotson of Dutchess wrote forebodingly that New York had "a strong Democratic Spirit prevailing that will some day not far off give a stab to its happiness. . . . The people want nothing but to be a little more impoverished to prepare them for it. The first stroke would be at the Tenanted estates. . . ." [8]

This conflict perceived by contemporaries was real. The egalitarian "spirit" which Smith called republican and Tillotson democratic was not a figment of the Federalist imagination. Historians who so regard it often assume that pre-Revolutionary society was, in fact, substantially democratic. [9] But whatever may have been the case in Massachusetts, Dutchess County before the American Revolution was a harsh, hierarchical community of which one complainant said with much justice that there was "no law for poor Men." [10] It was a society in which an heiress married "under a crimson canopy emblazoned with the family crest in gold—a demi-lion crowned issuing from a coronet," and, "as on rent day, the tenants gathered before the manor hall to feast and wish happiness to the bride while within a lavish banquet was spread for the Van Cortlandts, Livingstons and other river families." [11] It was a society, too, in which the leader of a tenant rebellion on the lands of this same heiress was sentenced to be hanged, drawn, and quartered for high treason. At mid-century, Henry Beekman, Jr., had "ruled the rapidly growing population of Dutchess County almost as if he had been its manor lord," a state of affairs condensed in the fact that Beekman's rent-collector doubled as manager of his invariably successful campaigns for election to the New York Assembly. [12] Even after Beekman's son-in-law, Judge Robert Livingston of Clermont, had been defeated in the Assembly elections of 1768 and 1769, the chief appointive positions continued to go to the great landlords until the Revolution.[13]

Landlordism was stronger in some parts of the county than in others. In all parts of Dutchess men made a living by raising "good, sweet, merchantable winter wheat" (and, in the eastern section farthest from the Hudson, cattle) for the New York City market. Socially, however, north, south, and central Dutchess were distinct communities.

In northern Dutchess, resident large landlords set the social tone. They had their great homes or "places," in the eighteenth as in the nineteenth century, in the northwestern township of Rhinebeck. Margaret Beekman Livingston, herself representing the union of two great families, owned six large houses and land assessed at £1500 in Rhinebeck, and at election time she sent her bailiff round to the tenants.[14] The social atmosphere in this part of the county is suggested by the Old Red Dutch Church, erected on the eve of the Revolution at Red Hook. It had special pews along the sides of the church for the landlords and their families, designed so that only the head of a seated occupant could be seen from the center of the building where the common people worshiped.[15]

In the south (the 200,000 acre region which later became Putnam County) the land and the people were poorer. "Mountainous and fit only for iron works," William Smith called the area in 1756.[16] The per capita tax assessment of the townships there, Frederickstown and Philipstown, was less than half that of Rhinebeck; taxpayers assessed at less than £5 made up over 90 per cent of the taxpaying population in Frederickstown and Philipstown, less than 40 per cent in Rhinebeck.[17] In contrast to the Germans and Dutch predominant in northern and central Dutchess, the inhabitants in the southern part were almost entirely from New England and Long Island.[18] They had come, said a Moravian missionary, in search of "cheap farms, and . . . religious liberty." [19] For a time they had found both, squatting on land which Adolph Philipse claimed but had done nothing to develop. But in the 1750's the Philipse heirs had become more aggressive, ejecting tenants who would not accept onerous leases; and it was here that the formidable riots of 1766 had begun, when two thousand armed tenants refused to pay rents, rescued comrades from the Poughkeepsie jail, marched on New York City for the same purpose, and were finally dispersed only by redcoats with cannon. In 1775, all of south Dutchess was held in tenancy rather than freehold. Every officer of the Revolutionary militia in this section was a tenant.[20]

The substantial freeholders of central Dutchess were—socially and politically as well as geographically—a group intermediate between the landlords of Rhinebeck and the tenants of the south. From Fishkill, Amenia, and Poughkeepsie came the popular politicians who courted tenant votes but who themselves belonged to "a rising middle-class of freeholders which disliked the domination of the landed aristocracy." [21] They included Dirck Brinckerhoff (who had defeated Judge Livingston in the Assembly elections of 1768 and 1769), Ephraim Paine, Melancton Smith, Gilbert Livingston, and Zephaniah Platt. These were the men who in 1779–80 led the struggle for price regulation and the confiscation of Loyalist lands, and in 1787–88, the struggle against the United States Constitution. From 1760 to 1790 and beyond, northern Dutchess voted for the landlords' candidates and southern Dutchess against them, while central Dutchess oscillated between the two.[22] In 1788, the leading men of northern Dutchess were Federalists; the two Dutchess delegates at the New York ratifying convention who voted against the Constitution came from the south; while the four delegates who were elected as anti-Federalists but voted for the Constitution in the end, came from central Dutchess.

The still-smoldering tenant discontent in southern Dutchess helps to explain why, in the spring of 1775, the northern townships under the leadership of Judge Robert Livingston elected delegates to a provincial congress, while the south was "almost unanimously opposed." [23] British agents in the county, complained a Whig leader, "have corrupted the minds of many of the ignorant and baser sort of men among us, maliciously telling them the whigs were in rebellion; the King would conquer them, and their estates be forfeited; and if they take up arms against them, the King for their services will give them the whigs' possessions." [24] Two years later William Smith was told that the neighborhood of Quaker Hill, where the tenant rioters of 1766 had made their last stand, was forty to one "agt. Independency." [25] But not all tenants were Tories. Outright Toryism shaded off into Whig discontent. Later in the Revolution the Colonel of a regiment of Dutchess militia classified his men as "good Whigs," "Tories," and "middling Whigs." The last category was the largest.[26] Moreover, when the War for Independence began to develop social-revolutionary dimensions, allegiances wavered and changed. By 1779–80 many landlords had become Tories or reluctant rebels, while tenants pressed for drastic measures to seize and distribute Loyalist estates.

II

After Lexington and Concord a "coalition of parties" took place.[27] From 1775 to 1777, the Dutchess delegations to the Provincial Congresses and Convention were a mixed bag of men made up from the old governing group (including notorious landlords like Beverly Robinson and Robert G. Livingston, and James Livingston, the Dutchess sheriff at the time of the tenant rebellion) and the new, popular leaders. In these first years of the Revolution, there were few signs of the later division of the Whig leaders. Indeed, in the Convention debates over the proposed New York constitution in the spring of 1777, Gilbert Livingston and Zephaniah Platt voted with Robert R. Livingston against universal manhood suffrage in Assembly elections, and against the compulsory introduction of the secret ballot at the end of the war.[28]

As the war dragged on, future Federalists and anti-Federalists labored together on a variety of overlapping Revolutionary committees in Dutchess. Striving to cope with endless administrative emergencies, they found themselves attacked from behind, as it were, by a rising popular discontent. The discontent involved a series of grievances painfully interlocked. High taxes, frequent militia duty, and the burden of refugees from southern New York were singled out by Robert R. Livingston in a letter to George Washington. In 1781 the New York legislature, in a letter to its constituents, mentioned "the Weight of Taxes, the rigorous Measures that have been used to restrain the Disaffected, Exertions oppressive to Individuals by which Supplies have been obtained, the Wants of the Army, the Calls upon the Militia, and the Destruction of our Frontiers. . . ." [29]

In these first years of the war, militia duty was perhaps the heaviest burden. Conservative Whigs viewed the militia with some distrust from the outset. James Duane wrote to Robert Livingston (the Lord of Livingston Manor) in 1775:

I am much pleased that young Mr. Livingston is raising a company in the Manor. I wish he may extend his View's further, in the only plan, which, independent of the grand Contest, will render landed property Secure. We must think in Time of the means of assuring the Reins of Government when these Commotions shall subside. Licenciousness is the natural Object of a civil [here the word, "war," was crossed out by Duane in the manuscript] discord and it can only be guarded against by placing the Command of the Troops in the hands of Men of property and Rank who, by that means, will preserve the same Authority over the Minds of the people which they enjoyed in the time of Tranquillity.[30]

But the men of property and rank did not control the militia in Dutchess. The highest-ranking officer in the county, Jacobus Swartwout, was the son of a tenant. Colonel Henry Luddington, commanding the south Dutchess regiment, was a tenant himself, as were all his officers. The Whig leaders in Dutchess, wrote William Smith in 1776, had "a general Suspicion of the lower Classes of the People" and no great confidence in the militia.[31]

If the officers were uncertain, the men were much more so. The chairman of the Dutchess Committee of Safety, writing ten days after the Declaration of Independence, warned that the county's militia was untrustworthy and should not be called out. Of the four hundred militiamen in Rhinebeck, one hundred had been disarmed for suspected disloyalty, and he doubted whether there were two townships in the county with less disaffection. He concluded: "We have always thought we should be happy if we were capable of combating our internal foes, and leave those from without to be resisted in some other way." [32]

The reason for the soldiers' dissatisfaction is not far to seek. A private received $6.66 a month. Bounties promised to supplement the basic pay were late in coming. In August 1776, Zephaniah Platt wrote that "there is great complaints amongst the troops concerning this bounty, many of them having no money to purchase necessaries, having left at home what little they had for the use of their families." [33] A year later Governor George Clinton protested that "the Continental Pay and Rations being far below the wages given for ordinary Labor the Difference becomes a Tax rendered by personal Service and as the Train Band List from the Exemptions arising from Age Office & other Causes consists chiefly of the Middling & lower Class of People this extraordinary Tax is altogether paid by them." [34] Frequent advertisements for the apprehension of deserters appeared in the Dutchess newspapers.

The "tax" of militia service bore with particular severity on the poor tenant militiamen of south Dutchess. Their colonel, Henry Luddington, complained that "at best the Regiment are verry poor when compared with other Regiments and are call'd on to raise an eaquil number with the others, when I can affirm that ten farmers in Coll. Brinckerhoff's Regiment is able to purchase the whole of mine. In this uneaquil way, I have been obliged to turn out my men untill they are so much impoverish'd that they almost dispair." [35] This was written in 1781; but as early as the spring of 1777, the commissioners for detecting conspiracies were laboring to enforce discipline in Luddington's regiment, and one Captain Delavan told the Provincial Convention that southern Dutchess was largely disaffected. At the same time a traveler reported to William Smith that "the Drafts in Dutchess were few and would not serve [because] the People were wore out last year. Those in the Army lost the opportunity of seeding their Ground and were now starving for Bread." [36]

III

The Provincial Convention which heard these disquieting reports in early 1777 was also attempting to draft New York's Revolutionary constitution. Abraham Yates, Jr., of Albany, antiquarian and future anti-Federalist, believed that discontent in the militia had much to do with the democratic features of the new government. "The Yeomanry of the Country," he wrote, "were wanted to fight and the Militia Duty which equally affected the poor and the rich (a Man of £10 had the same Duty as the one of 10,000) upon the Principal of Personal Service was Become very Burthensome to the yeomanry and if the Rich Intended the other should continue to fight for there Estates it was Necessary to show that they did not make any Difference but w[h]ere it was unavoidable." [37] While the Convention defeated the proposal to give the franchise in Assembly elections to all taxpaying resident freeholders over twenty-one years of age, the property requirement for the vote was decreased. Perhaps even more significant were the institution of annual rather than septennial Assembly elections and certain changes in electoral procedure. Whereas elections to the colonial Assembly and to the Provincial Congress and Convention had been held at the county seat by viva-voce voting, the gubernatorial election of June 1777 was held at five different places in Dutchess County, and in at least one precinct by secret ballot. That precinct was Rhinebeck, the stronghold of landlord influence, and the election inspector was Melancton Smith! [38]

It has recently been suggested that the absence of the secret ballot in pre-Revolutionary New York may not have seriously impaired democracy.[39] If this were so, why did John Morin Scott fight for the secret ballot in all elections at the New York Convention? Why did Charles DeWitt charge the Livingstons that "when the De-Lanceys were to be quelled down they were Advocates for Elections by Ballot and now their Power was broke were opposed to it"?[40] Yates, again, testified eloquently to what the late Sir Lewis Namier, speaking of England in 1760, called "the inevitable result of open voting by people in dependent positions."[41] "What material difference is there," Yates asked, "whether one elector by his own voice sends a Member to parliament, or a manour settled with a hundred or a thousand Tenants, under the influence of one Person (and moved by his insinuation, nod or at least a letter . . . the Tenant [gives] his vote against his inclination, against his most intimate friend or relation, to a person the landlord was pleased to nominate)." If the "landed Gentlemen" agreed on a candidate, Yates continued, the election was a foregone conclusion; if not, "the public houses in every quarter were opened and a trial made who had the most influence and the largest purse."[42]

The common folk of Dutchess, as they went to the polls in June 1777, must have pondered the fact that in the earlier, viva-voce voting for Dutchess delegates to the Provincial Congress, universally-hated landlords like Beverly Robinson and Robert G. Livingston had been returned.[43] For in this first election after the creation of the new Constitution, politics in Dutchess took a sharp swing to the left. George Clinton was decisively elected Governor. In Dutchess his margin was 206–132.[44] William Smith was told that resentment toward the Livingstons was the dominant passion behind the vote: Philip Schuyler, he noted just before the elections, "says Ulster and Dutchess are jealous of the Livingstons who have already got all the valuable Places and that they will not vote Ph: L [Philip Livingston, sheriff of Dutchess County] for Govr. . . ."; another informant told him that "the People of Dutchess and Ulster were perswaded in chusing a Govr. to name no Livingston nor any in Connection with that Family & hence Clinton was preferred to Jay & Schuyler."[45]

The election of Clinton was indeed a blow to the Livingstons' control over the Revolutionary ferment. On the eve of election, Robert R. Livingston had argued "the propriety of swimming with a stream, which it is impossible to stem." Contrasting the position of the Pennsylvania conservatives with that of his own group in New York, he continued: "Wilson will remember that I long ago advised that they shd. yield to the torent if they hoped to direct its course—you know that nothing but well timed delays, indefatigable industry, & a minute attention to every favourable circumstance could have prevented our being exactly in their situation." [46] After Clinton's election, it began to seem that Pennsylvania and New York might not be so different. In August 1777, Livingston wrote Gouverneur Morris concerning the first signs of a popular movement which was to bulk large in Dutchess two years later: "You have seen the attempts of the county of Albany to imitate the Philadelphia Committee in [price] regulations etc. tho' they have not been followed by the other Counties yet they have excited a spirit that will be troublesome." By early 1778 his tone had become acid. No doubt thinking of the Dutchess situation at his doorstep as well as of Governor Clinton, Livingston wrote Morris that "the ignorance of some, & the wickedness of others are hourly perverting the constitution," and, "you know too much of some people in power here to think the State safe in their hands." In April, Livingston lamented to Morris that the legislature wanted to regulate prices, prohibit the export of flour, and lay "a most unprecedented tax . . . on all Traders & Manufacturers who have made more than £1000." In the same letter, less than a year after his philosophical reflections on swimming with the stream, he announced that he was considering retirement from New York politics.[47]

Thus the events of 1777—the adoption of a compromise but still significantly more democratic constitution, Clinton's victory, Livingston's dismay—marked the first decisive fragmentation of the Whig coalition in New York. In the state, Yates and Scott aligned themselves against Rensselaer, Schuyler, and Livingston. In February 1778, William Smith noted that there was "a Severance between the Popular & the landed Interest and they will mutually pull each other down." In Dutchess, the landlords ceased to seek election. Robert G. Livingston, a member of the Dutchess delegation to the second Provincial Congress, became a passive Tory, and when the British fleet sailed up the Hudson to Kingston and burned the manor houses of Rhinebeck, Livingston's was left conspicuously untouched. Beverly Robinson, a delegate at the same Congress, became an active Tory, an officer in the British army. *His* house was Benedict Arnold's base of operations in the spring of 1780. As for Robert R. Livingston, he, together with Duane, John Jay, Duer, Gouverneur Morris, and Schuyler, began a powerful, co-ordinated campaign to strengthen and to capture the national government.

IV

Conservative Whigs had hoped that the creation of a state constitution would put an end to the irregular activities of local committees—what William Smith called an "Infinity of Lawgivers" [48] —and restore an orderly political and judicial structure which they could control. But just as discontent in the militia had influenced the politics of 1777, so now new grievances rose up from below to push the popular leaders on to still more extreme positions and ultimately, in 1779–81, to call forth a revival of the local committees. As Scott, Platt, and Brinckerhoff made proposals to regulate prices and to sell confiscated and unappropriated lands, "the basis of their popularity," [49] Robert R. Livingston and his friends could only strive to undo at Philadelphia what was enacted at Albany. In March 1780, when the New York legislature finally passed a bill to sell the Loyalist lands, the Congress in Philadelphia staved off price regulation and took the first step in the conservative financial program by devaluing the Continental currency. This was the last act of a drama which had begun in the winter of 1777–78, when John Morin Scott introduced bills in the New York legislature to regulate prices and wages, and to confiscate Loyalist lands.[50]

In Dutchess, pressure for price regulation and land confiscation rose with the cost of living. Figures in the papers of the Dutchess Commissioners of Sequestration suggest the magnitude of price inflation: a Negro slave girl sold for £50 on December 23, 1777, and for £3,680 on October 5, 1780; on August 16, 1780, a pair of oxen was sold for £1,040. As currency depreciated and prices rose, taxes and requisitions became ever heavier. Some Dutchess farmers left their wheat unground rather than accept the worthless quartermasters' certificates. Looking back years later on the hardships of those days, a group of Dutchess tenants recalled that while some had fled to the enemy, they themselves had "remain'd stedfast on . . . determined to defend the right of [our Co]untry as well as our own Property." They had suffered particularly, they said, from the nearness of the troops, "who were constantly Cantoned & encamped around us, notwithstanding our willingness at all times to supply their reasonable wants but how inadequate was our little property to the Support of an Army often hungry, Naked and distressed for the necessary Comforts of life, which consequently, at times, by living so contiguous to them Reduced us to the same predicament." [51]

The common man personalized his grievances and blamed financial distress on the malevolence of speculators. Henry Luddington and others inveighed against the "wicked, mercenary intrigues of a number of ingrossing jockies, who have drained this part of the State of the article of bread to that degree, that we have reason to fear there is not enough left for the support of the inhabitants." [52] The "petition of the freeholders and inhabitants of Dutchess County" told the New York legislature that speculators were selling provisions to the enemy for specie and refusing to sell to Whigs for paper, and asked for action against "a vile set of Men whose God is their Gain. . . ." [53]

To many a perplexed householder, not only in New York but throughout all the struggling states, the revival of local committees seemed, ultimately, to be the way to check the monopolistic practices of merchants and the dishonesty of public officials. Direct action on the spot, so ran the argument, would check what no mere law was competent to prevent. "At length," proclaimed a correspondent to the Poughkeepsie newspaper, "is the virtuous part of the community alarmed, and the old and true friends to their country again step forth to remedy evils the laws cannot reach, by the exertion of Committees, the terror of all villains. . . . As soon as the authority of your Committees ended, knavery shewed its head, villains of every class came forth and practiced with impunity. . . . Let no time be lost then, my countrymen, in forming your Committees." [54]

Before the catastrophic year 1779, in which the Continental currency sank from about one-eighth to about one-fortieth the value of specie, the Dutchess committees were somewhat diffident in taking direct action without approval from above. The chairman of the Rhinebeck committee wrote to the president of the New York Convention in March 1777 that a local speculator was debasing the currency but that the committee did not know whether it was authorized to act; in November he complained of the high price of Robert Livingston's iron and the revival of horse racing, adding, "it is not as we recollect in our power to prevent it." [55] Far different was the manner of the Dutchess committees revived in 1779 in response to Philadelphia's call for committees "in every State and county." [56] The committee of Rombout precinct, chaired by future anti-Federalist Jacobus Swartwout, announced that traders were to buy goods only at prices fixed by the committee and sell them only at designated rates of profit, after invoices had been exhibited to the committee or its chairman. The committee of Poughkeepsie, under the chairmanship of future anti-Federalist Gilbert Livingston, called for the immediate confiscation and sale of forfeited estates. A county-wide committee, meeting in August 1779, resolved to "diligently inquire into the conduct of all public officers." [57] At the same time the committees recognized the need for more centralized action by the state legislature and the Continental Congress. When Governor Clinton addressed the legislature in August 1779, he acknowledged the flood of local petitions concerning price and currency problems by referring to "the Sense that your Constituents loudly express of the Necessity of applying some suitable Remedy to this growing Evil." [58]

Meantime an even more controversial issue had loomed up. In the same issues of the newspapers which told of price-fixing committees started in Philadelphia, Boston, and Williamsburg in 1779, Dutchess farmers read of the confiscation of Loyalist lands in Pennsylvania, New Jersey, and Vermont. John Morin Scott had introduced a bill for this purpose in the New York Senate the year before, and dark rumors had begun to circulate in Dutchess. William Smith was told that "a Man in the Secrets of the Leaders" of the Dutchess and Ulster Clintonians had commented—on the Tory literature promising the estates of Whig landlords to their tenants —that "it was half right but the Tenants would not get the Lands in that Way meaning from the Crown but that when the Independency is established the Manors would be parcelled out to such Tenants as were in Favor with the New established Government." [59] In October 1778, "the respectful address and petition of the freeholders and others, inhabitants of the county of Dutchess" made it plain that tenant unrest as well as the government's need for money underlay the agitation for confiscating and selling Loyalist lands. Pleading with the legislature to speed passage of such a bill, the petition warned: "The delay of this act to another session is big with uncertainty of its passing at all, and therefore of the most dangerous consequences to this State. Especially as it will occasion universal uneasiness and in all probability produce tumults and insurrections, and tend to a domestic tyranny and confusion as much to be dreaded as the evils brought upon us by our connections with Great Britain." [60]

For if Whigs throughout the country saw in Loyalist property a potential prop to Revolutionary finance, the tenants of southern Dutchess had their own reasons for wanting the confiscation and sale of Loyalist estates. Two-thirds of south Dutchess belonged to Beverly Robinson and Roger Morris, attainted by the act of October 1779. The tenants had been reluctant rebels in 1775–76, but the opportunity of acquiring their farms as freeholds would appear to have worked mightily on their convictions. For Simon Calkins and other south Dutchess tenants whom Beverly Robinson had dispossessed in the 1760's, the legislation to confiscate and sell Loyalist lands was an opportunity to rehearse the history of their grievances and to lay claim to their inheritance. They had, they told the legislature in a 1779 petition,

settled a wild uncultivated Tract of Land . . . and turned it into comfortable Habitations [with an] Expectation of Reaping the Benefit, and enjoying [the fruits of] their Labour and Toil in the Decline of Life; being [confident] . . . that whoever should be the proper Owner . . . would have Justice Goodness and Compassion . . . to allow them the Priviledge of enjoying those Habitations [and] Farms which they had made comfortable and in some measure profitable by the sweat of their Brows, upon their paying an equitable and reasonable Rent.—But contrary to this . . . as soon as their farms were in any measure made comfortable convenient or profitable by their Industry, one Beverly Robinson instigated by his associates Philip Philipse and Roger Morris, and assisted by a Banditti of Kings Troops . . . in the Year 1766 . . . obliged them to quit their Houses and Farms and commit themselves naked unto Providence. . . .

Therefore, this much-charred and barely-legible document concludes, they desired the legislature to "enact such Laws or adopt Measures as may effect the Restoration of these your Petitioners. . . ." [61]

The course of the Revolutionary War brought to the tenants of the Dutchess Highlands not only the opportunity of acquiring freeholds, but the threat of being dispossessed from what precarious tenure they had already achieved. This much-troubled region was the southern boundary of the area controlled by the New York Revolutionary government and hence, the natural place for the Whig refugees from southern New York to accumulate. In March 1777, the legislature created Commissioners of Sequestration to sell the personal effects of Loyalists "under moderate rent from year to year to persons friendly to the cause of America," giving first priority to refugees.[62] This meant that a tenant of a Loyalist landlord like Beverly Robinson could himself be dispossessed to make way for a refugee. To those tenants who, like James Cox, received letters from the Commissioners ordering them to remove for this reason, the spirit of '76 may have suddenly seemed less important, and the spirit of '66 more real.[63]

By the fall of 1779 a formidable tremor of unrest was shaking the ground beneath the feet of the Whig leaders. Tenants, at least in Dutchess County, had passed from the withholding of rents [64] to mutterings about more aggressive action. "The people have become very licentious," Thomas Tillotson wrote Robert R. Livingston in December.[65] In the same month Livingston's mother, Margaret Beekman Livingston, capped a complaint about oppressive taxes (levied by another future anti-Federalist, John DeWitt) with the prayer for deliverance from the "persecutions of the Lower Class" already quoted.[66] Not only in Dutchess but all over America, it would seem, the pressure on legislative bodies from the people "out of doors" reached a high point in this winter of 1779–80. October 1779, when the New York legislature enacted the permanent confiscation (though not yet the immediate sale) of Loyalist estates, was also the month when resentment against profiteering culminated in the "attack on Fort Wilson" in Philadelphia.

The grave state of civilian morale was more than duplicated in the military. The commanding general of the northern army, William Heath, wrote in quiet desperation that the troops had been eight days without bread, "a universal uneasiness" prevailed, and mutiny seemed immanent. On December 16 he wrote that two-thirds of one Dutchess regiment had simply gone home, but he recommended leniency for the mutineers because of the shortage of food.[67]

As the legislators struggled through unprecedented snows and temperatures as low as eighteen degrees below zero to reach the January session in Albany, politicians of both parties voiced alarm. "I have not felt equal Distress at the Situation of our Affairs at any Period since the commencement of the War," wrote Clinton; "the Garrison of Fort Schuyler," echoed Philip Schuyler, "has been on half allowances, that Fort George so distressed they have been on the point of Evacuating"; and John Sloss Hobart summed up what all felt in the phrase: "this winter . . . is the most important to us of any that will fall within our age." [68]

Screwed to this pitch of tension, what bonds of confidence remained between the radical and the conservative New York Whigs were stretched and snapped. In this 1780 session of the New York legislature, when the immediate sale of Loyalist lands was enacted,[69] one sees in full operation the opposing parties which, in 1787–88, would take the names Federalist and anti-Federalist. Egbert Benson of Dutchess, himself already under attack in the Dutchess County newspapers for Tory sympathies, wrote at the end of the session that it had "been the most disagreeable and troublesome one I have known; almost a continual Wrangle from first to last. It certainly is the first in which I have known either Men or Measures lay under the Imputation of Disaffection. At our first sessions the Debates ran high . . . but we still believed each other Whigs and so far there was a perfect Confidence; at the last Meeting however our Proceedings were poisoned by a Distrust, and without Cause, if not of Toryism at least of cool dispirited Whiggism, equally injurious." [70] Benson's statement confirms the judgment of Allan Nevins and E. Wilder Spaulding that it was at this time, and over this issue, that "the patriots were clearly divided into moderate and extremist factions." [71]

It was symbolic that Benson, the future leader of Dutchess Federalism, led the fight in the Assembly against sale of the confiscated estates, while the favoring faction was guided by Dirck Brinckerhoff, the anti-landlord champion of 1768 and 1769. In September 1779, Benson moved to delay the sale of forfeited lands until the next meeting of the legislature and to prohibit the sale of unimproved lands in the confiscated estates. In each case Brinckerhoff and the majority of the Dutchess delegation voted against Benson. But the bill was sent back to committee and came up for final action at the next session. [72]

The committee reported out on February 4, 1780, stating that memorials had been received from several counties imploring the speedy sale of confiscated lands. Again the Assembly voted on whether to proceed to immediate sale; again Brinckerhoff and most of the Dutchess delegation were in favor, again Benson was opposed. The crucial division came on March 10, when the Senate returned the bill to the Assembly, urging that sales be postponed until further attempts had been made to raise money by loan: a third time Benson voted for delay by supporting the Senate suggestion, and a third time Brinckerhoff and the bulk of the Dutchess representatives joined the now-victorious majority. [73]

What lay behind these votes was not a contest of good men and bad men. On February 25, at the same Assembly session, a bill was introduced which provided that slaves who voluntarily enlisted for three years with the consent of their masters should thereby become free. Brinckerhoff moved to reject; Benson voted in favor. [74] What distinguished Benson from Brinckerhoff in the crisis of 1779–80 was a different relation to the popular movement for land confiscation and price regulation. Benson came from the conservative constituency of Rhinebeck. Throughout the session he consulted Robert R. Livingston, who thought the confiscation law "a most ill judged" bill: "never," Livingston wrote, "was there a greater compound of folly avarice & injustice." [75] Behind Brinckerhoff, who lived in Fishkill, stood the agitated voters of southern Dutchess, searching the newspapers for their representatives' votes, in order "to know before every new election, by the votes of the old one, in what manner they have acquitted themselves, and how well they are entitled to our future choice, which surely no one can have the least pretension to who voted against the confiscation bill." [76] Whatever his personal views may have been, Brinckerhoff, like Scott, bent with the storm and courted the good opinion of local committeemen like Gilbert Livingston and Peter Tappen. [77] It paid off at the polls. In 1781 Benson, hitherto the dominant figure in the legislature, [78] lost his Assembly seat and did not recover it until 1787. Brinckerhoff, on the other hand, served in five of the eight Assemblies which preceded the adoption of the United States Constitution.

Democratic in its origins, the confiscation law was also democratic in its results. Of the 496 forfeited lots sold under the law of March 10, 1780, in Dutchess County, 455 were in southern Dutchess, and 414 had belonged to Beverly Robinson and Roger Morris. [79] The 455 lots were sold directly to 401 persons: rarely, obviously, did a purchaser acquire more than one farm. Almost without exception the lots sold were small, under the five-hundred-acre maximum specified by the law. Moreover, not only were the lots small and shared among many hands, but in almost half the sales the purchasers were tenants in possession of the land at the time of confiscation. Of the 401 purchasers of forfeited farms in south Dutchess, 166 had paid taxes in these townships in 1777. [80] Of forty tenants actually in possession of a group of Robinson's lots offered for sale in July 1780, twenty purchased the land that they were farming. [81] William Pelletreau is certainly very near the mark in his conclusion that "in a large number of cases, in fact a majority, the lands were sold to the parties who were already in possession of the various farms, as tenants of Beverly Robinson and Roger Morris." [82] As in the case of the tenanted estates of Westchester County, the confiscation of Loyalist lands in Dutchess County helped to democratize the structure of society. [83]

V

After passage of the confiscation legislation, the popular ferment continued, but that legislation remained its most significant concrete achievement. Almost a year later Robert R. Livingston wrote that "the people are clamorous[;] the whole County of Dutchess have chosen precinct & County committees to instruct their members." At the same time he wrote to George Washington of the unrest among the common people: "sore and dissatisfied[,] their discontents begin to break out in complaints against their rulers in committees and instructions." [84] After still another year, Margaret Beekman Livingston worried that wheat continued at the low price of five shillings a bushel: "I know not what will become of our farmers"; [85] and Thomas Tillotson, as quoted earlier, wrote that "the people want nothing but to be a little more impoverished to prepare them" for violent action. But by 1781–82 the radical program for meeting the financial emergency had (in its decentralized form of local committee action) been shown impractical, and (in its centralized aspect at the Continental Congress) been defeated. What remained of the radical impulse was not a practical program for the nation, but a seedbed of stubbornly democratic attitudes which the 1780's would vainly try to cultivate and bring to harvest.

Then, amid the cut and thrust of controversy over the adequacy of the Confederation, rival mythologies of what happened in the Revolution were perfected. Both Federalists and anti-Federalists claimed to be the exclusive inheritors of the American Revolution. In 1787, Robert R. Livingston, in an Independence Day oration to officers of the Cincinnati, more than a little implied that the true Whigs of '76 had all become Federalists. On the other side, Abraham Yates, Jr., argued that "the Characters that Now are called Aristocratic were then called high prerogative Gentlemen." "It is admitted," Yates went on, "that there are poor as well as rich Tories . . . yet we know by experience that there would not have been a Tory in fifty in our late struggles if they had not been disaffected by the rich." [86]

These mythologies linger on in rival historical interpretations of the Revolutionary era, but the reality would appear to be different from either version. Neither the Federalist nor anti-Federalist leaders of Dutchess had been Tories. Politicians of democratic and aristocratic bent could join in support of independence because the American Revolution as a social movement was not intended or foreseen.

It developed as a pragmatic outcome of the practical crises which had to be surmounted if the war was to be won. As Merrill Jensen and Oscar and Mary Handlin, writing from different standpoints, agree, the new forces which arose in the years after Lexington "were the products of the problems of those years." [87]

And yet that is only half of the story. The responses evoked by the successive Revolutionary crises, for example the alternate programs brought forward to cope with the financial emergency of 1779–80, had deep roots in the colonial past. The antagonisms which rose to the surface of Dutchess politics as the war went on were long-standing and familiar. Far from springing full-grown from the brow of revolution, these antagonisms centered on the old conflict between the ruling families of the landed aristocracy and the tenants and small freeholders of the county. It was this linkage of the concrete wartime struggles over militia service and Revolutionary finance to traditional and easily-mobilized popular sentiments that made it certain democracy would emerge from the struggle, as de Tocqueville was told, paramount.

Such at least is the model suggested by the events of the Revolution in Dutchess County, New York. For a few years after Lexington and Concord, landlord-tenant conflict was partially overlaid by the concord in Whiggery of all Dutchess political leaders, aristocratic and popular. While their future constituents were refusing to form Revolutionary committees or to elect delegates to the Provincial Congress, Zephaniah Platt was defending a liberty pole erected in Poughkeepsie, and Melancton Smith, an ardent Whig since the 1760's, was raising the first Revolutionary militia company in Dutchess.[88] But by 1777–78, still more by 1779–80, the old alignments had revived. And when, at the New York ratifying convention of 1788, Melancton Smith rose to confront Robert R. Livingston and defend the participation in politics of the middling and humble sort of people,[89] he only echoed the poem of a twelve-year-old boy, written in the heated elections of the late 1760's, which told the Livingstons that "not a vote would you get if it wan't for your land." [90]

Not that the popular leaders—Melancton Smith, Dirck Brinckerhoff, Zephaniah Platt, Gilbert Livingston, Jacobus Swartwout, Ephraim Paine, and their like—were typical of the poor farmers who elected them. On the contrary, they were well-to-do and represented (to borrow a term from another controversy) the "entrepreneurial" element in the Dutchess democracy.[91] But these men chose, no

doubt in part because of their own humble origins, to ride rather
than to contend with the whirlwind of popular feeling. Whereas
Robert R. Livingston, in George Dangerfield's fine phrase, stood for
the "politics of privilege," the Smiths, Platts, and Brinckerhoffs of
Dutchess politics represented the "politics of opportunity." [92]
While never entirely at ease with the presence in politics of the
really poor, these popular leaders developed a democratic philosophy
of politics which called for the election to office of men of a
"middling sort," frequent elections, rotation of office, small election
districts, and a large representative branch.[93] Their brief hour of
dominion over Dutchess politics foreshadowed the decline of the
aristocracy in the politics of New York a generation later.

Looking back, it is easy to underestimate the meaning of the confiscation and sale of Loyalist estates, the major legislative achievement of Dutchess County's internal revolution. No doubt, the
confiscation laws only accelerated a long-run trend toward freehold
tenure. Hard-bitten landlords like Robert G. Livingston still sold
off a farm here, a farm there, finding it more convenient to hold
mortgages on freeholds than to try to control a tenant's management
of the land.[94] The Revolution did not "abolish the leasehold system." [95] Even in south Dutchess, where the bulk of the confiscations
occurred, many farms purchased by tenants slipped out of their
hands again in the 1780's as they failed to meet payments and were
forced to resell.[96] With the coming of peace, landlords like Robert
G. Livingston and his son Henry took the oath of loyalty and resumed their trade: "I have wrote several letters to William Devine
[a tenant]. . . . I must order him to be arrested please to write him
a line threaten him perhaps that may prevail on him to do something"; "Dirck has run off and left his son in possession. . . . Poppy
desired me to turn him off as he used him ill by sending him inso-
lent Messages such as refusing him rent and saying he would pay to
the King etc. etc." [97] The county's economy had not been revolutionized.

So it seems looking back. But to contemporaries, living through
the event and making it, the confiscation of Loyalist lands had a
more comprehensive significance. It was the first major break-
through of the independence struggle into social change. It brought
to political expression the trend toward freehold tenure which, in
time, would destroy the neo-feudal society of the Hudson Valley.

The best objective measure of the change wrought by the Revolution in the county is the disappearance of the old ruling families

from political office. Thus Beverly Robinson was replaced as first judge by Ephraim Paine, a self-taught lawyer who dressed so plainly he was often mistaken for a laborer; Sheriff Philip Livingston gave way to Melancton Smith, who had clerked in a retail store and was a mere "Mister" among a flock of "Esquires" in the Dutchess delegation to the first Provincial Congress.[98] Between 1777 and 1788 not one member of the old ruling families held an important elective or appointive position in Dutchess County.[99] For a decade it seemed that the Revolution had settled not only the question of home rule, but also—and just as decisively—the question: Who should rule at home?

NOTES

1. Alexis de Tocqueville, *Journey to America*, ed. J. P. Mayer (New Haven, 1960), 20.

2. The Livingstons of Clermont were the most powerful landlord family in Dutchess in the third quarter of the 18th century. Their influence was based on land acquired by strategic marriages with descendants of Henry Beekman, Sr., the largest landholder in early Dutchess history. The three most important Clermont Livingstons at the time of the Revolution were: Judge Robert Livingston, who died in 1775; his wife, Margaret Beekman Livingston; and their son, Chancellor Robert R. Livingston. They must be distinguished from two other branches, also involved in Dutchess affairs. Philip Livingston, Dutchess sheriff in 1775, belonged to the Livingstons of Livingston Manor, whose interests lay primarily in Albany (later Columbia) County. Robert G., Henry, and Gilbert Livingston belonged to a third and distinctly less prominent branch; their sphere of action was Dutchess County, and politically they often allied themselves with freeholders of the county opposed to the Livingston "interest."

3. Carl L. Becker, *The History of Political Parties in the Province of New York, 1760–1766* (Madison, 1909), 14.

4. Henry Noble McCracken, *Old Dutchess Forever! The Story of an American County* (New York, 1956), 234.

5. George Dangerfield, *Chancellor Robert R. Livingston of New York, 1746–1813* (New York, 1960), Pt. ii, chaps. 1–3, especially pp. 60, 81–82.

6. William Smith, *Historical Memoirs from 12 July 1776 to 25 July 1778 of William Smith*, ed. William H. W. Sabine (New York, 1958), 280, 306.

7. Margaret Beekman Livingston to Robert R. Livingston, Dec. 30, 1779, Robert R. Livingston Papers, New-York Historical Society, New York City. Hereafter cited as R. R. Livingston Papers.

8. Thomas Tillotson to Robert R. Livingston, June 17, 1782, R. R. Livingston Papers.

9. E.g., Robert E. Brown, *Middle-Class Democracy and the Revolution in Massachusetts, 1691–1780* (Ithaca, 1955), passim; Louis Hartz, *The Liberal Tradition in America . . .* (New York, 1955), 67–86.

10. Testimony at the trial of William Prendergast, leader of the tenant rebellion of 1766 (Irving Mark and Oscar Handlin, "Land Cases in Colonial New York, 1765–1767: The King v. William Prendergast," *New York University Law Review,* XIX [1942], 191). The court which condemned Prendergast to death consisted "wholly of important landowners and land speculators" (*ibid.,* 167); for the attitude of the judges, see William Smith, *Historical Memoirs,* 40. The tenants petitioned the King that they had attempted to pursue their grievances by legal means, but had "found that every Attorney at law in that whole Province was previously retained on the other side" (Brief of Daniel Ninham before Chancery, 1767, quoted in William S. Pelletreau, *History of Putnam County, New York* [Philadelphia, 1886], 79).

11. Alice C. Desmond, "Mary Philipse: Heiress," *New York History,* XXVIII (1947), 26.

12. Philip L. White, *The Beekmans of New York in Politics and Commerce, 1647–1877* (New York, 1956), 159. The correspondence of Henry Beekman, Jr., with his agent, Henry Livingston, is in the Henry Livingston Papers, Franklin Delano Roosevelt Library, Hyde Park, New York, and New York State Library, Albany, New York, and the Beekman Papers, N.-Y. H. S.; it is summarized by White, *ibid.,* 191–207.

13. The great landlords of Dutchess before the Revolution were, in the north, the intermarried Beekmans and Livingstons (note 2, above), and in the south, the heirs of Adolph Philipse. The latter were Philip Philipse, the son of Adolph Philipse, and Roger Morris and Beverly Robinson, who married Adolph Philipse's daughters. In 1775 these families owned about one-half of the millions acres in Dutchess County. The Philipse patent comprised 200,000 acres, while the whole of the present townships of Beekman and Pawling represented only a part of the holdings of Henry Beekman, Sr.

14. For the houses, see "A Particular List or Description of Each Dwelling-house . . . in Rhynbeck Town . . .," Gilbert Livingston Land Papers, New York Public Library, New York City. For the tax: Margaret Beekman Livingston to Robert R. Livingston, Dec. 30, 1779, R. R. Livingston Papers. For electioneering: Robert Livingston to James Duane, Apr. 30, 1788, Duane Papers, N.-Y. H. S.; Thomas Tillotson to Robert R. Livingston, Mar. 23, 1787, and Margaret Beekman Livingston to Robert R. Livingston, Apr. 1789, R. R. Livingston Papers.

15. Philip Smith, *General History of Dutchess County from 1609 to 1876 Inclusive* (New York, 1877), 382–383. An anti-Federalist later made use of this manner of church design to exemplify the kind of society which, he thought, the United States Constitution would foster: see the allegory by "A Countryman" in the *New York Journal* (New York City), Dec. 6, 1787, with its description of the "large high pews for the better sort of people to sit in, so that they might not be troubled with the common people, or rabble as they fained to call them."

16. William Smith, *History of the Late Province of New York from its Discovery to . . . 1762* (New York, 1830), I, 311.

17. The total assessment and number of taxpayers for each township in 1771 are printed in James Smith, *History of Dutchess County, New York* (Syracuse, 1882), 119. The percentages of taxpayers in different assessment categories were computed from "Copy of Assessment Rolls of the Freeholders and Inhabitants of Dutchess County . . . 1786," N. Y. S. L.

18. Regarding south Dutchess, McCracken states that in the 1800 Census only 2 per cent of the names in the southern townships were Dutch (Mc-

Cracken, *Old Dutchess Forever!*, 471). As to northern Dutchess, Richard Smith, traveling up the Hudson in 1769, landed at Henry Beekman's manor in Rhinebeck and found no one who could speak English (Francis W. Halsey, ed., *A Tour of Four Great Rivers . . . in 1769* [New York, 1906], 10); while the historian of northeastern Dutchess states that before 1770 nine-tenths of the inhabitants were Palatine Germans (Isaac Huntting, *History of Little Nine Partners . . .* [Amenia, 1897], I, 133).

19. Journal of Abraham Rhinke, quoted in Philip Smith, *Dutchess County*, 112.

20. Pelletreau, *Putnam County*, 120; Henry Lud[d]in[g]ton to George Clinton, Feb. 20, 1778, *Public Papers of George Clinton* (New York and Albany, 1899–1914), II, 784–785. Hereafter cited as *Clinton Papers*.

21. White, *Beekmans*, 206. Whereas more than 90 per cent of the tax-payers in southern Dutchess were assessed at £4 or less in 1786 (note 17, above), Zephaniah Platt was assessed at £16 in 1771 and at £46 in 1786, besides heading a speculative group which bought up soldiers' claims to 30,000 acres of land near Lake Champlain; Dirck Brinckerhoff was assessed at £27 in 1786 and lent £7664 on mortgages between 1768 and 1785 (H. W. Reynolds, ed., *Eighteenth Century Records of . . . Rombout Precinct*, Dutchess County Historical Society, *Collections*, VI [Poughkeepsie, 1938], 55, 59, 71, 72, 73, 80, 81, 96, 97, 112, 128–131, 229, 270, 283); Gilbert Livingston collected rents for his notorious uncle, Robert G. Livingston, and owned at least £7540 worth of real estate (H. W. Reynolds, "James Kent," Dutchess County His-torical Society, *Yearbook*, VIII [1923], 23); Jacobus Swartwout owned state and continental securities valued at approximately $7600 (Forrest McDonald, *We, The People; The Economic Origins of the Constitution* [Chicago, 1958], 307); Melancton Smith speculated in soldiers' warrants, Loyalist lands, and in a number of the speculative projects of William Duer (Israel Smith to Melancton Smith, Feb. 21 and 22, 1782, Daniel TerBoss to Jonathan Law-rence & Co., Mar. 4, 1782, Lawrence and Smith Papers, N.-Y. H. S.; Robert A. East, *Business Enterprise in the American Revolutionary Era* [New York, 1938], 94, 108, 117, 118, 146, 225, 275, 318).

The affluence of these popular leaders, however, was not in the same class with that of landlords like Henry Beekman, Jr., who in 1760 was assessed at £400 (McCracken, *Old Dutchess Forever!*, 73). The popular politicians were indeed, as they described themselves, of a "middling" rank.

22. See McCracken, *Old Dutchess Forever!*, 447, 464, 472. A few ex-amples: in the Congressional election of 1790, Rhinebeck went Federalist 215–13, Philipstown and Frederickstown went Clintonian, 15–0 and 69–42; in the Congressional election of 1800, Rhinebeck again voted Federalist 226–119, Philipstown and Frederickstown again voted Clintonian, 110–19 and 75–3 (*New York Daily Advertiser* [New York City], May 21, 1790; New York Secretary of State, "Certificates of Election, 1799, 1800," Miscellaneous Rec-ords, XXV, N. Y. S. L.).

23. Letters from Dutchess County correspondents to the *New-York Gazette: and Weekly Mercury* (New York City), Apr. and May 1775, Peter Force, ed., *American Archives*, 4th Ser., II (Washington, 1839), 304–305; Dangerfield, *Chancellor Livingston*, 57.

24. Samuel Dodge to the President of the New York Provincial Congress, Dec. 5, 1775, *Journals of the Provincial Congress, Provincial Convention, Committee of Safety and Council of Safety of the State of New-York* (Albany, 1842), II, 106. Hereafter cited as *Jour. Prov. Cong.*

25. William Smith, *Historical Memoirs*, 118. See in confirmation Nathan Pearce to the Provincial Congress, Jan. 5, 1777, *Jour. Prov. Cong.*, I, 766–767.

26. "Return of Delinquents in Col. Hopkins' Regiment . . . June 10, 1779," *Clinton Papers*, V, 71–73.

27. Letter from Dutchess County to *New-York Gazette: and Weekly Mercury* (New York City), May 15, 1775, *American Archives*, 4th Ser., II, 305.

28. *Jour. Prov. Cong.*, I, 867, 891–892.

29. Robert R. Livingston to George Washington, Jan. 8, 1781, R. R. Livingston Papers; *Votes and Proceedings of the Senate* (Fishkill, 1781), 71.

30. James Duane to Robert Livingston, June 7, 1775, quoted in Beverly McAnear, "Mr. Robert R. Livingston's Reasons against a Land Tax," *Journal of Political Economy*, XLVIII (1940), 76.

31. William Smith, *Historical Memoirs*, 27, 34.

32. Egbert Benson to the New York Provincial Convention, July 15, 1776, *Jour. Prov. Cong.*, II, 309.

33. Willis Fletcher Johnson, *Colonel Henry Luddington; A Memoir* (New York, 1907), 19; Zephaniah Platt to the New York Provincial Convention, Aug. 24, 1776, *Jour. Prov. Cong.*, II, 279.

34. George Clinton to the Committee of Safety of the Continental Congress, July 31, 1777, *Clinton Papers*, II, 142–143. On the difficulty of recruiting because of low militia pay, see also Egbert Benson to the New York Committee of Safety, Mar. 19, 1776, *Jour. Prov. Cong.*, I, 384–385.

35. Henry Lud[d]in[g]ton to George Clinton, May 1, 1781, *Clinton Papers*, VI, 817.

36. "General Jacobus Swartwout," Dutchess County Hist. Soc., *Yearbook*, XIII (1928), 68; *Jour. Prov. Cong.*, I, 910; William Smith, *Historical Memoirs*, 119.

37. "Notes on Early History of New York, etc.," Abraham Yates Papers, Box 3, N. Y. P. L.

38. On voting in colonial New York, see Michael N. D'Innocenzo, Voting in Colonial New York (unpubl. M.A. thesis, Columbia University, 1959); on voting for the Provincial Congresses and Convention, Becker, *New York*, 227, 252; on the Convention's provision for the gubernatorial election of 1777, *Jour. Prov. Cong.*, I, 918; and on the way the election was actually conducted in Rhinebeck, William Smith, *Historical Memoirs*, 159–160. Smith says that the instructions of the Convention as to voting were ambiguously worded, and that Melancton Smith interpreted them to require the use of the secret ballot. In 1778 the legislature made it clear that voting for governor was to be by ballot, and "not by counties but by boroughs towns manors district and precincts. . . ." (1st Session chap. 16).

39. Milton Klein, "Democracy and Politics in Colonial New York," *New York History*, XL (1959), 231–232.

40. So Peter R. Livingston reported to William Smith (William Smith, *Historical Memoirs*, 129, 157). Smith also states that Thomas Tredwell of Suffolk voted against the constitution of 1777 because it did not require the ballot in all elections (*ibid.*, 121). A draft of the Constitution providing for the secret ballot in Assembly elections is in the Abraham Yates Papers, Box 2, N. Y. P. L. Both Tredwell and Yates were anti-Federalists in 1788.

41. Lewis Namier, *The Structure of Politics at the Accession of George III*, 2d ed. (London, 1957), 70.

42. "Speeches to Delegates in Congress, 1786," Abraham Yates Papers,

Box 4. The importance assigned to the introduction of the secret ballot is supported by contemporary sources. But it would seem that, even before the Revolution, an intense popular feeling sometimes expressed itself at the polls despite all obstacles. Thus in the Assembly election of 1768, following close on the heels of the tenant rebellion of 1766, Judge Livingston "had so far lost the esteem of the Freeholders in that County, that he gave up before half the Freeholders then present had given in their votes, tho' he had every thing in his favour, which power could give him" (Cadwallader Colden to the Earl of Hillsborough, Apr. 25, 1768, in E. B. O'Callaghan, ed., *Documents Relative to the Colonial History of the State of New York* [Albany, 1856–87], VIII, 61). When he lost again in the following year, he was said to have been defeated by the votes of tenants "notwithstanding all the pains was taking with them" (Peter R. Livingston to Philip Schuyler, Feb. 27, 1769, quoted in Dangerfield, *Chancellor Livingston*, 40).

43. For the reputation of these landlords, see McCracken, *Old Dutchess Forever!*, 433. Beverly Robinson was the most active of the Philipse heirs in prosecuting ejectments in southern Dutchess in the 1760's; for the tenants' feeling about him, see note 61, below.

44. Professor Alfred Young of Paterson State College, New Jersey, discovered the returns for this election in the Van Cortland Papers, Sleepy Hollow Restoration Library, Tarrytown, N. Y., and kindly made them available to me.

45. William Smith, *Historical Memoirs*, 151, 326.

46. Robert R. Livingston to William Duer, June 12, 1777, R. R. Livingston Papers.

47. Robert R. Livingston to Gouverneur Morris, Aug. 8, 1777, Jan. 1778, Jan. 29, 1778, and Apr. 6, 1778, *ibid.* Morris attempted to rally Livingston to action: "Take a Survey of the Ground you have to act on. Where are the Eminences? They must be gained—*They* must be *gained.* . . . Will not some of their Forces revolt? . . . Take Ceres Bacchus and Minerva to your Aid" (Morris to Livingston, Jan. 21, 1779, *ibid.*).

48. William Smith, *Historical Memoirs*, 149.

49. Robert R. Livingston to Gouverneur Morris, Sept. 10, 1778, R. R. Livingston Papers.

50. *Votes and Proceedings of the Senate* (Fishkill, 1777), 17, 199.

51. Papers of the Commissioners of Sequestration, Dutchess County, N.-Y. H. S.; Ephraim Paine to Robert R. Livingston, Feb. 12, 1779, R. R. Livingston Papers; Robert R. Livingston to John Penn, Jan. 28, 1780, *ibid.*; petition of tenants on the "Water Lotts," Dutchess County, Sept. 6, 1784, New York Assembly Papers, XXVI, N. Y. S. L.

52. Henry Luddington and others to the New York Council of Safety, Dec. 3, 1776, *Jour. Prov. Cong.*, II, 355.

53. "The Petition of the Freeholders and Inhabitants of Dutchess County," undated, N. Y. S. L.

54. *New York Journal* (Poughkeepsie), Aug. 16, 1779. The price-fixing movement in the various states and the Continental Congress is described by Richard B. Morris, "Labor and Mercantilism in the Revolutionary Era," *The Era of the American Revolution: Studies Inscribed to Evarts Boutell Greene*, ed. Richard B. Morris (New York, 1939), 76–139.

55. Herman Hoffman to the President of the New York Convention, Mar. 17, 1777, and Jacob Heermance to the President of the Council of Safety, Nov. 21, 1777, *Jour. Prov. Cong.*, II, 409, 457.

56. *New York Packet* (Fishkill), July 15, 1779.

57. *Ibid.,* Sept. 16, 1779; *New York Journal* (Poughkeepsie), Aug. 9, Aug. 16, 1779.

58. Speech of Aug. 24, 1779, *Clinton Papers,* V, 210. The price-fixing movement alarmed and frightened the conservative New York Whigs. See, for example, Gouverneur Morris to Robert R. Livingston, Mar. 27, 1778: "Is it possible my friend that the State of New York can think of passing a *regulating Act.* How hath this madness got hold upon them" (Livingston-Bancroft Transcripts, II, N. Y. P. L.); John Sloss Hobart to Robert R. Livingston, Nov. 15, 1779: "The liberty of acquiring property is, probably, the greatest incentive to action in the whole moral system . . . Man is, by nature, a lazy beast. . . . Exert yourself therefore to prevent our resolves [the resolves of the Hartford Convention, favoring a general limitation of prices] from obtaining the sanction of congress, let there be no convention at Philadelphia" (R. R. Livingston Papers).

59. William Smith, *Historical Memoirs,* 326.

60. This petition is quoted by Johnson, *Luddington,* 153–156. It could not be located at the N. Y. S. L., and was presumably destroyed in the great fire there, which totally consumed several volumes of petitions that had been removed from the Assembly Papers. The reception of the petition is noted in the Assembly and Senate Journals.

61. Petition of Simon Calkins and others, Sept. 2, 1779, New York Assembly Papers, XXVI, N. Y. S. L. The continuity of the spirit of tenant unrest in Dutchess County from 1766 to 1780 is illustrated by a comparison of this petition with those of the 1760's, for example, "A petition for a Confirmation of our inheritance together with our associates," Nov. 10, 1763, Miscellaneous Manuscripts—Dutchess County, N.-Y. H. S.

62. For the steps leading up to this legislation, see Harry B. Yoshpe, *The Disposition of Loyalist Estates in the Southern District of the State of New York* (New York, 1939), 13–15. The work of the Dutchess Commissioners of Sequestration is described at length in my *Anti-Federalism in Dutchess County* (Chicago, 1962).

63. Theodorus Van Wyck to James Cox, Jan. 26, 1779, Papers of the Commissioners of Sequestration, Dutchess County, folder 1. Needless to say there were two sides to the situation. John Campbell wrote to Van Wyck, Jan. 31, 1780: ". . . those two Families have Twelve Children the Oldest not Eleven Years old and to my knowledg one of those Families have been six weeks this winter without Bread—and when the small remains is gone I brought out of New York this must be my situation unless you relieve me" (*ibid.,* folder 2).

64. For the widespread withholding of rents, see Robert R. Livingston to the Trustees of Kingston, Mar. 1, 1778, R. R. Livingston Papers; the advertisements of Robert G. Livingston, *New York Journal* (Poughkeepsie), Jan. 4, Aug. 16, 1779, and *New York Packet* (Fishkill), Aug. 19, Sept. 2, 1779, directed "to those tenants in arrears, from four, eight or ten years in particular"; Henry B. Livingston to Robert R. Livingston, May 1775: "The Tenants here are Great Villains. Some of them are resolved to take advantage of the times & make their Landlords give them Leases forever" (quoted in Bernard Mason, Organization of the Revolutionary Movement in New York State, 1775–1777 [unpubl. Ph.D. diss., Columbia University, 1958], 60).

65. Thomas Tillotson to Robert R. Livingston, Dec. 13, 1779, R. R. Livingston Papers.

66. Two years later Mrs. Livingston was still complaining of DeWitt's

taxes (Margaret Beekman Livingston to Robert R. Livingston, July 16, 1782, *ibid.*). It is evident from her letters that this great absentee owner was for the first time being assessed for holdings in eastern Dutchess and for the Dutchess poor tax.

67. William Heath to George Clinton, Dec. 3 and Dec. 16, 1779, Jan. 25, 1780; Clinton to Heath, Dec. 23, 1779, *Clinton Papers*, V, 396–398, 421–422, 429–430, 463–467. See Dangerfield, *Chancellor Livingston*, 119.

68. George Clinton to Robert R. Livingston, Jan. 7, 1780, R. R. Livingston Papers. Philip Schuyler to Robert R. Livingston, Jan. 18, 1780, *ibid.* John Sloss Hobart to Robert R. Livingston, Feb. 15, 1780, *ibid.* Two years later the contractor Jacob Cuyler referred to the year "Seventy nine Eighty when they were ready to Disband for want of Provisions" (Jacob Cuyler to James Duane, Aug. 31, 1782, Duane Papers).

69. The long struggle over Loyalist lands can be properly understood only when it is divided into three stages. First, Loyalist lands were sequestered (Mar. 1777); then confiscated (Oct. 1779); and then sold (Mar. 1780). Each step in this process provoked a separate legislative battle. More property was sequestered than confiscated, and more confiscated than sold. In Poughkeepsie, for example, the personal belongings of 45 persons were sold under the sequestration law, but only 1 of the 45 lost his land (Edmund Platt, *The Eagle's History of Poughkeepsie from Earliest Settlement, 1683 to 1905* [Poughkeepsie, 1905], 301); and that one, Bartholemew Crannell, recovered his land in the late 1780's with the help of his Whig son-in-law, Gilbert Livingston. George Clarke, with large holdings in northeastern Dutchess, went to England and "not wishing to lose this vast landed property . . . sent his son to America to take charge of it and at the same time to profess deep sympathy with the Whig element" (James Smith, *Dutchess County*, 214).

70. One correspondent accused Benson of saying in 1779 that "for two years past, the Whigs have done the State more damage than the Tories" (*New York Journal* [Poughkeepsie], Mar. 15 and Mar. 22, 1779). This would tend to confirm the chronology suggested by the text: 1775–77 as the period of Whig unity; 1777–79 as the period of developing tension; 1779–80 as the moment of open division.

Benson's remarks on the session are in Egbert Benson to Robert R. Livingston, Mar. 20, 1780, R. R. Livingston Papers. Livingston commented to Duane: "I was this day distressed by a letter from Benson, in which he mentions the mad lengths to which a party spirit arising, as far as I can find, from no real cause, has hurried our Legislature. It is much to be lamented that internal factions should break out before we had driven the enemy from our doors" (to James Duane, May 2, 1780, Duane Papers).

71. The phrase quoted is from Allan Nevins, *The American States During and After the Revolution, 1775–1789* (New York, 1924), 268. E. Wilder Spaulding says: "The Confiscation Act for the first time aroused a conservative Whig opposition to the extreme measures of the government" (*New York in the Critical Period, 1783–1789* [New York, 1932], 122).

72. *Votes and Proceedings of the Assembly* (Fishkill, 1779), 26, 28.

73. *Ibid.*, 95, 150.

74. *Ibid.*, 127.

75. Egbert Benson to Robert R. Livingston, Feb. 20, Mar. 20, June 28, July 8, 1780, R. R. Livingston Papers; Robert R. Livingston to John Jay, Mar. 4 and Apr. 20, 1779, *ibid.*

76. "A Country Man" in the *New York Journal* (Poughkeepsie), May 18, 1779.

77. See Robert R. Livingston to John Jay, Apr. 20, 1779, with its reference (crossed out in the manuscript) to "Scotts desire to satisfy the ship carpenters of Poughkeepsie" (R. R. Livingston Papers). The "ship carpenters of Poughkeepsie" were Gilbert Livingston and Peter Tappen, who were building ships for the Revolutionary government.

78. Alexander Hamilton later called Benson the pre-eminent figure in the Assembly during the Revolution (writing as "H——— G———" in the *New York Daily Advertiser* [New York City], Mar. 12, 1789); Walter Livingston wrote to Robert R. Livingston on Jan. 7, 1781, of Benson as the man who "is supposed to govern the politicks of this State" (R. R. Livingston Papers).

79. Except where indicated, the facts in this paragraph are derived from the Abstract of Forfeited Lands for Dutchess County, N.-Y. H. S. This volume corresponds exactly with Ledger A of Deeds in the basement of the county clerk's office at Poughkeepsie, New York.

80. The assessment rolls for southern Dutchess in 1777 are printed in Pelletreau, *Putnam County*, 122–128.

81. *New York Journal* (Poughkeepsie), July 24, 1780.

82. Pelletreau, *Putnam County*, 92–93. This is not to deny either that tenants were often cruelly dispossessed, or that speculators acquired many of the farms. The former is suggested by a petition, Jan. 15, 1781: "We the subscribers beg leave to represent the circumstance of Daniel Hunt who is now eighty-seven years of age. He lives on a small farm that did belong to Col. Robinson not more than twenty acres of improved land. He has always been friendly to the country he has lived on the place twelve years. If you will be pleased to order that the place may not be sold but let him continue the few days he has to live it can't be long and he is not able to buy it. . . ." (Miscellaneous Manuscripts—Dutchess County, N.-Y. H. S.). Speculation is well illustrated by that prince of speculators, William Duer, who bought two of Robinson's farms for himself and Robert Morris; assuring his partner that since the purchase could be made in money worth only 1/22 of its face value, they could expect a profit of 4 per cent on the investment in rent and a 200 per cent profit when they sold out (East, *Business Enterprise*, 112). Radical politicians like John Lamb, Zephaniah Platt, John Morin Scott, Jacobus Swartwout, Mathew Patterson, and Melancton Smith each picked up a farm or two. See also note 96 below.

83. Yoshpe, *Loyalist Estates*, 115, concluded that in the Southern District "patriotic profiteers contrived to get the bulk of the loyalist estates into their own hands." But Spaulding, in reviewing Yoshpe's book, correctly pointed out that Yoshpe slighted his own evidence that many tenants on the Philipse Manor in Westchester acquired their farms (this evidence is at *ibid.*, 50–63; Spaulding's review is in the *American Historical Review*, XLV [1939–40], 899–900). The entire literature on confiscation in New York is crisply summarized by Catherine Snell Crary, "Forfeited Loyalist Lands in the Western District of New York—Albany and Tryon Counties," *New York History*, XXV [1954], 239–258. The Dutchess and Westchester evidence, considered as a whole, suggests that where confiscation involved large, tenanted estates, the results may have been substantially democratic, while speculators found their pickings primarily in scattered, urban, or unoccupied parcels.

84. Robert R. Livingston to Gouverneur Morris, Jan. 18, 1781, and to George Washington, Jan. 8, 1781, R. R. Livingston Papers.

85. Margaret Beekman Livingston to Robert R. Livingston, Dec. 22, 1781, *ibid.*

86. Draft of oration to the Society of the Cincinnati given, New York, July 4, 1787, *ibid.*; "Speeches to Delegates in Congress, 1786," Abraham Yates Papers, Box 4.

87. The phrase quoted is from Oscar and Mary Handlin, "Radicals and Conservatives in Massachusetts after Independence," *New England Quarterly*, XVII (1944), 355. For Jensen's argument that "the American Revolution was a democratic movement, not in origin, but in result," see his "Democracy and the American Revolution," *Huntington Library Quarterly*, XX (1957), 321–341.

88. For Smith's political views before 1775, see his letters of Dec. 2, 1769, and Jan. 2, 1771, Melancton Smith Papers, N. Y. S. L.

89. The famous exchanges between Smith and Livingston laid particular stress on the question: From what socio-economic groups should the legislative representatives of a republic be recruited? At one point Livingston asked Smith if he intended to go out among the hedgerows and enlist the blind, sick, and lame as representatives; at another, switching tactics, he proclaimed, "We are all aristocrats." This theme, underlying the entire debate, is brilliantly characterized by Dangerfield, *Chancellor Livingston*, 222–233. Far from being rhetorical, it was the essential point at issue in Dutchess politics throughout the Revolutionary era.

90. This little verse, which begins, "One night in my slumbers, I saw in a dream / Judge Livingston's party contriving a scheme," will be found in "A Packet of Old Letters," Dutchess County Hist. Soc., *Yearbook*, VI (1921), 36 *n.*

91. See note 21, above.

92. Dangerfield, *Chancellor Livingston*, 88.

93. See the program of a meeting of Amenia freeholders (*Poughkeepsie Country Journal*, Dec. 22, 1785), which also calls for paper money and the repudiation of debts to Tories.
The attitude prompting these proposals is well suggested by Melancton Smith's notes for a speech at the New York ratifying convention: "The Senate will be a small Body, distant from ye people in a situation not to be observed by them—Men are apt in this condn. to forget their dependence—to lose their sympathy—to contract selfish habets . . . A Senator will be most of his time from home—will associate with none but his own class—will become a stranger to the condn. of the people—He should return and be obliged to live with the people . . ." (Melancton Smith Papers). In view of the frequency with which anti-Federalists expressed democratic sentiments of this sort, it is difficult to avoid the conclusion that Cecelia Kenyon's study of the anti-Federalist ideology ("Men of Little Faith: The Anti-Federalists on the Nature of Representative Government," *William and Mary Quarterly*, 3d Ser., XII [1955], 3–43) presents a very one-sided picture.

94. "Only let the farm year to year because I will sell them both as soon as possible"; "If any body would be in earnest about it I would agree about the price for I had better sell them almost at any rate than to have them out for they want repairs" (Robert G. Livingston to Gilbert Livingston, Apr. 6, 1773, and Mar. 22, 1775, Gilbert Livingston Papers, Box 1, N. Y. P. L.).

95. This is the judgment of the distinguished Dutchess antiquarian Helen W. Reynolds, "The Story of Dutchess County," Dutchess County Hist. Soc., *Yearbook*, XVIII (1933), 32; and of McCracken, *Old Dutchess Forever!,*

425, 430, 433. But it is refuted by the electoral census of 1790, which lists 1115 40 s. tenants along with 2780 £20 and £100 freeholders (*New York Daily Advertiser* [New York City], Jan. 15, 1791), figures which if anything underestimate the extent of tenancy, since tenants were often classified as freeholders for electoral purposes. The correct generalization is that of David Maldwin Ellis, *Landlords and Farmers in the Hudson-Mohawk Region, 1790–1850* (Ithaca, 1946), 28: "Dutchess County . . . presented a checkered pattern of land tenure with numerous leaseholds interspersed among the predominant freeholds."

96. For a struggle between several mortgage lenders to gain ownership of a confiscated Dutchess farm, see Henry G. Livingston to Gilbert Livingston, Mar. 4, 1781, Gilbert Livingston Papers, Box 1. Several petitions of tenants who had made deposits on their farms but could not meet the installment payments are in the New York Assembly Papers, XXV, XXVI, N. Y. S. L. Provision for installment payments was not included in the confiscation legislation in order to benefit speculators. On the contrary, the Council of Revision twice warned that unless a provision for installment payments were included, the lands would be monopolized by speculators, who alone had quantities of ready cash (*Votes and Proceedings of the Senate* [Fishkill, 1777], 214; *Votes and Proceedings of the Assembly* [Fishkill, 1779], 144–145). But many tenants were so short of cash in the mid-1780's that they petitioned to pay part of their payments in wheat and beef.

Another difficulty faced by the south Dutchess tenants in attempting to purchase their farms was that the confiscation legislation required tenants to pay all arrears of rent. This was a heavy burden: on May 1, 1777, Beverly Robinson's tenants had owed him £2753, two-and-a-half times their total annual rent. The tenants contended that the requirement to pay back rent prevented them, "a very few excepted," from purchasing their farms. See the petitions of Reuben Ferris and 93 others, June 26, 1781; Alexander Kidd and 102 others, Mar. 1782; and 61 residents of Philipstown, Mar. 1782 (*New York Senate Papers*, X, Box 2, and XI, Box 1); for the arrears of rents on Robinson's farms, see Frederick C. Haacker, *Early Settlers of Putnam County, New York* (1946), typescript at N. Y. S. L., 2. A law of Apr. 14, 1782 (5th Session, chap. 45) eased the tenants' situation by permitting them to pay half of their arrears in securities rather than specie.

97. Robert G. Livingston to Gilbert Livingston, Oct. 26, 1785, Henry G. Livingston to same, Feb. 1, 1785, Gilbert Livingston Papers, Box 1.

98. For Ephraim Paine, see Newton Reed, *The Early History of Amenia* (Amenia, 1875), 72, 102–103, and Philip H. Smith, *Dutchess County*, 121–122. For Melancton Smith, see "Committee of Dutchess County to the New-York Congress," *American Archives*, 4th Ser., II, 834.

99. Franklin B. Hough, *The New York Civil List* (Albany, 1861), 62–65, 74, 109–111, 122–130, 183–193, 420, 446, 457. Henry and Gilbert Livingston might seem exceptions to this generalization. But they belonged to the non-propertied branch of the Livingston family descended from Gilbert, one of the three sons of the first Robert. Whereas for the Manor and Clermont Livingstons politics was an avocation, "for the Gilbert line . . . local public offices tended to be a means of livelihood": the clerkship of Dutchess County was perennially in this family (Joan Gordon, *Kinship and Class: The Livingstons of New York* [unpubl. Ph.D. diss., Columbia University, 1959], 264–265).

Part II

—

TRANSFORMATION
OF THE ECONOMY
1790 - 1870

5

Public Policy

THE EARLY NINETEENTH CENTURY was long commonly regarded as the high point of *laissez faire* policy in the United States. Private business operated without significant government interference, the argument ran, and public policy consisted largely of beneficent inactivity. A series of recent scholarly studies of government policy before the Civil War has forced revision of the conventional view. These studies reveal that state government took an active role in conditioning the course of economic development. The federal government itself by no means withdrew from the field after the Hamiltonian economic program had been enacted in the 1790's. By providing engineering expertise to the states and private corporations, building roads and other public works such as river and harbor facilities, extending aid to the states by means of land grants for canals, and regulating banking practices both directly (through the Treasury Department) and indirectly (through the national banks), the federal government continued to exert a major influence on the economy. The state governments made their major contribution by providing social-overhead capital in the form of transport and banking facilities and by enforcing regulatory legislation controlling banking and corporate enterprise. Even local and county government, especially through regulation of markets and harbors and through public aid to railroads, performed significant economic functions.

In the following essay, Henry W. Broude weighs the significance of government activity in the economy during the years 1820–1890 and attempts to quantify the economic impact of federal spending in the more limited period 1821–1845. Taking as his reference point sociologist Bert F. Hozelitz's statement that there was "minimal interference by the state in economic activity" in the nineteenth century, Broude summarizes the newer interpretation and defines some important issues for future investigation.

THE ROLE OF THE STATE
IN AMERICAN ECONOMIC DEVELOPMENT,
1820–1890

Henry W. Broude

Economic change in the United States during the nineteenth century followed a pattern which, although set at an early stage by Great Britain, soon became distinctly American in characteristics and timing. The rate of growth increased with an impetus stemming from the simultaneous emergence of new technology and expansion of the domain under the aegis of the United States. The period has been described as typifying extensive and independent growth. Hoselitz has characterized the American setting as expansionist (almost unlimited natural resources), dominant (relatively self-sufficient, self-reliant approach to economic development), and autonomous (minimal intervention by the state in economic activity).[1] The appropriateness of the characterization as expansionist is evident not only as reflected in the advance of the frontier,[2] but also in the burgeoning "American system of manufacturing," unique in itself.[3]

Categorizing the United States of the nineteenth century as dominant may be acceptable, but certain remarks should accompany this designation. Dominance, in the sense used, is open to the qualification that insofar as European capital was used throughout the century American economic development did receive stimulus from abroad.[4] Also, questions arise concerning the pace of development in the absence of such immigration (and movement of goods

Reprinted by permission of the author and the Social Science Research Council from *The State and Economic Growth*, edited by Hugh G. J. Aitken (New York: Social Science Research Council, 1959), pp. 4–25.

to European markets) as took place. In particular, the critical period in the early decades of the century, when the country was evolving from a nondominant status, should not be overlooked.

It is to the third classificatory term, autonomous, that attention is given in this paper. Is the term appropriate when applied to American growth from 1820 to 1890? Rather than a complete catalogue of state activity in the economic sphere, we present material which, it is suggested, should temper the characterization of American growth in the nineteenth century as autonomous. Although one may well be wary of assigning weights to the "evidence" (and thereby appearing to tilt with the image of the American economy of that century), it seems worth while to attempt an appraisal of the role of the state in American development. The contemporary vogue in "economics of growth" of recommending policy based on analogy with past experience justifies detailed research on an example so frequently cited in present-day studies of underdeveloped areas. The more we relate the specific and detailed aspects of American economic development to each other and to the context of the period, the more sensitive and operationally significant any attempts to use this historical material may be.

The strategic location in the economy of governmentally induced activity may prove to have leverage implications for development well in excess of what highly aggregative studies may indicate. This may be true not only in the sense of specific impact at spatially and temporally strategic points, but also in the sense that the mere *presence* of government gives rise to activity that appears in history as purely autonomous; in actuality the effects of government may be cloaked in the data left behind.

The first part of the discussion below is concerned with the character and degree of governmental intervention in the economy. Next we present evidence on what might be termed positive aspects of the state's role. Finally, observations are made regarding the validity of the characterization and the potential usefulness of the American example in a framework of typical growth patterns.

CHARACTER AND DEGREE OF INTERVENTION

An appraisal of the degree of private enterprise in the development of a given economy might begin with specification of its industry sectors and estimates of each sector's share of output originating under the control of private establishments. For America in the nineteenth century, this would give a picture of overwhelming proportionate dominance of the private sphere. It might be desirable to supplement such an appraisal with a more qualitatively oriented survey of the sources of initiative in innovational activity. Both approaches would be needed to support the picture of America (undoubted here) as a society geared to individual enterprise, to general conformity to the profit maximization model, and to a growth pattern attuned to adopting new techniques as they emerge.[5] But what of the additional attribute of a minimal *role* for government? [6]

It is on this question that the evidence becomes less clear, and it is on the interpretation of what constitutes "government intervention" in economic life that the outcome of a judgment will depend. Hoselitz, for example, states: "Governmental practice may not coincide with the norms stipulated for the conduct of the political authorities. In other words, the relations between government and private individuals in the economic sphere may be so conceived as to leave, ideally, all significant decisions to the private individuals, yet government may impose narrow limits within which private initiative may be exercised or may use various forms of subsidies, so that, in practice, the process of growth depends primarily upon the government's 'inducements' rather than upon autonomous private decisions." He goes on to conclude, however: "If, therefore, we draw our line of distinction between induced and autonomous patterns of growth in such a way as to include in the former only those types of governmental action which have the aim of consciously allocating productive factors in a specified direction, the policies of almost all governments in the period before 1914 should be regarded as permitting an autonomous process of growth." [7]

Definition of the limits within which governmental intervention is considered to be passive and minimal plays an important part in evaluating the American situation, for the really significant role may be found to lie outside the defined function of "consciously allocating productive factors in a specified direction." One finds in aggregated data on governmental shares of national wealth (Table 1) or income realized from the government sector (Table 2) that the proportionate shares of government were relatively low, although on the rise during the nineteenth century.[8] An examination of federal finances shows federal expenditures to be a small portion of gross national product, and years in which budgetary surpluses existed were frequent in the earlier part of the century.[9]

TABLE 1. PERCENTAGE SHARES OF GOVERNMENT IN TOTAL
REPRODUCIBLE WEALTH, UNITED STATES *

	Structures		Equipment	
Year	Current prices	1929 prices	Current prices	1929 prices
1805	3.4	3.9	–	–
1850	2.9	3.1	–	–
1880	2.4	2.7	0.8	0.6
1890	2.8	2.8	0.9	1.0
1900	3.5	3.5	1.2	1.2

Source: Raymond W. Goldsmith, "The Growth of Reproducible Wealth of
the United States of America from 1805 to 1950," Table I, pp. 306–307, in
International Association for Research in Income and Wealth, *Income and
Wealth of the United States: Trends and Structure,* Income and Wealth
Series II (Cambridge, England: Bowes & Bowes, 1952).
* Including nonprofit institutions, but excluding military; inventory data
not available.

All of this substantiates the assertion of an autonomous climate.
Yet even at the outset of the period there are signs of conflict regarding the assumed ideological basis of this pattern. Jefferson and

TABLE 2. REALIZED INCOME FROM GOVERNMENT, BY KIND,
UNITED STATES, 1799–1900

Year	Realized income from government (million $)	Percentage of total realized national income	Production income from government (million $)	Other income from government (million $)
1799	6	0.9	6	–
1809	11	1.2	11	–
1819	17	1.9	15	2
1829	21	2.2	20	1
1839	39	2.4	37	2
1849	58	2.4	57	1
1859	101	2.3	100	1
1869	290	4.2	271	19
1879	322	4.5	284	38
1889	558	5.2	486	72
1899	1,005	6.5	910	95
1900	1,052	6.5	957	95

Source: Robert F. Martin, *National Income in the United States, 1799–
1938* (New York: National Industrial Conference Board, 1939), p. 87.

Jackson were clear about federal intervention, and there is a record of relative absence of "federalism" in fiscal matters in the United States up to and after the Civil War.[10] The patterns of minimal expenditure, however, during the administrations of Madison, Monroe, and John Quincy Adams obscure what was in reality a period of conflict in defining the *intended* role of government in the American economy in terms of both degree and level. These presidents, although in favor of federal expenditures for internal improvements, for example, were constrained either by their own doubts as to constitutionality or, in the case of Adams, by the impossibility of getting measures through Congress.[11]

From the early differences regarding governmental intervention there emerges a picture of men with ideological appetites for a laissez-faire menu, but one highly seasoned with the selective exceptions. The record shows that up to the end of the nineteenth century the wage and price system, usage of resources, credit creation, and provision of capital,[12] as well as other elements of the entrepreneurial function were kept within and held to be within the province of the private sector of the economy. Government effected a land tenure policy for the country, controlled immigration policy (conditioning the supply of labor), maintained intervention in the banking system (varied over the period),[13] established protection of trade through tariff and patent legislation, performed the roster of services "rightfully" governmental, and represented and strengthened the particular legal framework within which private business was organized.[14] Despite the acknowledged dominance of the autonomous sector of the economy, however, the record does indicate that at the end of the century calls for governmental aid had resulted in the holding by government of approximately 7 percent of the nation's capital assets and the employment by government of approximately 4 percent of the national labor force.[15]

Although the intent of this paper is to comment on the actual manifestations of state intervention rather than to discuss history of doctrine, one point regarding the intellectual climate of the period may be emphasized. There was tacit acceptance of an ideology; yet within it there were notable internal paradoxes and there were extensive departures from it in practice on a "selective" basis. This perhaps stresses the obvious but indicates the linked relationship, typically traced in discussions of economic growth, between investment (as the focal point in a dynamic industrial economy) and entrepreneurial action (responsive to expectations and the accessibility of usable funds).[16] Interwoven in such analysis is a link between ideology and growth and, hence, between the attitude of the entrepreneur toward the political climate and the state's role as it relates to the economic sphere. The pertinent question is whether the internal paradoxes and departures from the ideal that existed in the nineteenth century were at variance with the American entrepreneur's economic objectives or supplemental to them. Departure from a laissez-faire ideology means, of course, intervention of government. What must be established is whether intervention left the "representative" entrepreneur hostile, neutral, or perhaps with positive sentiments. If it appears that most "interventions" were compatible with the goals of the entrepreneur, it may be suggested that in evaluating the role of the state in economic growth we cannot consider only (or merely) the amount of income generated in the government sector of the economy, or the cases where impediments to activity in the private sector had been removed by government. Rather we must consider what the entrepreneur saw as the accommodation potential of the political structure in aiding him in his pursuit of his "special" needs along an uncertain and hazardous course.[17]

The next section presents examples of three aspects of government's positive role: giving specific and direct support to industry in the private sector; taking initial risks, leading the way, and removing bottlenecks; and creating a favorable climate which had salutory effects on expectations in the private sector.

POSITIVE ASPECTS OF THE STATE'S ROLE

The range of possible government actions affecting the economy is so wide that any discussion could become a mere exercise in cataloguing. It seems preferable, therefore, to consider particular episodes that illustrate "positive" action. Positive is here contrasted with passive or minimal, and a complete roster of such positive action in the nineteenth century would include attempts to modify the physical environment and the level and skill of the labor force, the introduction of new techniques, and the direct undertaking of business ventures, as well as support of industry in the private sector.[18]

A survey of the many dimensions of economic participation open to political units in the nineteenth century impresses one with the extensive functional range of these activities at all levels of government. Yet discussions of governmental intervention often implicitly emphasize government at the federal level. It is advisable, therefore, to differentiate explicitly between state and federal action as their effects were felt during the century.

Before the Civil War, government intervention in economic life was widespread but it was concentrated at the state level. The recent studies by the Handlins, Hartz, Heath, Pierce, and Primm [19] all present evidence not only of the extent of government intervention but of the fact that respective states held the center of the stage.[20] In his study of expenditures on railroads in the South, Heath concludes that public investment should be credited with more than 55 percent of total investment in that area (based on the total value of its railroads in the Census of 1860). He indicates that 4.7 percent of total public expenditures were federal, 56.7 percent were state, 26.0 percent municipal, and 12.6 percent county. In addition to direct expenditures, there was aid in the form of services of public officials and property, grants of rights of way, public lands and building sites, materials, tax exemptions, banking facilities, and other privileges.[21] There was activity at the local level also. Martin, in his study of living standards in 1860, points out that before 1860 local government expenditures were called forth, in part at least, by increased needs for goods and services.[22]

The nature and scope of the role of the respective states in the earlier part of the century is reflected in conclusions by Hartz:

. . . the mixed enterprise program . . . , embracing both profit and control objectives, . . . had more than simply a promotional significance. Originating in the banking field in the late eighteenth century, it flourished with increasing strength for half a century, eventually being extended to transportation and embracing various types of enterprise there. In 1844 over one hundred and fifty mixed corporations were currently listed in the official records of Pennsylvania, with public investments ranging from a few shares of stock to several thousand. It is hard to view such a policy as an incidental phase of state action worthy of only marginal notice.

Nor is it easy to regard as incidental the role of the state as entrepreneur exclusively in its own right. . . . It was with the inception of the public works in the 1820's, where a process of steady expansion and increasing investment was premised at the outset, that the entrepreneurial function of the state assumed major proportions.[23]

Writing of government action at the various levels in unlocking the reservoirs of national wealth, Potter calls attention to the rejection of "public capitalization of a great economic asset" in favor of "widespread access to wealth." Yet, as he notes, the potential for economic development depended not only on the now available land, but also on access to markets. Government participation in providing such access was extensive, taking the form of furthering internal improvements to facilitate communication with markets. Sometimes the federal government directly undertook projects, such as construction of the Cumberland Pike; sometimes the state government took responsibility, as New York did with the Erie Canal; and there were many cases of indirect participation, through offers of public credit or the power of eminent domain, as well as direct financial support of entrepreneurs.[24] Hibbard has pointed out that land grants as part of a program of internal improvements were "a major part of the whole episode of conscious development of the nation through public action. It was believed that private action was likely to be too uncertain and too slow." [25] Indeed there was an approach to conscious economic planning, which is reflected in President Fillmore's assertion, on signing the Land Grant Act in 1850, that it could be "expected to help undeveloped regions of West and South."

Controversy has long existed over how to evaluate a policy that transferred the disposal of resources to one industrial sector at the expense of alternative uses. Welfare criteria brought to bear on this discussion would have to weigh against the rapid expansion of a transportation system and the unifying effects on the nation such considerations as the episodes of waste, mismanagement, and erratic growth patterns.[26]

Characterization of specific activities and policies in an appraisal of the state's role must take account of continuing governmental action to make resources and areas more readily accessible as the economy developed. Initially, reference was made to internal improvements with emphasis on communication. However, as changing technology brought new resources (coal, iron, waterpower, oil) and new methods of production into use, government's role in "facilitating growth" covered the range of activities typically discussed in a survey of American developmental history: a legal structure conducive to corporate ownership of production units with guarantees of equal advantage in internal competition and, through tariff barriers, protection against competition from abroad.[27] Aitken has suggested that the temptation to minimize the role of tariffs in this respect should be resisted for two significant reasons: they have the effect of redistributing income among sectors of the economy and serve as means of reducing the uninsurable risks for private investment. Inclusion of these considerations in the American picture would depend on whether tariff protection effectively blocked sources of competition for American producers, whether entrepreneurial willingness to undertake certain amounts of production would have been affected at the margin by a risk element removed by the existence of the tariff barrier, and whether protection did not insulate enterprise from stimuli to greater growth than took place. The last possibility appears to be the one on which the firmest assertion can be made: it seems reasonable to say that stimulus to growth was not wanting and that, unlike France for example, the existence of protection did not result in stifling the dynamic potential of the period. Also, assurance of domination of domestic markets and the ensuing reduction of risk and promise of increased returns affected the rate of capital formation and the areas of the economy to which it was directed. However, in these latter developments one would be reluctant to assign a weight to the "importance" of protection. It does seem appropriate to say, with Aitken, that tariff protection deserves to be considered as among the "nonminimal" functions of government.

To fill out the picture, two other "types" of intervention should be examined. Manufacturing, commerce, and agriculture continually faced bottlenecks. Use of this term denotes short-run, "isolated" barriers to or inhibitors of development, as contrasted with continuing problems on a broad front of economic change. Removal of such barriers by government should be treated separately because, as in any bottleneck situation, coping with the critically placed obstacle may call for expenditure of relatively insignificant amounts with consequences of major importance.[28] Where government is the only source of initiative and action to remove such obstacles, assessment of the "importance" of this aspect of government's role is essential.

Examples range from the literal bottleneck to the psychological. On one hand, the raft of the Red River might be cited; on the other, the "presence effect" of government—i.e., the effect of government activity in an area, giving moral support to undertakings in the wilderness (geographic and technological) that would be too risky in the absence of nearby recourse to aid. We have an indication of one of many such literal bottlenecks:

At the date of the report just cited, the accumulations of drift at the head of the raft in the main river had been multiplied to such an extent that the navigation was rendered impracticable nearly to the head of Red bayou, which then had become the only channel or out-let through which the entire navigation of the river must be conducted, and fears were entertained that a few more accumulations of drift would effectually and entirely destroy the navigation of the entire river in its passage through the district of the present raft.

Agreeably to the latest information received concerning the raft, this catastrophe, if it has not already occurred, is likely to take place on the occurrence of the next considerable river freshet, when the abundant and valuable commerce of this important river will unavoidably be incommoded and obstructed by a difficult and expensive land portage of many miles in extent.

In view of what has already been stated on numerous occasions, in reference to the importance of keeping open a navigable channel through the district of the Red river raft, it is manifest that the fostering aid of Congress should be again extended to this object in the way of continued appropriations for its accomplishment.[29]

Government records give abundant evidence of the part played in removal of such obstacles as those in the Red River. Examples of providing links and easing the way are easy to find. The following items are typical: [30]

Constructing two piers and improving the navigation at the mouth of Vermilion river, Ohio	$10,777	(1839)
Improving navigation of the Arkansas river	17,452	(1839)
Road from Milwaukie [sic] by way of Madison, to Mississippi river opposite Dubuque	10,000	(1839)
Improving the harbor of Mobile	52,184	(1840)

There is evidence also in the sponsorship by Congress of scientific expeditions and surveys throughout the period. This pathfinding was certainly motivated in part by military needs,[31] but also by the desire to open areas for settlement and to increase communication and commerce. In these efforts should be included river surveying, well digging, resource surveying, wagon-road building, as well as cartography and other aspects of scientific exploration.[32] Congress approved a survey, largely under Army leadership, of a possible railroad route between the Mississippi and the West Coast; and during 1853–55 five surveys were made between the 32nd and the 49th parallels. The resulting empirical material was not only useful for railroad building but also added much to scientific knowledge of the area.[33]

In an attempt to gauge the pattern of government expenditures with reference not only to internal improvements but also to other outlays of specific significance in the growth of the economy, the Reports on the Finances of the respective Secretaries of the Treasury, 1821–45, have been examined.[34] Listings of so-called "selected" expenditures have been made for each of the years containing those items of federal expenditure that appeared to have particularly direct impact on the facilitation of economic activity. A summary of the relation of the selected items to total federal outlays is shown in Table 3. Because of the arbitrariness of selection, the lists should perhaps be characterized as impressionistic. All items covering pay and subsistence as well as most ordnance, arsenals, and armories, are excluded from the expenditures for the military establishment. The resulting figures should understate the extent of expenditures.[35] The breakdown is useful in indicating lower limits on the share of expenditures that affected the aspects of intervention under discussion here. The percentage figures indicate the extent of governmental involvement in economic pathbreaking and in activity which may have resulted, though only as a by-product, in positive contributions to development. The years 1836–38 show outlays greater than the trend would suggest. These can be explained largely by expenditures incurred in dealing with the Indians as is indicated, for example, in this item for 1837: "Carrying into effect treaty with Cherokees of 29th Dec., 1835 – act 2d July, 1836 . . . 1,132,834.81." In the same year, $4,010,162 was listed for "Preventing and suppressing Indian hostilities." [36] These items are included in the selected expenditures since efforts to remove hostile Indians were significant in making an area safe for economic development. The lands taken through treaties, of course, became part of the resources made available in the government land and settlement programs.

Finally, there is the somewhat elusive factor—the psychological impact of government's presence. Fleeting references in historical material acknowledge that this influence was of critical importance in conditioning the rate of growth. Part of the effect was due to the "credit standing" of the government. For example, commenting on the inability of private corporations to command a supply of capital in the years before 1840, Callender pointed out that "There was no body of private individuals in the country well enough known and with sufficient influence in the business world to establish the credit of a corporation so that it could command the confidence of both these classes of investors. The only securities that could do this were public securities, or the securities of corporations which were

TABLE 3. FEDERAL EXPENDITURES: COMPARISON OF TOTALS WITH
SELECTED EXPENDITURES FACILITATING ECONOMIC ACTIVITY,
UNITED STATES, 1821–45
(in thousands of dollars)

	Civil, foreign, miscellaneous			Military establishment		
	Expenditures		Selected as % of total	Expenditures		Selected as % of total
Year	Total	Selected	total	Total	Selected	total
1821	2,241.9	440.2	19.6	5,162.4	537.8	10.4
1822	1,968.0	180.1	9.2	5,635.2	797.8	14.2
1823	2,022.1	197.8	9.8	5,258.3	904.3	17.2
1824	7,155.3	221.8	3.1	5,270.3	1,011.2	19.2
1825	2,748.5	419.4 *	15.3	5,692.8	1,602.0	28.1
1826	2,600.2	406.7 *	15.6	6,243.2	1,768.9	28.3
1827	2,713.5	150.5 *	3.7	5,675.7	1,824.2	32.1
1828	3,676.1	203.3 *	5.5	5,719.6	1,821.1	31.8
1829	3,101.5	563.0 *	18.2	6,250.2	2,219.6	35.5
1830	3,237.4	403.5 *	12.5	6,752.7	2,427.9	36.0
1831	3,064.7	206.1 *	6.7	6,943.2	2,542.4	36.6
1832	4,577.2	473.5 *	10.3	7,982.9	2,841.5	35.6
1833	5,716.3	831.6	14.5	13,096.2	3,690.3	28.2
1834 †	3,584.1	222.7	6.2	8,349.4	2,115.7	25.3
1835	3,705.4			9,507.6		
1836 ‡	3,850.1	714.8	18.6	13,010.1	6,878.2	52.9
1837 ‡	4,024.8	736.5	18.3	16,310.2	8,554.6	52.4
1838 ‡	4,029.7	414.8	10.3	15,731.3	7,779.9	49.5
1839 ‡	3,649.4	470.9	12.9	10,791.8	3,545.3	32.9
1840 ‡	4,175.8	315.6	7.6	8,750.8	2,333.4	26.7
1841 ‡	4,615.4	222.6	4.8	10,834.1	3,756.5	34.7
1842 ‡	4,372.0	233.8	5.3	7,065.0	1,764.8	25.0
1843 §	2,867.3	96.5 ‖	3.4	4,158.4	974.9 ‖	23.4
1844 ⧧	5,231.8	320.6 ‖	6.1	8,231.3	2,064.3 ‖	24.9
1845 **	5,618.2	281.3 ‖	5.0	9,533.2	2,555.7 ‖	26.8

Source: Reports of the Secretary of the Treasury of the United States, for
the respective years. See pp. 123–124 supra for elaboration of "selected expenditures" category.

* The "selected expenditures" shown for the years 1825–32 include amounts
subscribed to stock in various canal companies, such as the Chesapeake & Delaware, the Dismal Swamp, the Louisville & Portland, and the Chesapeake &
Ohio.

† Three quarters, January 1 – September 30. Aggregate figures for the year
were: civil, foreign, miscellaneous, 4,404.7; military, 10,064.4; navy, 3,956.3;
total federal expenditures, 24,602.0.

‡ Three quarters, January 1 – September 30.

§ Six months, January 1 – June 30.

‖ Selection based on less disaggregated data.

⧧ Fiscal year, July 1, 1843 – June 30, 1844.

** Fiscal year, July 1, 1844 – June 30, 1845.

TABLE 3—*Continued*

| Year | Navy establishment Expenditures | | Selected as % of total | Total †† Expenditures | | Selected as % of total |
	Total	Selected		Total	Selected	
1821	3,319.2	.2	.01	19,090.6	978.2	5.1
1822	2,224.5			17,676.6	977.9	5.5
1823	2,503.8	6.0	.2	15,314.2	1,108.1	7.2
1824	2,904.6	4.4	.2	31,898.5	1,237.4	3.9
1825	3,049.1	1.9	.1	23,585.8	2,023.3	8.6
1826	4,218.9	1.3	.03	24,103.4	2,178.2	9.0
1827	4,263.9	6.8	.2	22,656.8	1,981.5	8.7
1828	3,925.9	1.1	.02	25,485.3	2,025.5	7.9
1829	3,308.7			25,044.4	2,782.6	11.1
1830	3,239.4			24,585.3	2,831.4	11.5
1831	3,856.2			30,038.4	2,748.5	9.1
1832	3,956.4	3.8	.1	34,356.7	3,315.0	9.1
1833	3,901.4	1.2	.03	24,257.3	4,521.9	18.6
1834 †	2,913.2			16,545.3	2,338.4	14.1
1835	4,917.0			18,189.2		
1836 ‡	3,931.2			20,791.4	7,593.0	36.5
1837 ‡	5,061.9			25,418.9	9,291.1	36.6
1838 ‡	4,325.6			28,427.2	8,194.7	28.8
1839 ‡	4,713.7			29,061.4	4,016.2	13.8
1840 ‡	4,620.3			21,188.1	2,649.0	12.5
1841 ‡	4,230.0	8.7	.2	24,734.4	3,987.8	16.1
1842 ‡	6,717.1	10.7	.2	26,264.9	2,009.3	7.7
1843 §	3,672.7	4.0 ‖	.1	11,560.0	1,075.4 ‖	9.3
1844 #	6,497.0			32,958.8	2,366.9 ‖	7.2
1845 **	6,228.6			29,968.2	2,837.0 ‖	9.5

† Three quarters, January 1 – September 30. Aggregate figures for the year were: civil, foreign, miscellaneous, 4,404.7; military, 10,064.4; navy, 3,956.3; total federal expenditures, 24,602.0.
‡ Three quarters, January 1 – September 30.
§ Six months, January 1 – June 30.
‖ Selection based on less disaggregated data.
Fiscal year, July 1, 1843 – June 30, 1844.
** Fiscal year, July 1, 1844 – June 30, 1845.
†† Including expenditures related to the public debt.

guaranteed or assisted by the government. American public credit had been raised to the highest pitch by the debt-paying policy of the federal government; and it was inevitable that the American people should turn to the only means in their power to provide for their needs." [37]

The psychological factor affected entrepreneurial expectations. The individual investor was reluctant to venture into the West alone; but his attitude was different with the government at his side, or more likely ahead of him. The effect was to encourage more and larger entrepreneurial undertakings. Many of the ventures that preceded the government into "uncharted" territory were unsuccessful, and this lesson was heeded by the entrepreneur. Certainly at early stages in American economic expansion, the presence of the government, usually in the form of the army, meant a tie with less primitive aspects of society. This tie was evidenced through the exchange of physical goods with governmental outposts, but it had a psychological impact as well in sustaining those who had moved to remote areas. This is reflected, for example, in the diary of a Minnesota farmer, William R. Brown, who wrote in 1845:

Friday 26th   Haskell & I went to Fort Snelling   took my pork Brot home my Flour 4 Barrels, 4 Barrels Beans 7 Bushels Corn Bot. a Buffaloe Robe at $2.50 bot 40 lbs of Harness leather for Charley at (Henry H.) Sibleys. learned of Steel that the Black & White cow of the Doe (?) Cattle that I sold to F. Steel weighed lighter than 400 lbs. Bot 7 Bushels Beans of Lieutenant (Robert S.) Granger   paid $1.50 per Bushel   took a Receipt of him   arrived at home at about 7 oclock. . . .
Saturday 24th   I borrowed J. A. Fords train and went to Fort Snelling   bot. 1 Barrel Beans @ 3.50   Bot Cloth for 2 Vests   one for myself & 1 for Harrison   Bot ⅔ of a Bushel fine salt . . .
. . . March 2nd . . . I went up to the Fort & carried up 40⅓ bushels of Oats   Steel was well pleased with them   they were Clean & the grain well filled. [38]

LEVERAGE EFFECTS OF GOVERNMENTAL INTERVENTION

Several observations on the general nature of American economic development seem important within the context of the present discussion; and in discussion of comparative development one must say something about *uniqueness*—particularity, rather than generality, emerges from a survey of the nineteenth-century American scene. [39] The word "pattern" should perhaps be avoided. As must be clear from preceding sections, the West, the revolution in transportation, and the continuing flow of new techniques in production dominate the picture. In the literature various hypotheses provide general developmental frameworks and direct special attention to a particular aspect or factor, for example, the frontier and abundance.[40] Taken separately or looked on as parts of a "total explanation," they provide a basis for illustrating the uniqueness of the American situation. They delineate development of a country with an expanding geographical area, in a position to use the know-how gained through the pathbreaking of another country, and to do so in an environment with a growing labor force and a growing market— all in what appears to be nearly optimal concomitance. The highly special set of circumstances that existed over the period should make one hesitant to generalize from the American experience. The constraint becomes all the more forbidding when, to these contextual factors, a series of specific *events* unique in character and having immediate impact on the course of economic change in America are added. These events include, of course, the conflicts arising from regional tensions (East vs. West, as well as Civil War and reconstruction), the pattern of settlement of the West, the role of foreign capital, the emergence of combinations in business, and the events conditioning the social and political milieu. These episodes and factors affected the attitudes of the entrepreneur and resulted in a conception of his social role quite different from that in other cultures. These ramifications reinforce the aspect of uniqueness.[41]

After reference to the role of the state in the development of the American West, there remains the task of pulling together the characterization of the West's impact on the East and hence on national economic growth. This can be done without re-evaluating the issues in the Turner controversy.[42] Nevertheless, in the literature on the Turner thesis there is implicit acknowledgment of the accelerator impact of the West on the East, with little recognition of what might be called the leverage effects of Eastern expenditures on the Western border and in areas newly opened to settlement.[43] Ready availability of land and the emergence of markets did act as stimuli to expansion of plant in the East, but more than this was involved: as Duesenberry has pointed out, it is likely that the *extension* of national economic activity over a wide and geographically remote area resulted in the need to duplicate as well as enlarge capacity.[44] Thus there were induced increments to national wealth. Along with the activity that generated income in areas that had been dormant (the West), there was stimulus for the already active areas with associated multiplier effects throughout—all as a result of the regionally focused expansion.[45]

Martin states that "to introduce the question of whether additional expenditures for military purposes would have 'raised' the level of living is futile." [46] This seems somewhat harsh; if the raw data were available and if the multiplier effects seemed conceptually useful enough to warrant a quantitative indication of the force of new expenditures in the area,[47] available analytical tools could aid in this research.

In more descriptive terms, evidence can be found in the multiplier effects of various governmental undertakings (in addition to railroad building and land policy): for example, in exploration and survey; in the use of local facilities to sustain governmental operations, as in the purchase of forage and subsistence items for the Army from farmers in the vicinity of a post; and in sutlers' activities.[48] All these were responsible to some degree for the introduction of new money into the remoter areas, giving rise to higher expectations and to subsequent investment activity.

In the light of the foregoing discussion and in conclusion, it may be well to return to the appropriateness of the designation "autonomous." The question does arise whether the factor so central to our discussion, i.e., the presence of the West, the advancing frontier, and its impact on the American experience, may not be the very condition that contributed most to the aptness of the general and ultimate characterization of the American pattern as one of autonomous growth. It is the view of some, for example, that because of the particular circumstances of expansionism in America (the open frontier combined with the ideological biases that were part of nineteenth-century America), the role of the central government was smaller than it might otherwise have been. They would argue that the very factors that placed America in the expansionist category were functionally linked in the case of the United States with placing it in the autonomous category. This suggests that the expansionist attribute in itself might contribute to minimization of the government's positive role in the economic life of the country. There is need for further study of this question.

There is, of course, need for detailed analysis of the functional role of government at different periods, not only of the various aspects of a positive role, but also in terms of changing functions and possible negative effects on development. Further study may show that the effects on allocation were more significant than the leverage effects.

Nevertheless, and even in the light of the argument referred to above, there appears to be good reason to hesitate before allowing the United States experience for the period 1820–90 to be placed, without qualification, in the autonomous category. For reasons suggested in this paper, it seems advisable to use caution in applying the American experience in analogies of growth; to emphasize the need for qualitative interpretation of governmental activity at both the state and federal levels, particularly because of the possible leverage effects of government action; and finally, to assert that the role of the state in American economic development in the nineteenth century was surely more than minimal. The effects of the action and presence of government on growth were significant and were manifested throughout the period.

NOTES

1. Bert F. Hoselitz, "Patterns of Economic Growth," *Canadian Journal of Economics and Political Science*, 21:416–431 (November 1955).

2. From Turner's vantage point (in 1893), "The fall line marked the frontier of the seventeenth century; the Alleghanies that of the eighteenth; the Mississippi that of the first quarter of the nineteenth; the Missouri that of the middle of this century (omitting the California movement); and the belt of the Rocky Mountains and the arid tract, the present frontier."—Frederick J. Turner, *The Frontier in American History* (New York: Henry Holt and Company, 1921), p. 9.

3. John E. Sawyer, "The Social Basis of the American System of Manufacturing," *Journal of Economic History*, 14(4):361–379 (1954), especially 368ff.

4. The test would be in whether potential existed internally to generate investment funds sufficient to satisfy demand for them, and whether these funds would have caused the rate of expansion that occurred (if such a rate is regarded as having been desirable).

5. Hoselitz [makes the assertion] that economic growth means a rise in the output of an economy and specifies that an increase in real product per worker signifies growth. In this connection Leontief has pointed out that if some assessment were made of the relative "importance" of (1) the extensive application of capital-using techniques as economic societies expand, as opposed to (2) the introduction of new methods leading to higher productivity of the capital that is either in use or is introduced, the latter—i.e., the changing production function—would be credited with the more far-reaching significance. Thus study of economic change should reveal technological innovation rather than capital accumulation as the motive force where these alternatives, as categories, are compared. For present purposes, however, it is worth noting that inducement to investment as a consequence of expanding

markets is an aspect of "growth" that may not initially involve technological change, but nevertheless has the requisite significant effects on output.

6. Government here refers to both state and national government. The differing influence of state versus federal intervention is discussed on pp. 119–120 infra.

7. "Patterns of Economic Growth," *op. cit.*, p. 425

8. Limitations of the data available for periods before 1880 are well known; nevertheless, reference to early series for an indication of relative magnitudes is useful for our purposes.

9. Cf. Albert S. Bolles, *The Financial History of the United States from 1789 to 1860* (New York: D. Appleton and Company, 1883), especially pp. 203–216, 538–566, 576–609.

10. Cf. James A. Maxwell, *The Fiscal Impact of Federalism in the United States* (Cambridge: Harvard University Press, 1946).

11. Fabricant writes of a later period: "Even a Democratic president, vetoing the appropriation for seed corn . . . could state: 'I can find no warrant for such an appropriation in the Constitution, and I do not believe that the power and duty of the general government ought to be extended to the relief of individual suffering which is in no manner properly related to the public service or benefit. A prevalent tendency to disregard the limited mission of this power and duty should, I think, be steadfastly resisted, to the end that the lesson should be constantly enforced that, though the people support the government, the government should not support the people.' [His citation: "Veto of the Texas Seed Bill, Feb. 16, 1887, *The Writings and Speeches of Grover Cleveland*, edited by G. F. Parker (Cassel Publishing Co., 1892)."] He goes on to state: "Yet efforts were constantly being made by every group 'seriously dissatisfied with the results of private enterprise, or of private enterprise as regulated by local or state governments,' to use the federal government as an agency for attaining what it desired."—Solomon Fabricant, *The Trend of Government Activity in the United States since 1900* (New York: National Bureau of Economic Research, 1952), pp. 6–7.

12. As to facilitating the availability of capital, Spengler has noted: "The state can contribute to the augmentation of equipment per worker by preventing waste of resources, by creating a milieu favorable to saving and capital formation, by facilitating the provision of an efficient banking system, by emphasizing investment rather than consumption expenditures in its anticyclical policies, and in general by fostering the increase of per capita output and of the fraction of this output devoted to capital formation. It should be noted that, for technical and economic reasons, a state's power to increase equipment through the importation of capital is quite limited."—Joseph J. Spengler, "The Role of the State in Shaping Things Economic," *Journal of Economic History*, Vol. 7, Suppl. (1947), p. 135.

13. Early discussion of government intervention in this sphere is cited by Victor S. Clark: "After the War of 1812, when other means to promote manufacturing than the tariff were under discussion, attention was drawn mainly to the difficulty of procuring capital for their support. 'Some thought it would be best for the Government to establish manufacturers and carry them on at public expense by managers and superintendents to be appointed by the Executive.' [Quoted from the *Aurora* undated, in Carey Clippings, VI, 281.] The Secretary of the Treasury suggested the expedient of a Government circulating capital, to be loaned without interest to manufacturers and to be repaid by them as conditions admitted [*American State Papers, Finance,* II,

430, 431]."—*History of Manufactures in the United States*, Vol. I, 1607–1860 (Washington: Carnegie Institution, 1916), p. 369.

14. Fabricant classifies government services "in terms of their ultimate objectives: (1) maintenance of order; (2) promotion of economic activity; (3) production to meet current needs; (4) development of the nation's capacity to defend itself and satisfy its needs; and (5) distribution of the nation's income."—*Op. cit.*, p. 48.

15. *Ibid.*, p. 7. Assets cited are "exclusive of roads and streets and most military and naval equipment."

16. "Further analysis seems to be called for, at least so far as American capitalism is concerned, analysis that will come to closer grips with the special features of American social structure and the various influences which made for a strong entrepreneurial bias in the 'social character' of the nineteenth-century American.'"—Leland H. Jenks, "Railroads as an Economic Force in American Development," in Frederic C. Lane and Jelle C. Riemersma, eds. *Enterprise and Secular Change* (Homewood, Ill.: Richard D. Irwin, 1953), p. 179.

17. Spengler has provided a basis for examining governmental effect on national income aggregates, dividing the range of state action into three subcategories. He states that distribution of income "is governed (a) by the functional division of net output among the co-operating productive agents, which depends, under simple competition, upon the comparative rates of growth of the several classes of human and nonhuman productive agents, and upon the elasticity of substitution of each type of productive agent for other agents; (b) by the distribution of the ownership of economically significant talents, output-creating factors, and income-generating institutional relations not otherwise covered; and (c) by the changes produced, by gifts and taxation, in income distribution as determined by (a) and (b) alone."—*Op. cit.*, p. 132.

18. A condensed survey of government activity in business (1789–1932) was made by Warren Persons, who was concerned with evaluating the relative "success" of undertakings (he found them unsuccessful); in the course of this evaluation he surveyed the range of activity. See his *Government Experimentation in Business* (New York: John Wiley & Sons, 1934).

19. Oscar and Mary F. Handlin, *Commonwealth: A Study of the Role of Government in the American Economy: Massachusetts, 1774–1861* (New York: New York University Press, 1947); Louis Hartz, *Economic Policy and Democratic Thought: Pennsylvania, 1776–1860* (Cambridge: Harvard University Press, 1948); Bray Hammond, "Banking in the Early West: Monopoly, Prohibition, and Laissez Faire," *Journal of Economic History*, 8:1–25 (May 1948); Milton S. Heath, "Public Railroad Construction and the Development of Private Enterprise in the South Before 1861," *Journal of Economic History*, Vol. 10, Suppl. (1950), pp. 40–53, and *Constructive Liberalism: The Role of the State in Economic Development in Georgia to 1860* (Cambridge: Harvard University Press, 1954); Harry H. Pierce, *Railroads of New York: A Study of Government Aid, 1826–1875* (Cambridge: Harvard University Press, 1953); James N. Primm, *Economic Policy in the Development of a Western State: Missouri 1820–1860* (Cambridge: Harvard University Press, 1954). Material presented in Pierce's study shows intervention well after the Civil War. Cf. Howard R. Lamar, *Dakota Territory, 1861–1889: A Study of Frontier Politics* (New Haven: Yale University Press, 1956).

20. For a nineteenth-century perspective on the relative success of state aid to early railroad development (and of attempts at internal improvements

by the states), see John L. Ringwalt, *Development of Transportation Systems in the United States* (Philadelphia: published by the author, 1888), pp. 79–82.

21. Heath, "Public Railroad Construction and the Development of Private Enterprise in the South Before 1861," *op. cit.*, pp. 40–43.

22. "The old voluntary fire and police departments were totally inadequate. A municipal water supply was essential to a crowded population, and sewers had to be provided. Greater distances and heavier traffic called for better streets and sidewalks, bridges, and (in other local divisions) roads."—Edgar W. Martin, *The Standard of Living in 1860: American Consumption Levels on the Eve of the Civil War* (Chicago: University of Chicago Press, 1942), pp. 280–281.

23. Hartz, *op. cit.*, p. 290.

24. Cf. David M. Potter, *People of Plenty: Economic Abundance and the American Character* (Chicago: University of Chicago Press, 1954), p. 124; also Carter Goodrich, "American Development Policy," *Journal of Economic History*, 16:449–460 (1956).

25. He continues: "Beginning with wagon road and canal grants in the twenties, followed closely by river improvement grants, the plan of granting the land to the states was devised. These specific grants extended over a period of about forty-five years, from 1823 to 1869. A more general plan was embodied in the half-million acre grants, mainly for the same, or at least similar, purposes in the act of 1841. . . . The grants for railroads, the most liberal donations ever made for the encouragement of private enterprise, reached the figure of 129,000,000 acres, and even this is somewhat short since other lands granted to states, not specifically for railroads, were turned over to them nevertheless. Minor grants, and grants to states for miscellaneous purposes, run well into the millions."—Benjamin H. Hibbard, *A History of the Public Land Policies* (New York: P. Smith, 1939), p. 267. Cf. James A. Maxwell, *Federal Grants and the Business Cycle* (New York: National Bureau of Economic Research, 1952).

26. Gates makes the point: "At the very moment when Congress was promising free land to settlers, it was enacting measures which gave to railroads, in order to aid in their construction, an area three times the size of New York State. Congress was also giving lands to states as subsidies for education in universities, vocational, and grade schools. These lands were not to be given to settlers but instead were to be sold at the highest possible price. Furthermore, despite the advent of free homesteads in 1862 Congress neglected to repeal measures providing for unrestricted sale of public lands. Consequently, many million acres continued to be sold to speculators, lumber barons, cattle kings, and land companies, who secured the profits in rising land values that the Homestead Act had intended to assure the small man. In keeping old policies and superimposing upon them the new and more generous policies, Congress was moving away from the well-organized, consistent, and coherent policies of the past into a complex maze of inconsistent and inharmonious measures that minimized greatly the benevolent character of the new program."—Paul W. Gates, *Fifty Million Acres: Conflicts over Kansas Land Policy, 1854–1890* (Ithaca: Cornell University Press, 1954), pp. 13–14. Cf. also his "The Homestead Act in an Incongruous Land System," *American Historical Review*, 41:652–681 (July 1939); Thomas C. Cochran, "Land Grants and Railroad Entrepreneurship," *Journal of Economic History*, Vol. 10, Suppl. (1950), especially pp. 55, 64, 67; and Jenks, *op. cit.*

27. Cf. Potter, *op. cit.*, pp. 124–125.

28. Aubrey comments on this problem in regard to European experience: "Time was of the essence, partly to cope with existing or threatened shortages, partly to 'catch up and keep up' in competitive trade. It was, therefore, important that a few fortunate or shrewd individuals who managed to smuggle information out of England should not hold a monopoly. Thus, in many instances, the government set up foreign technicians in the business of making the new machines and paid them premiums or subsidies for each machine they sold. By such means a fairly wide distribution was achieved in a relatively short time. In other cases, the government needed only to make a gift of prototypes of new machines. In this manner the state assumed risks and cost beyond the capacity of many entrepreneurs. It made, thus, an important contribution toward the private investment decision."—Henry G. Aubrey, "The Role of the State in Economic Development," *American Economic Review*, 41:268 (May 1951).

29. "Annual report of Lieutenant Colonel S. H. Long, topographical engineers, for the year ending June 30, 1859, and continued till the 5th October following," Appendix C to *Report of the Secretary of War*, U.S. Senate, 36th Congress, 1st Session, Ex. Doc. No. 2, Vol. 2 (1860), p. 749.

30. Reports of the Secretary of the Treasury of the United States, for the respective years.

31. Cf. William A. Ganoe, *The History of the United States Army* (rev. ed.; New York: D. Appleton-Century Company, 1942).

32. Cf. William H. Goetzmann, "The Corps of Topographical Engineers in the Exploration and Development of the Trans-Mississippi West," unpublished Ph.D. dissertation, Yale University, 1957.

33. "Payments from the Treasury, expenditures on account of public lands, surveys, administration, salaries, &c. from January 1, 1785, to June 30, 1880, were (estimated) $46,563,302.07. . . . The expenses of the Indian Department, on account of holding treaties, &c. and including yearly payments for annuities and other charges, which are, in fact, in consideration for surrender of occupancy-title of lands to the Government, from July 4, 1876, to June 30, 1880, was $187,328,903.91."—Thomas C. Donaldson, *The Public Domain: Its History, with Statistics* (Public Land Commission, 1881), pp. 18, 20. Cf. Forest G. Hill, "Government Engineering Aid to Railroads before the Civil War," *Journal of Economic History*, 11:235–246 (Summer 1951).

34. Federal expenditures on internal improvements amounted to approximately $15,000,000 over the period 1791–1820 and rose to $54,000,000 during 1829–40.

35. Heath refers to a similar problem in his discussion of the effects of land grants: "The estimates on public land grants are tentative, and other items are subject to further refinements through additional studies. It does not represent the total of the public effort, since no account is taken in this summary of the investment values of the many important public and quasi-public contributions in services, the uses of public streets and other properties, tax exemptions, and banking privileges. An adequate appraisal of these must await further research."—"Public Railroad Construction . . . ," *op. cit.*, p. 40.

36. Report of the Secretary of the Treasury of the United States on the Finances, September 1837.

37. Guy S. Callender, "The Early Transportation and Banking Enterprises of the States in Relation to the Growth of Corporations," *Quarterly Journal of Economics*, 17:45 (November 1902).

38. "The Diary of William R. Brown, 1845–46," in Rodney C. Loehr, ed., *Minnesota Farmers' Diaries*, Minnesota Historical Society Narratives and Documents, Vol. 3 (St. Paul, 1939), pp. 52, 59, 64–65.

39. Cf. Simon Kuznets, "Measurement of Economic Growth," *Journal of Economic History*, Vol. 7, Suppl. (1947), pp. 29–30; and Warren C. Scoville, "Discussion—Factors in Modern Industrial Development," *American Economic Review*, 41:275 (May 1951).

40. Turner, *op. cit.*; Potter, *op. cit.*

41. Sawyer, *op. cit.*

42. See bibliography in Oscar Handlin and others, *Harvard Guide to American History* (Cambridge: Harvard University Press, 1954), p. 21.

43. For an exception to this see Clarence H. Danhof, "Economic Validity of the Safety-Valve Doctrine," *Journal of Economic History*, Vol. 1, Suppl. (1941), p. 106.

44. "It is to be emphasized that the services in question [specialized medical, legal, and personal] cannot be imported. The facilities for producing them have to exist in the region in which the demand exists. The existence of such facilities in the East was of no use to the farmers of the Midwest. In consequence of this situation trading communities sprang up in strategic locations throughout the developing area. The people of these communities provided services to their agricultural hinterland."—James S. Duesenberry, "Some Aspects of the Theory of Economic Development," *Explorations in Entrepreneurial History*, 3:98–99 (December 1950).

45. Aitken suggests that perhaps the very act of acquisition of new territory constituted "the most important single contribution of the government to economic growth."

46. Martin, *The Standard of Living in 1860*, pp. 280–281.

47. ". . . the multiplier for any sector is the ratio of the final change in its receipts to the initial disturbance. If each sector's marginal propensity to spend to every sector is known, it is possible, mathematically, to calculate the value of the multiplier."—John S. Chipman, *The Theory of Inter-Sectoral Money Flows and Income Formation* (Baltimore: Johns Hopkins Press, 1951), p. 22.

48. For a description of the extent of sutlers' operations, see William N. Davis, Jr., "Post Trading in the West," *Explorations in Entrepreneurial History*, 6:30–40 (1953–54), especially p. 31.

6

Agriculture and Regionalism

THE TWO ESSAYS in this section represent complementary approaches to the study of agricultural history. The first, by the late Mildred Throne, is an intensive study of farming in one northern Corn Belt state. The second, by Eugene D. Genovese, deals with an entire region, the South, and appraises the role of the plantation system in conditioning southern economic development.

Miss Throne's essay treats the period of most rapid development of southern Iowa. A number of the features of commercialization that she identifies in Iowa were characteristic of development patterns in other agricultural areas of the North: prior to the advent of arable farming, there took hold a cattle industry based on availability of free grazing land; a rapid movement into cash crops manifested itself as soon as markets were accessible to pioneer settlers; corn-fed livestock provided a large part of the agricultural surplus, while the rise of local packing centers gave impetus to improved livestock-breeding practices; and construction of new transport facilities altered the position of local farmers in the national market, forcing agricultural readjustment.

Underlying the agricultural economy of Iowa was the widespread ownership of land by independent, generally small-scale farmers. This social structure was in striking contrast with that of the pre-Civil War South. Some recent studies of pre-1860 southern development have attempted to prove, by quantitative techniques, the profitability of slavery to plantation owners; but Genovese's essay goes beyond the economics of the individual plantation unit and evaluates the system itself in terms of its impact on southern economic growth.

SOUTHERN IOWA AGRICULTURE, 1833–1890:
THE PROGRESS FROM SUBSISTENCE
TO COMMERCIAL CORN-BELT FARMING

Mildred Throne

American agriculture, during the nineteenth century, underwent a series of rapid changes which transformed farming from a way of life to a business.[1] Many factors contributed to this development. First, the westward movement reached full tide, and new farms were being opened throughout the Middle West. Second, industrial expansion and the resulting growth of cities increased the number of people dependent on others for their food supply. Third, new and better agricultural machinery and methods were increasing the output of the farms and supplying the needed surplus. Fourth, railroads were spreading across the country, offering a quick means of transportation for carrying this farm surplus to the city markets. Farmers could concentrate their production on the crops best suited to their locality and still be assured of a market and also of a supply of the goods which they themselves no longer produced.[2]

For a detailed study of one segment of American agriculture, the southern third of the State of Iowa has been selected. Since the State is a geographic and economic unit, the development of this area is not, except in small details, any different from that of the State as a whole, nor, for that matter, is it any different from the entire Corn Belt area. Although various sections today show a differing emphasis, the basic pattern is the same—corn and grass, hogs and cattle.[3]

Reprinted by permission from *Agricultural History*, XXIII (April, 1949), pp. 124–130.

Iowa was opened to settlement in 1833 on the eve of these great changes in farming. In 1833, Cyrus McCormick was working on his reaper, and the Baltimore and Ohio Company had already built 133 miles of railroad.[4] Within twenty-one years, in 1854, the first railroad had reached the east bank of the Mississippi River, and McCormick was selling three-fourths of his annual production of reapers in Illinois, Wisconsin, Missouri, and Iowa.[5] Iowans who broke the first prairie sod in the mid-thirties lived to see farming transformed by the steel plow, the corn planter, the wheat drill, the reaper, and the thresher. The men who crossed the Mississippi in canoes lived to see the railroads cross the State. Iowa's geographic position made it the inevitable path of the transcontinental railroads, building rapidly west from Chicago in the fifties and sixties.[6] The pattern of Iowa agriculture, thus, was changed almost within a lifetime from subsistence to commercial farming.

In the thirties and forties the subsistence farms of the Iowa frontier followed a similar pattern. The farmer, after first breaking the tough prairie sod with the newly-invented prairie plow, sowed a field of wheat, a field of corn, and possibly some oats, barley, or flax. He had a few hogs and cattle, of no known breed, a horse or two, or possibly a yoke of oxen. His tools consisted of a wooden plow, the share sheathed with iron, a sickle, a cradle, and a flail. His axe cut logs for his house and for fuel. His wife tended the small vegetable garden, wove the linen and woolen cloth needed for her family, made the clothes, cared for a small flock of chickens, and churned the butter. What luxuries were purchased, such as coffee, tea, or sugar, were obtained from a village store in exchange for surplus wheat, corn, eggs, or butter.

The fact that villages and market towns sprang up in Iowa, almost on the heels of the first settlers, is an indication of the rapidity of the development of the State, the increasing speed of the westward movement. By covered wagon and by steamboat farmers and businessmen were converging on the new Territory by the thousands in the thirties, by the tens of thousands in the forties.[7] The first to come by the river were usually the storekeepers, men who brought a stock of goods with them and opened a general store which would supply the settler with the manufactured luxuries he could not himself provide. Storekeepers were closely followed by mechanics, men with tools, who found a rapidly expanding market for their labors. Carpenters, blacksmiths, millers—all could find eager purchasers for their work.

The Iowa market towns all followed a similar pattern of growth. From the nucleus of a general store the town expanded rapidly under the impetus of the flood of migration on the one hand and the growing surplus crops on the other. Within a few years a full-scale village economy had developed, revolving around the farmers' needs and products. At Burlington, for instance, there were two general stores before the end of 1833. In 1834 a grocery and a third general store had appeared; in 1835 a hotel and a law office were opened; [8] by 1838 S. Sherfy & Company was manufacturing plows.[9] By 1841— nine years after the opening of Iowa—John B. Newhall, a bookseller in Burlington, reported at length on the bustling town:

Burlington contains a population of 1,300 inhabitants. It contains the offices of the executive and secretary of the territory, the United States land office for the southern district of Iowa, several commodious brick churches, a jail, six spacious hotels . . . a mutual fire-insurance company, two printing-offices, from each of which is issued a weekly journal, two steam ferryboats, three livery stables, two extensive drug stores, five forwarding and commission houses, twenty wholesale and retail mercantile establishments, one crockery and glass warehouse, two hardware stores, one jewelry, two cabinet and chair making establishments, one cabinet warehouse, three blacksmiths, one carriage-maker, three beef and pork packers, two butchers, three bakers, five tailoring establishments, six practicing physicians, eight lawyers, three acting magistrates, one hatter, two shoemakers, six coffeehouses, a reading-room and mechanics institute, several primary schools for both sexes, an agricultural and a temperance society, &c. &c.[10]

Even in the interior, as the settlers moved into the State and away from the river highways, small towns sprang up out of the prairies almost overnight. Within three months Oskaloosa in Mahaska County grew from an idea into a small settlement of a dozen log cabins, one of which was the general store, marked with the usual sign of such businesses, a piece of red flannel hung over the door. A month later "dozens of frame houses had been built," and a tavern, another general store, two blacksmith shops, and a tailoring establishment had appeared.[11] Mahaska and Wapello counties had been opened to settlement on May 1, 1843. The steamboat *Agatha* was grounded on a ledge of rock in the Des Moines River at Appanoose Rapids in Wapello County from 4 o'clock on the afternoon of May 1 until daylight of May 2. One of the polemen on the keelboats with the *Agatha* reported: "Before we left that vicinity they had commenced staking off the town of Ottumwa and that city was born on the 2d day of May, 1843." [12] Thus, the Iowa pioneer was not a trail breaker, a subsistence farmer, for very long. Seldom was he dependent on his own resources for more than a season or two in any one locality.

Another indication of this speed is seen in the fact that by 1836 —three years after the Territory had been opened—lumber was coming into Burlington and Fort Madison from as far east as Pittsburgh. Later the lumber for Iowa homes came down the Mississippi from Wisconsin. This supply was very soon augmented by local sawmills set up on the rivers and creeks of the interior. By 1849 it was possible to build a four-room frame house, 19 by 25 feet, with the necessary doors, windows, plastering, and steps "both front and rear," for $294.50. The same house of brick cost $325.00.[13]

With civilization so close on his heels, the Iowa farmer could concentrate on crops which would bring him a cash return, or at least on crops which could be used in trading at the numerous general stores so close at hand. The staple crops were corn, wheat, the smaller grains, and livestock. Corn, the traditional American frontier crop, from the first far outstripped other grains both in area and yield. Climate and soil were ideal for this crop. Between 1840 and 1860 Iowa's corn production increased over 400 percent, and in the latter year southern Iowa accounted for about 58 percent of the total.[14] Planting and cultivation were fairly simple. The fields were plowed in May, weather permitting. (By 1850 the steel plow was used almost exclusively on the prairies, replacing the cheaper but less effective cast-iron implement.) [15] After plowing, the corn was planted by hand, harrowing was done several times with double-shovel plows or iron-tooth harrows, or both, and then the crop was left to the usually kind mercies of the Iowa summer climate. Without much more attention, yields varied from 40 to 60 bushels per acre as a rule, and often in ideal situations or because of careful cultivation to over 100 bushels. By these methods Iowa's corn crop increased faster than that of any other corn-producing State, according to the 1860 United States census.[16]

Husked in the field, the corn was stored in rail bins.[17] The river counties, before the advent of the railroads, could ship their corn to Saint Louis and the East fairly cheaply.[18] Farther west the cost of carrying the bulky crop to market was almost prohibitive.[19] Streams of new settlers, moving west during this period, offered a good market at the farmer's door, however.[20] But the best use the Iowa farmer found for his corn was as a feed for his livestock. By feeding his cheap and plentiful grain to his hogs and cattle he could produce a saleable and easily transportable crop—more accurately, a crop which transported itself to market. Thus, livestock came to be the most important marketable crop on the Iowa frontier, as it had proved to be on every frontier since the first crossing of the Alleghenies. Iowa farmers were following a familiar pattern when they began to specialize more and more in corn, hogs, and cattle.

Iowa's climate, ideal for corn, was often injurious to wheat. Fall wheat, which made the best flour, was often killed by the harsh Iowa winters; while spring wheat was just as often blasted by the heat of the Iowa summers or rusted by a too-wet spring. The yield, where successful, was large and encouraging for the first few years.[21] But crop failures, chinch bugs, and the instability of the wheat markets were factors which soon reduced the popularity of wheat as a major crop. Furthermore, the cultivation and harvesting of the crop, before the introduction of mowers and reapers, required a great amount of labor. Sown broadcast on a newly-broken field, or on a field previously broken by a crop of sod corn, the wheat was reaped with a cradle and threshed out with a flail or tramped out by horses or oxen, and the grain separated from the chaff by the age-old method of tossing it into the wind or into the breeze made by a sheet waved vigorously. This time-consuming process was still in use in some places in the late fifties, in spite of the introduction of reaping machinery, implements which speeded the harvesting of the grain but also made it increasingly expensive.[22]

The instability of the wheat market was perhaps the factor most discouraging to the farmer. Prices might range from 40 cents to $1.00 per bushel within a year, depending on the season, the quality of the wheat, nearness to market, or just general business conditions. The price of $1.00 per bushel, offered in May of 1857 in Washington County, would mean, at the average yield of 12 bushels per acre reported for that year, a return of $12.00 per acre for wheat. But few farmers had wheat in May, unless they had been able to hold their previous years' crop, and few farmers had enough of a surplus to do this. In October, when the crop of spring wheat was ready, the price had fallen to 40 cents, which meant a return of only $4.80 per acre.[23] These variations in price, coupled with the uncertainty of the crop—two factors always present in wheat farming—made wheat growing a precarious venture.

Corn, on the other hand, was a fairly certain crop, only an unusually dry or wet year affecting the yield seriously. Thus, corn came more and more to be the sure and reliable crop for the Iowa farmer. Farmers' letters in the agricultural journals and in the newspapers bring out graphically the growing emphasis on corn and hogs. In 1860 Calvin Allyn of Cedar Rapids wrote to the *Country Gentleman:* "Iowa farmers are turning their attention to raising hogs and cattle, as the best business which they can follow." [24] According to a Polk County farmer in 1863, corn, which cost 10 cents per bushel to raise, would bring only 12½ to 15 cents per bushel on the Des Moines market; 20 bushels of corn, if used to fatten a 200-pound hog, would bring from $6.00 to $6.50 in the same market, a profit of $4.00 to $4.50 on 20 bushels of corn, which, if sold as grain, would have brought a top profit of only $1.00.[25] In 1870 a letter to the *Iowa Homestead* read: "A farmer in Iowa can make more money on a dozen of eggs than he does on raising a bushel of wheat. A farmer in Iowa can make more money on one hog than he can on one acre of wheat." [26] Many similar letters show that the Iowa farmer was concentrating on the crops which would bring the highest profits—in other words, the Iowa farmer was rapidly becoming a businessman.

The 1856 State census, the first which reports the acreage of the various grains, shows that of the acres cultivated in the three leading crops in southern Iowa—wheat, oats, and corn—23 percent was in wheat, 18 percent in oats, and 59 percent in corn.[27] This roughly approximates the State acreage, which was 29 percent for wheat, 15 percent for oats, and 56 percent for corn.[28]

During the first two decades swine and cattle on the Iowa farms were raised mainly for home consumption or for sale to immigrants crossing the State. As the acreage in corn increased, a proportionate increase in the number of hogs and cattle is evident. By the time the farms of the southeastern counties in Iowa were established, the packing industry in Chicago had become a reality. With this market close at hand, plus the river markets of Saint Louis and New Orleans, it was natural that the Iowa farmer should pay increasing attention to the production of more livestock. With two of the active river market towns, Burlington and Keokuk, situated in southern Iowa, that section had a strong incentive to produce stock which would sell readily. The farmer could drive his stock overland to Burlington or Keokuk, where they could be shipped by river steamboat to Saint Louis and New Orleans; or the stock could be driven to Chicago by the farmer himself or by drovers who made a business of traveling through the countryside buying up cattle.[29]

A further market soon appeared—local packing plants in the river and interior towns.

At first packers bought any livestock presented for sale, paying for it by weight. Thus, there was little need to improve the breeds—the main task was to produce fat stock, and this was easily done by plentiful feeding of corn. When the packers began to distinguish between types of hogs and cattle and to pay better prices for better stock, the incentive was added for improving breeds. Wherever markets distinguished and graded either grain or livestock, the farmers, feeling the distinction in their pocketbooks, took steps to improve their products. The movement for better farming and better stock, present in Iowa since the thirties, at last began to have effect. Iowa farmers were, by the fifties, businessmen, awakening to the fact that quality paid better returns than quantity.

The coming of the railroads in the late fifties did not change Iowa's economy—rather, it merely speeded it on the path already taken. In 1856 the Burlington and Missouri River Railroad, later to become a part of the Chicago, Burlington, and Quincy Railroad system, began building across southern Iowa.[30] By 1859 the road had reached Ottumwa on the Des Moines River,[31] where construction was halted by the coming of the Civil War. Building was resumed after the close of the war, and the road reached the Missouri River in September of 1869.[32]

The many influences of the coming of the railroad were not all evident by 1860 in southeastern Iowa. Certain new emphases are noticeable, however. Corn, which had been fed to the livestock, now had an independent market.[33] In Washington County dealers bought unusual quantities of corn in 1859. According to the local newspaper, this was "an article our farmers have never been able to sell for shipment before, and for which they are now indebted to railroad transportation." [34] On the other hand, railroads presented new facilities for transporting cattle and hogs in a more highly finished state, thus increasing the profits from this branch of husbandry.[35] The coming of the railroads, then, did not radically change Iowa's agricultural pattern, but rather re-emphasized certain phases of that economy.

The Civil War decade brought other changes to Iowa's farming. The closing of the Mississippi River cut off Iowa's southern sugar and molasses supply, and the cultivation of sorghum thus attracted more interest than it had in the past. The demand for wool, to replace southern cotton, caused a rapid increase in sheep raising.

The needs of the army produced an enlarged market for both horses and livestock. The grain crops increased in area during this decade. Iowa's rank in corn production rose from seventh to second place in the Nation, and in wheat from eighth to second place.[36] The number of farms and the number of improved acres also increased. Part of this development, of course, can be attributed to the natural growth of a new country, but the speed of these changes can in large part be credited to the artificial stimulation of the war. Every crop showed an increase in production and acreage; the number of hogs, cattle, and horses more than doubled.[37]

Perhaps the greatest change in Iowa farming during the sixties was the increasing use of farm machinery. With so many men called to the army, the need for laborsaving machinery was great. With food prices rising rapidly, the farmers were easily encouraged to go into debt for machines they could not have afforded in the previous decade. In seven years, from 1860 to 1867, the value of Iowa's farm machinery more than doubled, and in the two years from 1867 to 1869 it almost doubled again.[38] Machines enabled the farmer to cultivate more land with fewer farm laborers. Reapers, mowers, planters, the sulky and riding plow—these and many others—made it possible to farm faster and with less labor. The level and rolling prairies of the Middle West were particularly well adapted to the use of such implements.[39] Early in the sixties the harvester had begun to replace the reaper. Self-binders to be attached to reapers were also developed in the seventies.[40] Mowers for cutting both prairie and tame hay were popular.[41] Improvements in reaping machines naturally led to dissatisfaction with the walking plow; the sulky and gang plows were greeted with pleasure. Sulky rakes and harrows added to the ease and speed of cultivation.[42] Corn cultivation, which had not been benefited by the reapers and mowers, now began to experience the advantages of the mechanical revolution. Riding and double shovel plows enabled the farmer to prepare his field quickly. Hand planters were used widely by the middle sixties, and in 1867 Cornelius Skiff of Grinnell had invented a combination corn plow and seeder.[43] Corn shellers and cornstalk cutters further lightened the farmers' labor.[44] In the decade of the sixties the value of machinery in southern Iowa rose from $2,300,000 to over $6,500,000.[45] As in the case of the railroads, machinery did not change Iowa's agricultural pattern; rather, the new tools merely enabled the farmer to continue his established methods at a faster pace.

On the whole, the seventies were years of continued rapid expansion—expansion in population, in acres under cultivation, in grain production, and in number of livestock. The eighties, on the other hand, were years of leveling-off and of consolidation. During the decade of the seventies the number of farms in southern Iowa, for instance, increased from almost 45,000 to well over 66,000; improved acreage almost doubled; the production of corn and of oats trebled; the number of swine and cattle doubled; and twice as much hay was produced in 1880 as in 1870.[46] A large part of this increase can be credited to the sale of the Burlington railroad land grant, which was put on the market in April of 1870.[47] The railroad sold its lands, as far as possible, to actual farmers on better terms than could be obtained from the land agents.[48] The farms, averaging between 75 and 80 acres, were sold on a 10-year credit plan at 6 percent interest. "No part of the principal due for two years, and afterwards only one-ninth annually," read the advertisements.[49] These contracts provided that at least one-tenth of the acreage purchased must be improved yearly for the first 3 years of the contract.[50] Thus, the railroad attracted many potential farmers to Iowa.

These new farmers quickly settled into the general pattern of Iowa farming—corn and hogs, grass and cattle. The production of corn and swine increased rapidly, while the production of better grades of cattle showed a marked increase after the advent of the railroad. Reports of shipments of "fancy fat cattle" from various counties became common.[51] Coupled with the improvement in cattle came an increased interest in the tame grasses and also in dairying. Since cattle require plenty of good pasture land, and since the wild prairie grass was nearly exhausted, practically all the counties of southern Iowa were reporting large areas planted to grass by 1879.[52] Dairying never became popular in southern Iowa except for a flurry of interest in the eighties.[53] Of the 478 creameries in the State in 1887, only 13 percent were in southern Iowa, where the majority of the farmers continued to concentrate their attention on beef cattle—the stock they knew best and for which they had a continuing and reliable market.[54] Wheat acreage declined steadily after the price slump of the postwar years; by 1890 the total production had fallen to the level of that of 1860.[55] Meanwhile, oats were gaining in popularity, both as a food for the increasing number of horses in Iowa and for use in the manufacture of oatmeal, grandly described by the makers as "a farinaceous food . . . highly esteemed for its nutritious qualities." [56] Horses for the new horse-drawn farm machines were much in demand, and a further market was found in the cities of the Middle West and the East where drayage and the new horsecar presented a steady market.[57]

As always, the demands of eastern markets influenced and guided Iowa agricultural production. Iowa farming, from 1870 to 1890, improved, consolidated, and came of age. The machine had made commercial farming probable, but the railroad had made it possible. The third factor in Iowa's development, more scientific farming, long urged by farm leaders, would now be the important force in Iowa's development. Without better farming, the use of machinery and the heavy market demands brought by the railroad would have completely exhausted even the rich soil of Iowa. By 1890 the public domain of Iowa was practically all in private hands. A new era was opening. Farmers had to make the best of the land they owned, since there was no "new frontier" left, either in Iowa or in the West. Agricultural education, the activities of State and national agricultural departments, and of the many types of farmers' organizations were to be the agencies of progress in the future.

NOTES

1. This article was presented at the meeting of the Agricultural History Society and the Mississippi Valley Historical Association at Rock Island, Illinois, on Apr. 24, 1948.

2. Louis Bernard Schmidt, "The Agricultural Revolution in the Prairies and the Great Plains of the United States," *Agricultural History*, 8:178 (1934); Wayne Caldwell Neely, *The Agricultural Fair* (New York, 1935), 76.

3. See C. L. Holmes, "In Which of the Iowas Is Your Farm?" *Wallaces' Farmer*, 54:459, 464 (1929), and "Five Farm States in Iowa: What Is Responsible for These Divisions of the State?" *ibid.*, 542–543.

4. William T. Hutchinson, *Cyrus Hall McCormick* (New York, 1930), 1:79; Robert E. Riegel, *The Story of the Western Railroads* (New York, 1926), 3.

5. Riegel, *The Story of the Western Railroads*, 6; and Hutchinson, *Cyrus Hall McCormick*, 1:352.

6. Riegel, *The Story of the Western Railroads*, 27.

7. *Hawk-Eye and Iowa Patriot* (Burlington, Iowa), Oct. 17, 1839.

8. *History of Des Moines County, Iowa* . . . (Chicago, 1879), 472.

9. *Wisconsin Territorial Gazette* (Burlington, Iowa), Apr. 28, 1838.

10. John B. Newhall, *Sketches of Iowa, or, The Emigrants Guide* (New York, 1841), 113

11. Mrs. T. G. Phillips, "Mahaska County's First School," *Annals of Iowa*, ser. 3, 3:219 (1897).

12. Tacitus Hussey, "History of Steamboating on the Des Moines River, from 1837 to 1862," *ibid.*, ser. 3, 4:334 (1900).

13. Charles A. White, "The Early Homes and Home-Makers of Iowa," *ibid.*, ser. 3, 4:181 (1899); Hawkins Taylor, "Recollections of Thirty-Four Years Ago," *ibid.*, ser. 1, 8:336 (1870); *Valley Farmer*, 1:4–5 (1849).

14. U.S. Census Office, 8th Census 1860, *Agriculture of the United States in 1860*, xlvii; and the Iowa census publication entitled *1836–1880 Census of Iowa* (Des Moines, 1883), 278–280.

15. Percy W. Bidwell and John I. Falconer, *History of Agriculture in the Northern United States, 1620–1860* (Washington, 1925), 283; Leo Rogin, *The Introduction of Farm Machinery in Its Relation to the Productivity of Labor* . . . (Berkeley, Calif., 1931), 33–34.

16. U.S. Census Office, 8th Census, 1860, *Agriculture of the United States in 1860*, xlvii.

17. Iowa State Agricultural Society, *Report*, 1857, 241, 435.

18. *Ibid.*, 259.

19. *Ibid.*, 225; *ibid.*, 1858, 424.

20. *Ibid.*, 1857, 355, 365, 372; *ibid.*, 1858, 200; *ibid.*, 1859, 168.

21. *Prairie Farmer*, 2:75 (1842); *Iowa Farmers' Advocate*, 1:70 (1847).

22. William M. Donnel, "The Pioneers of Marion County," *Annals of Iowa*, ser. 1, 7:41 (1869); David C. Mott, ed., "William Savage: Iowa Pioneer, Diarist, and Painter of Birds," *ibid.*, ser. 3, 19:100 (1933), Bidwell and Falconer, *History of Agriculture in the Northern United States*, 281.

23. *Washington Press* (Washington, Iowa), May 27, Oct. 14, 1857.

24. *Country Gentleman*, 15:83 (Feb. 2, 1869).

25. *Ibid.*, 21:90 (Feb. 5, 1863).

26. Quoted in *Warren County Banner* (Indianola, Iowa), Dec. 8, 1870.

27. Wheat, 156,211 acres; oats, 185,517 acres; corn, 409,067 acres; total, 690,795 acres. Figures compiled from *1836–1880 Census of Iowa*, 278–280, 284–286, and 296–298.

28. Wheat, 388,080 acres; oats, 190,922 acres; corn, 737,213 acres. *Ibid.*

29. E. Z. Russell, *et al.*, "Hog Production and Marketing," U.S. Department of Agriculture, *Yearbook*, 1922, 187, John A. Hopkins, Jr., *Economic History of the Production of Beef Cattle in Iowa* (Iowa City, 1928), 165–166.

30. Richard C. Overton, *Burlington West: A Colonization History of the Burlington Railroad* (Cambridge, Mass., 1941), 71.

31. *Ottumwa Weekly Courier*, Aug. 18, 1859.

32. Overton, *Burlington West*, 231.

33. Charles T. Leavitt, "Transportation and the Livestock Industry of the Middle West to 1860," *Agricultural History*, 8:27 (1934).

34. *Washington Press*, Nov. 9, 1859.

35. Leavitt, "Transportation and the Livestock Industry . . . ," 27–28; Hopkins, *Economic History* . . . *of Beef Cattle in Iowa*, 3, 24–25.

36. *1836–1880 Census of Iowa*, 64, 66.

37. *Ibid.*, 278, 281, 284, 287, 348, 350–351, 360, 362; Louis Bernard Schmidt, "Farming in Iowa in the Sixties," *Wallaces' Farmer*, 53:1581 (1928).

38. 1860—$5,327,033; 1867—$11,362,402; 1869—$20,540,977. *1836–1880 Census of Iowa*, 270.

39. Howard Hall, The Development of Agricultural Machinery in the Seventies (unpublished M. A. thesis, State University of Iowa, 1940), 5.

40. *Ibid.*, 12, 15; William T. Hutchinson, "The Reaper Industry and Midwestern Agriculture, 1855–75," in *Essays in Honor of William E. Dodd*, ed. by Avery Craven (Chicago, 1935), 116–117.

41. *Hawkeye Flag* (Winterset, Iowa), Aug. 26, 1864; *Keokuk County News* (Sigourney, Iowa), May 17, 1861; Iowa State Agricultural Society, *Report, 1868,* 412.

42. Iowa State Agricultural Society, *Report, 1866,* 357; Paul H. Johnstone, "Old Ideals Versus New Ideas in Farm Life," U.S. Department of Agriculture, *Yearbook,* 1940, 126; Rogin, *The Introduction of Farm Machinery* . . . , 36.

43. Iowa State Agricultural Society, *Report, 1867,* 226.

44. *Ibid.,* 1867, 221, 259; *ibid.,* 1870, 273–311, with illustrations of all types of farm machinery.

45. *1836–1880 Census of Iowa,* 270–273.

46. Totals compiled from *ibid.,* 197–199, 240–243, 244–247, 266–269, 296–298, 311–313, 350–353, 360–361, and 362–364; U.S. Census Office, 11th Census, 1890, *Report on Population of the United States,* 1:18–19, and *Report on the Statistics of Agriculture,* 138–140, 207–208, 246–247, 285–286, 327–328, 364–365, and 430–431.

47. Overton, *Burlington West,* 314.

48. *Country Gentleman,* 36:293 (1871).

49. *Osceola Republican,* July 18, 1872.

50. Overton, *Burlington West,* 296; Iowa State Agricultural Society, *Report, 1871,* 39.

51. Iowa State Agricultural Society, *Report,* 1874, 335; *Ottumwa Democrat,* June 17, 1875.

52. See Iowa State Agricultural Society, *Report,* 1879, 302–308.

53. *Adair County Reporter* (Greenfield, Iowa), June 28, 1881; *Iowa Homestead,* 26:4 (1881).

54. Iowa State Agricultural Society, *Report,* 1877, 568; *ibid.,* 1880, 19; *ibid.,* 1887, appendix 19–36; *ibid.,* 1890, 569.

55. *1836–1880 Census of Iowa,* 284–289; and U.S. Census Office, 11th Census, 1890, *Report on the Statistics of Agriculture,* 364–365.

56. Iowa State Agricultural Society, *Report,* 1882, 21.

57. *Ibid.,* 1887, 51–52, 465; *Prairie Farmer,* 53:117 (1882), 58:292 (1886).

THE SIGNIFICANCE
OF THE SLAVE PLANTATION
FOR SOUTHERN ECONOMIC DEVELOPMENT

Eugene D. Genovese

Historians are no longer sure that plantation slavery was responsible for the economic woes of the Old South. The revisionist doubts rest on two propositions of dubious relevance. The first is that slave labor could have been applied successfully to pursuits other than the raising of plantation staples; the second is that slave agriculture was possibly as profitable as were alternative industries and can not be held responsible for the unwillingness of Southerners to use their profits more wisely.[1] The first confuses slave labor and its direct effects with the slave system and its total effects; it is the latter that is at issue, and the versatility of slave labor is a secondary consideration. The second rests on the assumption that the master-slave relationship was purely economic and not essentially different from an employer-worker relationship. Yet, when confronted with the issue direct, who could deny that slavery gave rise to a distinct politics, ideology, and pattern of social behavior and that these had immense economic consequences?

We need not examine at the moment the precise relationship between slavery and the plantation. Certainly, plantation economies presuppose considerable compulsion, if only of the *de facto* type now prevalent in Latin America. The historical fact of an ante bellum plantation-based slave economy is our immediate concern, although, undoubtedly, post bellum developments preserved some of the retardative effects of ante bellum slavery.

Those retardative effects were too many even to be summarized here. A low level of capital accumulation, the planters' high propensity to consume luxuries, the shortage of liquid capital aggra-

Reprinted from *The Journal of Southern History,* XXVIII, No. 4 (November, 1962), pp. 422-37, by permission of the Managing Editor.

vated by the steady drain of funds out of the region, the low productivity of slave labor, the need to concentrate on a few staples, the anti-industrial, antiurban ideology of the dominant planters, the reduction of Southern banking, industry, and commerce to the position of auxiliaries of the plantation economy—all these are familiar and yet need restudy in the light of the important work being done on the economics of underdeveloped countries. For the present let us focus on another factor, which in itself provides an adequate explanation of the slave South's inability to industrialize: the retardation of the home market for both industrial and agricultural commodities.

Thirty years ago Elizabeth W. Gilboy complained that economic historians studying the process of industrialization were too much concerned with supply and insufficiently concerned with demand.[2] Her complaint was justified despite brilliant work on the problem of markets by a few outstanding men from Karl Marx to R. H. Tawney and Paul Mantoux. Since then, demand has received much more attention, although possibly not so much as it deserves. Important essays by Maurice Dobb, Simon Kuznets, H. J. Habakkuk, and Gunnar Myrdal, among others, have helped to correct the imbalance,[3] as has new research on European industrialization and the economics of underdeveloped countries. If there is one lesson to be learned from the experience of both developed and underdeveloped countries it is that industrialization is unthinkable without an agrarian revolution which shatters the old regime of the countryside. While the peasantry is tied to the land, burdened with debt, and limited to minimal purchasing power, the labor recruitment and market pre-conditions for extensive manufacturing are missing. "Land reform"—*i.e.* an agrarian revolution—is the essential first step in the creation of an urban working class, the reorganization of agriculture to feed growing cities, and the development of a home market.

There are several ways in which agricultural reorganization can provide markets for manufactures; for our immediate purposes we may consider two. First, when the laborers are separated from the land, as they were during the English enclosures, they necessarily increase the demand for clothing and other essentials formerly produced at home. Paradoxically, this expansion of the market is compatible with a marked reduction in the laborers' standard of living. Second, the farmers left on the countryside to produce for growing urban markets provide an increased demand for textiles, agricultural equipment, and so forth.

The rapid extension of the rural market was the way of the North, but the slave plantations dominated the South until such time as reorganization was imposed from without by a predatory foe interested primarily in a new system of rural exploitation. An adequate home market could not arise in the ante bellum South and has only evolved slowly and painfully during the last century.

In 1860 about seventy-five per cent of the Southern cotton crop was exported; during no ante bellum year did the grain exports of the United States exceed five per cent of the grain crop. No doubt, cotton profits were an important element in the financing of America's economic growth. The question is, were the profits syphoned off to build up the Northern economy? We know that the credit mechanisms alone, to a considerable extent, did just that. The South's dependence on the export trade, in contradistinction to the North's primary reliance on its home market, indicates not merely a social division of labor but the economic exploitation of the exporting South.

Robert G. Albion, in his excellent examination of the colonial bondage of the South to the North, concludes that the South's lack of direct trade with Europe constituted an irrational arrangement secured by the impudence of New York's aggressive entrepreneurs. We can agree that, had the South imported from abroad as much as the North and West, there could have been no sensible reason to route through New York either the South's cotton or its share of European goods; but Albion's assumption of a rough equality of imports, an assumption shared by contemporaries like George McDuffie and T. P. Kettell, can not be substantiated. The slave South's total market for manufactured goods was small relative to that of the free states; and even though the South depended upon Europe as well as the North for manufactured goods, its imports from Europe were smaller in value than imports into the North and West and smaller in bulk than the staples it exported. If the ships carrying cotton had sailed from Southern ports direct to Europe and back, they would have had to return in ballast,[4] New York's domination of the South's export trade was, therefore, not accidental. Furthermore, if the South's share in American imports had been as Albion suggests, and if the coastal trade had been as large as he implies, the greater part of the goods sent from New Orleans to the plantation areas would have originated in Europe and been reshipped through New York rather than being—as is known—of Western origin.[5]

Albion's acceptance of the assumption of nearly equal imports is the more surprising in view of the evidence of restricted Southern demand. The Southern cotton, iron, paper, wool, and railroad industries—to mention a few—struggled with indifferent results against a low level of Southern patronage. Antislavery leaders like Henry Ruffner and Cassius M. Clay made slavery's effects on the home market a cardinal point in their indictment. Thoughtful proslavery Southerners also commented frequently on the market problem. The opinion of the editor of the *Southern Agriculturalist* in 1828 that the South lacked sufficient customers to sustain a high level of manufacturing was echoed throughout the ante bellum period. The speech of Col. Andrew P. Calhoun to the Pendleton, South Carolina, Farmers' Society in 1855, for example, was strikingly similar in tone and content. On the other side, someone like Beverley Tucker would occasionally argue that Northerners would never risk a war "which, while it lasted, would shut them out from the best market in the world." [6] It is difficult to imagine that many, even those who adopted such arguments for political purposes, took seriously a proposition so palpably false.

Alfred Glaze Smith, Jr., and Douglass C. North have traced the low level of Southern demand, in part, to plantation self-sufficiency. This view is not borne out by the data in the manuscript census returns from the cotton belt, which reveal only trivial amounts of home manufactures on even the largest plantations and which bear out the judgments of Rolla M. Tryon and Mary Elizabeth Massey on the weakness of Southern household industry.[7] In De Soto and Marshall counties, Mississippi, the big planters (those with thirty-one or more slaves) averaged only seventy-six dollars worth of home manufactures in 1860, and farmers and small planters averaged much less. In Dougherty and Thomas counties, Georgia, the small planters (those with from twenty-one to thirty slaves) led other groups of slaveholders with one hundred and twenty-seven dollars, and the big planters produced only about half as much. Most of the planters in both clusters of counties recorded no home manufactures at all.[8] Sample studies from Virginia's tobacco area, wheat area, and tidewater reveal the same situation. Plantation manuscripts show surprisingly frequent, and often quite large, expenditures for artisans' services and suggest that plantations were much less self-sufficient and exhibited much less division of labor than is generally appreciated.[9] The root of the insufficient demand must be sought in the poverty of the rural majority composed of slaves, subsistence farmers, and poor whites.

In nineteenth-century America as a whole both capital and labor were in short supply. Industrial development was spurred by farmers who provided a large market for goods and tools, and manufacturing arose on the foundation of this immense rural demand. Eastern manufacturers gradually awoke to their dependence on this rural market and by 1854 were supporting homestead legislation not only to gain support for higher tariffs and for purposes of speculation but to expand the market for their goods. Farmers in New England saw their futures linked with industrial development, and their hostility toward commercial middlemen was not usually transferred to the manufacturers.[10] The same was true in the West. As the shrewd Achille Murat noted in the 1830's, the manufacturing interest of the West "is not constituted by the manufactories which exist, but those which they look forward to in prospective." [11] An agrarianism uncompromisingly hostile to industry and urbanization—to what was called "manufacturing as a system"—existed only in the South and can not be separated from the ideological leadership of the slaveholding planters. Even there, those seriously interested in economic progress saw the link between agricultural reform and industrialization and tried to work out proposals for increased manufactures that would be palatable to their fellow slaveholders.[12]

The West was able to import capital because Eastern manufacturers and European creditors were confident of her growth and prosperity. Outside credits at that time had to be accumulated by the importation of commodities and the maintenance of an unfavorable trade balance. The immense internal market guaranteed the West an import surplus until 1850. Its insatiable demand for manufactured articles contributed to the unfavorable trade balance of the United States, but on the whole this was not a serious problem for the country because American importers were strong enough to obtain long-term credits on relatively easy terms; and, during the 1850's, profits from shipping and other invisible gains largely restored the balance.[13] Thus, on the one hand, the national economy was sufficiently strong to overcome the worst effects of a trade deficit, and, on the other hand, the agrarian West was able to obtain the credits required for industrial development. The South did not benefit from this arrangement. It provided an exportable surplus, which, although of great help to the national economy in offsetting the large quantity of imports, was exploited by Northern capital. The invisible gains that were so important to national growth were made partly at the expense of the South.

The population statistics for 1860 offer a clue to the structure of the market. If we exclude Maryland, in which slavery was declining, and Delaware, which was a slave state in name only, the median population per square mile in the slave states was 18, and Kentucky was high with 31. In comparison, Massachusetts had a population of 158 per square mile; Rhode Island, 138; Connecticut, 98; New York, 84; New Jersey, 81; and so forth. In the West, Ohio had 59; Indiana, 40; and Illinois, 31.

These figures do not tell the important part of the story. A country that is sparsely settled, in absolute terms, may have a high population density, in economic terms, if its system of transportation and commodity production are well developed and integrated. For example, the Northern states in 1860 had a much higher population density—from an economic point of view—than the thickly populated countries of Asia. When we consider the superiority of Northern transportation and economic integration, relative to those of the South, we must conclude that the difference in the magnitude of the market greatly exceeded that suggested by the population figures.

Historians have long appreciated—at least since the pioneer researches of U. B. Phillips—that the Southern transportation system tied the staple-producing areas to the ports and that this was the best possible arrangement for the planters. The planters controlled the state legislatures in an era in which state participation was decisive in railroad construction and generally refused to assume the tax burden necessary to open the back country and thereby encourage and strengthen politically suspect farmers. Without a fully developed railroad network tying the South into an economic unit, the absorption of nonstaple producers into the market economy, except in a peripheral way, was impossible. Poor transportation was, for example, one important factor in the retardation of the Southern cotton textile industry.[14]

With good reason, alert Southerners spoke of the connection among railroads, markets, diversified agriculture, and manufacturing. James Robb pointedly described improved transportation and greater industry as necessary ingredients in the process of unifying the South. Oscar M. Lieber noted that without an adequate transportation system South Carolina farmers were prevented from entering the market as corn producers. John Bell warmly supported federal land grants to railroads to strengthen the bonds of commodity production.[15] Within the South these men could, at best, expect to be received with an impatient silence. Where their message was sometimes listened to attentively was in the upper South, as for example in what came to be West Virginia; the subsequent construction of road and railroad links to existing markets generally bound parts of the upper South to the free states and helped remove them from the slaveholders' domain.

In the slave South the home market consisted primarily of the plantations, which bought foodstuffs from the West and manufactured goods from the East. The planters needed increased Southern manufacturing but only for certain purposes. They needed cheap slave clothing, cotton gins and a few crude agricultural implements, rope for cotton bagging, and so forth. This narrow market could not compare with the tremendous Western demand for industrial commodities of all kinds, especially for agricultural implements and machinery on the more capital-intensive Western farms. The Northeast had the capital and skilled labor for fairly large-scale production and had established its control over existing markets in the North and West. Southern manufacturers could not hope to compete with Northern outside the South, and the same conditions that brought about Northern control of the Northern market made possible Northern penetration of the Southern market despite the costs of transportation.

The South was caught in a contradiction similar to that facing many underdeveloped countries today. On the one hand, it provided a market for outside industry. On the other hand, that very market was too small to sustain industry on a scale large enough to compete with outsiders who could draw upon wider markets. Only one fifth of the manufacturing establishments of the United States were in the South, and their average capitalization was well below that of the manufacturing establishments of the free states. Consider the situation in two industries of special importance to the South—cotton textiles and agricultural implements. New England had almost three times as many cotton factories as the entire South in 1860, and yet the average capitalization was almost twice as great. The concentration in this industry had proceeded so far by 1850 that of the more than 1,000 cotton factories in the United States only forty-one had one half the total capital investment. As for the agricultural implement and machinery industry, New York, Pennsylvania, Ohio, and Illinois each had a greater total capital invest-ment than did the entire South, and in three of these the average capitalization was between two and two and a half times as great as the average in the South.[16] This Northern advantage led Edmund Ruffin and T. L. Clingman, among others, to look forward to a Southern confederacy protected by high tariffs against Northern goods.[17]

In view of the nature of the plantation market it is not surpris-ing that data on the cotton textile industry almost invariably reveal that Southern producers concentrated upon the production of the cheapest and coarsest kind of cloth to be used in the making of slave clothing.[18] Even so, local industrialists had to compete for this market with Northerners who sometimes shipped direct and some-times established Southern branches and who had facilities for the collection and processing of second-hand clothing.[19] Just as New England supplied much of the South's "Negro cloth," so it supplied much of the boots and shoes. Firms like Batchellor Brothers of Brookfield produced cheap shoes especially for the Southern market and as early as 1837 opened a branch at Mobile to consolidate its Southern market.[20]

Producers of better cotton goods had little hope of making a living in the South. Occasionally, a William Gregg could penetrate Northern markets successfully, but Southern demand for such goods was too small to have much effect on the industry generally. North-ern firms like the Pepperell Manufacturing Company or A. A. Lawrence Company did little business in the South. On the other hand a rising demand for textiles in the agrarian West had greatly influenced the New England cotton industry since 1814.[21]

The Southern iron industry, hampered as it was by the restricted railroad development in the slave states, also had a poor time of it. American iron producers generally were handicapped because much of the country's railroad iron was being imported. The small scale of operations and resultant cost schedule, which hurt the industry nationally, hit the Southern manufacturers especially hard. De-pendent upon a weak local market, Southern iron manufacturers had great difficulty holding their own even during the prosperous 1850's.

No wonder the Augusta, Georgia, Commercial Convention added to its demand that Southerners buy Southern goods the qualifica-tion, unless you can get Northern cheaper. And no wonder the proposal was ridiculed as amounting to "Never kiss the maid if you can kiss the mistress, unless you like the maid better." [22]

We can not measure precisely the extent of the Southern market nor even make a reliable, general, quantitative comparison between the Southern and Western rural markets, but we can glean from various sources some notion of the immense difference. For example, Phelps, Dodge & Co., a prominent cotton shipping firm that also distributed metals, tools, machinery, clothing, and an assortment of other items, reported at the beginning of the Civil War that only five percent of its sales were to the South and that those were primarily to the noncotton states. We do not know the extent of the firm's participation in the cotton export trade, but it was considerable. Phelps, Dodge & Co. was in an excellent position to exchange industrial goods for cotton, but the Southern demand for imported goods could not compare in bulk or value with the supply of cotton. In the West, on the other hand, farmers and townsmen provided a growing and lucrative market, and the firm had more customers in Ohio than in any state except New York.[23]

An examination of the 1860 manuscript census returns and other primary sources pertaining to two representative cotton counties in Mississippi and to two in Georgia permits us to judge roughly the extent of the market in the cotton belt by estimating the expenditures made by planters and farmers in these counties. (See page 162, note 8.) The estimates are the most generous possible and exaggerate the extent of the Southern rural market in relation to the Western in two ways: There were far more rural poor with little or no purchasing power in the cotton belt than in the West, and the concentration of landholdings in the South resulted in fewer landowners than could be found in a Western area of comparable size. Thus, even if the estimate of the expenditures made by these Southern planters and farmers had been larger than the expenditures of a similar group of individual proprietors in the West— which was by no means true—the total purchased in each county would still have been far less than in a comparable Western area. Furthermore, as food was a major item in the expenditures of the Southerners, the market for industrial commodities was much smaller than might appear.

The concentration of landholding and slaveholding in the Mississippi counties meant that six percent of the landowners commanded one third of the gross income and probably a much higher percentage of the net. That is, the majority of landowners were faced with a disproportionately small portion of the total income accruing to the cotton economy as a whole.

Only the largest planters—ten per cent of the landowners—spent more than $1,000 a year for food and supplies, and they rarely spent more. These expenditures include the total purchases for the slaves. The slaveholding farms and plantations in Mississippi annually spent about thirty or thirty-five dollars per person for food and supplies; nonslaveholders spent about twenty-five dollars per person. In Georgia slaveholding farms and plantations spent about twenty-five dollars per person, and nonslaveholders were just about self sufficient.[24] In contrast, Philip Foner reports that contemporary newspapers and other sources indicate that the small farmers who made up the great majority of the rural population of the West accumulated store bills of from one hundred to six hundred dollars.[25] Even if we allow for considerable exaggeration and assume that the accounts were generally closer to the lower estimate, these figures, which are exclusive of cash purchases, mail orders, payments to drummers, and so forth, are at least a clue to the impressive purchasing power of the Western countryside.

However imprecise the estimates for the South may be, they indicate the lack of purchasing power among the rural population of the cotton belt and demonstrate how greatly the situation there differed from that in the West. With such a home market the slave economy could not sustain more than the lowest level of commodity production apart from that of a few staples. The success of William Gregg as a textile manufacturer in South Carolina and the data produced by Professor John Hebron Moore showing that a cotton textile industry could and did exist in ante bellum Mississippi would seem to contradict this conclusion; but Gregg, who was aware of the modest proportions of the home market, warned Southerners against trying to produce for local needs and suggested that they focus on the wholesale market. His own company at Graniteville, South Carolina, produced fine cotton goods that sold much better in New York than in the South. Gregg's success in the Northern market could not easily be duplicated by others, and when he discussed the Southern market, he felt compelled, as did Benjamin L. C. Wailes and other astute observers, to advocate production of cheap cotton goods for the plantations.[26] Moore's conclusion that his data prove the adaptability of manufacturing to the lower South requires for substantiation more than evidence of particular successes, no matter how impressive;[27] it requires evidence that Southern producers were strong enough to drive out Northern competition and, more important, that the market was large enough to sustain more than a few firms.

The plantation system did have its small compensations for industry. The planters' taste for luxuries, for example, proved a boon to the Petersburg iron industry, which supplied plantations with cast-iron fences, lawn ornaments, balconies, fancy gates, and other decorative articles.[28] A silk industry emerged briefly but was destroyed by climatic conditions as well as by a shortage of capital.[29] The hemp industry, which supplied rope for cotton baling, depended heavily on the plantation market.

Some Southern industrialists, especially those in the border states, did good business in the North. Louisville tobacco and hemp manufacturers sold much of their output in Ohio. Botts and Burfoot of Richmond, Virginia, reported the sale of $1,000-worth of straw cutters in the North during a six-month period. The more successful Southern iron producers were those of the upper South, who were able to sell outside the slave states. Smith and Perkins of Alexandria, Virginia, began production of locomotives and railroad cars in the 1850's and obtained a good many orders from the North; but the company failed because shipping costs made consolidation of its Northern market difficult and because only a few orders were forthcoming from the South. Similarly, the paper industry in South Carolina did well until the 1850's, when Northern orders dropped and no Southern orders appeared.[30] The political dangers of these links with the free states were widely appreciated. The Virginia Commercial Convention, for example, reported that West Virginia was being cut off from the South in this way.[31] During the Civil War, William Henry Holcombe, a thoughtful doctor from Natchez, listed in his diary various reasons for the adherence of the border states to the Union and placed close commercial ties high on the list.[32] One suspects that there was more than hindsight here, for politically sophisticated Southerners were alert to the danger well before 1861. But what could they have done about it?

The inability of the slave South to generate an adequate rural market inhibited industrialization and urbanization, which in turn limited the market for agricultural produce and undermined attempts at diversification. With the exception of New Orleans and Baltimore, the slave states had no large cities, and few reached the size of 15,000. The urban population of the South could not compare with that of the Northeast, as is generally appreciated; but, more to the point, it could not compare with that of the agrarian West either. The urban population of the lower South in 1860 was only seven per cent of the total population, and in the western part of the lower South, embracing most of the cotton belt, there was a relative decline during the preceding twenty years. In New England, the percentage was thirty-seven; in the Middle Atlantic states, including Ohio, thirty-five; and perhaps most significantly, in Indiana, Illinois, Michigan, and Wisconsin, fourteen.[33]

The urban market in the South was even less developed than these figures suggest. If we except New Orleans, which was a special case, three cities of the lower South had a population of 15,000 or more: Mobile, Charleston, and Savannah, with a combined population of 92,000. Of this number, thirty-seven per cent were slaves and free Negroes, who may be assumed to have represented only minimal purchasing power. In the 1850's American families certainly did not spend less than forty per cent of their incomes on food, and the importance of a large urban market for foodstuffs may be judged accordingly.[34]

Eugene W. Hilgard, state geologist of Mississippi, explained his state's failure to develop a cattle industry largely by the absence of a local market. Similarly, Oscar M. Lieber, state geologist of South Carolina, warned farmers in a state that was never comfortably self-sufficient in corn not to produce more corn than they could consume, for there was no place to market the surplus. Charles Yancey of Buckingham County, Virginia, wrote that planters and farmers would not grow oats because the only possibility of disposing of them lay in person to person barter.[35]

The weakness of the market for agricultural produce had many detrimental consequences for the South, of which we may mention only two. First, those sections of the border states which found markets in the Northern cities were increasingly drawn into the political-economic orbit of the free states at the very moment when the slave states required maximum solidarity to preserve their system. Second, the weakness of the market doomed the hopes of agricultural reformers and transformed their cry for diversification into a cry for a backward step toward natural economy.

When that great antislavery Kentuckian, Cassius M. Clay, finally receives from historians the honor and attention that he deserves, he will surely be recognized as one of the most penetrating commentators on the economics of slavery. Consider his remarks on the problem of markets, with which we are presently concerned:

Lawyers, merchants, mechanics, laborers, who are your consumers; Robert Wickliffe's two hundred slaves? How many clients do you find, how many goods do you sell, how many hats, coats, saddles, and trunks do you make for these two hundred slaves? Does Mr. Wickliffe lay out as much for himself and his two hundred slaves as two hundred freemen do? . . . All our towns dwindle, and our farmers lose, in consequence, all home markets. Every farmer bought out by the slave system send off the consumers of the manufacturers of the town: when the consumers are gone, the mechanic must go also . . . . A home market cannot exist in a slave state.[36]

Plantation slavery, then, so limited the purchasing power of the South that it could not sustain much industry. That industry which could be raised usually lacked a home market of sufficient scope to permit large-scale operation; the resultant cost of production was often too high for success in competition with Northern firms drawing on much wider markets. Without sufficient industry to support urbanization, a general and extensive diversification of agriculture was unthinkable. Whatever other factors need to be considered in a complete analysis, the low level of demand in this plantation-based slave society was sufficient to retard the economic development of the South.

NOTES

1. See, for example, the well known writings of R. R. Russel, including his "The General Effects of Slavery upon Southern Economic Progress," *Journal of Southern History*, IV (February 1938), 34–54, or the more recent statement of Alfred H. Conrad and John R. Meyer, "The Economics of Slavery in the Ante-Bellum South," *Journal of Political Economy*, LXVI (April 1958), 95–130.

2. Elizabeth W. Gilboy, "Demand As a Factor in the Industrial Revolution" in *Facts and Factors in Economic History; Articles by the Former Students of Edwin F. Gay* (Cambridge, Mass., 1932), 620–39.

3. Maurice Dobb, *Studies in the Development of Capitalism* (New York, 1947), 6 ff, 87 ff, 98 ff, 290–96; Simon Kuznets, "Toward a Theory of Economic Growth" in Robert Lekachman (ed.), *National Policy for Economic Welfare at Home and Abroad* (New York, 1955), 12–77; H. J. Habakkuk, "The Historical Experience on the Basic Conditions of Economic Progress" in L. H. Dupriez (ed.), *Economic Progress* (Louvain, Belgium, 1955), 149–69; Gunnar Myrdal, *Rich Lands and Poor* (New York, 1957), *passim*, 23–38 especially.

4. See Robert Greenhalgh Albion, *The Rise of New York Port, 1815–1860* (New York, 1939) and Albion, *Square-Riggers on Schedule; the New York Sailing Packets to England, France, and the Cotton Ports* (Princeton,

1938). For similar arguments presented by contemporaries, see James E. B. De Bow (ed.), *The Industrial Resources, etc., of the Southern and Western States* . . . (3 vols., New Orleans, 1852–1853), 125, 365; and *De Bow's Review*, IV (1847), 208–25, 339, 351. For a perceptive Northern reply, see the anonymous pamphlet, *The Effects of Secession upon the Commercial Relations Between the North and South and upon Each Section* (New York, 1861), 15. For the weakness of the Southern import trade, see George Rogers Taylor, *The Transportation Revolution, 1815–1860* (New York, 1951), 198; Philip S. Foner, *Business & Slavery; the New York Merchants & the Irrepressible Conflict* (Chapel Hill, 1941), 6–7; and Samuel Eliot Morison, *The Maritime History of Massachusetts, 1783–1860* (Boston, 1921), 298–99. Many of the lines carrying cotton from Northern ports were deeply involved in bringing immigrants to the United States, which was one of the reasons why their ships did not have to return from Europe in ballast. John G. B. Hutchins, *The American Maritime Industries and Public Policy, 1789–1914; an Economic History* (Cambridge, Mass., 1941), 262–63.

5. Emory R. Johnson and others, *History of the Domestic and Foreign Commerce of the United States* (2 vols., Washington, 1915), I, 242; R. B. Way, "The Commerce of the Lower Mississippi in the Period 1830–1860," Mississippi Valley Historical Association, *Proceedings*, X (1918–1919), 62; Louis Bernard Schmidt, "The Internal Grain Trade of the United States, 1850–1860," *Iowa Journal of History and Politics*, XVIII (January 1920), 110–11.

6. *Southern Agriculturalist* (Charleston), I (September 1828), 404; *Farmer and Planter*, VI (December 1855), 270–71; *Southern Quarterly Review*, XVIII (September 1850), 218.

7. Alfred G. Smith, *Economic Readjustment of an Old Cotton State: South Carolina, 1820–1860* (Columbia, S.C., 1958), 134; Douglass C. North, *The Economic Growth of the United States, 1790–1860* (Englewood Cliffs, N.J., 1961), 132–33; Rolla M. Tryon, *Household Manufacturers in the United States, 1640–1860; a Study in Industrial History* (Chicago, 1917); Mary Elizabeth Massey, *Ersatz in the Confederacy* (Columbia, 1952), 80, 98.

8. From the five Mississippi and the five Georgia cotton belt counties regarded as typical by Lewis C. Gray in his *History of Agriculture in the Southern United States to 1860* (2 vols., Washington, 1933), I, 334–35, II, 918–21, I have analyzed for each state the two that come closest to the mode in the only variable for which there is clear evidence, the size of slaveholdings. A review of the economic and natural conditions of the South reveals nothing to suggest that the four counties so chosen are not roughly typical of the cotton belt. I have used the four counties primarily for an investigation of purchasing power—to gain clues to the general structure of the market—and the insignificant expenditures recorded indicate that even with due allowance for the possibility of a wide, say 50%, deviation in other counties and for incorrect reporting in the census returns, the results could not conceivably be substantially different.

As a random sample, I selected the first ten names on each page of U.S. Census, 1860, Georgia, Schedule 4, Productions of Agriculture, Dougherty and Thomas counties (Library, Duke University, Durham, North Carolina) and U.S. Census, 1860, Mississippi, Schedule 4, De Soto and Marshall counties (Mississippi State Archives, Jackson). From the U.S. Census, 1860, Georgia, Schedule 2, Slave Inhabitants, Dougherty and Thomas counties, and U.S. Census, 1860, Mississippi, Schedule 2, De Soto and Marshall counties (National Archives, Washington), I determined the number of slaves held by each agriculturist in my sample. Where Schedule 4 gave the amount of produce but not its monetary value, I used a specially prepared price schedule in order to translate the amounts into dollar values. See Eugene D. Genovese, *The Limits of Agrarian Reform in the Slave South* (unpublished Ph.D. thesis, Columbia University, 1959), appendixes.

9. These expenditures were for blacksmiths' services, road building, cabin building, and even for such trivial tasks as the erection of door frames. The accounts often run into hundreds of dollars. See, for example, Moses St. John R. Liddell and Family Papers (Library, Louisiana State University, Baton Rouge), Haller Nutt Papers (Library, Duke University, Durham, N.C.), Everard Green Baker Papers (Southern Historical Collection, University of North Carolina, Chapel Hill), I, 139; Killona Plantation Journals (Mississippi State Department of Archives and History, Jackson), I, 60 ff.

10. Roy M. Robbins, *Our Landed Heritage; the Public Domain, 1776–1936* (New York, 1950), 177; Joseph Brennan, *Social Conditions in Industrial Rhode Island, 1820–1860* (Washington, 1940), 18; Samuel Rezneck, "The Rise and Early Development of Industrial Consciousness in the United States, 1760–1830," *Journal of Economic and Business History*, IV (1932), 784–811; Isaac Lippincott, *A History of Manufactures in the Ohio Valley to the Year 1860 . . .* (New York, 1914), 63–65; Grace Pierpont Fuller, *An Introduction to the History of Connecticut As a Manufacturing State* (Northampton, Mass., 1915), 45; James Neal Primm, *Economic Policy in a Development of a Western State, Missouri* (Cambridge, Mass., 1954), 56–59; Frank W. Taussig, *The Tariff History of the United States* (7th ed., New York, 1923), 68–108; and Bray Hammond, *Banks and Politics in America, from the Revolution to the Civil War* (Princeton, 1957).

11. Achille Murat, *America and the Americans* (New York, 1849), 19.

12. For examples, see the remarks of M. W. Philips and John J. Williams, *Mississippi Planter and Mechanic*, II (May 1858), 157–58; of Thomas J. Lemay, *Arator*, I (November 1855), 237; and of Andrew Johnson, *Congressional Globe*, XXIII, 312.

13. See Simon S. Kuznets, *Economic Change; Selected Essays in Business Cycles, National Income, and Economic Growth* (New York, 1953), 307 ff; and Charles F. Dunbar, *Economic Essays* (New York, 1904), 268.

14. See Milton S. Heath, *Constructive Liberalism; the Role of the State in Economic Development in Georgia to 1860* (Cambridge, Mass., 1954), 290–91, and Seth Hammond, "Location Theory and the Cotton Industry," *Journal of Economic History*, II (1942), Supp., 101–17. The opposition of entrenched landowning classes to the extension of transportation has been general in colonial, underdeveloped countries. See George Wythe, *Industry in Latin America* (New York, 1945), 4.

15. De Bow (ed.), *Industrial Resources*, II, 154; Oscar M. Lieber, *Report on the Survey of South Carolina . . . 1857* (Columbia, 1858), 106; *Congressional Globe*, XXI, pt. 1, 867–68.

16. U.S. Census Office, *Manufactures of the United States in 1860 . . .* (Washington, 1865), xxi, ccxvii, lxxiii, 729–30; Evelyn H. Knowlton, *Pepperell's Progress; History of a Cotton Textile Company, 1844–1945* (Cambridge, Mass., 1948), 32. The average capitalization of manufacturing establishments was in 1850 more than 25% higher in the free states and territories than in the slave states, and the gap widened in the 1850's when the increase in average capital investment was 68% in the free states and terri-

tories and only 51% in the slave states. The lower South (North Carolina, South Carolina, Georgia, Florida, Alabama, Mississippi, Louisiana, and Texas) fell even further behind. The average capitalization here, 38% less than in the free states in 1850, was 47% less by 1860. Furthermore, the rate of increase in the number of establishments during this decade was appreciably greater in the North than in the South.

17. Edmund Ruffin, Incidents of My Life, 19–20, in Edmund Ruffin Papers (Southern Historical Collection, University of North Carolina); T. L. Clingman's speech to the House of Representatives, January 22, 1850, in Selections from the Speeches and Writings of Hon. Thomas L. Clingman of North Carolina . . . (Raleigh, N.C., 1877), 233–54, especially 250.

18. See Patent Office, Annual Report, 1857, Agriculture, Senate Exec. Docs., 35 Cong., 1 Sess., No. 30, pt. 4 (Serial 928), 308–309, 318; and Richard H. Shryock, "The Early Industrial Revolution in the Empire State," Georgia Historical Quarterly, XI (June 1927), 128.

19. Jesse Eliphalet Pope, The Clothing Industry in New York (Columbia, Mo., 1905), 6–7.

20. Blanche Evans Hazard, The Organization of the Boot and Shoe Industry in Massachusetts Before 1875 (Cambridge, Mass., 1921), 57–58.

21. Knowlton, Pepperell's Progress, 83–84; Caroline F. Ware, The Early New England Cotton Manufacture; a Study in Industrial Beginnings (Boston, 1931), 48, 55.

22. Herbert Wender, Southern Commercial Conventions, 1837–1859 (Baltimore, 1930), 25.

23. Richard Lowitt, A Merchant Prince of the Nineteenth Century, William E. Dodge (New York, 1954), 31 ff, 37.

24. In Mississippi a sample of 584 units with 7,289 slaves and an estimated 2,480 whites spent about $316,500; in Georgia a sample of 100 units with 2,354 slaves and an estimated 710 whites spent about $73,300.

25. Foner, Business & Slavery, 143.

26. William Gregg, Essays on Domestic Industry; or An Inquiry into the Expediency of Establishing Cotton Manufactures in South-Carolina (Graniteville, S.C., 1941), 4; Benjamin L. C. Wailes, Address Delivered in the College Chapel Before the Agricultural, Horticultural and Botanical Society, of Jefferson College (Natchez, Miss., 1841), 22–23; De Bow's Review, XXIX (October 1860), 496–97; Broadus Mitchell, William Gregg, Factory Master of the Old South (Chapel Hill, N.C., 1928), 106.

27. John Hebron Moore, "Mississippi's Ante-Bellum Textile Industry," Journal of Mississippi History, XVI (April 1954), 81.

28. Edward A. Wyatt, IV, "Rise of Industry in Ante-Bellum Petersburg," William and Mary College Quarterly, s. 3, XVII (January 1937), 32.

29. Southerners were very much interested in silk cultivation and manufacture and saw fine market possibilities. See Charles G. Parsons, Inside View of Slavery; or a Tour Among the Planters (Boston, 1855), 71 ff; C. O. Cathey, "Sidney Weller: Ante-Bellum Promoter of Agricultural Reform," North Carolina Historical Review, XXI (January 1954), 6; Spaulding Trafton, "Silk Culture in Henderson County, Kentucky," Filson Club History Quarterly, IV (October 1930), 184–89.

30. Lippincott, Manufactures in the Ohio Valley, 64; Southern Planter, III (April 1843), advertisement on back cover; Lester J. Cappon, "Trend of the Southern Iron Industry Under the Plantation System," Journal of Economic and Business History, II (February 1930), 361, 371, 376; Carrol H.

Quenzel, "The Manufacture of Locomotives and Cars in Alexandria in the 1850's," *Virginia Magazine of History and Biography*, LXII (April 1954), 182 ff; Ernest M. Lander, Jr., "Paper Manufacturing in South Carolina Before the Civil War," *North Carolina Historical Review*, XXIX (April 1952), 225 ff.

31. De Bow (ed.), *Industrial Resources*, III, 465.

32. William Henry Holcombe Diary (Southern Manuscript Collection, University of North Carolina), entry for September 6, 1855, but obviously written in 1861.

33. Urban area defined as incorporated places of 2,500 or more. See U.S. Bureau of the Census, *Urban Population in the U.S. from the First Census (1790) to the Fifteenth Census (1930)* . . . (Washington, 1939).

34. This estimate is from Edgar W. Martin, *The Standard of Living in 1860* (Chicago, 1942), 11–12, and may greatly underestimate the situation in urban households. According to Richard O. Cummings, laborers in Massachusetts probably spent about three fourths of their weekly wages on food in 1860. R. O. Cummings, *The American and His Food; a History of Food Habits in the United States* (Chicago, 1941), 266.

35. Eugene W. Hilgard, *Report on the Geology and Agriculture of the State of Mississippi* (Jackson, 1860), 250–51; Lieber, *Report*, 106. See also Patent Office, *Annual Report, 1849, Agriculture*, Senate Exec. Docs., 31 Cong., 1 Sess., No. 15, pt. 2 (Serial 556), 137.

36. Horace Greeley (ed.), *The Writings of Cassius Marcellus Clay* . . . (New York, 1848), 179, 227. For a recent biography, see David L. Smiley, *Lion of White Hall: The Life of Cassius M. Clay* (Madison, Wis., 1962).

7

Foreign Trade and Domestic Growth

"THE ABSENCE OR REDUCTION of government intervention in the movement of goods, people, and capital made the nineteenth century unique in history," asserts Douglass North in the following essay. Given this set of conditions, and in light of American economic interdependence with Great Britain, North argues, American development before 1860 must be considered in the context of the Atlantic economy. Like Frederick Jackson Turner and a generation of American historians since Turner, Professor North attributes a major formative influence to the occupation of the western frontier. But North insists that western development was dependent upon the southern market for surplus crops of the West, and the South's ability to purchase western surpluses depended in turn upon the British market for southern cotton. Like George Rogers Taylor, who has characterized the years 1815–1860 as the period of the "transportation revolution," North acknowledges the key role of new transport in permitting regional specialization and development of a truly national economy. But North gives much weight to the fact that construction of American transport facilities was financed, to a large extent, by British and other European investment; and the magnitude of investment from Europe was closely tied to the counter-flow of American agricultural exports, foremost among which was cotton. Thus the Anglo-American cotton trade receives a central place in North's analysis, especially since southern and western development provided markets for rising eastern manufactures.

Professor North's studies of nineteenth-century American development have evoked much controversy among students of the period. Perhaps the most telling criticism has been that North gives too little emphasis to internal determinants of growth such as public economic policy, technological innovation, and the favorable social climate of enterprise in America. Whether or not such reservations are justified, North's work remains valuable for its systematic treatment of international economic relations as one of the strategic factors affecting the quality and pace of this country's early growth.

INTERNATIONAL CAPITAL FLOWS AND THE DEVELOPMENT OF THE AMERICAN WEST

Douglass C. North

When the Chairman asked me to undertake this **paper** he reminded me that the general theme was the West as an underdeveloped area and suggested that some comparison be made with underdeveloped areas today. However, it should be made clear at the outset that the problems of the development of the American West in the nineteenth century are very different from the problems of achieving sustained growth in the underdeveloped areas today. The underdeveloped areas today are most typically characterized by a factor combination of abundant labor with scarce capital and land (and resources), usually complicated by a social and political structure not geared to economic advance. America in the nineteenth century, in contrast, was characterized by scarce labor and capital combined with seemingly endless land (and natural resources) set in a framework of social and political institutions that was highly favorable to economic growth.

Reprinted by permission from *The Journal of Economic History*, XVI, No. 4 (December, 1956), 493–505.

Yet one point deserves emphasis here because it strikes me as being vastly underrated in contemporary analysis of economic growth; that is, the primary role of land and resources which, in contemporary theoretical analysis, usually take a back seat to capital, labor, or entrepreneurship as a critical factor in economic growth. Certainly the case of United States growth in the preceding century offers abundant evidence of the primary significance of this factor. Indeed the substance of this paper may be summarized as follows: Given the favorable institutional framework that existed and the characteristics of the Atlantic economy described below, then a critical limiting problem in growth was the opening up and development of land and resources. In this connection it is important to keep in mind that land cannot be thought of as an undifferentiated productive factor but must be considered in terms of its quality[1] and accessibility. The quality of land and resources in the West was unmatched and therefore the fundamental problem was one of overcoming distance. The point I should like to make clear is this: it was the natural resource wealth of the American West that served as the fundamental determinant of our extensive growth in attracting capital and labor to America; it was the rich quality of the land that gave America such a substantial share of this vast international movement of people and capital during this century.

The argument of this paper is that surges in westward development were initiated by long-run favorable movements of the prices of key staple commodities. However, an increased supply of these staples could only be obtained by heavy capital expenditure in internal improvements and plantation development. Long-term foreign capital played an important role in meeting this need by directing real resources into the needed social overhead investment and making possible an important surplus of consumer and capital goods during these expansive periods.

A presentation limited to twenty minutes has required some drastic limitations in the scope of this paper. Accordingly, the time span is limited to the period 1820–1860 and the focus is primarily theoretical.[2] In a paper of this length it is clearly impossible to present either the quantitative data or material evidence necessary to substantiate the relationships suggested here.[3]

II

It was the special characteristics of the international economy and conditions in Europe that were critical in the opening up and development of the West, particularly in the first half of the nineteenth century. In the light of the historian's preoccupation with the pervasive influence of the frontier on American development, it perhaps needs stressing that the rate at which the West was developed was basically a function of (1) the changing characteristics of consumer demand in the English and European market, (2) the international mobility of capital and labor that made possible emigration from England, Ireland, and the Continent, and (3) the international flow of technological information, with the particular significance, insofar as this paper is concerned, of the development of the steam engine and its application to land and water transportation. A brief elaboration of the first two factors will serve to clarify their influence upon American development.

The changing characteristics of demand came about as a result of the continuing economic growth of English and European economies and concomitant expansion in population and income. Two factors were particularly significant for American development; they were the growth in cotton textile manufacturing and the increasing per capita consumption of bread made from wheat flour (reflecting both a rise in income and a shift in taste from rye to wheat flour in leavened bread).

The unprecedented international movement of people appears to have reflected not only differential expectations as to income and employment between the country of emigration and immigration, but also differential expectations as among the alternative countries to which to immigrate.[4] An additional contributing factor was the decline in shipping fares.

The international flow of capital was possible as a result of the earlier growth in income of England and European countries. An aspect of this growth that was important in this capital flow was the substantial income inequality and resultant large volume of savings concentrated in a small segment of the population and responsive to differential rates of return (discounted for risk).

The absence or reduction of government intervention in the movement of goods, people, and capital made the nineteenth century unique in history.[5]

III

In a classic article written more than fifty years ago, G. S. Callender discussed the opening of the West in these terms: "By the opening of the West I do not mean the early settlement of the region west of the Mountains, which took place on a large scale during the thirty years after the Revolution. This in itself, as I shall attempt to show, had very little influence on the economic life of the Country. I refer rather to that improvement in the economic condition of the West which set in about the time of the second war with England, and which in a decade or two entirely changed the relationship of that region to the rest of the country. . . ." [6] The development of the West that Callender had in mind was not the subsistence agriculture of the early pioneer but that which came about as a result of a new region being able to produce goods in demand in existing markets at a cost competitive with alternative sources of supply. The essential requirements for this growth were (1) a market for primary goods and (2) rich land and resources that could be combined with the scarce productive factors of labor and capital to produce these goods at a comparable cost with alternative sources of supply. The limiting factor was the relative inaccessibility of the land and resources.

Under the nineteenth-century conditions of international mobility discussed above, capital and labor can be considered responsive on a world-wide basis to the quality and accessibility of land and resources. An examination of American internal expansion in the first 60 years of the nineteenth century in terms of these considerations will then make possible an assessment of the role of foreign capital in this western expansion.

In striking contrast to present times, the major market for goods in the first part of the nineteenth century lay outside America. The changing characteristics of demand in the European market, and to a lesser extent in the West Indies, South American, and other external markets, affected fundamentally the fortunes of America. As far as the westward movement was concerned, it was primarily the demand for cotton and then wheat (and flour) that was critical.

It is difficult to exaggerate the role of cotton in American growth in the first half of the nineteenth century. Not only was it the major part of America's external trade, but it was also a fundamental factor influencing internal trade as well. The nature of the trade between the agricultural West and the South and the increasingly industrialized East has been described many times.[7] The importance of this trade, insofar as this paper is concerned, lay in the dependence of the West upon cotton expansion in the South during the first half of the nineteenth century. Thus westward expansion during this period was primarily a function of expansion into land for cotton production in the South [8] or into land in the western states [9] capable of producing corn, hogs, and wheat (which would provide pork, lard, bacon, corn, cornmeal, flour, and whisky) to provision the South. While the West Indies, South America, and the eastern seaboard were markets for these staples, the expansion of the cotton South was the most critical determinant of the market for western provisions during the period from 1820 to 1850. Although this demand appears to have been somewhat income-inelastic and domestic trade fluctuated less violently than foreign trade,[10] nevertheless the fortunes of the West were tied to the cotton trade.

As early as 1825, with the opening of the Erie Canal, the western trade along the Great Lakes and the northern areas bordering thereon had been diverted to the East. While the Pennsylvania Canal furthered this east-west trade, it was not until the end of the 1840's that the basic pattern of trade changed. The growth of manufacturing and resultant urbanization in the New England and Middle Atlantic states substantially increased the demand for western staples. This expanded domestic demand was reinforced by increased foreign demand for wheat and flour. The rate of expansion of the West became increasingly dependent on the eastern and European market, and the rapid development of the 1850's in Minnesota, Iowa, Michigan, Illinois, Wisconsin, and Missouri reflected primarily this expansion in demand for foodstuffs.[11]

Although the development of both the Southwest and Northwest associated with this expanding demand for staple commodities was a continuous process, the pace of the westward movement varied significantly. There were notable surges in this expansion, followed by periods of assimilation in which the pace was markedly slower.[12] Thus the early 1820's, following the land boom of 1818–1819, was a period of slower expansion: there was a gradual acceleration of the tempo in the late 1820's and early 1830's, culminating in the surge of 1835 to 1839.[13] The early years of the 1840's paralleled the 1820's and then gradually the pace quickened and culminated in a sharp surge between 1854 and 1856. The pace was sharply reduced in the intervening years before the Civil War.

An explanation of these surges of expansion is clearly to be found in the expected profitability of western lands. It was the expected return upon cotton in the Southwest and upon the wheat, corn, and hogs (and the manufactures thereof) in the Northwest that was the most fundamental factor affecting the pace of western development. It was actual or anticipated prices of these staple commodities that exercised the most decisive influence.[14] If we take the volume of public land sales as the measure of western development,[15] then we may note a close correlation between the price of cotton on the one hand and the volume of public land sales in the five southern states of Alabama, Louisiana, Mississippi, Arkansas, and Florida on the other hand.[16] A similar correlation exists between the price of wheat (and corn) and public land sales in the seven western states of Ohio, Illinois, Indiana, Michigan, Iowa, Wisconsin, and Missouri.[17] Since the price of cotton on the one hand and of wheat, corn, and provisions on the other did not always move together, although the long-run movements were roughly parallel as indicated above, it is not surprising that accelerated westward movement was at times associated more with the Southwest than the Northwest and vice versa. Thus, while the price of cotton drifted down throughout most of the 1820's, the price of wheat improved after 1827, and the sales of western land in Ohio, Indiana, Illinois, and Michigan picked up markedly after the middle of the 1820's. Cotton prices began to rise after 1832, and only thereafter did public land sales in the southern states increase significantly. Similarly while cotton prices were depressed throughout most of the 1840's, wheat prices improved, and western land sales expanded from the middle forties. Finally, the boom period of the 1850's was primarily associated with the Northwest in which the rising price of wheat and corn was paralleled by a tremendous land boom, whereas cotton prices and land sales in the Southwest increased very moderately.

While the very sharp increases and subsequent declines in prices from 1835 to 1839 and from 1854 to 1857 reflected the speculative boom that overlaid each expansive period, the underlying real factors affecting these price movements were the character of shifts in demand and supply for these commodities. Shifts in demand appear by and large to have been more uniform, reflecting increased demand for cotton textiles and, in the American South and East, fairly steady growth in demand for provisions.[18] Yet there are notable exceptions, such as the expansion in demand for wheat with the Irish famine, which was a critical influence resulting in the rise in wheat prices and the accompanying land expansion in the Northwest in the mid-forties. Moreover, the periods of expansion were accompanied by rising incomes leading to increased demand for consumption goods, once the boom was under way. This rise was reinforced in the 1850's by the volume of immigration.[19] However, it was primarily the response of supply that led to these long-run price movements.[20] The increased supply of these primary commodities was a function of accessibility in the Northwest and of both accessibility and the necessary outlays for land, slaves, clearing the land, buildings, and getting the crop planted in the cotton South. The capital expenditure necessary for transport facilities in the Northwest and for both transport and plantation development in the Southwest were high. In consequence it is not surprising that supply did not shift smoothly with demand. Rather it moved irregularly in spurts, resulting in relative overexpansion, followed by consequent lengthy periods of depressed prices until the gradual increase in demand caught up. This was followed by slowly rising prices which induced another period of accelerated westward expansion and development of new lands.[21]

There were two factors responsible for the radical shifts in supply that took place. The first is inherent in the nature of transport developments to make new land accessible. The opening up of a canal or making a river navigable in the 1830's or the construction of a western railroad in the 1850's did not gradually open up new land but made land available in vast amounts where it had heretofore been simply inaccessible for commercial production.

The second factor involved in the shifts in supply resulted from the impetus of rising prices of these key commodities upon the capital market. The optimism engendered by these favorable price movements in the context of the special characteristics of the banking system and the supply of international capital led to a vast expansion of investment in internal improvements and plantation development during these periods of extensive development.

IV

It should be clear from the preceding discussion that the role of international capital was not in initiating these surges in expansion. The previous analysis suggests that movements in the prices of key staple commodities were the most important impetus in these surges of expansion. Foreign capital, however, did play a vital role in making possible each expansion and in its duration and character.

The importance of foreign capital lay in directing real resources into transportation and plantation expansion and sustaining this expansion by making possible an import surplus.

Although there are significant differences in the character of capital inflows in the 1830's as compared with the 1850's [22] the influence upon the balance of trade in each case was similar. In both expansive periods the volume of foreign trade increased substantially and the United States incurred an import surplus typical of a young debtor nation.[23] The increase in imports in the 1830's was in part in capital goods but primarily in consumption goods, with a substantial expansion in the imports of luxury goods. In the 1850's, as one would expect, the import of capital goods, particularly railroad iron, played a far more important part, although there was a significant increase in consumption goods.

Initial expansion in the late 1820's and middle 1840's was at a moderate pace [24] and took place with little rise in prices because of the unemployed and underemployed resources available. Once the expansion had begun, the actual or anticipated development of internal improvements implied a reduction in transfer costs. This made it possible for vast new areas to market their commodities and therefore further to accelerate the westward movement and demand for land.[25] Bank expansion played the most significant role in supplying capital, and foreign investment was selective and limited. The significant flow of foreign funds came later as a result of the increased opportunities associated with each expansive period. These opportunities were associated not only with the favorable prospects of the significant staple commodities but also with the regional expansion that would result from the concomitant development of new cotton areas in the South or new areas producing provisions in the Northwest. The necessary growth of facilities to market these commodities, as well as of those to supply the local needs of planters or settlers in new areas, led to a construction boom. In turn this expansion reacted back upon the East in expanded demand for goods and services,[26] particularly for English imports.

It was the inflow of capital during each expansive period that enabled the expansion to be sustained for a number of years rather than its merely erupting into an inflationary spiral and collapse.[27] Although bank expansion initially provided capital for the crucial investment in transport and plantation expansion that could open up and develop new lands, it was capital inflows that maintained the expansion by permitting a level of imports of consumption goods and capital goods without deterioration of foreign exchanges.

Thus the period from 1830 through 1834 was characterized by a slow but persistent rise in commodity prices,[28] an acceleration in the pace of internal improvements in the West, and an increase in the note issue of state banks from 61 million dollars in 1830 to 103 million dollars in 1835.[29] It was a period of real expansion interrupted only by the interval of contraction by the Second Bank of the United States during Biddle's struggle with Jackson. The bonds issued by the several states in order to build canals in the North or to finance expansion of cotton production in the South found their way for the most part into the hands of English holders of securities. During this period approximately 40 million dollars of American state securities were purchased abroad. At the same time the United States incurred an import surplus of merchandise trade as well as net specie imports of approximately 20 million dollars.[30]

After 1834 the pace increased and was overlaid with speculation, aided and abetted by the uninhibited expansion of the state banks and the policies of the Jacksonian administration.[31] More than 107 million dollars in state securities went abroad and the states pursued an unrestrained expansion in internal improvements, with their bonds finding a ready market among English investors. With the economy already at full employment, the effect was to shift labor out of agriculture and other activities and into construction of canals and their internal improvement. This redirection of productive factors out of consumer goods into social overhead investment was partially offset by the increased importation of consumer goods made possible by English capital. However, the expanded consumer demand associated with rising aggregate income inevitably led to rapidly rising prices. The result was ultimate collapse,[32] yet the extraordinary era between 1835 and 1839 is too often dismissed as one of wild and unproductive speculation without recognizing that substantial real expansion took place during these years. Although land sales were mostly to speculators for resale rather than cultivation, nevertheless this was a part of the process by which land ultimately got in the hands of cultivators [33] and by which the West was developed. Moreover, despite the many half-completed projects that were abandoned in the early 1840's, transport development and plantation expansion had made possible a large increase in the supply of cotton and wheat.

If foreign capital had sustained the boom of the 1830's, the lack of it helped to extend the depressed years of the 1840's. During a number of these years the United States had an export surplus when securities were being returned from Europe and interest payments on existing debt were a significant, if not always honored, obligation. The marked regional differences in economic well-being during the early forties lent support to the arguments presented above. The severely depressed price of cotton and western staples reflected the tremendous increase in supply resulting from the previous expansive era. In contrast, industrial prices in the East declined less severely.[34] The dependence of western expansion upon foreign capital was reflected in almost a cessation of internal improvements. In contrast, railroad construction in the East was significant and, while western railroad and bank stocks were severely depressed, those of the New England area declined only moderately.[35]

The gradual westward expansion that began in the mid-1840's was associated more with the Northwest and wheat than with the Southwest and cotton. The impetus was not only the extraordinary foreign demand for wheat in 1847 but the steady growth in demand by the increasingly urbanized East, reinforced by the first great wave of transatlantic migration that went on from the mid-1840's to 1860 and had its peak from 1849 to 1854.[36] As in the earlier period, initial expansion was mostly effected by domestic capital, with selective purchase of railroad securities by German investors. Beginning in 1850, the United States incurred a large import surplus and a substantial volume of railroad securities went abroad.

Immigration of capital and labor was a prominent feature of the real expansion that took place between 1849 and 1854. Both factors played an important part in the railroad development of the period, providing the additional labor and capital necessary without too significant a redirection of resources from other parts of the domestic economy. The import surplus of consumption goods again provided a cushion against rapid inflation. In addition, the large volume of railroad iron brought in directly contributed to the boom. Railroad mileage tripled from 1849 to 1856. Most of this increase was in the West or in lines connecting the East with the West.

While there is no doubt that the capital inflow during this period was a valuable contributing factor to the extensive expansion of the country, it did not play as important a part as it had in the 1830's. The large volume of gold exports from California, together with the earnings of the merchant marine, were more significant credit items than earlier in balancing the import surplus of the United States. This was particularly true after the advent of the Crimean War.

While railroad securities sold abroad may have totaled as much as $160 to $200 million for the decade, the composition of our balance of payments would indicate that most of the purchases after 1854 represented a shift out of mercantile credit rather than a net addition to our aggregate indebtedness.[37] Gold exports alone were sufficient to balance the import surplus of the United States.

While the speculative boom from 1854 to 1857 in some respects paralleled the earlier one, the peak in land sales occurred in 1855–1856. The increase in the supply of wheat had been so substantial that despite record exports the price of wheat was already declining in 1856, and the land boom in the seven western states was over well before the crisis of 1857.[38]

V

This paper has been concerned with the pace of westward development and the influence of the international economy, and particularly the supply of long-term capital, upon that development in the years from 1820 to 1860. The long-run impetus in this economic development was the expanding demand for certain staple commodities in the European and domestic market. The surges in westward expansion were the processes by which the supply of these commodities adjusted to this increasing demand. With the rich quality of the seemingly endless land available in western America, the essential requirement was for social overhead investment to make this land accessible. Although the initial impetus in each period of rapid extensive development was provided by the issuance of bank notes, foreign capital played the important role of directing real resources into the needed social overhead investment and of sustaining an import surplus of consumer and capital goods which made possible the prolonged periods of rapid development.

NOTES

1. The quality of land and resources is of course relative to the state of technology.

2. A further limitation of this paper is that it does not deal with the British financing of American trade. It should perhaps be emphasized here that the financing of a substantial part of our export trade, and some domestic trade as well, was probably as important in American development as were the long-term capital movements that are the subject of this paper.

3. The quantitative data on American capital imports in the nineteenth century will be presented in as much detail as possible in my forthcoming paper at the Conference on Income and Wealth in the Nineteenth Century, jointly sponsored by this Association and the National Bureau of Economic Research. [Ed. note: See Bibliography No. 7, p. 567, below.]

4. Brinley Thomas' view of the Atlantic economy as an evolving unit provides a useful perspective upon the movement of people and capital in the course of nineteenth-century development. See his *Migration and Economic Growth* (Cambridge: Harvard University Press, 1954), Ch. 3.

5. The uniqueness of this period with respect to its relative freedom from government intervention makes nineteenth-century international development very different from that of the twentieth century. See Ragnar Nurkse, "International Investment Today in the Light of Nineteenth-Century Experience," *The Economic Journal*, LXIV, No. 255 (December 1954).

6. "The Early Transportation and Banking Enterprises of the State in Relation to the Growth of Corporations," *Quarterly Journal of Economics*, XVII (November 1902), 115.

7. See Emory Johnson and others, *History of the Domestic and Foreign Commerce of the United States* (Washington: Carnegie Institute, 1915) for the classic account of this trade.

8. The expansion was primarily into Alabama in 1816–1819; into Alabama, Mississippi, Louisiana, Arkansas, and Florida in the 1830's; and into the same five southern states and Texas in the 1850's.

9. These states were Ohio, Indiana, Illinois, and Missouri in 1816–1819, to which must be added Michigan and Wisconsin in the 1830's.

10. Arthur H. Cole and Walter B. Smith, *Fluctuations in American Business, 1790–1860* (Cambridge: Harvard University Press, 1935), p. 73.

11. By 1850 east-west railroads were an important factor in this development and began seriously to eat into canal revenues. See E. L. Bogart, *Internal Improvements in Ohio* (New York: Longmans, Green & Co., 1924), ch. 2.

12. These surges in westward expansion are most carefully analyzed in T. S. Berry's *Western Prices Before 1861* (Cambridge: Harvard University Press, 1943).

13. The panic of 1837 caused only a temporary lull in the westward movement and it was not until 1839 that the movement collapsed.

14. Actual or anticipated reductions in production or transfer costs also played a role that will be described below.

15. Despite the speculative character of public land sales, they appear to be a rather good measure of westward development. A. H. Cole's study of the course of public land sales and population movements in several states indicates a close relationship. "Cyclical and Sectional Variations in the Sales of Public Lands, 1816–1860," *The Review of Economic Statistics*, IX (January 1927), 50. An analysis of land sales and production in five southern states from 1835 to 1842 indicates a lag of 4 to 5 years between surges in land sales and expanded production. Considering the time it took to clear land and plant a crop or two of corn, the actual lag indicated was not so substantial. The significance of the lag lies in its effect on prices as will be described below.

16. Data on the price of cotton may be found in M. B. Hammond, *The Cotton Industry* (Publication No. 1, American Economic Association, 1897), Appendix I. The data on land sales by states are found in Arthur Cole's "Variations in the Sale of Public Lands."

17. Prices of wheat and corn were obtained from A. H. Cole's *Wholesale*

Commodity Prices in the United States, 1700–1861 (Cambridge: Harvard University Press, 1938).

18. R. C. O. Mathews stresses that there is no evidence of an increase in the rate of growth of British demand for cotton in the 1830's over the 1820's. *A Study in Trade Cycle History* (Cambridge: The University Press, 1954), p. 53. Berry also reached the conclusion that demand for foodstuffs was less susceptible to variation than supply. *Western Prices Before 1861,* p. 535.

19. See the following section for amplification of this point.

20. It should be made clear that this paper is not concerned with the cyclical disturbances that affected prices but with the long swings in prices that are clearly evident by applying a nine-year moving average to prices. While the peak of these long swings is roughly coincidental with the peak of a cycle, nevertheless the decline in wheat prices and western expansion had already set in at least a year before the collapse of 1857.

21. An illustration will serve to clarify the process: Expansion into new cotton land was moderate as prices of cotton stabilized around 10 cents a pound in New York in the late 1820's. After 1832 the price began increasing and land sales rose rapidly in the five new cotton states than earlier. The peak was reached in 1835 and 1836, when more than five million acres of land were taken up in each year. However, the time interval involved in transferring land from speculator to cultivator, clearing the land, and getting it into production resulted in 1840 being the first year in which the production from these new states was felt. The crop in these five states jumped from 911,913 bales in 1839 to 1,538,904 bales in 1840. The lengthy period of depressed prices in the 1840's followed (data from M. B. Hammond, *The Cotton Industry*).

22. In the 1830's the British purchased primarily the securities of States that were floated for internal improvements (the bulk of them for canal construction) in the North and for commercial bank development for plantation expansion in the South. In the late 1840's the Germans provided the initial impetus and the British displayed a notable and understandable reluctance; however it was not long before the British were again purchasing American securities in volume. In this case, however, it was the private securities of railroads.

23. This was in contrast to the periods of borrowing after 1873, when the United States continued to have a favorable trade balance.

24. However, the extraordinary demand for wheat in 1847, the heavy influx of immigrants, and the gold discoveries accelerated the pace in the latter period.

25. Thus the opening of the Erie Canal and the construction of the Pennsylvania Canal gave an early impetus to development in the Northwest in the late 1820's. Similarly the land boom in Indiana from 1845 to 1852 was primarily a response to the opening of the Wabash and Erie Canal. A. H. Cole, "Variations in the Sale of Public Lands," p. 49.

26. The induced investment in manufacturing during these expansive periods contributed substantially to the process of industrialization that was going on in the East.

J. S. Dusenberry describes this multiplier-accelerator process resulting from westward development in his article "Some Aspects of the Theory of Economic Growth," *Explorations in Entrepreneurial History,* III, No. 2 (December, 1950).

27. The land boom in 1818 appears to have been of this character.

28. Smith and Cole, *Fluctuations in American Business,* p. 60.

29. Charles J. Bullock, John H. Williams, and Rufus S. Tucker, "The Balance of Trade of the United States," *The Review of Economic Statistics*, I (July 1919), 218.

30. Smith and Cole, *Fluctuations in American Business*, p. 79.

31. The peculiarities of banking in the 1830's deserve more than passing attention. The cessation of deposit of government funds in the Second Bank of the United States and the distribution of surplus revenues among the States played an important part in this inflation.

32. There is no room in this paper to discuss the immediate causes of the panic of 1837 and the ultimate collapse in 1839. See however, R. McGrane, *The Panic of 1837* (Chicago: University of Chicago Press, 1924). For a recent able analysis see R. C. O. Mathews, *A Study in Trade Cycle History*, ch. 5.

33. See footnote 15.

34. Smith and Cole, *Fluctuations in American Business*, p. 65.

35. Smith and Cole, *Fluctuations in American Business*, p. 50.

36. Brinley Thomas, *Migration and Economic Growth*, p. 89, and Appendix IV, Table 96.

37. See the summary account in Bullock, Williams, and Tucker, "The Balance of Trade," p. 223.

38. For an account of the Panic of 1857 and the circumstances surrounding it see George Van Vleck, *The Panic of 1857* (New York: Columbia University Press, 1943).

8

The Rise of Industry

AMONG THE THEMES which traditionally have concerned historians of early American industry are the "industrial consciousness," or "will to industrialize," that marked popular attitudes toward manufacturing; the rise of corporate business organization in industry and its relationship to changes in scale of production; expansion of domestic markets for American manufactures; origins, recruitment and discipline of the labor force; and the impact on industry of governmental policies such as tariff and patent legislation. The recent work of Lance Edwin Davis has illuminated still another feature of early industrial enterprise in America: sources of capital and patterns of stock-ownership in manufacturing firms, a subject which lends itself well to precise quantification. The eminent English scholar, Sir John Clapham, once wrote that the economic historian has (or ought to have) a more highly developed "statistical sense" than other types of historians. The kinds of data with which he deals permit a high degree of accuracy in answering such basic questions as: "how large? how long? how often? how representative?" * Professor Davis's article, reprinted here, deals with the New England textile industry, cradle of the industrial revolution in America; and Davis's method illustrates both the strengths and limitations of the quantitative approach. In this case, data relating to investment are concrete enough, for the records of eleven important firms were made available to Professor Davis. Yet the historian has had to resort to informed speculations to explain significant shifts in the

* Sir John Clapham: "Economic History as a Discipline," *Encyclopedia of the Social Sciences*, Vol. V (New York, 1930), pp. 328 ff.

perceived patterns of stock-ownership—a type of difficulty which the best quantitative studies, such as Davis's, explicitly recognize.

The article by William A. Sullivan deals with a classic problem in industrial history, the social cost of industrialization. How did the factory system, when first introduced on a large scale, affect real wages, working conditions, and the structure of power in industrial-labor relations? Did early-nineteenth century factory employment leave "not a single hour for social converse, . . . no time for anything but toil, toil, toil, enervating, ceaseless, destructive toil," as some contemporary observers contended? * Or was the idyllic, if puritanical, life of workers at Lowell, Massachusetts, in the early 1830's more typical? † Professor Sullivan's article, which is one product of his intensive study of Pennsylvania's industrial workers in the period 1800–1840, supports a harsh judgment of the social impact of industrialization.

STOCK OWNERSHIP IN THE EARLY NEW ENGLAND TEXTILE INDUSTRY

Lance Edwin Davis ‡

Students of American economic development have generally agreed that the New England cotton textile industry, and particularly that portion characterized by the large "Massachusetts Type" mills, was the first branch of American industry to feel the full impact of the

Reprinted by permission from the Business History Review, XXXII (Summer, 1958), pp. 204–22.
* New-Hampshire Patriot and State Gazette (Concord), Sept. 11, 1845.
† See Michael Chevalier: Society, Manners, and Politics in the United States, edited by John William Ward (Anchor Books edition, Garden City, N.Y., 1961), pp. 134 ff.
‡ The author wishes to express his thanks to his colleagues at Purdue University—and in particular Professors Irving Morrissett, Jared Sparks, and Duncan McDougall—for their help and advice on matters of both content and grammar. Moreover, the author wishes to acknowledge the aid of the Department of Political Economy of The Johns Hopkins University and of the Purdue Research Foundation that together financed the research on which this paper is based.

industrial revolution.[1] In 1800 few American firms produced textiles; but by 1860 cotton manufacturing represented a capital investment of over $65 million in the six New England states alone.[2] Since capital was far from abundant in ante-bellum America, the process by which this relatively large sum was accumulated and mobilized is an interesting subject for analysis.

A recent study of the large "Massachusetts" mills has shown that the sale of equity was the most important single source of finance. This examination of firm records indicates that sale of stock provided the mills with almost all of their original finance; and, even after the firms had been in existence for a quarter century, the study shows that contributed equity still represented over one-half of their total capital.[3] Still unanswered, however, are two basic questions: who were the stockholders, and from what sources did they garner the funds that they invested in the textile industry? This study attempts to provide at least partial answers to these questions.

The answers are based on the records of eleven cotton textile mills of the "Massachusetts Type": the Amoskeag, Boston, Dwight, Cabot, Perkins, Hamilton, Nashua, Lyman, Lawrence, Lancaster, and Massachusetts Cotton Mills. Analyses were made of the stockholder records of these firms for the date of the original stock subscription and for the fourth and ninth years of each decade in the period 1829–1859. The fourth and ninth years were chosen because more stockholder records were available for these years than for any other five-year intervals; but even so, the records are incomplete. However, the records for every selected year are complete for at least two firms up to 1839, and for at least six firms thereafter. Table 1 shows the firms and years for which information is available, together with the total value of their outstanding stock.[4] Although the survey was limited to stockholders who, at some time during the period, had investments of $2,500 or more in the industry, this restriction resulted in the exclusion of less than one-fifth of the total value of the equity (see Table 2).[5]

The company records listed the stockholders only by name and city of residence, and it was necessary to obtain further identification from city directories, university alumni records, local histories, and other similar sources. These chronicles provided information about the occupation and business connections of most stockholders, but they seldom identified the sources of their invested wealth. Lacking better information, it was assumed for the purposes of this analysis that the invested capital originated in the occupation in which the buyer was engaged at the time of his purchase, or, in the case of retired persons, in the last occupation in which he was engaged prior to his retirement. In a few instances in which the actual sources of capital were known, this arbitrary assumption proved to be reasonably realistic.[6]

THE STOCKHOLDERS

The Mercantile Groups

The most important and numerous group of stockholders were nontextile merchants purchasing shares in their own name, or, less commonly, in the name of their firm. In all, some 234 nontextile merchants and 17 nontextile mercantile firms owned shares in one or more of the eleven firms; however, the importance of the individual contributions within this group varied greatly. Its membership ranged from individuals whose holdings totaled a bare $2,500 on the one hand to persons whose personal investments ran as high as $200,000.

Over the period studied, the average investment per nontextile merchant per firm remained remarkably constant while the average total investment per merchant in the eleven firms rose slowly from $11,000 to $17,000.[7] However, the *proportion* of equity held by this group has a very different pattern. This ratio rose between 1829 and 1834, from about 30 to almost 40 percent, then declined steadily throughout the remainder of the period. By 1859, these merchants owned less than one-quarter of the equity included in the sample. The relative distribution of shares owned by these merchants and by other occupational groups is shown in Table 6.[8]

Not only do the nontextile merchants bulk large among stockholders in each of the cross-section years, but also they appear to have made a substantial contribution to new equity. The group subscribed to over one-third of all new issues; and, although their average investment per firm was only $11,600, the average individual investment was in excess of $16,000. Nor did their contribution to new issues diminish perceptibly over time. As late as 1854 this mercantile group contributed 32 percent of the equity capital of the newly organized Lyman Company.

In many ways the textile merchants represent the most interesting single group.[9] They are set apart from the other merchants not only by the size of their investments, but also by their investment motives. While other merchants could look at textile stock as only one more of a series of investment alternatives, the textile merchants must also have seen such investment as a method of securing their raw material sources.

During the entire period, only 45 textile merchants and 7 textile firms were identified among the stockholders included on the sample; however, their contribution to textile finance was far out of proportion to their numbers. Only once during the entire period did this group represent more than 8 percent of the total number of investors; but during the middle years of the survey their holdings represented about 16 percent of the total equity.[10] During the 1830's their holdings rose from 6 to 18.5 percent of the total stock surveyed; but after 1840 their importance gradually diminished; and in 1859 they owned only 7 percent. Although the records show an increase in the number of textile merchant owners during the 1830's, this increase was small; and the group's increasing importance among occupational groups can be traced almost entirely to the increasing size of the individual merchant's investments. In 1829 the average investment of textile merchants in each firm was less than $11,000; ten years later, however, this figure had more than doubled (see Table 4). Even more striking is the rise in the average investment per individual. In the same period this figure increased by almost 200 percent, from $12,800 to $36,800 (see Table 5). Similarly, the post-1844 decline in the importance of the textile merchants' investments can in large part be attributed to a fall in the average investment per individual. By 1859 the average textile merchant held equities totaling only about $20,500, and in each mill he had less than $16,000.[11]

In new issues, too, the textile merchants made a contribution far out of proportion to their small numbers. Although the group represented only a little more than 8 percent of the new stock purchasers, they purchased about 17 percent of the new equity issues. Moreover, the average investment of each purchaser in the new issues of the mills was in excess of $35,000.

If the eleven firms studied here are typical of the large "Massachusetts Type" mills, this analysis tends to substantiate the belief that a large portion of the equity capital of the early American textile industry was drawn from mercantile sources. However, the same evidence casts some doubt on several corollary assumptions that are often made about the causes and nature of this transfer from mercantile to industrial investment.

An examination of the contribution of the entire mercantile sector attests to the importance of trade-born capital in the financing of American textiles. The mercantile groups together contributed over one-half of the original equity and represented over one-third of the total holdings in almost every cross-section year.[12]

Most writers have recognized the importance of mercantile capital, but many have attributed the transfer of capital from trade to industry almost entirely to the declining returns in commerce that followed the post-Napoleonic depression.[13] Although such a decline may have triggered the first capital emigration, the evidence suggests that such a decline is not a satisfactory explanation of the continued transfer. While the stock holdings of the nontextile mercantile groups declined in relative importance over the period, the estimates of their total contributions to equity capital (Table 3) indicate that the absolute size of these holdings continued to increase, at least until 1860. Moreover, similar steady increases in the number of investors and in the average size of the individual's investment also seem to indicate that the transfer was not a short-run phenomena induced by a sudden sharp decline in commercial profits, but, instead, a long-term process lasting at least until the Civil War.

Undoubtedly, declining profits provided some impetus to *push* capital from trade, but it is difficult to ignore the *pull* supplied by the high expected profits and the supposed safety of textile investment. If the decline of the returns to investment in trade had been the only cause of the transfer to industrial capital, it is reasonable to assume that an increase in commercial profits would have caused a withdrawal of merchants' investments in industry and a reinvestment in trade, or at least a cessation of new transfers from trade to industry. But it appears that mercantile capital continued to flow into textile production even during periods of commercial prosperity.[14]

Although high expected profits may be largely responsible for the transfers of mercantile capital to the textile industry during the 1830's, some other factor must be adduced to explain the continued flow during the 50's when textile profits were low and the expectation of future prospects dim.[15] It appears likely that this flow can, in part, be explained by the merchants' search for a reasonably safe investment that did not require their personal attention rather than an investment chosen to maximize their short-run monetary profits. Except for the issues of railroads (never known for their safety), private bonds were largely unknown; and, aside from the flotations of railroads, commercial banks and textiles, there were few available equity issues. Thus, since men of wealth were usually prohibited from investing in Savings Banks and Trust Companies, the only investment alternatives aside from textiles that combined safety and impersonality were the bond issues of government bodies —and these were often rather unrewarding and at times not even safe.

Finally, the evidence indicates that the transfer process cannot be correctly described as a flight of capital from trade to industry. No doubt some merchants withdrew completely from trade and invested large portions of their fortunes in industry; however, the evidence suggests that this was not the usual case. Instead, it appears that the merchants only gradually withdrew their funds from trade and transferred them to industry. Table 5 shows that the merchants' average investment increased gradually through the period, and an examination of the accounts of individual stockholders also confirms the gradual nature of their investment.

The investments of the textile merchants appear to have rested on the three legs of profits, wealth, and economic control. Before 1820 textile merchants were largely engaged in the import and sale of foreign cloth, and, as a result, the merchants were not particularly concerned with the infant textile industry. As the industry grew, however, established merchants shifted from foreign to domestic goods and new merchants entered the domestic field. Profits were frequently large and capital began to accumulate in the hands of those merchants specializing in the sale of American goods. At the same time, two forces combined to draw the group's capital into the manufacture of textiles. In the industry's early years the large mills were highly profitable. Because of their close association with textile manufacture, the textile merchants must have been able to recognize this profitability and have been in a position to subscribe to the new equity issues.[16] Moreover, the merchants must have realized that their own prosperity depended on a continued supply of finished cotton. Although no direct evidence can be marshaled to support the belief that textile merchants attempted to cement their sources of supply by investment in textile production, indirect evidence makes this conclusion seem reasonable. The records show that members of textile mercantile firms invested much more heavily in those mills served by their firms than they did in the remainder of the eleven mills. Moreover, studies of the structure of the early textile industry have shown that most of the original Massachusetts Type mills were established as noncompetitive operations with each mill specializing in one particular textile product.[17] Since the textile merchants were faced with an almost monopolistic group of mill suppliers, it seems reasonable to assume that the necessity of maintaining a source of supply must have dictated their investment in textiles.

The high profits of the mid-forties brought many new firms into the industry; and entry apparently did much to reduce the strength of the forces that had combined to draw the capital of textile merchants into the mills. The influx of new firms drove profits below the returns in alternative investments. The textile merchants, because of their position, should have been among the first to sense the effects of increased competition. At the same time, entry caused increased sales competition among the mills and reduced the merchants' need for ties of ownership to maintain their sources of supply. The result was a withdrawal of capital by the textile merchants.

Financial Institutions

Among the records of stockholders appears the names of 35 commercial banks, 7 savings banks, 5 fire and marine insurance companies, 5 brokerage firms, 2 private banks, 1 life insurance company, and 1 trust company. Two conditions set these financial intermediaries apart from the other occupational classes. First, since these institutions often served only as intermediaries, the true capital source remains partly obscured; and, second, the intermediaries apparently acquired their holdings for a wide variety of reasons. Although no exhaustive study of motivation is possible, it appears that the insurance companies purchased equity as a permanent part of their investment portfolio; that at least some of the commercial and savings banks acquired their holdings in the process of loan creation (i.e., the shares were signed over to them as collateral or they were received in partial payment of the forfeited loans); and that the brokers frequently purchased their shares for resale.[18] Despite this variety of motives, these financial institutions did provide capital, either directly (through the deliberate investment of their own or their customers' funds) or indirectly (by permitting individuals to hypothecate stock and thus invest in the industry without forfeiting their other enterprises).[19] In its ultimate effect there is little difference between direct and indirect investment. In the former case, the intermediaries make a direct capital grant to the recipient firm. In the latter, the institution interposes an added guarantor (the borrower) between itself and the capital recipient. Thus potential investors who otherwise would be forced to hold surplus funds in liquid reserves are allowed to invest in industrial equity. For these investors know that the intermediaries would be willing to convert equity shares into liquid reserves by substituting their capital for the funds of the investor if the need should arise. The history of the Massachusetts Hospital Life Insurance Company provides evidence of the importance of indirect lending. While the Mass. Hospital never purchased textile equity as a permanent earning asset, the company did, as a result of its loan policy, become the registered owner of a large quantity of the issues of the eleven firms. In no cross-section year did that institution hold less than $8,000 in stock in the eleven companies, and in 1854 the holdings totaled $390,500.

Just as the motives for shareholding of these financial intermediaries differed from those of the merchants, so the pattern of their investment also differed markedly from that of the mercantile investors. Although these intermediaries accounted for a sizable share of the equity in every cross-section year, the group made only a small (2 percent) contribution to original sales. Moreover, despite the evidence of substantial fluctuation, there appears to have been no significant trend in their relative contribution, their relative importance among the total number of stockholders, the average investment per firm, or in the average size of the individual institution's investment.[20]

That the relative holdings of the financial intermediaries did not increase despite the rapid increases in the size and numbers of these institutions, can probably be traced to two related circumstances. First, only the insurance companies purchased textile stock as a permanent part of their portfolio; and, although their rate of growth was high in the two decades before Lincoln's election, their absolute size was never large. Thus, the majority of the textile shares held by the group reposed in the hands of the trust companies and the commercial and savings banks—institutions that acquired their holdings in the course of their loan activities. And, although these latter institutions were rapidly increasing their loans during the 40's and 50's, this expansion was occurring in real estate and personal security loans and not in loans on intangible securities.[21]

Although the five-year cross-sections do not permit a complete analysis of cyclical fluctuations, some evidence suggests that the intermediaries' holdings may have been affected by fluctuations in business activity. In 1834 (a year of panic) and in 1844 (after a prolonged depression) the relative contribution of the financial institutions fell precipitously (see Table 6).[22] Since these fluctuations are more pronounced in the holdings of the commercial and savings banks than they are in the portfolios of the other financial institutions, they probably reflect shifts in loan policy induced by deteriorating business conditions.

Financiers

Persons engaged in financial enterprises appear on the textile companies' books as stockholders almost as frequently as financial institutions. The sample yields the names of 59 persons who could be termed financiers; these include 19 commercial bank officers, 17 officers of insurance companies, 15 brokers, 4 trust officers, and 4 private bankers.

Although the proportion of stock held by these financiers was only about two-thirds that held by the textile merchants, over time the two series appear to have moved closely together. The relative contribution of the financiers rose from 6 percent in 1829 to almost 11 percent ten years later. After that date, the trend was reversed, and the ratio displays a gradual decline reaching 6 percent again in 1854.[23] Unlike the movements of the textile merchants' holdings, the fluctuations in the relative importance of financiers can be attributed both to changes in the relative number of investors and to changes in the average investment of each individual.[24]

The contribution of the financial group to new equity issues did not diverge far from the pattern of their holdings in a typical cross-section year. They purchased about 9 percent of the new equity included in the survey, and their individual investments in these new issues averaged slightly over $16,000.

These figures seem to indicate that the financiers were as aware of the actual levels of profit as were the textile merchants. The financiers' entry coincides closely with the years of high profits, and their exit follows swiftly on the heels of declining profits.[25] It is not difficult to believe that the "men of money" would be acutely aware of the industry's true profit prospects, and that these men would not be bound to textiles by any nonprofit considerations. However, their apparent re-entry in the late 50's is more difficult to rationalize. It may have reflected some astute guesses about the proximity of hostilities coupled with an awareness of the profit potential of the textile industry in wartime.

Out-of-State Contributions to Equity

In the entire study, no characteristic stands out more plainly than the almost total absence of foreign capital. Even if the category "foreign capital" is used to include all non-Massachusetts investors, the contribution is insignificant.

Among the stockholders included in the survey were 59 persons who did not live in Massachusetts and 2 firms whose offices were outside the Commonwealth. Of the 59 out-of-state stockholders, 7 were residents of foreign countries, 29 were Nashua and Amoskeag owners residing in New Hampshire, and 27 did not live in either Massachusetts or the state in which their mills were located.[26] The two out-of-state businesses were Paddleford and Far, the Savannah cotton house, and Baring Bros., the English private bankers.

Until 1839 no out-of-state owners can be identified on the list of stockholders; and, although their importance gradually increases during the ensuing twenty years, by 1859 they owned only slightly more than 2 percent of the total equity surveyed. The individuals in the group seldom held stock in more than a single firm and their average investment ($5,500 to $7,300) was lower than that of any other class.

Nor was the out-of-state group important in the financing of new firms. Of the nine new issues included in the survey the out-of-state group subscribed to only .3 percent (.003).

Although foreign capital made significant contributions to other sectors of the American economy, the textile industry appears to have drawn little direct benefit from this source. The 7 alien holders (3 Englishmen, 3 Germans, and 1 Canadian) subscribed to no new stock issues, and holdings of the largest investor never exceeded $16,000.

Today the corporate form of business is often thought of as an instrument designed to depersonalize capital and thus free it of its geographic ties; however, there is nothing in the pattern of equity ownership of these early mills that would attest to the importance of that feature.[27] The dependence upon local capital is so strong that it seems to suggest that the location of the early textile industry in New England might be traced not only to immobile labor and power sources but also to the existence of a substantial quantity of immobile capital.

Women and Trustees

Although accounts held in the name of women or trustees were rare in the industry's formative years, maturity brought with it increased participation by these two groups.[28] Their individual investments remained small; but each succeeding survey included a greater number of their accounts; and, by 1859, women and trustees together held almost one-fourth of the total shares surveyed (and, of course, this is one-quarter of a much larger total).[29]

A comparison of the records of the individual firms shows that the increase in the importance of women and trustees was linked not only with the passage of time, but also with the age of the firm. The two groups appear earlier and become important sooner in the three older firms (the Boston, Hamilton, and Nashua) than they do in the remaining eight mills. Moreover, the contribution of the women and trustees was important in the original financing of only one mill—the Lyman—and here the new issue did not represent a voluntary purchase of shares, but merely a substitution of shares in the new mill for those in an already-established enterprise (the Hadley Falls Company).

In her excellent monograph on the New England textile industry, Miss Ware has attributed the rising proportion of holdings of women and trustees to the industry's high profits and increasing stability that made investment appear both safe and lucrative.[30] While there is no certain method of verifying this hypothesis, some evidence indicates that at least a part of the increase can be attributed not to voluntary investment by widows and orphans, but to the deaths of the original investors and the distribution of their estates, including textile shares, to their heirs.[31] An examination of the women listed on the individual stockholder accounts indicates that well over two-thirds of the new women holders had the same surname as men who had previously held shares but whose names had ceased to be listed. Furthermore, the notation "widow of ...." not infrequently followed the name of the new shareholder. In a few cases, the trustee accounts carried the notation "Josiah Quincy trustee for Paschal Pope." In these cases, investigation usually showed that Paschal Pope had held stock in the company in an earlier year. Finally, the fact that the size of the women's and trustees' holdings were related to the age of the firm (as well as the historical year) also supports the view that inheritance helped determine ownership. If safety and profitability had been the cause of the increased investment, the investments should have moved into all firms in the same chronological period. If, however, the stock were acquired by inheritance, the women and trustees could be expected to appear first in the oldest firms, since the owners of older firms could be expected to die earlier than the owners of newer companies, on the average. An examination of the holdings by firms does in fact show a marked positive partial correlation between firm age and women and trustee holdings.

Other Groups

Little industrial capital found its way to the textile industry through investment by persons earning a living in nontextile manufacturing. In the 30-year span, 71 such persons (31 artisans, 27 managers and officers in manufacturing companies, and 13 owners of manufacturing companies) and 1 manufacturing company held stock in one or more of the 11 mills. However, their holdings represented only about 5 percent of the total. They typically invested only a small amount and in only a single concern, and they did not increase their relative contribution over the period.

The failure of the nontextile industrial group to increase its relative share appears as something of a surprise. Given the industrial development that marked the first half of the century, it appears reasonable to expect manufacturing capital to have become more important as the period progressed. That this did not occur, indicates, perhaps, that manufacturing wealth did not increase more rapidly than the accumulation of capital in the economy as a whole; or, perhaps, in the later years falling profits caused a withdrawal of capital from textiles that offset the increase that otherwise would have occurred; or, perhaps most likely, almost all industrial capital was reinvested in the business in which it originated.[32]

The 100 professional persons who owned stock in the 11 firms made a greater contribution than the nontextile industrialists, but their proportionate share of holdings declined over the period, from 12 to 7 percent.[33] However, if the estimates of absolute capital are reliable, the decline does not indicate a withdrawal of capital, but merely a rate of increase lower than the rate of the industry's expansion.

SUMMARY AND CONCLUSIONS

Recent studies have indicated that the sale of equity shares pro-vided the American textile industry with most of its original capital. This study utilizes the records of 11 Massachusetts Type textile mills to trace the source of the equity capital. These records, sup-plemented by local histories, city directories, and university alumni records, served to identify the majority of the stockholders by occu-pation. A comparison of the holdings of the occupational groups at five-year intervals permitted an estimate of the trends in the relative importance of each group to be made; and, in addition, it provided some insights into the investment behavior of the members of each group.

If the 11 firms were typical of the early cotton manufacture, mer-cantile wealth appears to have been the most important single source of textile finance—at least one-third of the total in every year except 1859. The evidence also suggests that the shift from mercantile to industrial capital was a slow process, with merchants only gradually withdrawing their funds from trade and investing them in industry. Moreover, although the first movement of capital from trade to in-dustry may have been instigated by a decline in trading profits, the transfer process appears to have continued even during periods of mercantile prosperity.

During the 1830's, textile merchants were by far the heaviest in-vestors in the textile industry. This propensity to invest can prob-ably be attributed to their knowledge of, and close contact with, the textile manufacturing firms, and to their need to assure a source of domestic supply in a market that was not yet very competitive. During the 1840's textile merchants withdrew their capital from textile production. The withdrawal apparently resulted from falling profits in textile manufacture coupled with increasing competition among manufacturers.

Even in the industry's formative years, a significant portion of its equity shares was held by financial intermediaries; but despite the rapid growth in the resources of these financial institutions, there appears to have been no sustained increase in the proportion of equity supplied by them.

Unlike some other young industries of the ante-bellum period, New England textiles received only a negligible amount of capital from abroad and very little from other parts of the country. Al-though the equity holdings of non-Massachusetts owners increased with time, even at the end of the period they represented only 2 percent of the industry's capital. In the entire period only 7 aliens held stock in one or more of the firms; and the total holdings of the largest investor among the 7 never exceeded $16,000.

TABLE 1. TOTAL VALUE OF STOCK OUTSTANDING [a]
(*in thousands of dollars of par value*)

	First Year	1829	1834	1839	1844	1849	1854	1859
Amoskeag	$ 965			$ 988	—	$3,000	$3,000	$3,000
Boston	100	$600	$ 600	600	$ 600	540	450	450
Dwight	—				—	—	700	1,700
Cabot	400			—	—	—	b	
Perkins	360			—	—	—	1,000	c
Hamilton	—	—	—	—	1,200	1,200	1,200	1,200
Nashua	—	600	—	750	800	1,000	1,000	1,000
Lyman	1,470						1,470	1,470
Lawrence	1,200		1,200	1,500	1,500	1,500	1,500	1,500
Lancaster	100			—	117	—	—	—
Mass. Cotton	1,200			—	1,200	1,800	1,800	1,800

[a] Blank spaces indicate firms were not in operation; dash (—) indicates no stockholders' lists were available.

[b] Cabot merged with Perkins, 1852.

[c] Perkins merged with Dwight, 1856.

TABLE 2. VALUE OF CAPITAL STOCK OWNED BY STOCKHOLDERS INCLUDED IN THE STUDY
(*in thousands of dollars of par value*)

	First Year	1829	1834	1839	1844	1849	1854	1859
Amoskeag	$ 895			$ 950		$2,292	$1,862	$1,947
Boston	100	$474	$ 448	428	$ 390	381	343	308
Dwight	390						627	1,662
Cabot	354							
Perkins	348						937	
Hamilton					1,008	840	856	773
Nashua		600		692	755	776	861	862
Lyman	1,408						1,012	1,227
Lawrence	1,240		1,095	1,169	1,091	994	1,022	1,027
Lancaster	85				111			
Mass. Cotton	1,040				994	1,413	1,366	1,306
Per cent of total included in the sample		.946	.896	.857	.844	.803	.741	.733	.752

TABLE 3. ESTIMATED VALUE OF TOTAL EQUITY CONTRIBUTED BY
VARIOUS OCCUPATIONAL GROUPS TO EIGHT
COTTON TEXTILE FIRMS
(*in thousands of dollars*)

	1829	1834	1839	1844	1849	1854	1859
Merchants & Merc. Firms (excl. Textile)	$637	$1,237	$1,443	$2,315	$2,921	$2,744	$3,006
Textile Merchants & Tex. Merc. Firms	108	411	979	1,192	1,124	872	837
Manufacturers, Artisans & Mfg. Firms	180	112	237	249	347	483	648
Professional Persons	326	349	575	764	813	791	876
Misc. Persons & Firms	1	20	28	103	80	181	222
Financial Institutions	308	203	537	270	742	902	854
Financiers	99	183	572	756	657	629	976
Foreign Persons & Firms a	0	6	24	76	146	322	265
Women	49	93	94	292	436	588	742
Trustees	30	140	314	704	1,219	1,676	2,003
No Occupation	77	223	236	273	316	449	520
No Information	221	203	475	581	933	932	1,170

a Includes all non-Massachusetts residents.

TABLE 4. AVERAGE INVESTMENT PER STOCKHOLDER PER FIRM,
BY OCCUPATION OF STOCKHOLDERS
(*in thousands of dollars*)

	First Year 1829	1834	1839	1844	1849	1854	1859
Merchants & Merc. Firms (excl. Textile)	$11.6	$10.9	$12.8	$11.5	$11.3	$17.2	$12.2	$12.8
Textile Merchants & Tex. Merc. Firms	20.0	10.7	22.1	23.2	20.2	19.7	17.1	15.5
Manufacturers, Artisans & Mfg. Firms	7.9	14.5	16.0	11.8	6.9	9.4	11.2	10.5
Professional Persons	8.9	10.8	10.4	9.7	9.1	9.4	7.5	8.8
Misc. Persons & Firms	6.1	0	9.0	7.0	5.2	4.8	8.2	8.4
Financial Institutions	7.4	21.4	25.5	24.1	9.2	14.6	12.7	15.8
Financiers	11.0	12.0	8.4	14.9	7.2	11.2	13.0	16.5
Foreign Persons & Firms a	5.5	0	0	5.3	7.3	5.6	7.0	6.9
Women	6.1	7.5	9.5	4.5	8.4	6.8	7.9	7.2
Trustees	9.4	7.7	5.9	12.5	6.8	10.1	9.6	9.0
No Occupation	9.1	7.8	11.4	9.9	6.4	9.0	9.5	11.6
No Information	7.1	8.2	10.1	8.8	6.8	7.5	6.6	7.4

a Includes all non-Massachusetts residents.

TABLE 5. AVERAGE TOTAL INVESTMENT PER INDIVIDUAL
INCLUDED IN THE STUDY, BY OCCUPATION
(*in thousands of dollars*)

	First Year	1829	1834	1839	1844	1849	1854	1859
Merchants & Merc. Firms (excl. Textile)	$16.3	$10.9	$13.3	$14.6	$14.7	$17.6	$16.7	$17.4
Textile Merchants & Tex. Merc. Firms	35.7	12.8	31.6	36.8	32.1	28.9	24.5	20.5
Manufacturers, Artisans & Mfg. Firms	8.3	14.5	16.0	12.2	6.9	9.4	11.2	10.5
Professional Persons	12.1	10.8	12.0	12.3	13.5	12.9	10.6	12.3
Misc. Persons & Firms	12.2	0	9.0	7.0	6.3	7.7	15.4	16.9
Financial Institutions	7.4	34.2	25.5	30.7	11.6	21.3	24.6	28.2
Financiers	16.1	12.0	10.1	23.8	25.4	17.2	17.6	23.9
Foreign Persons & Firms[a]	5.5	0	0	5.3	7.3	5.6	7.0	6.9
Women	8.1	7.5	9.5	4.5	9.6	7.8	8.4	7.9
Trustees	9.4	7.7	5.9	12.3	6.8	10.3	9.6	9.0
No Occupation	11.0	7.8	11.4	19.9	8.1	9.0	10.2	11.6
No Information	7.1	7.2	10.1	8.8	6.8	7.6	6.6	7.7

[a] Includes all non-Massachusetts residents.

TABLE 6. PERCENTAGE DISTRIBUTION OF EQUITY HOLDINGS
BY OCCUPATIONAL GROUPS

	First Year	1829	1834	1839	1844	1849	1854	1859
Merchants & Merc. Firms (excl. Textile)	.360	.299	.393	.347	.300	.299	.276	.248
Textile Merchants & Tex. Merc. Firms	.166	.062	.142	.185	.163	.120	.080	.068
Manufacturers, Artisans & Mfg. Firms	.051	.085	.021	.055	.025	.032	.050	.054
Professional Persons	.105	.121	.100	.103	.111	.085	.076	.072
Misc. Persons & Firms	.009	.000	.017	.004	.014	.008	.014	.018
Financial Institutions	.020	.167	.066	.095	.041	.076	.077	.070
Financiers	.089	.059	.064	.107	.100	.066	.059	.080
Foreign Persons & Firms[a]	.003	.000	.000	.004	.010	.015	.027	.022
Women	.008	.015	.024	.012	.047	.043	.055	.061
Trustees	.045	.022	.041	.055	.089	.123	.155	.166
No Occupation	.031	.038	.072	.044	.029	.031	.043	.043
No Information	.112	.130	.059	.088	.070	.099	.088	.096

[a] Includes all non-Massachusetts residents.

TABLE 7. PERCENTAGE DISTRIBUTION OF THE NUMBER OF
SHAREHOLDERS BY OCCUPATIONAL GROUPS

	First Year	1829	1834	1839	1844	1849	1854	1859
Merchants & Merc. Firms (excl. Textile)	.322	.298	.379	.285	.258	.198	.227	.203
Textile Merchants & Tex. Merc. Firms	.085	.064	.079	.104	.074	.071	.047	.047
Manufacturers, Artisans & Mfg. Firms	.066	.064	.016	.044	.034	.034	.045	.053
Professional Persons	.137	.181	.118	.129	.120	.104	.102	.086
Misc. Persons & Firms	.015	.000	.008	.007	.025	.019	.018	.023
Financial Institutions	.028	.085	.032	.052	.080	.060	.061	.047
Financiers	.083	.053	.095	.092	.069	.068	.046	.051
Foreign Persons & Firms[a]	.006	.000	.000	.011	.014	.031	.040	.033
Women	.012	.000	.032	.033	.053	.073	.071	.089
Trustees	.049	.032	.087	.059	.126	.141	.163	.193
No Occupation	.035	.053	.079	.059	.044	.042	.046	.039
No Information	.160	.170	.071	.133	.099	.151	.134	.137

[a] Includes all non-Massachusetts residents.

TABLE 8. NUMBER OF PERSONS INCLUDED IN THE SAMPLE
BY OCCUPATION

	First Year	1829	1834	1839	1844	1849	1854	1859
Merchants & Merc. Firms (excl. Textile)	147	28	46	60	89	114	153	131
Textile Merchants & Tex. Merc. Firms	31	5	7	18	22	28	30	31
Manufacturers, Artisans & Mfg. Firms	41	6	2	12	20	23	41	47
Professional Persons	58	17	13	29	35	44	67	54
Misc. Persons & Firms	5	0	1	2	9	7	9	10
Financial Institutions	18	5	4	11	15	24	29	23
Financiers	37	5	10	16	17	26	31	31
Foreign Persons & Firms[a]	4	0	0	3	6	18	37	29
Women	8	2	4	21	37	61	71	
Trustees	32	3	11	16	57	80	150	170
No Occupation	19	5	10	8	15	24	39	34
No Information	104	16	9	36	45	87	123	115

[a] Includes all non-Massachusetts residents.

Over the period, the most significant increases in ownership are recorded for women and trustees. Although these two groups held almost no shares in 1830, by 1859 they accounted for almost one-fourth of the total. The evidence suggests, however, that the increases can be attributed not to the positive attractions of textile investment, but to the natural processes of death and inheritance.

NOTES

1. Students of the period divide textile producers into two categories. The small single-operation mills that were the American heirs to the English development are termed Rhode Island Type mills. These firms are typified by the Slater enterprises near Providence, Rhode Island, and by the development at Fall River in Massachusetts. The Massachusetts Type is the name given to the large integrated mill that grew out of the development of the Boston Manufacturing Company at Waltham, Massachusetts.

2. The Census of Manufactures in 1860 reported that total capital in cotton textile production in the United States amounted to $93,143,759. Of this amount more than two-thirds ($65,947,819) was invested in the six New England states. The total estimated capital in all industry in the entire U.S. was $1,009,855,715. Thus New England textiles represented about 7 percent of the total. These official figures probably underestimate the total actual investment. United States Secretary of the Interior, *Manufactures in the United States in 1860* (Washington, D.C., 1865), pp. 679, 735 and 742.

3. Lance E. Davis, "Sources of Industrial Finance: The American Textile Industry, A Case Study," *Explorations in Entrepreneurial History*, Vol. IX (April, 1957), pp. 190–192.

4. The figures displayed in Table 1 represent the par value of *all* outstanding stock, and no allowance has been made for purchases at prices above or below the par value nor has any attempt been made to deduct the shares received as stock dividends. The paucity of data on stock prices as well as the complexity of stock transactions make it all but impossible to adjust the figures for price changes. At the same time, without stretching the facts very far, stock dividends can be looked at as voluntary reinvestment in the business, since the typical stockholder then had much more to say about dividend policy than does the average stockholder today. The mill records, from which these figures and other data in this article come, are on deposit in the manuscript collection of the Baker Library, Graduate School of Business Administration, Harvard University.

5. If the occupational composition of the small stockholders differed greatly from that of the large purchasers the conclusions may be subject to some revision; however, a spot check on the small investors in particular mills does not seem to show any marked departure from the pattern established by the large investors.

6. Throughout this article, major dependence is placed on four measures of contribution. First, the relative proportion of the total equity that was held by the members of each occupational group included in the survey. Second,

the relative proportion of the total number of stockholders represented by each group included in the survey. Third, the average investment *per stockholder per firm* for each occupational group. And fourth, the average *total* investment of the individual members of each occupational group in the eleven firms. Some reliance is also placed on the estimates of total absolute contribution as displayed in Table 3; the reader should bear in mind that the latter are estimates only.

7. See Tables 4 and 5.

8. Estimates of the *absolute* amounts of equity owned by each of the occupational groups are shown in Table 3; they are less reliable than the estimates of proportionate shares shown in the text, because of the problems created by the changing number of firms and incomplete data. Most of the discussion of capital contributions has, therefore, been limited to the proportions of equity contributed. The estimates in Table 3 are based on the eight firms for which there are records for more than one-half the selected years. Data missing for these firms were estimated by a method based on Yates' "missing plots" technique. See F. W. Yates, "The Analysis of Replicated Experiments Where Field Results are Incomplete," *The Empire Journal of Experimental Agriculture*, Vol. I (1933), pp. 129–142. From the information displayed in Table 3, it appears that the decline in mercantile holding referred to above was only a *relative* decline caused by the industries' equity issue increasing more rapidly than the merchants' holdings. (Possibly for no other reason than that the number of merchants was increasing less rapidly than the population in general.) The estimates of absolute contribution show that the mercantile holdings increased in every year (except 1854) from 1829 to 1859.

9. Since only those merchants who could positively be identified as trading primarily in textiles are included, the category probably underestimates the actual contribution of this group.

10. See Tables 6 and 7.

11. If the estimates in Table 3 are correct, the reduction in the importance of textile merchants after 1839 represents not only a relative but also an absolute decline in their holdings. The table shows an increase in the holdings until 1844, but after that date there appears to have been an absolute withdrawal of capital amounting to $355,000 by 1859.

12. The total contribution of the two groups fell below one-third of the total surveyed only in 1859.

13. See, for example, Victor S. Clark, *History of Manufactures in the United States 1607–1860* (New York, 1929), Vol. VI, p. 367; or Caroline Ware, *The Early New England Cotton Manufacture* (Boston, 1931), p. 141.

14. Although no precise estimates of the returns from trade do exist, such returns are probably loosely correlated with the volume of trade, for which some evidence does exist. See, for example, Walter Buckingham Smith and Arthur Harrison Cole, *Fluctuations in American Business 1790–1860* (Cambridge, 1935), pp. 73 and 104.

15. An examination of the records of the nine firms possessing adequate financial data (Amoskeag, Dwight, Cabot, Perkins, Hamilton, Lancaster, Lawrence, Lyman, and Mass. Cotton) show that profits (as a percent of total capital stock) average 10.3 percent from 1830 to 1834; 9.4 percent from 1835 to 1839; 6.8 percent from 1840 to 1844; 12 percent from 1845 to 1849; 6.1 percent from 1850 to 1854; and 6.0 percent from 1855 to 1859.

16. The stock subscriptions were usually first opened to the friends and associates of the original promoters and public sale was atypical.

17. Other evidence of the noncompetitive market structure is found in the continual exchange of cost, price and labor information that passed between the mills. For a full discussion of the industry's organizational structure see Vera Shlakman, *Economic History of a Factory Town; A Study of Chicopee, Massachusetts* (Northampton, Mass., 1935).

18. The records of the New England Mutual Life Insurance Company make it very clear that stock was purchased as a part of the investment portfolio. Conversely, the records of the Provident Institution for Savings and the Massachusetts Hospital Life Insurance Company (a trust company) show that almost all of their holdings arose out of loan creation.

19. In the period under consideration, the hypothecation of stock resulted in ownership passing temporarily into the hands of the lender. The firm records, then, show the lending firm as the registered stock owner until the loan has been repaid and title again passed to the original owner.

20. See Tables 4, 5, 6, and 7.

21. See, for example, the balance sheets of the Provident Institution for Savings and the Massachusetts Hospital Life Insurance Company. In the case of the Provident Institution, security loans declined from $472,445 in Dec., 1840, to $37,500 in Dec., 1858.

22. The estimates of absolute holdings (see Table 3) also seem to bear out the contention that there is some relationship between the holdings of this group and the state of business activity. Both 1834 and 1844 show a sharp drop in the absolute holdings of the financial institutions.

23. See Table 6. The estimates of absolute contribution also show a pattern similar to that established by the textile merchants. Table 3 shows an increase until 1844 followed by a reduction in the succeeding years (except for an increase in 1859).

24. See Tables 5 and 7. Interestingly enough, however, there appear to have been no regular movements in the average size of the investment per firm (Table 4).

25. See footnote 15.

26. The Nashua and Amoskeag were located in New Hampshire, while the other nine firms were located in Massachusetts.

27. Nor for that matter does the corporate form even appear to have freed capital from personal ties in the Boston area. The records show that most stockholders regularly attended meetings and took an active part in the direction of the firm's activities. Their comments make it clear that many felt that their companies were as much their personal property as their own partnerships and sole proprietorships.

28. The estimates of absolute contribution show a steady increase throughout the period (see Table 3).

29. There is no way of estimating the number of estates that are represented by the trustee figures. The stockholder records most frequently list the trust account under the name of the trustee (followed by the note "trustee"), and the same persons often served as trustees for several estates.

30. Caroline Ware, *The Early New England Cotton Manufacture*, pp. 122 and 148.

31. Even if the original stock had been acquired through inheritance, it would still be possible to argue that continued ownership implied a belief in the safety and profitability of the investment. However, in the absence of a well-defined equity market, it is safe to infer that often the legatees could dispose of their shares only at a substantial loss.

32. If the equity figures had been disaggregated and those shares representing stock dividends assumed to represent reinvestment in textiles, the figures
would show a substantial increase in industrial capital during the 1840's.

33. The 100 included 60 lawyers, 19 doctors, and 21 judges, ministers,
dentists, and teachers.

THE INDUSTRIAL REVOLUTION AND
THE FACTORY OPERATIVE IN PENNSYLVANIA

William A. Sullivan

Industrial processes, revolutionized by the harnessing of water and
steam, wrought transformations in our society whose ends are not
yet in sight. Inexorably, with the advent of the factory system
the geography of America was altered, and American life in its
moods and its ideals underwent a profound change. Drab factories
with their clusters of squalid tenements destroyed the serenity of the
American countryside; shattered, too, was Jefferson's idyllic agrarian
dream.

The promise of America—advancement and riches—was there for
those of enterprise and ambition who would seize it. Especially was
this true in Pennsylvania in the first half of the nineteenth century.
Capital flowed ceaselessly and in ever-increasing quantities into the
mills and factories of the Keystone State.[1] Artisans, mechanics, and
laborers of all kinds were in great demand throughout most of this
period.[2]

For the ambitious and thrifty American workingman, success appeared inevitable. Man could be the master of his own fate. If fortune smiled upon him, it was of his own making; if he failed, the
responsibility was his alone. An article reprinted in Hazard's *Register of Pennsylvania* gave credence to this idea when it asserted that
"as a general rule, with few exceptions, frugal industrious journey-
men, unencumbered with families, may save so much of their wages,
as in a few years, to be enabled to commence business on their own
account on a moderate scale." [3]

Reprinted by permission from *The Pennsylvania Magazine of History and
Biography*, LXXVIII (1954), pp. 476–94.

There is often a large gap between appearances and realities. And although there were apparent signs of opportunity for the working-man to improve his status (and in many instances the opportunities were real), in actuality he shared but slightly in the general business progress of the first half of the nineteenth century. By the thousands workers flocked to the cities to meet the demands of new industries, and these urban manufacturing centers teemed with masses of land-less, job-hunting wage carners.

Factory operatives absorbed the first shocks and suffered most grievously from the dislocations brought on by the industrial revolution. Cheerless, unventilated dwellings did little to brighten their monotonous existence. The deplorable circumstances in which large numbers of the factory population lived almost defies description. In the summer of 1832, a citizens committee of Philadelphia, determined to awaken the social consciences of the City Fathers, investigated and made the following report of the living conditions which prevailed among large segments of the working class in Upper Delaware Ward: [4]

The result of this investigation shows, that the whole number of tenements is sixty-four; total number of inhabitants, four hundred and seventy-three. Of these, there are thirty tenements containing fifty-five families, and two hundred and fifty-three individuals, that have not the accommodation of a privy for their use! They are compelled to make use of vessels of various descriptions; the contents of which are daily thrown into the neighbouring docks or into the streets! It will be observed, that the buildings in this block (with one or two exceptions) occupy the whole ground belonging to the premises. The privies [of 34] are situated either in the cellars, or in the vaults under the streets. Of the thirty tenements above mentioned, there are four with three, two with four, and two with six families in each.

Nor was the situation any better in Pittsburgh.[5] Poverty, wretched-ness, and squalor went hand in hand with the growth of industries.

If his home surroundings were depressing, the conditions under which the factory operative labored were infinitely worse. The introduction of power machinery and the spread of the factory system had imposed upon the American worker a regimentation and a discipline which were both foreign and repugnant to him. In those mills propelled by steam, the engineer "regulates the speed of the machinery, and all the operatives, adults and children must keep pace with it." [6] The operative was merely another machine in this vast and complex system. The *New York American* declared that "the 'personel' of a large factory is a machine. . . . A strict and almost superstitious discipline is necessary to keep this vast instrument going for a single day." [7]

Much of the ill will which developed among factory hands grew out of the regulations and methods adopted to enforce and maintain this discipline and ensure the smooth operation of the plant. One mill owner, Charles V. Hagner, confirmed this. He related that "a frequent bone of contention between the employer and the employed in manufactories, is certain rules, in the nature of a contract, established in all well-regulated mills, and which are chiefly indispensable for their good management." [8]

Arbitrary labor contracts, usually verbal in form but understood by all, enabled the entrepreneurs and the managers of the factories to maintain a rigid control over their employees. The operatives had no voice either in the adoption or in the enforcement of the rules and regulations under which they worked. Acceptance of employment was assent to the rules. Typical were these general rules which prevailed at the Silesia factory: [9]

1. The hours of work shall be from sunrise to sunset, from the 21st of March to the 20th of September inclusively; and from sunrise until eight o'clock, P.M., during the remainder of the year. One hour shall be allowed for dinner, and half an hour for breakfast, during the first mentioned six months; and one hour for dinner during the other half year; On Saturdays, the mill shall be stopped one hour before sunset, for the purpose of cleaning the machinery.

2. Every hand coming to work a quarter of an hour after the mill has been started, shall be docked a quarter of a day; and every hand absenting him or herself, without absolute necessity, shall be docked in a sum double in amount of the wages such hand shall have earned during the time of such absence. No more than one hand is allowed to leave any one of the rooms at the same time,—a quarter of a day shall be deducted for every breach of this rule.

3. No smoking or spirituous liquors shall be allowed in the factory, under any pretence whatsoever. It is also forbidden to carry into the factory, nuts, fruits, &c.: books or papers, during the hours of work. . . .

7. Every hand (excepting those who rent a tenement belonging to this concern,) shall give at least two weeks' notice of his or her intention to depart from or cease working in this factory, and the said hand shall continue to work in it, if required so to do, during and until the expiration of the said two weeks. In case of failure herein, the said

hand shall forfeit all the wages which may be due to him or her at the time of leaving the mill.

Adam Smith was the prophet of the new order. In the laissez-faire ideal which he so brilliantly postulated, the emergent princes of industry found sustenance for their cherished belief of freedom of contract. To them, freedom of contract was one of those simple, ineluctable natural laws, which, if observed, would ensure progress and happiness for all mankind. And when in 1837 the industrial peace of Philadelphia was threatened, the *Public Ledger*, one of the early penny newspapers, observed that recognition by labor and management of the contractual nature of their ties would go far toward eliminating friction and strife: [10]

The relation between . . . proprietor or overseer and the operatives, whether minors or of full age, is strictly one of contract, in which nothing beyond the terms of the contract can be required by either party. The one agrees to perform labor, the other to pay money; and so far they are on perfectly equal terms. If the operative agrees to labor for a certain price, and to conform to certain rules, the employer has no right to alter these rules without the consent of the other. If he does so alter them, the laborer is absolved from his part of the contract, and may depart immediately, with the right to payment for labor already performed, according to the price stipulated. This is the legal ground on which such contracts rest, and if it were generally understood, both by employers and operatives, many disputes, contentions, strikes and other proceedings mischievous to both parties, would be avoided.

This idyllic interpretation of freedom of contract had little relation to the facts, for capital was hardly prepared to accept labor as its equal.

The mill hands resented the lopsided nature of the labor contract. Occasionally, their smoldering anger flared into open rebellion. Especially critical were they of the rule requiring them to give their employers two weeks' notice when leaving, but imposing no similar obligation upon the latter. "In some factories," complained one operative, "one of these rules is, that if any of the hands leave the factories, the proprietors retain from one to two weeks' of their wages, under the pretence that the hands must give two weeks' notice before leaving; but the proprietors discharge the hands without notice." [11] Some factory owners affirmed the charge. Others asserted that if any of their hands were discharged without notice "they are entitled to a week's wages in advance," and several employees who had been summarily dismissed corroborated this.[12]

The blacklist was one of the most effective weapons which the employers possessed in disciplining their hands, and they were not reluctant to use it. Obviously not a part of the wage contract, it was a tacit agreement among various mill owners not to hire any workers who could not produce a certificate of discharge from their previous employers.[13] William Blackstock, a Pittsburgh manufacturer, explained that the "reason for the establishment of this rule, [was] to prevent hands from leaving without notice, and to prevent tampering with hands, by the employers themselves." [14] Not only was a certificate of discharge made a prerequisite for securing another position, but the employers also made it a general practice to inform "all the employers in the vicinity, whenever a hand [had] been discharged." [15] So oppressive were these practices that the state Senate committee investigating factory conditions in the Pennsylvania textile mills concluded that "these regulations, taken together, leave scarcely an alternative to the operative, but unconditional submission." [16]

Collective bargaining, although not unknown, was hardly the accepted mode for formulating a wage contract. Management determined the wages, the hours, and the general working conditions. Wage negotiations were carried on between the individual wage earner and the boss, leaving the worker free to accept the conditions proffered or to move on.[17]

But he was beginning to resent the arbitrary character of these labor negotiations. The surge of democracy which swept America in this first half of the nineteenth century was partially an expression of the unrest and dissatisfaction which permeated the laboring masses. The "weavers . . . in America pay very little deference to their employers in general," noted one visitor from England.[18] Even more important, the men were organizing into trade unions and collectively voicing their protests. Strikes were becoming common, and factory hands were appointing committees to make their wishes known to employers.

The employers met this threat with customary harshness. Two employees of William Blackstock's factory who had been delegated to voice a demand for a ten-hour day were discharged without notice and proscribed. Mr. Blackstock explained that these two employees "had taken rather too efficient a part in the business." [19] At Samuel McBride's factory in Philadelphia, where a serious difficulty had arisen between labor and management because of the careless manner in which the warps had been handled, "three of his best hands" were dismissed "for taking an active part in favor of their fellow workers." [20] Thus, with these two formidable weapons—the right of arbitrary dismissal and the blacklist—employers were able to hold the initiative in their relations with their hired hands.

Indicative of the one-sided nature of the labor contract was the system of fines and punishments devised by the mill owners to maintain factory discipline. Heavy fines were meted out for a variety of reasons, most commonly for lateness. The accepted practice among most of the factories was to deduct as much as one quarter of a day's earnings for those who failed to report within five minutes of the opening of the plant.[21] This issue played a prominent part in the protest of the citizens of Pittsburgh which led to an investigation of factory conditions throughout the state. "The [cotton mill owners] have been uniformly in the practice of deducting one quarter from each day's labour, when they were but five minutes late," complained the factory hands of that city.[22] Matthew M'Candless, an operative, charged that "if the hands come in more than five minutes after the bell, they are docked." Dismissal was the penalty for a repetition of this offense.[23]

Physical punishment as a disciplinary measure was confined almost solely to children, both male and female, but occasionally grown women felt the sting of the lash.[24] A factory girl from one of the Pittsburgh mills swore that she had "seen poor innocent females not only 'docked' of a half day's wages for going to work a few minutes after set time, but beat over the shoulder by a rope with knots on the end, until their backs were black and blue; and if they left on that account they would be docked a week's wages." [25] One of the witnesses before the Senate committee testified that "those superintendents who are severe are preferred by employers." [26]

It was the children who suffered most from this form of maltreatment by their employers. George Low, a thirteen-year-old factory hand, stated that he "was frequently punished by having [his] ears pulled; at one time the foreman pulled them until they bled." This punishment, the boy explained, was "because I could not take the laps off." [27] In the Northern Liberties, a suburb of Philadelphia, a superintendent of one of the cotton mills was haled into court and convicted for having unmercifully beaten a boy for arriving "a few minutes too late in the morning." [28]

Fines and punishments, debasing and burdensome as they were, paled into insignificance when compared with the questions of hours and wages. Trending lower wages and interminably long hours convinced the factory operative of the degradation of his status in society. Seldom, if ever, were these wage and hour contracts in writing, and the employer's voice was as arbitrary and final in these matters as in all the other factors affecting the conditions of employment.

The actual wage and hours records extant for the cotton factories are few and fragmentary, but those that are available tell the distressing story of the factory operative. The accounts of William Whitaker's cotton mill in the northeastern section of Philadelphia, if typical, disclose an actual decline in wages and an increase in the hours of labor. In 1820, the weavers at this mill received one dollar per cut making tickings.[29] The price, by 1832, had been reduced to seventy-five cents per cut, and in the following year was seventy cents. Late in the summer of 1837, the mill hands were out on strike to restore a wage cut, but without success. By 1840, the price per cut had been reduced to sixty cents, and the hours of work had been increased. The hands weaving cords suffered similar wage setbacks. In 1830, these mill hands had been paid sixty cents per cut, and ten years later the records reveal that they were being paid only fifty cents for the same work.[30]

Wage reductions throughout the 1830's were the source of considerable friction between the weavers and their employers. At the Schuylkill Cotton Factory in 1834, the operatives, whose wages averaged only three dollars a week, were threatened with a twenty-five percent reduction in their wages.[31] The handloom weavers of Corlies' mill in 1839, faced with a twenty percent reduction in their wages, appealed to the public in an effort to stay the action of their employers. They disclosed the pittance which was their wage prior to this proposed reduction: [32]

. . . —18 yards of Superfine Check is considered a day's work, which, at 4½ cents per yard, amounts to 81 cents per day, or $4.86 per week —out of which is to be deducted 75 cents per week for winding, leaving a balance of $4.11; for house rent, fuel, light, loom and tackling repairs, &c. $1.37½ per week—leaving a balance of $2.73½ for finding food and raiment for a family of four or five members. The proposed reduction being $1.08 per week, in exact ratio to the above, would reduce the amount for finding food and raiment for the family to $1.65 per week.

Nor did the decade of the 1840's reveal any improvement in the status of the weavers. "God knows," caustically wrote one journal, "some of the poor fellows had great cause to feel rebellious. Empty stomachs and empty purses are not the best advocates of good order. At the prices paid, some of them, we are told, a man and his wife, with constant and close application sixteen hours per day, could not earn over $2.50 per week." [33]

Declining wages and a longer workday were the lot not only of the handloom weavers, but of the other operatives in the mills. The mule spinners at Whitaker's mill were, in 1820, paid at the rate of thirty cents per one hundred hanks, and the highest wages of the best hands amounted to twenty-two dollars per month. [34] Niles, in 1828, reported that the mule spinners in the neighborhood of Philadelphia received about two dollars per day, which, if true, would have meant a considerable advance in their wages. [35] But in that same year, the spinners of that city went on strike against a proposed reduction of their wages. They complained that even at the old prices a spinner could make only "from $7.50 to $8.50 per week for himself by working the full period of twelve hours daily." [36] James Montgomery, a Britisher who had a wide familiarity with the American textile industry, wrote in 1840 that "the rate at which the mule spinners are paid in this country [*the United States*] would average from eight to ten cents per one hundred hanks." [37] If this assertion is correct, it would indicate a substantial reduction in their pay rates.

Widespread exploitation in the textile mills of women and children, who made up almost two thirds of the labor force, added to their burdens. In their dependent status they not only drove wages down, but kept them at low levels. The legislative committee investigating factory conditions in Pennsylvania concluded that one third of the employees in the cotton mills were men and two thirds were women. [38] As Edith Abbott has pointed out in her study of the employment of women as mill hands, there was no initial displacement of men by women, nor any great prejudice against women in the mills. Until the introduction of the power loom, the early factories were spinning mills, and spinning had always been "women's work." [39] More women, Tench Coxe reported in his *Statement of the Arts & Manufactures of the United States*, prepared in 1814, were turning to the "operations of the weaver . . . while the male weavers [employed] themselves in superintendence." [40] They worked the same long hours, but their wages fell considerably below those of their male coworkers. According to the information supplied by various mill owners throughout Pennsylvania in 1832, the wages of the female workers ranged from fifty cents per week to two dollars and sixty-two and one-half cents per week.[41] Other sources indicate that these estimates of the earning power of the women employed in the mills were in all probability correct. In the late 1830's, the women at Whitaker's mill were averaging between one dollar and two dollars per week.[42]

Although many indignities had been inflicted upon men and women mill hands, and although their losses had been both material and psychological, it was the children, who made up a large part of the labor force in the textile mills, who suffered most from the factory system. According to one estimate, one fifth of all the factory workers in Pennsylvania were children under twelve years of age.[43] "There can be no doubt," remarked an early student of the labor movement, "that the introduction of machinery was at first extremely injurious to those whose means of living were affected." [44] This was especially true for the many young boys and girls who daily made their dreary way to take positions alongside grown men and women.

They came to add their meager pittance to the family income. The mill owners often contended that they made no profit out of the children, and that the children were forced on them by the poor, and, in many instances, by worthless parents. Mill owner Joseph Ripka declared: "I employ twenty-five children under twelve years of age, and they are pressed on me by widows, or by mothers of dissipated husbands; and when I do employ them, it is for mere charity than any thing else." [45] Other mill owners made substantially the same assertions.[46] Undoubtedly it was true that needy and greedy parents did send their children to the mills at an early age; nonetheless, the fact that many mill owners solicited for children would lead one to believe that their claim of not profiting from the employment of children was disingenuous.

Occasionally, advertisements for factory help announced that "a family that could furnish 4 or 5 hands, would be preferred." [47] The same Joseph Ripka who had stated that he hired children only out of charity advertised in the *Public Ledger*: "Men with families, who can work either as Power Loom Weavers or Card Room Hands, will be preferred." [48] Many of the witnesses before the Senate committee investigating factory conditions pointed out that if the labor of children under a certain age were prohibited, "it would cost the employers more for larger hands, who could not be had without larger wages." [49] Robert Kerr, a factory hand, contended that the employment of children more than twelve years of age "would increase the wages paid by the factory—as children over twelve could not be had for wages as low as those under." [50]

It was the long hours of work and the pitifully low wages which drew the attention of the public to the miserable status of children in factories. One of the great humanitarian drives characteristic of the Jackson era was the movement for free public education. Great concern was voiced for the factory children who could not enjoy the benefits of education, free or otherwise, because of the long hours of work.

Sunrise to sunset had been the traditional workday in America, and the practice in the 1830's of illuminating the factories with lamps enabled the owners to increase the working hours. At the Whitaker factory during the late thirties, the men began to work at 5:30 in the morning and remained at the job until 7:30 in the evening. The machines were stopped at seven in the morning, allowing thirty minutes for breakfast, and again at noon, allowing thirty minutes for lunch.[51] In 1839, the *Public Ledger* disclosed that the hours of labor in the factories at Norristown were nearly fifteen in the summer months. Although twelve hours was considered the usual workday, it was not unusual for factory operatives to work thirteen and fourteen hours daily.[52] The working people of Manayunk, very much aggrieved by the conditions under which they labored, complained that they were "obliged by [their] employers to labor at this season of the year, from 5 o'clock in the morning until sunset, being fourteen and a half, with an intermission of half an hour for breakfast, and an hour for dinner, leaving thirteen hours of hard labor." [53] Seventy-two hours was considered to be the average work week in most of the mills throughout the state. In its report concerning the time of labor in the factories of Pennsylvania the committee stated that

There is nothing which deserves the name of a system in the time of labor, in the factories in Pennsylvania, so far as the investigation of the committee extended. In the vicinity of Philadelphia, for instance, where the cotton mills are numerous, eleven hours of labor, per day, are exacted in some establishments; twelve in others, and in one, at least, it has exceeded fourteen hours per day; the humanity, or cupidity of employers, being the only motive by which it is regulated.[54]

One employer, when queried by the committee as to the evils of the factory system as it prevailed in Pennsylvania, replied, "I know of no evil worth notice, except that which arises from the refractory, factious spirit of some of the men, and they are mostly foreigners." [55] The same man, when asked if he thought that the hours of work were too long and the labor of children excessive, blandly answered, "Far from it—it approaches nearer to amusement." [56]

Such myopia was not characteristic of all mill owners. It was generally agreed even among many of the manufacturers that one of the greatest evils of the factory system was the long hours of work. Most of the ills associated with the textile industry, especially as they affected the children, stemmed from the long workday.

Although many of the mill owners frowned upon the employment of children under twelve, they were at the same time apprehensive of any reduction in the hours of labor or of the prohibition of child labor. John P. Crozer, a manufacturer, testified that "small operatives have often been scarce, and employers were therefore desirous to retain the children in the factories." [57] The Senate committee, sifting through the testimony of both factory hands and mill owners, concluded that "the labor of children under twelve years of age, in factories, is not desirable or profitable; and that no injury would result to employers, by the enactment of a law to prohibit the employment of all children under that age." [58]

What should have made life particularly wretched for these infants, who labored through an intolerably long workday in a dirty and dusty atmosphere, was the pittance they received in return for their labors. Their wages varied according to age, and some of them received only twelve and one-half cents a day or seventy-five cents a week, which is roughly equivalent to a cent an hour.[59] Wages of the older children generally averaged from one dollar to two dollars per week. While the more highly paid workers, that is, the mule spinners and those employed in the cardroom of the Whitaker mill, had suffered from a reduction in their wages, the records reveal no similar decline in the earnings of the children and lesser-paid workers.[60]

From all that has been written, it would appear that the position of the factory operative was an unenviable one. Not only were his oppressions many and his wages low, but what proved particularly irksome to him was the difficulty he often experienced in collecting the earnings due him. It was a practice of many mill owners to combine a store with their mill operations, and the wage contract occasionally stipulated that a portion of the wages was to be paid in store orders. One contemporary observed that "in general, the conductors of the factories keep a shop or store; and it is stipulated that one half of the wages shall be paid in groceries, &c." [61] A mill owner at Morrisville, Pennsylvania, paid his hands in store orders, and his profit was reported to be from ten to fifteen percent. Others paid their hands in depreciated bank notes, which meant, at times, a loss of at least ten percent of their wages.[62] In addition, the general practice of paying the factory hands only once in every four weeks, and at the same time withholding a portion of their wages, left the operatives in a continual state of financial insecurity.[63]

The American operative could derive scant satisfaction from the fact that his wages were better than those of his fellow workers in England and on the Continent, for it was generally recognized that he worked harder and faster than did his brethren across the sea. Harriet Martineau, who had been favorably impressed by the congenial atmosphere which prevailed in the American mills, emphatically asserted that "there seems to be no doubt among those who know both England and America that the mechanics of the New World work harder than those of the old." [64] James Montgomery, thoroughly familiar with the operations of cotton factories in both countries, noted that "the manufacturers here can afford to pay higher wages than the British, because they run their factories longer hours, and drive their machinery at a higher speed from which they produce a much greater quantity of work." [65] An operative who had worked in both England and America stated: "I consider the operation of the factory system upon persons employed, is more oppressive in this country than in England." [66] The *Public Ledger* concurred: [67]

The great evil which laborers are subject to in this country, is the amount of work they have to perform. Though receiving a higher rate of wages than those of Europe, and better paid for their services, yet the length of the time they are obliged to keep at their work, to receive this compensation, makes the task they have to perform fall heavier upon them.

Operations which in England required the services of two and three individuals were performed in the United States by a single adult worker. A conviction was beginning to pervade a large number of the factory hands that their situation was no better than that of the depressed workers abroad.[68]

That the grievances of these artisans who worked in the mills and factories were real is obvious. But far more serious was that overpowering sense of degradation which was beginning to be felt by large masses of these working people. "The losses of the individual worker in the first half of the century," wrote an astute student of the labor movement, "were not comfort losses solely, but losses, as he conceived it, of status and independence and no comfort gains could cancel this debt." [69]

This theme was aired again and again at meetings of wage earners. "What," they were asked, "is the cause of [their] degeneracy?" And why should it be "more degrading to turn a spinning wheel in a factory, than a spinning wheel at home?" A growing pessimism permeated the minds of many—a feeling of frustration, a loss of hope, a conviction that there was no escape. "Those who are toiling day after day, spending their strength, and wasting their health in the production of wealth are doomed not only to poverty with all its attendant inconvenience, but even to contempt," gloomily predicted a mechanic of Philadelpiha. [70]

Nor was this a matter of concern to the wage earners alone. When the rumblings of protest and discontent over hours and wages and all the other attendant evils of the factory system began to be heard throughout Pennsylvania, one of the conservative Philadelphia papers pointedly reminded its readers that although "labouring in the field or in a workshop cannot confer any distinction . . . it ought not to be a degradation." [71] This editorial struck close to the heart of the issue, since the problems of the working classes were social as well as economic, and transcended the comparatively narrow struggle for better wages and shorter hours.

Long hours of work combined with the constant fear of unemployment and the depreciation in the value of human labor had a demoralizing effect upon the wage earner. It was the artisans who suffered most from the dislocations and adjustments which beset American business in the early stages of the industrial revolution. During the great panic of 1819 unemployment reached epidemic proportions. Various estimates placed the unemployment in Philadelphia from 5,000 to 20,000. [72] In Pittsburgh, the number of employed had fallen from 1,960 in 1815 to 672 in 1819. [73] No enumeration of the unemployed, no calculation of the pecuniary loss to the nation could adequately reveal the heart-rending tragedy inherent in this great panic. The story of the stirrings, the doubts, the fears, which gripped the hearts and minds of men, was left untold. A citizens committee of Philadelphia, investigating the effects of the great crisis, suggested that the losses were not material losses alone: [74]

> But who can calculate the injuries of another description that flow from it? The demoralization that necessarily results from want of employment, and its attendant dissipation: the heart rending pangs felt by parents, whose prospects of supporting their families are blighted and blasted? the numerous estimable females accustomed to earn a subsistence by spinning, and other employments adapted to their sex, and whose wants and distresses may force them to a life of guilt and wretchedness.

Insecurity and fear were the lot of the factory operative. One business recession followed closely upon another—1824, 1829, 1833.[75] The business recession of 1833 was but a prelude to the great debacle of 1837. Barely had the laboring classes recovered from the economic dislocation of the previous layoff than they once again had to endure the misery of unemployment, privation, and want.[76]

Probably never before had the complacency of thinking Americans been so rudely shattered. What is to be done? queried the *Ledger.* "The pecuniary difficulties which have for some time afflicted our community continue in almost undiminished severity." What were its effects upon the poor man, who in his "daily struggle with want and penury . . . [knows] that even when he sleeps to gain strength for the toil of to-morrow; that the enemy he contends against is sleepless and never rests"? [77] Some, like the *Ledger,* felt that the nation's economy had reached the peak of its expansive possibilities and saw little hope for improvement in the future: [78]

> There begins to prevail, among the more reflecting of our citizens, an apprehension that the present troubles are not temporary in their nature—are not the eruptions of high health, but the settled symptoms of a cankered and cureless disease—are not mere ripples on the advancing tide of our national prosperity, but the agitations of a certain and rapid ebb.

There can be no doubt that recurrent crises, bringing widespread unemployment and declining living standards, caused many men seriously to doubt the efficacy of the factory system. According to some workers, it was merely an efficient means of robbing them of the fruits of their labor. One mechanic complained that

> The factory system is that system by which, with the aid of machinery, a small company of men, possessing a large stock of money and

sometimes aided by legislative enactments, are enabled to avail themselves of the labor of hundreds and frequently thousands of men, women, and children, to increase the wealth of the company, while the men, women, and children are generally worked to the utmost possible number of hours a day and paid for their work the smallest possible compensation which will enable them to keep life in the body and sufficient strength to return to their daily task.[79]

The factory system, more than any other single factor, convinced the workers of the degradation of their social status. They resented the willingness of some mill owners to equate human labor with that of the machine, and in the machines they found a cause for their oppression and degeneration. When one statistically minded individual estimated that "Philadelphia loses $1000 every time the mechanics quit to go to dinner," the *Public Ledger* denounced him as belonging to "that hard hearted school which considers man a mere laboring machine, whose value is to be estimated by the amount of labor which can be forced from him." [80]

Man and machine were becoming indistinguishable, and it was the conviction of one who purported to speak for the working classes that the effect of the establishment of manufactories was "to sink and degrade the actual manufacturer into a necessary piece of machinery." This same individual argued that "in a great manufactory the laborer is qualified to be what he is—a part of the machinery." [81]

It was difficult to convince the workingman of the beneficial aspects of machinery when he was experiencing greater hardships than ever before. He was not yet willing to listen dispassionately to the argument that machinery would greatly reduce the costs of manufacture and spread its benefits to all. "We see," protested a critic of laborsaving machinery, "that the more assistance our Mechanics and Working Men derive from machinery, and consequently, the *more* rich and comfortable they *ought to be*, the *less* rich and comfortable they *are*." [82]

The factory operative, along with most of the other wage earners of Pennsylvania, was deeply disturbed. He had seen the machine make threatening inroads into his way of life. His hours of work had increased, but his wages had not increased proportionately, and more and more he saw women and children entering into occupations which formerly had been monopolized by men. No slide rule could calculate the human misery and suffering which had accompanied the new industry. The operative searched frantically for a solution to his dilemma, but in vain. Recurrent crises swept away the few gains which he had won through stubborn struggle and left him to flounder among the forces which were transforming America into a great industrial nation.

NOTES

1. According to estimates gleaned from the Fourth and the Sixth Censuses of the United States, capital invested in manufacturing enterprises in Pennsylvania more than quadrupled in twenty years.

2. Pennsylvania newspapers carried innumerable "men wanted" advertisements, and featured articles on the chronic labor shortage, which affected most of the industries of the state. See *Miner's Journal* (Pottsville, Pa.), July 21, 1827; *Niles' Weekly Register*, Vol. 34, 376 (Aug. 2, 1828); *United States Gazette*, Apr. 18, 1835; *Aurora and Pennsylvania Gazette*, June 16, 1828; *Lycoming Gazette*, May 20, 1829; *Pennsylvania Inquirer*, Sept. 18, 1831; *Juniata Telegraph*, Oct. 19, 1831; *Public Ledger*, June 1, 1837.

3. Hazard's *Register of Pennsylvania*, VIII, 55 (July 23, 1831).

4. Report to the Select and Common Council of the City of Philadelphia by a Citizens Committee of Upper Delaware Ward (signed by Thomas Taylor, Daniel Barr, Samuel J. Robbins, William Rush, Powell Stackhouse and John Perkin, Philadelphia, July 23, 1832), cited in Thomas Brothers, *The United States of North America as They Are* . . . (London, 1840), appendix V, 403; see also Mathew Carey, *Essays on the Public Charities of Philadelphia* (Philadelphia, 1830), 27.

5. In 1837–1838 a Pennsylvania Senate committee undertook to investigate factory conditions in the state, particularly with reference to the employment of children. Dr. L. Callaghan of Pittsburgh, testifying before that committee, presented a distressing tale of the circumstances in which too many of the factory operatives lived. *Journal of the Senate of the Commonwealth of Pennsylvania, Session of 1837–38* . . . (Harrisburg, 1837–1838), II, 348–350, hereafter cited as *Pa. Senate Journal*.

6. *Ibid.*, I, 324.

7. Quoted in *Niles' Weekly Register*, Vol. 52, 393 (Aug. 19, 1837).

8. *Pa. Senate Journal*, II, 326.

9. *Germantown Telegraph*, Nov. 6, 1833. Compare with testimony given before the Pennsylvania Senate investigating committee, *Pa. Senate Journal*, I, 324; II, 291, 296, 301, 309, 330, 338, 353. See also *Daily Chronicle* (Philadelphia), Jan. 7, 1830.

10. *Public Ledger*, June 1, 1837.

11. *Pa. Senate Journal*, II, 296, 297; see also *Allegheny Democrat and Workingman's Advocate*, Oct. 21 and Dec. 9, 1836.

12. *Pa. Senate Journal*, II, 334, 345, 353.

13. *Ibid.*, 334, 342, 343, 344, 353; J. Lynn Barnard, *Factory Legislation in Pennsylvania: Its History and Administration* (Philadelphia, 1907), 13, 14.

14. *Pa. Senate Journal*, II, 334, 342, 343.

15. *Ibid.*, I, 325.

16. *Ibid.*

17. *Germantown Telegraph*, Oct. 30 and Sept. 4, 1833.

18. Peter Neilson, *A Six Years' Residence* (Glasgow, 1830), 155.

19. *Pa. Senate Journal*, II, 344, 345.

20. *National Laborer* (Philadelphia), Oct. 1, 1836.

21. *Pa. Senate Journal*, II, 338.

22. *Allegheny Democrat and Workingman's Advocate*, Oct. 21, 1836.

23. *Pa. Senate Journal*, II, 330; I, 324.

24. See Richard B. Morris, *Government and Labor in Early America* (New York, 1946), 480 ff., for a discussion of physical punishment of servants in colonial America.

25. *Allegheny Democrat and Workingman's Advocate*, Dec. 9, 1836.

26. *Pa. Senate Journal*, II, 330.

27. *Ibid.*, 346.

28. *Public Ledger*, June 1, 1837.

29. A one-quarter cut was fifty yards long and thirty-six inches wide; a seven-eighths cut was fifty yards long and thirty-one and one-half inches wide.

30. Whitaker Account Books, 1820, 1821, 1830, 1833, 1834, 1835, 1836, William Whitaker & Sons, Inc., Philadelphia.

31. *Man*, May 3, 1834; *Pennsylvanian*, May 9, 1834. Compare with Neilson, 152, 153, 157.

32. *Public Ledger*, Aug. 30, 1839.

33. *Annual Report of the Secretary of Internal Affairs of the Commonwealth of Pennsylvania: Part III: Industrial Statistics, 1880–81* (Harrisburg, 1882), 268.

34. Whitaker Account Book, May 26, 1821.

35. *Niles' Weekly Register*, Vol. 34, 281 (June 28, 1828).

36. Hazard's *Register of Pennsylvania*, Jan. 17, 1829, as quoted in John R. Commons, *et al.*, *History of Labour in the United States* (New York, 1918), I, 418.

37. James Montgomery, *Practical Detail of the Cotton Manufacture of the United States of America* (Glasgow, 1840), 75.

38. *Pa. Senate Journal*, I, 323.

39. Edith Abbott, "Employment of Women in Cotton Mills," *Journal of Political Economy*, XVI (1908), 603.

40. Tench Coxe, A *Statement of the Arts & Manufactures of the United States of America* (Philadelphia, 1814), xxiv.

41. *Documents Relative to the Manufactures in the United States . . . ,* House Doc. No. 308, Twenty-second Congress, 1st Session (Washington, 1833), II, 206, 221, 337, 338, 394, 395, 396, 420, 421, 430, hereafter cited as *McClane's Report*.

42. Whitaker Account Books, October, 1838, January, 1839, and January, 1840.

43. *Pa. State Journal*, I, 323.

44. William Trant, *Trade Unions, Their Origin and Objects* (Washington, 1915), 10.

45. *Pa. Senate Journal*, II, 358.

46. *Ibid.*, 302; Barnard, 14, 15.

47. *Mechanic's Free Press*, Aug. 7, 1830; *Union Times and Republican Herald* (New Berlin, Pa.), July 1, 1831; *Huntingdon Journal*, May 8, 1839.

48. *Public Ledger*, July 19, 1839.

49. *Pa. Senate Journal*, II, 283, 287, 291.

50. *Ibid.*, 287.

51. Whitaker Account Books, October, 1838, September, 1839, and October, 1840.

52. *Allegheny Democrat and Workingman's Advocate*, Oct. 7, 1836; *Public Ledger*, June 27, 1839; *Germantown Telegraph*, Aug. 28, 1833; *Working Man's Advocate*, Mar. 24, 1833; *Pa. Senate Journal*, II, 338; *McClane's Report*, 204, 207, 225, 226, 450; Whitaker Account Book, January, 1840.

53. *Pennsylvanian*, Aug. 28, 1833; see also the report on manufactures in Hazard's *Register of Pennsylvania*, I, 157–158 (Mar. 8, 1828).

54. *Pa. Senate Journal*, I, 322.

55. *Ibid.*, II, 354.

56. *Ibid.*, 355.

57. *Ibid.*, 305.

58. *Ibid.*, I, 324.

59. Whitaker Account Books, 1820, 1821; *McClane's Report*, 200, 201, 206, 221, 430, 431; *Pa. Senate Journal*, II, 281, 283, 309, 311, 315, 319, 351.

60. Whitaker Account Books, 1834–1837.

61. Isaac Holmes, *An Account of the Untied States of America* . . . (London, 1823), 201.

62. *Pennsylvania Reporter*, June 20, 1834; *Mechanic's Free Press*, Oct. 9, 1830; *Germantown Telegraph*, Apr. 15, 1835; *Public Ledger*, June 8, 1837, and Feb. 23, 1839.

63. *Pa. Senate Journal*, II, 297.

64. Harriet Martineau, *Society and Manners in America* (New York, 1837), II, 251–252; Montgomery, 126.

65. *Ibid.*, 138.

66. *Pa. Senate Journal*, II, 316.

67. *Public Ledger*, June 27, 1839.

68. *Pennsylvanian*, Aug. 28, 1833; *National Trades' Union*, Dec. 19, 1835.

69. Norman Ware, *The Industrial Worker* (New York, 1924), i, xi, xiv. See Sidney and Beatrice Webb, *The History of Trade Unionism* (London, 1911), 47, for a discussion of the situation of factory workers in Great Britain at this time.

70. *Philadelphia Mercury*, Dec. 29, 1827.

71. *Poulson's Daily American Advertiser*, Aug. 18, 1830.

72. *Aurora and General Advertiser*, July 22 and 29, and Oct. 5, 1819; Mathew Carey, *Address Before the Philadelphia Society for Promoting Agriculture*, 25, 26, 30; Hazard's *Register of Pennsylvania*, IV, 169 (Sept. 12, 1829).

73. *Ibid.*, VII, 280 (Apr. 30, 1831); Erasmus Wilson, *Standard History of Pittsburg* (Chicago, 1898), 217.

74. *Aurora and General Advertiser*, Oct. 15, 1819.

75. *Poulson's Daily American Advertiser*, Jan. 7, 1824; *United States Gazette*, Feb. 12, 1824; *Free Trade Advocate* (June 20, 1829), 399; *Niles' Weekly Register*, Vol. 36, 281 (June 27, 1829).

76. For the most penetrating short study of the great depression of 1837, see Samuel Rezneck, "Social History of an American Depression, 1837–1843," *American Historical Review*, XL (1935), 662–687.

77. *Public Ledger*, Sept. 20, 1839.

78. *Ibid.*, Sept. 19, 1839.

79. *Working Man's Advocate*, Mar. 24, 1832.

80. *Public Ledger*, Jan. 23, 1837.

81. *National Laborer*, Apr. 23, 1836.

82. *Mechanic's Free Press*, May 8, 1830.

9

The Civil War and Industrial Growth

As THOMAS COCHRAN indicates in his introduction to the following article, historians have long ascribed great importance to the Civil War as an event that gave impetus to American industrialization. According to the standard interpretation, the purchase of war matériel by the Union during mobilization generally favored large-scale producers, thus encouraging concentration and mass-production in certain key industries; the war brought reorganization of the northern railroads, whose financial structure had been shattered by the panic of 1857; and wartime inflation stimulated investment in the newer industries. Some scholars contend also that southern secession in 1861 left the industrial class of the North in control of the federal government. As a result, they argue, Congress passed a high protective tariff, a national banking act, a contract labor law and similar pro-business legislation during the war years; and these measures were in the long run critical to the increased pace of industrialization in the post-war period. All of these contentions are subjected to re-examination by Professor Cochran.

Basing his study on federal census data and commodity-output series constructed by Robert Gallman, Cochran asserts that the war deranged the economy, interrupting what had been an impressive, upward secular trend in industrial production dating from the 1840's. Thus Cochran emphasizes the significance of pre-war industrial development, identifying the 1840's and early 1850's as the critical period, when conditions necessary for accelerated, self-sustaining growth were established.

Cochran's article has already become controversial. It has been criticized especially for giving inadequate weight to political changes of the war period that allegedly transformed the climate of enterprise. But two difficulties stand in the way of a definitive interpretation: the lack of reliable, detailed statistical data susceptible to regional breakdown; and the problems inherent in speculation on the course industrialization might have taken had there been no war.

DID THE CIVIL WAR
RETARD INDUSTRIALIZATION?

Thomas C. Cochran

In most textbook and interpretative histories of the United States the Civil War has been assigned a major role in bringing about the American Industrial Revolution.[1] Colorful business developments in the North—adoption of new machines, the quick spread of war contracting, the boost given to profits by inflation, and the creation of a group of war millionaires—make the war years seem not only a period of rapid economic change but also one that created important forces for future growth. The superficial qualitative evidence is so persuasive that apparently few writers have examined the available long-run statistical series before adding their endorsement to the conventional interpretation. The following quotations taken from the books of two generations of leading scholars illustrate the popular view.[2]

"The so-called Civil War," wrote Charles A. and Mary R. Beard in 1927, ". . . was a social war . . . making *vast changes* in the arrangement of classes, in the accumulation and distribution of wealth, *in the course of industrial development.*"[3] Midway between 1927 and the present, Arthur M. Schlesinger, Sr., wrote: "On these tender industrial growths the Civil War *had the effect of a hot-*

Reprinted by permission from *The Mississippi Valley Historical Review,* XLVIII (September, 1961), pp. 197–210.

house. For reasons already clear . . . nearly every branch of industry grew lustily." [4] Harold U. Faulkner, whose textbook sales have ranked near or at the top, said in 1954: "In the economic history of the United States the Civil War was extremely important. . . . In the North *it speeded the Industrial Revolution* and the development of capitalism by the prosperity which it brought to industry." [5] The leading new text of 1957, by Richard Hofstadter, William Miller, and Daniel Aaron, showed no weakening of this interpretation: "The growing demand for farm machinery as well as for the 'sinews of war' led to American industrial expansion. . . . Of necessity, *iron, coal, and copper* production boomed during the war years." [6] A sophisticated but still essentially misleading view is presented by Gilbert C. Fite and Jim E. Reese in a text of 1959: "The Civil War proved to be a boon to Northern economic development. . . . Industry, for example, was not created by the war, but wartime demands *greatly stimulated and encouraged industrial development* which already had a good start." [7] In a reappraisal of the Civil War, in *Harper's Magazine* for April, 1960, Denis W. Brogan, a specialist in American institutions, wrote: "It may have been only a catalyst but the War *precipitated the entry* of the United States *into the modern industrial world,* made 'the take-off' (to use Professor W. W. Rostow's brilliant metaphor) come sooner." [8]

In all of these reiterations of the effect of the Civil War on industrialism, statistical series seem to have been largely neglected. None of the authors cited reinforce their interpretations by setting the war period in the context of important long-run indexes of industrial growth. Since 1949, series for the period 1840 to 1890 that would cast doubt on the conventional generalizations have been available in *Historical Statistics of the United States, 1789–1945.*[9] In 1960 a new edition of *Historical Statistics* and the report of the Conference on Research in Income and Wealth on *Trends in the American Economy in the Nineteenth Century* have provided additional material to support the argument that the Civil War retarded American industrial development.[10] These volumes give data for many growth curves for the two decades before and after the war decade—in other words, the long-run trends before and after the event in question. The pattern of these trends is a mixed one which shows no uniform type of change during the Civil War decade, but on balance for the more important series the trend is toward retardation in *rates* of growth rather than toward acceleration. This fact is evident in many series which economists would regard as basic to economic growth, but in order to keep the discussion within reasonable limits only a few can be considered here.

Robert E. Gallman has compiled new and more accurate series for both "total commodity output," including agriculture, and "value added by manufacture," the two most general measures of economic growth available for this period. He writes: "Between 1839 and 1899 total commodity output increased elevenfold, or at an average decade rate of slightly less than 50 percent. . . . Actual rates varied fairly widely, high rates appearing during the decades ending with 1854 and 1884, and a very low rate during the decade ending with 1869." [11] From the over-all standpoint this statement indicates the immediately retarding effect of the Civil War on American economic growth, but since most of the misleading statements are made in regard to industrial growth, or particular elements in industrial growth, it is necessary to look in more detail at "value added by manufacture" and some special series. Gallman's series for value added in constant dollars of the purchasing power of 1879 shows a rise of 157 percent from 1839 to 1849; 76 percent from 1849 to 1859; and only 25 percent from 1859 to 1869. [12] By the 1870's the more favorable prewar rates were resumed, with an increase of 82 percent for 1869–1879, and 112 percent for 1879–1889. Thus two decades of very rapid advance, the 1840's and the 1880's, are separated by thirty years of slower growth which falls to the lowest level in the decade that embraces the Civil War.

Pig-iron production in tons, perhaps the most significant commodity index of nineteenth-century American industrial growth, is available year-by-year from 1854 on. Taking total production for five-year periods, output increased 9 percent between the block of years from 1856 to 1860 and the block from 1861 to 1865. That even this slight increase might not have been registered except for the fact that 1857 to 1860 were years of intermittent depression is indicated by an 81 percent increase over the war years in the block of years from 1866 to 1870. [13] If annual production is taken at five-year intervals, starting in 1850, the increase is 24 percent from 1850 to 1855; 17 percent from 1855 to 1860; 1 percent from 1860 to 1865; and 100 percent from 1865 to 1870. While there is no figure available for 1845, the period from 1840 to 1850 shows 97 percent increase in shipments, while for the period 1870 to 1880 the increase was 130 percent. To sum up, depression and war appear to have retarded a curve of production that was tending to rise at a high rate.

Bituminous coal production may be regarded as the next most essential commodity series. After a gain of 199 percent from 1840 to 1850 this series shows a rather steady pattern of increase at rates varying from 119 to 148 percent each decade from 1850 to 1890. The war does not appear to have markedly affected the rate of growth.[14]

In the mid-nineteenth century copper production was not a basic series for recording American growth, but since three distinguished authors have singled it out as one of the indexes of the effect of the war on industry it is best to cite the statistics. Before 1845 production of domestic copper was negligible. By 1850 the "annual recoverable content" of copper from United States mines was 728 tons, by 1860 it was 8,064 tons, by 1865 it was 9,520 tons, and by 1870 it was 14,112 tons. In this series of very small quantities, therefore, the increase from 1850 to 1860 was just over 1,000 percent, from 1860 to 1865 it was 18 percent, and from 1865 to 1870 it was 48 percent.[15]

Railroad track, particularly in the United States, was an essential for industrialization. Here both the depression and the war retarded the rate of growth. From 1851 through 1855 a total of 11,627 miles of new track was laid, from 1856 through 1860, only 8,721 miles, and from 1861 through 1865, only 4,076 miles. After the war the rate of growth of the early 1850's was resumed, with 16,174 miles constructed from 1866 through 1870. Looked at by decades, a rate of over 200 percent increase per decade in the twenty years before the war was slowed to 70 percent for the period from 1860 to 1870, with only a 15 percent increase during the war years. In the next two decades the rate averaged about 75 percent.[16]

Next to food, cotton textiles may be taken as the most representative consumer-goods industry in the nineteenth century. Interference with the flow of southern cotton had a depressing effect. The number of bales of cotton consumed in the United States manufacturing rose 143 percent from 1840 to 1850 and 47 percent from 1850 to 1860, but *fell* by 6 percent from 1860 to 1870. From then on consumption increased at a little higher rate than in the 1850's.[17]

While woolen textile production is not an important series in the over-all picture of industrial growth, it should be noted that, helped by protection and military needs, consumption of wool for manufacturing more than doubled during the war, and then *fell* somewhat from 1865 to 1870. But Arthur H. Cole, the historian of the woolen industry, characterizes the years from 1830 to 1870 as a period of growth "not so striking as in the decades before or afterwards." [18]

Immigration to a nation essentially short of labor was unquestionably a stimulant to economic growth. Another country had paid for the immigrant's unproductive youthful years, and he came to the United States ready to contribute his labor at a low cost. The pattern of the curve for annual immigration shows the retarding effect of both depression and war. In the first five years of the 1850's an average of 349,685 immigrants a year came to the United States. From 1856 through 1860 the annual average fell to 169,958, and for the war years of 1861 to 1865 it fell further to 160,345. In the first five postwar years the average rose to 302,620, but not until the first half of the 1870's did the rate equal that of the early 1850's. Had there been a return to prosperity instead of war in 1861, it seems reasonable to suppose that several hundred thousand additional immigrants would have arrived before 1865.[19]

In the case of farm mechanization the same type of error occurs as in the annual series on copper production. "Random" statistics such as the manufacture of 90,000 reapers in 1864 are frequently cited without putting them in the proper perspective of the total number in use and the continuing trends. Reaper and mower sales started upward in the early 1850's and were large from 1856 on, in spite of the depression. William T. Hutchinson estimates that most of the 125,000 reapers and mowers in use in 1861 had been sold during the previous five years.[20] While the business, without regard to the accidental coming of the war, was obviously in a stage of very rapid growth, the war years presented many difficulties and may actually have retarded the rate of increase.[21] Total sales of reapers for the period 1861–1865 are estimated at 250,000—a quite ordinary increase for a young industry—but the 90,000 figure for 1864, if it is correct, reinforces the evidence from the McCormick correspondence that this was the one particularly good year of the period. During these years William S. McCormick was often of the opinion that the "uncertainties of the times" made advisable a suspension of manufacturing until the close of the war.[22]

For a broader view of agricultural mechanization the series "value of farm implements and machinery" has special interest. Here the census gives a picture which, if correct, is explicable only on the basis of wartime destruction. Based on constant dollars the average value of machinery per farm *fell* nearly 25 percent in the decade of the war and showed nearly a 90 percent gain in the 1870's.[23] Differing from these census figures is a series prepared by Marvin W. Towne and Wayne D. Rasmussen based on the production of farm machinery. While this obviously does not take account of destruction of existing equipment or the rapid increase in the number of farms, the record of new production is hard to reconcile with the census figures. The production of implements and machinery reckoned in constant dollars is a sharply rising curve from 1850 on, with increases of 110 percent from 1850 to 1860; 140 percent from 1860 to 1870; and 95 percent from 1870 to 1880.[24] Meanwhile the number of farms increased by about one third in each of the decades of the 1850's and 1860's and by one half in the 1870's.[25] Whatever interpretation is given to these figures, it does not appear that the war greatly increased the trend of agricultural mechanization. The series for gross farm product in constant dollars shows wide variations in increase from decade to decade, with the 1860's in the low group. The gains were 23 percent, 1840 to 1850; 42 percent, 1850 to 1860; 21 percent, 1860 to 1870; 52 percent, 1870 to 1880; and 20 percent, 1880 to 1890.[26]

Much American business expansion was financed by short-term bank loans continuously renewed. Thus major increases in business activity should be mirrored in increases in bank loans, both for financing short-term transactions and for additions to plant and working capital that would, in fact, be paid off gradually. If there was a really great Civil War boom in business activity it should be indicated in the series "total loans" of all banks. But it is not. In constant dollars, bank loans fell slightly between 1840 and 1850, and rose nearly 50 percent by 1860. It should be noted that none of these three decadal years were periods of high prosperity. During the war Confederate banking statistics were not reported by the comptroller of the currency, but by 1866 there is a comparable figure for the nation as a whole, and in constant dollars it is some 35 percent below that of 1860. Even by 1870 the constant dollar value of all loans was more than 15 percent lower than just before the war. If instead of examining loans one looks at total assets of all banks the decline in constant dollars from 1860 to 1870 is reduced to 10 percent, the difference arising from a larger cash position and more investment in government bonds.[27]

Net capital formation would be a more proper index of economic growth than bank loans or assets. Unfortunately, neither the teams of the National Bureau of Economic Research nor those of the Census Bureau have been able to carry any reliable series back of 1868. From colonial times to 1960, however, the chief single form of American capital formation has undoubtedly been building construction. Farm houses, city homes, public buildings, stores, warehouses, and factories have year-by-year constituted, in monetary value, the leading type of capital growth. Gallman has drawn up series for such construction based on estimating the flow of construction materials and adding what appear to be appropriate markups.[28] Admittedly the process is inexact, but because of the importance of construction in reflecting general trends in capital formation it is interesting to see the results. The rate of change for the ten-year period ending in 1854 is about 140 percent; for the one ending in 1859 it is 90 percent; for 1869 it is 40 percent; and for 1879 it is 46 percent. Taking a long view, from 1839 to 1859 the average decennial rate of increase was about 70 percent, and from 1869 to 1899 it was about 40 percent.[29] The *rate* of advance in construction was declining and the war decade added a further dip to the decline.

Since the decline in rate is for the decade, the exact effect of the war years can only be estimated, but the logic of the situation, reinforced by the record of sharp cut-backs in railroad building, seems inescapable: the Civil War, like all modern wars, checked civilian construction. The first year of war was a period of depression and tight credit in the Middle West, which checked residential and farm construction in the area that grew most rapidly before and after the war. In both the East and the West the last two years of the war were a period of rapid inflation which was regarded by businessmen as a temporary wartime phenomenon. The logical result would be to postpone construction for long-term use until after the anticipated deflation. The decline in private railroad construction to a small fraction of the normal rate exemplifies the situation.

Lavish expenditure and speculation by a small group of war contractors and market operators gambling on the inflation seem to have created a legend of high prosperity during the war years. But the general series on fluctuations in the volume of business do not bear this out. Leonard P. Ayres's estimates of business activity place the average for 1861 through 1865 below normal, and Norman J. Silberling's business index is below its normal line for all years of the war.[30] Silberling also has an intermediate trend line for business, which smooths out annual fluctuations. This line falls steadily from 1860 to 1869.[31] Much of Silberling's discussion in his chapter

"Business Activity, Prices, and Wars" is in answer to his question: "Why does it seem to be true that despite a temporary stimulating effect of war upon some industries, wars are generally associated with a long-term retarding of business growth . . . ?" [32] He puts the Civil War in this general category.

Collectively these statistical estimates support a conclusion that the Civil War retarded American industrial growth. Presentation of this view has been the chief purpose of this article. To try to judge the non-measurable or indirect effects of the war is extremely difficult. But since further discussion of the conventional qualitative factors may help to explain the prevailing evaluation in American texts, it seems appropriate to add some conjectural obiter dicta.

Experience with the apparently stimulating effects of twentieth-century wars on production makes the conclusion that victorious war may retard the growth of an industrial state seem paradoxical, and no doubt accounts in part for the use of detached bits of quantitative data to emphasize the Civil War's industrial importance.[33] The resolution of the paradox may be found in contemporary conditions in the United States and in the nature of the wartime demand. The essential wastefulness of war from the standpoint of economic growth was obscured by the accident that both of the great European wars of the twentieth century began when the United States had a high level of unemployment. The immediate effect of each, therefore, was to put men to work, to increase the national product, and to create an aura of prosperity. Presumably, the United States of the mid-nineteenth century tended to operate close enough to full employment in average years that any wasteful labor-consuming activities were a burden rather than a stimulant.

By modern standards the Civil War was still unmechanized. It was fought with rifles, bayonets, and sabers by men on foot or horseback. Artillery was more used than in previous wars, but was still a relatively minor consumer of iron and steel. The railroad was also brought into use, but the building of military lines offset only a small percentage of the over-all drop from the prewar level of civilian railroad construction. Had all of these things not been true, the Confederacy with its small industrial development could never have fought through four years of increasingly effective blockade.

In spite of the failure of direct quantitative evidence to show accelerating effects of the war on rates of economic growth, there could be long-run effects of a qualitative type that would gradually foster a more rapid rate of economic growth. The most obvious place to look for such indirect effects would be in the results of free-ing the slaves. Marxists contended that elimination of slavery was a necessary precursor of the bourgeois industrialism which would lead to the socialist revolution. The creation of a free Negro labor force was, of course, of great long-run importance. In the twentieth century it has led to readjustment of Negro population between the deep South and the northern industrial areas, and to changes in the use of southern land.

But economically the effects of war and emancipation over the period 1840 to 1880 were negative. Richard A. Easterlin writes: "In every southern state, the 1880 level of per capita income origi-nating in commodity production and distribution was below, or at best only slightly above that of 1840. . . . [This] attests strikingly to the impact of that war and the subsequent disruption on the southern economy." [34] In general the Negroes became sharecroppers or wage laborers, often cultivating the same land and the same crops as before the war. In qualification of the argument that free Negro labor led to more rapid industrialization it should be noted that the South did not keep up with the national pace in the growth of non-agricultural wealth until after 1900.[35]

Two indirect effects of the war aided industrial growth to degrees that cannot accurately be measured. These were, first, a more satis-factory money market, and, secondly, more security for entrepre-neurial activity than in the prewar period. The sharp wartime inflation had the usual effect of transferring income from wage, salary, and interest receivers to those making profits. This meant concentration of savings in the hands of entrepreneurs who would invest in new activities; and this no doubt helps to explain the speculative booms of the last half of the 1860's and first two years of the 1870's which have been treated as the prosperity resulting from the war. Inflation also eased the burdens of those railroads which had excessive mortgage debts. But a great deal of new re-search would be needed to establish causal connections between the inflationary reallocation of wealth, 1863 to 1865, and the high rate of industrial progress in the late 1870's and the 1880's.

The National Banking Act, providing a more reliable currency for interstate operations, has been hailed as a great aid to business expansion although it would be hard to demonstrate, aside from a few weeks during panics, that plentiful but occasionally unsound currency had seriously interfered with earlier industrial growth.[36]

The existence of two and a half billion dollars in federal bonds also provided a basis for credit that was larger than before the war. This led to broader and more active security markets as well as to easier personal borrowing. But two qualifications must be kept in mind. First, local bank lending to favored borrowers had probably tended to be too liberal before the war and was now put on a somewhat firmer basis. In other words, since 1800 a multiplication of banks had made credit relatively easy to obtain in the United States, and in the North this continued to be the situation. Second, the southern banking system was largely destroyed by the war and had to be rebuilt in the subsequent decades. It should also be remembered that by 1875 some 40 percent of the banks were outside the national banking system.[37]

Because of a few colorful speculators like Jay Gould, Daniel Drew, and Jim Fisk, and the immortality conferred on them, initially by the literary ability of the Adams brothers, the New York stock exchange in the postwar decade appears to have mirrored a new era of predatory wealth. But one has only to study the scandals of the London and New York stock exchanges in 1854 to see that there was little growth in the sophistication or boldness of stock operators during these fifteen years.[38] In any case, the exploits of market operators were seldom related in a positive way to economic growth. Even a record of new issues of securities, which is lacking for this period, would chiefly reflect the flow of capital into railroads, banks, and public utilities rather than into manufacturing. Very few "industrial" shares were publicly marketed before the decade of the 1880's; such enterprises grew chiefly from the reinvestment of earnings.

There was strong government encouragement to entrepreneurial activity during the Civil War, but to ascribe to it unusual importance for economic growth requires both analysis of the results and comparison with other periods. Government in the United States has almost always encouraged entrepreneurs. The federal and state administrations preceding the Civil War could certainly be regarded as friendly to business. They subsidized railroads by land grants, subscribed to corporate bond issues, and remitted taxes on new enterprise.[39] Tariffs were low, but railroad men and many bankers were happy with the situation. Whether or not American industrialism was significantly accelerated by the high protection that commenced with the war is a question that economists will probably never settle.

The building of a subsidized transcontinental railroad, held back by sectional controversies in the 1850's, was authorized along a northern route with the help of federal loans and land grants when the southerners excluded themselves from Congress. Putting more than a hundred million dollars into this project in the latter half of the 1860's, however, may have had an adverse effect on industrial growth. In general, the far western roads were built for speculative and strategic purposes uneconomically ahead of demand. They may for a decade, or even two, have consumed more capital than their transportation services were then worth to the economy.

To sum up this part of the obiter dictum, those who write of the war creating a national market tied together by railroads underestimate both the achievements of the two decades before the war and the ongoing trends of the economy. The nation's business in 1855 was nearly as intersectional as in 1870. Regional animosities did not interfere with trade, nor did these feelings diminish after the war. By the late 1850's the United States was a rapidly maturing industrial state with its major cities connected by rail, its major industries selling in a national market, and blessed or cursed with financiers, security flotations, stock markets, and all the other appurtenances of industrial capitalism.

But when all specific factors of change attributable to the war have been deflated, there is still the possibility that northern victory had enhanced the capitalist spirit, that as a consequence the atmosphere of government in Washington among members of both parties was more friendly to industrial enterprise and to northern-based national business operations than had formerly been the rule. It can be argued that in spite of Greenbackers and discontented farmers legislation presumably favorable to industry could be more readily enacted. The Fourteenth Amendment, for example, had as a by-product greater security for interstate business against state regulation, although it was to be almost two decades before the Supreme Court would give force to this protection. By 1876, a year of deep depression, the two major parties were trying to outdo each other in promises of stimulating economic growth. This highly generalized type of argument is difficult to evaluate, but in qualification of any theory of a sharp change in attitude we should remember that industrialism was growing rapidly from general causes and that by the 1870's it was to be expected that major-party politics would be conforming to this change in American life.

Massive changes in physical environment such as those accompanying the rise of trade at the close of the Middle Ages or the gradual growth of industrialism from the seventeenth century on do not lend themselves readily to exact or brief periodization. If factory industry and mechanized transportation be taken as the chief indexes of early industrialism, its spread in the United States was continuous and rapid during the entire nineteenth century, but in general, advance was greater during periods of prosperity than in depressions. The first long period without a major depression, after railroads, canals, and steamboats had opened a national market, was from 1843 to 1857. Many economic historians interested in quantitative calculations would regard these years as marking the appearance of an integrated industrial society. Walt W. Rostow, incidentally, starts his "take-off" period in the 1840's and calls it completed by 1860.[40] Others might prefer to avoid any narrow span of years. Few, however, would see a major stimulation to economic growth in the events of the Civil War.

Finally, one may speculate as to why this exaggerated conception of the role of the Civil War in industrialization gained so firm a place in American historiography. The idea fits, of course, into the Marxian frame of revolutionary changes, but it seems initially to have gained acceptance quite independently of Marxian influences. More concentrated study of the war years than of any other four-year span in the nineteenth century called attention to technological and business events usually overlooked. Isolated facts were seized upon without comparing them with similar data for other decades. The desire of teachers for neat periodization was probably a strong factor in quickly placing the interpretation in textbooks; thus, up to 1860 the nation was agricultural, after 1865 it was industrial. Recent study of American cultural themes suggests still another reason. From most standpoints the Civil War was a national disaster, but Americans like to see their history in terms of optimism and progress. Perhaps the war was put in a perspective suited to the culture by seeing it as good because in addition to achieving freedom for the Negro it brought about industrial progress.

NOTES

1. This article is based on a paper presented by the author at the annual meeting of the Mississippi Valley Historical Association in Louisville in April, 1960.

2. These particular authors are cited merely as examples of historical opinion, not because they are more in error than others. The reader needs only to take down other texts from his own shelf to find similar statements.

3. *The Rise of American Civilization* (2 vols., New York, 1927), II, 53. In this and the following quotations the italics are mine.

4. Homer C. Hockett and Arthur M. Schlesinger, *Land of the Free: A Short History of the American People* (New York, 1944), 355. Schlesinger wrote the section beginning with the Civil War.

5. *American Economic History* (7th ed., New York, 1954), 345. The same statement appears in a later edition (New York, 1960), 345.

6. *The United States: The History of a Republic* (Englewood Cliffs, N.J., 1957), 381.

7. *An Economic History of the United States* (Boston, 1959), 284.

8. "A Fresh Appraisal of the Civil War," *Harper's Magazine* (New York), CCXX (April, 1960), 140.

9. U.S. Bureau of the Census, *Historical Statistics of the United States, 1789–1945* (Washington, 1949).

10. U.S. Bureau of the Census, *Historical Statistics of the United States: Colonial Times to 1957* (Washington, 1960); *Trends in the American Economy in the Nineteenth Century* (Princeton, 1960), published by the National Bureau of Economic Research as Volume XXIV of its *Studies in Income and Wealth*.

11. *Trends in the American Economy*, 15.

12. *Historical Statistics* (1960 ed.), 402. "Constant" or "real" means dollars adjusted to eliminate price changes. It should be remembered that all series expressed in current dollars need to be corrected for rather violent price movements during these fifty years. Precise adjustments would vary with every series, and would involve many problems, but the movement of wholesale prices in general (Warren-Pearson Index) may be roughly summarized as follows. In 1850 prices were 12 percent lower than in 1840, but by 1860 they were 11 percent higher than in 1850. From 1860 to 1865 prices rose 99 percent, but by 1870 the increase for the decade was only 46 percent. By 1880 the decline for the decade was 26 percent, and for the decade ending in 1890 it was 18 percent. *Ibid.*, 115. In other words, current dollars are a very unreliable indicator, particularly as applied to wholesale prices.

13. *Ibid.*, 365–366.

14. *Ibid.*, 357.

15. *Ibid.*, 368.

16. *Ibid.*, 427–428.

17. *Historical Statistics* (1949 ed.), 187. This table is not carried back to 1840 in the 1960 edition.

18. Arthur H. Cole, *The American Wool Manufacture* (2 vols., Cambridge, 1926), I, 392.

19. *Historical Statistics* (1960 ed.), 57.

20. William T. Hutchinson, *Cyrus Hall McCormick* (2 vols., New York, 1930–1935), II, 67.

21. *Ibid.*, II, 67–95.

22. *Ibid.*, II, 88.

23. *Historical Statistics* (1960 ed.), 285. For price index see note 12, above.

24. *Trends in the American Economy*, 276.

25. The percentage increases were 41 percent (1860 over 1850); 30 percent (1870 over 1860); and 51 percent (1880 over 1870). *Historical Statistics* (1960 ed.), 278.

26. *Ibid.*, 284.

27. *Ibid.*, 624. The reader is again warned that deflation of current dollar values for this early period is an inexact process.

28. *Trends in the American Economy*, 60–64.

29. *Ibid.*, 24. Gallman has two alternate series which I have averaged. For the purposes of this paper either series leads to the same conclusions.

30. Leonard P. Ayres, *Turning Points in Business Cycles* (New York, 1939), 14; Norman J. Siberling, *The Dynamics of Business* (New York, 1943), 50.

31. Silberling, *Dynamics of Business*, 61.

32. *Ibid.*, 66.

33. Ayres, Silberling, and some other students of economic activity such as Herbert Hoover, however, blame the breakdown of the 1930's on the dislocations caused by World War I. *Ibid.*, 65–66. See also *The Memoirs of Herbert Hoover: The Great Depression, 1929–1941* (New York, 1952), 105.

34. *Trends in the American Economy*, 85.

35. Simon Kuznets (ed.), *Population Redistribution and Economic Growth: United States, 1870–1950* (2 vols., Philadelphia, 1957–1960), I (*Methodological Considerations and Reference Tables*), 729–32; II (*Analysis of Economic Change*), 109.

36. See Bray Hammond, *Banks and Politics in America. From the Revolution to the Civil War* (Princeton, 1957), 663–67, 670.

37. *Historical Statistics* (1960 ed.), 628, 638.

38. See James K. Medbury, *Men and Mysteries of Wall Street* (Boston, 1870), 319 ff.; Margaret G. Myers, *The New York Money Market* (2 vols., New York, 1931), 1, 140.

39. Myers, *New York Money Market*, I, 296; National Bureau of Economic Research, *Capital Formation and Economic Growth* (Princeton, 1955), 382. See also Carter Goodrich, *Government Promotion of American Canals and Railroads, 1800–1890* (New York, 1960).

40. W. W. Rostow, *The Stages of Economic Growth* (Cambridge, Eng., 1960), 95.

Part III

—

EMERGENCE OF THE
MODERN ECONOMY
1870 - 1920

Part II

IO

Determinants of Regional Development

ONE OF THE major influences on nineteenth-century American economic development was the settlement of a vast area of fertile, unoccupied land. The policy adopted by the federal government for disposal of the public domain inevitably would be of critical importance in fashioning the pattern of landownership from the Alleghenies westward to the Pacific; and throughout the pre-Civil War years land policy was one of the foremost issues in national politics. While eastern leaders generally jealously guarded the principle that land policy should be designed to maximize revenues, western spokesmen pressed for lower land prices, rapid alienation of the public domain, and guarantee of pre-emption rights for squatters who settled on public lands. Some western politicians and a group of articulate land reformers in the East went further, advocating a policy by which the government would grant a tract of land free of cost to any actual settler. This policy was finally embodied in legislation when the Civil War Congress passed the Homestead Act in 1862.*

* One recent student of the subject has said that the Homestead Act was the product of two reform "visions." The eastern reformers were primarily interested in making land available free to actual settlers, whereas western supporters of the law sought "the enticement of a numerous population to the West, the rapid alienation of federal title, and the passage of the land into a taxable status so as to support community development and subsequent prosperity." Lawrence B. Lee: "The Homestead Act: Vision and Reality," *Utah Historical Quarterly,* XXX (1962), p. 220.

Until publication in 1935 of Paul W. Gates's article, which is reprinted here, the Homestead Act was commonly eulogized as the cornerstone of federal land policy after 1862, and as a law which assured a pattern of democratic landownership in the West. As a result of the work of Professor Gates and others, it is widely recognized today that the Homestead Act was only one law of many by which large areas of the public domain were alienated in the late nineteenth century. Whereas the stereotyped view of the Homestead Act has been discarded, a key interpretive question remains: though the "incongruous land system" permitted large-scale acquisitions of western lands by speculators, railroad companies and other private agencies, did federal land policy in practice retard or stimulate the pace of western development and national development?

In September 1956, the Economic History Association devoted its annual meeting to questions such as this one, the theme of the sessions being "The American West as an Underdeveloped Region." Douglas F. Dowd's study of western and southern development was first presented at this meeting. In this essay, Dowd argues that institutional factors explain the regional differential between West and South in the pace and quality of economic growth. The West, he asserts, was never "underdeveloped" (in the conventional sense of the term) whereas the South has chronically lagged behind the rest of the nation and has failed to realize its economic potential. Delineated here in sharp historical perspective are the peculiarly southern institutions and mores which have continued to plague that region's economic development well into the twentieth century.

THE HOMESTEAD LAW IN AN INCONGRUOUS LAND SYSTEM

Paul Wallace Gates

The Homestead Act of 1862 is one of the most important laws which have been enacted in the history of this country, but its significance has been distorted and grossly misinterpreted.[1] An important misconception concerning the Homestead Act is that its adoption marked a more or less complete break with the past, in that the lands which previously had been considered as a source of revenue were now to be given free to settlers. As part of this interpretation it is held that direct land sales virtually ceased except for transactions under the Pre-emption Law, the commutation clause of the Homestead Act, the Timber and Stone Act, and the Desert Land Act. Each of the first three of these acts permitted the purchase by individuals of 160 acres and the Desert Land Act permitted the purchase of an additional 640 acres, making a total which could be acquired under them of 1120 acres. Aside from this maximum which was open to purchasers, the accepted view is that speculators[2] in lands were barred from direct transactions at the land offices and that, to secure large tracts, they were forced to operate through dummy entrymen or buy from states and railroads.

To state this view differently, it is held that after 1862 the chief way in which settlers and speculators alike acquired land from the government was through the Pre-emption and Homestead laws and their subsequent modifications. Indeed, some writers have maintained that the region beyond the Mississippi was largely settled by homesteaders taking up free land under the Act of 1862. Congressman Harvey B. Ferguson stated in 1914, "It was great statesmanship that created the homestead laws under which such a State as Iowa developed."[3] Another writer made an even broader statement as follows: "Under the homestead law were taken up the rich agricultural alluvial lands of the central Mississippi basin. . . ."[4] Even

Reprinted by permission from *The American Historical Review*, XLI, No. 4 (July, 1936), pp. 652–81.

Professor Hibbard, the authority on American land policies, has misunderstood the developments in land matters after 1862. He states that land sales made after 1862 were "only in connection with preemption and miscellaneous parcels of land, the preemptions covering by far the larger part of the operations." He also states that a congressional resolution, expressing opposition to the further sale of agricultural lands, which passed the House in 1868 but failed of adoption in the Senate, was virtually "tantamount to a law." [5] As these views have been widely accepted it is essential to examine briefly their source and then to test their accuracy.

The principle of free homesteads for settlers had long been the goal for which the West had struggled, and as each succeeding land law, more liberal than its predecessor, was passed, that goal came constantly nearer until, in 1862, it was attained. So generous seemed this policy in contrast with the earlier one of regarding the lands as a source of revenue, and so significant did it appear prospectively, that it became the subject of eulogy at the outset. Furthermore, the measure had been sponsored by the Republican party, and when this party was later accused of representing the interests of large capitalistic combines and of neglecting the farmers, its leaders pointed to the Homestead Act as a refutation of the accusation.[6] Consequently there was built up around the law a halo of political and economic significance which has greatly magnified the importance to be attributed to it and which has misled practically every historian and economist who has dealt with land policies. The Homestead Law has been considered the capstone of an increasingly liberal land policy, and to it has been ascribed the rapid settlement of the West and the large percentage of farmer owners in the United States. It has also been regarded as providing an outlet for the discontented and surplus labor of the East with the result that, as compared with European countries, high wage rates have prevailed in that section. The influence of free land has been blithely discussed by writers who have never taken the time to examine the facts with which they dealt so lightly.[7]

The source of most of these ideas concerning the Homestead Law is, of course, the *Congressional Globe*, later the *Record*, upon which so many writers completely depend. A careful reading of the congressional debates should, however, lead one to question the general conception above outlined. Professor Hibbard bases his generalizations upon even more untrustworthy evidence. He quotes from the *Report* of the Commissioner of the General Land Office for 1863 wherein it is stated that it is not the design of Congress "to look to the public lands as a source of direct revenue," [8] and, from the exceedingly small amount of sales reported in the first year that the Homestead Law was in operation, draws the inference that cash sales were thenceforth of no importance. Professor Hibbard may also have been depending upon a statement made by that great compiler of land statistics, Thomas Donaldson, in his book, *The Public Domain,* originally published in 1880, in which it is stated that lands available for cash entry are few and isolated, except for those in the five Southern states of Alabama, Louisiana, Florida, Arkansas, and Mississippi. The statement was correct in general in 1880, in so far as it applied to the lands ordinarily described as "public domain," [9] but there were many million acres of rich agricultural lands which at that time were rapidly being brought into the market for cash sale by the Federal government.[10] It would not apply at all to the period prior to 1880 when large areas of the best agricultural lands in the country were subject to sale.

It is the purpose of this paper to show that the Homestead Law did not completely change our land system, that its adoption merely superimposed upon the old land system a principle out of harmony with it, and that until 1890 the old and the new constantly clashed. In presenting this view it will appear that the Homestead Law did not end the auction system or cash sales, as is generally assumed, that speculation and land monopolization continued after its adoption as widely perhaps as before, and within as well as without the law, that actual homesteading was generally confined to the less desirable lands distant from railroad lines, and that farm tenancy developed in frontier communities in many instances as a result of the monopolization of the land. The efforts to abolish cash sales will also be outlined briefly.

The moderate land reformers of the mid-nineteenth century believed that the enactment of a homestead measure would retard if not end speculation in public lands.[11] They argued that once free homesteads were available to settlers speculators would no longer have a market for their lands and all inducements to purchase in advance of settlement would be ended. Parenthetically, similar arguments have been advanced by certain historians to prove that there was little or no profit in land speculation.[12] The land reformers reckoned too lightly, however, with the astuteness of the speculators who in the past had either succeeded in emasculating laws inimical to their interests or had actually flouted such laws in the very faces of the officials appointed to administer them.

From the outset the cards were stacked against the efficient and successful operation of the Homestead Law. Other acts in existence in 1862 greatly limited its application and new laws further restricting it were subsequently enacted. The administration of the law, both in Washington and in the field, was frequently in the hands of persons unsympathetic to its principle,[13] and Western interests, though lauding the act, were ever ready to pervert it. The existence of the Pre-emption Law and its later variations, the Desert Land Act, the Timber Culture Act, the Timber and Stone Act, the land grants to railroads and states, the cash sale system, the Indian land policy, the acts granting land warrants to ex-soldiers or their heirs, and the Agricultural College Act of 1862, which granted millions of acres of land scrip to Eastern states, tended to make it practically as easy for speculators to engross huge areas of land after 1862 as before.

The retention of the Pre-emption Law and the commutation clause of the Homestead Law made it possible for timber dealers,[14] cattle graziers, mining interests, and speculators to continue to acquire lands through the use of dummy entrymen, false swearing, and, often, the connivance of local land officers. That this was done on a large scale is evident by the frequent and sometimes pathetic admissions of the apparently helpless land commissioners. The Desert Land Act, the Timber Culture Act, and the Timber and Stone Act provided even greater opportunities for dummy entrymen to enter lands and assign them to hidden land engrossers.[15] The palpable frauds committed and the large areas transferred under these acts and their interference with the homestead principle lead one to suspect that their enactment and retention were the results of political pressure by interested groups.

It was not entirely necessary, however, for speculators to resort to these illegal and fraudulent methods of acquiring land since Congress proceeded to aid their schemes by enacting a series of laws which went far toward vitiating the principle of land for the landless. By continuing after 1862 the policy of granting lands to railroads to encourage their construction, Congress from the outset struck a severe blow at the principle of free homesteads. In the eight years after the passage of the Homestead Law five times as much land was granted to railroads as had been given in the twelve preceding years; 127,628,000 acres were granted between 1862 and

1871 to aid in the extension of the railroad net and 2,000,000 acres were granted for wagon roads and canals. Such imperial generosity was at the expense of future homesteaders who must purchase the land.[16] As it was necessary to withdraw all lands from entry in the regions through which such roads were projected to prevent speculators from anticipating the railroads in making selections of land, and as the routes were rarely definitely established when the grants were made, more than double this amount of land was withdrawn from entry and remained unavailable to settlement for a long period of years.[17]

The railroads were, of course, built through undeveloped regions and, other things being equal, routes were selected which would ensure to the companies the largest amount of what was then considered to be the best agricultural land. When the alternate government sections were finally restored to market settlers were frequently outbid for them by speculators.[18] Moreover, the provision in the Homestead Law which confined the homesteader to eighty acres within the limits of a railroad grant [19] was sufficient to send many homeseekers farther afield. On the railroad sections, of course, no free homesteading was permitted and thus the prospective settler found it necessary to go far from transportation facilities in order to take advantage of the government's bounty. In numerous instances the land policies of the railroads encouraged speculative and large-scale purchases with the result that millions of acres were turned into bonanza farms, such as those found in Dakota Territory,[20] or were rented or leased to incoming settlers who had expected to find free land available to them.

These grants to railroads after 1862 were a limitation on the homestead principle and indicate cynical indifference to the idealistic expressions constantly voiced concerning the principle. That some doubt existed among members of Congress as to the propriety of continuing to make grants for railroads is revealed by a resolution adopted by the House in 1870 [21] which stated:

> That in the judgement of this House the policy of granting subsidies in public lands to railroad and other corporations ought to be discontinued; and that every consideration of public policy and equal justice to the whole people requires that the public lands of the United States should be held for the exclusive purpose of securing homesteads to actual settlers under the homestead and preëmption laws, subject to reasonable appropriations of such lands for the purposes of education.

Although adopted without any debate the resolution was just a bluff, for within the next twelve months Congress made one of the largest and most indefensible of the railroad grants which, together with a number of smaller ones, totaled nearly 20,000,000 acres.[22] The anti-railroad feeling which swept over the West in the early seventies finally brought these grants to an end. After 1871 no more grants were made [23] although various interests were at the time seeking additional grants which, if made, would have required practically all the valuable lands remaining to the government.

The continuation of the policy of granting to the states Federal lands within their borders was likewise contrary to the homestead principle. With the exception of the swamp land grants, the purpose of these donations was to provide the states with a valuable commodity, the sale of which would produce revenue or endowment for educational and other state institutions. Over 72,000,000 acres were granted to states which came into the Union after 1862 while other states had their grants increased subsequent to the enactment of the Homestead Law.[24] It is safe to say that over 140,000,000 acres of land were in the hands of the states for disposition after 1862.[25] The philosophy behind the grants, and frequently the conditions embedded in the donations, required their sale at the highest market price. The states were prevented, therefore, from giving homesteads to settlers and the prices asked for their lands, with the exception of the swamp lands which were generally sold at low prices or granted to railroads, made them the prey of speculators. It is true that limitations were sometimes placed on the amount of land which individuals could purchase, but dummy entrymen were usually employed to circumvent such restrictions.[26] The states, like the railroads, naturally endeavored to secure the best possible lands in order to ensure large returns therefrom. The following table,[27] showing the land sales of and the prices received by representative states, reveals clearly that persons seeking cheap or free lands found little encouragement from state officials.

State	Net amount of land sold to date	Average price per acre
Idaho [28]	838,140	$16.90
Kansas	3,064,547	3.22
Minnesota	2,306,600	6.53
Montana	1,587,488	15.50
North Dakota	1,686,436	16.73
South Dakota	873,960	35.22
Utah	3,448,876	2.44

The maintenance of the cash sale system after the Homestead Law went into operation did even greater violence to the principle of free lands. It is not generally appreciated that there were available in 1862 for cash sale 83,919,649 acres of land.[29] Contrary to the views of Hibbard and others, this figure was later increased to well over 100,000,000 acres by the opening up of new lands to the auction and cash sale system.[30] Throughout the sixties and seventies and, indeed, until 1888 the government continued to offer land at auction in Oregon, Washington, California, Kansas, Nebraska, Colorado, New Mexico, and in practically all of the states in the Lakes region and in the Mississippi Valley where it still had land. It is true that after 1870 most of the land so offered was timbered but by then a goodly portion of the arable lands had been surveyed and opened to sale. The richest and most fertile sections of Kansas, Nebraska, Missouri, California, Washington, and Oregon were thus open to the cash purchaser after the enactment of the Homestead Law and, as will be seen later, great landed estates were acquired through outright purchase in these states.

Little attention has been devoted by historians to the Indian lands and yet there is a story involved in their disposition totally at variance with the conventional account of the era of free land. At the time the Homestead Law was passed the government was following the policy of concentrating the Indians on reservations where they would be in less conflict with white settlers. The rights of the Indians in lands claimed by them were recognized and, when they were persuaded to leave a hunting area over which they claimed ownership to dwell in a reservation, they were generally compensated for their lands either by the Federal government or by a purchaser acting with the consent of the government. Some of the lands were ceded outright to the government for a consideration; others were ceded in trust, the lands to be sold for the benefit of the Indians; the disposition of still others to railroads was authorized in a number of treaties. As these Indian lands were frequently the very choicest and contained some improvements they were much desired by speculators. No uniform policy concerning their final disposition was worked out—both legislative and administrative regulations as to their disposal varying widely—and consequently speculators were able to get their grasp on them more easily than if the lands had been subject to a clearly defined policy. The only consistent rule concerning them was that they must be sold for a consideration, which, of course, denied to the homesteader the right to enter them free. The obligation of the government to compensate the Indian for his land did not necessitate a policy of sale to settlers but the revenue complex with reference to the public lands was still prevalent in spite of the Homestead Law, and the Indian lands were reserved for cash sale.

The amount of land in Indian reservations or claimed by the Indians in 1862 was probably 175,000,000 acres.[31] The land was scattered throughout the Western states, but large amounts were concentrated in the states of Kansas and Nebraska and the Dakota and Indian territories into which settlers were eagerly pressing in the sixties, seventies, and eighties, or where they looked longingly for lands. At the outset, these lands were sold in large blocks to groups of capitalists and railroads, as is seen below, without being offered in small lots. Slightly later they were appraised, generally at high valuations, offered at auction and sold to the highest bidders. Still later, some of the Indian lands were sold in small tracts to settlers, a slight concession to the homeseekers.[32]

The Indian Allotment Act of 1887, as modified by the Burke Act of 1906 [33] and subsequent measures, was undoubtedly in part the result of Western pressure to have the lands of the Indians made available to white settlement. These acts provided for the allotment of Indian lands and eventually for their sale. The Dawes Act continued the policy whereby the government purchased the surplus lands from the Indians and subsequently resold them, but it provided that lands so acquired in the future should be reserved for actual settlers in tracts of 160 acres. This provision did not apply to ceded lands transferred before 1887 nor did it open the ceded lands to free homesteading. Congress has been consistent at least in requiring payment for Indian land. Between 100,000,000 and 125,000,000 acres of Indian land have been sold since 1862, practically one half as much as the total acreage which has been entered under the Homestead Law.[34]

With over 125,000,000 acres of railroad lands,[35] 140,000,000 acres of state lands, 100,000,000 acres of Indian lands, and 100,000,000 acres of Federal lands for sale in large or small blocks, and with the opportunities for evasion of the Homestead and Pre-emption laws and their variations outlined above, it is obvious that there were few obstacles in the way of speculation and land monopolization after 1862. As before, it was still possible for foresighted speculators to precede settlers into the frontier, purchase the best lands, and hold them for the anticipated increase in value which the succeeding wave of settlers would give to them. It has heretofore been maintained that the existence of free land after 1862 greatly diminished the speculators' chances of profit and consequently limited their activities. This view will not bear careful scrutiny. Except for the squatters' claims, the speculators were generally able to secure the most desirable lands, that is, those easily brought under cultivation, fertile and close to timber, water, markets, and lines of communication. The subsequent settler had the choice of buying at the speculators' prices, from the land grant railroads which held their alternate tracts at equally high prices, from the states whose land policies were less generous than those of the Federal government, or of going farther afield to exercise his homestead privilege where facilities for social and economic intercourse were limited. The fact that their lands were more advantageously situated was effectively advertised by the land companies. Thus the American Emigrant Company in advertising its Iowa lands in the sixties summed up under the caption "Better than a Free Homestead" all the disadvantages of free land:

Under the homestead law the settler must, in order to get a good location, go far out into the wild and unsettled districts, and for many years be deprived of school privileges, churches, mills, bridges, and in fact of all the advantages of society.[36]

Settlers arriving in Kansas—to consider a typical state—between 1868 and 1872 were greeted with advertisements announcing that the choicest lands in the state had been selected by the State Agricultural College which was now offering 90,000 acres for sale on long term credits. The Central Branch of the Union Pacific Railroad offered 1,200,000 acres for prices ranging from $1.00 to $15.00 per acre; the Kansas Pacific Railroad offered 5,000,000 acres for $1.00 to $6.00 per acre; the Kansas and Neosho Valley Railroad offered 1,500,000 acres for sale at $2.00 to $8.00 per acre; the Capital Land Agency of Topeka offered 1,000,000 acres of Kansas land for sale; [37] Van Doren and Havens offered 200,000 acres for $3.00 to $10.00 per acre; T. H. Walker offered 10,000 (or 100,000) acres [38] for $5.00 to $10.00 per acre; Hendry and Noyes offered 50,000 acres; and even the United States government was advertising for bids for approximately 6000 acres of Sac and Fox Indian lands.[39] That virgin lands in Kansas were selling for substantial prices in this period is shown by the following tables:

Table showing Sales of State Lands [40]

		Acres	Average price per acre
Common School lands	(1865–1882)	450,764	$4.00
Agricultural College lands	(1868–1882)	48,465	4.78
University lands	(1878–1882)	6,224	2.88
Normal School lands	(1876–1882)	4,966	4.72

Table showing Land Sales of Atchison, Topeka, and Santa Fe Railroad [41]

Total Sales from March 1, 1871, to Dec. 31, 1879

Year	Acres	Principal	Average price per acre
1871	71,801.51	$ 425,013.75	$5.91
1872	45,328.81	269,627.66	5.94
1873	133,507.30	748,977.25	5.61
1874	200,459.96	900,973.30	4.49
1875	75,415.33	416,409.85	5.52
1876	122,201.17	665,455.17	5.44½
1877	85,047.78	423,477.49	4.98
1878	267,122.47	1,206,527.64	4.52
1879	104,744.41	494,353.73	4.72
Total	1,105,628.74	$5,550,815.84	$5.02

Such sales—and many others might be cited—are evidence that free homesteads on the most desirable land were not available in this state to incoming settlers.

A strong impulse to speculation was provided by the existence of large amounts of land warrants, chiefly those of the Act of March 3, 1855,[42] which were to be had in the market at prices of a dollar an acre or less.[43] They could be used to locate solid blocks of land wherever the surveyed area of the public domain was open to cash entry. In addition, it is startling to find a provision in the Agricultural College Act of July 2, 1862, whereby 7,672,800 acres in land scrip,[44] which likewise could be used to locate surveyed lands open to cash entry, were thrown on the market. Within a comparatively short time this scrip depreciated greatly in value. Some states sold their scrip for an average price of less than fifty cents an acre and such prices tempted many individuals to purchase and locate large areas in the Western states.[45] Probably no other scrip or warrant act was used so extensively by speculators to build up large holdings as was this Agricultural College Act. Other special acts were passed after 1862 creating smaller amounts of Indian land scrip and other compensatory scrip, part of which possessed the special privilege of being subject to location on any part of the public domain, whether or not it was surveyed or had been offered for sale.[46]

The existence of large areas of rich lands open to speculative entries and the availability of warrants and scrip at depreciated prices made possible large-scale engrossment after the Homestead Law was passed. Some of the richest and most fertile sections of Iowa, Kansas, Nebraska, Missouri, California, Washington, and Oregon were thus open to cash or warrant entry and after the adoption of the Homestead Law they were quickly engrossed by speculators.

Some of the land entries [47] made after 1862 are interesting to note. Senator John Sherman, who, like most politicians of his day, was not averse to speculating in lands, located with Agricultural College scrip 2560 acres in Missouri in 1868; Robert Mears with the same kind of scrip located 29,280 acres in the Boonville district of Missouri; Amos Lawrence, prominent among the promoters of the Emigrant Aid Company at an earlier date, located 58,360 acres in Kansas in 1866 with Agricultural College scrip; Charles and Henry Stebbins and Henry M. Porter entered 53,760 acres in Kansas and Nebraska in 1866, 1867, and 1868 with the same kind of scrip; John C. Work and Rufus Hatch of New York, John J. Blair of New Jersey, and James C. Cusey of Sioux City, Iowa, entered in western Iowa in 1869 and 1870, 12,200, 28,671, 20,970, and 9280 acres respectively; John P. Crothers, of Berks County, Pennsylvania, later of Clark County, Ohio, entered with scrip and cash 44,140 acres in Nebraska; William Scully, one of the greatest landed proprietors in the United States whose relations with his tenants have been the subject of much hostile comment and legislation,[48] purchased for cash in a single land district in Nebraska in 1870, 41,421 acres; Ira Davenport of Steuben County, New York, whose land operations extended throughout most of the Northwestern states entered with cash and land warrants 16,949 acres in the Dakota City district of Nebraska. Perhaps the largest purchasers of land in Nebraska were a group of Providence, Rhode Island, speculators, consisting of Robert H. Ives, John Carter Brown, Charlotte R. and Moses B. J. Goddard. Ives alone had previously purchased 82,431 acres in Illinois, 50,000 acres in Iowa, and smaller amounts in Minnesota and

Missouri, while Brown had acquired over 30,000 acres in Iowa and Illinois. These four individuals entered with cash over 96,000 acres in the Dakota City district. Between 1862 and 1873, twenty-seven other persons entered a combined area of 250,000 acres in Nebraska. Numerous other illustrations could be cited to indicate that speculation in agricultural lands in the Great Plains area did not cease with the passage of the Homestead Law.

Not only were the best agricultural lands being snapped up by speculators but the richest timber lands remaining in the possession of the United States were being rapidly entered by large dealers during the post-Civil War period. There were three areas in which vast amounts of timber land were still owned by the Federal government, the Lake states, the Gulf states with Arkansas, and the Pacific Coast states. In each of these three regions millions of acres of pine, spruce, hemlock, and fir were available for cash entry and in the Pacific area lands covered with the rich redwood and other trees peculiar to that region had been or were just being brought into the market. In the timber lands of these three sections some of the largest purchases by speculators or lumber men took place. Many thousands of acres in Wisconsin and Michigan were located by Isaac Stephenson, Philetus Sawyer, and Russell A. Alger, influential lumber dealers, who were subsequently to become members of the Senate of the United States. Ezra Cornell located 385,780 acres in the Eau Claire, Wisconsin, land district, 76,180 acres in the Bayfield district, 29,200 in the Stevens Point district, 12,480 acres in Minnesota, and 4000 acres in Kansas, all with Agricultural College scrip of New York. A group of New York magnates, Thomas F. Mason, George B. Satterlee, and William E. Dodge, entered 232,799 acres in the Marquette, Michigan, district, 10,850 acres elsewhere in that state, and 10,359 acres in Wassau, Wisconsin. Francis Palms purchased in Wisconsin and Michigan 286,208 acres, and with Frederick E. Driggs entered in the eighties about 200,000 acres more in the Marquette district. Three Ithaca, New York, lumber dealers, Henry W. Sage,[49] John McGraw, and Jeremiah W. Dwight, like Ezra Cornell benefactors of Cornell University, entered 277,000 acres in Michigan, Wisconsin, and Minnesota, and 75,000 acres in Mississippi, Alabama, and Arkansas. Other large timberland entrymen in the Northwest were Calvin F. Howe of New York who acquired 105,000 acres in Minnesota, Thomas B. Walker[50] who alone and with others acquired 166,000 acres in the St. Cloud, Minnesota, district, George M. Wakefield who accumulated 110,000 acres in the Marquette district, and Jesse Spaulding and H. H. Porter of Chicago who purchased 113,000 acres in the same district. Fifty-six other persons purchased a total of 1,514,000 acres in Michigan, mostly in the Marquette district.

The same concentration of ownership of timber lands developed in the South after 1877. Some of the large purchases in this section were Daniel F. Sullivan's purchase of 147,000 acres in the Montgomery, Alabama, district in 1880–1882; Jabez B. Watkins's purchase of 145,000 acres in the New Orleans district; Delos A. Blodgett's purchase of 136,000 acres in the Jackson, Mississippi, district in 1885 to 1888; Lutcher and Moore's purchase of 108,000 acres in Louisiana in the eighties; and Franklin Head's and Nathan B. Bradley's purchases of 110,000 and 111,200 acres respectively in the New Orleans district. Sixty-eight other persons entered 2,110,000 acres in the Southern districts. Altogether, over five and one half million acres of land were sold in the five Southern states between 1880 and 1888, exclusive of pre-emption sales. Practically all of this area went to large land and lumber dealers. These lands comprised some of the very choicest timbered areas in the South and within less than a generation were selling at prices which brought enormous profits to the owners. It is worthy of note that many of the large timber dealers in Wisconsin, Michigan, and Minnesota made great acquisitions in the South.

The engrossment of timber and agricultural lands on the Pacific Coast proceeded at an even more rapid rate than in other sections of the country. Here in the years immediately following the Civil War a relatively small group of speculators sought to monopolize the best timber and agricultural lands. A group of Eastern speculators consisting of W. W. Corcoran of Washington, ex-Senator Bright of Indiana, and Elisha and Lawrason Riggs, whose land acquisitions in the Middle West had been very profitable, purchased over 7000 acres in Washington and Oregon in the early seventies; another group of San Francisco speculators purchased 59,000 acres in the Olympia, Washington, district; J. W. Sprague of Minnesota purchased 24,000 acres in the same district, and five other persons acquired 42,000 acres. More spectacular were the huge entries in California.

Land monopolization in California dates back to the Spanish and Mexican periods when large grants were made to favored individuals. After investigation by an American commission, 588 of these claims amounting to 8,850,143 acres, or an average of 15,051 acres each, were confirmed.[51] Following 1848 there came a rapid influx of settlers which, together with the large profits realized from the grazing industry in the interior valleys, created a land boom and led to extensive purchases. With great areas of land in the San Joaquin and Sacramento valleys open to cash purchase the opportunity for speculative profits was unparalleled elsewhere; nor was the opportunity neglected. From 1862 to 1880 land sales and warrant and scrip entries in California were on an enormous scale, surpassing all other states for the period and in some years comprising well over half of the sales for the entire country. In the single year, ending June 30, 1869, 1,726,794 acres were sold in this state by the Federal government, and for the entire period from 1862 to 1880 well over 7,000,000 [52] acres were entered with cash, warrants, or scrip. It should also be remembered that the State of California which received 8,426,380 [53] acres from the Federal government was disposing of its most valuable holdings at this time.

Greatest of all the speculators operating in California was William S. Chapman whose political influence stretched from Sacramento to St. Paul, Minnesota, and Washington, D.C. Of him it was said, with apparent justice, that land officers, judges, local legislators, officials in the Department of the Interior, and even higher dignitaries were ready and anxious to do him favors, frequently of no mean significance. Between 1868 and 1871 Chapman entered at the Federal land offices approximately 650,000 acres of land in California and Nevada with cash, scrip, and warrants. At the same time he entered additional land through dummy entrymen, purchased many thousands of acres of "swamp" lands from the State of California, and otherwise added to his possessions till they totaled over 1,000,000 acres. Fraud, bribery, false swearing, forgery, and other crimes were charged against him but he passed them off with little trouble.[54] The most remarkable feature about his vast acquisitions is that when plotted on a land-use map today they appear to be among the choicest of the lands. Chapman was not able to retain this vast empire for long. He became deeply involved in a grand canal project and eventually lost his lands, many of them going to a more constructive but equally spectacular land plunger, Henry Miller.[55]

Miller, unlike Chapman, bought lands for his cattle business which was his main interest. As the activities of his firm—Miller and Lux, of which he was the chief promoter—expanded, he pushed its land acquisitions until they mounted to over a million acres.

One hundred and eighty-one thousand acres of this amount were acquired directly from the Federal government, with cash, Agricultural College scrip, and military warrants; large amounts were purchased from Chapman and other big land speculators and from the State of California. Miller's lands were slowly irrigated, parts were disposed of to small farmers, and upon them today exists a veritable agricultural empire.[56]

Other large purchasers of land in California were Isaac Friedlander, E. H. Miller, and John W. Mitchell, who acquired 214,000, 105,000, and 78,000 acres respectively. The total amount purchased from the Federal government by Chapman, Miller and Lux, Friedlander, E. H. Miller, and Mitchell was one and a quarter million acres. Forty-three other large purchasers acquired 905,000 acres of land in the sixties in California. Buying in advance of settlement, these men were virtually thwarting the Homestead Law in California where, because of the enormous monopolization above outlined, homesteaders later were able to find little good land.

Further details concerning the widespread speculative activity in public lands—both agricultural and timbered—after the passage of the Homestead Act are unnecessary; it is clear that speculation and land engrossment were not retarded by the act. Homeseekers in the West, being unwilling to go far afield from means of transportation or to settle upon the inferior lands remaining open to homestead, and lacking capital with which to purchase farms and to provide equipment for them, were frequently forced to become tenants on the lands of speculators. Thus farm tenancy developed in the frontier stage at least a generation before it would have appeared had the homestead system worked properly. In the states of Kansas and Nebraska, in which large-scale land monopolization has been revealed, sixteen and eighteen percent respectively of the farms were operated by tenants in 1880, the first year for which figures are available, and in 1890 twenty-eight and twenty-four percent respectively were operated by tenants.[57] This continued monopolization of the best lands and the resulting growth of farm tenancy led reformers and others who feared the establishment of a landed aristocracy similar to that existing in many European countries to advocate the ending of the cash sales system entirely. Their demands were expressed in petitions to Congress, agitation in the press, and union of effort with other antimonopoly groups which were coming into prominence in the last third of the nineteenth century. Their agitation and the growing seriousness of the monop-

oly movement led to a series of halting steps toward the abandonment of cash sales, which frequently were offset by movements in
the opposite direction.

The first step in the direction of abolishing the cash sale system
was taken in June, 1866, when Congress provided that all public
lands in the five Southern states of Alabama, Arkansas, Florida,
Louisiana, and Mississippi should be reserved from sale and subject
only to entry under the Homestead Law.[58] The avowed purpose of
this apparent discrimination against land speculation in the South
while it was permitted to flourish elsewhere, was to prevent speculators from monopolizing the land when it was restored to market—
all land transactions had of course ceased in these states during the
Civil War—and to encourage the growth of small holdings among
the freedmen. By the South, the act was regarded, perhaps rightly,
as a punitive measure. Certain it is that much of the 46,398,544
acres [59] thus reserved from cash entry was unsuited to small-scale
farming and the freedmen showed no great desire to take advantage
of the homestead privilege thus safeguarded. Nevertheless, the act
was the first attack on the cash sale system.

Two backward steps were tried the same year, however. In the
same month that the law was passed restricting Southern public
lands to homestead entry an apparently innocuous measure slipped
through Congress without much debate or opposition, giving to the
New York and Montana Iron Mining and Manufacturing Company
the right to purchase at $1.25 per acre twenty sections—12,800 acres
—of unsurveyed and unopened lands in the territory of Montana,
three sections of which might contain iron ore or coal and the remaining sections would presumably be timber lands. This measure
was put through by Benjamin Wade of Ohio and Thaddeus Stevens
of Pennsylvania of whom it cannot be said that the interests of the
homesteaders were nearest to their hearts.[60] It gave a gross extension
of privilege to a group of speculators or land monopolists. Never
had such a *carte blanche* grant been made before, though frequently
petitioned for, and it aroused the indignation of President Johnson
who, in a ringing veto message, declared that the privileges conferred by the act "are in direct conflict with every principle heretofore observed in respect to the disposal of the public lands." [61] If
the measure had been signed, the principle of granting lands free or
for the minimum price to mining companies and other industrial
organizations might have been established and the remaining portion of the public domain might have been divided among such

capitalistic groups, just as millions of acres were being parceled out among the railroads. In placing himself squarely against the law, President Johnson aided in preserving the lands from speculators.

President Johnson's opposition to the granting of such special privileges to private business groups did not end the matter, however, for a similar measure passed the Senate in 1870. This second measure would have authorized the Sierra Iron Company of California to purchase 640 acres of land containing iron ore in the vicinity of Gold Lake, California, and 3200 acres of timber lands for $2.50 per acre. As originally proposed by Senator Cole of California it would have permitted the purchase of 10,000 acres of timber lands at $1.25 per acre but was amended as above. The measure was rushed through the Senate at a night session when there was a very small attendance, but was later reconsidered, amended to provide further safeguards, and sent to the House where the opponents of land monopoly succeeded in preventing its adoption.[62] Eternal vigilance on the part of true friends of the homesteaders was essential to prevent such laws being slipped through without adequate consideration.

The second backward step was a series of Indian treaties and administrative measures by which substantial areas of land in the Great Plains were sold to railroad companies and other speculative groups. When railroads were projected through Kansas and Nebraska, it was found that they must run through Indian reservations. Congressional land grants did not apply to such lands and the railroad officials therefore sought to purchase the lands which they could not receive as a gift. Instead of asking for alternate sections, however, as in the grants, they sought to purchase solid areas which would enable them to secure the entire benefits resulting from the construction of the railroads. As the Granger period had not yet arrived, railroads were still popular throughout most sections of the country. Furthermore, they possessed great influence at the seat of power and it was not difficult for them to prevail upon the proper officials to make treaties for the cession or sale of Indian lands. The Senate at this time was far more friendly to the railroads than to the homeseekers, as shown by its generous land grants and financial subsidies to the former and its refusal to place restrictions upon speculative purchases of land. Apparently it saw little difference between making donations of alternate sections of the public domain to the railroads and selling solid blocks of Indian lands to them for a low price. It therefore ratified such treaties with little hesitation.

In the years immediately following the enactment of the Homestead Law, a number of such treaties and subsequent sales contracts were ratified, providing for the sale of several million acres in Kansas to railroad companies.[63] That which aroused the greatest local opposition was the sale of some 800,000 acres of Cherokee Indian lands in southeastern Kansas. A treaty was negotiated with the Cherokees which permitted the sale of 800,000 acres to a single individual or corporation for $1.00 per acre, and which completely disregarded the white settlers already on the lands. Before ratification, the treaty was amended to permit the sale of tracts of 160 acres to the squatters.[64] In the meantime, the Secretary of the Interior had sold this great tract to the American Emigrant Company. This company was organized to operate under the nefarious contract labor law of 1864 but quickly saw that larger profits were to be realized in land speculation and it began to deal in lands. Its record of land deals is obscure but is accompanied by sufficient evidence to indicate that the transactions were not always legitimate.[65] The purchase of 800,000 acres of Cherokee lands at $1.00 per acre on long credit was the result of secret negotiations; the lands were not offered at public sale, and the settlers were given no opportunity to purchase the tracts upon which they were squatting. The sale was, then, an outrageous violation of the principle of land for the landless and was immediately attacked as a gross fraud upon the public. Subsequent investigations revealed much that could not be satisfactorily explained and the Attorney General held that it was not in conformity with the treaty with the Cherokees.

Meantime, the Cherokee tract, through widely circulated rumors as to its fertility and desirability for settlement, was attracting the attention of many interested people. Following 1866 settlers flocked to the area in large numbers so that by 1867 there were reported to be 10,000 or 12,000 people there [66] and the number was shortly increased to 20,000. The settlers expected from the government the same lenient attitude toward their intrusions upon land not open to settlement as was being rendered to other people in similar circumstances elsewhere. Unfortunately for them the value of the tract was appreciated by a number of railroad groups which desired to secure ownership of the entire area as a means of financing the construction of their lines. Concrete proposals for the purchase of the tract were made by three railroads—the Tebo and Neosho Railroad Company of Missouri,[67] the Atlantic and Pacific Railroad, and the Kansas City, Fort Scott, and Gulf Railroad. Prominent Missouri and Kansas politicians, John C. Fremont and James F. Joy— "The Railroad King"—were interested in these lines and each sought to secure the much coveted lands for his company. Although not the highest bidder, the sale was finally awarded to James F. Joy who purchased the land for the Kansas City, Fort Scott, and Gulf Railroad. After the sale was made and the rival proposals turned down, the lenient officials of the Department of the Interior permitted Joy to surrender his contract and to substitute the original but less exacting contract with the American Emigrant Company which was now assigned to him. This necessitated a supplementary treaty with the Cherokees to validate a contract previously held to be illegal. The contract was modified, however, to permit settlers who resided upon the land in 1866 to purchase their tracts at the appraised value.[68] Joy was required to pay but $1.00 an acre and generous credit was allowed him, while the settlers were asked to pay an average of $1.92 per acre in cash.[69]

The second sale was an equally great violation of the principle of free homesteads, and, it should be noted, was ratified by the Senate the same year that the House resolution frowning upon the further sale of agricultural land was passed. Secretary Browning who, as Harlan's successor, had negotiated the sale, came in for as bitter accusations as had his predecessor and, it must be admitted, with some justification. The sale was made to his brother-in-law, Joy; his partner was at the time employed by Joy to negotiate the transaction; Browning himself had earlier represented Joy, and the following year was again retained by him in a series of important cases.[70] Furthermore, as was pointed out in a joint resolution adopted by the House on July 13, 1868,[71] the sale failed to consider the rights of a large number of people who had settled upon the tract between 1866 and 1868 and who were subsequently forced to purchase their lands from the railroad. Petitions from settlers upon the Cherokee tract demanding the abrogation of the sale poured in upon the Interior Department;[72] the governor of Kansas denounced the sale as "a cheat and a fraud in every particular, and should have been encircled with hell's blackest marks," a "gigantic swindle";[73] and in 1868 both the Republican and Democratic state conventions condemned the policy of disposing of Indian lands to "speculators and foreign corporations."[74] The campaign to have the second sale annulled was unsuccessful but, combined with the opposition to similar sales of Indian lands, it was eventually to end the policy.

Equally inconsiderate of the rights of settlers were the sales of the lands of the Delaware, Pottawatomie, Kickapoo, and Sac and Fox of the Mississippi Indians in Kansas. Treaties authorizing the sale of the surplus Delaware and Pottawatomie lands to the Leavenworth, Pawnee, and Western Railroad for $1.25 per acre were proclaimed on August 22, 1860, and April 19, 1862, respectively.[75] This railroad was unable to carry through the purchase of the Pottawatomie lands but did succeed in negotiating a sufficiently liberal contract for the Delaware lands whereby it acquired title to 223,966 acres of rich farming lands in Leavenworth, Atchison, and Jefferson counties for $286,742 paid in its own bonds, instead of cash as originally required.[76] In 1866, the Delaware Indians having decided to abandon their diminished reserve in Kansas, which had been allotted in severalty, accepted a second treaty which provided for the sale of the 92,598 acres contained in the reserve to the Missouri River Railroad for $2.50 per acre, exclusive of improvements, which were to be appraised and sold at a fair valuation.[77]

The Pottawatomie lands were subsequently sold, in 1868, to the Atchison, Topeka, and Santa Fe Railroad. This sale called for the payment of $1.00 per acre, not $1.25 as the earlier treaty provided, and five years' time was given during which no payments were required except advance interest of six percent annually upon the purchase sum. The government thus not only denied to settlers the right to acquire the land directly but gave the railroad company the use of 340,180 acres of rich agricultural lands for annual payments of $20,410 for five years. At the end of this time a payment of $340,180 was required, which could be paid in greenbacks.[78] The policy of making land sales to settlers on credit had been abandoned in 1820 and Congress had resisted all efforts to restore the credit system but credit was extended to railroads in the sixties. The Atchison, Topeka, and Santa Fe Railroad proceeded to sell the lands at prices well over double their cost, and charged seven percent interest on delayed payments. By 1873 it had received in cash and notes $646,784 and valued the remaining lands at $507,366,[79] no small profit for the times. A substantial part of the amount due the government in 1873 was paid from cash sales. The mortgage bonds based on these lands, obtained for only $20,410 down, enabled the railroad to begin construction without the promoters having to supply any capital of their own worth mentioning.

A treaty similar to that with the Pottawatomie Indians was concluded with the Kickapoo Indians under the terms of which 123,832 acres were sold in 1865 to the Atchison and Pike's Peak Railroad for $1.25 per acre, on generous credit.[80] This treaty was negotiated with a railroad whose president, Samuel C. Pomeroy, was not only senator from Kansas and thus in a position to support its adoption, but was also very close to the administration of the Indian Office and the Department of the Interior. Pomeroy represented the attitude of his state in demanding the speedy removal of the Indians and the disposal of their lands but he went against popular opinion in supporting the sale of the Cherokee, Delaware, Pottawatomie, Kickapoo, and Osage lands to railroads.

The sale of the Sac and Fox Indian lands differs somewhat from those previously mentioned. These lands, comprising 272,000 acres, were advertised for sale to the highest bidders but, unlike the public land auctions, the bids were to be submitted by letter. This of course had the effect of preventing settlers upon the lands from combining into a claims association and preventing outsiders from bidding as was done at the public auctions. As a result most of the land was acquired at low prices by speculators, among whom the largest buyers were John McManus,[81] William B. McKean, Fuller and McDonald, Robert S. Stevens, and the Hon. Hugh McCulloch who acquired respectively 142,915, 29,677, 39,058, 51,689, and 7014 acres.[82]

The treaty providing for the largest sale of Indian lands was negotiated in 1868 between the Osage Indians of Kansas and representatives of the Department of the Interior, according to which 8,000,000 acres of land were to be sold to the Leavenworth, Lawrence, and Galveston Railroad for $1,600,000.[83] This was at the rate of twenty cents an acre for lands to which settlers were eagerly looking for homes. Characterized by Governor Crawford as "one of the most infamous outrages ever before committed in this country," it was indeed a most disgraceful and unjustified action. If adopted it would have deprived the State of Kansas of 500,000 acres of school lands, robbed the Indians of a fair price for their lands, and would have killed a number of rival railroads, including the Atchison, Topeka, and Santa Fe. Worst of all, the treaty ignored the rights of settlers already on the lands. Furthermore, it was stated that a substantially higher bid had been turned down in order to accept that of the Leavenworth, Lawrence, and Galveston Railroad. The hand of James F. Joy was again seen, for the latter road had already come under his control as part of the great transportation system he was constructing. The Osage treaty brought to a climax the utter disregard shown by the officials of the Department of the Interior for the rights of settlers and aroused a storm of criticism, both in Kansas and in Washington.[84]

Representative George W. Julian, than whom no one had the interests of the homesteader more at heart, saw the iniquity in these Indian treaties and subsequent land sales to railroads and others. He introduced a resolution into the House of Representatives to the effect that these sales were a usurpation of power by the Senate which was endangering the entire land system and urged upon the Senate the advisability of ratifying no more such treaties. He pointed out that by using the treaty making power in this way it was possible for the Senate to transfer all the public lands to the Indians and then by other treaties to arrange for their sale to railroads or other speculative groups, thus completely frustrating the Homestead Law and subverting the land system. Julian succeeded in winning the support of the House for his view and the resolution was adopted.[85] The enactment of this resolution and the storm of criticism which rained upon the Senate apparently had some effect, for the treaty with the Osage Indians, although urgently supported by the Commissioner of Indian Affairs, was not ratified and Congress later provided for the sale of the Osage lands to actual settlers.

One may plainly see from events in Congress during 1867 and 1868 how insincere that body was in rendering lip service to the homestead principle. In this year Representative Julian introduced two measures into the House, the action on which throws a flood of light on the question. The first was a resolution that:

In order to carry into full and complete effect the spirit and policy of the preëmption and homestead laws of the United States, the further sale of the agricultural public lands ought to be prohibited by law and that all proposed grants of land to aid in construction of railroads, or for other special objects, should be carefully scrutinized and rigidly subordinated to the paramount purpose of securing homes for the landless poor, the actual settlement and tillage of the public domain, and the consequent increase of the national wealth.[86]

The second was a bill to prevent any further sale of the public lands except as provided for in the Pre-emption and Homestead laws.[87] In support of these measures Julian made a number of strong speeches in which he described the evils resulting from speculation in lands, showed that, except for the Southern states, free homesteading was restricted to the least attractive lands, and denounced the land monopoly which was rapidly being created by the lavish grants to the railroads. Julian was followed by two congressmen from Michigan districts in which lumbering was the chief industry. They favored large grants to railroads and no restrictions on land sales, and argued that Julian's bill, if passed, would ruin the lumber industry, increase speculation and fraudulent entries, and thus frustrate its own purpose.[88] Although unanimously reported by the Committee on Public Lands, nothing further was heard from the bill to end cash sales. The resolution, on the other hand, which had no binding effect but which favored exactly the same policy toward cash sales as the bill, passed the House without any important opposition.[89] Congress was far from ready in 1868 to end cash sales, and the passage of the resolution was certainly not "tantamount to a law." [90]

Between the enactment of this resolution in 1868 and 1876, the forces interested in opening up the public domain to large-scale purchases were fighting the advocates of the homestead principle on two grounds; they struggled to repeal the Act of 1866 which placed restrictions on cash sales in the South, and they tried to prevent further limitations on land engrossment in the West.

The discriminatory character of the restrictions upon cash sales in the South and its obviously punitive features rankled with the Southern congressmen who sought to repeal the act of 1866. They were vigorously supported by representatives from other sections who were either interested in the lumber industry themselves or whose constituents looked with longing eyes upon the rich pine lands of the South. In the early seventies the movement for repeal gained headway. Its leaders harped on the discriminatory features of the Act of 1866, its retarding effects upon immigration and the lumber industry, and argued that it led to the public lands being stripped of their only valuable commodity—timber. In 1875 the commissioner of the General Land Office came to the support of the repealists. Indeed, the land commissioners in their reports of 1875, 1876, and 1877 favored opening up all public lands to cash sale.[91] Strong opposition was voiced against the repeal measure by the Northern radicals for political purposes and by land reformers who foresaw the effects of such a backward step, but the combination of Southern resentment and Northern economic interests was too strong, and the measure became a law on July 4, 1876, without the approval of President Grant.[92] Southern lands were again made subject to cash entry, the unfortunate results of which have already been seen in the large-scale monopolization by lumber interests, mostly from the Northern states.

Although defeated in the South, the land reformers, under the leadership of Senator Harlan of Iowa and Representative Julian of Indiana, continued the fight to limit or end cash sales to large purchasers. In the House three measures were passed in 1870, one to end cash sales in California, another to end cash sales in Dakota Territory, and the third to prevent cash sales in Nebraska, Nevada, California, Arkansas, and Utah.[93] Similar measures were introduced in the Senate but were uniformly unsuccessful, because here the interests of lumber men, mining groups, and large speculators were well represented. In 1872 a congressman from California proposed an amendment to the Constitution which would have prohibited the further disposal of the public lands except to actual settlers but it made no progress.[94]

From the date of the repeal of the restrictions on cash entry in the South until 1889 there was not a session of Congress in which the question of reserving all the public lands for homestead entry was not fiercely debated. Continued efforts were made to end the cash sale system. Following 1880, the Pre-emption, Timber and Stone, Timber Culture, and Desert Land acts came in for much criticism since it was apparent that, like the commutation clause of the Homestead Law, they lent themselves to abuse and fraud. In the eighties the movement was given a great impetus by the discovery of enormous frauds in which foreign corporations and titled noblemen were engaged for the purpose of building up vast estates. The fact that most of this alien ownership was English [95] was used effectively by the Anglophobes and, added to the antimonopoly movement which was rapidly gaining in strength, it made easy the conversion of many politicians to the cause of land reform.

President Cleveland's land commissioner, William A. J. Sparks, dramatically brought the issue to the front by revealing with overwhelming evidence that "the public domain was being made the prey of unscrupulous speculation and the worst forms of land monopoly through systematic frauds carried on and consummated under the public land laws." [96] In cold, biting language, he accused the administration of the General Land Office of being either extraordinarily inept in its management or directly involved in the great frauds which he unearthed. So general were the illegal or fraudulent entries that within a month after his accession to office he suspended all final entries under the Timber and Stone Act and the Desert Land Act, and in Colorado, Dakota, Idaho, Utah, Washington, New Mexico, Montana, Wyoming, Nevada, and parts of Minnesota, Kansas, and Nebraska suspended all entries except those made with cash and scrip. The evidence of fraud continued to come in, and, as the demand for complete suspension of all non-homestead entries stimulated speculators and monopolists to feverish activity, Sparks in desperation, in 1886, ordered the land officers to accept no further applications for entries under the Pre-emption, Timber Culture, and Desert Land acts.[97] This precipitate action stirred up a veritable hornets' nest of opposition and the order was rescinded, but its effect remained.

The onslaught of the antimonopolists had the effect of stimulating the speculators, cattlemen, lumber and mining companies to prompt action before the public domain should be closed to them. Land sales and entries under the Pre-emption, Timber Culture, Timber and Stone, and Desert Land acts and the cash sale system shot up to a high point in 1888, exceeding those of any year since 1856 and being surpassed only four times in our entire history.

This enormous speculation, added to the widespread frauds which were being uncovered, produced a demand for reform which swelled to a tremendous volume. Hundreds of petitions with innumerable signatures flooded Congress urging changes in land policy and administration. They made it plain that public opinion had been aroused and could no longer be ignored.

Measure after measure providing for repeal of the objectionable laws passed the House in the eighties only to be defeated in the Senate. Finally, under the stimulus of Sparks's dramatic gesture, repeal measures passed both houses in 1886 and again in 1887, but were defeated through failure to harmonize conflicting views. These were to be the last defeats, however, because Congress was rapidly being forced into a position where it had to take action. In May and July, 1888, two measures were passed by which land sales in the five Southern states were temporarily suspended, and the Act of 1876 was reversed. This was followed, on March 2, 1889, by an act ending all cash sales of public lands except in Missouri where the remaining lands were mostly mineral in character or scattered fragments of little value for agriculture. In 1890 a rider was attached to an appropriation act by which it was stipulated that henceforth no person should acquire title to more than 320 acres in the aggregate under all of the land laws.[98] Finally, in 1891 a combination of antimonopoly land reformers and conservationists placed upon the statute books a law which was as far reaching, as important, perhaps, as the Homestead Act of 1862. This law [99] repealed the Pre-emption and Timber Culture acts and placed additional safeguards in the Desert Land Act and the commutation clause of the Homestead Act. Except for Indian lands and small isolated tracts the speculators could no longer purchase whole counties for the minimum price and land engrossment by fraudulent means was at least made more difficult. Unfortunately these land reforms were not enacted until the best of the area suitable for farming without irrigation had passed into private ownership.

The most important section of the Act of 1891 was that which authorized the creation of forest reservations on the public lands. Here was the first fundamental break with the underlying philosophy of our land system—the desire to dispose of the lands and hasten their settlement. The conservationists had now convinced the country that a part of our natural resources must be retained in public ownership and preserved for the future. Unfortunately, conservation, when first adopted, was embedded in an outworn laissez-faire land system of a previous age just as the free homestead plan had been superimposed upon a land system designed to produce revenue. In both cases the old and the new clashed with disastrous effects.

NOTES

1. The material for this article was gathered in part while the writer was Fellow of the Social Science Research Council in 1933 and 1934. Grateful acknowledgments are due to the Council and especially to Donald Young of its staff for many kindnesses. The article was completed while the writer was engaged in a study of Recent Land Policies of the United States for the Land Policy Section of the Agricultural Adjustment Administration, later the Resettlement Administration.

2. The word "speculator," as used in this article, refers to large-scale land operators, and does not include many farmers who speculated in a small way.

3. "Grazing Homesteads and the Regulation of Grazing on the Public Lands," *Hearing before the Committee on the Public Lands*, House of Representatives, 63 Cong., 2 sess., pt. 1, p. 358.

4. Leifur Magnusson, *Disposition of the Public Lands of the United States with Particular Reference to Wage-Earning-Labor* (Washington, 1919), p. 29. See also Arthur C. Cole, *The Irrepressible Conflict, 1850–1865* (New York, 1934), pp. 119, 357; John Ise, *The United States Forest Policy* (New Haven, 1920), p. 56.

5. Benjamin Horace Hibbard, *History of the Public Land Policies* (New York, 1924), pp. 111, 112.

6. The shallowness of this contention was pointed out by George W. Julian in 1884 (*Political Recollections, 1840 to 1872*, Chicago, 1884, p. 218). Speaking of the continuation of cash sales, railroad grants, and disposal of the Indian lands as fatal to the homestead principle, he said that they furnished "a remarkable commentary upon the boasted friendship of the Republican party for the landless poor."

7. In contrast, Herbert Heaton ventures the view that the importance of free land in drawing immigrants to America has been overestimated while the influence of high wages has been underestimated. "Migration and Cheap Land—the End of Two Chapters," *The Sociological Review*, XXVI (July, 1934), 237.

8. *Report*, 1863, p. 7. See also *Report*, Secretary of the Interior, 1862, p. 4.

9. 1884 edition, pp. 25, 415. It is worth noting that a total of 4,851,296 acres was entered in Michigan, Wisconsin, and Minnesota in the eighties with cash, scrip, and warrants. This is exclusive of pre-emption, homestead, and other limited entries.

10. These lands, which were being ceded by the Indians, are neglected by both Donaldson and Hibbard.

11. The more advanced reformers demanded that all sales should be discontinued, grants to railroads and other special interests ended, and all the public lands reserved for actual settlers under the provisions of the homestead measure. The differences between what may be called the moderate and the radical land reformers is apparent in the congressional debates. See also George M. Stephenson, *The Political History of the Public Lands from 1840 to 1862* (Boston, 1917), p. 166 and elsewhere; Roy M. Robbins, "Horace Greeley: Land Reform and Unemployment, 1837–1862," *Agricultural History*, VII (Jan., 1933), 26, *passim*; St. George L. Sioussat, "Andrew Johnson and the Early Phases of the Homestead Bill," *Mississippi Valley Historical Review*, V (Dec., 1918), 253, *passim*; Hibbard, p. 347, *passim*; John Bell Sanborn, "Some Political Aspects of Homestead Legislation," *Am. Hist. Rev.*, VI (Oct., 1900), 19, *passim*.

12. Speaking of the period from 1836 to 1876 Professor Joseph Schafer writes: "It was, in this period, a rare thing for an outside speculator in wild lands to make any profit on his speculation." *Wisconsin Magazine of History*, XIII (June, 1930), 428. See also his *The Wisconsin Lead Region, Wisconsin Domesday Book*, "General Studies," III (Madison, 1932), p. 153; *Wisconsin Domesday Book, Town Studies* (1924), I, 10.

13. Wm. A. J. Sparks, commissioner of the General Land Office, in his *Report* for 1885 (pp. 3–4), writes as follows concerning the administration of the land laws:

> I found that the magnificent estate of the nation in its public lands had been to a wide extent wasted under defective and improvident laws and through a laxity of public administration astonishing in a business sense if not culpable in recklessness of official responsibility.
>
> The widespread belief of the people of this country that the land department has been very largely conducted to the advantage of speculation and monopoly, private and corporate, rather than in the public interest, I have found supported by developments in every branch of the service. It seems that the prevailing idea running through this office

and those subordinate to it was that the government had no distinctive rights to be considered and no special interests to protect; hence, as between the government and spoilers of the public domain, the government usually had the worst of it. I am satisfied that thousands of claims without foundation in law or equity, involving millions of acres of public land, have been annually passed to patent upon the single proposition that nobody but the government had any *adverse* interest.

The vast machinery of the land department appears to have been devoted to the chief result of conveying the title of the United States to public lands upon fraudulent entries under strained constructions of imperfect public land laws and upon illegal claims under public and private grants.

14. Ise, *passim*, has drawn together and summarized the published information concerning the vast frauds committed by the lumber interests in their efforts to acquire great areas of timber lands. See also Jenks Cameron, *The Development of Governmental Forest Control in the United States* (Baltimore, 1928), *passim*.

15. The commissioners of the General Land Office from 1875 onward recommended annually the repeal of the Pre-emption Law; in 1883 the commissioner recommended the repeal of the commutation clause of the Homestead Law and the Timber Culture Act (*Report*, 1883, pp. 6–7); in 1884 the commissioner suggested the repeal of these laws and the Desert Land Act and the Timber and Stone Act. *Ibid.*, 1883, pp. 6–8. These documents are cited hereafter as G.L.O. *Report*.

16. Computed from Donaldson, pp. 258–273. The best criticism by a contemporary of the railroad land grant policy, is found in Henry George, *Our Land and Land Policy, National and State* (San Francisco, 1871). See also George W. Julian, "Railway Influence in the Land Office," *North American Review*, CXXXVI (Mar., 1883), 237–256, and his "Our Land-Grant Railways in Congress," *International Review*, XIV (Feb.-Mar., 1883), 198–212.

17. G.L.O. *Report*, 1885, pp. 26, *passim*. As late as 1883, twelve years after the last land grant was made to railroads, it was estimated that more than 100,000,000 acres were withdrawn from settlement pending selection of the railroad sections. Julian, N. *Am. Rev.*, CXXXVI, 252.

18. For large speculative purchases within the limits of the Illinois Central Railroad grant, see Paul Wallace Gates, *The Illinois Central Railroad and its Colonization Work* (Cambridge, 1934), pp. 107, 123 ff.

19. This provision was practically repealed by the acts of Mar. 3, 1879 (20 U.S. Stat., 472), July 1, 1879 (21 U.S. Stat., 46), and June 15, 1880 (*ibid.*, p. 238).

20. James B. Hedges, "The Colonization Work of the Northern Pacific Railroad," *Mississippi Valley Hist. Rev.*, XIII (Dec., 1926), 327; Harold E. Briggs, "Early Bonanza Farming in the Red River Valley of the North," *Agricultural History*, VI (Jan., 1932), 26, *passim*; Alva H. Benton, "Large Land Holdings in North Dakota," *Journal of Land and Public Utility Economics*, I (Oct., 1925), 405–413.

21. *Cong. Globe*, 41 Cong., 2 sess., p. 2095.

22. Donaldson, p. 272.

23. Lewis H. Haney, A *Congressional History of Railways in the United States* (Madison, 1910), II, 20–22; Stephenson, p. 122, n.

24. Computed from G.L.O. *Report*, 1932, pp. 45–50.

25. A total of 230,088,219 acres have been patented to the states of which

38,206,487 acres were given for railroads, 3,359,188 acres for wagon roads, and 6,842,921 acres for canals. Most of these special grants were quickly transferred to construction companies or disposed of by the states. The total also includes 7,672,800 acres in land scrip which was granted to the states in which there were no remaining public lands for the endowment of agricultural colleges. The scrip could not be located by the states and had to be sold promptly. Of the remaining lands granted, or which were subsequently granted to the states, it seems safe to say that at least 140,000,000 acres were still unsold to 1862.

26. U.S. Department of Commerce and Labor, Bureau of Corporations, *The Lumber Industry* (1913), pt. 1, p. 252.

27. Computed from reports of the land offices of the respective states.

28. To 1918.

29. G.L.O. *Report*, 1862, p. 8.

30. Volumes of "Proclamations for Public Land Sales," General Land Office; G.L.O. *Reports*, 1862 and following. It is true that 46,000,000 acres in the South were withdrawn from cash entry under the Act of June 21, 1866, but these lands were restored to sale in 1876 and during the interval the amount of land disposed of was small, amounting to only 2,000,000 acres by 1871. Computed from G.L.O. *Report*, 1871, p. 343.

31. Indian reservations and claims were not sharply defined in 1862, much of the area not having been surveyed. In 1875 the Commission of Indian Affairs (*Report*, 1875, p. 142) gave the acreage in Indian reservations as 165,729,714 acres. The amount of Indian lands sold directly to individuals and corporations and that sold through the General Land Office during the years 1862–1875 would bring this figure to 175,000,000 acres for 1862.

32. There is little available information on the Indian lands and their disposition, the most important published source being the *Annual Reports* of the Commissioners of Indian Affairs during the years after the Civil War.

33. 24 *U.S. Stat.*, 388; 34 *U.S. Stat.*, 182.

34. Recent addresses by John Collier, commissioner of Indian Affairs, and Senator William H. King have called attention to the alienation of Indian lands since the Allotment Act of 1887, but they have not been concerned with the previous crowding of the Indians on the reservations and the forced cession or sale of their surplus lands which antedated that act. See the speech of Senator King on "Condition of Indians in the United States," *Senate Document*, 72 Cong., 2 sess., no. 214. It is difficult to estimate the total amount of Indian land which was sold prior to 1887 and after 1862 but it would certainly bring the total Indian land sales since 1862 to over 100,000,000 acres.

35. The railroads have received 132,425,574 acres of land directly from the Federal government or from grants originally given to the states for railroad construction. *Report, Secretary of the Interior*, 1934, p. 73. This amount would be greatly augmented by grants made by the State of Texas from its public lands and by other states from the swamp lands received from the Federal government, and also by the lands purchased by railroads from the Indians. As used here only the 132,425,574 acres are considered. Only a small part of this vast area was sold prior to 1862. Not all of it was available for sale even by 1871 but this total represents all the land which the railroads received from congressional land grants.

36. Pamphlet: *Two Thousand Families Wanted For Iowa*, n.d., n.p.

37. Letterhead of letter of W. C. Fitzsimmons, a member of the firm,

July 15, 1871, to E. S. Parker, commissioner of Indian Affairs, file of material on Indian land sales, Indian Office.

38. In June, 1870, Walker was advertising 10,000 acres of Kansas land for sale (Leavenworth *Bulletin*, June 13, 1870), while in February, 1871, he was advertising 100,000 acres for sale (*ibid.*, Feb. 7, 1871). Thaddeus H. Walker of Topeka, Kansas, formerly of Washington County, New York, had entered in 1855 to 1859 in the Kickapoo, Kansas, Land District 16,000 acres, 46,000 acres in the Lecompton, Kansas, Land District, 14,000 acres in the Junction City, Kansas, Land District, and 4600 acres in the Decorah, Iowa, Land District. The lands were entered mostly with military land warrants. See the abstract and entry books of the above-mentioned land districts in the General Land Office.

39. The advertisements appeared in the *Kansas Farmer*, the Leavenworth *Bulletin*, the Lawrence *Republican Daily Journal*, the *Cultivator and Country Gentleman*, and the *American Agriculturist*.

40. *Biennial Report*, Auditor of State, Kansas, 1882, pp. 359–360.

41. Compiled from *Annual Reports* of the Atchison, Topeka, and Santa Fe Railroad, 1873–1880.

42. 10 *U.S. Stat.*, 701–702. It should be pointed out that prior to the adoption of the prospective pre-emption principle public lands were not subject to disposal until they had been surveyed and offered at public auction. Lands then remaining unsold were subject to private entry for cash, scrip, or warrants. After prospective pre-emption was adopted settlers could make claims upon surveyed but unoffered lands, thus preceding the speculators. When the homestead idea was being debated its advocates argued that its effects would be largely mitigated unless all lands were withdrawn from speculative entry upon its passage. Such a radical proposal was too much for many homestead advocates and it failed of serious consideration. Nevertheless, it was expected by many people that no additional lands would be offered at auction after 1862 and therefore the area open to private entry would become progressively smaller as time passed. Unfortunately, additional land was put up at auction in the sixties, seventies, and eighties, thus increasing the areas open to speculative and large-scale entries. At the same time land was being opened to homestead and pre-emption entry which was not offered at auction and therefore not subject to private entry for cash, scrip, or warrants.

43. G.L.O. *Report*, 1862, p. 9. In 1862 there were 7,123,380 acres of military warrants outstanding.

44. 12 *U.S. Stat.*, 503–505; "Report of the Public Lands Commission," 1905, *Sen. Doc.*, 58 Cong., 3 sess., no. 189, p. 361.

45. Of course the Southern states did not receive their scrip until after the Civil War but it took some time for the Land Office to handle the details involved in issuing it and consequently most of it was located between 1864 and 1868. The price which each state received for the sale of its scrip is given in *History of the Agricultural College Land Grant of July 2, 1862, together with a Statement of the Conditions of the Fund derived therefrom as it now exists in each State of the Union* (Ithaca, 1890), pp. xvi, xvii.

46. G.L.O. *Report*, 1875, p. 69; *Public Land Statutes of the United States*, Daniel M. Greene, compiler (Washington, 1931), pp. 637–639.

47. These land entries were compiled from hundreds of volumes of abstracts in the General Land Office, Department of the Interior, Washington, the listing of which would be almost impossible and equally futile. Following are the chief types of entry books: Abstracts of Lands Entered (for cash),

Military Warrant Abstracts, Agricultural College Scrip Abstracts, Indian and other miscellaneous scrip abstracts, and Registers of Receipts.

48. See C. F. Taylor, ed., *The Land Question from Various Points of View* (Philadelphia, 1898), pp. 44, *passim.*

49. The land empire of Henry W. Sage alone is said by a local historian to have included over 500,000 acres. John H. Selkreg, ed., *Landmarks of Tompkins County, New York* (Syracuse, 1894), pt. 2, p. 4.

50. Walker acquired 700,000 acres of valuable sugar pine and western pine timber land in California, chiefly through the use of dummy entrymen. Bureau of Corporations, *The Lumber Industry*, pt. 2, p. 91.

51. "Report of the Public Lands Commission," 1905, *op. cit.*, p. 140.

52. G.L.O. *Reports*, 1862–1880.

53. G.L.O. *Report*, 1932, p. 46.

54. There is a mass of testimony offered to prove these charges in *Reports of the Joint Committees on Swamp and Overflowed Lands, and Land Monopoly*, presented at the Twentieth Session of the Legislature of California (Sacramento, 1874).

55. Edward F. Treadwell, *The Cattle King* (New York, 1931), p. 73.

56. The story of Henry Miller is interestingly told in Treadwell, *op. cit.* A more detailed and objective study of the land and cattle business of Miller and Lux would shed much light on the history of the Far West.

57. *Eleventh Census*, 1890, "Statistics of Agriculture," p. 4. There is some detail on the relation of land policy and farm tenancy in an article by the present writer on "Recent Land Policies of the Federal Government" which is to appear in part VII of the Supplementary Report of the Land Planning Committee to the National Resources Board, entitled "Certain Aspects of Land Problems and Governmental Land Policies."

58. Act of June 21, 1866, 14 *U.S. Stat.*, 66–67.

59. *Cong. Globe*, 39 Cong., 1 sess., pp. 715 ff.; p. 2736.

60. *Ibid.*, pp. 2193, 2218, 2219, 2303, 2965, 2966.

61. Message of June 15, 1866, *Senate Journal*, 39 Cong., 1 sess., p. 532.

62. *Ibid.*, 41 Cong., 2 sess., pp. 3659–3670, 4543–4546.

63. These treaties are included in *United States Statutes-at-Large*, vols. XII, XIII, XIV. They are analyzed and the areas conveyed by them are pictured on maps in Charles C. Royce, *Indian Land Sessions in the United States* (Eighteenth Annual Report of the Bureau of American Ethnology to the Secretary of the Smithsonian Institution, 1896–1897), pt. 2.

64. 14 *U.S. Stat.*, 799–809.

65. The sale of 18,000 acres of "swamp lands" in Wright County, Iowa, to the American Emigrant Company for $1500 and the subsequent recovery of a portion of the land is described by W. J. Covil in the Webster City *Freeman-Tribune*, July 13, 1904, republished in *Annals of Iowa*, 3d ser., VII (1905), 360.

66. Governor S. J. Crawford, Topeka, Kansas, Aug. 19, 1867, to Secretary Browning, file of material on Indian land sales, Indian Office.

67. P. A. Ladue, St. Louis, Missouri, Jan. 19, 1867, to L. C. Bogy, commissioner of Indian Affairs, *ibid.*

68. The sale of the Cherokee lands is discussed in a letter of Charles Mix, acting commissioner of Indian Affairs, Apr. 21, 1869, to J. D. Cox, secretary of the Interior, Cherokee File, Indian Office. Secretary Harlan's interpretation of the sale may be read in *Cong. Globe*, 40 Cong., 3 sess., pp. 409 ff., and 41 Cong., 1 sess., pp. 21–23; also in Johnson Brigham, *James Harlan* (Iowa City,

1913), pp. 235 ff. See also Eugene F. Ware, "The Neutral Lands," Kansas State Historical Society, *Transactions*, VI (1900), 147–169.

69. *Report*, Commissioner of Indian Affairs, 1869, p. 502.

70. Theodore Calvin Pease and James G. Randall, eds., *Diary of Orville Hickman Browning* (Illinois State Historical Library, *Collections*, vols. XX, XXII, 1925–1933), I, 645–646; II, 219, 239, 257, 276, *passim*.

71. *Cong. Globe*, 40 Cong., 2 sess., pp. 4000–4001.

72. These petitions are filed in the Indian Office, Cherokee File.

73. Samuel J. Crawford, *Kansas in the Sixties* (Chicago, 1911), p. 310. Crawford, as governor, took an active part in the campaign to end the sale of large tracts of Indian lands to railroads and other speculative groups. Aside from his interest in the settlers who were being deprived of the right of buying their holdings directly from the government he opposed the Indian land policy on the ground that it deprived the state of the 16th and 32d sections which it would otherwise get for its public schools.

74. D. W. Wilder, *Annals of Kansas* (Topeka, 1886), pp. 481, *passim*. In this book are found a number of items indicating the emotions which were aroused in the settlers of the Cherokee tract by the arbitrary sale of the lands.

75. 12 *U.S. Stat.*, 1129, 1193. This railroad later became the Union Pacific Railway Company, Eastern Division, and still later the Kansas Pacific Railroad.

76. *Ibid.*, p. 1177.

77. 14 *U.S. Stat.*, 793–794; O. H. Browning, Secretary of the Interior, Oct. 21, 1867, to C. E. Mix, Commissioner of Indian Affairs, Delaware Files, Indian Office.

78. 15 *U.S. Stat.*, 535–536; *Report*, Commissioner of Indian Affairs, 1869, p. 504.

79. *Report*, Atchison, Topeka, and Santa Fe Railroad, 1873, p. 10. It is true that in later reports the meager data given indicate the estimate of return contained in the *Report* for 1873 as somewhat optimistic.

80. 13 *U.S. Stat.*, 623 ff.; *Cong. Globe*, 40 Cong., 2 sess., p. 1715; Royce, *passim*.

81. John McManus, of Reading, Pennsylvania, was a director of the Kansas Pacific Railway Company which had the largest land grant in Kansas. *Report*, Kansas Pacific Railway Co., 1870.

82. *Report*, Commissioner of Indian Affairs, 1865, p. 549 ff. See also speech of Representative Julian in *Cong. Globe*, 40 Cong., 2 sess., p. 1715.

83. *Report*, Commissioner of Indian Affairs, 1868, p. 5.

84. Crawford, pp. 299 ff.

85. *Cong. Globe*, 40 Cong., 2 sess., pp. 2753, 2814, 3278–3279.

86. *Ibid.*, p. 97.

87. *Ibid.*, p. 371.

88. *Ibid.*, pp. 1712–1715, 2380–2387.

89. *Ibid.*, p. 1861.

90. See p. 653 of this article.

91. *Cong. Globe*, 41 Cong., 3 sess., pp. 539–540; *Cong. Record*, 43 Cong., 1 sess., pp. 4633, *passim*; 44 Cong., 1 sess., pp. 815 ff., 1090, 3655. G.L.O. *Report*, 1875, pp. 8–9, 17–19; 1876, p. 7; 1877, p. 34.

92. *Cong. Record*, 44 Cong., 1 sess., p. 4469; 19 *U.S. Stat.*, 73–74. The debates on the repeal measure are discussed in Ise, pp. 49–53.

93. *Cong. Globe*, 41 Cong., 2 sess., pp. 738–739, 5129.

94. *Cong. Globe*, 42 Cong., 3 sess., p. 84.

95. In 1884 the Senate called for an investigation of the foreign land holdings and the resulting report contains some interesting information on the practices and holdings of a number of well-financed British land and cattle companies. See *Sen. Doc.*, 48 Cong., 1 sess., no. 181.

96. G.L.O. *Report*, 1885, p. 48.

97. *Report*, 1886, p. 43, 135.

98. 25 *U.S. Stat.*, 622, 626; 854–855; 26 *U.S. Stat.*, 371, 391.

99. 26 *U.S. Stat.*, 1095–1103.

A COMPARATIVE ANALYSIS OF ECONOMIC DEVELOPMENT IN THE AMERICAN WEST AND SOUTH *

Douglas F. Dowd

I

In 1930, the West—for present purposes, Kansas, Nebraska, the Dakotas, Montana, Idaho, Wyoming, Utah, and Colorado—had a level of per capita income payments that stood at 79 percent of the national figure. In that same year, the figure for the South—Kentucky, Tennessee, Virginia, the Carolinas, Georgia, Florida, Alabama, Mississippi, Louisiana, and Arkansas—was 51 percent.[1]

This West was part of what used to be called the Great American Desert. The South, physically, has been thought of since the beginning as "the garden spot of America." Although it is not true that the West is a desert, nor the South a garden spot, the South has the better resources—in the combined terms of soils, waterways, climate, terrain, minerals, timber—and, of course, a much more abundant labor supply. And yet, the economic development of the West surpassed that of the South, using almost any criteria of economic development.

Because of the divergent characteristics of past economic developments in the West and the South, using the time period 1865–1930,

Reprinted by permission from *The Journal of Economic History*, XVI, No. 4 (December, 1956), 558–74.

* The author expresses his gratitude to John A. Brittain, A. E. Kahn, Emmett Rice, and Peter Vukasin, his colleagues at Cornell University, for their very helpful and stimulating criticisms of this study while it was in process.

their comparative treatment may enable us to tighten up our notion of the meaning of "underdevelopment," and extend our understanding of the process of development by illuminating those aspects of the developmental process that are fundamental and those that are incidental, either as obstacles or stimuli. There will be no pretense here of uncovering new data; rather, I shall attempt to reorganize what is well known.

Unintentionally, a by-product of this analysis will appear as a repudiation of the theme of these meetings. For, taking the development of the West at any time, and through time, it is difficult to conceive of it as being, in any acceptable sense, an underdeveloped region. Up until 1930, at least, quite the contrary is true of the South.

The argument here will be a familiar one, which nonetheless requires continuous reiteration, and which certainly can stand further substantiation: namely, that the core of the developmental problem is institutional.[2] This is not to overlook the obvious fact that resources, natural and human, must be obtainable if things are to be produced. But the mere presence of a "good" resource base does not insure economic development, as witness the difference between Russia and the Soviet Union; and the presence of a relatively "poor" resource base does not preclude substantial achievements in production, per capita income, health, education, and the whole run of other advantages associated with development, as witness, say, Japan. This is merely another way of saying that the nature and the extent of resources are of course meaningless apart from the social context within which they exist. And it is differences in social context that so strikingly set apart the West from the South.

The social context, in the West, was such that its resources were exploited rapidly and successfully (ignoring conservation criteria), and apparently close to their potential, given time and circumstance. The South, with a markedly better and more diversified resource base, lagged miserably, not only behind the nation as a whole, but also well behind the West. The basic reason for these disparate, and on resource grounds unintelligible, developments is that western development was *ancillary* to that taking place to the east of it; that the physical differences between West and East were, Webb's "institutional fault" to the contrary notwithstanding,[3] unmatched so far as key institutions *affecting development* were concerned. In the last analysis, the economic development of the West cannot be looked upon as a regional development; it is the physical extension of dynamic developments taking place to the east and overseas.

The South, on the other hand, was *not* an extension, or, in an important sense, even a part of an industrializing America. The South was one of America's colonies; it was, as Cash has put it, "another land, sharply differentiated from the rest of the American nation, and exhibiting within itself a remarkable homogeneity." It is the component parts of that "homogeneity" that deserve extended treatment, for they were antithetical to healthy, sustained economic development. If, as seems to be true, the South is currently engaged in a process of rapid economic growth, it is precisely because its "homogeneity" is crumbling, largely under the combined impact of two world wars, a major depression and a long world-wide boom.

II

Out of the hubbub over underdeveloped areas that has sounded for the last decade or two, we should be in a position to state simply the major defining characteristics of such areas, in terms of quantity, quality, and process. Quantitatively, underdevelopment is expressible in terms of per capita income, the degree of surplus (savings and investment), levels and patterns of consumption and investment, and productivity; in measures of health, education, etc., where the bias is heavily toward lowness and inadequacy. Qualitatively, the underdeveloped society exhibits a structure of production, ownership, and control which, taken together with thin and shallow markets, and an absence of adequate financial institutions and the factors making for external economies, combines to keep the quantitative achievements of the society at a low level. Often there is an associated population problem that holds back growth and wipes out gains. In terms of process, the underdeveloped society is one that is spinning its wheels in the mud; which, to use the more common metaphor, is revolving slowly and helplessly within a series of intertwined vicious circles.

Did the American West fit this definition? Of course not. We may note that the productive structure of the West has been dominated by primary production; that much of the ownership (particularly in railroads, mining, cattle, and timber) was nonwestern; that Westerners were faced with unfavorable terms of trade in their dealings with the more powerful East; that the per capita income of Westerners throughout our period and to this date is lower than that of those to the east of them above the Mason and Dixon line, and lower than those in the Far West. These and other particular characteristics often associated with underdevelopment may be found in the West. What *cannot* be found is the over-all quality of underdevelopment: the matrix of inhibiting institutional relationships is almost totally absent. The West, from its inception as a settled area, was possessed of vitality; it continually changed and expanded.[4]

The West was settled and exploited in a series of *booms*: railroad booms, cattle booms, farming booms, mining and timber booms. These booms were in time followed by the rise of commercial and financial nuclei, and by the growth of secondary industries. That much of the profitability of the booms may have drained out to eastern (and some foreign) owners is true, but because the West was an integral part of the society to which the largest part of it went, the drain did not have a long-run negative impact on development possibilities, although it did affect the distribution of income as between West and East.

In its critical period of development, the thirty years or so following the Civil War, the West was of course subjected to falling prices for its goods—as was the rest of the nation, and the rest of the world. As is well known, price drops were a consequence of newly opened food lands, and a connected rapid improvement in technology, transportation, and communications. Western resources were exploited ruthlessly and often stupidly, as were western miners, farm workers, and loggers; and many western farmers sank into tenancy or were pushed out of farming. But through it all western production and productivity grew, so much so as to provide simultaneously a rising level and improving quality of life for Westerners, cheap food and raw materials for the rest of the country, and a surplus of foodstuffs that played a crucial role in our balance of payments.

In brief, the West was never a region faced with a development *problem*. It developed as an outcome of the needs of the rest of the nation, and out of its inherent possibilities as an area empty of people (except the easily brushed-aside Indians), and relatively well equipped with natural resources. Extravagant and some not so extravagant hopes pulled people and capital out of the regions of the East and from Europe—both on the make, the people ambitious and relatively flexible, the capital speculative and always forthcoming, albeit at high rates.

The story of the impact of technology on western farming has been told frequently and well. The point of it, for present purposes, is that the West was quick to adopt relevant new techniques on a general scale.[5] If settlement was to take place in the West, it had to take place with a more capital-intensive agriculture than had existed in the regions to the east and south. Fencing and barbed wire, deep wells and windmills, seeds and agricultural science; all had to be experimented with if the Plains were to be cultivated. Given the climate and soils, a labor-extensive agriculture had to be practiced, and cultivation had to be mechanized. The needs were faced, the technical problems were solved, and settlement rapidly followed the solutions. What is true of agriculture—the necessity of adopting new techniques—is true of cattle raising, of mining, and of timber exploitation, though fewer people and therefore less drama were involved. This was an area that innovated quickly and extensively, held back only briefly by preconceived notions, driven on by a "boomer" optimism and a materialistic social philosophy.

Puritanism in Kansas and Mormonism in Utah, to mention the most striking cases, combined religion and economics to promote rapid development. For the region as a whole, it is clear that the social outlook of the people was completely in harmony with sustained economic growth, particularly with the prodding of an East and a world hungry for raw materials and food. Though we may deplore wheat cultivation in lands better suited to grazing, though many "busted" in Kansas and points west and north, though we may muse on the ultimate meaning of wasted mineral and timber resources, we cannot argue, at this point in our history, that economic growth was sickly, or its results unfortunate, in the West.

Perhaps it was the relatively lower levels of income in the West that led to the notion that it was underdeveloped. Perhaps it is the still wide-open spaces. But if underdevelopment is to have any serious meaning, that meaning must lie in the realm of comparing actual with potential. Looking back at the West, it is hard to imagine how, given the technology and markets of the period 1865–1930, much more could have been made of the area.

III

The West remained empty until its resources could fit the needs of the vigorous East. As such, vested interests and inhibiting forms of economic and social organization were absent. There were no significant institutional obstacles to the maximum development of western resources. And when settled, the West was thinly settled, by people whose eyes were fixed on the main chance.

The South, of course, stands in sharp contrast. As the southern region moved through time, it developed a set of institutions and accompanying attitudes which, intensified by the shock and chaos flowing from the Civil War, produced a formidable barrier to the achievement of rational economic organization. At the terminal year of this study, 1930, the South presented an almost classic picture of an underdeveloped society.[6]

Per capita income in the South in 1929 was $365, the lowest of any region in the nation—about 60 percent of the West's, and about 39 percent of the Far West's. Illiteracy rates for the eleven southern states were among the highest fourteen in the country (the other three were in the Southwest); the nine western states (with the exception of Colorado) ranked among the twelve lowest in illiteracy. Estimated tangible wealth per capita in the South did not rise above $2,000 for any state in 1930; no state in the West fell below $3,000. Value added per wage earner in the South in 1929 was 60 percent of that in the West. With 40 percent of the nation's farms in 1930, the South had 56 percent of the nation's tenants. With a sixth of all the nation's croplands, in 1929, the eroded lands of the South used two thirds of the fertilizer used in the nation; with a fifth of the agricultural income, the South paid three fifths of the nation's fertilizer bill. The South ranked lowest in terms of health, with a particularly high incidence of diseases associated with malnutrition and poverty, such as pellagra and tuberculosis. Malaria alone was estimated as late as 1938 to have reduced the industrial output of the South by one third.[7] And so on, with other measures of underdevelopment. These were the "fruits" of the southern industrialization process up to 1930.

"The nation's No. 1 economic problem," as Roosevelt called the South in 1938, was also the nation's No. 1 political problem, and, of course, the nation's No. 1 social problem. All grew from the same core of institutions; and these, in combination, retarded and stultified southern development. What was that core?

It consisted of three elements: cash crop monoculture, the plantation system, and Negro slavery. All these elements were present in some degree in the colonial period, when the major crops were tobacco, rice, and indigo. But during the colonial period, and for a generation or so after independence, the South possessed a relatively diversified economy. Its peak in diversification—in agriculture and industry—was probably reached between 1810 and 1820.[8] With the cotton gin, cotton could not but become king. King Cotton brought about the decay of small manufactures and what diversification there had been in agriculture, and ineluctably eliminated meaningful protests against slavery.[9]

Negro slavery and the plantation became simultaneously the roots from which stemmed the economic, social, and political life of the South. The planter naturally took over the best lands, whether for cotton, rice, sugarcane, or tobacco, and the small farmer was squeezed into the pine barrens, the hills, or out of the South. If he stayed in the South, the onetime small farmer might become a planter's overseer, or he might, rarely, become a planter himself. Most likely, he added to the ever-growing poor white group. There was no place else to go for most whites but down, or out.

As the American version of the *latifundia*, plantations were the ganglia of the southern economy. The plantation did its own marketing and buying (operating through the factor, the commercial and financial representative of nonsouthern interests), often produced, and always distributed the goods needed for all people and functions on the plantation. The growth of a middle class was thus stunted. There was, of course, no wage system on the plantation. Nor was there much work to be had for those off the plantation. The Negro did the agricultural work on the plantation, and he was also the skilled and unskilled artisan on and off the plantation.

As is well known, the plantation was only formally disrupted by the southern defeat in the war. Large-scale ownership remained the dominant characteristic; what changed was the identity of the owner. Increasingly, after the Civil War, the owner was absentee in location, northern in origin, and a commission house or banker in function. But the abolition of slavery required that a new means of getting the work done be found.

The attempt was made, in the first two years or so following the War, to utilize the freedmen on a free, wage-labor basis, but it miscarried. The freedmen, logically enough, could not be counted on to be around at the critical harvest time, voluntarily. Neither they, nor their poor white brethren, possessed land or tools or seed, and the planters wanted a guaranteed labor force. By 1867 the sharecropping and tenancy system began to spread rapidly throughout the South, as a natural and easy outgrowth of the combined needs of the propertied and propertyless. "Guarantees" for labor were provided by the commercial and financial system that grew up simultaneously with cropping and tenancy: the furnishing and supply system, and the crop lien.[10] Once begun, there was no turning back, for cropper, tenant, planter, merchant, or creditor (where the latter three were often two, and sometimes one).

The differences between the plantation-cum-slavery system of the ante-bellum South and the system just described were that the Negroes were now debt slaves, or peons, rather than chattel slaves, and probably lived less well; the growing class of poor whites, who had at least not been enslaved before the War, now joined the Negroes, and in numbers ultimately outstripped them. Of the approximately 1,800,000 tenants (including croppers) in the cotton belt in 1930, over 1 million were white, slightly under 700,000 were colored.[11]

The furnishing and supply system extended credit to cropper, tenant, and planter, for guano, food, and, for those who could afford them, clothes and other articles.[12] Money rarely changed hands, and indebtedness was permanent and growing. Foreclosures, which were frequent (and unpublicized), changed the form but not the functioning or the results of the system, which was highly exploitative. Illiterate and ignorant Negroes and poor whites had neither the information nor the power to recognize or demand honest bookkeeping. Even with honesty—and there appears to have been some—the risks for the lender were high, and interest rates were accordingly oppressive, often running between 40 and 80 percent per annum. With poor techniques, low productivity, mined soil, and high fertilizer costs, with continually fluctuating and secularly falling prices for their crops, the agriculturalists in the South (often including the planter) fell ever more hopelessly into a vicious downward spiral: deadening commitment to the cash crop, rising costs, falling prices, increasing indebtedness, poverty and, for most, peonage. The movement toward the deconcentration of land ownership after the Civil War was reversed. By 1930, it is estimated that 30 percent of cotton lands were owned by insurance companies and banks.[13]

Apart from the legal commitment to the cash crop required in the crop-lien contract, the Southerner was in any event unable to diversify. Away from the rivers, the road system, if the lack of roads may be called a system, prevented the marketing of anything but the cash crop, which did not perish with time and heat. And had there been roads, there were no marketing arrangements. Add to it all the lack of substantial opportunities in secondary and tertiary industry even during the "industrial revolution in the South," and the highest rate of population growth in the nation, the South found itself in the familiar pattern of overcrowding on the land, fragmentation, increasing pressures, and rural idleness. By the 1880's the social situation in the South had become explosive.

IV

Railroads, mines, and mills had of course existed in the South before the 1880's and they had been profitable. But around 1880 there began a rapid expansion of all three, at a rate that was unprecedented for the South. The "industrial revolution" in the South was given its impetus by many factors, including eager capital from the North and from England, and the favorable location of raw materials and power sources, but the most important were the tinderbox social situation and a large, unused labor pool. The latter made it possible for wages to be kept low and hours long, and the former made it imperative that some outlets for the labor of impoverished poor whites be found. The two were of course but different sides of the same coin.

Railroad mileage more than doubled in the South in the 1880's. The public lands were thrown open for sale for a decade or so after 1877, and were swallowed up almost completely in vast tracts by predominantly nonsouthern railroad and timber interests.[14] Pig iron production in the Birmingham area rose by seventeen times in the space of twenty-five years, and coal mining expanded in rhythm. Tobacco processing and cigarette manufacturing became a big business, particularly in North Carolina, and, of course, it was in the 1880's that the southern cotton mills began their spectacular rise.[15]

In 1870 there were 151 cotton mills in the South, in 1880 there were 161, in 1890 there were 239, and by 1900 there were 401 mills. In that period, capital invested had risen from $11.1 millions to $124.6 millions; the cotton processed had risen from about 34 million pounds to about 708 million pounds, and the number of factory operatives had risen from a little over 10 thousand to almost 98 thousand. By 1930 there were 280,000 cotton-mill workers, and the South had over half the active spindles in the country.[16] The associated cottonseed oil industry also grew rapidly, immediately stimulated by the great need for fertilizers in the area; ultimately to be used for oleomargarine and other products. As time went on, the

South's great forest resources were to be turned to furniture-making and paper products, and its phosphates, zinc, and bauxite were to be actively exploited.

Surely this growth defies the notion that the South remained underdeveloped, throughout the period under examination? Not at all. For the quality of the development, the control over it, and its consequences cannot be said to have benefited or affected the majority of the people, nor to have furnished a basis for a sustained process of expansion. In 1930 only 19.6 percent of Southern employment was in manufacturing and mechanical occupations, and one third of this was in the cotton mills.[17]

Listen to Cash, a Southerner, as he tells us of the benefits to the mill worker of his new-found job:

By 1900 the cotton-mill worker was a pretty distinct physical type in the South; a type in some respects perhaps inferior to even that of the old poor white, which in general had been his to begin with. A dead-white skin, a sunken chest, and stooping shoulders were the earmarks of the breed. Chinless faces, microcephalic foreheads, rabbit teeth, goggling dead-fish eyes, rickety limbs, and stunted bodies abounded— over and beyond the limit of their prevalence in the countryside. The women were characteristically stringy-haired and limp of breast at twenty, and shrunken hags at thirty or forty. And the incidence of tuberculosis, of insanity and epilepsy, and, above all, of pellagra, the curious vitamin-deficiency disease which is nearly peculiar to the South, was increasing.[18]

We may doubt that the cephalic index or the shape of the Southerner's chin had changed within a few generations, but the general picture was still valid as late as the 1930's in and around the mill towns.

Of all the industrial workers the southern cotton-mill workers were perhaps the worst off, and the source of the greatest profits to southern and northern owners. It can scarcely be argued that the New England mill worker was well off; but it was the even greater exploitation of the mill worker in the South that acted as the most important justification of the new location of cotton textile mills. And this may be expressed in terms of lower wages and longer working days, and the extensive use of child labor.

In 1900 the average wages of cotton-mill workers in the South were about half of those in New England; in 1927, average weekly earnings in the five leading New England states were still 47.8 percent higher than those in the five leading southern states. In

1900 the work week in the South was sixty-eight to seventy-two hours; in New England, it was fifty-six to fifty-eight.[19] Children labored for from twelve to fourteen hours a day, and in the poor-white family all able-bodied children worked. Without the work of the entire family, wages were insufficient for subsistence. And, if it be thought that the cost of living was lower in the South than in New England, and this seems to be the generally accepted notion, it is at least startling to read that a National Industrial Conference Board study of the cost of living in 1919 and 1920 found that the higher cost of food, clothing, and sundries in the South offset the lower cost of shelter, so that it cost a southern family anywhere from one to three hundred dollars more a year to live, in the towns studied (Fall River and Lawrence, Mass., and Greenville and Pelzer, South Carolina and Charlotte, North Carolina).[20] Perhaps these figures are deceptive, because of the years or the manner in which they were gathered, but at worst they argue against any clear-cut lower cost of living in the South.

How was the poor white held in the thralldom of low wages, long hours, miserable health, illiteracy, and the gamut of conditions that led him to be called "trash"? By several factors: the always great abundance of labor; the fact that he had been lifted from the brink of starvation to a position perhaps an inch or two removed; the fact that life in the mill town was in its basic essentials a continuation of plantation life, with not only the exploitation but the paternalism thereby implied; and by the "race issue." The conditions of the mill worker were matched by those of his farming counterpart, and by a comparable situation for the entire South, which was an economic colony of the North.

Some have been tempted to compare the "industrial revolution" in the South with the industrial revolution in England. The differences are so great, however, that it is doubtful that the term can be applied sensibly to what took place in the South. The process in England was dynamic and pervasive, ultimately bringing forth an economy widely diversified in its production. Industrial England had arisen from a previously advanced commercial, financial, and efficient agricultural nation.

Compare the South. There a transition was made from a virtually one-crop agrarian economy to a virtually one-product industry embedded in a still heavily agrarian, backward society. Cotton textile production in England was but one step, and not the first step, in a long series, the upshot of which was to make England the industrial, political, financial, and military leader of the world. The South's industrial development was as lopsided as its agrarian development. The South did not become less, but more heavily dependent on outside capital. It did not develop a modern political system, but continued, even worsened, the nature and structure of political control of the ante-bellum period—minus whatever dignity might have been found in the earlier period. The South did not develop an empire on the basis of new-found strength; it became even more a colony of the North than it had been before the Civil War. Apart from its internal politics, the political position of the South in the nation was down, not up, from the earlier period. And so on.

How can all this be explained? I have already argued that the three elements of the southern past that were decisive in its development after the Civil War were cotton monoculture, the plantation, and Negro slavery. Here I believe it is necessary to bring the role of the Negro in the South more sharply into focus. For after all else is said, it was the treatment of the Negro, and his numbers, that led all in the South—whether powerful or weak—to behave in such a fashion that the South could not emerge from its economically desperate situation—until sucked out of its isolation by unprecedentedly powerful national and international developments.

V

What has been the role of the Negro in the South? Simply this: he was the basis of the southern labor system before the Civil War; he was, taken together with the land he worked, the wealth of that same South; owning him was the basis of the social prestige of the southern aristocracy; and the Negro's existence, last but by no means least, enabled the poor white to feel somehow elevated. The Negro slave was the depth below the depth. After the Civil War, the freedman remained the rock on which the white's respectability was based. But the Negro was also part of the enormous agricultural and industrial labor pool in the South. As such, the economic competition of Negro and white kept both impoverished, and ate away at the poor white's illusions of respectability—thereby intensifying the race issue.

The Emancipation Proclamation transformed the legal status of the Negro, without bringing in its wake a lasting change in the substantive economic, political, and social life of the overwhelming majority of the Negroes. Indeed, it has been the attempts of whites to prevent such substantive changes that have given the Negro question its importance in southern life, and have been so important in conditioning the entire quality of southern development.

The profits of southern industry were dependent upon cheap and abundant labor. The self-respect of the mass of southern whites was dependent, to a critical degree, upon the existence of the underprivileged and oppressed position of the Negro. The power of southern business and political leaders rested on the creation and maintenance of the one-party system, a post-bellum development in the South. The maintenance of the South as an economic preserve of the North was dependent to an important degree on the continued political sterility of the South in national affairs. All these, of course, were interconnected.

The basic nature of the southern economy owes its origins to cash cropping and the plantation system, with consequent weaknesses, stresses, and backwardness. But the *prolongation* of this situation, in an area contiguous to, and presumably part of, a nation that in the same period outstripped the world in its economic development, rested on the dominance of southern economic, political, and social affairs by the "race question." Let me elaborate.

When, in the late 1880's and early 1890's American labor and farmers heated to the boil that ultimately became Populism, they were joined by workers and farmers in the South, where, indeed, the demands were greater, the shouting more strident—for a while. Unions and farmers' political groups would have been weak in the South in any event, given the general surplus position of people in the South, and their isolation and ignorance. But in the South, the shapers of public opinion—newspapers and political leaders—had one weapon not available in the North: for the underprivileged in the South to achieve success, white and Negro had to combine forces. And when, for a short time, they did so, all the forces of the southern race mythology were brought to bear. Protest dissolved, and its place was taken by increased race violence, and continuing mass impoverishment.[21]

That impoverishment was itself another potent obstacle to the development of southern industry, of course, and one that needs no elaboration here. Southern industrial and farm workers were a market for only the barest of necessities, symbolized in the three M's: meat (i.e., sowbelly), meal, and molasses. On the farm and in the town, the plantation tradition dominated all, in the sense that a genuine money economy existed neither in the ante-bellum nor the post-bellum South. The planter had provided all; the landowner, or the supply merchant, and the mill owner provided all. And the "all" in neither period constituted a market sufficient to justify the growth of industry in the South.

What of the upper crust in the South? The middle class was stunted both before and after the Civil War, but that does not mean there was none. Rather, the *size* of the middle class necessary to provide the South with the enterprise and capital needed for balanced development was lacking. But a middle class existed, and it was its members who held both economic and political power. It was this group, made up of bankers, merchants, landowners, lawyers, speculators, and publicists, that fought for southern political autonomy and won it in the Compromise of 1877.[22] It was this group that gave, as a *quid pro quo*, easy access to the natural riches of the South to those on the outside, a process that greatly furthered the economic domination of the South by the North. And it was this group whose political power was ultimately dependent upon the continuation of the one-party system. That meant the continuation of the Democratic Party as the white man's party: i.e., the single-minded focusing upon the race issue as the dominant and persistent issue in southern politics.

The North's role in this power play was to sacrifice what had remained of abolitionist idealism for the right to plunder the South, and to look the other way in the long decades after 1877 when the common principles of American government were violated.

The South got its railroads after 1877—one of its goals in the Compromise—but the price it paid was ownership and control by the North, and rates that fostered northern and inhibited southern development. The South, with the best natural location for a steel industry in the nation, saw its developed capacity in Birmingham bought up and restricted by U.S. Steel, in 1907, with the connivance of trust-buster Roosevelt.

The North gave up political control of the South; the South gave up political interference in the affairs of the nation, to keep political control of itself. For North and South alike this meant stability, for a genuinely democratic, represented South would dull the Gilded Age, and free the Negro and the poor whites.

VI

This paper began with the hope that a comparative treatment of West and South would enable us to shed some light on the manner in which institutions affect economic development. After one has pointed to the initial "emptiness" of the West, and the long history of cash crop monoculture in the South, there seem to be at least three general remarks worth making.

First, it may be noted that both West and South were short of capital, and thus had to rely on outsiders if investment was to take place. Both areas became, in some sense of the word, economic colonies. It is the difference in the "sense" as between West and South which is fundamental, however. For the West, "colonial" status meant that some of the cream was skimmed off; that is, had ownership and control been indigenous to the area, more of the income generated would have stayed in the area. For the South, "colonial" status meant that the cream was skimmed off, too; but it also meant that development there was seriously unbalanced.

The explanation for this difference leads to a second point. The West was exploited primarily because of the abundance of its physical resources. The South was exploited because of the abundance of its physical and its *human* resources. The individual and national advantages to be gained from exploiting the potentialities of the West—in cattle, timber, minerals, and grains—did not require a superabundant pool of labor. Moreover, those who went to the West—from further east, or Europe—were geared to social mobility and, obviously, geographic mobility. When times worsened for Westerners, some fell into tenancy, but more left for the Far West, returned to the East, or became migratory, i.e., hobo labor. There was no such geographical mobility of the abundant labor in the South. Not until World War I, the depression of the 1930's, and, particularly until World War II, does substantial geographic migration of Southerners take place. The poverty and indebtedness of whites and Negroes is one explanation for their immobility. But certainly of equal importance is the uniqueness that white Southerners attached to themselves—to leave the South would be to leave for another and an enemy country.[23]

It seems to be undisputed that the major factor that attracted industry to the South was its cheap labor (which is not to overlook favorable resource factors). Cheap labor as a stimulus to industrial location may be counted as a favorable factor in the early stages of industrialization. But when cheapness takes on the overwhelming proportions it did in the South, it appears to act as a decisive obstacle to *balanced* development. For, under such conditions, the ability to attract industry becomes geared to the maintenance of general impoverishment.

There was, of course, a "crusade"—and so it was called—to attract capital in the South, particularly from the 1890's on. The crusade, from that day to this, self-consciously stressed the docility of southern workers, whether white or Negro. That docility can be explained in part by the abundance of the people, but a full explanation requires that the "race issue" be given its due. Terrorism must be added to explain the "docility" of Negroes; the doctrine of white supremacy and the associated lack of sustained focus on economic issues must be added to explain the economic docility of the whites.

Finally, one further difference between West and South may be drawn. Politically, the West was part of the nation; the South was not. The West was never a powerful political region in our history, but it has been listened to, and it has been part of the mainstream of American economic and social advancement. The West had no reason to become or remain a separate region; it had every reason to catch up with, to become *like* the rest of the nation, and to fight legislatively toward that end.

The South chose, both before and after the Civil War, to remain "another land." The South's participation in the political affairs of the nation has been more in the nature of keeping it apart from than of drawing it closer to the rest of the country—that is, the cardinal issue in the South, the issue that has absorbed its energies, its emotions, and its intellect, has been the negative one of maintaining a color caste society. But the ultimate price paid for the second-class citizenship of Negroes was the second-class status of the South in the nation. There is no reason to believe that the "price" will decline in the future; there is, however, some reason for believing that the willingness to pay the price is decreasing.

NOTES

1. U.S. Bureau of the Census, *Statistical Abstract of the United States, 1954* (Washington, D.C.: U.S. Government Printing Office, 1954), p. 306. The "West" may of course mean any area west of Manhattan, the Appalachians, the Mississippi, or whatever. Had I chosen to include in my "West"

the Far West, and/or states east of Kansas, my argument would have been made easier, for of all regions called "West," the area I have chosen is the poorest. In delineating the South, I have left out the "Southwest." To have done otherwise would have unnecessarily blurred, without adding to or weakening, the analysis. I stop at the year 1930 because of the periods of depression and war that followed, during which national crises overwhelmed regional characteristics.

2. My attention was first drawn to the South as a clear illustration of this position by Professor Sanford A. Mosk. For a brief and useful statement of the "institutionalist" position, see Mosk's "Latin America versus the United States," *Papers and Proceedings of the American Economic Association,* XLI, No. 2 (May 1951), 367–383.

3. Walter Prescott Webb, in his well-known *The Great Plains: A Study in Institutions and Environment* (New York: Ginn and Company, 1931), dealt with an area not coextensive with my "West," but one that included it, and a good deal more. It was his view that the physical environment of the Great Plains "bent and molded Anglo-American life . . . destroyed traditions, and . . . influenced institutions in a most singular manner" (p. 8). This is certainly wrong on matters affecting economic development. Shannon would add that it is probably wrong on almost all but the most trivial institutional relationships. See the latter's lengthy critique of Webb (and Webb's rejoinder) in *Critique of Research in the Social Sciences: III, An Appraisal of . . . "The Great Plains"* (New York: Social Science Research Council, 1940), by Fred A. Shannon, pp. 3–135.

4. The literature on the West is abundant, but largely unsystematic, and highly romanticized. Comprehensive bibliographical materials may be found in Ray Allen Billington, *Westward Expansion* (New York: the Macmillan Co., 1950), and in Fred A. Shannon, *The Farmer's Last Frontier* (New York: Rinehart and Co., Inc., 1945).

5. The development and adoption of agricultural machinery is given a lucid and detailed treatment in Leo Rogin, *The Introduction of Farm Machinery in its Relation to the Productivity of Labor in the Agriculture of the United States During the Nineteenth Century* (Berkeley: University of California Press, 1931). Rogin was concerned with a longer time period and a broader area than the West as here defined.

6. Howard W. Odum, *Southern Regions of the United States* (Chapel Hill: The University of North Carolina Press, 1936) is a most valuable study, containing well-arranged data on almost every conceivable technological, cultural, and physical characteristic of the South, most of which are compared on a state-wide basis for the entire nation. I have relied heavily on Odum for the factual material in this paper.

7. National Emergency Council, *Report on Economic Conditions of the South* (Washington, D.C.: U.S. Government Printing Office, 1938), pp. 29–30. In 1938, two million people were presumed to have malaria in the South.

8. There seems to be little dispute over this point. For a fuller discussion, see Harriet L. Herring, "Early Industrial Development in the South," *The Annals,* 153 (January 1931), pp. 1–10. This issue of *The Annals* is wholly devoted to industrialization in the South.

9. Broadus Mitchell and George Sinclair Mitchell, *Industrial Revolution in the South* (Baltimore: The Johns Hopkins Press, 1930), pp. 1–7, contains a brief summary of this process.

10. On the persistence of the plantation system, see Roger Wallace Shugg, "Survival of the Plantation System in Louisiana," *Journal of Southern History*, III, No. 3 (August 1937), 311–325. For the post-bellum labor system, see Oscar Zeichner, "The Transition from Slave to Free Agricultural Labor in the Southern States," *Agricultural History*, XIII, No. 1 (January 1939), 22–32.

11. Charles S. Johnson, Edwin R. Embree, and W. W. Alexander, *The Collapse of Cotton Tenancy* (Chapel Hill: The University of North Carolina Press, 1935), p. 4.

12. For an extended discussion of this system, see Thomas D. Clark, "The Furnishing and Supply System in Southern Agriculture Since 1865," *Journal of Southern History*, XII, No. 1 (February 1946), 24–44.

13. Johnson, Embree, and Alexander, *The Collapse of Cotton Tenancy*, p. 33.

14. See Paul Wallace Gates, "Federal Land Policy in the South, 1866–1888," *Journal of Southern History*, VI, No. 3 (August 1940), 303–330. For a decade or so after the War, southern public lands were restricted to homesteading. In the following decade, they were thrown open to public sale. Following that, the lands were again taken off the market; by that time there was little left, qualitatively or quantitatively.

15. C. Vann Woodward's *Origins of the New South, 1877–1913* (Baton Rouge: Louisiana State University Press, 1951) is a penetrating study of the period and the area. Chapter V, "The Industrial Evolution," is an excellent brief summary of the pace and quality of the industrial movement, narrowly defined.

16. Broadus Mitchell's *Rise of the Cotton Mills in the South* (Baltimore: The Johns Hopkins Press, 1921) is the definitive work on this movement.

17. J. J. Spengler, "Population Problems in the South—Part III," *Southern Economic Journal*, IV, No. 2 (October 1937), 131 ff. Spengler's "South" is a broader concept than that used above, which strengthens the point I am trying to make.

18. W. J. Cash, *The Mind of the South* (New York: Doubleday and Company, 1954), pp. 205–206. Originally published by Knopf, in 1941.

19. Mitchell and Mitchell, *Industrial Revolution*, p. 13.

20. *Ibid.*, pp. 14–15.

21. See Jack Abramowitz, "The Negro in the Populist Movement," *Journal of Negro History*, XXXVIII, No. 3 (July 1953), 257–289; also, see Woodward, *Origins of the New South*, chs. 8 and 9.

22. C. Vann Woodward, *Reunion and Reaction* (New York: Doubleday and Company, 1956), provides a detailed and solid explanation of this important question. Originally published by Little, Brown and Company, 1951.

23. Although I am unable to document it, I have heard of countless instances where Negroes were forcibly prevented from migrating—through, e.g., the refusal to sell them railroad tickets.

II

The Agrarian Problem: Its World Context

SETTLEMENT OF THE vast trans-Mississippi area, together with a revolution in farm technology, provided the United States with an agricultural surplus for export during the years 1870–1914, despite the rapid enlargement of the domestic urban market that accompanied industrialization. Though acreage in production and average yield per acre constantly increased, farm prices failed to keep pace with rising costs of farming. Even during periods of favorable economic conditions in the 1880's and in 1910–14, prices of several major crops did not significantly exceed the levels achieved in the late sixties and early seventies.

As the market position of the American farmer deteriorated, agrarian discontent found expression in reform and protest movements, culminating in the Populist uprising of the 1890's. Contemporary farm spokesmen identified federal monetary policy, private mortgage-lending practices, the tariff, and operating practices of railroad companies and middlemen as the major sources of the farmers' difficulties. Since that time, historians have tended to explain the farm problem of the nineties in the terms first set forth by farm-protest spokesmen of that era. In the following article, Morton Rothstein reappraises the traditional version of late-nineteenth century agricultural history. He does not offer an apology for all the marketing practices of the agricultural middleman, but he does take a hard look at the farm problem in its world context and offers a dispassionate evaluation of marketing organization.

AMERICA IN THE INTERNATIONAL RIVALRY FOR THE BRITISH WHEAT MARKET, 1860–1914 *

Morton Rothstein

Whatever its political significance may have been, the repeal of the British Corn Laws in 1846 signaled the emergence of a large-scale international wheat market with England as its center. The next two decades marked the transition from relatively small shipments in response to scarcity prices to a situation where large imports from all parts of the world were regularly handled with relatively little regard for price levels.[1] In this period the American wheat economy was becoming fully committed to production for the English market, a dependence that later became stronger and more constant. The accelerated expansion of American agriculture after the Civil War saw a continuous growth in wheat acreage and production until the turn of the century and created a large, steady surplus. Great Britain provided by far the most important market for that surplus, just as she did for other major products of America's farms. From 1870 to 1914 Britain absorbed about half of the wheat and flour exported from the United States, and in some years she took as much as two thirds. Conversely, in the last three decades of the nineteenth century Britain came to regard the United States as her most dependable source of breadstuffs, purchasing about half of her annual imports from Americans.[2]

The annual volume of breadstuffs exported from the United States fluctuated widely before the 1870's. During the "corn crisis" of 1846, the Crimean War years, and the first three years of the Civil War, shipments of American wheat and flour were heavy and made up a large proportion of British and continental imports, yet

Reprinted by permission from *The Mississippi Valley Historical Review*, XLVII (December, 1960), pp. 401–18.

* Grateful acknowledgment is made to the Social Science Research Council for a fellowship which helped make possible research of which this paper is one result.

they fell to comparatively low levels during the intervening periods. Adjustments in the domestic market after the Civil War kept exports to a minimum for a few years, and not until 1870 did they resume the dimensions of the previous peak years. Even at this level, little more than 10 percent of the crop entered foreign trade.[3]

The big push in production and exportation came in the decade from 1873 to 1882, which Thorstein Veblen called "the most remarkable period that has been seen in American wheat growing." [4] Acreage rose from 29 to 41 million, production from 368 to 555 million bushels, and exports from 40 to 150 million bushels. Fortuitously, the rapid growth of production was matched by a quickening and urgent demand in Europe, which in turn helped stimulate further expansion. The climax came in the three years from 1879 to 1881, when both Britain and western Europe were confronted with disastrous harvests. Plentiful supplies and low prices were maintained primarily by increased purchases in the United States.

Even before these critical years, the American surplus had come to be regarded as the principal factor in the international wheat trade.[5] The crop failure of 1879 heightened English consciousness of their dependence on overseas supplies and elicited a comment which exemplifies the British attitude for the next three years: "America, this year more than ever, will be the staff of life on which Europe will have to lean. The month of August, therefore, has not failed the world; it has brought its golden store of corn, only it has distributed it niggardly here, lavishly there, impoverishing our farmers, enriching those of America." [6] The trade was no less vital to American producers, for during this three-year period the foreign market absorbed over 30 percent of the crop, a higher proportion than for any three-year span down to World War I.

In a sense, this relationship was the fulfillment of earlier prophecies. Spokesmen for western farmers in the period before the Civil War had been confident that the development of the interior would make the United States the world's leading wheat exporter. The boastful vision of the Mississippi Valley as the "Garden of the World" had been an inextricable part of the thinking of many Americans before the first plow cut through the prairie sod. If the realities of an agriculture drawn more closely into the commercial nexus brought disillusionment to some, to many others the promise of America as the "Granary of the World" still seemed valid.[7]

The consequences of this commitment to a foreign market soon became apparent. Until the 1880's the volume and price of American exports of breadstuffs had been influenced primarily by the size and condition of the British harvests. Increasingly, however, the *total* available supply in a more closely knit world market became the major determinant.[8] The United States had achieved leadership largely by supplanting Russia as the chief purveyor of cereals to western Europe, in part because Russian exports in the 1870's dropped off after emancipation and the troubles in the Near East.[9] With the resumption of heavy Russian shipments in the early 1880's, and the simultaneous advent of a new and seemingly formidable competitor in India, the challenge to that position became more serious. American exports fell somewhat during the price decline of the 1880's, though they were still much higher than the average of the previous decade and accounted for about one fourth of the national harvest.[10]

Widespread crop failures in Russia and India in 1890 and 1891 brought an additional boom to the American trade. Wheat exports reached new heights, then fell sharply during the five years of depression that followed. More normal shipments from Russia and India, and the appearance of Argentina as a major factor in the market, produced a surplus which depressed prices to the lowest levels of the century. During most of the preceding seasons a bountiful crop in one region of the world had been offset by rather poor harvests in another, but from 1893 to 1895 all the major exporting nations enjoyed plentiful yields.[11]

From 1897 to 1903 the volume of breadstuffs exported from the United States once more reached the high level established in earlier years, although world prices as set at Liverpool had recovered only slightly. But America's share of the steadily growing international market had begun to decline. When the poor crops of 1904 and 1905 drastically curtailed shipments from the Atlantic and Gulf ports, Britain and other importing nations had no difficulty in finding other sources of supply. From that time until 1914 American exports of wheat played a relatively minor role in the world market. Furthermore, both acreage and production dropped from the high point reached at the turn of the century. With domestic demand growing faster than ever before, the United States seemed to be moving into an era in which production and consumption would achieve a balance, and the old problem of disposing of surplus wheat would finally vanish.[12]

A host of interacting factors account for the persistence of America's wheat surplus in the latter third of the nineteenth century. Wheat was not only pre-eminent as the major cash crop of pioneer settlements, but was securely fixed in the crop rotation schemes of established agricultural communities. In addition, every new area on the agricultural frontier where wheat was a possible crop was hailed as a great granary, which, if developed, would become the richest region on the continent. Whatever the effect of such blandishments, or the additional lure provided by the example of successful "wheat millionaires," many westerners became disillusioned with the results of specialization in the production of this cereal.[13]

The non-agricultural groups in American society took a more sanguine view of our surplus in breadstuffs. To the business community there was an obvious connection between abundant wheat harvests and improved business conditions. Mercantile interests came to regard the volume of wheat produced and exported as an economic bellwether during the 1870's and 1880's.[14] This idea carried over into the twentieth century, but its validity became highly questionable as the causal connection between prosperous agriculture and prosperous industry weakened.

To such interested groups the desirability of a high level of wheat exports, no matter what the returns to the producer, remained axiomatic. During the price decline of the 1880's, grain trade journals and commercial newspapers alike urged that farmers sell at lower prices so that America could retain her proper share of the English market. They argued that when farmers held back their wheat for higher prices rival nations took away much of the trade, whereas continued sales would enable America to drive out the competition. Then the United States could quickly reap the benefits of the inevitable future price rise.[15]

Some observers were unconcerned about low prices because they were confident that American wheat growers could profitably expand production despite decreasing returns, an idea astonishing to many Europeans. One of the more influential and prolific commentators of the period, Edward Atkinson, provoked a storm of controversy in Britain and the United States in the late 1880's with his reiterated claims that American farmers were still raising wheat at a profit and would continue to do so if prices went even lower.[16] From the Civil War to the turn of the century many persons expressed unqualified gratification that the United States maintained her position as the leading wheat exporter, and that Great Britain remained dependent on the farmers of America for much of her food supply.[17]

Others held deep misgivings over the close link between the American wheat farmer and the British consumer. Such persons, including many in the grain business itself, were at first reluctant even to admit the influence of foreign markets on the domestic wheat economy, and heated debates on the extent to which Liverpool regulated prices in America filled agricultural and grain trade journals in the late 1870's and early 1880's.[18] By the mid-1880's there was almost universal acknowledgment of the crucial role of the British market in fixing prices. As a result, members of the wheat trade began to agitate for new markets in other parts of the world. Flour millers, for example, repeatedly urged diplomatic measures to open Latin America to their products. By 1900 leading spokesmen for western wheat growers were urging the development of Far Eastern markets in order to escape the dominance of Liverpool.[19]

A growing disenchantment with Anglo-American interdependence was no less evident in Britain. Before 1880 few adverse comments appeared and these were generally unnoticed in the chorus of approval. This was particularly true in periods of political tension between Britain and Russia, her other major source of breadstuffs.[20] The 1880's, however, witnessed a growing uneasiness on the part of several groups of Britishers watching the flood of American wheat pouring into their country. Critics of free trade policies were quick to use this sentiment in condemning the American tariff, which blocked British exports while the United States was given such free access to the British market. Others expressed apprehension about the wisdom of depending on a country where "corners" and other manipulations were so prevalent, and denounced American middlemen for attempting to extort higher prices from the British consumers. Finally, there were those who feared too great a dependence on any foreign source of breadstuffs because they felt that it made the United Kingdom more vulnerable in terms of its military security. As international tensions mounted toward the end of the century, this last point received increasing emphasis.[21]

Among the several solutions offered by such critics was a policy of developing greater wheat production within the British Empire. Measures to stimulate wheat exports from India received considerable attention in the 1880's and 1890's from the English public, government officials, and grain trade organizations. Proposals for subsidizing railroad construction in Australia and Canada were frequently defended on the ground that the regions involved would become granaries for the United Kingdom and relieve her of reliance on American wheat.[22] Such arguments bordered on the absurd when British expansion in central Africa was in part justified as a measure to create a wheat supply by developing agriculture in such places as the Sudan.[23]

All of these proposals were given full, indeed exaggerated, attention by Americans. The strong reaction to them, and to a later trans-Atlantic debate on the limits of wheat production in the United States, reveals a continuous sensitivity of Americans to the competition, real or imaginary, of other wheat-growing nations. Reports from countries that were actual or potential rivals were constantly discussed and circulated. Though most interested Americans probably remained unconcerned in their pride in the nation's supremacy, a series of scares generated by such reports provided ammunition to the opponents of surplus production and to several leaders of the agrarian movement.[24]

As early as the 1860's sagging wheat prices were attributed to exports from Russia and Egypt, where the low standard of living of the peasants and fellahin presumably threatened to undermine the prospects of American wheat growers.[25] Such fears subsided in the 1870's when both of these countries dropped to relatively minor positions. In 1878 American journalists crowed over the defeat of Russia, "our most formidable rival" for world leadership in this field.[26] However, the expansion of India's wheat trade and the expectation of its rapid growth soon came to be treated as a veritable bugbear by many American writers, and provoked excited discussions that reached their climax from about 1884 to 1887.[27] As the Indian threat seemed to fizzle the resurgence of Russia brought a rash of predictions about the threat from that nation, which were given additional weight by the fact that from 1888 to 1890 Russia surpassed the United States in supplying wheat to the British market, America retaining her over-all lead by virtue of heavy shipments of flour.[28] The serious famine in Russia during 1891, which all but eliminated her as a rival for the next two seasons, prompted a renewal of American optimism. A leading grain trade journal looked back on previous scares with a smug air in 1892:

Long ago English economists saw that they would in the future have to buy most of their breadstuffs in foreign countries and the development of agriculture at the ends of the earth was hailed with delight as affording inexhaustible supplies of the necessaries of life. Once India was the land of promised plenty, then Australia, then Russia, but the broad prairies of the United States still continue to supply Johnny Bull's right and tight little island with the major portion of the breadstuffs imported. England may as well accept the inevitable, for America is the granary of the importing world.[29]

This rosy outlook faded once more with the rude shocks of the mid-1890's. Many Americans believed that the sharp downturn was largely the result of the apparently sudden emergence of Argentina as a major producer. A prominent Pacific Coast exporter was speaking for many members of the grain trade when he stated that "the Argentine farmers are the most serious competitors that the American wheat growers have." [30] The contemporaneous advance of wheat cultivation in Australia and Canada, however, thoroughly reinforced the growing conviction that America was not faced with any single "rival" but was now simply part of an international market in which the total world supply and demand determined conditions.[31]

Many of these and other discussions of the grain trade were imbued with the prevalent hostility to middlemen. Farmers in the wheat belts of the United States, unable to deal with most of the basic factors responsible for their weak position in the market, directed their discontent against the nearby agencies which controlled their access to consumers. Railroads, local grain dealers, terminal elevator owners, and grain speculators came under successive attacks during the course of the so-called agrarian crusade.[32]

There can be no denial that there were very real abuses, and many of the complaints of the farmer against these agencies gained widespread sympathy among other segments of American society. Yet friction between farmers and representatives of a market system are as old as civilization. The intensity to which it developed in the United States was perhaps an inevitable outcome of the extraordinary degree to which agriculture had become commercialized.[33]

With all its imperfections, it was the highly developed and tightly organized grain business, along with additional advantages in transportation, that accounted in large measure for the unique position of the American wheat trade in the last three decades of the nineteenth century. This is less valid for the important Pacific Coast trade, where there were no elevators and transport facilities were often comparatively poor.[34] But east of the Rockies the business of assembling, handling, financing, and transporting grain was vastly superior to that of any other nation. Once American supremacy had been established, other countries sent a stream of official and quasi-official missions to the United States to study the operation of the grain trade in the hope of emulating its efficiency. In most cases they sought to introduce the technology involved—such as grain elevators and systems of grading and inspection—but were anxious to forego the establishment of futures markets.

Yet futures trading, which was introduced into the grain trade by Americans and reached its highest development in the United States, was fundamental to the system as a whole. In spite of the almost universal condemnation of grain speculators it was this group which reduced many of the risks inherent in a free market. On the whole they endured heavy losses down to 1896 and made relatively modest gains from the rise in prices after 1897. By protecting millers, dealers, and exporters from losses, they helped to narrow the difference between the average price paid to farmers and the average price charged to the ultimate consumer.[35]

The impact of futures trading, and the presence of large financial resources with which it must be articulated, was especially discernible in the foreign wheat trade. In most of the major exporting regions, the annual volume of shipments was determined almost entirely by the size of the previous harvest, and had remarkably little correlation with movements of prices. The American trade was far more sensitive to the prices established at Liverpool, and it showed a smaller correlation than any other major exporter between the size of the crop and the amount shipped abroad. The enormous storage system and the trade in futures permitted American shippers to carry over a large percentage of the surplus in years when low prices prevailed on the British market, and to reduce these stocks when prices rose.[36]

The wheat economy east of the Rockies had a further advantage in the comparatively low cost of ocean shipping. In most other grain-exporting regions, the shipments to Britain or the Continent were usually the most profitable part of the voyage for the owners of the tramp vessels that carried most of the wheat. In the California trade, for example, where shipments to Britain went almost entirely in sailing vessels, owners usually charged relatively low rates for the voyage from the home port to San Francisco and earned their real profit from the higher rates charged for carrying wheat around Cape Horn to the United Kingdom or the Continent.[37] Similar conditions were often found in the Black Sea, Australia, and India. But in the heavily traveled lanes of the North Atlantic, the situation was often quite the reverse. Steamer lines, whether devoted primarily to pas-senger or freight traffic, were eager to carry grain as ballast in this era before the adoption of the water ballast tank. The ease and speed with which grain could be loaded and unloaded, and its fluid quali-ties when handled in bulk, made it particularly desirable. Conse-quently, liners vied with tramp vessels for grain at Atlantic ports, offering berth rates that often made this manner of shipment cheaper than assembling full cargoes for a tramp ship. Sometimes, when rates were unusually low, liners carried grain free in order to secure ballast.[38]

These factors were generally overlooked by the host of foreign visitors investigating the American grain trade after the late 1870's. Those from the larger importing countries of western Europe were concerned for the most part with the possible future expansion of production, and with the conditions under which the surplus was created. The avalanche of American grain, accepted with compara-tive equanimity by the British, had brought consternation to large and powerful agrarian interests in France and Germany.

In 1880, when the well-known British Parliamentary Commis-sion was engaged in its inspection of American agriculture, the French government ordered a similar undertaking devoted exclu-sively to the question of wheat. The ensuing report placed unusual emphasis on the superior organization of the grain trade in the United States, and concluded:

It is not without legitimate pride that the Americans have been able to say of their business in grain that it is becoming one of the marvels of modern commercial history. More than anywhere else the trader in grain in the United States has contributed to domestic and foreign traffic and to the development of the nation's agricultural resources. Encouraged by today's growing needs in the markets of Europe, the foreign grain trade of the Atlantic States, which was concentrated in a few cities of the seaboard, is being extended over a greater area, to the point of becoming the predominant element of the national pros-perity and one of the real causes of the influence of the American Union on the rest of the world.[39]

For the most part, however, French observers were more concerned with ascertaining the dimensions of the American threat to their wheat growers, and after a series of protective measures largely solved that problem the question of the American trade was left to theoretical discussions by economists.[40]

The German response of the 1880's was along the same lines, with several experts, most notable among them being Dr. Max Sering, making exhaustive studies of the American wheat-growing potential.[41] By the 1890's, however, German economists gave increasing attention to the methods and organization of the grain trade in all the major exporting nations. A typical assessment of the United States appeared in 1898 in a study which compared the techniques of America, India, and Russia with those employed in Germany. Although the author took cognizance of such factors as fertile soils, the efficiency of the transportation network, and "intelligent farmers willing to adopt modern methods," he concluded that the elevator system—including inspection and grading, transferable elevator receipts, bulk-handling, and futures trading—was the real key to American leadership.[42]

These features received even greater attention from nations which were competing with the United States. To Austria-Hungary, whose Danubian provinces were heavily dependent on the British market as an outlet for their wheat and high-grade flour, the advent of large-scale American competition was regarded as catastrophic. In 1881 the Hungarian government sponsored a world tour of wheat regions and flour-milling centers by Professor Emil Pekar, who was deeply impressed by the efficiency of grain-handling in the United States. On the basis of his report, the Hungarian government sent an outstanding engineer, Miklos Oedon, to study the construction of American terminal elevators, and built one according to his design in Pest. But within two years it had come to be regarded as obsolete in comparison with the new elevators on the American seaboard. Additional visits were made in the next fifteen years, including a joint tour by an engineer and an economist in 1895.[43]

In the wheat exporting nations outside Europe there were equally anxious attempts to copy aspects of the elevator system. As early as the mid-1870's concerted efforts were made by government leaders in London and India to adopt the grading methods of American traders, including the use of warehouse receipts and bulk handling, to the wheat trade of the Asian subcontinent. Local officials felt that it would be impossible to get the native dealers to make the change, and the idea was abandoned. In the late 1880's a proposal was made by private parties to introduce the elevator system along the railroads being built into the major wheat-growing districts of northern India. They asked for government support in the venture and justified their plea on the grounds that successful elevator lines would enable India to compete more easily with America on the British market, where buyers were accustomed to purchasing on the basis of elevator certificates and designated grades. However, they failed to gain the subsidy and dropped the project. A more widely supported campaign by government officials was undertaken in 1909 but achieved few results before World War I.[44]

In the 1880's the Department of Agriculture of New South Wales, Australia, initiated its campaign to have the bulk handling of wheat adopted. It sent Dr. Nathan A. Cobb to the United States in 1900 to report on the methods used, and he, too, came to consider the use of elevators and the associated commercial techniques as the elements which made American competition so vigorous.[45] Similar investigations were conducted for the Victoria Department of Agriculture between 1895 and 1920. In spite of these efforts, Australia moved very slowly in implementing the resultant suggestions, primarily because of political difficulties.[46]

Of all the countries affected by American participation in the world wheat economy, Russia showed the most intense and sustained interest in meeting the competition. This was understandable, since Russia was America's major rival, and of all the leading wheat producers was most dependent on this commodity as a component of her foreign trade. Consequently, for the last quarter of the nineteenth century the grain export trade was treated as "the pet child of the Russian financial administration." [47] As early as 1879 the Russian government sent "a well known political and agricultural economist," Professor Robert Orbinsky, to the United States. He explained the reason for his trip in a letter to the St. Louis *Republican:*

The last year your country has furnished no less than 51 per cent of the want of England [for wheat] and we only 22. Ten years ago it was exactly the contrary of that proportion.

Then it was very natural for my government to inquire in what manner and by what way such a change could take place.[48]

Orbinsky's report placed the greatest emphasis on American advantages in transportation and in efficient handling of grain by the elevator system, which he urged should be adopted at once.[49]

The continued high level of American exports in the early 1880's increased the concern of many Russian observers. Much of the previous decline in the Russian trade had been attributed to the disruptions of the Turkish War and the succession of bad harvests that followed. Although the bumper crop of 1882 brought an increase in exports, they were still dwarfed by the volume of American shipments. The resulting low prices created a veritable "grain crisis" for Russian merchants and dealers.[50]

There was fairly wide agreement that the solution of Russia's difficulties had to include modernization of the grain trade along American lines, but changes were painfully slow. In 1884 a bill was placed before the Imperial Council authorizing the construction and operation of American-style elevators by a joint-stock company along railroads in the wheat regions. The promoters of this venture were rumored to have been two Americans and the Duc de Morny of France. Though the project gained a favorable vote in the council, nationalist sentiment caused hostility to the scheme and fears were widespread that such a monopoly would do more harm than good.[51] The plan was dropped. A similar undertaking, in which elevators were to be built and operated by the government, was drawn up in 1888, and given additional sanction by a special commission of inquiry.[52]

In connection with this second project, Spenisky Carnitt, a prominent engineer, made a thorough study of the grain elevators of the United States and Canada in 1889. That year saw the Russian government begin construction of terminal elevators at Odessa and other Black Sea ports.[53] Two more Russian engineers visited the United States in 1893, and included among their aims was the study of terminal elevators.[54]

In addition, Russian officials were sent to Britain to establish better relations with British buyers, so that the latter might approve the proposed standards of grading and other commercial features connected with the planned system, as well as to gather information on the flour-milling industry of the United Kingdom. All this in the hope that Russia could then better compete with America.[55] Few of these inquiries, however, were followed by action, and the Russian trade remained backward and inefficient until the eve of World War I.[56]

With the rise in prices after 1897 and the loss of American leadership in wheat exports a few years later, other nations ceased to be so desperately concerned with the foreign grain trade of the United States. New rivals entering the scene were beginning to show the same kind of dynamic agricultural development that had been almost uniquely American until the turn of the century. Distinct parallels can be drawn between the over-all expansion of wheat growing in Canada, Australia, and Argentina at this time with the earlier phases of production in the United States. Moreover, these newcomers were adopting techniques in marketing which compared favorably with those in the American trade. Canada, for example, already had a system of inspection and grading that surpassed that of the United States.[57]

Compared with its chief rivals of the last three decades of the nineteenth century, India and Russia, which had underdeveloped economies and primitive trade organization, the United States had been in an extremely favorable position. Whatever the difficulties of the wheat farmer, he had enjoyed far better circumstances than his counterparts among the depressed and exploited peasantry in those countries. One might say that the American wheat grower, with his higher standard of living and greater costs of production, had found it difficult to compete in the world market because these nations had used their wheat exports, often at tragic cost to their farmers, in a strenuous effort to gain capital for industrial growth. America's success in maintaining her leadership in the trade resulted in large measure from the fact that here the expansion of agriculture took place in an economy in which commerce and industry were developing with at least equal speed. Industrialization, which in itself bred discontent for farmers, and the unique commercial institutions of the grain trade, about which they and other groups complained bitterly, provided a vital cushion against the effects of world competition and helped postpone its disastrous impact until the 1920's.

NOTES

1. William Ashworth, A Short History of the International Economy, 1850–1950 (London, 1952), 29, 62–70; Asa Briggs, The Age of Improvement (London, 1959), 286–343; Carl J. Fuchs, "Der englische Getreidehandel und seine Organisation," Jahrbücher für Nationalökonomie und Statistik (Jena), XX, Neue Folge (January, 1890), 5–15.
2. Statistical information for this period is far from satisfactory, and for the purposes of this paper only rough computations have been made from American and British sources. For acreage and production, I have used Holbrook Working, "Wheat Acreage and Production in the United States since 1866: A Revision of Official Estimates," Wheat Studies of the Food Research Institute (Stanford University), II (June, 1926), 237–64, and Revisions of Wheat Statistics (mimeo.), U.S. Department of Agriculture (Washington, 1936). Export and import figures are derived from "The Grain Trade of the United States," Monthly Summary of Commerce and Finance (Washington),

January, 1900, pp. 1955–2075; *Statistical Abstract of the United States* (Washington) for the period after 1900; and "Annual Returns of Trade and Navigation," *British Parliamentary Papers*, for the period from 1865 to 1914.

3. Herbert J. Wunderlich, "Foreign Grain Trade of the United States, 1835–1860," *Iowa Journal of History and Politics* (Iowa City), XXXIII (January, 1935), 27–29, 63; Eli Ginzberg, "The Economics of British Neutrality during the Civil War," *Agricultural History* (Washington), X (October, 1936), 147–56.

4. Thorstein Veblen, "The Price of Wheat since 1867," *Journal of Political Economy* (Chicago), I (December, 1892), 77–78.

5. *Northwestern Miller* (La Crosse, Wis.), October 4, 1878.

6. *London Miller*, September 5, 1879.

7. Thomas Stirton, "Free Trade and the Wheat Surplus of the Old Northwest, 1839–1846" (M.A. thesis, University of Chicago, 1952), *passim*; Thomas P. Martin, "The Staff of Life in Diplomacy and Politics during the Early Eighteen Fifties," *Agricultural History*, XVIII (January, 1944), 1–15; Richard O. Cummings, "American Interest in World Agriculture, 1861–65," *ibid.*, XXIII (April, 1949), 116–23; Henry Nash Smith, *Virgin Land: The American West as Symbol and Myth* (Vintage ed., New York, 1957), 138–89.

8. Veblen, "The Price of Wheat since 1867," *Journal of Political Economy*, I (December, 1892), 77–94.

9. Vladimir P. Timoshenko, "The Agrarian Policies of Russia and the Wars," *Agricultural History*, XVII (October, 1943), 192–210; *Northwestern Miller* (Minneapolis), December 8, 1882.

10. "The Grain Trade of the United States," *Monthly Summary of Commerce and Finance* (January, 1900), 1955.

11. Helen W. Farnsworth, "The Decline and Recovery of Wheat Prices in the 'Nineties," *Wheat Studies of the Food Research Institute*, X (June and July, 1934), 289–336.

12. Yves Guyot, "Le Rôle Économique des Céréales," *Journal des Économistes* (Paris), Series 6, XXXVI (October, 1912), 3–24; John C. Williams, "The Wheat Situation in the United States," *Science* (New York), New Series, XXI (March 24, 1905), 458–59; Mark A. Carleton, "The Future Wheat Supply of the United States," U.S. Department of Agriculture, *Yearbook, 1909* (Washington, 1910), 259–70.

13. For an analysis of the pressures for continued specialization in wheat production on the frontier see U.S. Commissioner of Agriculture, *Report, 1884* (Washington, 1885), 506, and *Northwestern Miller*, November 8, 1878. An example of wheat in an older region is thoroughly discussed in Oren L. Whalin, "Commercial Red Winter Wheat of the Cornbelt, An Economic Study" (Ph.D. dissertation, University of Illinois, 1931), Chapter I. On the booster spirit in touting various regions as future granaries see Theodore Saloutos, "The Spring-Wheat Farmer in a Maturing Economy, 1870–1920," *Journal of Economic History* (New York), VI (November, 1946), 173–75; T. B. Thorpe, "Wheat and Its Associations," *Harper's Magazine* (New York), XV (August, 1857), 301–13; Richard E. Edmonds, "Our Exports of Breadstuffs," *International Review* (New York), XI (November, 1881), 458–62. *Northwestern Miller*, August 30, 1878, January 24 and September 5, 1879, and May 7, 1880, contains examples of western opposition to continued reliance on wheat as a major crop.

14. Rendigs Fels, "The American Business Cycle of 1879–1885," *Journal*

of Political Economy, LX (February, 1952), 68–69; *Northwestern Miller*, December 22, 1882; *American Elevator and Grain Trade* (Chicago), February 15, 1886, and February 15, 1888. On the question of wheat exports and business prosperity see Farnsworth, "The Decline and Recovery of Wheat Prices in the 'Nineties," *Wheat Studies of the Food Research Institute*, X (June and July, 1934), 328–36; A. Piatt Andrew, "Influence of the Crops upon Business in America," *Quarterly Journal of Economics* (Boston), XX (May, 1906), 323–53.

15. A variety of stories in this vein, reprinted from such papers as the St. Paul *Pioneer Press*, Baltimore *Journal of Commerce*, and others, appeared in the *Northwestern Miller*, November 4 and December 9, 1881, August 25, 1882, October 17, 1884, June 5, 1885, April 23, 1886, and March 22, 1889. For another long discussion of this position see *Grain Review* (St. Louis), June, 1882.

16. Harold F. Williamson, *Edward Atkinson: The Biography of an American Liberal* (Boston, 1934), 163–66, 237; *Northwestern Miller*, October 14 and November 18, 1887.

17. Edmonds, "Our Exports of Breadstuffs," *International Review*, XI (November, 1881), 450–62; James D. Whelpley, "American Control of England's Food Supply," *North American Review* (New York), CLXXIV (June, 1902), 796–806; Andrew Carnegie, *Triumphant Democracy* (New York, 1887), 192; *American Elevator and Grain Trade*, November 15, 1890, and November 15, 1892; *New York Produce Exchange Reporter* (New York), May 26, 1883.

18. An early discussion of this point appeared in the Chicago *Inter-Ocean*, reprinted in the *Northwestern Miller*, August 16, 1878. For a later example of such a debate see the issues of *New York Produce Exchange Reporter*, July to September, 1883.

19. The *Northwestern Miller* periodically revived the campaign for wider Latin American markets in the 1880's. See issues of March 15, April 12, and October 18, 1889. The same attitude is replete in the testimony of farmers and millers before the Cullom Committee, "Report of the Senate Select Committee on Interstate Commerce," *Senate Reports*, 48 Cong., 1 Sess., No. 46, Part 2 (Serial 2173), 358, 791, 865, 1253. On the quest for oriental markets see U.S. Industrial Commission, *Report*, X (Washington, 1901), 288, 712–16; *Proceedings of the Tri-State Grain Growers Association* (Fargo, N.D., 1900), 6–8, 16–17.

20. At first even the *Mark Lane Express* (London), spokesman for English farming interests, viewed the prospect of American exports calmly, stating that "should the folly and presumption of any particular nation keep the continent of Europe in war, we have an unfailing resource in the regions peopled and cultivated by our own Anglo-Saxon race, and what would be Europe's time of need would most surely prove to be America's opportunity." *Ibid.*, August 1, 1870. For other views of approval see Augustus Mongredien, *Free Trade and English Commerce* (London, 1879), 93–96; Stephen Bourne, *Trade, Population, and Food* (London, 1880), 95–99, 110–13; Robert Giffen, *Essays in Finance, Second Series* (London, 1887), 130–34; London *Times*, May 21, 1884.

21. *The Economist* (London), XXXIX (August 20, 1881), 1044; *Saturday Review* (London), LVII (April 12, 1884), 478–79; *American Elevator and Grain Trade*, April 15, 1888. For later arguments on the national defense issue, see R. B. Marston, *War, Famine, and Our Food Supply* (London,

1897), *passim;* Charles J. Irving, *An Essay on Public Granaries* (London, 1898), *passim;* "London Letter," *Northwestern Miller,* September 10, 1897; *Spectator* (London), LXXX (June 18, 1898), 854–55; Albert Humphries, "The Production of Wheat in the British Empire," *Journal of the Royal Society of Arts* (London), LVII (February 12, 1909), 230–53.

22. William Fowler, "India, Her Wheat and Her Railways," *Nineteenth Century* (London), XV (February, 1884), 274–92; *Saturday Review,* LVII (March 29, 1884), 411–13; *The Influence of English Trade and American Protection by the Development of India* (Anonymous pamphlet, n.d., n.p. [1883 ?]), 5–17; T. T. V. Smith, "Our New Wheat Fields in the Northwest," *Nineteenth Century,* VI (July, 1879), 10–22; *Northwestern Miller,* September 3, 1880, May 15 and 29, 1885.

23. *Northwestern Miller,* May 2 and August 18, 1884. In the first of these reports Sir Samuel Baker is quoted as saying: "If the Soudan were in English hands in a very few years you would be entirely independent of the United States both for cotton and corn."

24. For the debate on the future position of the United States as a wheat exporter, see Sir William Crookes, *The Wheat Problem* (New York, 1900), v–vii, 8–29, 55–56; Joseph S. Davis, "The Specter of the Dearth of Food: History's Answer to Sir William Crookes," *Facts and Factors in Economic History* (Cambridge, Mass., 1932), 733–54; C. Wood Davis, "Wheat: Crookes vs. Atkinson, Dodge, et al.," *Forum* (New York), XXVII (March, 1899), 101–13. For the use of the threat of foreign competition by the opponents of wheat production for export see U.S. Commissioner of Agriculture, *Report, 1884* (Washington, 1885), 505, and *Report, 1885* (Washington, 1886), 569–82; Thomas H. Dudley, *Competition of Indian Wheat* (Camden, N.J., 1885), *passim; Northwestern Miller,* November 9, 1888, May 17 and November 1, 1889.

25. U.S. Commissioner of Agriculture, *Report, 1871* (Washington, 1872), 297, 453; Henrietta Larson, *The Wheat Farmer and the Market in Minnesota, 1858–1900* (New York, 1926), 167–68.

26. Chicago *Inter-Ocean,* reprinted in *Northwestern Miller,* November 29, 1878, October 15 and 29, 1880; *Grain Review,* December, 1882.

27. U.S. Department of Agriculture, *Report of the Secretary for 1891* (Washington, 1892), 304–305; "Report of the Secretary of State [1885]," *Senate Exec. Docs.,* 49 Cong., 1 Sess., No. 108 (Serial 2340), 11–14; *Northwestern Miller,* August 11, 1882, July 25 and November 14, 1884. The discussion was accompanied by a heated controversy between the *Northwestern Miller* and the *London Miller* over the quality of Indian wheat and its value in flour-making. For some reprints of the English stories and American rejoinders see *Northwestern Miller,* August 17, 1883, July 11, 1884, October 23, 1885, and July 8, 1887.

28. *Northwestern Miller,* November 9, 1888, May 17, 1889, November 1, 1889; *American Elevator and Grain Trade,* November 15, 1890.

29. *American Elevator and Grain Trade,* November 15, 1892.

30. Portland (Ore.) *Commercial Review,* November 8, 1894. This was the report of an interview with Alexander Guthrie, of Balfour, Guthrie & Co., one of the most important firms in the West Coast grain trade. A brief discussion of the special connection between Argentina and the British wheat market is contained in H. S. Ferns, "Investment and Trade between Britain and Argentina in the Nineteenth Century," *Economic History Review* (Cambridge, Eng.), Second Series, III (1950), 216–17.

31. U.S. Industrial Commission, *Report*, IV (Washington, 1900), 195, 395, 411; U.S. Department of Agriculture, *Report of the Secretary of Agriculture for 1891* (Washington, 1892), 298–304; *American Elevator and Grain Trade*, November 15, 1893; *Northwestern Miller*, September 27, 1895.

32. On the succession of targets of the grain producers' agitations see Joseph B. Kenkel, *The Cooperative Elevator Movement* (Washington, 1922), 133–38.

33. Saloutos, "Spring-Wheat Farmer in a Maturing Economy," *Journal of Economic History*, VI (November, 1946), 173–75, and "The Agricultural Problem and Nineteenth Century Industrialism," *Agricultural History*, XXII (July, 1948), 156–74; James Mavor, "The Economic Results of the Specialist Production and Marketing of Wheat," *Political Science Quarterly* (New York), XXVI (December, 1911), 663–75.

34. Horace Davis, "Wheat in California, A Retrospect and Prospect," *Overland Monthly* (San Francisco), Second Series, XXXII (July, 1898), 60–63; Donald W. Meinig, "Wheat Sacks out to Sea: The Early Export Trade from the Walla Walla Country," *Pacific Northwest Quarterly* (Seattle), XLV (January, 1954), 13–18; Rodman W. Paul, "The Wheat Trade between California and the United Kingdom," *Mississippi Valley Historical Review* (Cedar Rapids), XLV (December, 1958), 391–412.

35. Holbrook Working, "The Financial Results of Speculative Holding of Wheat," *Wheat Studies of the Food Research Institute*, VII (July, 1931), 405–38. On the narrowing of the difference in prices see Larson, *Wheat Farmer and Market in Minnesota*, 243–56, and J. Chester Bowen, "Wheat and Flour Prices from Farmer to Consumer," U.S. Department of Labor, *Bureau of Labor Statistics, Bulletin No. 130* (Washington, 1913), *passim*.

36. Holbrook Working, "Annual Fluctuations in the International Situation," *Wheat Studies of the Food Research Institute*, VI (September, 1930), 438 ff. For a comparison of the American and Russian trade in these terms see I. M. Rubinow, "Russian Wheat and Flour in European Markets," U.S. Department of Agriculture, *Bureau of Statistics, Bulletin No. 66* (Washington, 1908), 60–81.

37. Benjamin C. Wright, *San Francisco's Ocean Trade, Past and Future: A Story of the Deep Water Service of San Francisco, 1848 to 1911: Effect the Panama Canal Will Have Upon It* (San Francisco, 1911), 161–62; Joseph Nimmo, Jr., "Report on the Internal Commerce of the United States, Submitted May 6, 1885," *House Exec. Docs.*, 48 Cong., 2 Sess., No. 7, Part 3 (Serial 2295), 60–63.

38. Joseph Nimmo, Jr., "First Annual Report on the Internal Commerce of the United States, Submitted June 30, 1877," *House Exec. Docs.*, 44 Cong., 2 Sess., No. 46, Part 2 (Serial 1761), Appendix, 73; V. D. Wickizer, "Shipping and Freight Rates in the Overseas Grain Trade," *Wheat Studies of the Food Research Institute*, XV (October, 1938), 53; Frank Andrews, "Ocean Freight Rates and the Conditions Affecting Them," U.S. Department of Agriculture, *Bureau of Statistics, Bulletin No. 67* (Washington, 1907), 25, 30–31. On liners carrying grain free see *Mark Lane Express*, October 15, 1888, and Frederic A. Ogg, "Railroad Rates and the Flow of Our Foreign Trade," *Review of Reviews* (New York), XXXIII (April, 1906), 458–63.

39. A. Ronna, *Essai sur L'Agriculture des États-unis d'Amerique: Le Blé aux États-unis d'Amerique, Production, Transports, Commerce* (Paris, 1880), 205.

40. Édouard Picard, "La Production et l'Exportation des Blés aux États-

unis," *Révue d'Économie Politique* (Paris), XVI (December, 1902), 913–25; Yves Guyot, *Le Blé et les Autres Céréales aux États-Unis* (Paris, 1905), *passim.*

41. Max Sering, *Die Landwirthschaftliche Konkurrenz Nordamerikas in Gegenwart und Zukunft* (Leipzig, 1887), *passim.* For an earlier, briefer estimate of some note see Friederich Kapp, *Die Amerikanische Weizenproduktion* (Berlin, 1880).

42. Otto Böhm, *Die Kornhäuser: Eine Studie über die Organisation des Getreideverkaufes in Amerika, Indien, und Russland, sowie in einigen Deutschen Staaten* (Stuttgart, 1898), 40–41. Similar conclusions were reached in Herman Schumacher, "Die Getreidehandel in den Vereinigten Staaten von Amerika und seine Organisation," *Jahrbücher für Nationalökonomie und Statistik,* LXV (March and December, 1895), 361–92, 801–22; and in Walther Lotz, "Die Organisation des Getreideverkaufes in den Vereinigten Staaten von Nordamerika," *Bayerische Handelszeitung* (Munich), November 11, 1893.

43. I have been unable to locate a copy of Pekar's book about his journey (*Weizen und Mehl unserer Erde,* Budapest, 1882), but a series of long excerpts in translation appeared in the *Northwestern Miller* throughout the summer of 1883. Later interviews indicated that Pekar had graded wheat with Chicago grain inspectors and had carefully studied every aspect of the elevator system. *Northwestern Miller,* December 4, 1896, and January 29, 1897. Other journeys on behalf of the Austro-Hungarian government are described in Rudolph H. Meyer, *Ursachen der amerikanischen Concurrenz* (Berlin, 1883), *passim,* and *Northwestern Miller,* April 16, 1886. In the visit of 1895, the men came to "study the elevator system, methods of constructing and equipping them and handling the grain." *American Elevator and Grain Trade,* July 15, 1895.

44. "The Wheat Production and Trade of India," *Selections from the Records of the Government of India, Home, Revenue, and Agricultural Department,* No. CLX (Simla, 1879), 302–57; "Papers Relating to the Introduction of the System of Grain Elevators in Vogue in the United States of America and in Canada, 1890–91," *British Parliamentary Papers* (1894), LVIII (East India, III), 4–9; Frederick Noel-Paton, *Indian Wheat and Grain Elevators* (Calcutta, 1913), i–ii, 2–17.

45. Nathan A. Cobb, "Grain Elevators," Department of Agriculture, New South Wales, *Miscellaneous Publication No. 452* (Sydney, 1901), *passim;* A. R. Callaghan and A. J. Millington, *The Wheat Industry in Australia* (Sydney, 1956), 374–75.

46. James M. Sinclair, *Report on Wheat Production in the United States, Canada, and the Argentine* (Victoria Department of Agriculture: Melbourne, 1895), 41–53. Sinclair's conclusion after an inspection of the American trade was that Australia could produce wheat at lower cost, but that "this advantage is wiped out by the economy of cheaper handling through elevators."

47. Isaac A. Hourwich, "Russia in the International Market," *Journal of Political Economy,* II (March, 1894), 284. For a perceptive analysis of the role of wheat exports in Russia's struggle to attain a gold standard and increase her capital imports see Olga Crisp, "Russian Financial Policy and the Gold Standard at the End of the Nineteenth Century," *Economic History Review,* Second Series, VI (December, 1953), 156–72.

48. Reprinted from St. Louis *Republican* in *Northwestern Miller,* August 29, 1879.

49. *Northwestern Miller,* September 17, 1880.

50. *Ibid.*, December 17, 1880, and December 8, 1882.

51. *Ibid.*, April 4 and 11, 1884.

52. *Ibid.*, June 25, 1886, and July 20, 1888.

53. *J. E. Beerbohm's Corn Trade News* (London), Supplement, November 25, 1889; *Board of Trade Journal* (London), October, 1889, p. 399.

54. *Northwestern Miller*, July 28, 1893.

55. *Ibid.*, October 2, 1891, and March 5, 1895; *Beerbohm's Corn Trade News*, May 18, 1892.

56. Rubinow, "Russian Wheat and Flour in European Markets," U.S. Department of Agriculture, *Bureau of Statistics, Bulletin No. 66*, pp. 98–99; Edward T. Peters, "Russian Cereal Crops," U.S. Department of Agriculture, *Bureau of Statistics, Bulletin No. 84* (Washington, 1911), *passim*.

57. Vernon C. Fowke, *The National Policy and the Wheat Economy* (Toronto, 1957), 108–11, 153–64.

12

State Intervention:
The Granger Laws

PASSAGE OF THE Granger laws in the 1870's has long been regarded
as a pivotal event in American economic and political history. According to the standard interpretation, these state laws for regulation of warehouses and railroads comprised the first major attempt
at governmental control of business practices, following a lengthy
period of *laissez faire* policy in the United States. They have commonly been identified, therefore, as marking the beginning of the
modern regulatory state. Moreover, as the term "Granger laws"
connotes, it has commonly been assumed that an organized farm
movement, the Grange, was the political pressure group chiefly
responsible for this legislation.

Recent historical scholarship has modified this conventional interpretation in two respects. First, Frederick Merk and others have
demonstrated that as early as the 1850's, during the first wave of
major railroad consolidations, the state governments acted to regulate railroad rate practices. Even in the canal period of the 1830's,
it has been argued, the state governments manipulated public canal
tolls for special purposes (thereby regulating markets indirectly)
and imposed prescribed rate schedules on private turnpike companies. Some scholars therefore now perceive considerable continuity
in the history of regulatory action by the states, and they have discarded the notion that the Granger laws marked a clear-cut break
with tradition.

The following article by George H. Miller represents the second

recent revision in interpretation of the Granger laws. Miller questions the notion that these laws were of purely agrarian political
origins. In certain localities, Miller argues, businessmen as well as
farmers were injured by railway rate discriminations, and both business and agricultural leaders responded to this threat by demanding
state regulation. Miller's interpretation, which emphasizes the
interplay of conflicting local interests, supercedes the older view that
portrayed the Granger laws as a victory of agrarian over industrial
and commercial interests.

ORIGINS OF THE IOWA GRANGER LAW

George H. Miller

The Granger laws are prominent mileposts in the history of American public-service law. Their enactment in the 1870's precipitated
a constitutional crisis from which there emerged a fundamental re-
statement of state rights with respect to "private enterprise." [1] As
contributions to substantive and procedural law they figured prominently in the evolution of a system of railroad rate regulation which
later was embodied in the pioneer Interstate Commerce Act of
1887.[2] To their adoption has been traced the very beginnings of
modern industrial control in the interest of the public welfare.[3]

The body of state legislation referred to as the Granger laws
derives its common name from the farmers' organization known as
the Patrons of Husbandry or Grange. The standard interpretation
as to the origin of these measures holds that during the decade
following the Civil War, "militant farmers," oppressed by the ex-
orbitant and discriminatory charges of railroads and warehousemen,
"seized control" of Western state legislatures and enacted a series
of radical and stringent rate-control statutes. The "militant farmers"
were generally called Grangers whether they belonged to that organization or not; the laws were known almost from the beginning as
Granger laws even though the Patrons disclaimed any political
objectives.[4]

Reprinted by permission from *The Mississippi Valley Historical Review*, XL
(March, 1954), pp. 657–80.

But the farmers' movement which brought the Grange into national prominence during the early 1870's was by no means coextensive with the movement leading to the adoption of the Granger laws. Solon J. Buck has pointed out in his authoritative account of the Granger movement that "the agitation for the regulation of railways began long before the Patrons of Husbandry arose to importance." [5] It would seem to follow, therefore, that the historical importance of the Granger laws cannot properly be assessed without reference to the non-Granger elements in the movement for their adoption.

It can be shown conclusively that the Granger railroad laws passed by the states of the upper Mississippi Valley between 1871 and 1874 were all concerned primarily with the problem of rate discrimination. "The uprising of the people of the Western States . . . ," wrote a contemporary observer, "was not against the aggregate amount of the rates being collected by the railways, but against the discrimination they were practicing in collecting their revenues. This fact should be thoroughly mastered by every mind which desires to comprehend the meaning of the so-called Granger legislation." [6] The primary target of these measures was discrimination against localities, a form of unequal treatment against which the existing common law of carriers offered no protection. [7] They are part of a chain of historical development which begins with the introduction of prorata bills in New England state legislatures during the 1840's and 1850's and continues through the adoption of the Interstate Commerce Act of 1887. [8] This series of proposals for rate-law reforms, sponsored for the most part by merchants and businessmen, can scarcely be interpreted as agrarian attacks upon the business community. On the contrary, they were designed to protect vested commercial interests in the face of disruptive economic forces engendered by discriminatory railroad rate-making practices; and to this general rule the Granger laws were no exception. [9] The legislative history of the Iowa law of March 19, 1874, provides abundant evidence in support of this thesis.

During the early years of railroad operation in the United States the power to regulate the charges of common carriers by statute was freely exercised by state legislatures. It is quite probable that most of the railway mileage of the United States in the year 1850 was being operated under some form of legislative restriction with regard to rate levels. [10] As far as the courts were concerned rate fixing was a normal operation of the police power and was exercised without benefit of judicial review unless the right to regulate was specifically granted away by charter.[11] The two decades between 1850 and 1870, however, were marked by a general curtailment of the regulatory function. In the interest of railway promotion many state legislatures refrained from using their power of police over rates, and in some cases made outright grants of immunity from statutory control. For a short time the established practice of carrier rate restriction gave way to a liberal policy of freedom and encouragement for railroad development.[12]

It was during the expansive 1850's, when the spirit of promotion was in the ascendancy, that railroad operation was first undertaken in the State of Iowa. At the outset the policy of the Iowa legislature was generous to a fault. Construction was encouraged by a favorable program of taxation and local aid, and by an openhanded distribution of public lands. Although the railroad land-grant act of 1856 reserved the traditional right of regulation for all roads receiving benefits from the act, and the new state constitution of 1857 provided for the amendment of all corporate charters subsequently granted, there was no attempt to impose statutory regulations upon rates and fares.[13] There was, in fact, an overwhelming popular sentiment against such restrictions. The reservation of the right of control over railway franchises was impelled by a general distrust of corporate power; it indicated no immediate demand in Iowa for controls over rates. The reluctance of outside capitalists to invest their money in Western enterprises subject to such legislative interference was too well known; and Iowa, because she lacked adequate financial resources of her own, was courting the favor of outside capitalists.[14] Even though no constitutional barriers to regulation were raised, the state offered ample guarantees of operational freedom in the form of an insatiable demand for the benefits of railroad transportation.[15]

The first Iowa railroads—those put into operation during the 1850's—were planned as feeder lines for the towns along the Mississippi River. They were conceived as connecting lines between the River and the interior—as improved highways over which the grain of the prairies could be brought to the mills and landings at McGregor, Dubuque, Clinton, Davenport, Muscatine, Burlington, Fort Madison, Keokuk, and other ports along the banks of the great north-south waterway.[16] Prior to 1860 the primary market for Iowa grain was St. Louis, and the Iowa river towns were in fact its subsidiary collecting points. They served Iowa as Chicago served Illinois and as Milwaukee served Wisconsin; they were terminal collecting points, wholesale markets, banking centers, mill towns; and the railroads had promised each one of them a wide and prosperous future.[17]

But to the river towns of Iowa the railroad soon proved a mixed blessing. Beginning in 1854, Chicago and Milwaukee rail lines reached the River at points opposite the Iowa terminals. The Milwaukee, the Illinois Central, the Northwestern, the Rock Island, and the Burlington laid their tracks to the River's edge, contemplated the bridging of the great barrier, and established running connections with roads on the other side. The impact of the Chicago and Milwaukee "invasion" upon the commercial life of the state was tremendous. The easy-going collection and distribution system established by merchants serving the older river trade was no match for the aggressive, highly competitive organizations serving the Great Lakes ports. Ignoring the existing terminals, Eastern grain buyers and wholesale merchants moved into the interior, going straight to the rural markets. Lumber for prairie farmhouses began to roll westward from Chicago to interior Iowa communities without using the facilities of the river-town markets. In like manner grain and hogs were billed through directly to the Lakes from local Iowa collecting points. Virtually overnight, the Mississippi ports had become mere way points on trunk lines serving the lake cities. Dubuque, Davenport, and Burlington in their position as primary markets were forced into direct competition with Chicago for the business of their own state.[18]

The market price of grain at each step in the chain of sale was that offered at the next terminal collecting point minus freight charges and the customary dealer's commission. Dubuque merchants, in other words, paid either St. Louis or Chicago prices less the cost of transportation to these markets; the grain buyers at Waterloo, Iowa, now paid either Dubuque or Chicago prices less the cost of shipment to one of these two points. If Dubuque were to compete with Chicago for the grain of Waterloo and realize the profits of a primary grain market, it obviously had to pay a price equal to that offered by Chicago; but its ability to do so depended in large measure upon the structure of rates on the Illinois Central and its Iowa connection.

During the late 1850's Chicago was replacing St. Louis as the principal market for Iowa grain. Under these circumstances the river-port grain buyers and wholesale merchants were bound to have trouble in maintaining their position. But their difficulties were compounded after 1858 by railroad rate-making policy. Freight charges between rural collecting points and the River, when added to separate charges between the River and Chicago, were totaling considerably more than the through charges for the same shipment between interior points and the Lake. An expanding system of preferential long-haul rail rates was depriving the Iowa commercial centers of their former economic importance. The state was in danger of becoming a mere agricultural province of Chicago.[19]

At the session of the Iowa general assembly held in 1860, a number of petitions and resolutions were presented inquiring into the propriety of compelling Iowa railroads to charge the same rate per mile for transportation within the state as they did for passengers and freight destined beyond the state line. The representative from Jefferson County introduced a rate-control measure with additional provisions designed to correct the evil tendencies of absentee ownership; the representative from Des Moines County presented a prorata bill requiring that all rates be fixed in strict accordance with the distance covered; the mayor and aldermen of Burlington submitted the draft of a measure to regulate freight and passenger tariffs in the interest of Iowa commerce.[20] The beginnings of the movement to impose statutory limitations upon Iowa railroad rates clearly stemmed from the discrimination practiced against local trading interests.

The reaction of the state assembly to the introduction of the railroad rate problem into Iowa politics was decidedly hostile. The majority felt strongly that it would be "state suicide" to legislate in an unfriendly manner with respect to railroads at that time. Since Iowa was unable to supply sufficient capital to build her own roads and since no Eastern capitalist would invest money in a railroad over which he and his associates could not exercise control, rate restrictions were considered inimical to the best interests of the state. The need of the day was for more railroads. Accordingly each of the rate-control measures was rejected.[21]

In 1861 the Civil War closed the Southern market and further intensified the subservience of the river towns to the Lake Michigan ports. Although the great prosperity of the war years was shared by Iowa as by all states of the agricultural West, the native commercial interests of the state did not lose sight of their growing dependence upon Chicago and Milwaukee. During the war years they worked out a program calculated to restore their economic independence.

Their demands came to include improved water routes to and from the East which would permit boats from the Great Lakes to come through to the river ports. When the war came to an end, this plan was enlarged to include the rejuvenation of the Southern market with its promise of trade with the Eastern seaboard and Europe by way of New Orleans. Plans were made for the improvement of the Mississippi north of Keokuk where the Des Moines and Rock Island rapids hindered river traffic and added greatly to the cost of water shipment. Enthusiastic support was given to such projects as the improvement of the Illinois and Michigan Canal and the construction of a Wisconsin-Fox River waterway. In fact any improvement which promised to open direct water routes between Iowa and her Eastern markets was sure to win the favor of the river communities.[22]

The plan for establishing a flourishing commerce by natural and artificial waterways, however, presupposed a system of railroad rates which would give favorable treatment to the river towns. Dubuque would still be hard put to compete with Chicago as a primary market if the Illinois Central asked a greater total charge for freight carried between interior points and Dubuque than it did for that shipped over the longer distance to Chicago. Produce would not stop at a river port if it could go at lower cost to a lake port. In order to restore the river towns to a favorable position on the trade routes of the West it would be necessary to level the rate structures on the various trunk lines leading to the Lakes. That this was a problem of interstate commerce was a fact that Iowa commercial and political leaders were quick to perceive. From a very early date, Iowa was in the vanguard of the campaign for federal regulation of railroad rates.[23] But national control was too improbable at the time to promise quick relief. A system of state regulation capable of producing the same result was the requirement of the moment.

It was impossible, of course, to raise the rates between interior towns and Chicago because Iowa had no control over the Illinois segments of the trunk lines involved. For the same reason a simple prorata law or a long-and-short-haul measure would have been of no benefit to the river ports. The base rate in either case would have to be an intrastate rate and would not necessarily be affected by the Chicago rate. The only available solution was to lower charges between interior points and the Mississippi by imposing mandatory schedules of fixed maximum rates on all intrastate traffic. A program of this sort was prepared and presented to the general assembly of 1866.[24]

Governor William Stone's message to the legislature of 1866 warned the senators and representatives that the people were still clamoring for more railroads. He claimed to speak for the farmers of the state when he advised the encouragement of additional competing routes of transportation in place of hostile legislation as the best solution to the transportation problem.[25] Nevertheless, the river interests, led by W. T. Barker of Dubuque and Samuel McNutt of Muscatine, put forward a plan for statutory control of the rate level for all Iowa railroads. Thomas Wilson of Dubuque sponsored a second reform bill placing the regulatory power in the hands of an independent commission. Wilson hoped to prevent the alienation of Eastern capital, but the more radical element was extremely suspicious of halfway measures of this sort.[26]

The first significant vote on the rate question came with the introduction by the house committee on commerce of a bill designed to place a legal maximum upon Iowa rail rates and thereby to prevent discrimination against the river towns in favor of Chicago. When Wilson tried to amend it in such a way as to give the rate-fixing authority to a commission, Barker asked if this idea had not originated with a railroad official. Wilson admitted that it had. The upshot of the debate was that Wilson's amendments were decisively defeated and the commerce committee bill was adopted by the house.[27]

But the house majority does not give an accurate picture of Iowa sentiment. The representatives of the western counties—the "have nots" in so far as railroads were concerned—had supported the more radical bill only because it would have even less chance of passing the senate. There was neither surprise nor alarm when the measure died in the files of a senate committee.[28]

When the general assembly next convened, in January, 1868, Governor Stone, who was retiring from office, delivered a farewell address full of references to the prosperity of the state. The railroads, he reported, were doing a splendid job of opening vacant areas to settlement and were giving rise to numerous towns and cities. The legislature, by all means, should continue to encourage new construction and should avoid measures hostile to railroad development. Stone recognized, of course, that there were abuses in the management of railroads that ought to be prevented. Injudicious and discriminatory tariffs had become a subject of almost universal complaint, and there was undeniably a need for cheaper means of transportation to the Eastern seaboard. But in his opinion the solution best calculated to solve both problems was the opening of rival water routes. Remove the obstructions from the Mississippi between Rock Island and Keokuk, and the Northwest would no longer be at the mercy of the railroad corporations.[29]

Governor Stone's successor in 1868 was Samuel Merrill, a Republican merchant and banker from the river town of McGregor. Merrill's ideas on the railroad problem were set forth in a special message to the assembly on January 24, 1868. Assuring his audience that he was fully aware of the dangers of discouraging construction, he recommended the insertion of a clause in every future railway charter which would prohibit discrimination in the arrangement of freight tariffs and passenger fares. It seemed only reasonable to the Governor that transportation charges should be made prorata according to distance. He explained in a subsequent message that he was not in favor of absolute legal maxima since this could easily deter new enterprise, but he was in favor of enforcing equal charges —just how he did not say—and of reserving the right to regulate wherever possible.[30]

Merrill's views were vigorously supported by his attorney general, Henry O'Connor. In an opinion upholding the constitutionality of proposed legislation to regulate the rates of railroads already chartered, O'Connor urged the prohibition and punishment of rate-making abuses. Unjust discrimination which builds up one city and destroys the trade of another, he declared, "shocks the most elementary notions of law. It is wholly inconsistent with the plainest notions of our institutions, and at war with the whole theory of our government." By virtue of the reservation clause in the state constitution, he said, the general assembly had full power to prevent such discrimination.[31]

The general assembly of 1868 considered a number of bills to prevent railways from discriminating "against the trade and commerce of the state." Proposals for investigatory commissions that might examine the nature and scope of the discrimination problem were also discussed.[32] But immediate regulation was defeated once again by the representatives of the western counties. In Iowa the early months of 1868 were "a season of Railroad Conventions"—to encourage construction and not to restrict rates. The railroad fever of the postwar era was at its peak and would not tolerate legislation hostile to its purpose.[33]

The most that could be obtained from the assembly of 1868 was a series of reservation clauses known as the Doud amendments.

These provisions for future legislative control were inserted in a number of private acts referring to the extension and transfer of land grants. Under the leadership of Representatives McNutt of Muscatine and James Wilson of Tama, and of Senators Eliab Doud of Van Buren and B. B. Richards of Dubuque, the amendments were pushed through the general assembly without much difficulty.[34] As measures designed to limit individual trunk lines each of which had acquired the backing of important Eastern interests, the Doud amendments did not have to buck the unified hostility of the have-not areas.

By 1870, Iowa was well integrated into the national railway net and more than ever tributary to the Chicago market. The railroads continued to defeat the commercial ambitions of the river towns by their rate-making policies and by their political strength in the state assembly. By steadily reducing their rates from interior points to Lake Michigan they had virtually neutralized the competitive possibilities of the River; and by playing upon the promotional aims of the have-not areas they had helped to prevent the adoption of active control laws and charter provisions.[35] The rapid development of the railroad system, however, was giving rise to other forms of local inequalities in the rate structures of the different roads. The wave of discontent was moving westward across the state in the wake of railroad construction.

Most elementary of all types of local rate discrimination which gave rise to the rate-law reform movements of the last half of the nineteenth century was that practiced against way points—the towns served by but one line of railroad without the benefit of competition for their trade. Just as the earliest railroad towns attracted business and population away from unserved communities, so the towns at the junction of two or more rival lines drew trade and settlers away from the way points. Because competitive rail rates meant higher prices for the farmer's crops and lower prices for his supplies, the producers, wherever possible, took their business to the competitive centers. The grain buyers, retail merchants, bankers, lawyers, and other businessmen at the way points saw their trade diminished, their land values lowered, the return on their local investments threatened. The Iowa merchants of the prairie way points added powerful voices to the complaints of the river towns as the effects of local discrimination became more and more evident in the interior.[36]

In the Iowa state legislature, however, the representatives of the river towns, and especially those of Dubuque, maintained their position of leadership in the movement for railroad rate restrictions. The general assembly of 1870 was the recipient of scores of petitions demanding regulation of railroad rates and fares. The petitions poured in from every part of the state, but the legislative debates revealed that the bulk of them had been printed by the merchants of Dubuque and distributed along the rights of way of the major trunk lines. By January, 1870, many thousands of signatures had been obtained from the merchants and shippers of the collecting points. In the same month Dubuque further demonstrated her intention of leading the rate-control movement by calling a convention of protest with respect to local and terminal rate discrimination.[37]

The 1870 session of the legislature witnessed a determined bid to obtain a maximum-rate law. In the house of representatives a bill introduced by William Mills, a Dubuque lawyer, became the focal point of debate. The measure was frankly designed to prevent the diversion of trade from the River to Chicago and, according to the Iowa City *State Press,* was prepared by former Senator B. B. Richards, also of Dubuque. Early in February, Richards appeared in person before the house committee on railroads. He cited examples of discrimination against the river towns and indicated the effect of current rate-making practices upon the commercial and industrial interests of the state. Flour mills along the Mississippi, he claimed, were being forced out of business; farmers in the interior were being deprived of their "natural outlets" down the River; grain buyers were being compelled to move to Chicago in order to make a living; the river ports were losing their "natural advantage" as lumber markets and all because of unequal freight rates. He asked for immediate adoption of the Mills bill as the only means of saving Iowa trade from complete destruction.[38]

The committee then took testimony from representatives of the railroad companies. The latter took the position that their schedules were prepared in the interests of the farmers, and they pointed to the fact that low through rates to Chicago were the only means whereby the inland farmer could compete in the Eastern market. As far as discrimination against trade within the state was concerned, they insisted that "long experience" had shown these distinctions to be both necessary and just. The differences in rates were simply the result of variations in traffic and cost conditions. The proposed legislation, they concluded, would be extremely burdensome and would probably necessitate the abandonment of through-freight service.[39]

After hearing both sides a majority of the house committee reported in favor of the Mills bill. A minority, to be sure, thought that such matters should be left to the workings of natural laws and challenged the expediency of the measure for the usual have-not reason that it might deter capital from coming into Iowa. But the house adopted the bill with a solid majority of 62 to 28 and with even greater ease passed a companion measure dealing with passenger fares.[40]

The senate, however, was less willing to follow the lead of the river interests. Although a number of control measures, including the Mills bill, were vigorously defended by Frank T. Campbell of Jasper County, John P. Irish of Iowa City, Samuel McNutt of Muscatine, Samuel H. Fairall of Iowa City, and M. B. Mulkern of Dubuque, all were doomed to failure. In the course of the debates members from several inland counties became bitter in their denunciation of the selfishness displayed by the river communities. They accused them of deliberately trying to prevent the construction of north-south lines and insisted that there was no popular demand in the interior for control legislation. The petitions, they asserted, meant nothing since they originated for the most part from a single source. The people of Iowa wanted railroads; they did not want regulation.[41]

There were other critics of both house and senate control bills who now based their opposition upon the intricacies of the rate problem. Senator Homer Newell, with slight exaggeration, called attention to the fact that every state in the Union from Maine to Iowa had considered the prorata principle and pronounced it unworkable. Senator William Larrabee pointed to the impossibility of fixing a just maximum rate for all the railroads in the state.[42] The latter point, in fact, was becoming of more and more political consequence. Senator Larrabee had broached the strong-weak road problem, a continuing factor in the determination of rate-control legislation. The disparity in earning power of the different roads within the state made the imposition of a single effective maximum rate completely impossible. Obviously a rate that would be fair and just for a strong, east-west line would be entirely unremunerative for a new, north-south road. And since the river-town interests were concerned primarily with the trunk lines, the stringency of their maximum-rate proposals had brought forward a weak-road faction willing to accept anti-discrimination laws but hostile to rigid statutory limitations which might bankrupt the smaller lines. In 1870 the combined forces of have-not and weak-road interests in the upper house prevailed. By very close margins the house measures were tabled, and a senate rate-control bill, introduced by Dubuque's Senator Mulkern, was defeated on its third reading.[43]

The state election of 1871 produced a Republican landslide and brought to the governorship Cyrus C. Carpenter of Fort Dodge.[44] Carpenter's views on the railroad question were moderate, well informed, and geared to the best interests of the interior collecting points. He did not doubt for a moment the right of the assembly to impose restrictions upon rates, and he recognized competition as the source rather than the cure for prevailing ills. Nevertheless, he was not prepared to endorse arbitrary fixed maxima. His own solution in 1871 was to abolish all discrimination between individuals and localities without reference to the rate level and to open up improved water routes to the seaboard.[45]

But the Dubuque contingent returned to Des Moines in 1872 with renewed intentions of securing their maximum rate law. Representative Frederick O'Donnell, acting as their spokesman, reintroduced the so-called "Dubuque bill" which had been sponsored by Mills at the previous session, and proceeded to steer it through the house. An effort to have rate-fixing powers vested in a commission was easily brushed aside; a similar fate awaited a weak-road amendment exempting roads with annual gross earnings of less than $3000 per mile. But the Dubuque bill did not get through completely unscathed. A group claiming to represent the interior collecting points succeeded in inserting a long-and-short-haul clause which would prevent a railroad from charging more for any short haul than it did for a longer haul on the same line. The chief complaint of the inland counties, they maintained, was discrimination against way points and not excessive rates. O'Donnell and his supporters hastened to assure the house that the original bill would accomplish the same purpose and hoped that the chance of obtaining a rate-control measure at this session would not be jeopardized by the inclusion of a measure distasteful to the competitive centers. But the latter argument proved unfounded, for the amended bill passed the house by a vote of 80 to 13.[46]

The Dubuque bill of 1872 went to the senate where it once again came under attack from the more moderate exponents of control. Senator John Y. Stone of Mills County proposed an amendment which would provide for a popularly elected commission. According to his plan the legislature would fix rates in the first instance, but the commissioners would be authorized to modify them from time to time as they saw fit. The friends of the Dubuque measure rallied to the defense of untrammeled statutory control, claiming first that the legislature could not delegate its police powers and secondly that the remedy demanded by all the petitions presented at that session was *fixed* uniform rates. Stone countered with an appeal to the have-nots and finally succeeded in gaining his point. The senate concurred in the house bill amended by Stone and sent it back to the house of representatives.[47]

The house immediately rejected the Stone amendment as equivalent to a complete emasculation of the original measure. The radicals were convinced that a commission would be little more than an agency of the railroad companies and implied that the amendment must have been dictated by the corporations themselves. In the weeks that followed three separate efforts were made to find a satisfactory compromise, but the deadlock remained unbroken.[48] Toward the end of April the general assembly adjourned without reaching any agreement whatsoever. Although a large majority of both houses had recognized the need for immediate regulation in some form, the unwillingness of the fixed-maximum-rate group to withdraw from its original position had made compromise impossible. By the same token the have-not and weak-road elements had flatly refused to yield.[49]

The general assembly of 1872, however, was to have another chance at solving the railroad rate problem. In January, 1873, it reassembled for the purpose of recodifying the laws of the state, a process which permitted amendments and additions equivalent to new legislation. During the intervening winter of 1872–1873, it should be noted, the state of Iowa had been shaken by the first rumblings of the coming farmers' revolt. The movement for rural organization, highlighted by the rise of the Patrons of Husbandry, was sweeping across the Middle West with amazing success. In Iowa the Grange undeniably was becoming a force with which to be reckoned, and it quickly made known its intentions of influencing political opinion by holding its convention at Des Moines during the special session of the assembly. The Grangers put forward a comprehensive program of reform. They asked for a government-built, double-track, all-freight railroad to the seaboard; state-owned, narrow-gauge feeder routes in Iowa; an end to railway land grants; and legislative regulation of intrastate rates.[50] But they took no

definite stand on the matters of dispute within the larger issue
of control which had prevented the legislature from adopting rate
legislation at its previous meeting. It was not until the following
year that the Grange actually committed itself to a precise program.
The session of 1873, meanwhile, seems to have been little affected
by the emergence of the militant farmer.

The squabble between house and senate of the previous year was
repeated with only slightly improved results. The lower chamber,
led once again by Representative O'Donnell of Dubuque, tried to
insert a schedule of maximum rates into the section of the code dealing with internal improvements. The addition of a long-and-short-
haul clause, distasteful to competitive centers, was forestalled by an
agreement, made in caucus by the advocates of control, to exempt
roads whose gross annual earnings did not exceed $4000 per mile.
With the weak-road faction pacified in this manner, the hopes of
the radicals soared.[51]

But once again the senate proved adamant. McNutt's efforts
to place a similar schedule of rates in the senate's version of the
internal improvement section were frustrated by a tie vote. He
succeeded in inserting a three and one-half cent maximum passen-
ger-fare law and added a section protecting the "Doud amendments" with respect to the right of regulation; but these features
were the only innovations in the railroad rate law of the code of
1873. Once again the senate rejected the house proposal and refused
to allow any changes in its own.[52]

Because of divisions of opinion among the proponents of rate
regulation in Iowa, the legislature of 1872–1873 had accomplished
very little in the way of rate-law reform. Generally speaking, the
representatives of eastern and southern "have" areas had supported
direct legislative control, while the western and northern members
from unserved and weak-road districts had held out for the more
flexible commission system; but the more numerous haves were
divided in turn between the river interests who were determined
to have fixed legal maxima and the men from way-station areas
who were more concerned with obtaining a long-and-short-haul
measure. The river towns had succeeded thus far in retaining the
initiative, and because of the regional appeal of their program with
its insistence that Iowa railroads must serve Iowa interests, plus
their promise that maximum charges would level the structure of
rail rates in much the same way as would a prorata law, they had
won the largest body of supporters. A shift of one vote in the senate

of 1873 might have resulted in victory for the Dubuque schedule. But the maximum-rate group had yet to find a satisfactory means of pacifying the have-not and weak-road areas. The fear that rigid schedules would ruin the newer lines, halt construction, and drive capital from the state was sufficiently strong in 1873 to merit the attention of the most rabid advocate of legislative control.

The state elections in the fall of 1873 saw the appearance on Iowa ballots of a new party label. In an effort to capitalize on defections from the Republican ranks during the Grant administration and current rumblings of rural discontent, a new opposition party known as the Anti-Monopolists was founded on the apparent ruins of the Democracy. The "new" party made notable gains in the general assembly and, although failing to win the governorship, cut deep into Carpenter's majority of 1871. But the railroad question can hardly be considered a decisive factor in the campaign. Since 1870 both Republican and opposition platforms had contained planks endorsing state regulation without any important distinctions as to principle.[53] Moreover, in the state legislature from 1860 on, party affiliation had not played a visible part in the voting on control measures. The conclusion would seem to be justifiable that the railroad problem remained fundamentally sectional and did not become a party issue.

Governor Carpenter's biennial message to the new general assembly together with his second inaugural, delivered four days later, included a careful analysis of the railroad problem as of January, 1874. He pointed out that railway construction had fallen off sharply in the past two years, destroying the hopes of many that competition from new roads would bring an adequate remedy. It had been claimed, of course, that fear of hostile legislation was the cause of the cessation, and no doubt this was partly true; but this, said the Governor, was all the more reason to pass a rate law. A sensible, conservative measure would remove the fears of capitalists and encourage whatever new development was needed. The law should prevent railroads from making unjust discriminations against places and individuals and prevent them from discouraging local trade and manufacturing. Freight should not be deterred from reaping the advantages of water communication. The most effective form of control, he now thought, would be a maximum-rate law based on a system of classification that would provide a fair return on the actual paid-in capital of each road.[54]

The principle of classification suggested by Carpenter had helped to secure the adoption of the Illinois Granger laws of 1871 and 1873. It was now to prove helpful in breaking the deadlock which had existed in the Iowa assembly. Although the moderate reformers still pressed for commission control with the new Illinois system as their model, and a small group continued to work for a simple anti-discrimination law, the great majority of the representatives in the legislature of 1874 were ready to accept the Dubuque formula as soon as it had been modified by a system of classification based on earnings.[55] A committee of the Iowa State Grange, it is true, now came out in favor of the long-and-short-haul plan supplemented by commission control.[56] Strangely enough the railroad lobby, in the hope of obtaining a compromise settlement, was pressing for precisely the same measure.[57] The Grangers, in fact, seem everywhere to have favored the more moderate system of regulation adopted by Illinois even though this system with its so-called strong commission had been rejected repeatedly by the radicals as too susceptible to railroad influence.[58] The Grange in Iowa was actually a conservative force on this particular issue. Delegations of businessmen, on the other hand, appeared at Des Moines to urge the enactment of a maximum-rate law.[59] The latter seemed to have spoken with louder voices.

The final statute adopted on March 19, 1874, was the product of deliberation in the railroad committee of both houses. In contrast with previous sessions there was relatively little debate on the floor, and no conference committee was necessary to settle the inevitable differences between senate and house. Its adoption by overwhelming majorities in both houses was almost anticlimactic.[60] The heart of the law of 1874 was a detailed schedule of maximum rates graduated according to distance for all classes of freight. Its authorship was credited to Senator Frank T. Campbell, a Republican merchant and journalist from Jasper County who had been a staunch supporter of the Dubuque bills. The schedule was based on the table of maximum rates issued by the Illinois Railroad and Warehouse Commission for the year 1874.[61] On the basis of annual earnings Iowa railroads were divided into three classes and were limited to 90 percent, 105 percent, and 120 percent of the established legal tariff according to their classification. Passenger fares were restricted to three, three and one-half, and four cents per mile, depending on the earning power of the road.[62]

The schedule was obviously prepared in the interest of local Iowa commerce, and to a limited extent it seems to have had the desired effect. On some classes of freight it brought about a reduction of rates between interior points and the River amounting to as much as 50 percent. But the continuing decline of through rates after 1873 seems to have made the schedule obsolete soon after it was prepared. Furthermore, the hoped-for development of water routes to the seaboard—the essential complement of rate restriction according to the original river-town program—had failed to materialize. The course of Western trade in 1874 was running irresistibly eastward over iron rails that extended clear to the Atlantic ports. The percentage of trade stopping at the River remained relatively small.[63] Thus, the primary goal of the first proponents of rate restriction was not to be realized. Beyond this, the Iowa Granger law of 1874 was entirely too rigid and too inadequate with respect to procedural guarantees to prevent the other forms of local discrimination. It was repealed by the general assembly of 1878.[64]

The legislative history of the Iowa Granger law shows clearly that the movement to impose legislative restrictions upon intrastate railroad rates in Iowa grew out of complaints of unjust discrimination against the trade and commerce of the state. It shows further that the hardships inflicted by the carriers upon certain mercantile interests remained a decisive factor in the movement down to the time of legislative enactment. Neither the agrarian revolt of 1873–1874 nor the appearance of the Anti-Monopoly party in 1873 can be credited with any decisive influence upon the course of the movement in the legislature or upon the substance of the law. The issue was decided by the extension of the railway net over the unserved part of the state and by a political compromise of the strong-weak road problem. This does not mean that agrarian interests were without influence in the movement for rate regulation. It means simply that the organized or "militant" farmers were not in control of the movement and that a rate-control measure would almost certainly have been adopted by the general assembly of 1874 had there been no Granger revolt.

These conclusions with respect to Iowa find added confirmation in the parallel experiences of neighboring states. In Illinois and Minnesota the pattern of protest is found to be very similar, and the origins of the railroad rate legislation enacted by these states between 1869 and 1874 are different only in detail. Here, too, the merchants and shippers complained of uneven rate structures and were the first to ask for Granger-type legislation. The organized farmers and Anti-Monopolists joined the movement only after it was well under way and in no instance came to dominate it. In Iowa the leadership of the river-town interests gave to the movement a special character which led to the adoption of fixed statutory maxima. In Illinois and Minnesota the interior way-point interests came to dominate and brought about the passage of long-and-short-haul measures supplemented by commission control.[65]

In Wisconsin, where the most radical of all the Granger laws was adopted, the movement for regulation had similar beginnings but followed a different course from 1867 on. Strong agitation for controls virtually disappeared from the political scene for a period of six years and then suddenly re-emerged in the election campaign of 1873. The passage of the famous Potter law by the state legislature of the following year was so confused by partisan politics that it is difficult to determine the true objectives of the sincere advocates of controls. The Potter law was little more then a Republican trick designed to embarrass a Reform party administration. It was neither sponsored nor approved by the Grangers.[66]

If the Grangers and Anti-Monopolists contributed in any significant way to the adoption of these laws it was in their promotion of a public attitude which was hostile to certain railroad practices and which was sufficiently strong to overbalance for a time that hunger for more railroads which had led to freedom from regulation in the first place. In an atmosphere charged with anti-railroad sentiment it was difficult for state legislators to find a satisfactory solution to the rate problem. Consequently much of the Granger legislation was premature and ill-advised, and only the Illinois law of 1873 survived the reaction of the late 1870's. Such a contribution is of considerable historical importance. But it does not alter the fact that rate discrimination, a source of discontent in nearly every state, was primarily a problem for merchants and shippers and that the remedies adopted in all of the Granger laws were geared to the needs of commercial interests. The same remedies had been and were being demanded in areas unaffected by the farmers' crusade.

The Iowa Granger law, then, was a local manifestation of the same problem which had given rise to prorata movements in the East and which would eventually produce the federal act to regulate commerce in 1887. Merchants and shippers, supported at times by local farmers and manufacturers, were rebelling against the depressing effect which local rate discrimination had upon their trade at unfavored commercial centers. Since the common law of carriers offered no remedy for this form of abuse, they sought through legislation to provide themselves with legal protection. The Iowa law was no more radical in intent than Massachusetts legislation passed between 1869 and 1871; [67] in its political and economic origins it was scarcely more agrarian.

NOTES

1. Carl B. Swisher, *American Constitutional Development* (Boston, 1943), 397–401.

2. Isaiah L. Sharfman, *The Interstate Commerce Commission: A Study in Administrative Law and Procedure*, 4 vols. in 5 (New York, 1931–1937), I, 16.

3. Allan Nevins, *The Emergence of Modern America, 1865–1878* (New York, 1927), 176.

4. The standard work on the origins of the Granger laws is Solon J. Buck, *The Granger Movement* (Cambridge, Mass., 1913); but see the following paragraph above for that author's qualifications. Bolder statements of the accepted thesis may be found in Nevins, *Emergence of Modern America*, 162–77, and Fred A. Shannon, *The Farmer's Last Frontier: Agriculture, 1860–1897* (New York, 1945), 309–11.

5. Buck, *Granger Movement*, 124.

6. Alpheus B. Stickney, *The Railroad Problem, with Many Illustrative Diagrams* (St. Paul, 1891), 24. Similar statements may be found in Illinois Railroad and Warehouse Commission, *First Annual Report* (Springfield, 1871), 19; "Report of the Select Committee on Transportation Routes to the Seaboard," *Senate Reports*, No. 307, 43 Cong., 1 Sess., Pt. II, 40, 682; William Larrabee, *The Railroad Question; A Historical and Practical Treatise on Railroads, and Remedies for Their Abuses* (Chicago, 1893), 84; Shelby M. Cullom, *Fifty Years of Public Service; Personal Recollections* (Chicago, 1911), 306; and Jonathan Periam, *The Groundswell: A History of the Origin, Aims, and Progress of the Farmer's Movement* (St. Louis, 1874), 453–54.

7. Joseph H. Beale and Bruce Wyman, *Railroad Rate Regulation* (2nd ed., by Bruce Wyman, New York, 1915), 657–58.

8. Thorough studies of the early prorata movements are lacking. For an introduction to the subject, see Frederick Merk, "Eastern Antecedents of the Grangers," *Agricultural History* (Washington), XXIII (January, 1949), 1–8. On New England in general, see Edward C. Kirkland, *Men, Cities, and Transportation: A Study in New England History, 1820–1900*, 2 vols. (Cambridge, Mass., 1948), I, 344–57; on Rhode Island in particular, see John K. Towles, "Early Railroad Monopoly and Discrimination in Rhode Island," *Yale Review* (New Haven), XVIII (November, 1909), 299–319. The best account of the New York prorata movement of 1858–1860 is in Henry V. Poor, *Manual of the Railroads of the United States for 1881* (New York, 1881), xxxi–xxxvii. Material on the movement in Pennsylvania can be found in Louis Hartz, *Economic Policy and Democratic Thought: Pennsylvania, 1776–1860* (Cambridge, Mass., 1948), 272–73, 296, and Allan Nevins, *John D. Rockefeller*, 2 vols. (New York, 1940), I, 259–64. For Ohio, see William F. Gephart, *Transportation and Industrial Development in the Middle West* (New York, 1909), 184–89.

9. For a fuller development of this thesis, see George H. Miller, "The Granger Laws: A Study of the Origins of State Railway Control in the Upper Mississippi Valley" (Ph.D. Dissertation, University of Michigan, 1951).

10. "Were gentlemen willing to grant an unlimited discretion to all [railroad] companies of charging such toll as they may think proper? . . . It seemed to him that a wise legislation would . . . limit the exercise of that power. Such, at any rate, had been the universal practice." Statement of Richard Stillwell in *Report of the Debates and Proceedings of the Convention for the Revision of the Constitution of the State of Ohio, 1850–51,* 2 vols. (Columbus, 1851), I, 347. See also Dionysius Lardner, *Railway Economy* (New York, 1850), 424, and Edward C. Kirkland, *A History of American Economic Life* (3rd ed., New York, 1951), 259–60.

11. The leading case is Beekman *v.* Saratoga and Schenectady Rail Road Co., 3 Paige 45 (N.Y. Ch., 1831), 75. See also Olcott *v.* The Supervisors, 16 Wall. 678 (1873), 694. Early rate regulation is discussed in [Charles F. Adams, Jr.], "Railroad Legislation," *Merchants' Magazine and Commercial Review* (New York), LVII (November, 1867), 339–55; Balthasar H. Meyer, *Railway Legislation in the United States* (New York, 1903), 56–69, 80–96; and Walter C. Noyes, *American Railroad Rates* (Boston, 1905), 214–16.

12. On early railroad promotion, see "Public Aids to Domestic Transportation," *House Documents,* No. 159, 79 Cong., 1 Sess., 105–87, *passim;* and Carter Goodrich, "The Revulsion against Internal Improvements," *Journal of Economic History* (New York), X (November, 1950), 145–69.

13. Peter A. Dey, "Railroad Legislation in Iowa," *Iowa Historical Record* (Des Moines), IX (October, 1893), 540–41; Ivan L. Pollock, *History of Economic Legislation in Iowa* (Iowa City, 1918), 40–41; Earl S. Beard, "Local Aid to Railroads in Iowa," *Iowa Journal of History* (Iowa City), L (January, 1952), 1–17; Iowa Constitution of 1857, Article 8.

14. *Debates of the Constitutional Convention of the State of Iowa, Assembled at Iowa City, Monday, January 19, 1857,* 2 vols. (Davenport, 1857), I, 108–14, 144–61, 167, 171.

15. Dubuque *Weekly Herald,* March 21, 1866; reports of "railroad conventions" in Des Moines *Iowa State Weekly Register* for the first quarter of 1866; Benjamin F. Gue, *History of Iowa,* 4 vols. (New York, 1903), III, 25–26, 58. For examples of antirestriction petitions, see Iowa General Assembly, *House Journal,* 1868, pp. 216, 364, 379. As late as 1865, Iowa had only 891 miles of railroad. Illinois, in the same year, had 3,157 miles.

16. Edgar R. Harlan, *A Narrative History of the People of Iowa,* 5 vols. (Chicago, 1931), I, 301; Robert E. Riegel, "Trans-Mississippi Railroads during the Fifties," *Mississippi Valley Historical Review* (Cedar Rapids), X (September, 1923), 153–55, 165, 171–72.

17. Harlan, *History of Iowa,* I, 299.

18. Wyatt W. Belcher, *The Economic Rivalry between St. Louis and Chicago, 1850–1880* (New York, 1947), *passim;* Bayrd Still, "Patterns of Mid-Nineteenth Century Urbanization in the Middle West," *Mississippi Valley Historical Review,* XXVIII (September, 1941), 198–99; Franklin T. Oldt (ed.), *History of Dubuque County, Iowa* (Chicago, n.d.), 133, 142.

19. Oldt (ed.), *History of Dubuque County,* 133, 142. At times the aggregate rate between an interior town and the River was said to exceed the aggregate rate between the same town and Chicago.

20. Iowa General Assembly, *Senate Journal,* 1860, pp. 167, 423; *House*

Journal, 1860, pp. 297, 304; Des Moines *Iowa State Daily Register*, February 28, March 3, 1860.

21. Des Moines *Iowa State Daily Register*, February 14, 23, 24, March 15, 1860.

22. Iowa State Agricultural Society, *Annual Report of the Secretary*, 1862 (Des Moines, 1863), 7, 126; Iowa General Assembly, *Senate Journal*, 1864, pp. 92, 114, 142, 484; *House Journal*, 1864, pp. 79, 85, 89, 102, 223–24, 511; "Report of the Northwestern Ship Canal Convention," *House Miscellaneous Documents*, No. 23, 38 Cong., 2 Sess.; *Proceedings of the Mississippi River Improvement Convention, Held at Dubuque, Iowa, February 14 and 15, 1866* (Dubuque, 1866); Des Moines *Iowa State Weekly Register*, January 17, 1866; Harlan, *History of Iowa*, II, 21; *Memorial of the Twelfth General Assembly of the State of Iowa to the United States Congress, Relative to Water Communication between the Atlantic and Mississippi*, in Iowa, *Legislative Documents*, 1868, II; Iowa State Agricultural Society, *Annual Report of the Secretary*, 1869 (Des Moines, 1870), 27.

23. National Board of Trade, *Proceedings of Second Annual Meeting* (1869), 71; Iowa General Assembly, *Senate Journal*, 1873, pp. 29–30; *House Journal*, 1874, p. 420; *Senate Journal*, 1874, pp. 290, 313.

24. Railroad rate control was not an issue in the Iowa general assemblies of 1862 and 1864.

25. Benjamin F. Shambaugh (ed.), *Messages and Proclamations of the Governors of Iowa*, 7 vols. (Iowa City, 1903–1905), III, 56–57.

26. Iowa General Assembly, *House Journal*, 1866, pp. 235, 440–41; Dubuque *Weekly Herald*, March 14, 21, 1866; Des Moines *Iowa State Weekly Register*, March 7, 14, 1866; Iowa City *Weekly State Press*, March 21, 1866.

27. Des Moines *Iowa State Weekly Register*, March 7, 14, 21, 1866. It is interesting to note that those representatives who had voted for the Wilson amendment voted against the committee bill; the opponents of commission control, on the other hand, proved to be supporters of the statutory maximum. In Iowa, as in all of the Granger states, commission control bore the stigma of railroad support and consequently was not acceptable to the radical proponents of regulation. Iowa General Assembly, *House Journal*, 1866, pp. 454–55, 763–64.

28. Dubuque *Weekly Herald*, March 21, 28, 1866; Iowa General Assembly, *Senate Journal*, 1866, pp. 495, 540–41, 661. For a fuller development of the thesis that opposition to regulation came chiefly from the unserved western counties, see Earl S. Beard, "The Background of State Railroad Regulation in Iowa," *Iowa Journal of History*, LI (January, 1953), 1–36.

29. Shambaugh (ed.), *Messages and Proclamations*, III, 98–99, 118–21.

30. William H. Fleming, "Governor Samuel Merrill," *Annals of Iowa* (Des Moines), 3rd Series, V (April, 1902), 337–41; Harlan, *History of Iowa*, II, 22, 25; Shambaugh (ed.), *Messages and Proclamations*, III, 398–99, 413–15.

31. Henry O'Connor, *Opinion of the Attorney General of the Powers of the Legislature to Regulate Tariffs on Railroads in the State of Iowa*, in Iowa, *Legislative Documents*, 1868, II.

32. Iowa General Assembly, *Senate Journal*, 1868, pp. 227, 435; *House Journal*, 1868, pp. 116, 487, 581.

33. Iowa General Assembly, *Senate Journal*, 1868, p. 283; *House Journal*, 1868, pp. 216, 364, 379, 490; Des Moines *Iowa State Weekly Register*, January 1, 1868.

34. Des Moines *Iowa State Weekly Register,* February, 1868, *passim;* Harlan, *History of Iowa,* II, 22. The amendments provided that each of the railroads in accepting the land grants would become subject "to such rules, regulations and rates of tariff for the transportation of freight and passengers as may from time to time be enacted and provided for by the General Assembly." *Laws of Iowa, 1868,* Chap. 13, sec. 2; Chap. 57, sec. 3; Chap. 58, sec. 1; Chap. 124, sec. 7.

35. In 1869, a carload of lumber could be shipped from Chicago to Independence, Iowa (75 miles west of Dubuque), for $11. It cost $10 to ship a similar load from Dubuque to Independence on the Illinois Central. Wheat could be shipped from Ft. Dodge, Iowa, to Chicago (340 miles) for 40 cents a hundredweight. It cost 35 cents to send the same wheat from Ft. Dodge to Dubuque (150 miles). In neither case could the Dubuque merchants compete with their Chicago rivals. Statement of T. M. Monroe of Dubuque in National Board of Trade, *Proceedings of Second Annual Meeting* (1869), 70. See also Chicago *Tribune,* December 10, 1869, and Belcher, *Economic Rivalry between St. Louis and Chicago,* 168. On the political influence of the railroads, see Larrabee, *Railroad Question,* 221.

36. Iowa State Agricultural Society, *Annual Report of the Secretary,* 1868 (Des Moines, 1869), 7–8; Frank H. Dixon, *State Railroad Control with a History of Its Developments in Iowa* (New York, 1896), 24; Milo Smith, "Answers to Inquiries in Relation to Commercial Movements to and from the State of Iowa . . . ," in Joseph Nimmo, Jr., *First Annual Report on the Internal Commerce of the United States . . . for the Year 1876* (Bureau of Statistics, Treasury Department, Washington, 1877), Appendix No. 5, p. 95.

37. Iowa General Assembly, *Senate Journal,* 1870, pp. 54, 117, 121, 129, 193, 203, 211, 219–21, 239, 246, 247, 251, 252, 454; *House Journal,* 1870, pp. 90, 114–15, 170, 180, 187, 196, 218, 224, 225, 272, 280, 300, 434–37; Des Moines *Iowa State Daily Register,* January 28, March 18, 26, 1870.

38. Iowa City *Weekly State Press,* February 23, 1870; Des Moines *Iowa State Daily Register,* February 5, 1870. Richards claimed that it cost 60 cents to ship a barrel of flour from Downing, Iowa, to Davenport (42 miles) and only 35 cents to ship one from Downing to Chicago (260 miles). *Ibid.,* February 5, 1870.

39. Des Moines *Iowa State Daily Register,* February 5, 1870. Sponsors of the Mills bill insisted that it would work no hardship on the railroads since it would not prevent them from raising their through rates to Chicago. *Ibid.,* March 24, 1870.

40. Iowa General Assembly, *House Journal,* 1870, pp. 218, 241, 400–401, 428, 442–43; Iowa City *Weekly State Press,* February 23, 1870.

41. Des Moines *Iowa State Daily Register,* March 12, 18, 26, 1870.

42. *Ibid.,* March 26, 1870.

43. Iowa General Assembly, *Senate Journal,* 1870, pp. 163–64, 224–26, 363, 378.

44. The railroad problem was not a major issue in the campaign. Mildred Throne, "Electing an Iowa Governor, 1871: Cyrus Clay Carpenter," *Iowa Journal of History,* XLVIII (October, 1950), 368–69.

45. Shambaugh (ed.), *Messages and Proclamations,* IV, 14–17, 20–23; Iowa State Agricultural Society, *Annual Report of the Secretary,* 1872 (Des Moines, 1873), 201–14.

46. Iowa General Assembly, *House Journal,* 1872, pp. 80, 429, 473, 477,

481–83, 486–87; Iowa City *Weekly State Press*, March 20, 27, April 3, 10, 1872; Des Moines *Iowa State Daily Register*, March 20, 21, 22, 1872.

47. Iowa General Assembly, *Senate Journal*, 1872, pp. 414–16; Des Moines *Iowa State Daily Register*, March 29, 1872.

48. Iowa General Assembly, *Senate Journal*, 1872, pp. 466–67, 480, 482, 522, 612–14, 654–56; Des Moines *Iowa State Daily Register*, April 4, 5, 6, 10, 18, 20, 1872.

49. Gue, *History of Iowa*, III, 58.

50. For an excellent study of the Granger movement in Iowa, see Mildred Throne, "The Grange in Iowa," *Iowa Journal of History*, XLVII (October, 1949), 289–324. The convention of 1873 is described in Periam, *Groundswell*, 264–65. The report of the State Agricultural Society for 1872 (issued early in 1873) gives an impression of general satisfaction with market conditions. The reports of local societies mention the transportation problem but none suggests rate regulation as a cure. The remedies proposed are more railroads and diversified industry.

51. Des Moines *Iowa State Daily Register*, February 8, 9, 11, 12, 1873. The issue of February 11 quotes the Council Bluffs *Nonpareil* as warning that the house schedule was designed for the benefit of the river towns only.

52. Iowa General Assembly, *Senate Journal*, 1873, pp. 132–37; *House Journal*, 1873, pp. 112–19; Des Moines *Iowa State Daily Register*, February 6, 1873; *Iowa Code of 1873*, Sections 1297, 1304, 1305, 1306. See also statement by Samuel McNutt, in D. C. Cloud, *Monopolies and the People* (Davenport, 1873), 168–69.

53. The Republican state ticket had won by a majority of 60,000 votes in 1872. In 1873 the Republican majority was cut to about 20,000. The new senate was composed of 34 Republicans, 16 opposition. The new house had 50 members from each party. Solon J. Buck, "Independent Parties in the Western States, 1873–1876," *Essays in American History Dedicated to Frederick Jackson Turner* (New York, 1910), 149–57; Frederick E. Haynes, *Third Party Movements since the Civil War with Special Reference to Iowa* (Iowa City, 1916), 67–73; Herbert Fairall, *Manual of Iowa Politics, State and National Conventions, Platforms, Candidates, and Official Vote of All Parties from 1838 to 1884* (Iowa City, 1884), 83–84, 86–87, 91–92; James D. McCabe (Edward Winslow Martin, *pseud.*), *The Grange Movement; or the Farmer's War against Monopolies* (Chicago, 1874), 513–14.

54. Shambaugh (ed.), *Messages and Proclamations*, IV, 90–92, 112.

55. Iowa General Assembly, *House Journal*, 1874, pp. 247, 399–402; *Senate Journal*, 1874, pp. 39, 65, 211–18.

56. Iowa City *Weekly State Press*, February 25, 1874. The report of the State Agricultural Society for 1873 again speaks of prosperity. Local societies mention the need for improved water routes but none suggests rate control.

57. "Mr. Morse and myself did all that we could to procure the substitution of the Grangers bill (the one you preferred)." William P. Hepburn to President James M. Walker of the Burlington Railroad, March 10, 1874, James M. Walker, In-letters, June, 1873–August, 1874, Burlington Archives (Newberry Library).

58. Buck, *Granger Movement*, 170–71. The Illinois law of 1873 made long-and-short-haul discrimination only *prima facie* unjust. Similarly the schedule of rates prepared by the Illinois Railroad and Warehouse Commission was only *prima facie* evidence that such rates were reasonable. The system of

judicial review provided by these measures must be considered a concession to the railroads. See Miller, "The Granger Laws," 164–92.

59. Gue, *History of Iowa*, III, 66.

60. Iowa General Assembly, *Senate Journal*, 1874, pp. 138, 197, 215–19, 277, 292, 294–95, 305.

61. Gue, *History of Iowa*, III, 66–71; Dey, "Railroad Legislation in Iowa," *Iowa Historical Record*, IX (October, 1893), 556–57.

62. Iowa, *Laws of 1874*, Chap. 68. In some cases the legal rates were actually higher than those charged by the railroads before the passage of the act. For opinions that they were both moderate and just, see Dey, "Railroad Legislation in Iowa," *Iowa Historical Record*, IX (October, 1893), 556–57; and Larrabee, *Railroad Question*, 332.

63. *First Annual Report on the Internal Commerce of the United States*, Appendix No. 5, pp. 93–97.

64. Pollock, *History of Economic Legislation in Iowa*, 47–48; Charles R. Aldrich, "Repeal of the Granger Law of Iowa," *Iowa Journal of History and Politics* (Iowa City), III (April, 1905), 256–70; Mildred Throne, "The Repeal of the Iowa Granger Law, 1878," *Iowa Journal of History*, LI (April, 1953), 97–130. Miss Throne shows that the opposition to repeal came largely from the river towns.

65. Illinois, *Public Laws*, 1873, 136–40; Minnesota, *General Laws of 1874*, Chap. XXVI. The schedules of rates prepared by the Illinois and Minnesota Commissions were also formed with the help of "shippers and businessmen generally." Minnesota Railroad Commissioners, *Annual Report for the Year 1874* (St. Paul, 1875), 4–5; Illinois Railroad and Warehouse Commission, *Third Annual Report*, 1873 (Springfield, 1874), 26.

66. The origins of the Potter law are treated in detail by Herman J. Deutsch, "Disintegrating Forces in Wisconsin Politics of the Early Seventies," *Wisconsin Magazine of History* (Madison), XV (December, 1931, March, June, 1932), 168–81, 282–96, 391–411. The law is printed in Wisconsin, *Laws*, 1874, Chap. 273.

67. Kirkland, *Men, Cities, and Transportation*, II, 280–83.

13

The Rise of Big Business

WHETHER OR NOT one accepts Thomas Cochran's assertion that the Civil War interrupted an established pattern of industrial growth, it is evident that the most phenomenal surge of American industrialization occurred in the late nineteenth century. In the four decades after the war, the railway network was extended westward to the Pacific, while east of the Mississippi transport lines were built into localities that had remained outside the railroad system. The enlarged transport network opened once-remote natural resources to exploitation and made the rapidly growing urban markets accessible to domestic manufacturers and farmers, while a series of inventions in processing and extraction of minerals set off a revolution in manufacturing technology. Application of electrical power to industrial purposes and development of long-distance transmission at the turn of the century provided energy resources sufficient to sustain the rapid pace of industrialization. As shipping, distribution, and manufacturing became progressively more specialized, a new class of entrepreneurs supplanted the "merchant capitalist" type that had dominated American business since the colonial era.*

These developments inevitably had a profound impact upon business organization. In the following essay, Alfred D. Chandler, Jr., attempts the difficult task of explaining the dynamics of the movement toward combination and "big business" in American enterprise. Chandler closely analyzes the various forces that gave impetus to combination in several types of industry, forces such as techno-

* The last chapter of George Rogers Taylor: *The Transportation Revolution, 1815–1860* (New York, 1951), surveys the national economy in 1860.

logical change and the dominant role of financiers in industry after 1897. However, he singles out the growing urban market as the key challenge to which innovators in industrial organizations responded in the 1880's and early 1890's. Most intriguing, perhaps, is Chandler's contention that in long-range terms the most important single innovation of that period "was the creation of the great corporations in American industry."

THE BEGINNINGS OF "BIG BUSINESS" IN AMERICAN INDUSTRY *

Alfred D. Chandler, Jr.

CRITERIA FOR SELECTION AND ANALYSIS

The historian, by the very nature of his task, must be concerned with change. What made for change? Why did it come when it did, and in the way it did? These are characteristically historians' questions. For the student of American business history, these basic questions can be put a little more precisely. What in the American past has given businessmen the opportunity or created the need for them to change what they were doing or the way they were doing it? In other words, what stimulated them to develop new products, new markets, new sources of raw materials, new ways of procuring, processing, or marketing the goods they handled? What encouraged them to find new methods of financing, new ways of managing or organizing their businesses? What turned them to altering their relations with their working force, their customers and competitors, and with the larger American public?

The question of what constitutes the dynamic factors in American business history, dynamic in the sense of stimulating change and in-

Reprinted by permission from the *Business History Review*, XXXIII (Spring, 1959), 1-31

* This study was supported by the Sloan Research Fund of The School of Industrial Management and the Center for International Studies, Massachusetts Institute of Technology.

novation, can be more clearly defined if the country's land, natural resources, and cultural patterns are taken as given. Land and resources were the raw materials with which the businessmen had to work, and the cultural attitudes and values helped set the legal and ethical rules of the game they had to play. Within this cultural and geographic environment a number of historical developments appear to have stimulated change. These provide a framework around which historical data can be compiled and analyzed.

The following major dynamic forces are visible in the American business economy since 1815: the western expansion of population; the construction and initial operation of the national railroad network; the development of a national and increasingly urban market; the application of two new sources of power: the internal combustion engine and electricity, to industry and transportation; and the systematic application of the natural and physical sciences, particularly chemistry and physics, to industry through the institutionalizing of research and development activities.

The first, the westward expansion, appears to have provided the primary impetus, except possibly in New England, to business innovation in the years from 1815 to about 1850; the building of the railroads appears to have been the major factor from the 1850's to the late 1870's; the growth of the national and urban market from the 1880's until a little after 1900; the coming of electricity and the internal combustion engine from the early 1900's to the 1920's; and, finally, the growth of systematic and institutionalized research and development since the 1920's.

These five factors are essentially aspects of fundamental population changes and technological advances. There were, of course, other factors that encouraged business innovation and change. The coming of the new machines and mechanical devices may have been a more important stimulant to innovation in New England than the growth of her markets and sources of supply in the expanding South and West. Wars usually precipitated change. The business cycle, flow of capital, government policy and legislation all played a significant part in business innovation. But such political and financial developments appear to have intensified or delayed the more basic changes encouraged initially by fundamental population shifts and technological achievements.

The purpose of making such a list is, however, not to argue that one development was more dynamic than the other. Nor are these five factors to be considered as "causes" for change; nor are they "theses" to be argued as representing reality, nor "theories" to provide an over-all explanation of change or possibly of predicting change. They are, rather, a framework on which historical information can be tied and inter-related. They provide a consistent basis upon which meaningful questions can be asked of the data.

This framework and these questions are, it should be emphasized, concerned only with fundamental changes and innovation in the business economy. They do not deal with the day-to-day activities to which businessmen must devote nearly all of their time. They are not concerned with the continuous adaptation to the constant variations of the market, sources of supply, availability of capital, and technological developments. Nor do they consider why some businesses and businessmen responded quickly and creatively to the basic population and technological changes and others did not. But an understanding of the continuous response and adjustment would seem to require first an awareness of the meaning of the more fundamental or "discontinuous" changes.

Since historical compilation and analysis must be selective, it is impossible to undertake any historical study without some criteria either implicit or explicit for selection. Further study and analysis, by indicating the defects of this approach and framework, will suggest more satisfactory ones. In the process, an analysis and interpretation of change in the American business past should come a little nearer to reality.

The purpose of this article then is, by using the framework of basic, dynamic forces, to look a little more closely at the years that witnessed the beginnings of big business in American industry. What types of changes came during these years in the ways of marketing, purchasing, processing, and in the forms of business organization? Why did these changes come when they did in the way they did? Was the growth of the national market a major prerequisite for such innovation and change? If not, what then was? How did these innovations relate to the growth of the railroad network or the coming of electricity and the internal combustion engine?

In addition to secondary works on this period, the data used in seeking answers to these questions have been annual and other corporation reports, government documents, articles in periodicals, histories, and biographies concerning the 50 largest industrial companies in the country in 1909. Nearly all these companies, listed in Table I, had their beginnings in the last years of the nineteenth century.

MAJOR CHANGES IN AMERICAN INDUSTRY AT THE
END OF THE NINETEENTH CENTURY

Between the depression of the 1870's and the beginning of the twentieth century, American industry underwent a significant transformation. In the 1870's, the major industries serviced an agrarian economy. Except for a few companies equipping the rapidly expanding railroad network, the leading industrial firms processed agricultural products and provided farmers with food and clothing. These firms tended to be small, and bought their raw materials and sold their finished goods locally. Where they manufactured for a market more than a few miles away from the factory, they bought and sold through commissioned agents who handled the business of several other similar firms.

By the beginning of the twentieth century, many more companies were making producers' goods, to be used in industry rather than on the farm or by the ultimate consumer. Most of the major industries had become dominated by a few large enterprises. These great industrial corporations no longer purchased and sold through agents, but had their own nation-wide buying and marketing organizations. Many, primarily those in the extractive industries, had come to control their own raw materials. In other words, the business economy had become industrial. Major industries were dominated by a few firms that had become great, vertically integrated, centralized enterprises.

In the terms of the economist and sociologist a significant sector of American industry had become bureaucratic, in the sense that business decisions were made within large hierarchical structures. Externally, oligopoly was prevalent, the decision-makers being as much concerned with the actions of the few other large firms in the industry as with over-all changes in markets, sources of supplies, and technological improvements.

These basic changes came only after the railroads had created a national market. The railroad network, in turn, had grown swiftly primarily because of the near desperate requirements for efficient transportation created by the movement of population westward after 1815.[1] Except for the Atlantic seaboard between Boston and Washington, the construction of the American railroads was stimulated almost wholly by the demand for better transportation to move crops, to bring farmers supplies, and to open up new territories to commercial agriculture.

By greatly expanding the scope of the agrarian economy, the railroads quickened the growth of the older commercial centers, such as New York, Philadelphia, Cincinnati, Cleveland, and St. Louis, and helped create new cities like Chicago, Indianapolis, Atlanta, Kansas City, Dallas, and the Twin Cities. This rapid urban expansion intensified the demand for the products of the older consumer goods industries—particularly those which processed the crops of the farmer and planter into food, stimulants, and clothing.

At the same time, railroad construction developed the first large market in this country for producers' goods. Except for the making of relatively few textile machines, steamboat engines, and ordnance, the iron and nonferrous manufacturers had before 1850 concentrated on providing metals and simple tools for merchants and farmers. Even textile machinery was usually made by the cloth manufacturers themselves. However, by 1860, only a decade after beginning America's first major railroad construction boom, railroad companies had already replaced the blacksmiths as the primary market for iron products, and had become far and away the most important market for the heavy engineering industries. By then, too, the locomotive was competing with the Connecticut brass industry as a major consumer of copper. More than this, the railroads, with their huge capital outlay, their fixed operating costs, the large size of their labor and management force, and the technical complexity of their operations, pioneered in the new ways of oligopolistic competition and large-scale, professionalized, bureaucratized management.

The new nation-wide market created by the construction of the railroad network became an increasingly urban one. From 1850 on, if not before, urban areas were growing more rapidly than rural ones. In the four decades from 1840 to 1880 the proportion of urban population rose from 11 percent to 28 percent of the total population, or about 4 percent a decade. In the two decades from 1880 to 1900 it grew from 28 percent to 40 percent or an increase of 6 percent a decade. Was this new urban and national market, then, the primary stimulant for business innovation and change, and for the coming of big business to American industry?

CHANGES IN THE CONSUMERS' GOODS INDUSTRIES

The industries first to become dominated by great business enterprises were those making consumer goods, the majority of which were processed from products grown on the farm and sold in the urban markets. Consolidation and centralization in the consumers' goods industries were well under way by 1893. The unit that appeared was one which integrated within a single business organization the major economic processes: production or purchasing of raw materials, manufacturing, distribution, and finance.

Such vertically integrated organizations came in two quite different ways. Where the product tended to be somewhat new in kind and especially fitted for the urban market, its makers created their businesses by first building large marketing and then purchasing organizations. This technique appears to have been true of the manufacturers or distributors of fresh meat, cigarettes, high-grade flour, bananas, harvesters, sewing machines, and typewriters. Where the products were established staple items, horizontal combination tended to precede vertical integration. In the sugar, salt, leather, whiskey, glucose, starch, biscuit, kerosene, fertilizer, and rubber industries a large number of small manufacturers first combined into large business units and then created their marketing and buying organizations. For a number of reasons the makers of the newer types of products found the older outlets less satisfactory and felt more of a need for direct marketing than did the manufacturers of the long-established goods.

Integration via the Creation of Marketing Organization

The story of the changes and the possible reasons behind them can be more clearly understood by examining briefly the experience of a few innovating firms. First, consider the experience of companies that grew large through the creation of a nation-wide marketing and distributing organization. Here the story of Gustavus F. Swift and his brother Edwin is a significant one. Gustavus F. Swift, an Easterner, came relatively late to the Chicago meat-packing business. Possibly because he was from Massachusetts, he appreciated the potential market for fresh western meat in the eastern cities.[2] For after the Civil War, Boston, New York, Philadelphia, and other cities were rapidly outrunning their local meat supply. At the same time, great herds of cattle were gathering on the western plains. Swift saw the possibilities of connecting the new market with the new source of supply by the use of the refrigerated railroad car. In 1878, shortly after his first experimental shipment of refrigerated meat, he formed a partnership with his younger brother, Edwin, to market fresh western meat in the eastern cities.

For the next decade, Swift struggled hard to carry out his plans, the essence of which was the creation, during the 1880's, of the nation-wide distributing and marketing organization built around a network of branch houses. Each "house" had its storage plant and its own marketing organization. The latter included outlets in major towns and cities, often managed by Swift's own salaried representatives. In marketing the product, Swift had to break down, through advertising and other means, the prejudices against eating meat killed more than a thousand miles away and many weeks earlier. At the same time he had to combat boycotts of local butchers and the concerted efforts of the National Butchers' Protective Association to prevent the sale of his meat in the urban markets.

To make effective use of the branch house network, the company soon began to market products other than beef. The "full line" soon came to include lamb, mutton, pork, and, some time later, poultry, eggs, and dairy products. The growing distributing organization soon demanded an increase in supply. So between 1888 and 1892, the Swifts set up meat-packing establishments in Kansas City, Omaha, and St. Louis, and, after the depression of the 1890's, three more in St. Joseph, St. Paul, and Ft. Worth. At the same time, the company systematized the buying of its cattle and other products at the stockyards. In the 1890's, too, Swift began a concerted effort to make more profitable use of by-products.

Before the end of the 1890's, then, Swift had effectively fashioned a great, vertically integrated organization. The major departments —marketing, processing, purchasing, and accounting—were all tightly controlled from the central office in Chicago. A report of the Commissioner of Corporations published in 1905 makes clear the reason for such control: [3]

Differences in quality of animals and of their products are so great that the closest supervision of the Central Office is necessary to enforce the exercise of skill and sound judgement on the part of the agents who buy the stock, and the agents who sell the meat. With this object, the branches of the Selling and Accounting Department of those packing companies which have charge of the purchasing, killing, and dressing and selling of fresh meat, are organized in the most extensive and thorough manner. The Central Office is in constant telegraphic correspondence with the distributing houses, with a view to adjusting the supply of meat and the price as nearly as possible to the demand.

As this statement suggests, the other meat packers followed

Swift's example. To compete effectively, Armour, Morris, Cudahy, and Schwarzschild & Sulzberger had to build up similar integrated organizations. Those that did not follow the Swift model were destined to remain small local companies. Thus by the middle of the 1890's, the meat-packing industry, with the rapid growth of these great vertically integrated firms had become oligopolistic (the "Big Five" had the major share of the market) and bureaucratic; each of the five had its many departments and several levels of management.

This story has parallels in other industries processing agricultural products. In tobacco, James B. Duke was the first to appreciate the growing market for the cigarette, a new product which was sold almost wholly in the cities.[4] However, after he had applied machinery to the manufacture of cigarettes, production soon outran supply. Duke then concentrated on expanding the market through extensive advertising and the creation of a national and then world-wide selling organization. In 1884, he left Durham, North Carolina, for New York City, where he set up factories, sales, and administrative offices. New York was closer to his major urban markets, and was the more logical place to manage an international advertising campaign than Durham. While he was building his marketing department, Duke was also creating the network of warehouses and buyers in the tobacco-growing areas of the country.

In 1890, he merged his company with five smaller competitors in the cigarette business to form the American Tobacco Company. By 1895 the activities of these firms had been consolidated into the manufacturing, marketing, purchasing, and finance departments of the single operating structure Duke had earlier fashioned. Duke next undertook development of a full line by handling all types of smoking and chewing tobacco. By the end of the century, his company completely dominated the tobacco business. Only two other firms, R. J. Reynolds & Company and P. Lorillard & Company had been able to build up comparable vertically integrated organizations. When they merged with American Tobacco they continued to retain their separate operating organizations. When the 1911 antitrust decree split these and other units off from the American company, the tobacco industry had become, like the meat-packing business, oligopolistic, and its dominant firms bureaucratic.

What Duke and Swift did for their industries, James S. Bell of the Washburn-Crosby Company did during these same years in the making and selling of high-grade flour to the urban bakeries and housewives, and Andrew J. Preston achieved in growing, transporting, and selling another new product for the urban market, the banana.[5] Like Swift and Duke, both these men made their major innovations in marketing, and then went on to create large-scale, departmentalized, vertically integrated structures.

The innovators in new consumer durables followed much the same pattern. Both Cyrus McCormick, pioneer harvester manufacturer, and William Clark, the business brains of the Singer Sewing Machine Company, first sold through commissioned agents. Clark soon discovered that salaried men, working out of branch offices, could more effectively and at less cost display, demonstrate, and service sewing machines than could the agents.[6] Just as important, the branch offices were able to provide the customer with essential credit. McCormick, while retaining the dealer to handle the final sales, came to appreciate the need for a strong selling and distributing organization, with warehouses, servicing facilities, and a large salaried force, to stand behind the dealer.[7] So in the years following the Civil War, both McCormick and Singer Sewing Machine Company concentrated on building up national and then world-wide marketing departments. As they purchased their raw materials from a few industrial companies rather than from a mass of farmers, their purchasing departments were smaller, and required less attention than those in the firms processing farmers' products. But the net result was the creation of a very similar type of organization.

Integration via Horizontal Combination

In those industries making more standard goods, the creation of marketing organizations usually followed large-scale combinations of a number of small manufacturing firms. For these small firms, the coming of the railroad had in many cases enlarged their markets but simultaneously brought them for the first time into competition with many other companies. Most of these firms appear to have expanded production in order to take advantage of the new markets. As a result, their industries became plagued with overproduction and excess capacity; that is, continued production at full capacity threatened to drop prices below the cost of production. So in the 1880's and early 1890's, many small manufacturers in the leather, sugar, salt, distilling and other corn products, linseed and cotton oil, biscuit, petroleum, fertilizer and rubber boot and glove industries, joined in large horizontal combinations.

In most of these industries, combination was followed by consolidation and vertical integration, and the pattern was comparatively consistent. First, the new combinations concentrated their manufacturing activities in locations more advantageously situated to meet the new growing urban demands. Next they systematized and standardized their manufacturing processes. Then, except in the case of sugar and corn products (glucose and starch), the combinations began to build large distributing and smaller purchasing departments. In so doing, many dropped their initial efforts to buy out competitors or to drive them out of business by price-cutting. Instead they concentrated on the creation of a more efficient flow from the producers of their raw materials to the ultimate consumer, and of the development and maintenance of markets through brand names and advertising. Since the large majority of these combinations began as regional groupings, most industries came to have more than one great firm. Only oil, sugar, and corn products remained long dominated by a single company. By World War I, partly because of the dissolutions under the Sherman Act, these industries had also become oligopolistic, and their leading firms vertically integrated.

Specific illustrations help to make these generalizations more precise. The best-known is the story of the oil industry, but equally illustrative is the experience of the leading distilling, baking, and rubber companies.

The first permanent combination in the whiskey industry came in 1887 when a large number of Midwestern distillers, operating more than 80 small plants, formed the Distillers' and Cattle Feeders' Trust.[8] Like other trusts, it adopted the more satisfactory legal form of a holding company shortly after New Jersey in 1889 passed the general incorporation law for holding companies. The major efforts of the Distillers Company were, first, to concentrate production in a relatively few plants. By 1895 only 21 were operating. The managers maintained that the large volume per plant permitted by such concentration would mean lower costs, and also that the location of few plants more advantageously in relation to supply and marketing would still reduce expenses further. However, the company kept the price of whiskey up, and since the cost of setting up a distillery was small, it soon had competition from small local plants. The company's answer was to purchase the new competitors and to cut prices. This strategy proved so expensive that the enterprise was unable to survive the depression of the 1890's.

Shortly before going into receivership in 1896, the Distillers Company had begun to think more about marketing. In 1895, it had planned to spend a million dollars to build up a distributing and selling organization in the urban East—the company's largest market. In 1898, through the purchase of the Standard Distilling & Distributing Company and the Spirits Distributing Company, it did acquire a marketing organization based in New York City. In 1903, the marketing and manufacturing units were combined into a single operating organization under the direction of the Distillers Securities Company. At the same time, the company's president announced plans to concentrate on the development of brand names and specialties, particularly through advertising and packaging.[9] By the early years of the twentieth century, then, the Distillers Company had become a vertically integrated, departmentalized, centralized operating organization, competing in the modern manner, more through advertising and product differentiation than price.

The experience of the biscuit industry is even more explicit. The National Biscuit Company came into being in 1898 as a merger of three regional combinations: the New York Biscuit Company formed in 1890, the American Biscuit and Manufacturing Company, and the United States Biscuit Company founded a little later.[10] Its initial objective was to control price and production, but as in the case of the Distillers Company, this strategy proved too expensive. The Annual Report for 1901 suggests why National Biscuit shifted its basic policies: [11]

This Company is four years old and it may be of interest to shortly review its history. . . . When the Company started, it was an aggregation of plants. It is now an organized business. When we look back over the four years, we find that a radical change has been wrought in our methods of business. In the past, the managers of large merchandising corporations have found it necessary, for success, to control or limit competition. So when this company started, it was thought that we must control competition, and that to do this we must either fight competition or buy it. The first meant a ruinous war of prices, and a great loss of profit; the second, a constantly increasing capitalization. Experience soon proved to us that, instead of bringing success, either of those courses, if persevered in, must bring disaster. This led us to reflect whether it was necessary to control competition. . . . we soon satisfied ourselves that within the Company itself we must look for success.

We turned our attention and bent our energies to improving the internal management of our business, to getting full benefit from purchasing our raw materials in large quantities, to economizing the expenses of manufacture, to systematizing and rendering more effective our selling department; and above all things and before all things to improve the quality of our goods and the condition in which they should reach the customer.

It became the settled policy of this Company to buy out no competition. . . .

In concentrating on distribution, the company first changed its policy from selling in bulk to wholesalers to marketing small packages to retailers. It developed the various "Uneeda Biscuit" brands, which immediately became popular. "The next point," the same Annual Report continued, "was to reach the customer. Thinking we had something that the customer wanted, we had to advise the customer of its existence. We did this by extensive advertising." This new packaging and advertising not only quickly created a profitable business, but also required the building of a sizable marketing organization. Since flour could be quickly and easily purchased in quantity from large milling firms, the purchasing requirements were less complex, and so the company needed a smaller purchasing organization. On the other hand, it spent much energy after 1901 in improving plant layout and manufacturing processes in order to cut production costs and to improve and standardize quality. Throughout the first decade of its history, National Biscuit continued the policy of "centralizing" manufacturing operations, particularly in its great New York and Chicago plants.

In the rubber boot, shoe, and glove industries, the story is much the same. Expansion of manufacturing facilities and increasing competition as early as 1874, led to the formation, by several leading firms, of the Associated Rubber Shoe Companies—an organization for setting price and production schedules through its board of directors.[12] This company continued until 1886. Its successor, the Rubber Boot and Shoe Company, which lasted only a year, attempted, besides controlling prices and production, to handle marketing, which had always been done by commissioned agents. After five years of uncontrolled competition, four of the five firms that had organized the selling company again combined, this time with the assistance of a large rubber importer, Charles A. Flint. The resulting United States Rubber Company came, by 1898, to control 75 percent of the nation's rubber boot, shoe, and glove output.

At first the new company remained a decentralized holding company. Each constituent company retained its corporate identity with much freedom of action, including the purchasing of raw materials and the selling of finished products, which was done, as before, through jobbers. The central office's concern was primarily with controlling price and production schedules. Very soon, however, the company began, in the words of the 1896 Annual Report, a policy of "perfecting consolidation of purchasing, selling, and manufacturing." [13] This was to be accomplished in four ways. First, as the 1895 Annual Report had pointed out, the managers agreed "so far as practicable, to consolidate the purchasing of all supplies of raw materials for the various manufactures into one single buying agency, believing that the purchase of large quantities of goods can be made at more advantageous figures than the buying of small isolated lots." [14] The second new "general policy" was "to undertake to reduce the number of brands of goods manufactured, and to consolidate the manufacturing of the remaining brands in those factories which have demonstrated superior facilities for production or advantageous labor conditions. This course was for the purpose of utilizing the most efficient instruments of production and closing those that were inefficient and unprofitable." The third policy was to consolidate sales through the formation of a "Selling Department," which was to handle all goods made by the constituent companies in order to achieve "economy in the distribution expense." Selling was now to be handled by a central office in the New York City headquarters, with branch offices throughout the United States and Europe. Of the three great new departments, actually manufacturing was the slowest to be fully consolidated and centralized. Finally, the treasurer's office at headquarters began to obtain accurate data on profit and loss through the institution of uniform, centralized cost accounting.

Thus United States Rubber, National Biscuit, and the Distillers Securities Company soon came to have organizational structures paralleling those of Swift and American Tobacco. By the first decade of the twentieth century, the leading firms in many consumers' goods industries had become departmentalized and centralized. This was the organizational concomitant to vertical integration. Each major function, manufacturing, sales, purchasing, and finance, became managed by a single and separate department head, usually a vice president, who, assisted by a director or a manager, had full authority and responsibility for the activities of his unit. These departmental chiefs, with the president, coordinated and evaluated the work of the different functional units, and made policy for the company as a whole. In coordinating, appraising, and policy-making, the president and the vice presidents in charge of departments came to rely more and more on the accounting and statistical information, usually provided by the finance department, on costs, output, purchases, and sales.

CHANGES IN THE PRODUCERS' GOODS INDUSTRIES

Bureaucracy and oligopoly came to the producers' goods industries somewhat later than to those making products for the mass market. Until the depression of the 1890's, most of the combinations and consolidations had been in the consumers' goods industries. After that, the major changes came in those industries selling to other businesses and industrialists. The reason for the time difference seems to be that the city took a little longer to become a major market for producers' goods. Throughout the 1880's, railroad construction and operation continued to take the larger share of the output of steel, copper, power machinery, explosives, and other heavy industries. Then in the 1890's, as railroad construction declined the rapidly growing American cities became the primary market. The insatiable demand for urban lighting, communication, heat, power, transportation, water, sewerage, and other services directly and indirectly took ever growing quantities of electric lighting apparatus, telephones, copper wire, newsprint, streetcars, coal, and iron, steel, copper, and lead piping, structures and fixtures; while the constantly expanding urban construction created new calls on the power machinery and explosives as well as the metals industries. Carnegie's decision in 1887 to shift the Homestead Works, the nation's largest and most modern steel plant, from rails to structures, symbolized the coming change in the market.[15]

Also the new combinations and consolidations in the consumers' goods industries increased the demand for producers' products in the urban areas. Standard Oil, American Tobacco, Swift and other meat packers, McCormick's Harvesting Machinery and other farm implement firms, American Sugar, Singer Sewing Machine, and many other great consumer goods companies concentrated their production in or near major cities, particularly New York and Chicago.

The changes after 1897 differed from the earlier ones not only in types of industries in which they occurred but also in the way they were promoted and financed. Combinations and vertical integration in the consumer goods industries before 1897 had been almost all engineered and financed by the manufacturers themselves, so the stock control remained in the hands of the industrialists. After 1897, however, outside funds and often outside promoters, who were usually Wall Street financiers, played an increasingly significant role in industrial combination and consolidation. The change reflected a new attitude of investor and financier who controlled capital toward the value of industrial securities.[16] Before the depression of the 1890's investment and speculation had been overwhelmingly in railroad stocks and bonds. The institutionalizing of the American security market in Wall Street had come, in fact, as a response to the needs for financing the first great railroad boom in the 1850's.

The railroads, however, had made a poor showing financially in the middle years of the 1890's when one-third of the nation's trackage went through receivership and financial reorganization. The dividend records of some of the new large industrial corporations, on the other hand, proved unexpectedly satisfactory. Moreover, railroad construction was slowing, and the major financial and administrative reorganizations of the 1890's had pretty well stabilized the industry. So there was less demand for investment bankers and brokers to market new issues of railroad securities.

Industrials were obviously the coming field, and by 1898 there was a rush in Wall Street to get in on this new business. The sudden availability of funds stimulated, and undoubtedly overstimulated, industrial combination. Many of the mergers in the years after 1897 came more from the desire of financiers for promotional profits, and because combination had become the thing to do, and less from the special needs and opportunities in the several industries. Moreover, as the financiers and promoters began to provide funds for mergers and expansion, they began to acquire, for the first time, the same type of control over industrial corporations that they had enjoyed in railroads since the 1850's.

The changes in the producers' goods industries were essentially like those in the consumer goods firms before the depression. Only after 1897 the changes came more rapidly, partly because of Wall Street pressures; and the differences that did develop between the two types of industries reflected the basic differences in the nature of their businesses. Like the companies making consumer goods, those manufacturing items for producers set up nation-wide and often world-wide marketing and distributing organizations, consolidated production into a relatively few large plants and fashioned purchasing departments. Because they had fewer customers, their sales departments tended to be smaller than those in firms selling to the mass market. On the other hand, they were more concerned with obtaining control over the sources of their supply than were most of the consumer goods companies.

Here a distinction can be made between the manufacturers who made semi-finished products from raw materials taken from the ground, and those who made finished goods from semi-finished products. The former, producing a uniform product for a few large industrial customers, developed only small sales departments and concentrated on obtaining control of raw materials, and often of the means of transporting such materials from mine to market. The latter, selling a larger variety of products and ones that often required servicing and financing, had much larger marketing and distributing organizations. These makers of finished goods, except for a brief period around 1900, rarely attempted to control their raw materials or their semi-finished steel and other metal supplies. They did, however, in the years after 1900, begin to buy or set up plants making parts and components that went into the construction of their finished products.

Except in steel, integration usually followed combination in the producers' goods industries. And for both makers of semi-finished and finished goods, integration became more of a defensive strategy than it was in the consumers' goods industries processing agricultural products. In the latter the manufacturers had an assured supply of raw materials from the output of the nation's millions of farms. In the former, on the other hand, they had to consider the threatening possibility of an outsider obtaining complete control of raw materials or supplies.

Integration and Combination in the Extractive Industries

By the early twentieth century nearly all the companies making semi-finished product goods controlled the mining of their own raw materials. The industries in which they operated can, therefore, be considered as extractive. This was also true of two consumers' goods industries: oil and fertilizer. The experience of these two provides a good introduction to the motives for integration and the role it played in the coming of "big business" in steel, copper, paper, explosives and other businesses producing semi-finished goods.

In both the oil and fertilizer industries, control over raw materials came well after combination and consolidation of groups of small manufacturing firms. The Standard Oil Trust, after its formation in 1882, consolidated its manufacturing activities and then created a domestic marketing organization. Only in the late 1880's, when the new Indiana field began to be developed and the older Pennsylvania ones began to decline, did the Trust consider going into the production of crude oil. Both Allan Nevins in his biography of John D. Rockefeller and the Hidys in their history of Standard Oil agree that the need to be assured of a steady supply of crude oil was the major reason for the move into production.[17] Other reasons, the Hidys indicate, were a fear that the producers might combine and so control supplies, and the desire of the pipeline subsidiaries to keep their facilities operating at full capacity. Although neither Nevins nor the Hidys suggest that the desire to obtain a more efficient flow of oil from the well to the distributor was a motive for this integration, both describe the committees and staff units that were formed at the central office at 26 Broadway to assure more effective coordination between production, refining, and marketing.

What little evidence there is suggests somewhat the same story in the fertilizer industry. Shortly after its organization in the mid-1890's, the Virginia-Carolina Chemical Company, a merger of many small southern fertilizer firms, began, apparently for the same defensive reasons, to purchase phosphate mines. Quickly its major competitor, the American Agricultural Chemical Company, a similar combination of small northeastern companies formed in 1893, responded by making its own purchases of mines. As the latter company explained in a later annual report: "The growth of the business, as well as the fact that available phosphate properties were being fast taken up, indicated that it was the part of wisdom to make additional provision for the future, and accordingly . . . available phosphate properties were purchased, and the necessary plants were erected and equipped, so the company now has in hand a supply of phosphate rock which will satisfy its growing demand for 60 years and upwards." [18] However, neither of these companies appeared to have set up organizational devices to guide the flow of materials from mine to plant to market; nor did the managers of a third large integrated fertilizer company, the International Agricultural Corporation, formed in 1909.

Defensive motives were certainly significant in the changes in the steel industry. Here the story can be most briefly described by focusing on the history of the industry's leader, the Carnegie Steel

Company.[19] That company's chairman, Henry C. Frick, had in the early 1890's consolidated and rationalized the several Carnegie manufacturing properties in and about Pittsburgh into an integrated whole. At the same time, he systematized and departmentalized its purchasing, engineering, and marketing activities. The fashioning of a sales department became more necessary since the shift from rails to structures had enlarged the number of the company's customers.

Then in 1896 the Carnegie company made a massive purchase of ore lands when it joined with Henry W. Oliver to buy out the Rockefeller holdings in the Mesabi Range. As Allan Nevins points out, the depression of the 1890's had worked a rapid transformation in the recently discovered Mesabi region.[20] By 1896, the ore fields had become dominated by three great interests: the Oliver Mining Company, the Minnesota Mining Company, and Rockefeller's Consolidated Iron Mines. A fourth, James J. Hill's Great Northern Railroad, was just entering the field. Frick's purchases, therefore, gave the Carnegie company an assured supply of cheap ore, as well as providing it with a fleet of ore ships. Next, Frick and Carnegie bought and rebuilt a railroad from Lake Erie to Pittsburgh to carry the new supplies to the mills.

Yet the steel company's managers did little to coordinate systematically the mining, shipping, and manufacturing units in their industrial empire. These activities did not become departments controlled from one central office but remained completely separate companies under independent managements, whose contact with one another was through negotiated contracts. This was the same sort of relation that existed between the Frick Coke Company and Carnegie Steel from the time Frick had joined Carnegie in 1889. If the Carnegie company's strategy had been to provide a more effective flow of materials as well as to assure itself of not being caught without a supply of ore and the means to transport it, then Frick and Carnegie would have created some sort of central coordinating office.

The steel industry responded quickly to the Carnegie purchases.[21] In 1898, Chicago's Illinois Steel Company, with capital supplied by J. P. Morgan & Company, joined the Lorain Steel Company (with plants on Lake Erie and in Johnstown, Pennsylvania) to purchase the Minnesota Mining Company, a fleet of ore boats, and railroads in the Mesabi and Chicago areas. Again, little attempt was made to coordinate mining and shipping with manufacturing and marketing.

In the same year, many iron and steel firms in Ohio and Pennsylvania merged to form the Republic and National Steel Companies. Shortly thereafter, a similar combination in the Sault Sainte Marie area became the Consolidated Lake Superior Company. These three new mergers began at once to set up their marketing organizations and to obtain control by lease and purchase of raw materials and transportation facilities. In 1900, several small firms making high-grade steel did much the same thing by the formation of the Crucible Steel Company of America. In these same years, the larger, established steel companies, like Lackawanna, Cambria, and Jones & Laughlin obtained control of more supplies of ore, coke, and limestone and simultaneously reorganized their manufacturing and marketing organizations. Like Carnegie and Federal, they at first made little effort to bring their mining and coke operations under the direct control of the central office.

In copper, defensive motives for integration appear to have been somewhat less significant. In the 1890's, mining, smelting and refining were combined on a large scale. During the 'eighties the railroad had opened up many western mining areas, particularly in Montana and Arizona; a little later the new electrical and telephone businesses greatly increased the demand for copper. Mining firms like Anaconda, Calumet & Hecla, and Phelps Dodge moved into smelting and refining, while the Guggenheims' Philadelphia Smelting & Refining Company began to buy mining properties.[22] In the copper industry, the high cost of ore shipment meant that smelting and—after the introduction of the electrolytic process in the early 1890's—even refining could be done more cheaply close to the mines. Of the large copper firms, only Calumet & Hecla and the Guggenheims set up refineries in the East before 1898, and both made use of direct water transportation.

After 1898, several large mergers occurred in the nonferrous metals industries. Nearly all were initially promoted by eastern financiers. Of these, the most important were Amalgamated Copper, engineered by H. H. Rogers of Standard Oil and Marcus Daly of Anaconda, the American Smelting and Refining Company which the Guggenheims came to control, and United Copper promoted by F. Augustus Heinze. United Copper remained little more than a holding company. Amalgamated set up a subsidiary to operate a large refinery at Perth Amboy and another, the United Metals Selling Company, with headquarters in New York City, to market the products of its mining and processing subsidiaries. The holding company's central offices in New York remained small and apparently did comparatively little to coordinate the activities of its several operating companies. The Guggenheims formed a much tighter organization with direct headquarters control of the company's mining, shipping, smelting and marketing departments. On the whole, there appears to have been somewhat closer coordination between mining and processing in the large copper than in the major steel companies.

Lowering of costs through more effective coordination appears to have been a major motive for consolidation and combination in three other businesses whose raw materials came from the ground: explosives, paper, and coal.[23] The mergers that created the Pittsburgh Coal Company in 1899 and greatly enlarged the Consolidation Coal Company in 1903 were followed by a reorganization and consolidation of mining properties and then by the creation of large marketing departments which operated throughout most of the country. The merger of close to 30 paper companies, forming the International Paper Company in 1899, was followed first by consolidation and reorganization of the manufacturing plants, next by the formation of a national marketing organization with headquarters in New York City, and then by the purchase of large tracts of timber in Maine and Canada. These three activities were departmentalized under vice presidents and controlled from the New York office. In all these cases, the central office was responsible for the flow of materials from mine or forest to the customer or retailer.

The explosive industries underwent a comparable sweeping change in 1902 and 1903. Since the 1870's, price and production schedules had been decided by the industry's Gunpowder Trade Association, and almost from its beginning, that Association had been controlled by one firm, the E. I. DuPont de Nemours & Company. However, the member concerns had retained their own corporate identities and managements. In 1902, the DuPonts bought out a large number of these independent companies through exchanges of stock, and then consolidated them into a single centralized organization. In the process, plants were shut down, others enlarged, and new ones built. A nation-wide selling organization was created, and centralized accounting, purchasing, engineering and traffic departments formed. Once the new organization was completed, then the company's executives obtained control of their raw materials through the purchase of nitrate mines and deposits in Chile.

Except possibly in paper, the control of price and production does not appear to have been a major motive for the initial combinations in the extractive industries making producers' goods. In steel before 1901, and in nonferrous metals and coal, there were several combinations, but none acquired as much as 20 percent of the market. Nor is there any evidence that the creators of the different mergers, while they were forming their organizations, were arranging with one another to set over-all price and production schedules. In explosives, control of competition could not have been a significant reason for the 1902 changes since the DuPont company had enjoyed such control since the 1870's. In coal and explosives, and possibly in copper, the major motive for combination, consolidation, and the integration of supply with the manufacturing and marketing processes seems to have been an expectation of lowered costs through the creation of a national distributing organization, the consolidation of manufacturing activities, and the effective coordination of the different industrial processes by one central office. In steel and possibly copper, the desire for an assured supply of raw materials appears to have been more significant in encouraging combination and integration.

Changes and Integration in the Finished Producers' Goods Industries

Control of price and production was, on the other hand, much more of an obvious motive for combination and resulting consolidation in the industries manufacturing finished products or machinery from the semi-finished materials produced by the extractive firms. Concern over supply, however, was also a cause for change, for after 1898 the users of steel, copper, coal, and other semi-finished materials felt threatened by the growing number of combinations among their suppliers. In any case, between 1898 and 1900 there was a wave of mergers in these industries, largely Wall Street financed, which led to the formation of American Tin Plate, American Wire & Steel, American Steel Hoop, National Tube, American Bridge, American Sheet Metal, Shelby Steel Tube, American Can, National Enameling & Stamping Company and a number of other combinations among steel-fabricating firms.[24] At the same time, there were many amalgamations in the power machinery and implement businesses, such as American Car & Foundry, American Locomotive, Allis-Chalmers, International Steam Pump, and International Harvester. The largest combination among the copper users, the American Brass Company, came a little later, in 1903, after the Guggenheims, Rogers, and Heinze had completed the major copper mergers.

Nearly all these combinations quickly consolidated their constituent companies into a single operating organization. Manufacturing facilities were unified and systematized, over-all accounting procedures instituted, and national and often world-wide distributing organizations formed. Many set up central traffic and purchasing departments; some even began to assure themselves control over supply by building up their own rolling mills and blast furnaces. As American Wire & Steel and National Tube began to make their own steel, they cancelled contracts with Carnegie and other semi-finished steel producers. This development, in turn, led Carnegie to develop plans for fabricating his own finished products.[25]

The resulting threat of overcapacity and price-cutting led to the formation of the United States Steel Corporation.[26] This giant merger, which included Carnegie, Federal and National Steel, and the first six of the fabricating companies listed above, continued on as a combination. Although the activities of the various subsidiaries were re-formed and redefined, there was no consolidation. United States Steel remained a holding company only, and the central office at 72 Broadway did comparatively little to coordinate the operations of its many subsidiary companies.

After 1901, the fabricators and the machinery manufacturers made little attempt to produce their own steel or copper. Nor did the makers of semi-finished products try, for some years to come, to do their own fabricating. Possibly the metal users realized that even with the formation of United States Steel they were fairly certain of alternative sources of supply. Also they may have found that once they had combined they had enough bargaining power to assure themselves of a supply of steel and other materials more cheaply than they could make it themselves.

While such firms no longer sought to control their basic materials, many, particularly the machinery makers like General Electric, Westinghouse, American Car & Foundry, International Harvester and, a little later, General Motors, began to purchase or set up subsidiaries or departments to make parts and components.[27] Here again the motive was essentially defensive. Since much of their manufacturing had now become mainly assembling, they wanted to be sure to have a supply of parts available at all times. The lack of a vital part could temporarily shut down a plant. However, they expected to take only a portion of the output; a major share was sold to outsiders. One outstanding exception to this pattern was Henry Ford. He came to control his raw materials as well as his parts and components, and rarely sold such parts to outside companies. But Ford's insistence on having a completely integrated organization from mine to market, concentrated largely in one huge plant, proved to be one of the most costly mistakes in American business history.

Control of parts and accessory units led to a diversification of the types of products these manufacturing companies made and sold. Such diversification brought, over time, important changes in business organization. Even more significant for stimulating product diversification was the new "full line" strategy adopted by a number of these recently consolidated concerns. Such a policy, initiated largely to help assure the maximum use of the new departments, encouraged technological as well as organizational change.

Pioneers in developing "full lines" in the producers' goods industries were the two great electrical companies: General Electric and Westinghouse. Unlike almost any other of the leading American industrial companies in 1900, these two had begun as research and development rather than manufacturing organizations. Because of their origins, they had the skilled personnel and the necessary equipment to move, in the mid-1890's, from making lighting equipment alone to manufacturing many lines of electric traction and power machinery products.[28] Allis-Chalmers, International Steam Pump, and American Locomotive began, shortly after their formation and subsequent consolidations, to develop new lines using electric and gasoline engines.[29] International Harvester, building up a number of farm implement lines, also started to experiment with the use of the gasoline engine for machinery on the farm. In this same first decade of the twentieth century, rubber, explosive, and chemical companies began to turn to industrial chemistry in their search to develop broader lines of products.

Continuing diversification came, however, largely in industries where science, particularly chemistry and physics, could be most easily applied. And it was in these industries, and in those which were directly affected by the coming of two new sources of power, electricity and the internal combustion engine, that the major innovations in American industry came after 1900. The chemical, automotive, power machinery, rubber, and petroleum industries led the way to the development of new processes and products, new ways of internal organization and new techniques of external competition as the new century unfolded. The metals industries and those processing agricultural goods have, on the other hand, changed relatively little since the beginning of the century. In these industries, the same firms make much the same products, use much the same processes, and compete in much the same manner in the 1950's as they did in the 1900's. For them the greatest period of change came in the last decade of the nineteenth century.

CONCLUSION: THE BASIC INNOVATIONS

The middle of the first decade of the new century might be said to mark the end of an era. By 1903, the great merger movement was almost over, and by then the metals industries and those processing agricultural products had developed patterns of internal organization and external competition which were to remain. In those years, too, leading chemical, electrical, rubber, power machinery and implement companies had initiated their "full line" policy, and had instituted the earliest formal research and development departments created in this country. In this decade also, electricity was becoming for the first time a significant source of industrial power, and the automobile was just beginning to revolutionize American transportation. From 1903 on, the new generators of power and the new technologies appear to have become the dominant stimuli to innovation in American industry, and such innovations were primarily those which created new products and processes. Changes in organizational methods and marketing techniques were largely responses to technological advances.

This seems much less true of the changes during the 20 to 25 years before 1903. In that period, the basic innovations were more in the creation of new forms of organization and new ways of marketing. The great modern corporation, carrying on the major industrial processes, namely, purchasing, and often production of materials and parts, manufacturing, marketing, and finance—all within the same organizational structure—had its beginnings in that period. Such organizations hardly existed, outside of the railroads, before the 1880's. By 1900 they had become the basic business unit in American industry.

Each of these major processes became managed by a corporate department, and all were coordinated and supervised from a central office. Of the departments, marketing was the most significant.

The creation of nation-wide distributing and selling organizations was the initial step in the growth of many large consumer goods companies. Mergers in both the consumer and producer goods industries were almost always followed by the formation of a centralized sales department.

The consolidation of plants under a single manufacturing department usually accompanied or followed the formation of a national marketing organization. The creation of such a manufacturing department normally meant the concentration of production in fewer and larger plants, and such consolidation probably lowered unit costs and increased output per worker. The creation of such a department in turn led to the setting up of central traffic, purchasing, and often engineering organizations. Large-scale buying, more rational routing of raw materials and finished products, more systematic plant lay-out, and plant location in relation to materials and markets probably lowered costs still further. Certainly the creators of these organizations believed that it did. In the extractive and machinery industries integration went one step further. Here the motives for controlling raw materials or parts and components were defensive as well as designed to cut costs through providing a more efficient flow of materials from mine to market.

These great national industrial organizations required a large market to provide the volume necessary to support the increased overhead costs. Also, to be profitable, they needed careful coordination between the different functional departments. This coordination required a steady flow of accurate data on costs, sales, and on all purchasing, manufacturing, and marketing activities. As a result, the comptroller's office became an increasingly important department. In fact, one of the first moves after a combination by merger or purchase was to institute more effective and detailed accounting procedures. Also, the leading entrepreneurs of the period, men like Rockefeller, Carnegie, Swift, Duke, Preston, Clark, and the DuPonts, had to become, as had the railroad executives of an earlier generation, experts in reading and interpreting business statistics.

Consolidation and departmentalization meant that the leading industrial corporations became operating rather than holding companies, in the sense that the officers and managers of the companies were directly concerned with operating activities. In fact, of the 50 companies with the largest assets in 1909, only United States Steel, Amalgamated Copper, and one or two other copper companies remained purely holding companies. In most others, the central office included the heads of the major functional departments, usually the president, vice presidents, and sometimes a chairman of the board and one or two representatives of financial interests. These men made major policy and administrative decisions and evaluated the performance of the departments and the corporation as a whole. In the extractive industries a few companies, like Standard Oil (N.J.) and some of the metals companies, were partly holding and partly operating companies. At Standard Oil nearly all important decisions were made in the central headquarters, at 26 Broadway, which housed not only the presidents of the subsidiaries but the powerful policy formulating and coordinating committees.[30] But in some of the metals companies, the subsidiaries producing and transporting raw materials retained a large degree of autonomy.

The coming of the large vertically integrated, centralized, functionally departmentalized industrial organization altered the internal and external situations in which and about which business decisions were made. Information about markets, supplies, and operating performance as well as suggestions for action often had to come up through the several levels of the departmental hierarchies, while decisions and suggestions based on this data had to be transmitted down the same ladder for implementation. Executives on each level became increasingly specialists in one function—in sales, production, purchasing, or finance—and most remained in one department and so handled one function only for the major part of their business careers. Only he who climbed to the very top of the departmental ladder had a chance to see his own company as a single operating unit. Where a company's markets, sources of raw materials, and manufacturing processes remained relatively stable, as was true in the metals industries and in those processing agricultural goods, the nature of the business executive's work became increasingly routine and administrative.

When the internal situation had become bureaucratic, the external one tended to be oligopolistic. Vertical integration by one manufacturer forced others to follow. Thus, in a very short time, many American industries became dominated by a few large firms, with the smaller ones handling local and more specialized aspects of the business. Occasionally industries like oil, tobacco, and sugar, came to be controlled by one company, but in most cases legal action by the federal government in the years after 1900 turned monopolistic industries into oligopolistic ones.

Costs, rather than interfirm competition, began to determine prices. With better information on costs, supplies, and market conditions, the companies were able to determine price quite accurately on the basis of the desired return on investment. The managers of the different major companies had little to gain by cutting prices below an acceptable profit margin. On the other hand, if one firm set its prices excessively high, the other firms could increase their share of the market by selling at a lower price and still maintain a profit. They would, however, rarely cut to the point where this margin was eliminated. As a result, after 1900, price leadership, price umbrellas, and other evidences of oligopolistic competition became common in many American industries. To increase their share of the market and to improve their profit position, the large corporations therefore concerned themselves less with price and concentrated more on obtaining new customers by advertising, brand names, and product differentiations; on cutting costs through further improvement and integration of the manufacturing, marketing, and buying processes; and on developing more diversified lines of products.

The coming of the large vertically integrated corporation changed more than just the practices of American industrialists and their industries. The effect on the merchant, particularly the wholesaler, and on the financier, especially the investment banker, has been suggested here. The relation between the growth of these great industrial units and the rise of labor unions has often been pointed out. Certainly the regulation of the large corporation became one of the major political issues of these years, and the devices created to carry out such a regulation were significant innovations in American constitutional, legal, and political institutions. But an examination of such effects is beyond the scope of this paper.

Reasons for the Basic Innovations

One question remains to be reviewed. Why did the vertically integrated corporation come when it did, and in the way it did? The creation by nearly all the large firms of nation-wide selling and distributing organizations indicates the importance of the national market. It was necessary that the market be an increasingly urban one. The city took the largest share of the goods manufactured by the processors of agricultural products. The city, too, with its demands for construction materials, lighting, heating and many other facilities, provided the major market for the metals and other producers' goods industries after railroad construction slowed. Without the rapidly growing urban market there would have been little need and little opportunity for the coming of big business in American industry. And such a market could hardly have existed before the completion of a nation-wide railroad network.

What other reasons might there have been for the swift growth of the great industrial corporation? What about foreign markets? In some industries, particularly oil, the overseas trade may have been an important factor. However, in most businesses the domestic customers took the lion's share of the output, and in nearly all of them the move abroad appears to have come after the creation of the large corporation, and after such corporations had fashioned their domestic marketing organization.

What about the investor looking for profitable investments, and the promoter seeking new promotions? Financiers and promoters certainly had an impact on the changes after 1897, but again they seem primarily to have taken advantage of what had already proved successful. The industrialists themselves, rather than the financiers, initiated most of the major changes in business organization. Availability of capital and cooperation with the financier figured much less prominently in these industrial combinations and consolidations than had been the case with the earlier construction of the railroads and with the financing of the Civil War.

What about technological changes? Actually, except for electricity, the major innovations in the metals industries seem to have come before or after the years under study here. Most of the technological improvements in the agricultural processing industries appear to have been made to meet the demands of the new urban market. The great technological innovations that accompanied the development of electricity, the internal combustion engine, and industrial chemistry did have their beginning in these years, and were, indeed, to have a fundamental impact on the American business economy. Yet this impact was not to be really felt until after 1900.

What about entrepreneurial talent? Certainly the best-known entrepreneurs of this period were those who helped to create the large industrial corporation. If, as Joseph A. Schumpeter suggests, "The defining characteristic [of the entrepreneur and his function] is simply the doing of new things, and doing things that are already done, in a new way (innovation)," Rockefeller, Carnegie, Frick, Swift, Duke, McCormick, the DuPonts, the Guggenheims, Coffin of General Electric, Preston of United Fruit, and Clark of Singer Sewing Machine were all major innovators of their time.[31]

TABLE I. THE FIFTY LARGEST INDUSTRIALS

(Numbers indicate relative size according to 1909 assets)

Consumers' Goods Companies

Agricultural Processing	*Extractive*	*Manufacturing*
3. Am. Tobacco	2. Standard Oil	4. Int'l. Harvester
8. Armour & Co.	26. Va.-Carolina Chem.	10. U.S. Rubber
9. American Sugar	35. Am. Agri. Chem.	12. Singer Mfg. Co.
13. Swift & Co.		
30. Nat'l. Biscuit		
33. Distillers' Securities		
50. United Fruit		

Producers' Goods Companies

Agricultural Processing	*Extractive*	*Manufacturing*
6. Central Leather	1. U.S. Steel	7. Pullman
18. Corn Products Co.	5. Amalgamated	15. Gen. Electric
21. Am. Woolens	(Anaconda) Copper	16. Am. Car &
	11. Am. Smelting &	Foundry
	Refining	19. Am. Can
	14. Pittsburgh Coal	22. Westinghouse
	17. Colo. Fuel & Iron	24. DuPont
	20. Lackawanna	29. Am. Locomotive
	23. Consolidation Coal	36. Allis-Chalmers
	25. Republic Steel	44. Int. Steam Pump
	27. Int'l. Paper	46. Western Electric
	28. Bethlehem Steel	
	31. Cambria Steel	
	33. Associated Oil	
	34. Calumet & Hecla	
	37. Crucible Steel	
	38. Lake Superior Corp.	
	39. U.S. Smelting & Ref.	
	40. United Copper	
	41. National Lead	
	42. Phelps Dodge	
	43. Lehigh Coal	
	45. Jones & Laughlin	
	48. Am. Writing Paper	
	49. Copper Range	

And their innovations were not in technology, but rather in organization and in marketing. "Doing a new thing," is, to Schumpeter a "creative response" to a new situation, and the situation to which these innovators responded appears to have been the rise of the national urban market.

There must be an emphasis here on the words "seem" and "appear." The framework used is a preliminary one and the data itself, based on readily available printed material rather than on business records are hardly as detailed or accurate as could be desired. More data, more precise and explicit questions, and other types and ranges of questions will modify the generalizations suggested here. For the moment, however, I would like to suggest, if only to encourage the raising of questions and the further compilation and analysis of data, that *the* major innovation in the American economy between the 1880's and the turn of the century was the creation of the great corporations in American industry. This innovation, as I have tried to show, was a response to the growth of a national and increasingly urban market that was created by the building of a national railroad network—the dynamic force in the economy in the quarter century before 1880. After 1900 the newly modified methods of interfirm and intrafirm administration remained relatively unchanged (as did the location of major markets and sources of raw materials) except in those industries directly affected by new sources of power and the systematic application of science to industry. In the twentieth century electricity, the internal combustion engine, and systematic, institutionalized research and development took the place of the national urban market as the dynamic factor in the American industrial economy.[32]

NOTES

1. The factors stimulating the growth of the American railroad network and the impact of the earlier construction and operation of this network on the American business economy and business institutions is suggested in Chandler, *Henry Varnum Poor—Business Editor, Analyst, and Reformer* (Cambridge, 1956), especially chaps. 4, 6–9.

2. Swift's story as outlined in Louis F. Swift in collaboration with Arthur Van Vlissingen, *The Yankee of the Yards—the Biography of Gustavus Franklin Swift* (New York, 1928). The United States Bureau of Corporations, *Report of the Commissioner of Corporations on the Beef Industry, March 3, 1905* (Washington, 1905), is excellent on the internal operations and external

activities of the large meat-packing firms. There is additional information in the later three-volume *Report of the Federal Trade Commission on the Meat Packing Industry* (Washington, 1918–1919). R. A. Clemen, *The American Livestock and Meat Industry* (New York, 1923) has some useful background data.

3. *Report of Commissioner of Corporations on the Beef Industry,* p. 21.

4. Some information on James B. Duke and the American Tobacco Company can be found in John W. Jenkins, *James B. Duke, Master Builder* (New York, 1927), chaps. 5–7, 10. More useful was the United States Bureau of Corporations, *Report of the Commissioner of Corporations on the Tobacco Industry* (Washington, 1909).

5. The story of Bell is outlined in James Gray, *Business Without Boundary, the Story of General Mills* (Minneapolis, 1954), and of Preston in Charles M. Wilson, *Empire in Green and Gold* (New York, 1947).

6. The early Singer Sewing Machine experience is well analyzed in Andrew B. Jack, "The Channels of Distribution for an Innovation: the Sewing Machine Industry in America, 1860–1865," *Explorations in Entrepreneurial History,* Vol. IX (Feb., 1957), pp. 113–141.

7. William T. Hutchinson, *Cyrus Hall McCormick* (New York, 1935), Vol. II, pp. 704–712.

8. The major sources of information on combination and consolidation in the distilling industry are Jeremiah W. Jenks, "The Development of the Whiskey Trust," *Political Science Quarterly,* Vol. IV (June, 1889), pp. 296–319; J. W. Jenks and W. E. Clark, *The Trust Problem* (rev. ed.; New York, 1917), pp. 141–149. The annual reports of the Distilling and Cattle Feeding Company and its various successors provide some useful additional data, as does the Industrial Commission, *Preliminary Report on Trusts and Industrial Combinations* (Washington, 1900), Vol. I, pp. 74–89, 167–259, 813–848, and Victor S. Clark, *History of Manufactures in the United States* (New York, 1929), Vol. II, pp. 505–506. Changes in taxes on liquors also affected the company's policies in the early 1890's.

9. *Annual Report of the President of the Distillers Securities Company* for 1903.

10. The information on National Biscuit comes largely from its annual reports.

11. *Annual Report of the National Biscuit Company for the Year Ending December,* 1901, January 3, 1902. References to centralizing of manufacturing facilities appear in several early annual reports. As this was written before Theodore Roosevelt had started to make the Sherman Act an effective antitrust instrument and Ida Tarbell and other journalists had begun to make "muck raking" of big business popular and profitable, the Biscuit Company's shift in policy could hardly have been the result of the pressure of public opinion or the threat of government action.

12. The background for the creation of the United States Rubber Company can be found in Nancy P. Norton, "Industrial Pioneer: the Goodyear Metallic Rubber Shoe Company" (Ph.D. thesis, Radcliffe College, 1950), Constance McL. Green, *History of Naugatuck, Connecticut* (New Haven, 1948), pp. 126–131, 193–194, and Clark, *History of Manufactures,* Vol. II, pp. 479–481, Vol. III, pp. 235–237. The company's annual reports provide most of the information on its activities.

13. *The Fifth Annual Report of the United States Rubber Company,* March 31, 1897, pp. 6–7.

14. This and the following quotations are from the *Fourth Annual Report of the United States Rubber Company, May 25, 1896*, pp. 4–5, 7–8.

15. Clark, *History of Manufactures*, Vol. II, chap. 19.

16. The story of the shift from rails to industrials as acceptable investments is told in Thomas R. Navin and Marian V. Sears, "The Rise of the Market for Industrial Securities, 1887–1902," *Business History Review*, Vol. XIX (June, 1955), pp. 105–138. Government securities were, of course, important in the years before 1850 and during and after the Civil War, but in the late 1870's and 1880's as in the 1850's, railroads dominated the American security exchanges. As Navin and Sears point out, some coal and mining firms were traded on the New York Exchange, but the only manufacturing securities, outside of those of the Pullman Company, were some textile stocks traded on the local Boston Exchange. The connections between the railroad expansion and the beginnings of modern Wall Street are described in detail in Chandler, *Poor*, chap. 4.

17. Ralph W. Hidy and Muriel E. Hidy, *Pioneering in Big Business, 1882–1911* (New York, 1955), pp. 176–188. Allan Nevins, *Study in Power, John D. Rockefeller, Industrialist and Philanthropist* (New York, 1953), Vol. II, pp. 1–3. Nevins adds that another reason for the move into production was "partly to limit the number of active wells and reduce the overproduction of crude oil," Vol. II, p. 2, but he gives no documentation for this statement.

18. *Annual Report of the American Agricultural Chemical Company, August 14, 1907* also the same company's *Annual Report* dated August 25, 1902. In addition to the annual reports of the two companies, Clark, *History of Manufactures*, Vol. III, pp. 289–291, provides information. There is a brief summary of the story of the International Agricultural Corporation in Williams Haynes, *American Chemical Industry—A History* (New York, 1945), Vol. III, p. 173.

19. The information on the Carnegie Steel Company is taken from Burton J. Hendrick, *The Life of Andrew Carnegie*, 2 vols. (New York, 1932), George Harvey, *Henry Clay Frick, the Man* (New York, 1928), James H. Bridge, *The Inside Story of the Carnegie Steel Company* (New York, 1903).

20. Nevins, *Rockefeller*, Vol. II, p. 252.

21. The experience of the other steel firms comes primarily from their annual reports and from prospectuses and other reports in the Corporation Records Division of Baker Library. A company publication, *J & L—The Growth of an American Business* (Pittsburgh, 1953) has some additional information on that company. Also, books listed in footnote 26 on the United States Steel Corporation have something on these companies. Two other steel companies listed in Table I made major changes somewhat before and after the period immediately following 1898. One, the Colorado Fuel & Iron Co., established in 1892, quickly became an integrated steel company in the Colorado area. The Bethlehem Steel Corporation was formed in 1904 when Charles F. Schwab, formerly of the Carnegie company and the United States Steel Corporation, reorganized the finances, corporate structure, and administrative organization of the bankrupt United States Shipbuilding Company.

22. Information on the mining companies came from their annual reports and from Isaac P. Marcosson's two books, *Magic Metal—the Story of the American Smelting and Refining Company* (New York, 1949), and *Anaconda* (New York, 1957), also Clark, *History of Manufactures*, Vol. II, pp. 368–369.

23. The story of the leading explosives, paper, salt and coal companies

comes from annual reports and also from Charles E. Beachley, *History of the Consolidation Coal Company 1864–1934* (New York, 1934), George H. Love, *An Exciting Century in Coal* (New York, 1955), the company-written, *The International Paper Company, 1898–1948* (n.p., 1948), William S. Dutton, *DuPont—One Hundred and Forty Years* (New York, 1940), and *U.S. v. E. I. DuPont de Nemours & Company et al. in Circuit Court of the United States for the District of Delaware, #280 in Equity* (1909), *Defendants' Record Testimony*, Vol. I, and for the paper industry, Clark, *History of Manufactures*, Vol. III, pp. 245–252. The American Writing Paper Company, though less successful, had many parallels to International Paper.

24. The best brief summary of these mergers and the formation of the United States Steel Corporation is in Eliot Jones, *The Trust Problem in the United States* (New York, 1924), pp. 189–200. The companies' annual reports and prospectuses provide additional material.

25. Hendrick, *Carnegie*, Vol. II, pp. 116–119.

26. The beginnings and the operation of the United States Steel Corporation are outlined in Abraham Berglund, *The United States Steel Corporation: A Study of Growth and Combination in the Iron and Steel Industry* (New York, 1907), Arundel Cotter, *The Authentic History of the United States Steel Corporation* (New York, 1916), Ida M. Tarbell, *The Life of Elbert H. Gary, the Story of Steel* (New York, 1925).

27. This generalization is based on the annual reports of the several companies.

28. As is well described in Harold C. Passer, *The Electrical Manufacturers* (Cambridge, 1953).

29. The development of new lines by Allis-Chalmers, International Steam Pump, and American Locomotive is mentioned in their annual reports in the first decade of the twentieth century. International Harvester's similar "full line" policies are described in Cyrus McCormick, *The Century of the Reaper* (New York, 1931), chaps. 6–9, and United States Bureau of Corporations, *The International Harvester Co., March 3, 1913* (Washington, 1913), especially pp. 156–158.

30. Hidys, *Pioneering in Big Business*, chap. 3 and pp. 323–388.

31. Joseph A. Schumpeter, "The Creative Response in Economic History," *Journal of Economic History*, Vol. VII (May, 1947), p. 151, and also his *Theory of Economic Development*, trans. Redvers Opie (Cambridge, 1934), pp. 74–94.

32. This point has only been considered briefly here, but has been developed at some length in my "Development, Diversification and Decentralization," in *Postwar Economic Trends*, ed. R. E. Freeman (New York, 1960).

14

Business Expansionism
in the Nineteis

THROUGHOUT THE NINETEENTH CENTURY, the boundaries of the United States were pushed westward by successive military and diplomatic triumphs. The "expansionist impulse" of the pre-Civil War years has been ascribed by various scholars to the quest for military security, the vision of a North American empire which "manifest destiny" decreed for the United States, and simple land hunger on the part of northerners and southerners alike. But students of expansionism recently have given increasing weight to commercial motives; for example, it has been argued that many statesmen who in the 1840's supported an aggressive posture against Great Britain in Oregon and against Mexico in the Southwest were primarily interested in acquiring West Coast ports and hoped to expand American trade with China and the Pacific Ocean area. Similarly, the colorful expansionist episodes of the decades immediately after the Civil War have been interpreted less in terms of the "diplomacy of adventure" and increasingly in terms of conscious pursuit of economic aims.

Although the new emphasis on economic motives of early expansionism may suggest considerable continuity in the objectives of nineteenth-century diplomacy, most students of the period acknowledge a significant qualitative change in expansionist designs, beginning in the mid-1880's. At that time, highly placed strategists and politicians began to advocate a more aggressive role for the United

States in world politics. American interests were global in scope, they argued, and American policy would have to be formulated in global terms; the power struggles of Europe's imperialist powers represented a threat to the vital interests of the nation; and pursuit of those interests required expansion of the navy and a willingness to use it in remote parts of the world. Some of the new expansionists were more directly concerned with economic advantage, preaching that the profits of foreign markets for manufactured goods and capital would be lost to European rivals unless the United States took an active role in Asia, Latin America and other developing areas.

President Grover Cleveland's unprecedentedly belligerent stand against a European rival in Latin America during the 1895 Venezuela crisis has often been explained as a product of American jingoism of the 1890's. In the following article, Walter LaFeber reassesses Cleveland's policy, suggesting the importance of the post-1893 depression and the rising belief in business and political circles that expanded foreign trade was vital to recovery and renewed industrial development. LaFeber argues that economic and strategic aims were inseparably combined in Cleveland's definition of American interests in 1895. Thus he places Cleveland (and prominent business spokesmen as well) squarely in the movement of the 1890's that later culminated in President William Howard Taft's explicitly business-oriented policy of Dollar Diplomacy.

THE BACKGROUND OF CLEVELAND'S
VENEZUELAN POLICY: A REINTERPRETATION

Walter LaFeber

The policy that Grover Cleveland's second administration formulated in the Venezuelan controversy of 1895–1896 was a direct answer to British encroachments on United States interests in Latin America. Political and business leaders believed these American

Reprinted by permission from *The American Historical Review*, LXVI, No. 4 (July, 1961), pp. 947–67.

interests to be economic, strategic, and political. The economic influence on the shaping of Cleveland's policy in this dispute has not received sufficient attention. After the 1893 depression paralyzed the domestic economy, United States attention focused increasingly on Latin America; indeed, it is significant that the controversy occurred during the depths of that business crisis.

American interests, both economic and strategic, were threatened during the 1893–1895 period by ominous British moves in Brazil, Nicaragua, the disputed area in Venezuela itself, and the small island of Trinidad off the Brazilian coast. During the same years Germany and France menaced United States advantages in Brazil and the Caribbean. Gravely concerned, the State Department finally forced a showdown struggle on the issue of the Venezuelan boundary. By successfully limiting British claims in this incident, the United States won explicit recognition of its dominant position in the Western Hemisphere.

This essay attempts to trace two developments: that international dangers motivated the Cleveland administration in formulating its Venezuelan policy; that the economic crisis arising out of the 1893 depression provided the context and played an important role in this policy formulation. This is not to say that the economic influence was the only motivating force, but that this factor, relatively overlooked by previous writers on the subject, greatly shaped the thinking of both the Cleveland administration and key segments of American society.

Five considerations should serve to establish the validity of this interpretation: timing played a key role in that the year 1895 witnessed a convergence of forces which brought the United States into the controversy (after the argument had simmered over half a century) and led it to assert control over the nations of the Western Hemisphere; the Cleveland administration and the American business community viewed foreign markets, especially those of Latin America, as providing a solution to the domestic depression; policy makers in Washington believed the Monroe Doctrine to be important primarily for what Secretary of State Richard Olney called its "practical benefits," that is, its potential strategic and economic benefits; [1] the State Department acted unilaterally in the affair, cared little for Venezuelan opinion or advice, and hoped to benefit American interests primarily, not Venezuelan; neither the political situation in the United States nor the newly discovered "psychic crisis" of the 1890's played important roles in key American decisions.

The events leading to the Venezuelan crisis were silhouetted against the somber and ominous background of the 1893–1897 depression. Economic crisis had threatened the United States since 1890 and 1891, when only unexampled American exports had averted financial trouble.[2] Despite these huge exports, American prices and wages continued their long downward swing which had begun in 1873. By late 1892 and early 1893 business observers recognized that the American economic system had reached a point of maturity which disrupted its relations with the markets of the world.[3] Panic struck the weakened nation in the spring of 1893 when the Philadelphia and Reading Railroad and the National Cordage Company collapsed.

Political and social uprisings, which were renewed and intensified by the economic breakdown, forced the Cleveland administration not only to face the problem of reviving a glutted industrial system, but to do so before radical political forces paralyzed the administration's initiative. Labor unrest manifested itself in the marches of Coxey's and Hogan's armies of the unemployed on Washington—marches which highly dramatized the fact that the great American frontier no longer attracted, but even repelled the discontented of the nation—and in the nearly successful attempt of the socialist wing of the American Federation of Labor to control that body. The threat posed by restless farmers (and many businessmen) in the West and South compounded the danger of labor dissatisfaction. Among others, James J. Hill and the assistant chairman of the Kansas State Democratic Committee warned Cleveland in 1893 that all the "isms" that had plagued society in the past were "now appearing in an organized and most formidable manner." [4]

Cleveland quickly reacted by calling a special session of Congress to repeal the Silver Purchase Act of 1890. The President hoped that the repeal would stabilize the country on a gold standard. Though this action had little immediate effect on the economy, the administration's reasons for the repeal pointed the way for further ameliorative action. Cleveland and his advisers assumed that the economic problems stemmed not from the lack of circulating medium (as the Populists and silverites charged), but from bad monetary laws and overproduction. Since a powerful Populist-silver bloc in Congress could sidetrack any legislation that would carefully regulate and restrict the amount of paper money, the administration emphasized overproduction as the causative factor of the depression. This, in turn, led to a quest for foreign markets.[5]

In a speech to the New York Chamber of Commerce in November 1893, Secretary of the Treasury John G. Carlisle explained the administration's belief that the gold standard and an expanded foreign trade went hand in hand. Carlisle declared that "our commercial interests are not confined to our own country; they extend to every quarter of the globe, and our people buy and sell in nearly every market of the civilized world. . . . Without exception these prices are fixed in the markets of countries having a gold standard." Carlisle's *Annual Reports* and many of Cleveland's public statements emphasized the administration's belief that foreign trade provided a key to America's economic revival and that the gold standard was necessary for such trade.[6]

Two other developments motivated the Cleveland administration to view enlarged foreign trade as a means to end the depression: the withdrawal of British investments and the closing of the American frontier. American political and business leaders believed the exodus of British capital from the United States to be a basic cause of the panic.[7] When the repeal of the Silver Purchase Act failed to attract new foreign investments, the administration and the business community turned to the hope of a large foreign trade surplus as a replacement for the withdrawn capital. Such a trade balance would not only provide fresh capital to invigorate stagnant American industries, but newly found markets would revive these industries to a point where they would again be appealing to outside investors.[8]

Cleveland and others in influential positions coupled this view of foreign capital with the belief that a mature American system had finally absorbed its western frontier. They viewed this occurrence with alarm.[9] Cleveland made special mention of this in his annual message in 1893 and later attempted to reopen western lands that had been claimed by speculators.[10] Obviously, if the closed frontier had been a leading cause in the glutting of the home market, the Republican protective tariff had to be revised. The Democrats thus proposed a tariff that they believed would stimulate the movement of domestic surpluses into world markets.[11]

In this desire to reinvigorate production instead of redistributing goods, Cleveland asked for a tariff bill that would include a long list of free raw materials.[12] He believed that if these industrial essentials entered the United States tariff-free, "the world [would] be open to our national ingenuity and enterprise." He related this hope of world markets to the growing labor unrest by noting that "the limited demand for . . . goods" on a "narrow market" inevitably led to industrial stagnation.[13] Carlisle expressed it more succinctly: "The demand for labor would steadily grow with the extension of trade." [14]

Cleveland's two congressional leaders, William L. Wilson of West Virginia in the House and Roger Q. Mills of Texas in the Senate, shared these opinions. Wilson introduced the tariff by observing that it had been devised "in the shadow and depression of a great commercial crisis." He declared that the free raw materials clauses would lead to "the enlargement of markets for our products in other countries, the increase in the internal commerce and in the carrying trade of our own country." All these factors would "insure a growing home market." In effect, Wilson believed that the United States had to rebuild its home market by enlarging its foreign market.[15] Mills echoed Wilson's statements, then added a new note by declaring that Great Britain would have to suffer economic setbacks since she blocked the path of America's economic manifest destiny. Mills believed that the British "saw with alarm the triumph of Mr. Cleveland as the representative of commercial expansion." [16] Many other congressmen repeated these arguments during the tariff debates.[17]

A group of protectionist senators gathered support to defeat the House bill and to substitute a quasi-protectionist measure of its own. This tariff measure resulted mainly from the lobbying of several trusts and from political and personal hatred for Cleveland. But during the congressional debate, the President continually reiterated the importance of the raw materials provisions. In disgust, he finally allowed the bill to become law without his signature, though only three free raw materials remained in the measure.[18]

The American business community followed the example of the administration in attempting to devise new means of expanding its foreign commerce. The depression reached its deepest trough in 1894–1895 as exports, especially staple agricultural products, failed to revive the economy. Business circles recognized this condition and called for drastic measures. The *Banker's Magazine* declared, "Small exports and agricultural depression are, therefore, now the chief remaining obstacles to a return of general prosperity." [19] The *Commercial and Financial Chronicle* concurred, stating that the "abnormal situation of the Treasury and of our foreign trade" had halted the growth of prosperity "several times" in 1894.[20] Perhaps Henry W. Cannon, president of the Chase National Bank, best summarized the American business community's position when he wrote in February 1895, "It is necessary, in order to restore complete prosperity, that we should compete in the markets of the world with our goods and commodities." [21] The New York correspondent of the *Economist* bluntly warned in September 1895: "Either goods or gold must go abroad to pay for our purchases there, and thus far this autumn our shipments . . . have not equalled expectations." [22] One authority explicitly prescribed the cure. A. S. Heidelbach, the senior member of a large international banking firm in New York, declared that in order to stop the gold outflow, merchandise exports would have to exceed merchandise imports by "at least" $350,000,000 per year. Some disputed his figures, but few disputed his solution.[23]

Unfortunately for the prospects of such a trade surplus, American agriculture, the main prop of the export trade, could not bear such a burden. Though the volume of exports for the 1894 fiscal year had been surpassed only twice before in American history, the four leading staples of the export trade—breadstuffs, provisions, cotton, and oil products—had decreased in value by almost six million dollars. This occurred because in order to find markets their producers had to accept extremely low prices, in some cases the lowest in history.[24]

Several astute observers, however, saw hope in these export tables. Worthington C. Ford, chief of the Bureau of Statistics, published an article in the summer of 1895 entitled "The Turning of the Tide." [25] Ford demonstrated that while exports of farm staples had slumped, American manufactured exports had rocketed to all-time highs. He emphasized this change by noting that the United States had imported less food in 1895, but that "more raw materials for domestic industries" had arrived.

Business journals quickly drew the lesson from such trade figures. *Banker's Magazine* and *Bradstreet's*, among others, declared that American agriculture could no longer compete with the newly exploited grain lands of Argentina and Russia.[26] The former journal foretold the consequences for the American economy: henceforth the United States must depend upon "our future manufacturing supremacy over Europe" rather than upon American "producers of food, feed, and raw materials." When this occurred, the business community's dream would be realized. There would be no more booms followed by depressions, but "slow and steady improvement . . . and our surplus manufacturing capacity turned to the production of goods we may be able to export hereafter at reduced cost and thus keep all our industries permanently employed, as England does, having the world's markets in which to unload any accumulation." [27]

In his article Ford further observed that this change in the nature of American trade had "political consequences," for it meant that the United States would need markets in the underindustrialized nations of Latin America and Asia rather than in Europe.[28] Translating these words into action, the American business community began systematically opening Latin American markets. Business journals devoted much space to the promotion of a Nicaraguan canal; *Bradstreet's* called for the immediate formal abrogation of the Clayton-Bulwer Treaty.[29] American investment, composed mainly of surplus capital accumulated from the home market's collapse, flowed into Latin America in increased amounts during the 1893–1898 period. New steamship lines, heavy investments in Latin American railroads, the movement of American bankers into Santo Domingo, and the expansion of the Guggenheim interests in Mexico exemplified this southward advance of the dollar.[30] The investor moved southward with a minimum of fanfare, but the manufacturer invaded Central and South America with the cheers of commercial manifest destiny ringing in his ears.[31]

James G. Blaine's intense interest in Latin American markets and tranquillity, symbolized by the Pan-American Conference of 1889, had directed American commercial attention to the southern nations. But the stagnation of 1893–1895 increased and sharpened the business community's interest. Before 1893 Blaine had led, and the businessmen had willingly followed. But after 1893 the businessmen played at least an equal role in focusing attention southward and in some instances blazed paths that the State Department then followed in formulating Latin American policies.

This intensified expansion of American industrialists into Latin American markets can be illustrated by three developments: the growth of and interest in expositions held in the southern United States, the development of commercial museums, and the formation and growth of the National Association of Manufacturers. Encouraged by such business journals as *Dixie* and the Chattanooga *Tradesman*, the South held several large industrial expositions during the depression.[32] The chairman of the Atlanta Exposition of 1895 informed Secretary of State Olney that "the foreign trade idea is the basic and uppermost feature of the Exposition." [33] Olney and his predecessor in the State Department, Walter Quintin Gresham, encouraged this exposition, while President Cleveland and several members of his cabinet found time to visit it.[34]

The full bloom of the commercial museum movement appeared in the flowering of the Philadelphia Commercial Museum in 1894–1897. New York City soon followed this example. Secretaries of State Gresham and Olney again displayed much interest. Speaking at the opening of the Philadelphia museum in June 1897, Olney declared that economic solidarity in the Western Hemisphere was "inevitable." American industrialists strove to make this prediction come true, for the president of the museum, William Pepper, wrote Olney in 1896 that he was "surprised and gratified at the rapid spread of interest" shown by United States industrialists.[35]

After the panic struck, the most publicized and concerted movement for the systematic opening of Latin American markets arose from the formation of the National Association of Manufacturers in January 1895. The depression operated as a direct cause of this movement, and the association's first convention met for the avowed purpose of enlarging the Latin American trade of the United States.[36] Three themes dominated that convention: the need for foreign, especially South and Central American markets; a strong anti-British feeling, revealed in bitter references to British control of international trade and finance; and the hope that the federal government would provide favors to American businessmen which would encourage overseas economic expansion.[37] After the convention the NAM sent a group of American industrialists and financiers to inspect potential market areas in Latin America. In 1897 the association established its first sample warehouse in Caracas, Venezuela.[38]

By late 1895 a concise economic analysis had led both the American business community and the administration to the conclusion that the United States industrial system needed more Latin American markets. Such a conclusion suggested that any expansion of European (especially British) influence in the area endangered not only America's security, but also its economic and political well-being.

In 1894 and 1895 these dynamic American policies clashed with expanding European claims in Brazil, Nicaragua, and Trinidad, a small island off the Brazilian coast. A revolution erupted in Brazil in September 1893. Rebels, led by promonarchist groups, hoped to end the four-year-old republic and restore the empire. But most important for American-Brazilian commercial relations, the insurgents included elements desiring to abrogate Brazil's reciprocity treaty with the United States—the most important one the United States possessed.[39] The rebels planned to cut off all outside aid to the besieged government by blockading the harbor of Rio de Janeiro; indeed, they had placed all their hopes of success in this one embattled area. Secretary of State Gresham did little more in the early months of the revolution than promulgate the rule that American merchants and traders could continue their commerce with Rio harbor unless their ships crossed the line of fire.[40]

Suddenly, in December 1893, the revolutionary cause grew stronger when a key Brazilian admiral, known for his promonarchist views, defected to the insurgents. Thus reinforced, the rebels announced that they would prevent all incoming trade from unloading in Rio harbor. This meant that all foreign ships would encounter "lines of fire." When German and British business interests endorsed the new rebel stand, the State Department feared that if the insurgent policy succeeded, American trading interests would lose their favored position.[41] Influenced by urgent letters from United States exporters, especially Crossman Brothers of New York and Standard Oil President William Rockefeller, and guided by his own fervent belief that American industry needed more foreign markets, Gresham reversed his position in early January 1894.[42] Sending a strong naval force to Rio harbor, the Secretary of State instructed the commander to protect with force the landing of American goods. This was accomplished, and the revolution collapsed. American congressional leaders, applauding Gresham's policy, portrayed Great Britain as the culprit in the rebellion. The republic had not only been saved from a monarchist inspired plot, but United States commercial interests (as the American minister to Brazil was quick to point out) had preserved intact their private inroads into the Brazilian market. The German minister to Brazil remarked, "The American dollar started to roll in order to break off the monarchist point of the revolution." [43]

Several months after the failure of this revolt, Gresham peacefully but firmly ejected British interests from the Mosquito Indian reservation in Nicaragua. This reservation occupied a crucial area, for it governed the eastern entrance to the proposed Nicaraguan canal. During the summer of 1894 the British hesitated leaving the region as they claimed that under an 1860 treaty they had obtained rights to protect the Indians from Nicaraguan injustices. Gresham disagreed and exerted continuous pressure on the British Foreign Office; and in the fall of 1894 the British surrendered their position.[44]

The American press disliked England's reluctance to leave this key area. When in the spring of 1895 British warships blockaded the Nicaraguan port of Corinto, American public and official opinion became aroused. An injury to a British citizen suffered during the 1894 trouble brought about the blockade. The State Department admitted the British right of blockade when it announced that the Monroe Doctrine had no relevance to the situation.[45] But American press and business circles, concerned over the future safety of an American-owned canal, deprecated the possibility that Great Britain would continue to rule over four million dollars worth of mushrooming American investment in bananas, timber, and inland trade in the reservation area.[46] Gresham shared this alarm, for although he disavowed the pertinence of the Monroe Doctrine, he nevertheless expressed deep concern to American Ambassador Bayard in London.[47] Then, with two strokes, the Secretary of State brought the reservation under United States control. First, Gresham implicitly agreed to protect the expanding American investments in the territory from Nicaraguan injustices. Second, he informed the British ambassador in Washington that henceforth the State Department would assume Britain's duties of guarding the rights of the Mosquito Indians.[48] By doing so, Gresham replaced England's control with that of the United States.

As Venezuelan matters moved to a climax in 1895, other British actions increased American apprehension. The Foreign Office attempted to force Nicaragua to reopen the delicate reservation problem. Though the outstanding points were soon settled, Alvey A. Adee, Second Assistant Secretary of State, told Olney that this irritation was "an important indication of the drift of British policy."[49] England further worried Washington by occupying the island of Trinidad; it hoped to use this uninhabited jut of rock off the Brazilian coast as a cable station. The American press loudly supported Brazil's protests. Adee wrote Olney that "the newspaper men are wild about the Trinidad business."[50] Under scrutiny of the State Department, Brazil and England reached an agreement in 1896.

Britain's multiplying claims in the Western Hemisphere caused

Adee to exclaim to Olney in August 1895 that the British were playing a "grab game" throughout North and South America.[51] But France also gave the State Department concern. In mid-1895 France and Venezuela severed relations over the French minister's alleged insult of the Venezuelan government. The United States stepped into the dispute and attempted to restore diplomatic connections. Bayard explained the State Department intervention when he wrote in August 1895 that the dispute was "of present interest" when viewed in "connection with the status of the existing Anglo-Venezuelan Boundary dispute." [52]

This situation had cooled when France attempted to occupy some 155,000 square miles of Brazil shortly after gold was discovered in the region. France had previously claimed the area, but had never forcibly tried to govern it. Olney and Bayard watched proceedings closely and even discussed the contingencies that might occur in case the United States assumed "a supervision of Brazilian boundaries, should French interests or ambitions prompt their invasion." [53] French and American interests also clashed in Santo Domingo. France demanded that the customs houses of the Caribbean nation guarantee a reparation payment which the French had demanded as a result of the murder of one of their citizens. A group of New York bankers shared the control of these customs houses and quickly asked for State Department aid. When a French naval squadron arrived at Santo Domingo, American Secretary of the Navy Hilary Herbert promptly instructed United States warships to proceed to the area and "watch carefully" over American interests. Fortunately the matter was soon adjusted.[54]

Congress and the Cleveland administration responded vigorously to these European encroachments. The character of this response can be briefly analyzed in the following incidents and personages: a congressional debate in the winter of 1894–1895 on the best means of protecting and expanding American commerce abroad; the naval appropriation debates of 1895 and 1896; a speech by Don Dickinson in May 1895; recognition by influential Americans that the Orinoco River was a vital pawn in the Venezuelan boundary dispute; Olney's concepts of American economic needs and power; statements of Cleveland and Olney during the Venezuelan boundary negotiations.

In the winter of 1894–1895 Congress became the center of an extended debate over American expansion into commercial and strategic areas and over the evolution of an anti-British policy. Henry Teller, leader of the Senate's silver bloc, sounded the keynote when he called England "our great commercial antagonist." [55] Conservative Nelson Aldrich of Rhode Island concurred as he warned that "there is a commercial warfare . . . going on among the great nations of the world for enlarged markets" and added that the United States could not "sit down silently and submissively." [56] In the House, Leonidas F. Livingston of Georgia proposed a resolution requesting Cleveland to invoke "friendly arbitration" to solve the Venezuelan-British Guiana boundary dispute. When weak opposition to the proposal appeared, William J. Coombs of New York quickly silenced it by replying, "Large American interests will be promoted by a friendly settlement of this question." Livingston added that the Orinoco River played a crucial role in the problem. Great Britain's claims endangered this waterway, which provided "the key to more than one-quarter of the South American continent." Livingston capped his argument by bluntly remarking, "This relates to a matter on our [sic] continent. Our trade and other relations with those people are involved in this settlement." [57] It is difficult to find much altruistic concern for Venezuela in this debate.

During this and the 1895–1896 session, Congress passed naval appropriation measures that provided money for the continued construction of the new American battleship fleet. The first three battleships had been authorized in 1890, and another had been added in 1892. Congress accelerated the construction program in 1895 and 1896 when it authorized the construction of five more battleships. Significantly, Congress provided money to begin building these vessels even though the Treasury suffered from an acutely depressed condition.

The cry for both commercial expansion and protection against British encroachments appeared frequently in these naval debates. Senator Orville Platt of Connecticut noted the importance of the frontier's closing when he declared: "It is to the ocean that our children must look, as they have once looked to the boundless West." Senator Anthony Higgins of Delaware urged the building of more battleships with the argument that the necessity of United States commercial expansion would have serious implications for the potency of the Monroe Doctrine and "the suzerainty of the American Republic over both American hemispheres." [58] Robert Adams, Jr., of Pennsylvania, an important member of the House Foreign Affairs Committee, was more specific: he announced that the Monroe Doctrine had become not only a political principle, but a notice to all nations that the American people would brook "no foreign interference either in the political affairs or the commercial relations of this hemisphere." Adams observed that Gresham's intervention in Brazil showed how the United States would have to uphold its new interpretation of Monroe's dictum.[59] J. Fred Talbott of Maryland, chairman of the House Naval Affairs Committee, declared that the American navy had to dominate the Western Atlantic and Eastern Pacific; if anyone disagreed with this proposition, he "was not worthy to represent his people in this Congress." Talbott pointed to the enemy when he said, "Great Britain never arbitrates with anybody except one who is ready to fight her." [60] John Van Voorhis of New York added that the United States could take care of itself, but that he wanted battleships to protect Latin America from Great Britain.[61] By 1896 such arguments had silenced almost all previous opposition to the building of a battleship fleet.[62]

Perhaps a speech delivered in May 1895 by Don Dickinson, a leader of the Democratic forces in Michigan and a close friend of President Cleveland, provided the most widely publicized commercial argument for American action in the Venezuelan dispute. One student of this episode calls Dickinson's speech "the most notable incident . . . indicating the desire of the Cleveland Democrats to assert their own lusty patriotism." [63] It should be emphasized, however, that Dickinson's address was more than a reflection of internal political pressure on the Cleveland foreign policies. The speech was important because it symbolized a wide and strongly held opinion that the United States had to obtain additional foreign markets. In a flaming peroration that summarized the speech, Dickinson declared, "We need and must have open markets throughout the world to maintain and increase our prosperity." He realized that such American expansion would conflict with "the settled policy of Great Britain." Consequently, Dickinson asked that England's "extraordinary claims and movements" be watched closely in Nicaragua and Venezuela.[64] The President applauded the speech in a personal letter to Dickinson.[65]

Cleveland had become interested in the Venezuelan dispute in early 1895, the importance of the Orinoco River especially attracting his attention. When Dickinson made a midnight call on the hardworking Chief Executive in April 1895, Cleveland displayed a large map showing the controversial boundary area. He explained that Great Britain had not previously formally included the mouth of the Orinoco in its territory, but recently the British Foreign Minister had entered such a claim. Cleveland expressed alarm since the control of the river meant the control of a rich section of the South American interior trade.[66]

The State Department shared the President's concern, for it also realized the importance of the Orinoco for American commerce. In late 1894 Venezuela closed the river in an alleged effort to end smuggling. By quickly exerting diplomatic pressure to reopen the waterway, Gresham demonstrated that the United States valued the Orinoco.[67] Venezuela took advantage of this incident to send a diplomatic note to Washington that stressed the dire consequences for American commerce if England gained control of the river's entrance.[68] Then, on April 5, 1895, the British formally claimed the Orinoco's mouth. Between this date and May 25 events moved rapidly. Cleveland told Dickinson of his concern over the control of the river; Gresham asked Venezuela to restore diplomatic relations with England in order that the United States would "be in a position" to mediate; and the President began an urgent search to find "someone . . . of a much higher grade than is usually thought good enough" to send to the vacant ministerial post in Venezuela. Gresham finally began composing a long note on the subject which he planned to send to Great Britain, but death cut short his task.[69] Olney picked up and supercharged this growing American concern, then exploded it in the British Foreign Office with his note of July 20.

The real origins of the boundary dispute dated from 1841, but the United States entered the controversy much later, in 1883 and 1886, and then only briefly. The State Department made the British-Venezuelan controversy a three-cornered affair only toward the close of Gresham's term of office.[70] Olney, former Attorney General, replaced Gresham upon the latter's death in May 1895. He possessed two beliefs that must be understood to comprehend American action in the dispute. First, he had a clear conception of the 1893 depression as a "labor revolution" which had resulted from the introduction of machine technology. With these new means of expanded production, more markets had to be found if Olney were to fulfill his hope of restraining this "revolution" to what he termed "peaceful and moderate channels." [71] Second, he believed that the United States had emerged from its century of internal development as a full-fledged world power. The natural corollary of this was that the United States could now exert its will almost any place in the world, particularly in the Western Hemisphere. As Olney stated this concept, "It behooves us to accept the commanding position" the United States occupies "among the powers of the earth." [72]

Olney embodied these beliefs in his July 20, 1895, note on the Venezuelan boundary question to British Prime Minister Lord Salisbury. The Secretary of State posited that American "honor and . . . interests" were involved in the controversy. He then tried to fit the Monroe Doctrine into the dispute. Historians might demonstrate that Olney made a poor fitting and that the doctrine, as defined by past use, did not apply to the question. This, however, does not lead to an understanding of either Olney's intentions or the aims of the Cleveland administration's foreign policy. Olney advanced the argument that American interests as well as Venezuelan territory were at stake. In essence, he interpreted the Monroe Doctrine as the catchall slogan that justified protecting America's self-interests. If the Monroe Doctrine had never existed, Olney's note would have been penned anyway; only the term "American self-interest" would have been substituted for the doctrine. [73]

Declaring that the United States had political and commercial stakes in Latin America, the Secretary of State proceeded to proclaim the ideal of extending the American form of democracy to the world in sentences that resemble those of Wilson in 1917. He interrelated American interests with the Orinoco River since it controlled "the whole navigation of the interior of South America." Of vital significance is the context within which Olney placed these points, for he emphasized that the Monroe Doctrine was positive as well as negative. Not only did the doctrine formulate the rule of European abstinence from the Western Hemisphere, but "It aimed at also securing the practical benefits to result from the application of the rule." Olney then defined these benefits as "popular self-government" in Latin America, the commercial and political relationship of South and Central America to the United States, and the unencumbered use of the Orinoco. The Secretary of State climaxed this argument with the blunt assertion that if necessary these benefits could be secured and preserved by American force: "Today the United States is practically sovereign on this continent, and its fiat is law upon the subjects to which it confines its interposition." [74]

When Lord Salisbury challenged these claims, Cleveland rephrased the American argument in his special message of December 17, 1895. The President first defined the Monroe Doctrine as a statement of self-interest. He then declared that the doctrine had to be maintained since it was "essential to the integrity of our free institutions and the tranquil maintenance of our distinctive form of government." Phrasing his message candidly, Cleveland warned that if Great Britain continued its course in the boundary dispute, the United States would regard this action "as a willful aggression upon its rights and interests." [75]

The causes and intentions of the administration's policy are given in a personal letter from Cleveland to Bayard. The President emphasized two points. He wrote that the Monroe Doctrine had been invoked because of "its value and importance *to our government and welfare*, and that its defense and maintenance involve its application when a state of facts arises requiring it" [Cleveland's italics]. The President next strongly disclaimed any idea that internal political pressure, especially jingoism, had inspired the American action; such influence was "entirely irrelevant to the case and . . . had absolutely nothing to do with any action I have taken." [76]

Throughout the ensuing negotiations, the United States acted unilaterally. Venezuela did not know that Olney had penned his July note until the newspapers printed the text. Even after this, the Cleveland administration did not consult Venezuela.[77] When, in January 1896, Great Britain proposed a court of arbitration that included a Venezuelan representative, Olney countered with an offer excluding Venezuelan membership. The Secretary of State took the same position when he opposed including the Latin American nation in the negotiations. He argued that he did not care to have Venezuela "consulted at every step." [78] Olney succeeded in including his plan for the court of arbitration in the treaty signed by England and the United States in November 1896. When the Caracas government learned of this, it demanded and obtained a representative on the tribunal. Even then Venezuela so intensely disliked both the treaty and the manner in which Olney had carried on negotiations that the legislature ratified the pact only after police ended threats of street rioting in Caracas.[79]

The United States obtained its two principal objectives: England submitted the dispute to an arbitral commission, and in the final disposition Venezuela retained control of the Orinoco River. But most important, by submitting its case to arbitration, England recognized Olney's claim of American dominance in the Western Hemisphere.

American historians have offered three interpretations to explain the Cleveland administration's policy in the boundary dispute. The most popular explanation states that domestic political attacks "must explain both the seriousness with which the administration came to consider a distant boundary dispute and also the aggressive tone which the Olney note and the Cleveland message displayed." [80] A second thesis traces the policy's roots to Olney's bellicose, stubborn temper.[81] A third interpretation declares that a "psychic crisis" struck influential segments of American opinion in the 1890's and that a new spirit of manifest destiny emerged from this "crisis." [82]

There can be little doubt that Cleveland took domestic political pressures into account, but defining these pressures as major causative elements leaves key questions unanswered and raises many others. Cleveland's bellicose policy could not have permanently won any political enemies to his side. The Republican jingoists and the Democratic silver bloc led the cheering for the December 17 message. Neither of these groups would have agreed with Cleveland on national political objectives. The President actually alienated many of his strongest supporters, especially the eastern financiers who had once saved the gold reserve, and who, at Cleveland's request, repeated the rescue operation shortly after the December message.[83] In other words, the administration's Venezuelan policy attracted groups that were irreconcilable in domestic politics, while repelling the administration's stanchest supporters. War might have united the nation behind him, but Cleveland certainly did not want to turn the controversy into an open conflict.

No reliable proof exists which shows that Cleveland hoped to benefit personally from the episode. It is extremely doubtful that with his conservative conception of the Chief Executive's duties and responsibilities he would have broken the third term tradition even if he had possessed the support. E. C. Benedict, who handled Cleveland's investments in stocks and bonds, testified three weeks before the Venezuelan message that the President had repeatedly said that he was "impatient" to end his term in office.[84]

An interpretation that stresses Olney's bellicose character misses two important points. First, Gresham worked on a diplomatic note concerning the Venezuelan situation several months before Olney assumed the top position in the State Department. Second, Cleveland probably initiated the dispatch of the Olney note, reworked the draft, and heartily endorsed his Secretary of State's language. The President played an extremely important part in the formulation of the policy, especially during the crucial incubation period of April–July 1895.[85]

A thesis which emphasizes that Cleveland bowed to the pressure of jingoism and a mass psychological need for vicarious excitement does an injustice to Cleveland. The President's greatest assets were his courage and a strong character.[86] After all, Cleveland defied public pressures exerted for Hawaiian annexation, the application of the Monroe Doctrine in the Corinto dispute, and compromises in the silver repeal act and the 1894 tariff. There is no reason to believe that he suddenly bent to the winds of jingoism in 1895, unless he had better reasons than pleasing irreconcilable political enemies. It would be difficult, if not impossible, to put Cleveland and Olney in the social groups that supposedly were undergoing this psychological dilemma.

Olney and Cleveland acted as they did because they feared that United States interests were in jeopardy. Both men said this at the time, and there is no reason to doubt their word. Such danger emanated from actual or threatened European encroachments in Latin America. This expansion not only endangered both areas held vital for American strategic purposes and existing or possible political democracies in the Western Hemisphere, but it also threatened present and potential commercial markets for American products. Both the administration and the business community proclaimed these markets to be necessary for American economic and political health. They reasoned that increased shipments of industrial products to less developed regions would have to replace faltering agricultural products as the staple of American export trade; and, as a member of the State Department observed in 1895, "It has been the task of Mr. Cleveland's foreign policy to prepare the way" for these manufactured goods.[87] One may speculate that Cleveland referred to both economic and security problems when he told a close friend late in 1896 that the Venezuelan affair was not a foreign question, but the "most distinct of home questions." [88] As Olney realized, the mature power of the United States could be used to harvest what the Secretary of State called "the practical benefits" of the Monroe Doctrine. Then these "home questions" could be solved.

NOTES

1. Olney to Thomas F. Bayard, July 20, 1895, Department of State, Instructions to Great Britain, State Department Archives, National Archives [hereafter cited as SDA]. The note is also in *Papers Relating to the Foreign Relations of the United States* [hereafter cited as FR] (2 vols., Washington, D.C., 1896), I, 545–62.

2. Alexander Dana Noyes, *Thirty Years of American Finance* (New York, 1898), 158–59, 200. The best accounts of the effect this depression had on the American economy are Charles Hoffman, "The Depression of the Nineties," *Journal of Economic History*, XVI (June 1956), 137–64; E. H. Phelps Brown with S. J. Handfield-Jones, "The Climacteric of the 1890's," *Oxford Economic Papers*, new ser., IV (Oct. 1952), 266–307; Frank S. Philbrick, "The Mercantile Conditions of the Crisis of 1893," *University Studies of the University of Nebraska*, II (1894–1902), 299–320; W. Jett Lauck, *The Causes of the Panic of 1893* (Boston, 1907); Gerald Taylor White, "The United States and the Problem of Recovery after 1893," doctoral dissertation, University of California, Berkeley, 1938.

3. Noyes, *Thirty Years of American Finance*, 200. For a summary of the factors influencing the new manifest destiny, see Samuel Flagg Bemis, *The Latin American Policy of the United States: An Historical Interpretation* (New York, 1943), 123–24.

4. Hill to Cleveland, June 24, 1893, and J. B. Crouch to Cleveland, June 23, 1893, Grover Cleveland Papers, Manuscript Division, Library of Congress.

5. Alfred Vagts believes the monetary situation directly affected Cleveland's Venezuelan policy since the policy not only silenced silverite expansionists temporarily, but also attempted to keep England away from Venezuelan gold fields which American interests had claimed. Alfred Vagts, *Deutschland und die Vereinigten Staaten in der Weltpolitik* (New York, 1935), 510, 1257.

6. Quoted in James A. Barnes, *John G. Carlisle: Financial Statesman* (New York, 1931), 299–302. See especially Carlisle's *Annual Report* of 1894 in which he declared that American "prosperity . . . depends largely" upon the ability of the United States to sell its "surplus products in foreign markets at remunerative prices." *Annual Report of the Secretary of the Treasury* (Washington, D.C., 1894), lxxii–lxxiii. See also Cleveland's letter to the Chicago Businessmen's Meeting, quoted in *Commercial and Financial Chronicle*, Apr. 20, 1895, 690; the President's letter to J. M. Stone, governor of Mississippi, Apr. 26, 1895, Cleveland Papers; and Carlisle's letter to Secretary of the Interior Hoke Smith, Aug. 11, 1894, *ibid.*

7. *A Compilation of Messages and Papers of the Presidents, 1789–1897*, ed. James D. Richardson (10 vols., Washington, D.C., 1900), IX, 402; R. H. Inglis Palgrave, "An English View of Investment in the United States," *Forum*, XV (Apr. 1893), 191–200. *Banker's Magazine*, XLIX (Aug. 1894), 97–98, supplements Cleveland's and Palgrave's views.

8. See again Carlisle's remarkable analysis in his 1894 *Annual Report*, lxxii–lxxiii; see also A. D. Noyes, "Methods and Leadership in Wall Street Since 1893," *Journal of Economic and Business History*, I (Nov. 1931), 3–4. A lack of markets for capital, not a lack of capital, caused the 1893–1897 depression in the United States. The administration paradoxically attempted to

attract foreign capital at the same time American investors placed their money in foreign markets. (See the discussion of United States investments in Latin America below.) This attitude can probably be traced to such vital sections of the American economy as railroads and cotton and wheat exporters—groups that believed the London Stock Exchange to be the best indicator of economic prosperity. Also, these years marked the early stage of the transitional period when control of the international money market swung from London to New York.

9. See Lee Benson, "The Historical Background of Turner's Frontier Essay," *Agricultural History*, XXV (Apr. 1951), 59–82; Herman Clarence Nixon, "The Precursors of Turner in the Interpretation of the American Frontier," *South Atlantic Quarterly*, XXVIII (Jan. 1929), 83–89; John R. Proctor, "America's Battle for Commercial Supremacy," *Forum*, XVI (Nov. 1893), 320–22.

10. *Messages and Papers of the Presidents*, ed. Richardson, IX, 454, 661–62.

11. *Ibid.*, 459; *Annual Report of the Secretary of the Treasury* (Washington, D.C., 1893), lxxx–lxxxi; see also Vagts, *Deutschland und die Vereinigten Staaten*, 1257.

12. See the excellent observations by Frank W. Taussig in "Rabbeno's American Commercial Policy," *Quarterly Journal of Economics*, X (Oct. 1895), 109.

13. *Messages and Papers of the Presidents*, ed. Richardson, IX, 459. It is important to note that Cleveland had wagered his political life on the tariff issue in his first administration, but did not emphasize this raw materials argument as he did after the 1893 depression struck. See *ibid.*, VIII, 589, 776.

14. *Annual Report of the Secretary of the Treasury*, 1893, lxxx–lxxxi.

15. *Congressional Record*, 53 Cong., 2 sess., XXVI, pt. 9, Appendix, 193–96 (Jan. 8, 9, 1894); Frank W. Taussig, *The Tariff History of the United States* (7th ed., New York, 1923), 309; Festus P. Summers, *William L. Wilson and Tariff Reform* (New Brunswick, N. J., 1953), 172–74.

16. Roger Q. Mills, "The Wilson Bill," *North American Review*, CLVIII (Feb. 1894), 235–44.

17. See *Congressional Record*, 53 Cong., 2 sess., XXVI, pts. 1, 2, 945 (Jan. 17, 1894), 776 (Jan. 12, 1894), 643 (Jan. 10, 1894), 1422 (Jan. 25, 1894), and Appendix, 79 (Jan. 16, 1894).

18. See esp. *ibid.*, 53 Cong., 2 sess., XXVI, pt. 8, 7712 (July 19, 1894). Cleveland's letters sharply criticizing protectionist senators are in *Letters of Grover Cleveland, 1850–1908*, ed. Allan Nevins (New York, 1933), 363, 365–66.

19. *Banker's Magazine*, XLIX (Nov. 1894), 326; see also *Bradstreet's: A Journal of Trade, Finance and Public Economy*, Feb. 16, 1895, 99. Henry L. Bryan of the State Department sent newspaper clippings to Ambassador Bayard in London (Aug. 23, 1895) which illustrated the great interest in increasing American export trade. Even some protectionist papers pointed out the need for more exports and thus opposed revising the 1894 tariff. Thomas F. Bayard Papers, Manuscript Division, Library of Congress.

20. *Commercial and Financial Chronicle*, Jan. 5, 1895, 9.

21. J. Sterling Morton, William M. Spring, and Henry W. Cannon, "The Financial Muddle," *North American Review*, CLX (Feb. 1895), 129–56, esp. 151. Another banker and merchant, A. B. Farquhar, said essentially the same thing to his good friend Cleveland (Nov. 9, 1894, Cleveland Papers).

22. *Economist*, Sept. 21, 1895, 1244.

23. Alfred S. Heidelbach, "Why Gold Is Exported," *Forum*, XVIII (Feb. 1895), 647–51; see also *Yale Review*, IV (Aug. 1895), 136; *Commercial and Financial Chronicle*, Mar. 30, 1895, 542–43.

24. *Ibid.*, July 21, 1895, 93–95.

25. Worthington C. Ford, "The Turning of the Tide," *North American Review*, CLXI (Aug. 1895), esp. 188–95.

26. *Banker's Magazine*, XLVIII (Mar. 1894), 649 ff; *ibid.*, XLIX (Dec. 1894), 31–32; *Bradstreet's*, Apr. 27, 1895, 259; *ibid.*, Oct. 26, 1895, 674; *Economist*, Mar. 3, 1894, 273.

27. *Banker's Magazine*, XLIX (Nov. 1894), 326–28; *ibid.* (Oct. 1894), 249. See especially the article in the Baltimore *Sun* of May 27, 1895, by Frederic Emory, a member of the State Department. Emory explained how manufactured products would have to replace raw materials as the backbone of United States exports. Copy in Bayard Papers.

28. Ford, "Turning of the Tide," 93–95.

29. *Economist*, Sept. 7, 1895, 1179; *Bradstreet's*, Dec. 28, 1895, 820.

30. Bureau of American Republics, *Special Bulletin* (Washington, D.C., Aug. 1896), 839–42; *ibid.* (May 1896), 626–27; *ibid.* (Sept. 1895), 145; James Morton Callahan, *American Foreign Policy in Mexican Relations* (New York, 1932), 508; *Bradstreet's*, Jan. 5, 1895, 14. By 1897 American investments in Cuba, the West Indies, Central and South America (excluding Mexico) amounted to $108,000,000. Cleona Lewis, *America's Stake in International Investments* (Washington, D.C., 1938), 606; see also Hoffman, "The Depression of the Nineties," 156–57.

31. See *Bradstreet's*, Apr. 27, 1895, 270; *Banker's Magazine*, XLIX (Mar. 1895), 498; *Public Opinion*, XVII (May 17, 1894), 159.

32. The *Tradesman* believed that "if the South shall push her advantages . . . her ports will soon have a monopoly of many lines of trade with the West Indies, Central and South America." Quoted in *Bradstreet's*, July 7, 1894, 430.

33. J. W. Avery to Olney, Nov. 8, 1895, Richard Olney Papers, Manuscript Division, Library of Congress.

34. *Public Opinion*, XVIII (Apr. 25, 1895), 436–37; *Bradstreet's*, Dec. 21, 1895, 808.

35. Pepper to Olney, Aug. 2 and Nov. 29, 1895, Olney Papers; Philadelphia Commercial Museum, *The Philadelphia Commercial Museum: What It Is, Why It Is* (Philadelphia, 1899); Olney's speech is dated June 2, 1897 (Olney Papers). For testimony to Gresham's interest in the commercial museum movement, see Pepper to Bayard, Aug. 11, 1895, Bayard Papers.

36. See Albert Kleckner Steigerwalt, "The National Association of Manufacturers: Organization and Policies, 1895–1914," doctoral dissertation on microfilm, University of Michigan, 1953, 24–26, 381; also National Association of Manufacturers, *Purposes of the National Associal Association of Manufacturers* (Philadelphia, 1896).

37. For the best summary of these themes, see Steigerwalt, "The National Association of Manufacturers," 41–42, 51–53.

38. National Association of Manufacturers, *A Commercial Tour to South America*, Apr. 25, 1896; National Association of Manufacturers, *Sample Warehouse for American Goods in Caracas, Venezuela* (2d ed., Philadelphia, 1897).

39. American action in the Brazilian revolt of 1893–1894 is analyzed in

detail in Walter LaFeber, "American Depression Diplomacy and the Brazilian Revolution, 1893–1894," *Hispanic American Historical Review*, XL (Feb. 1960). See also James Lawrence Laughlin and H. Parker Willis, *Reciprocity* (New York, 1903), 208.

40. Gresham to Thomas S. Thompson, American minister to Brazil, Nov. 1, 1894, Instructions to Brazil, SDA.

41. Gresham to Bayard, Dec. 18, 1893, Instructions to Great Britain, SDA.

42. Gresham to Isidor Straus, Jan. 6, 1894, Letterbooks, Walter Quintin Gresham Papers, Manuscript Division, Library of Congress; Rockefeller to Gresham, Jan. 4, 1894, Area 4 file, Navy Department Archives, National Archives [hereafter cited as NDA]. For Gresham's ardent belief in the need of foreign markets for the American industrial glut, see Gresham to Wayne MacVeagh, May 7, 1894, and Gresham to Judge Charles E. Dyer, May 2, 1894, both in Letterbooks, Gresham Papers; also Matilda Gresham, *Life of Walter Quintin Gresham, 1832–1895* (2 vols., Chicago, 1919), II, 797–98. For an opposing view of Gresham, see Vagts, *Deutschland und die Vereinigten Staaten*, 1918.

43. *Ibid.*, 1699–1700. On the effect of the American action, see *ibid.*, 1700; Lawrence F. Hill, *Diplomatic Relations between the United States and Brazil* (New York, 1932), 208.

44. Gresham to American minister to Nicaragua, Lewis Baker, June 13, 1894, Instructions to Central America, SDA; Gresham to Bayard, May 2, 1894, Letterbooks, Gresham Papers; Bayard to Gresham, May 28, 1894, Dispatches from Great Britain, SDA.

45. This episode and the reaction of American policy makers is best outlined in a "memorandum" prepared for Olney dated August 10, 1895, in the Olney Papers. See also Gresham to Bayard, Apr. 24, 1895, Instructions to Great Britain, SDA.

46. See *Review of Reviews*, XI (June 1895), 621–22; W. T. Stead, "Jingoism in America," *Contemporary Review*, LXVIII (Sept. 1895), 338; *Public Opinion*, XVIII (May 9, 1895), 502.

47. "Memorandum" enclosed in State Department's files with cable from Baker to Gresham, Dispatches from Central America, Apr. 13, 1895, SDA.

48. See especially Gresham's actions in restoring the rights of the Maritime Canal Company in Nicaragua and the protection he gave two American citizens who should have been dealt with by Nicaraguan law for attempting to lead a revolution in the reservation against Nicaraguan authorities: *Nicaraguan Canal . . . (Senate Executive Document*, No. 184, 54 Cong., 2 sess., 1897), 96–97; Gresham to Baker, Aug. 4, 1894, Instructions to Central America, SDA; see also Wilfred Hardy Callcott, *The Caribbean Policy of the United States, 1890–1920* (Baltimore, 1942), 77–78.

49. Note penned by Adee on dispatch from Baker to Olney, Nov. 18, 1895, Dispatches from Central America, SDA.

50. Adee to Olney, Aug. 2, 1895, Olney Papers.

51. Adee to Olney, Aug. 19, 1895, *ibid.*

52. Bayard to Olney, Aug. 8, 1895, Dispatches from Great Britain, SDA. German financiers were active in Venezuela during the 1890's (Vagts, *Deutschland und die Vereinigten Staaten*, 1525–29). Olney, Gresham, Cleveland, and key personnel in the State Department paid little attention to this infiltration, judging from their papers and diplomatic correspondence.

53. Bayard to Olney, Oct. 25, 1895, Dispatches from Great Britain, SDA.

54. Explanatory memorandum sent by Santo Domingo's chargé in Washington to the State Department, Feb. 5, 1894, Confidential Correspondence, NDA; Secretary of the Navy to Rear Admiral R. W. Meade, Mar. 9, 1895, *ibid.* German and American interests had clashed in Santo Domingo and Haiti before 1893. The State Department became active in pressuring Germany out of the area only after 1897. See Vagts, *Deutschland und die Vereinigten Staaten,* 1707–1709, 1788–93.

55. The essence of the debate is in the *Congressional Record,* 53 Cong., 3 sess., XVII, pt. 1, 157–626, *passim* (Dec. 1894–Jan. 1895).

56. *Ibid.,* pt. 3, 1889 (Feb. 7, 1895).

57. *Ibid.,* 1832–34. William Scruggs, former United States minister to Venezuela, had been hired by the latter country to interest the United States in the dispute. Livingston's introduction of the House resolution was one result of Scruggs's work. The interesting fact, however, is the argument used to support the resolution in debate.

58. *Ibid.,* 3045, 3109; see also *ibid.,* 1950, 2259, 3043.

59. *Ibid.,* 2307, 3106.

60. *Ibid.,* 2310–11.

61. *Ibid.,* 3105–3106.

62. This is illustrated by the action of the Quaker bloc in the House. Prior to 1896 this group opposed battleship appropriations. In the 1896 debates, however, one of the Quaker leaders, John B. Robinson of Pennsylvania, rose, quoted Tennyson's vision of universal peace, and then asked for four battleships. *Ibid.,* 3249.

63. Nelson W. Blake, "The Background of Cleveland's Venezuelan Policy," *American Historical Review,* XLVII (Jan. 1942), 267.

64. Clipping in Cleveland Papers from *Detroit Free Press,* May 10, 1895.

65. Cleveland to Dickinson, July 31, 1895, Cleveland Papers.

66. Note that this visit occurred before Dickinson's speech in May. Allan Nevins, *Grover Cleveland: A Study in Courage* (New York, 1933), 631. Nevins is one of the few historians who have given the Orinoco River any significance in explaining American concern in the dispute. For Cleveland's anxiety over the Orinoco, see his *Presidential Problems* (New York, 1904), 182–83.

67. See P. F. Fenton, "The Diplomatic Relations of the United States and Venezuela," *Hispanic American Historical Review,* VIII (Aug. 1938), 299–329; *Bradstreet's,* Apr. 27, 1895, 257.

68. Seneca Haselton to Gresham, Jan. 15, 1895, Dispatches from Venezuela, SDA. William L. Scruggs also widely publicized the importance of the Orinoco in *The Monroe Doctrine on Trial* (Atlanta, Ga., 1895), 24–25.

69. On April 5, 1895, Bayard learned from Lord Kimberley, the British Foreign Minister, that England claimed land inside the mouth of the Orinoco (Bayard to Gresham, Apr. 5, 1895, Dispatches from Great Britain, SDA). Gresham began drafting a note to England on the subject sometime during the last part of that month. There are good reasons to believe that Gresham's note would have been nearly as blunt and boastful as Olney's. As early as January 1895, Gresham told Bayard that Britain's position on the Orinoco question was "contradictory and palpably unjust" and that if England continued to encroach on Venezuelan territory "we will be obliged . . . to call a halt." Gresham to Bayard, Jan. 16, 1895, Instructions to Great Britain, SDA. For Cleveland's reaction, see Nevins, *Grover Cleveland,* 631; *Letters of Grover Cleveland,* ed. *id.,* 392; Cleveland, *Presidential Problems,* 251–52.

70. For the background of the boundary dispute, see Dexter Perkins, *The Monroe Doctrine, 1867–1907* (Baltimore, 1937), 44–60.

71. Significantly, Olney changed his mind about the depression's causes between June 1893 and 1894. In 1893 he believed the panic resulted from a cyclical movement in the economy. See his remarks prepared for Harvard commencement dinner, June 28, 1893, Olney Papers; clipping from Philadelphia *Daily Evening Telegraph*, June 20, 1894, *ibid*.

72. Richard Olney, "International Isolation of the United States," *Atlantic Monthly*, LXXXI (May 1898), 577–88; speech at national opening of the Philadelphia Commercial Museum, June 2, 1897, Olney Papers.

73. For an opposite view of the involvement of American interests, see Perkins, *Monroe Doctrine*, 155, 180.

74. Olney to Bayard, July 20, 1895, Instructions to Great Britain, SDA; the note is in *FR*, I, 545–62.

75. *Messages and Papers of the Presidents*, ed. Richardson, IX, 656–58.

76. Cleveland to Bayard, Dec. 29, 1895, Cleveland Papers; the letter is also in *Letters of Grover Cleveland*, ed. Nevins, 417–20.

77. See esp. George B. Young, "Intervention under the Monroe Doctrine: The Olney Corollary," *Political Science Quarterly*, LVII (June 1942), 251–52, 260, and Arthur P. Whitaker, *The United States and South America: The Western Republics* (Cambridge, Mass., 1948), 160–61.

78. Olney to Bayard, Jan. 22, 1896, Olney Papers. Bayard was very bitter at Olney's exclusion of Venezuela. See Bayard's personal memorandum, undated, but written sometime during March 1896 (Bayard Papers).

79. Young, "Intervention under the Monroe Doctrine," 276–78; London *Times*, Feb. 5, 15, 1897.

80. Blake, "Background of Cleveland's Venezuelan Policy," 275–76. Blake acknowledges that Cleveland did not "surrender to political pressure" and that "he became personally convinced that the Monroe Doctrine was at stake and that it was his duty to maintain it." But Blake then adds the statement quoted above. Bemis, *Latin American Policy of the United States*, 119; Vagts, *Deutschland und die Vereinigten Staaten*, 510–11.

81. Charles Callan Tansill, *The Foreign Policy of Thomas F. Bayard, 1885–1897* (New York, 1940), 776; see also Vagts, *Deutschland und die Vereinigten Staaten*, 1918.

82. Richard Hofstadter, "Manifest Destiny and the Philippines" in *America in Crisis*, ed. Daniel Aaron (New York, 1952), 173–200, esp. 176, 178.

83. *Wall Street Journal*, Dec. 21, 1895. Two weeks before the special Venezuelan message, Henry Villard personally pleaded with the President to prevent American "arguments with Europe" until the treasury reserve was restored. Vagts, *Deutschland und die Vereinigten Staaten*, 512, 1702.

84. *Wall Street Journal*, Nov. 27, 1895.

85. Cleveland, *Presidential Problems*, 257–59; *Letters of Grover Cleveland*, ed. Nevins, 392; Bemis, *Latin American Policy of the United States*, 119.

86. Nevins rightly emphasizes these traits in his *Grover Cleveland*.

87. Unsigned article by Frederic Emory in Baltimore *Sun*, May 27, 1895, sent to Bayard, May 28, 1895, Bayard Papers.

88. George F. Parker, *Recollections of Cleveland* (New York, 1909), 195. This conclusion differs from Vagts's belief that Cleveland's policy was one of "negative imperialism" or what Vagts describes as "eager for rule but not for gain." *Deutschland und die Vereinigten Staaten*, xi, 1416, 1701, 1702. It

should be noted, however, that numerous and influential voices of the American business community applauded Cleveland's vigorous use of the Monroe Doctrine to challenge British expansion in Latin America. Many of these businessmen based their support on the hope of increased commercial expansion into Latin America once British power was weakened in the area. See Walter LaFeber, "The American Business Community and Cleveland's Venezuelan Message," *Business History Review,* XXXIV (Winter 1960), 393–402.

15

Immigration

In 1917 Congress enacted a bill that began to close the door on Europe's "teeming masses" by requiring a literacy test for immigrants. In the 1920's, further restrictive legislation finally ended the traditional American policy of free immigration, substituting the system of quotas for people of each national origin. Pressure for restriction was not without precedent, for throughout the nineteenth century there had been sporadic efforts to limit immigration. Fearing the competition of foreigners in the labor market, American labor unions had agitated successfully for laws in the 1880's limiting Oriental immigration, and unions played a key political role in the struggle for a literacy-test law. At the same time, the doctrine of Anglo-Saxon racial superiority, then widely accepted, was strengthening the hand of nativists who opposed immigration on racial or religious grounds. On the other hand, most business spokesmen seem to have favored a liberal immigration policy, arguing that a serious labor shortage would occur should restrictions be imposed. When the 1917 bill reached President Woodrow Wilson's desk, he was besieged with letters and petitions expressing business opposition to the law.

During the debate over immigration, many American social scientists lent their influence to the restrictionist movement, both by their racial theories and by their assertions that immigrant labor depressed wages. In recent years, however, historians, demographers, and economists have reassessed earlier views of the great international migration of the nineteenth century and early twentieth century. Among the most prominent scholars now concerned with this issue is the

British demographer Brinley Thomas, whose study of *Migration and Economic Growth* (1954) has become a contemporary classic. Although, in the following essay, Thomas is interested only in the 'positive contribution" of immigrants, the viewpoint of the article accurately reflects the conclusions of *Migration and Economic Growth:* that on balance the immigrant made a significant, constructive contribution to American economic development.

THE POSITIVE CONTRIBUTION BY IMMIGRANTS: THE ECONOMIC ASPECT

Brinley Thomas

The various ways in which an inflow of migrants may benefit the economy of a country can be reduced to a few elements: we can study the impact on the labour market, the supply of first-class brains, the utilization of natural resources, the quality of enterprise, capital formation and real income per capita. Some of the questions arising under these headings are as follows:

1. Evidence of immigration enabling an economy to overcome rigidities and to redistribute its manpower more effectively in accordance with changes in technique and consumer demand or as a consequence of a major disturbance such as war.
2. Immigrants who have made outstanding contributions to research in science and technology which has had an important influence on the nation's economy.
3. Cases where an inflow of immigrants has made it possible for natural resources to be more effectively used.
4. The introduction of new crops, more advanced methods of soil cultivation, and new industrial techniques. Settlers contributing inventions and bringing new ideas, e.g. in methods of production, business management or industrial relations.

Reprinted by permission of the United Nations Educational, Scientific and Cultural Organization from *The Positive Contribution by Immigrants* (Paris: Unesco, 1955), pp. 166–174.

5. Making it possible for the country to acquire new social capital, e.g. extensions of its transport network, increasing the attractiveness of investment, and leading to a higher real income per capita. . . .

THE EXPERIENCE OF THE UNITED STATES

In the century ending in 1924 immigration played a considerable part in the economic growth of the United States. Within the compass of this survey it will be possible only to touch upon some of the salient features of her experience without attempting to do justice to the voluminous material available on this vast subject. No one will deny that the position occupied by the United States in the world today could never have been attained but for the periodic inflows of population over a long span.[1] Much of the significance of these inflows is overlooked if we concentrate on what happens in the short period; the positive contribution of immigrants to the United States cannot be assessed except in the light of experience in the period when entry was relatively unrestricted.

We shall begin with an analysis of the bearing of immigration on the growth of productivity and the standard of living in the United States. This will be followed by an account of some outstanding contributions of individual immigrants to science, technology and business enterprise in the era of freedom of movement. Finally, the economic significance of the recent influx of refugees will be discussed.

Between 1820 and 1930 the total number of immigrants recorded as having entered the United States was 37,762,000. When allowance is made for the probable size of the return movement of aliens from the country, it is estimated that the net increase through immigration during this period was 26,180,000.[2] The rate of inflow was not even; at certain times the number of immigrants was very considerable. There were five such periods of rapid absorption, namely, 1844–54, 1863–73, 1878–88, 1900–13, 1920–24. Strong evidence can be presented to show that there was a direct connexion between immigration and rapid economic growth.

A summary of relevant statistical data is set out in Table I.

In this table the period 1869–1913 is divided into overlapping decades, 1869–78, 1874–83, and so forth; and the course of immigration, real national income per capita and the volume of output of net producer durables is expressed in percentage rates of change from one decade to the next overlapping decade. There is a clear positive correlation between fluctuations in immigration on the one hand and rates of change in real national income per capita and capital investment on the other. Let us look, for example, at the decade 1874–83 compared with 1869–78; an increase of 26 percent in immigration was accompanied by a rise of 74 percent in investment and 29 percent in real income per head which is an index of the average standard of living. On the other hand, in the decade 1889–98 compared with 1884–93 we find a decrease of 20 percent in immigration associated with a decline of 8 percent in investment and only a small rise in real income per head, 4 percent—the lowest in the whole period. The decade 1899–1908 saw an expansion of 89 percent in immigration compared with the decade 1894–1903, and there was a corresponding rise of 75 percent in the index of capital investment and a rise of 14 percent in the average standard of living.

TABLE I. THE UNITED STATES: IMMIGRATION, NATIONAL INCOME
AND INVESTMENT: PERCENTAGE RATES OF CHANGE FROM
DECADE TO OVERLAPPING DECADE, 1869–1913

Decade (yearly average)	Total immigration [1]	Real national income, per capita [2]	Output of net producer durables [3] (at 1929 prices)
	%	%	%
1869–78	—	—	—
1874–83	26.4	29.3	73.5
1879–88	35.1	17.3	27.7
1884–93	−4.4	5.5	−4.2
1889–98	−19.7	3.8	−7.7
1894–1903	7.2	12.3	49.2
1899–1908	89.3	14.2	75.3
1904–13	25.2	9.6	9.4

[1] U.S. Department of Commerce, *Historical Statistics of the United States 1789–1945*, Washington, 1949, p. 33–4.

[2] S. Kuznets, *National Income: A Summary of Findings*, New York, National Bureau of Economic Research, 1946, p. 32.

[3] S. Kuznets, *National Product since 1869*, New York, National Bureau of Economic Research, 1946, p. 118.

Against this background it is interesting to observe the course of technical innovations in relation to immigration. A satisfactory statistical index is not easy to find, but for our purpose it is worth taking the annual number of patents granted for inventions, 1839–

1913. An examination of this series brings out the fact that the periods during which the number of patents granted for inventions rose most rapidly were periods during which the number of immigrants was relatively large. The data are set out in Table II.

TABLE II. THE UNITED STATES: IMMIGRATION AND PATENTS GRANTED FOR INVENTIONS

Years	Increase in annual number of patents granted for inventions [1]		Years	Increase in annual number of immigrants [2]	
1847–49	495	to 988	1846–50	154 000	to 369 000
1851–56	757	to 2 315	1851–54	379 000	to 428 000
1863–67	3 781	to 12 301	1863–66	176 000	to 319 000
1880–83	12 926	to 21 196	1879–82	178 000	to 789 000
1898–1903	20 404	to 31 046	1898–1903	229 000	to 857 000

[1] Historical Statistics of the United States 1789–1946, pp. 312–3.
[2] Ibid., pp. 33–4.

The steepest increases in the number of patents granted for inventions occurred in the *early phases* of the major upswings in immigration; during the intervals between these major upswings the number of patents granted for inventions was either stationary or increasing very slowly. It is reasonable to infer that each wave of immigrants (accompanied by capital imports) created conditions favourable to a high rate of capital investment, brisk industrial enterprise, the application of technical inventions, and consequently a relatively rapid increase in productivity and real income per head.

The average annual real income per head in the United States in the decade 1919–28 was $612; the corresponding figure for 1869–78 was $215.[3] Thus in 50 years the average standard of living of the American people had risen nearly threefold. The above analysis has shown that, in the process of attaining this goal, the longest strides were taken in the periods when there was heavy immigration.[4] This correlation between a big volume of immigration and a high standard of living also holds when we compare different regions of the United States. In 1946 the 10 states which had the largest proportion of foreign-born had an income per head of $1,344, while the 10 states which had the smallest proportion of foreign-born had an income per head of only $739. This disparity cannot be explained by differences in natural resources or climatic conditions; in areas where immigrants have been most numerous the pace of economic development has been most vigorous.

Immigration provides the receiving country with a supply of labour, the cost of whose upbringing has been borne elsewhere. It is a free gift of human capital, and the smaller the proportion of dependants among the new settlers, the greater the economic advantage. Of the 8,213,000 European immigrants who entered the United States in the years 1899–1909, no less than 83 percent were between 14 and 44 years of age; only 5 percent were over 44 and 12 percent were under 14. Of the 5,939,000 "new" immigrants (i.e. those from southern and eastern Europe) in the same period three out of every four were males. In the first decade of this century, when the greatest wave of immigration occurred, the addition to America's productive power was very considerable. From a strictly economic point of view the fact that 36 percent of the "new" immigrants in the period 1899–1909 could neither read nor write must not be regarded as a serious disadvantage. This enormous inflow of men in the prime of life coincided with a revolution in the sphere of technology; the age of electricity, chemistry and the automobile was beginning. The foundations of modern productivity were laid in the first few years of this century, and the United States was able to take the fullest advantage of that great opportunity chiefly because she was presented with a large addition to her labour force. In order to make use of it, it was necessary to introduce automatic machines and processes which reduced human skill to a minimum. The very fact that a third of the "new" immigrants were illiterate reinforced the need for mechanical devices which were fool-proof.

One of the chief reasons why America became the home of mass production and the pioneer of highly mechanized processes was that large periodic inflows of alien labour had made this evolution necessary. It was the technical price which had to be paid for effective and rapid economic assimilation; and one of its potent consequences was the development of a frame of mind—among workers as well as employers—alive to the advantages of scrapping out-of-date methods and adopting new techniques which increased productivity.

An argument used against the "new" immigration of 1899–1909 was that it contained a far smaller proportion of skilled workers than the "old" immigration. It was stated that the percentage of skilled among the immigrants from northern and western Europe was more than double the percentage among those from southern and eastern Europe.[5] This reasoning, however, is open to serious objection. It is not fair to compare the "new" immigrants of the years 1899–1909 with the "old" in the same period: after the turn of the century the unskilled from northern Europe were to a large extent displaced by those from southern Europe. Quite a different result is obtained if we compare the "new" immigration of 1899–1909 with the "old" immigration of an earlier period, 1871–82; there was not much difference between the proportion of skilled in these two groups, 22.9 percent in the "old" as against 18.1 percent in the "new." [6] In discussing the positive contribution to the American economy, it is easy to overestimate the importance of the proportion of the influx recorded as skilled. The majority of the newcomers were unskilled and unfamiliar with an industrial society, and they were absorbed into the lower-grade occupations which constitute the indispensable basis of the pyramid of production. Precisely for that reason there was no serious opposition from the native-born and the sons of the northern Europeans. The greater the inflow of unskilled, the greater the prosperity of the managerial, professional and executive grades; and, given the high degree of social mobility characteristic of America, the sons of the "new" immigrants had every opportunity to climb the ladder and enter the "white-collar" class.

The larger good is of course not without its mixture of evil. America could not have absorbed several millions of aliens in a few years without strains and stresses. The notorious sweating system in the clothing trade degraded thousands of the poorest workers; chronic overcrowding became a menacing social problem; and there was a downward pressure on the real wages of unskilled workers in the early years of the century. Moreover, the presence of such a large number of foreign-born in the coal mines must have been a major cause of the extraordinary increase in the number of mining accidents in the period 1900–10. It has sometimes been argued, even on high academic authority, that immigration accentuated unemployment.[7] Enough has been said in previous paragraphs to indicate that such a view is untenable. Countries of emigration suffered quite as severely, if not more severely, from cyclical unemployment as countries of immigration. The United States would have experienced the business cycle even if it had had no immigration, and if, in addition, the expansive influence of its population growth had been low its depressions would have had the chronic character associated with secular stagnation and its unemployment would have been correspondingly heavy. Indeed it was in the early thirties, a few years after the immigration barriers had been erected, that America ad its most catastrophic experience of unemployment. The outstanding fact is that immigration in its upward phases was a powerful actor pushing up the rate of growth of investment, income and employment, while in its downward phases, unlike internal population growth, it automatically contracted and thus relieved pressure in the labour market.

To do justice to the contribution of individual immigrants to the economic life of the United States would be to write an encyclopaedic history.[8] The record of achievement would fill many volumes. Had it not been for transatlantic migration in the nineteenth century many rich talents would have lain hidden and undeveloped in the Old World, and the United States and the world as a whole would have been immeasurably poorer. The bracing atmosphere of a new continent offering endless opportunities, the American creed with its accent on individual initiative and social equality, the spur of competition, the challenge of the frontier—all these factors combined to make the enterprising individual give of his best. In the previous section we discussed the impact on the American economy of immigration in the mass; we shall now select individual examples of the benefits brought by new settlers.

The following list is a small illustrative sample showing an extraordinary range of talent and variety of original nationality. It does not pretend to cover the most important or to include all countries.

These few examples are chosen at random. No-one could foresee which of the alien settlers would turn out to be outstanding inventors or pioneers; if America had not allowed freedom of entry to the millions she would never have received the precious few who possessed latent genius. From the initiative of each innovator there flowed countless benefits to the mass of the people. Three aspects of this record are worth emphasizing. First, the fact that in one wave after another America received a cross-section of the multifarious talents of Europe made it possible for inventions to appear in almost every sector of the economy. Secondly, a country in which the innovator was welcomed and allowed full scope attracted men of ability who might otherwise have been quite content to remain in their own countries; where the inventor was at a premium, economic progress was likely to be rapid. Thirdly, successive groups of immigrants of different nationalities implied a constant circulation of new ideas, and thus it became a habit to scrap old methods in favour of the new. In this respect America evolved in a different way from older countries.

Name of immigrant	Country of extraction	Contribution (industry or inventions associated with the immigrant)
Pupin	Serbia	Long-distance telephony
Tesla	Serbia	Electricity
Berliner	Germany	Telephone
Schwalbach	Germany	Typewriter
Steinmetz	Germany	Electricity
Bien	Germany	Mapmaker
Seemann	Germany	Sugar beet
Ericsson	Sweden	Ironclad ship and screw propeller
Eisen	Sweden	Horticulture
Lindquist	Sweden	Electric elevator
Swenson	Sweden	Cotton export and banking
Bendix	Sweden	Pioneer designer and builder of motor cars
Hoff	Norway	Underwater tunnels
Fahm	Norway	Subway construction
Holland	Norway	Holland tunnel
Dykstra (Theodore)	Holland	Potato expert
Bol	Holland	Bol lamp
Schilt	Holland	Schilt photometer
Goudsmit	Holland	Co-discoverer of 'spin of the electron'
Chanute	France	Glider
Garand	France	Automatic rifle
DuPont	France	Chemical industry
Bellanca	Italy	Aviation
Fermi	Italy	Nobel Prize physicist
Maramarco	Ireland	Vine growing
Ford	Ireland	Mass production of motor cars
Fulton	Ireland	Steamboat
O'Rourke	Ireland	Pennsylvania terminal

Since the Immigration Restriction Acts of the early twenties, the entry of aliens into the United States has been strictly limited. No longer does immigration play the part which it used to do in the economic development of America. The stream, however, has not completely dried up. One group of recent immigrants—the refugees —still deserves attention. . . . Referring to the aliens admitted from Germany (1933–41) and Austria (1930–41), Mr. Donald P. Kent wrote: 'In the entire history of immigration it is doubtful if there was ever so large a proportion of well-educated and talented persons among any large group of immigrants.' [9]

A thorough examination of the inflow of refugees was made by the Committee for the Study of Recent Immigration from Europe and published in 1947.[10] Commenting on its general quality, Professor Davie wrote: 'Not only did the refugees have a higher economic background than former immigrants but a higher educational background as well.' [11] Abundant data were collected about the businessmen and manufacturers among the refugees.[12] The proportion of Americans among the workers engaged in refugee undertakings was found to be considerable. The capital invested in 158 enterprises replying to the committee's special questionnaire amounted to between $10 and $12 million. Through this immigration America received certain trades and processes which had been unique features of Europe. The most striking is the diamond industry. As a result of the Nazi régime about 1,000 Belgian and Dutch diamond merchants and between 4,000 and 5,000 workers migrated to the United States, thereby transferring the centre of this highly specialized trade to New York City. There also came a number of high-grade jewellers particularly from France and Austria, who were outstanding as stylists and fashion designers. The picture as a whole can be seen from the Study Committee's enquiry into 158 refugee firms engaged in manufacturing; it was found that no less than 69, or 44 percent, of these were making things which had not previously been produced in America. Out of this sample, 50 firms had pioneered new products, 22 new processes, 16 patents, 7 secret formulas and 13 new skills.[13] Examples of the type of industry affected by these innovations are chemicals and synthetics, decorative arts, foods, furs, gloves, animal hair and hides, leather, novelties and toys, publishing, printing and photography, shoes and textiles. It would be inaccurate to infer that this migration was entirely urban: of the refugees replying to the Study Committee's questionnaire, 194 became farmer owners and 1,006 business owners.

It was a humanitarian impulse which prompted America, along with other nations, to extend a helping hand to the victims of persecution and the upheavals of war in Europe; those who were thus enabled to live a new life free from fear have conferred real economic benefits on the country which rescued them. Under the Displaced Persons Act of 1948, 400,000 displaced persons were admitted to America up to the middle of 1952 through the temporary relaxation of certain provisions of the immigration laws.[14] The results have been highly significant. In the words of the *Final Report:* 'This was immigration with a new look. Normal immigration was not interested in the contributions of the immigrant, but rather in the sponsor's financial responsibility. Here the skills, personal capacities, and the humanitarian efforts of Americans were the important factors.' [15]

Government agencies spent $19,000,000 of appropriated funds on the Displaced Persons Programme; but by the end of 1952 the wage earners among the 400,000 persons allowed to enter the United States had paid about $57,000,000 in federal income taxes alone. The report described it as a good investment and concluded in the following words. 'Reliable insurance company estimates indicate that it costs about $10,000 for an average American family to raise a child to the age of 18 years. Of the 400,000 persons admitted to the United States under the Displaced Persons Act, some 300,000 had reached 18 upon their arrival. Therefore, the United States was enriched by some $3,000,000,000 in productive human resources through the Act.' [16]

The action of the United States in opening the door to hundreds of thousands of refugees in the last 20 years has given a vivid demonstration of the economic value of immigration; it has brought to the notice of a generation which has grown up in the age of restriction the old truths which their forefathers held to be self-evident. As the *DP Story* put it, 'Here, a return was made to the faith of the Founders of the Republic that immigrants were assets and should be welcomed as valuable additions to the national wealth.' [17] What happened in the last few years was, on a small scale, analogous to those nineteenth-century waves of immigration which made America what she is today.

NOTES

1. It is impossible to take seriously the theory which used to be put forward in certain quarters in the United States, that immigration did not add anything to the population but simply replaced native by foreign elements. The exponents of this theory (e.g. F. A. Walker, 'Immigration and Degradation,' *Forum*, vol. 11, 1891) held that the gain through immigration was offset by a reduction in the birth rate in the receiving country and that the lower number of births was caused by the inflow of aliens. There is no solid evidence for this notion. See A. M. Carr-Saunders, *World Population*, Oxford University Press, 1936, p. 204–5; and W. F. Willcox, 'Immigration into the

United States,' *International Migrations,* vol. 11, ed. by W. F. Willcox, National Bureau of Economic Research, New York, 1931, p. 93–103.

2. W. F. Willcox, op. cit., p. 89.

3. See S. Kuznets, *National Income: A Summary of Findings* (1946), p. 32.

4. For an extended treatment of this theme see Brinley Thomas, *Migration and Economic Growth: A Study of Great Britain and the Atlantic Economy,* Cambridge University Press, 1954, chapters VII and X.

5. See J. W. Jenks and W. J. Lauck, *The Immigration Problem,* New York, Funk and Wagnalls, 1912, p. 31.

6. See Paul H. Douglas, 'Is the New Immigration more Unskilled than the Old?,' *Publications of the American Statistical Association,* vol. XVI, 1918–19, p. 401.

7. This was stated by Harry Jerome in his authoritative study, *Migration and Business Cycles,* National Bureau of Economic Research, New York, 1926, p. 209, in the following words: '. . . despite the sensitiveness of the flow of immigration to industrial conditions in the United States, the net effect of cyclical fluctuations in immigration is to aggravate, on the whole, the unemployment problem in the United States.'

8. For an instructive survey see Louis Adamic, *A Nation of Nations,* Harper, New York and London, 1944.

9. Donald P. Kent, *The Refugee Intellectual: The Americanization of the Immigrants of 1933–41.* New York, Columbia University Press, 1953, p. 82.

10. Maurice R. Davie, *Refugees in America,* Harper, New York and London, 1947.

11. Ibid., p. 44–5.

12. Ibid., chapter XIV.

13. Ibid., p. 246.

14. *The DP Story: Final Report of the United States Displaced Persons Commission,* Washington, 1952.

15. Ibid., p. 345.

16. Ibid., p. 350.

17. Ibid., p. 346.

Part IV

THE ECONOMY
SINCE 1920

16

The New Industrial Era

THE great stock-market crash of 1929 and the ensuing depression, the worst in American history, ended the fabled era of the twenties with a sense of finality that only complete economic and social disaster could have afforded. At the end of World War I, demobilization had taken place without benefit of coordination or planning by the federal government. After a brief postwar boom and a short but severe depression in 1920–21, economic expansion resumed its course, and it soon became evident that a new industrial order was emerging. The dominant Republican party interpreted its successive victories in national elections as a mandate to reverse the pre-war trend toward increased government control of economic life; and so the federal regulatory agencies took a benevolent view of corporate concentration in almost all the major industries. The electrical industry entered a spectacular boom period, new forms of mass communications were developed, and rapidly expanding automobile production exceeded even the wildest hopes of the industry's pioneers. Increased opportunity for white-collar and professional employment accompanied the rapid growth of the modern corporation, changing significantly the composition of the labor force. The emblem of the new industrial order, however, was the market for industrial securities, which is the focus of Giulio Pontecorvo's study of investment in the heyday of speculation.

If the stock market was emblematic of an earlier period, the aircraft industry is equally symbolic of a new industrial epoch, the post-World War II defense economy. The aircraft industry is today the nation's largest manufacturing employer. As G. R. Simonson demonstrates in the second selection, the structure of the industry and the course of its development (even in its early years) have been as much influenced by government policy as the securities market of the twenties was influenced by the absence of governmental restraints.

INVESTMENT BANKING AND SECURITY
SPECULATION IN THE LATE 1920's *

Giulio Pontecorvo

INTRODUCTION

The performance of the American economy in the 1920's has been analyzed by many observers, and while our over-all picture of the decade is reasonably clear, in several important areas we have, as yet, only limited information. This article attempts to throw some light on one of these areas by analyzing the capital market in the later part of the decade.

More specifically, we suggest for examination the following assertions:

(1) During the 1920's there was no effective regulation of the American capital market.

(2) The pattern of new security issues, both stocks and bonds, indicates that money capital was made available to a wide variety of business borrowers on progressively easier terms prior to the downturn in business activity in 1929. After the panic in the fall of 1929 only firms with the very highest credit ratings could obtain funds in the capital market. This behavior in the capital market was contrary to Federal Reserve policy.

Reprinted by permission from the *Business History Review*, XXXII (Summer, 1958), pp. 166–91.

* The author wishes to express his indebtedness for many helpful suggestions to Professors Darling and Storer of Bowdoin College, Professors R. A. Gordon and F. T. Morrissey of the University of California, Professor K. Ainsworth of Allegheny College, and to the Faculty Committee on Research of the University of Colorado.

(3) While the pattern of new security issues was not "acceptable" by orthodox standards of monetary policy, the volume
of new security issues did not as yet have any observable
quantitative effects on either aggregate consumption or investment in the United States.

We will begin our analysis by examination of the various possible
sources of regulation of the capital market: i.e., the Federal Reserve
System, institutional lenders, and the investment banking business.
We will then consider the pattern of financing, primarily the value
and number of security issues in the late 1920's. And finally, we
will look into the impact of the capital market on general business
conditions in the United States.

REGULATORY FORCES AND THEIR LIMITATIONS

The literature on the role of the Federal Reserve System and on
the money market in the 1920's is voluminous. Here we need only
to reassert the basic findings of that literature.

The primary motivation behind the formation of the Federal
Reserve System was to provide a solution to the monetary problems
that had plagued the country during the latter half of the nineteenth and the early twentieth centuries. The transition from the
intent of the founders to the Federal Reserve System of today was
a long and often painful one, and the performance of the Federal
Reserve System in the 1920's is best explained as part of this growth
process.

The prosperity of the 1920's, or to state it slightly differently,
the absence of any major monetary crisis from 1921 to 1927, permitted the Board of Governors gradually to consolidate its position
within the Federal Reserve System and to begin to work out its
broader policy objectives.[1] These processes were far from complete
when, after 1927, the Board was forced to come to grips with the
problems of inflation in the stock market. The inflation in stock
prices and the number of new security issues clearly raised the
question of whether or not a particular sphere of private interest
could or should be regulated in the public interest by the Federal
Reserve System. It cannot be said that the Board showed real
knowledge of the implications of the stock boom or that the steps
they took to end it were the decisive influences that brought stock
prices down. But it is clear that by 1929 the Board of Governors
had moved sufficiently far from a purely laissez-faire interpreta-

tion of their position that they were prepared to act during the crisis to the best of their ability to regulate the level of security prices and therefore indirectly the amount and kind of new security issues. However, while the Federal Reserve Board was moving in the direction of increased monetary regulation in the public interest, the deliberateness and the uncertainty of their actions meant that the Board did not during the 1920's have any significant restraining influence on the behavior of the capital market.

It might have been expected that some degree of regulation would have been imposed from the supply side of the capital market. However, in the decade of the 1920's there was no array of powerful institutional lenders such as one finds in today's market.[2] In the 1920's funds were supplied to the market primarily by a public which had a rising level of income and a historical interest in security speculation. Investment companies of various sorts became important late in the decade but, as we shall see, they tended to resemble and behave more like holding companies than modern investment companies. The close ties between some of these investment companies and speculative interests meant that by their policies they contributed more to market instability than to stability.[3]

The conclusion one may draw from these preliminary remarks is that the American capital market in the 1920's was still independent of any significant constraints on freedom of action that might have been imposed by the public at large or by the suppliers of capital. This freedom had been a characteristic of the American market since its inception early in the nineteenth century.[4]

Let us turn now to the question of self-regulation of the capital market by investment bankers. It was during the decade of the 1890's that investment banking reached maturity. From the end of the depression of the nineties until World War I the investment banking business was a highly concentrated oligopoly. The leadership in the business was competent, in its own terms, and aggressive. Entry was difficult primarily because money capital was scarce and also because of the nature of the business. Prestige and "the right connections" have always been an important part of the business, and these factors constituted a formidable barrier to entry.[5]

However, the structure created by the elder Morgan and his contemporaries was not stable. The most important contributing factor to the instability in investment banking was the rate of growth in the American economy. The increased capital needs of a rapidly growing and diversifying economy could only have been met by a small number of investment bankers with the greatest difficulty. And certainly these needs were not met by a group of investment banking firms that tended in time to lose both their aggressiveness and adaptability. The situation was further aggravated by the rapid growth in the supply of money capital as a result of the First World War and the impact of Federal Reserve policy on the supply of money during the 1920's.

The rate of growth of the American economy had two effects on investment banking. One was to increase the size and financial strength of business units, which reduced their dependence on investment bankers. While the impact of the tendency for firms to reach giant size has been most heavily felt in the 1940's and 1950's, it was also a factor in the 1920's.[6]

The other effect of economic growth was to create new opportunities for financing. Investment banking was and is a service industry. Historically, investment banking firms have had a tendency to specialize in the financial problems of specific industries. As the economy grew, the relative importance of various industries changed, and this in turn was, in part at least, reflected in the fortunes of those investment banking houses closely associated with specific industries. The failure of the leading firms to fill the financial needs of the rising industries created opportunities for the entry of new investment banking firms.[7]

A final factor that contributed to the instability in the structure of investment banking was the development of a wide market for securities, i.e., the upsurge of security retailing in the 1920's. It would appear that there were economies of scale in security retailing. These economies lay in increased specialization and in the advantage a connection between investment banking and commercial banking gave in the distribution process. This observation is based on the tendency for commercial banks to form investment banking affiliates, and for these affiliates to develop into the big volume houses in the 1920's. These two sources of entry, i.e., to finance new industries and to participate in a large number of issues which were widely distributed, were a basic source of instability in the industry.[8]

While the investment banking business of the 1920's was still a concentrated oligopoly, the effect of entry was to reduce the relative importance and the leadership role of the original firms. Furthermore, the industry developed a large competitive fringe. This fringe of highly competitive firms had a considerable effect on the behavior of the industry.

The over-all impact of these changes was the elimination of any internal controls that may have been present in the earlier period. The instability in the structure created by the rise of new firms was a factor in the security inflation that followed. In the face of entry by new firms, the older houses tended to differentiate themselves by emphasizing their prestige, by avoiding competition, and by their relatively more conservative practices. (This was especially true of J. P. Morgan and Kuhn, Loeb and Company.) Thereby these older houses abandoned the potential leadership which they might have exercised over their competitors: [9]

Mr. Kahn. Well, if you want a categorical answer, Mr. Pecora, I can only say it is always the other way around; has been with us for 50 years perhaps, or certainly for the last 30 or 40 years. It is not we that go to the corporations and ask them to do business with us. We hope that we have established a reputation which is our show window, which attracts customers. We hope that our trade mark, our sponsorship is recognized of some value to the corporation. We do not go after them. That may be conceited, but we do not. We would rather do less business. We do not go after them.

We may carry the analysis a step further and suggest that in the 1920's, within the concentrated sector of the industry, there were two groups of firms. The oldest firms with the greatest prestige and tradition of financial leadership were generally the most conservative; conservative in terms of not actively seeking new business on a competitive basis and also in maintaining relatively higher standards of conduct throughout the period.[10]

A second group of firms was aggressively engaged in expansion of their business.[11] This differentiation among investment banking firms is best illustrated by examination of the types of issues they sponsored.

A certain portion of the new issues in the late 1920's was created in order to provide the money capital necessary to protect existing properties and vested interests.[12] Here, the idea of control of real property was the basic consideration. Using the concept of control of real property as our criterion of differentiation between types of new issues we may establish at least one other alternative type of security issue. In this second group of issues there was no motivation toward control of real property or protection of a vested interest. This second group consisted of the issuance and sale to American

investors of foreign government bonds that the underwriting American investment banking house knew or strongly suspected to be
worthless or extremely risky. Control of real property was not a part
of this latter type of issue; it was just a question of having something attractive to sell in a sellers market.

Issues of the first type, i.e., those that were part of an attempt
to affect or protect the structure of an industry, were clearly in the
historical image or pattern of behavior in the American capital
market.[13] The following is an example of this type of issue. In the
late 1920's, the managements of the principal eastern railroads were
disturbed by the possibility of a reorganization of existing railroad
properties. (The reorganization was to be instituted by the Van
Sweringen Brothers assisted by J. P. Morgan and Company.) [14]
This threat caused concern among the other roads and the Pennsylvania Railroad, assisted by the investment banking house of Kuhn,
Loeb, took steps to protect its position.[15]

The struggle for the control of railroad properties was directly
responsible for the important Allegheny and Pennroad security
issues in 1929. These security issues were just a part of the power
struggle of private interests for control of important transportation
facilities. They grew out of the traditional use by the investment
banker of the capital market as the source of funds to be employed
in industrial reorganization. Issues for this purpose had appeared
in the market for at least the previous fifty years, whenever general
business conditions and the expectations of security buyers made
their sale possible.

The intensity of the sellers' market in the late 1920's is better
revealed, however, by the other group of new issues, i.e., those void
of any attempt at control of property, of which certain Peruvian
bonds sold by the National City Company will serve as an example.
Throughout the decade, the National City Company had been
interested in the possibilities of South American bonds. Unfortunately, in the case of Peru, the reports from their agents on economic
and political conditions in that country were so discouraging that
in the first half of the decade the matter was not pursued. However, by 1927, in spite of continued adverse reports on Peru, the
National City Company was willing to proceed with a $15,000,000
loan: [16]

Mr. Pecora.   Do you find any mention in it (the prospectus) whatsoever of the bad credit record of Peru which is embodied in the information I have read into the record from your files?

Mr. Baker. I should have to read this over, Mr. Pecora (after perusing document). No; I do not see anything. It is a secured loan. I do not see any statements in there.

Mr. Pecora. No statement or information was given to the American investing public in your circular corresponding to the information that your company possessed in writing among its files concerning the bad debt record of Peru and its being a bad moral and political risk?

Mr. Baker. No, sir.

In late December, 1927, a second $50,000,000 issue was offered to the public, and in October, 1928, a third issue of $25,000,000 was brought out. The National City Company persisted in these issues even though its foreign advisors continued to warn them of dangers in all phases of economic and political activity in Peru.[17]

The questionable circumstances surrounding these particular bond issues certainly did not represent any radical innovation in financial practices. The American public had been sold shoddy merchandise on many previous occasions. However, based on our criteria of control of real property, there is a decided distinction between the Allegheny incident and the sale of Peruvian bonds. By inference this distinction separates the issuing houses from each other. We may tentatively conclude, therefore, that the new issues boom was in part the product of the structure of the investment banking business. The changing attitude of the National City Company (i.e., the decision some time in 1927 to issue the bonds regardless of the reports received) toward these Peruvian issues is indicative of the increasing self-assurance and decreasing lack of any sense of public responsibility of an important "new" investment banking firm. It also clearly demonstrates the decline in lending standards in the market. We will develop this last point more fully when we discuss the pattern of new issues.

Further evidence on the structure of investment banking in the 1920's comes from examination of the number of business organizations involved in the issuance of securities in the year 1929.[18]

In 1929, out of slightly less than 1,000 organizations involved in security issues, about 87 percent participated in five or fewer issues; about 7 percent took part in from six to ten issues; 4 percent in from eleven to twenty issues; about 1 percent from twenty-one to thirty issues; and less than 1 percent in thirty-one or more issues. Significantly, the more conservative prestige-minded houses were far from the top in number of issues handled. The leaders in number of issues participated in were such firms as Halsey Stuart, National City Company, E. H. Rollins & Sons, and Harris Forbes.

The data on the number of potential issuers and the number of new issues (see below) tend to contradict the preconception that at least in the 1920's concentration in investment banking could seriously restrict the availability of money capital to business. The availability of money capital to business enterprises in the 1920's was a function of the greater ease of entry into the investment banking business, the easy money policy, and the high expectations of security purchasers. When expectations shifted as security prices collapsed in the fall of 1929, money capital was available only to the best situated borrowers. In effect there was a marked increase in concentration in investment banking and a reduction in the availability of money capital to business after the turning point in 1929.

THE SHIFTING PATTERN OF SECURITY ISSUES

Our second assertion relates the pattern of new security issues to the accepted norms of monetary policy. Accordingly, let us now examine in some detail the data on the value and number of new security issues in the period from 1926 to 1932.[19]

The principal conclusion indicated by the data on the value of new financing during the period is that while the over-all figures on the volume of "new capital issues by domestic corporations" followed a normal cyclical pattern by increasing until 1929 and then subsequently declining, the various subcomponents of this series did not. The rapid increase in the relative and "absolute" importance of common stock financing prior to 1929 indicates a progressive lowering of credit standards in the new issues market. Debt securities represent a contractual claim against income during operations, and a prior claim against assets in case of liquidation. Equity securities, whether common or preferred stocks, represent a contingent claim against income and a residual claim against assets. The shift in the market away from debt to stock financing meant that it was increasingly possible to sell securities which gave much less legal protection to the buyer. To put it the other way around, the public was willing to sacrifice a higher degree of certainty of income and repayment of principal in the hope of capital gains. Once the turning point was reached, this process was reversed, and credit standards went up rapidly in the market. At the depth of the depression, only debt securities were saleable in the market.[20]

It is worthwhile to review in greater detail the data on the various types of financing during the period. The total dollar volume

CHART I

VOLUME OF FINANCING—1926-1932 (In Millions of Dollars)

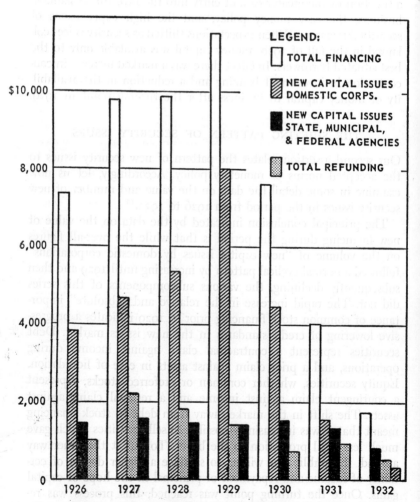

LEGEND:

☐ TOTAL FINANCING

▨ NEW CAPITAL ISSUES
DOMESTIC CORPS.

■ NEW CAPITAL ISSUES
STATE, MUNICIPAL,
& FEDERAL AGENCIES

▨ TOTAL REFUNDING

Source: *Banking and Monetary Statistics,* Board of Governors, Federal Reserve System (Washington, D.C., 1943), Table 137, pp. 488-489.

of financing, including refunding and foreign issues, increased as indicated on Chart I by 56 percent from 1926 to 1929. From 1929 to 1932, the volume fell by 85 percent.

"New capital issues by domestic corporations" increased by 113 percent from 1926 to 1929, or from $3,755,000,000 to $8,002,-000,000. From 1929 to 1932, the decline was 96 percent, or from $8,002,000,000 to $325,000,000. Taken as a percentage of the total dollar volume of new capital issues (i.e., total financing including domestic corporations, government subsidiaries, and foreign, less issues for refunding), this series became an increasingly larger percentage of that total up to 1929, and a declining proportion of the total thereafter. In 1926, 60 percent of the total new capital issues were made by domestic corporations. In 1929, new capital issues by domestic corporations amounted to 79 percent of the total new issues; in 1932, they were only 27 percent of the greatly reduced total. New capital issues by domestic corporations are classified by the *Chronicle* as either bonds and notes, preferred stock or common stock. The dollar value of bonds and note issues for new capital in 1926 was $2,665,000,000, and in 1929 it was $2,077,000,000, a decline of 22 percent. The peak year for new debt issues was 1927 ($3,182,000,000), and a secondary peak occurred in 1930, when new debt issues amounted to $2,979,000,000. The volume of new debt financing fell rapidly after 1930. However, as is shown on Chart II, the rate of decline in the debt series for the last two years was less than that of the common stock component. The dollar volume of preferred stock issued showed a fairly steady advance from 1926 to 1929, and a rapid decline thereafter. The rate of increase was less than that for common stock, but the decline occurred at a similar rate to the latter series. The common stock series shows only a moderate increase in 1927, but 1928 and 1929 represented spectacular advances. The total volume of common stock financing from 1926 to 1929 rose from $579,000,000 to $4,406,000,000, or a percentage increase of 661. The decline was from $4,406,000,000 to $11,000,000, or almost a 100 percent (99.8) decline from 1929 through 1932.

The next step is to examine the performance of the three components—bonds and notes, preferred stock, and common stock as percentages of the total "new capital issues by domestic corporations." Prior to the turning point, in September, 1929, the high percentage for the bonds and the notes was in the third quarter of 1926, when they represented 76 percent of the total new capital issues by domestic corporations. The low came in the third quarter of 1929 when only 15 percent of the total was in the form of debt issues. In yearly terms, it was 71 percent in 1926, and 26 percent in 1929. From the turning point in the new issues market to the depth of the depression, the percentage moved in the opposite direction. In 1930, 67 percent of all new issues were debt in some form; in 1931, 80 percent; and in 1932, 94 percent. In the second quarter of 1932, all issues (100 percent) were debt.

Percentagewise, the common stock series moved inversely with the debt series. In 1926, new common stock financing comprised 15 percent of the "total new capital issues by domestic corporations." This percentage fell slightly in 1927, then increased rapidly until 1929 when 55 percent of all new capital issues by domestic corporations were in the form of common stock. The high tide of common stock financing occurred in the third quarter of 1929, when common stock issues made up 65 percent of the total. After the turning point, the amount of common stock financing fell steadily

CHART II
SUMMARY OF FINANCING—1926-1932 BY QUARTERS
(In Millions of Dollars)

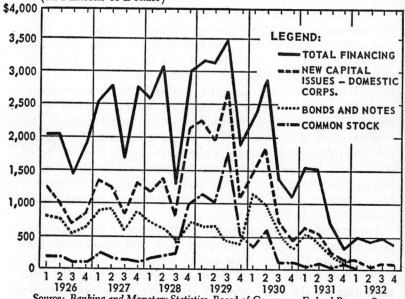

Source: *Banking and Monetary Statistics*, Board of Governors, Federal Reserve System (Washington, D.C., 1943), Table 137, pp. 488-489.

until 1932, when in that year only 3 percent of the new capital issues by domestic corporations consisted of common stock.

The preferred stock series showed considerable stability from 1926 to 1929. It was 14 percent in 1926, rose to 22 percent in 1928, fell slightly in 1929 to 19 percent, and then once past the turning point, the percentage fell sharply to 3 percent in 1932.

If we switch from examination of the value of new issues to the number and size distribution of new issues the same decline in lending standards noted above is observed.

From 1926 to 1929 (Chart III), the total *number* of new capital issues by domestic corporations which took the form of bonds and notes declined. (The year 1927 actually was the high point in the number of debt issues.) By size of issue, there was a marked decline in the issues in the smaller size category, and a small increase in the larger size category. The decline in the small size issues from 1926 to 1929 was directly related to the falling off in building activity, particularly after 1927.[21] Considerably more interesting is the period after the turning point, particularly the

CHART III
NUMBER OF NEW CAPITAL ISSUES
BY DOMESTIC CORPORATIONS FOR 1926-1932

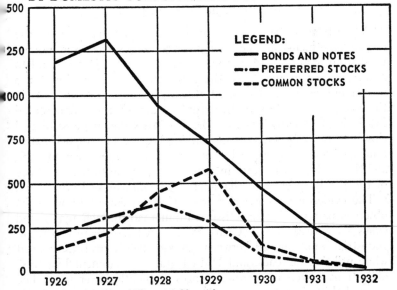

Source: *Commercial and Financial Chronicle.*

first half of 1930 which was characterized by debt issues of large size: [22]

New financing in the United States during January (1930) reached good sized proportions, reflecting a return to the normal after the setback occasioned by the stock market collapse in the autumn of 1929, though the total is large by reason of the bringing out of some issues of unusual size—such as the offering of $150,000,000 5's by the American Telephone and Telegraph Company, $87,500,000 Pacific Telephone and Telegraph stock, and $50,000,000 debenture 5's by the International Telephone and Telegraph—rather than being made up of a host of issues of ordinary size.

The tendency for debt issues to increase in size and to reduce in number, so noticeable in the first half of 1930, continued in 1931.[23] In 1931, the peak month for debt financing was March, and the *Chronicle* had the following comment: [24]

The point of most importance, however, in any broad consideration of the subject, is that the floating of a few issues of unusual size accounts for the bulk of the new financing for the month. This shows —and the feature has been noted on other recent occasions—that borrowing was on behalf of strong and powerful undertakings and organizations, and holdings, for one reason and another, exceptionally favored situations, and that as yet there is little indication of any widespread or general appeal to the investment market.

While bond issues declined in number and value prior to the crash, investment and holding company issues were surging upward from $271,000,000 in 1927 to $1,033,000,000 in 1928 and to $3,131,000,000 in 1929.[25] In the year 1929 there were almost 300 investment company issues, of which about 90 percent were in the first three-quarters of the year.[26] Many of these represented purely local undertakings, but the big issues dollarwise were tied closely to the large investment banking houses. The approximately fourfold increase in the value of these issues from 1927 to 1928 and the twelvefold increase in 1929 over 1927 are further evidence of the purely speculative character the boom assumed after 1927.

The evidence on bond and stock yields is consistent with the observed pattern of security issues. From 1926 through 1931, bond yields on a yearly basis (Chart IV), varied less than 1 percent. Industrial bonds moved between 4.8 and slightly over 5.5 percent while utilities, railroads, and United States government long-term obligations moved in narrower ranges at slightly lower rates. The internal shifts in rates among the various classes were very slight.

All bonds reflected the trend toward equity financing and higher interest rates by selling at higher yields in 1929. But in no instance was the 1929 high for bond yields markedly different from what it had been in 1928 or shortly before.[27]

CHART IV
BOND YIELDS AND EXPECTED STOCK YIELDS—1926-1932

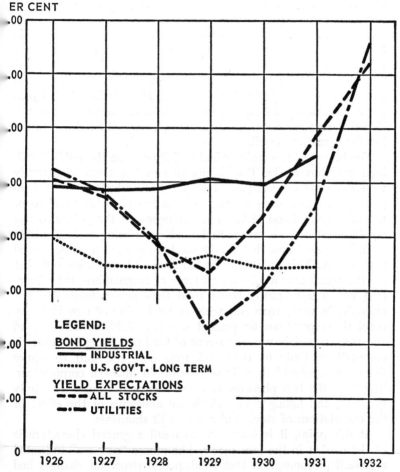

Source: Bond Yields—U.S. Dept. of Commerce, *Survey of Current Business, Annual Supplement,* 1932, p. 99.
Yield Expectations—*Cowles Commission Monograph No. 3. Common Stock Indexes, 1871-1937.* Bloomington, Indiana; Principia Press, Inc. 1938, p. 270.

On the other hand, stock yields reflect emphatically the shift to equity financing and the rapid increase in equity price levels. The *yield expectations* for all stocks fell from over 5 percent in 1926 to just over 3 percent in 1929.[28] For all stocks, the low yield expectation was 2.90 in September, approximately 2 percent less than the yield expectation in September, 1926, and almost 1 percent less than in 1928. Utility equities show the greatest decline in yield,[29] from over 5 percent in September, 1926, to slightly over 1½ percent in September, 1929.

The yield expectations for all categories of common stocks in September, 1929 (industrial yield expectation 3.16, utilities 1.68, railroads 3.75), were well below the yield on all private bonds, and with one exception (railroads) well below the yield on long-term government bonds (3.65 yield in 1929). The relationship between bond and stock yield expectations gives substance to the observation that in 1929 stock prices not only had discounted the future but the hereafter as well.

Tumbling yields seemingly had no influence on the public's willingness to buy stocks. The volume of new issues moved inversely with the yield expectations. The public absorbed (at least temporarily) an increasing amount of securities at yields equal to or less than going bond yields. The willingness of the public to buy equities on this basis meant that funds were being made available to business on terms that would not have seemed possible several years earlier. This point may be emphasized by pointing out that for the 1920's as a whole, for all types of corporations, debt financing was a significantly larger total than equity financing. For example, in 1926, 1927 and 1928, of total value of new issues by domestic corporations 62 percent was new debt, while for 1926 and 1927, new debt was 71 percent of total new issues by domestic corporations. Only in 1928 and 1929 does the shift to equity financing occur and there it is primarily in financial corporations. Together, the two phenomena of an increased volume of equity financing and falling equity yields are indicative of the effect of the expectations of stock traders on credit standards.

At this point, it is important to recall a general characteristic of the market in the late 1920's. The phrase "new era" indicated a general preconception that fundamental structural changes had occurred in the economic organization of the country which made prolonged hard times impossible. While there was little "real" evidence to this effect, the preconception was important and was tied to the increase in common stock financing.[30] The great collapse in the stock market in the last quarter of 1929 caused only the temporary end of the "new era." The period from the turning point until some time before the end of 1931 was a time of recurring optimism. Not until the second half of 1930 and then not completely until 1931, did the market accept the view that quick recovery could not be expected.

If the prosperity of the 1920's had come to an end in 1927, an index of stock prices comparing December, 1895, with December, 1927, would have shown an increase of 289 percent in the thirty-one year period (about 9 percent per year, or, if compounded annually, at a rate of 4.48 percent).[31] An increase of this type was not far out of line with the growth of industry and profits. But the moderate rate of increase in security prices changed quite suddenly into the violent stock boom of 1928–1929. The stock price average for the year 1929 was 190.3, an increase of 61 percent over the year 1927. Comparison of September, 1929 (225.2), with December, 1927, shows an increase of 69 percent in twenty-one months (a rate of 30.05 percent).[32] In terms of expectations, long-run business expectations were good (primarily because of the long period of expansion) and probably would have remained that way for some time regardless of short-run changes. But in the latter part of 1927, a change occurred and the general public became convinced that in the short run, at least, stock market prices would go up. Accordingly, an increasingly larger number of speculators entered the market, and those already in the market increased their existing holdings. It should be remembered that if margin requirements are relatively low and prices are rising, the leverage effect of margin trading makes it possible for a trader to pyramid, that is to increase both the number of shares held and his equity in those shares without expending additional funds.

The condition of expectations and the increasing stock prices meant that the attractions in the market place were not confined to trading. From September, 1927, through the first week in October, 1929, money rates increased. In September and October, 1927, ninety-day Stock Exchange loans ranged from 4 to 4.38 percent while new call loans varied from 3.5 to 4.18 percent. For the same period in 1928, the range for time loans was 6.5 to 7.38 percent and new call loans were slightly higher, ranging from 6.42 to 7.69 percent. In 1929 for the month of September and the first week of October, time rates varied from 8.88 to 9.13 percent, while new call money was quoted from 8.08 to 9.03 percent.[33] The more than doubling of rates on Stock Exchange loans attracted an increasing amount of money capital into the market. To a large extent this consisted of "loans on the account of others" rather than loans by the commercial banking system. (The "others" were foreign banking agencies, corporations with large cash balances, other brokers and individuals possessing idle funds seeking transitory employment.) These loans amounted to $1,680,000,000 on September 30, 1927, $3,610,000,000 on October 3, 1928, and $6,640,000,000 on October 4, 1929.[34]

The effect of these loans was to add an element of instability to the credit structure which was supporting the stock bubble. These lenders were attracted to the market by the optimistic short-run expectations, which made these loans seem safer than usual, and by the steadily increasing rates. When the serious break in the market in late October changed short-run expectations, these lenders deserted the market. By December 31, 1929, the value of these loans was only $2,450,000,000, a four-billion-dollar decline in three months.

What events in 1927 brought about the change in short-run expectations and the accompanying collapse in lending standards? Certainly the factors already mentioned—the prolonged prosperity, the self-assurance of the business community, especially the investment bankers, and the absence of effective regulation were decisive influences. But there were also two additional factors of great importance, one of which we may call the emotional climate of the times. We will not attempt to evaluate such diverse events as the Florida land boom and the effect of the automobile on the American home. However, taken collectively, these and other similar developments of the 1920's are an indication of social change and instability. This instability combined with the traditional American preoccupation with business, money making, and speculation contributed heavily to the public's lack of judgment.

The second important factor, security manipulation, has already been discussed briefly. Manipulation of stock prices to create the conditions that will ease the selling of securities is as old as security selling itself.[35] The first important corner on the New York Stock Exchange occurred in the 1840's, and throughout the nineteenth and early twentieth centuries manipulative practices of many kinds became an accepted part of the security business.

Security manipulation was such an important factor in the market in the twenties that we will examine two examples of manipulation to note the various aims of the manipulators. The first involves the maintenance of a market for the stock of a company so that additional issues could be sold. The second, a stock pool whose sole objective was to affect the price of a security in such a way that the "insiders" could make profits by trading.[36]

The relationship between Henry L. Doherty and Company and Cities Service Company may be used to illustrate the first case. In the late 1920's, Doherty and Company not only handled all new issues for Cities Service but they manipulated the market for Cities Service securities so that additional new issues could easily be marketed.[37]

If churning the market was a traditional device to assist in the selling of securities, it became in the late 1920's an important phenomenon in its own right, and the price increases generated by manipulation had an effect on the business community.[38]

The pool activities in Radio Corporation of America common stock in March, 1929, is our second example.[39] In the late 1920's, the Radio Corporation of America and all elements of the press kept up a steady flow of information about RCA. Radio was new, it had unlimited technological possibilities, and new technical developments were constantly called to the public's attention. Furthermore, RCA was a growing company and promised to grow even faster in the future. Earnings were high and were increasing. From March 1 to March 20, the *New York Times* carried seventeen press releases on RCA, the *New York Herald Tribune* sixteen, and the *Wall Street Journal* sixteen. RCA was continually plugged in this indirect fashion, and in addition, prior to the pool operation, the newspaper tipsters (such as "Trader" in the *New York Daily News*) constantly publicized the "coming fireworks" in RCA. They urged the public to jump on the bandwagon as the coming operation was to be a bull pool and that was the time to buy.

Manipulation intensified the public's interest in the market and, more than anything else, it brought about the change in the basis of valuation of securities. Until 1927, at least a fairly reasonable basis of evaluation had existed. After 1927, valuation was made largely on an irrational basis. Capital gains became a certainty as future values could only be higher than the current values. "Be bullish on America" was the slogan. This type of thinking is only completely irrational in the long run. In the short run, it is the only profitable way to "play the game." The game continued in 1928 and into 1929. Several times during this period, the market hesitated and sank back a little, but after each lull, it rose faster than before. The strength of each of these recoveries added credence to the popular myth of a continually rising market. But since a structure built primarily on expectations cannot endure forever, the eventuality of a price collapse gradually became a certainty.

EFFECT OF THE MARKET ON CONSUMPTION
AND INVESTMENT

The great panic in the fall of 1929 has become an important symbol in American history. It marks the end of the buoyant, reckless twenties and the beginning of the stagnant thirties. As a historical landmark, the stock bubble has great importance, but the crucial economic question that must be answered is what was the effect of the behavior of the market on general business conditions? What follows are some observations on our third assertion, i.e., the impact of the capital market on consumption and investment.

The progressive deterioration of credit standards in the capital market contributed to unwise security issues by certain business concerns. But it is very difficult to establish a direct connection between the ease with which funds were available and any unrealistic acquisition of *plant and equipment* or excessive *inventory* accumulation of business enterprise. Eddy has worked out the details of the amount of "real investment" resulting from issuance of new securities in 1929.[40] Out of approximately $8 billion worth of new security issues by domestic corporations only $2 billion were for productive purposes. Of this $2,001,550,000 total, $1,076,179,000, or about half was raised by the sale of stock, both common and preferred. This was, of course, far below the 74 percent of total new capital issues by domestic corporations which were in the form of common and preferred stocks. On this evidence, it would appear that in spite of the advantages of stock financing in 1929, corporations still relied heavily on debt instruments to finance "productive expenditures." [41]

Three classifications of business accounted for 68 percent of the productive investment: "Public Utilities," 29.7 percent; "other industrial and manufacturing," 18.1 percent; and "land and buildings," 20.2 percent. Of these, the industrial and manufacturing group did almost all their "productive" financing by means of stock issues, public utilities acquired slightly less than 60 percent of new

"productive" capital by stock issues, while land and building enterprises relied primarily on bonds and notes. Only in the case of
the industrial and manufacturing category is it likely that stock
market conditions, i.e., high equity prices and low equity yields,
contributed in any significant fashion to unwise acquisition of plant,
equipment, and inventory. And the aggregate amount of such unwise
borrowing in this last group even if all equity issues were for
unrealistic purposes was about $341 million.

This evidence indicates that conditions in the capital market did
not contribute in any significant manner to unwise investment by
business in real assets. However the low credit standards in the
market did make possible unwise corporate integration and the
creation of a holding company structure that was uneconomic.[42]
It appears that a portion of the funds that went into purely financial transactions in 1929 tended to create structural weakness (i.e.,
holding companies with insufficient earning bases, unsound mergers, etc.) in the American business system; weaknesses that were
revealed as soon as the level of corporate earnings fell by a significant amount. Specifically, the areas with large volumes of new yet
"unproductive" issues were the railroads, public utilities, industrial
and manufacturing, a miscellaneous category, and, of course, investment trust, trading, and holding company issues. How much firms
in these areas suffered during the downswing in business as a result
of their financial activity and how much they may have been
strengthened is unknown, but it seems likely that the effect was
mixed.

If we turn from investment to consumption we find that in the
aggregate, the flow of consumer goods shows steady increase
throughout the 1920's from $52.5 billion in 1920 to $76.4 billion
in 1929.[43] The two years of greatest growth were between 1922 and
1924 when the flow increased $9.5 billion. The increase from 1927
to 1929 was only $4.7 billion; from 1928 to 1929, it was $3.2 billion.

Consumers' outlays increased from $50.9 billion in 1920 to $77.0
billion in 1929.[44] Once again, as in the case of the flow of goods to
consumers, the increase from 1922 to 1924 was greater than the
increase in the late 1920's. From 1927 to 1928, the absolute increase
in consumers' outlays was $2.2 billion while from 1928 to 1929, it
was $3.2 billion. However, if we translate these absolute increases
into a marginal propensity to consume by comparing the changes
in consumers' outlays to the changes in aggregate payments to
individuals (including entrepreneurial savings),[45] in 1928 the mar-

ginal propensity was considerably greater than 1 (1.47), while in 1929, it was less than two-thirds (.64). (It may be that the sharp increase in aggregate payments to individuals in 1929—$5.0 billion over 1928 as compared with $1.5 billion for 1928 over 1927—was related to capital market activity.) The evidence of "expenditures on services rendered directly to consumers" is equally inconclusive.[46] Almost all categories of consumption increased in 1929, but in no case was the increase particularly different from the kinds of increases recorded throughout the decade.[47] For example, the increase in recreation and amusement spending was greater in 1929 than it had been in 1928 while, on the other hand, the outlays for personal services were less.[48]

Contradictory evidence of this kind reinforces the opinion that the capital market had little effect on short-run consumption.[49] On an *a priori* basis, it is reasonable that a steadily rising stock market would have only a small effect on the level of consumption. Personal consumption could be increased by the stock market in several ways. Increased activity in the market would result in higher incomes for those individuals directly employed in the field of finance. Capital gains might be realized by those trading in securities and these gains translated into higher levels of consumption. Interest in stock trading might persuade individuals to transfer other cash balances (or even postpone investment and consumption expenditures to acquire such cash balances) into security purchases to obtain higher yields which when realized would result in a higher level of consumption. In the first case, the number of people employed in finance has always been relatively small, and while they may have increased their spending on consumer items, it is unlikely that such a small number of individuals would have had a serious effect on the general level of demand for consumption items.[50]

In the aggregate it is unlikely that those who traded on their own account and who realized capital gains, increased their consumption in any significant amount. A rising market attracts funds so that paper profits tend to be kept in that form or, if realized, the resulting cash balances are quickly shifted into other securities. (The effect of a falling market on consumption expenditures is not symmetrical. It is quite likely that the capital losses which actually were realized after the crash were reflected in reduced consumer outlays. This effect may have been operative as soon as margin calls were made in any significant amount.) Those attracted toward stock speculation by the rising market are usually tempted to stay

on the band wagon. Margin traders would be particularly susceptible to this kind of thinking, especially if their remaining balances
due to brokers were very large. If the 1929 market had leveled off
for a prolonged period, then undoubtedly capital gains would have
been taken and in part, at least, consumed. But the rapid up and
then down of the stock bubble left traders (in the aggregate) no
time to withdraw at any given level of market activity.

Dividend payments to the increased number of individuals in
the market were another possible source of increased consumption;
however, stock yields were so low in the late 1920's that it is highly
unlikely that funds invested in stocks provided more current income
for consumers than did the same funds in bonds or some alternative investment. In fact, it is quite possible that some consumers
actually reduced their current consumption, or at least did not
increase consumption as their income rose, in order to obtain funds
with which to speculate in securities.

Although the data examined show no clear-cut indication that
the stock boom and credit conditions in the capital market were
important influences on general business conditions prior to the
crash, it is perhaps unwise to be too dogmatic about such a conclusion. The stock market was the symbol of the national prosperity
of the "new era" and the health and vigor of the market had a
tremendous effect on entrepreneurial expectations. The recovery
after the recession of 1927, in part, at least, may have been the
result of the general optimism in the business community.[51] As
we have noted, the stock boom was asymmetrical in its determin-
able effects on general business conditions. The collapse of stock
prices hurt short-run expectations; and although long-run optimism
did not die at once, the data on the kind of financing that took
place after 1929 indicate a basic change in the terms on which
funds were available to even the most favored borrowers. Furthermore, the purely financial transactions of the late 1920's (the missing $6 billion) may have created an unsound superstructure of
financial combinations, primarily holding companies, that were vulnerable to any decline in business activity.

By and large, however, the banks and stock exchange firms
withstood the panic in the fall of 1929. It was the prolonged liquidation of capital values from their inflated pinnacle to the depths
of the depression that compounded the monetary woes of the period
after 1929.

SUMMARY

The stock bubble in the late 20's stands out as a great landmark. It is symbolic to all observers of the American scene, although there are almost as many interpretations of the symbol as there are observers. In all probability, part of the importance generally attached to the stock boom of the 20's is due to the great changes in American life and our economy that came afterwards. From a distance the change in direction of movement of our society is clearly marked.

More specifically, the evidence presented is consistent with the assertions suggested. The absence of a strong central bank, the withdrawal of governmental influence from the market, and the increasingly competitive structure of investment banking meant that there was no possible effective regulation of the capital market, a condition that contributed heavily to the inflation in the number of new issues and in stock prices. The capital market clearly violated the norms of accepted monetary policy, but the effect of this violation on general business conditions is not clear since the adverse effects may have been outweighed by the additional liquid resources acquired by business firms in the market.

In all probability, the greatest impact of security inflation was on the expectations of the business community after 1927. And it may be that the more speculative nature of the business boom after 1927 was in part, at least, a function of the behavior of the capital market. Aside from this, the evidence does not indicate any close causal connection between the level of economic activity and the stock boom. However, given the complexities and interrelationships in economic affairs, it is best to accept this last conclusion as a tentative judgment.

NOTES

1. We may roughly generalize and say that, in the 1920's, the Board of Governors had as its basic aims restoration and maintenance of the international Gold Standard and the stability of the domestic price level.

2. For a résumé of the position of institutional investors during the late 1920's and early 1930's, see *The Security Markets* (New York: Twentieth Century Fund, 1935), Chap. VI.

3. It should be noted that the management of the New York Stock Exchange worked to improve the level of financial practices throughout the decade.

4. It was highly unusual for the capital market of a modern nation to

be virtually exclusively oriented toward private interests. In fact, in the 1790's it was the fiscal problems of the young American government that had been responsible for creating the financial business that led to the original organization of a stock market in New York. But the peculiarities of American development in the nineteenth century reduced the necessity for government financial activity, substituting a combination of state and local government and private financial transactions. In the 1860's, briefly in the 1890's, and during the First World War, the fiscal needs of the state suddenly rose to dominate the financial markets, but in each case the need was transitory and the influence of the government was subsequently withdrawn from the market place.

5. "In consequence of such policies and tactics, the great investment bankers, Morgan, Baker, Stillman, Kuhn, Loeb and Company, Lee Higginson and Company, and Kidder, Peabody and Company controlled large transactions almost to the complete exclusion of outsiders, i.e., minor houses which they did not approve. Between about 1900 and 1910 there was only one issue exceeding $10,000,000 that was floated without their participation, and even that (an issue of $13,500,000) had the Morgan blessing." Fritz Redlich, *The Molding of American Banking* (New York, 1951), Part II, p. 380.

6. See Lauchlin Currie, "The Decline of the Commercial Loan," *Quarterly Journal of Economics,* Aug., 1931.

7. Redlich, *op. cit.,* pp. 380 ff.

8. A discussion of entry into investment banking should consider not only the number of firms but the relationship of various firms to the generation of new security issues. Therefore the evidence presented below that about 1,000 firms participated in security issues in 1929 is only partly indicative of the importance of the entry of new firms. On a more qualitative basis the extent of the entry that took place from just before the First World War to 1929 is indicated by the fact that of the 17 firms named as defendants in the antitrust suit in 1949 some 7 firms or their predecessor firms began operations after 1910. Of even greater importance was the rate of growth in the firms which entered after 1910.

9. Hearings before the Committee on Banking and Currency, U.S. Senate, 73d Cong., 1st Sess. on S. Res. 84, Part 3, p. 968. For a similar statement of attitude and purpose, see *op. cit.,* Testimony of J. P. Morgan, Part 1, pp. 4, 5 and 6.

10. Because of the diverse and changing nature of investment banking firms, this categorization is only an approximation. For example, J. P. Morgan did participate in the formation of Standard Brands in 1929. For a comment on the absence of "glaring abuses" in the way the Morgan firm conducted itself during this period, see F. Pecora, *Wall Street Under Oath* (New York, 1939), p. 5 ff.

11. Typical representatives of this group of "new firms" of the 20's would be Dillon, Read and the National City Company. Dillon, Read & Company was formed as a joint stock association in New York in 1922. This firm had roots much further back but it only grew to national importance in the 1920's. The National City Company was formed in 1911. Charles E. Mitchell became president in 1916.

12. This discussion of new issues applies to those issues which were not aimed primarily at providing funds for real capital additions for domestic corporations, i.e., issues for financial purposes to consolidate firms or modify the structure of industries.

13. We are not directly concerned here with the problem of the investing public, but rather with the kind of issues put forward by investment banking houses and the insight the various kinds of issues offered give us about the motivation and orientation of the issuing house.

14. See the testimony by Mr. O. B. Van Sweringen, Hearings, *op. cit.*, Part 2, pp. 563 ff., especially his statement of the intent and purpose of the *Allegheny Corporation* on pages 564–569.

15. See testimony of Otto Kahn, Hearings, *op. cit.*, p. 1,246.

16. Stock Exchange Practices, Report of the Committee on Banking and Currency, Senate Report No. 1455, 73d Cong., 2d Sess., 1934, III, p. 128.

17. *Ibid.*, p. 129; Ilse Mintz, *Deterioration in the Quality of Foreign Bonds Issued in the United States, 1920–1930:* National Bureau of Economic Research, 1951, especially Chap. 6.

18. The data are from *American Underwriting Houses and their Issues,* New York City National Statistical Service, Serially 1926–1935, O. P. Schwarzchild, editor.

Since the data represent at best an approximation of the number of issuing organizations I have used percentage figures. Organizations are primarily commercial banks and investment banks. Some Canadian firms are included.

19. Data on the *number* of new issues and on specific security issues by companies come from the monthly summaries in the *Commercial and Financial Chronicle.* All data on the dollar volume of new issues are from *Banking and Monetary Statistics.* The basic source of data is the record of security issues compiled by the *Commercial and Financial Chronicle.* A complete description of the *Chronicle's* sources may be found in C. C. Abbot, *The New York Bond Market, 1920–1930* (Cambridge, 1937), p. 32, n. 5; and also in the *Commercial and Financial Chronicle*, Vol. CXII (March 26, 1921), pp. 1,216–1,218.

The figures from the monthly reports of the *Chronicle* have been summarized by the Board of Governors of the Federal Reserve System in *Banking and Monetary Statistics*, Washington, D.C., 1943. The Department of Commerce in the *Survey of Current Business*, February and April, 1938, published certain revisions of the data; and the figures given in *Banking and Monetary Statistics* reflect the adjustment so that there are certain differences in the monthly figures as originally given by the *Commercial and Financial Chronicle*, and as summarized by the Board of Governors.

The term "new issue" does not mean that these funds were used for new plant and equipment expenditures; a large part of these new funds were spent for purely financial transactions. See George A. Eddy, "Security Issues and Real Investment in 1929," *Review of Economic Statistics* (May, 1937). Eddy's data indicated that out of $8,002,000,000 new capital issues by domestic corporations in 1929, only $2,002,000,000 or approximately 25 percent went for real investments.

20. The phrase "lower credit standards" usually means less credit rationing. It applies to a loan market—quite often to borrowers from the commercial banking system—where there is at all times a "fringe of unsatisfied borrowers." One way to test for changes in credit standards would be to examine the quality of loans that are acceptable to lending institutions. In the case of the securities markets where the "lending institutions" are the entire range of stock and bond purchasers, an indication of the change in credit standards may be obtained by examination of the terms, conditions, and quality of the new securities purchased by the public.

21. "This enormous increase occurred before 1927; from then on construction declined. Thus the final spurt in economic activity during 1928–1929, vigorous enough to expand total capital formation by $3 billion, and to induce the largest single year's increase in gross national product since 1923, was in the face of deflationary pressures operating on the largest single component of total investment." R. A. Gordon, *Cyclical Experience in the Inter-War Period: The Investment Boom of the 'Twenties,* Bureau of Business and Economic Research, University of California (Berkeley, 1952), Reprint 8, p. 201.

22. *Commercial and Financial Chronicle,* Vol. 130, No. 3373 (Feb. 15, 1930), p. 1,030.

23. In 1929 the total number of debt issues was larger than in 1930, but the dollar volume was smaller.

24. *Commercial and Financial Chronicle,* Vol. 132, No. 3433 (April 11, 1931), p. 2,660.

25. F. C. Mills, *Economic Tendencies in the United States* (New York, 1932), Table 169, p. 427. The data, a special compilation from the *Chronicle,* are for the National Bureau and represent a series of issues for "unproductive" purposes. It should be recalled that in the 1920's the distinction between investment companies and holding companies was not as sharp as it is today.

26. Data are from *American Underwriting Houses and their Issues, op. cit.,* and are for issues listed as "Financial, Investment Trusts and Security Investment Companies."

27. It may be that the slight increase indicated had some effect on marginal borrowers, particularly those whose debt instruments were of low quality. Thus, bonds of poorer quality show slightly higher rates of increase than indicated on Chart IV. But in view of the amount of equity funds available in the market, this does not appear to have been a serious consideration.

28. Yield expectations: "the prevailing annual dividend rate, multiplied by the number of shares outstanding, is shown as a percentage of total stock values" *Cowles Commission Monograph number 3 Common Stock Indexes, 1871–1937* (Bloomington, Indiana, 1938), p. 3.

29. In spite of the almost incredibly low yields on utility stocks, the utility industry did not take advantage of the situation to increase plant and equipment significantly. The year 1929 for all utilities excluding railroads shows an increase of $274,000,000 in plant and equipment expenditures over 1928, but this was only $40,000,000 more than the increase from 1923 to 1924. The bulk of the increase came in telephone ($158,000,000) and electric power ($95,000,000). Even though utility stock yields remained low in 1930, expenditures on plant and equipment dropped by about $40,000,000. George Terborgh, *Federal Reserve Bulletin* (Sept., 1939), Table 2, p. 732, the sum of columns 3, 4, 5 and 6.

30. Perhaps the Federal Reserve System provided a false basis for estimating the strength and stability of the banking system.

31. The changes are slightly different if measured on an annual basis instead of from the December values.

| Value for December, 1895 | 34.2 | Value for year 1895 | 34.8 |
| " " " 1927 | 133.1 | " " " 1927 | 118.3 |

(230 percent or approximately 7 percent per year)
Cowles Commission, op. cit., p. 66 "All Stocks."

32. Ninety-two points in the index or about four points per month. In speculative issues, of course, the increases were much larger.

33. Partly because of the moral suasion exerted by the Federal Reserve Bank, a severe monetary stringency developed in late March, 1929. Call rates jumped to an average of 14.40 in the last week of March. The rate on the 26th was well above 15.5 percent. It was the next day that Charles E. Mitchell announced that the National City Bank was ready (in defiance of Federal Reserve Board wishes) to lend $20,000,000 in the market; $5,000,000 at 15 percent, $5,000,000 at 16 percent, etc. Mitchell's action apparently checked the precipitous decline of the 26th. The market regained confidence, money rates eased and prices began to move up again. Excessive manipulation of the market may have had an effect both on the supply of and demand for loan funds and so have been partially responsible for the credit tightness that developed in late March.

34. *Banking and Monetary Statistics, op. cit.*, p. 494.

35. For description of these practices in seventeenth- and eighteenth-century England, see W. R. Scott, *The Constitution and Finance of English, Scottish and Irish Joint-Stock Companies to 1720* (3 vols.; London, 1912), see especially Vol. III; see also Redlich, *op. cit.*, pp. 375 ff.

36. In this connection, *The Security Markets* (New York, 1935), pp. 443–508, gives an excellent description of techniques of security manipulations in the 1920's and 1930's.

37. F. T. C., Utility Corporations Report, No. 72–A, Senate Document 92, 70th Cong., 1st Sess (1935), p. 543.

For example, in the latter part of April, 1927, a clique of "bear" speculators sold Cities Service common stock short in large volume while spreading a rumor of the death of Mr. Doherty. The Doherty management resisted this bear raid, making purchases in large volume of the shares offered for sale on the exchange. On one day, April 30, 1927, Henry L. Doherty & Co purchased 25,373 shares of this stock at the total cost of approximately $1,086,000. Under the influence of the bear raid, the closing market quotation for this stock sagged from $51⅝ per share April 1, 1927, to $44 (or a low of $41) on April 30; but after the market support furnished by the Doherty management had overcome the effects of the bear raid, the market quotations again rose and continued to rise steadily to a close of $53¾ per share on December 31.
Ibid., pp. 544–545.

38. See Gordon, *op. cit.*, pp. 208–209.

39. *The Security Markets, op. cit.*, pp. 475–483.

40. See Eddy, *op. cit.*, p. 85.

41. This conclusion is based on Eddy's evidence for 1929, but it may not have general validity. If business conditions had remained good for a longer time, and if stock prices had continued at high levels while yields were very low, it is logical to assume a greater shift to equity financing. The 1928–1929 stock bubble did not allow sufficient time for a complete reorientation of business thinking.

42. An important offset to this, however, was the strengthening of the cash balances of certain firms as a result of new equity issues. What is needed is analysis and evaluation of the effect of the missing $6 billion "non-productive" new issues in 1929 on the structure of industry.

43. All data from S. Kuznets, *National Product Since 1869* (New York, 1946), p. 52. The flow of goods to consumers is a sum of commodities and

services. In essence it is the difference between national income and net capital formation.

44. This data from S. Kuznets, *National Income and its Composition, 1919–1938* (New York, 1941), Vol. I, p. 147, Table 5.

45. *Ibid.*

46. Harold Barger, *Outlay and Income in the United States* (New York, 1942), p. 227, Table 22.

47. There were, of course, exceptions such as radio sets, but these cases have a likely alternative explanation.

48. D. Hamberg, *Business Cycles* (New York, 1951) suggests that speculative profits from the stock market were a stimulus to consumption. See especially pp. 373 and 426. This may have been the case, although the effects of such a stimulus were probably local, i.e., limited to certain specific metropolitan areas. These local expenditures, as indicated above, were not sufficient to show in the aggregate data and so Hamberg offers an under-consumptionist, under-investment explanation of the downturn. See pp. 420–425 and 442–453. Both Hamberg and Gordon, *op. cit.,* suggest that rising stock prices and the condition of short-run expectations acted to shift the marginal efficiency of capital schedule to the right after 1927. This may well have been the case, but, as the Eddy evidence cited indicates, the effect did not show up in a new pattern of security sales for productive purposes.

49. If quarterly data were available, this conclusion might have to be modified. This is particularly true of the year 1929.

50. An interesting sidelight on this question is how did the brokers and dealers in securities actually behave during the period of the boom. There is constant reference in the literature on the South Sea Bubble of 1720 to the high and mighty ways of the directors of the South Sea Company. Their conspicuous consumption in the spring and summer of 1720 invited the same combination of disdain and envy that any nouveau riche group encounters.

51. See Gordon, *op. cit.,* p. 209.

THE DEMAND FOR AIRCRAFT AND THE
AIRCRAFT INDUSTRY, 1907-1958 *

G. R. Simonson

I

The invention of the airplane by Wilbur and Orville Wright in 1903 marked the beginning of an industry which has grown to be the largest single manufacturing employer in the United States.[1] Once the airplane was invented, there was wide-spread expectation that producing aircraft would be a very profitable business.

Even the Wright brothers, who previously were concerned only with proving that flight was a possibility,[2] became motivated by the profit prospects in the industry. In response to a request from the Ordnance Board of the United States War Department, on May 31, 1907, the Wrights submitted a formal offer to sell one of their flying machines for $100,000. The War Department did not accept this proposal. Later that year, however, the United States Army Signal Corps advertised for competitive bids on an airplane and accepted that of the Wrights. On February 10, 1908 the brothers signed a contract for the sale of an aircraft for $25,000.[3]

Although the Wrights applied for a patent on their flying machine early in 1903, enough variations in the structure of an airplane were believed possible to encourage others to enter the industry. The Curtiss Motor Company was formed in Hammondsport, New York, in November 1907 to manufacture airplanes as well as other motor vehicles. Actually Glenn H. Curtiss is credited with having built and sold the first "commercial" airplane in the United States.[4] The Wright Company was not founded formally until November, 1909

Reprinted by permission from *The Journal of Economic History*, XX, No. 3 (September, 1960), 361–82.

* This paper is a somewhat condensed version of the first chapter of my unpublished doctoral dissertation, "Economics of the Aircraft Industry" (Seattle: University of Washington, 1959). I am indebted to Dean A. Worcester, Jr. for helpful comments on a previous draft.

to operate the factory located in Dayton, Ohio, and about the same time the Glenn L. Martin Company was organized in Santa Ana, California.

Although these three companies stand out in early aircraft manufacturing, their prominence could not obscure the tremendous response in the rest of the industry. In 1911, private individuals built more than 750 airplanes. From 1911 through 1913 no less than 139 companies were formed to manufacture others.[5]

The expectations of the early manufacturers, however, were not justified; few airplanes were sold for either commercial or military purposes. Producers were further disillusioned when lawsuits developed over infringement of patent rights between the Wright brothers and other manufacturers, notably the Herring-Curtiss Company and Glenn H. Curtiss. These patent lawsuits were settled in most cases by 1914.

With impending war in Europe, as early as 1912, small orders for American aircraft and aircraft engines were being received from Russia, Roumania, Japan, and even Mexico. The value of aeronautical exports jumped from around $100,000 in 1912 to $226,149 in 1914.[6] In the latter year, out of a total of only 49 aircraft sold, 34 were exported. Aside from the foreign demand during this period, the market for aircraft was growing but slowly; commercial aviation had not yet developed, and the Federal government's demand increased only gradually with the recognition of the potential of a military air arm.

II

The aircraft industry experienced a period of tremendous growth during World War I. Prior to 1917 the increase in demand was principally for exports. In 1917 and 1918, when the United States was actively in the war, by far the greatest percentage of sales was to the United States Government and exports were relatively a much less important component of total demand. However, the number and value of all aeronautical exports, including engines and other aircraft parts, rose significantly as Table 1 indicates.

After the war got underway, the Allies appealed to the United States for 25,000 airplanes.[7] At the time this country had an estimated capacity to produce only 10 percent of that number. Only five of the companies had ever manufactured more than 10 airplanes, and the largest company, Curtiss Aeroplane and Motor Corporation, could turn out about 1,500 annually. Even by 1917 the

TABLE 1. UNITED STATES AIRCRAFT PRODUCTION AND EXPORTS
1914–1918

Year	Aircraft Produced	Aircraft Exported	Percent Exports of Production	Value of Aircraft Exports	Value of All Aeronautical Exports
1914	49	34	69	$ 188,924	$ 226,149
1915	178	152	85	958,019	1,541,446
1916	411	269	65	2,158,345	7,002,005
1917	2,148	135	6	1,001,542	4,135,445
1918	14,020	20	.1	216,120	9,084,097

Source: Civil Aeronautics Administration, CAA *Statistical Handbook of Civil Aviation*, 1957 (Washington: Government Printing Office, 1957), pp. 58, 65.

nation's manufacturers had capacity to produce only 7,200 airplanes per year.

When the United States entered the war on April 6, 1917 it had less than 300 military aircraft. This was an insignificant number in contrast to the 40,000 airplanes that the Joint Army and Navy Technical Board recommended should be produced by July 1, 1918.[8] Appropriations for military aviation increased from $1,800,000 in 1916 to $22,500,000 in 1917. But before manufacturers could expand production they had to make arrangements with the basic patent holders, the Wright Company and Curtiss Aeroplane and Motor Company, in order to produce aircraft of proven design. The Manufacturers Aircraft Association, organized in February 1917, provided membership for any aircraft builder and the issuance of licenses between members.[9]

Two factors led to extremely high corporate profits. The government lacked experience in dealings with the industry, and important government officials had close personal connections with it. For example, the Dayton Wright Company was granted a contract to produce Dehavilland airplanes at an estimated production cost plus a maximum profit of 12½ percent; the company was to retain 25 percent of the savings arising from lower production costs. Actual per unit cost turned out to be $4,400 instead of $7,000, which meant the company realized a net return of $1,525 per aircraft. Ford, Fisher Body, Packard, Lincoln, and others made fantastic gains in aeronautical production.[10] Post-war investigations of the industry's profits resulted in censure of the industry for its lack of responsibility in wartime.

At the time of the Armistice the United States was producing aircraft at the rate of 21,000 planes per year and employment in the industry had risen from 5,000 at the outset of the war to 175,-000. Between April 1917 and November 1918 a total of 13,894 airplanes was delivered to the government on contract at an aggregate cost of $113,721,043.[11] The aircraft industry, exclusive of other wartime producers of aircraft such as the automotive industry, produced 9,742 of these airplanes, and 14,765 of the 41,953 aircraft engines. The total expenditure on all aircraft components was approximately $350,000,000 of which about 70 percent was for engines.[12] The specialized aircraft manufacturers produced, therefore, approximately 70 percent of the aircraft and only about 34 percent of the aircraft engines.

III

Three days after the Armistice more than $100,000,000 of aircraft contracts were cancelled. Within three months the industry had contracted to 10 percent of its wartime strength. Few of the 24 aircraft companies existing at the time of the Armistice survived that contraction and those remaining liquidated surplus plants and cancelled subcontracts; the latter actions forced the automotive industry completely out of the aircraft business. Production shrank from 14,020 aircraft in 1918, to 780 in 1919 and to a post-war low of 263 in 1922. Controversy between the Army and Navy over the airplane versus the battleship resulted in failure to formulate a firm policy for the development of military aviation and whatever civilian demand existed was largely supplied by the disposal of surplus military aircraft.

The impact of the "barnstormers" and the record-breakers of the early 1920's was evidently not a significant factor in creating an increased demand for civil aircraft. When the War Department opened the first air mail route between New York and Washington in May 1918, the American Aviation Mission expressed the view that this move might ultimately provide a small market for planes. The industry's growth was impeded, however, by the lack of adequate airports and landing facilities, weather reporting, and air laws. Finally, the clamoring of the American Aviation Mission, the National Advisory Committee for Aeronautics, the Aeronautical Chamber of Commerce, and General William Mitchell moved President Coolidge to appoint Dwight W. Morrow to investigate airpower needs of the nation. The recommendations of the Morrow Board resulted in the passage of several acts which were to assist the industry significantly.

The first of these acts was the Kelley Bill or Air Mail Act of 1925. The purpose of the act was "to encourage commercial aviation and to authorize the Postmaster General to contract for air mail service." [13] The legislation removed the government from the operation of the air mail lines which it had undertaken since 1918 and turned the task over to private operators.

In 1926 a major step was taken with the passage of the Air Commerce Act.[14] This act, the forerunner of the Civil Aeronautics Act of 1938, charged the Secretary of Commerce with the responsibility for fostering air commerce through the establishment of airports, civil airways, and navigational aids. It also gave him authority to insure safe operations by providing for registration and certification of aircraft and flying personnel.

An increased demand for the products of the industry was assured with the passage of the Navy Five-Year Program [15] in June 1926 and the Army Five-Year Program in July of the same year. The Navy program provided for the procurement of 1,614 aircraft between the fiscal years 1927 and 1931. The Army program, included in the Air Corps Act of 1926,[16] authorized the Secretary of War to equip the Army with up to 1,800 serviceable airplanes in the same period. Federal expenditures for aircraft had increased from $6,000,000 in 1922 to $12,000,000 in 1926 and, with the growing prosperity, the output of civil aircraft had grown to represent 55 percent of the total output in the latter year.

IV

The next year, 1927, was one of history-making flights and almost overnight flying increased significantly in popularity, in part as a consequence of these feats. This development, coupled with the government support provided for in the legislation of 1925 and 1926, led to a notable expansion in aircraft manufacturing. Output increased from 1,186 aircraft in 1926 and reached a peak for the period of 6,193 in 1929, and aircraft sales had risen from $21,162,000 in 1927 to $71,153,000 in 1929.

The expansion of existing firms and the entry of new ones gave the industry capacity of between 15,000 and 20,000 planes per year by the end of the twenties. There were then an estimated 286 companies manufacturing airplanes. However, only about half of the

6,193 aircraft produced in 1929 were sold that year.[17] Although exports increased somewhat, the increase in production and domestic sales of civil aircraft was the outstanding development between 1927 and 1929. The growth in civil aircraft was from 652 units in 1926 to a high of 5,516 in 1929.

The prospects for increased profits from aircraft manufacturing which induced the expansion also led to vertical and horizontal integration. Although the interests of the major organizations in the aviation industry were very intertwined, it appears that five more-or-less definite interest groups existed; the Curtiss-Wright Corporation, the Detroit Aircraft Corporation, United Aircraft and Transport Company, the Cord Corporation, and General Motors.[18] Ownership or control of aircraft manufacturing firms along with those of air transport was the most prevalent form of vertical combination. Such organization was sought to secure financial strength for competition and expansion, and to assure markets for the manufacturers of aircraft. These combinations obviously had a survival value: when the industry underwent the violent contraction following the crash of 1929, those manufacturing firms integrated with air transport survived while most of the independents went into bankruptcy.

United Aircraft and Curtiss-Wright had by far the greatest share of total sales in the period 1927–1933 and the greatest proportion of government aircraft orders, as Table 2 indicates. Curtiss-Wright and

TABLE 2. AIRCRAFT AND ENGINE SALES, 1927–1933

Companies	Government Sales	Percent of Total Government Sales	Commercial Sales	Percent of Total Commercial Sales	Total Sales	Percent of Total Sales
U. A. & T. (Boeing, Chance Vought, Pratt & Whitney)	$50,184,443	39.7	$28,056,208	48.0	$78,240,651	42.3
Curtiss-Wright (Curtiss, Wright, Keystone)	44,755,590	35.4	26,813,517	45.9	71,569,107	38.7
Douglas	14,437,623	11.4	1,412,790	2.4	15,850,413	8.6
Glenn Martin	9,895,605	7.8	none	...	9,895,605	5.4
Consolidated	4,307,632	3.4	1,118,231	1.9	5,425,863	2.9
Great Lakes	2,451,993	1.9	905,719	1.5	3,357,712	1.8
Grumman	452,195	.4	153,492	.3	605,687	.3
Totals	$126,485,081	100.0	$58,459,957	100.0	$184,945,038	100.0

Source: Elsbeth Freudenthal, *The Aviation Business* (New York: The Vanguard Press, 1940), p. 120.

United had approximately 75 percent of the military business. The other 25 percent was divided largely among the five leading independents, and virtually nothing in the way of military sales went to the remaining 279 or more firms. Furthermore, the vertically integrated organizations, including the leading manufacturers, were getting practically all of the government air mail payments. In 1933 the United Aircraft combination received 36.45 percent of the total air mail payments; General Motors affiliates received 29.72 percent; and American Airways, which was controlled by Cord, had 23.67 percent.[19] The receipt of government air mail business not only strengthened the positions of the combinations directly but it was also an important factor in creating and sustaining a demand for the commercial aircraft produced by the manufacturers within these combinations.

Although per share earnings dropped after 1929, the profits as a percent of costs of the surviving large manufacturers were high for the entire period under consideration. Boeing made an average of 21 percent on its Navy contracts and 25 percent on Army contracts; Douglas made 21 percent on its Navy sales and 18 percent on Army sales. Pratt and Whitney, which together with Wright Aeronautical were practically the only producers of aircraft engines in the period, made profits which were usually in excess of 40 percent per year.[20] Following the stock market crash of 1929, however, sales of the aircraft industry contracted almost as rapidly as they had expanded during the "Lindbergh Boom." By 1933 they had fallen to $26,460,-000, and literally scores of companies were forced out of business. Military aircraft procurement dropped off upon completion of the five-year programs in 1931, but it was primarily the decreased demand for civil aircraft which brought the severe retrenchment in the industry. At the 1929 peak, 5,516 civil aircraft were produced; in 1932 there were only 802.

In part foreign demand helped to keep up the output. Exports increased during the period. From 63 aircraft valued at $848,568 in 1927, exports rose to 490 valued at $8,195,484 in 1934. This represented a considerable proportion of the 1,615 aircraft produced in the latter year. The exports in most cases during this period were for purposes of defense or waging war: "Where there were revolutions, wars, or threats of war, there were our aircraft customers." [21]

The interlocked positions of the major air transport companies and the large aircraft manufacturers had been under criticism for some time, but not much action was taken before the Crane Committee reported. It expressed the view that business combinations had prevented the free growth of aviation and had resulted in waste of public funds through higher air mail rates and the payment of huge salaries to company officials.[22] The Crane Report resulted in the passage of the Air Mail Act of 1934, the purpose of which was "to revise air mail laws, and to establish a commission to make a report to the Congress recommending an aviation policy." [23] Section 7 (a) of this act provided that after December 31, 1934, it would be unlawful for any party holding an air mail contract to have any other interests in the aviation industry other than those in direct support of its transport operation. The manufacturing and transport operations of the big aviation firms would have to be completely separated if they were to benefit by governmental subsidization of air transport operations. The aviation combinations responded in accordance with the legislation, rather than experience the loss of the government air mail business. As far as the principal airframe manufacturing companies were concerned, the Air Mail Act of 1934 had special significance as anti-trust legislation.

V

Production of aircraft diminished in 1932 and 1933. This was co-incident with a declining civil demand as the depression progressed and with the completion of the Army and Navy five-year programs. No new government program was devised until the middle of 1934.

After the Baker Board, appointed to investigate the status of American air power, stated that commercial demand was not adequate to maintain the industry,[24] new government encouragement followed. The Baker Board recommended an increase in the number of Army aircraft to 2,230 by 1940. The Vinson Act, passed in 1934, authorized the Navy to buy 1,200 planes by 1940. Table 3 illustrates the impact of the new five-year programs as they got well underway in 1936. When it became increasingly evident that the United States was lagging behind other countries in air power, new authorizations were made in 1938 and 1939 to increase the number of aircraft in the Navy to 3,000 and to 6,000 for the Army.

Finally, on May 16, 1940 President Roosevelt made what at that time appeared to be a fantastic request of the industry: "I should like to see this nation geared up to the ability to turn out at least 50,000 planes a year. Furthermore, I believe that this nation should plan at this time a program that would provide us with 50,000 mili-

tary and naval planes." [25] By the end of 1940 capacity was expanding
and military production had increased to 6,019 units.

Table 3. Aeronautical Production and Exports, 1935–1940

Year	Aircraft Production Military	Civil	Total	Aircraft Exported	Per-cent of Output Exported	Value of Aircraft and Parts Produced	Value of Aeronautical Exports	Percent Exports of Total Value
1935	459	1,251	1,710	333	20	$ 45,347,000	$ 14,291,000	32
1936	1,141	1,869	3,010	527	18	N.A.	23,143,000	..
1937	949	2,824	3,773	628	17	149,700,000	39,404,000	26
1938	1,800	1,823	3,623	875	24	N.A.	68,228,000	..
1939	2,195	3,661	5,856	1,220	21	279,497,000	117,807,000	42
1940	6,019 a	6,785	12,804	3,522	28	370,000,000 b	311,871,000	84

a Includes value of output of July through December only.
b Represents domestic civil only; data on new aircraft produced for export
not available.
N.A.—Not Available.
Sources: Civil Aeronautics Administration, CAA Statistical Handbook of
Civil Aviation, 1957, pp. 58, 65. Ben S. Lee, ed., Aviation Facts and Figures,
1957 (Washington: American Aviation Publications, 1957), p. 12.

The demand for aircraft exports from the United States increased
as international relations deteriorated. The rise in exports following
1935 was the result of several causes: difficulties within foreign
nations, difficulties between nations, and the slackening in foreign
competition. Great Britain, France, Germany, and Italy were building their own air defenses instead of competing with the United
States in foreign markets to the extent they had done previously.
Because of the unsettled conditions in Asia and Latin America from
1935–1938, these areas accounted for around two-thirds of American
aircraft exports. By the end of the first nine months of 1939, French
and British imports accounted for 71 percent of the value of United
States aircraft exports. In the short period of five years to 1940, the
quantity of our aircraft exports increased more than 1,000 percent
and aeronautical exports rose to more than 21 times their former
value.

The production of civil aircraft also gained significantly during the
period from 1935 to 1940. It increased almost fourfold to a total of
6,785. Production of civil aircraft for the domestic market increased
from 918 airplanes in 1935 to 3,263 in 1940. The gain in sales of
light planes can be attributed to the improvement of general business conditions, the better flying facilities provided by the government, and the lower prices of these aircraft.[26] At the same time,

commercial airlines were carrying more passengers and flying more revenue passenger seat miles as flying safety improved and air passenger rates decreased. Although air operations increased, the number of commercial aircraft in service declined for a time, from 363 in 1935 to a low of 260 in 1938, but it had increased again to 369 by 1940. Dollar sales of commercial aircraft had improved because of a general conversion toward larger, more expensive, twin-engined aircraft.[27]

On September 11, 1940, the War Department followed up President Roosevelt's request for 50,000 planes a year by informing aircraft manufacturers to tool up for mass production orders. From a rank, by value of product, of forty-fourth in 1939, the United States aircraft industry was soon to become the largest in the world.

VI

Almost three months after President Roosevelt's request for 50,-000 airplanes, orders had been placed for only 16,000. It was not until July 2, 1940 that emergency legislation gave the services the authority to grant contracts to manufacturers without going through the more lengthy procedure of obtaining competitive bids. The Vinson-Trammell Act, which restricted profits on contracts, was suspended in October 1940, and new legislation was passed providing for accelerated amortization of defense facilities.[28] With greater certainty concerning the status of costs and profits, the aircraft companies entered into production contracts and began to expand their facilities.

After the Japanese attack on Pearl Harbor, the Materiel Division of the Air Service got all aircraft factories to operate on three shifts, each on a 48 hour week.[29] It was estimated that this would boost output by 30 percent. As the scale of production increased, assembly line methods were used more extensively and greater specialization of labor was afforded.[30] As a consequence, and with the use of training programs, 80 percent of the workers were able to learn their jobs in six to twelve weeks.[31]

Between June and December of 1940, aircraft companies invested $83,000,000 in new plants and equipment. The government sought to facilitate the expansion by building and leasing plants to manufacturers through the Defense Plant Corporation, and by granting loans for constructing privately owned facilities through the Reconstruction Finance Corporation. The Defense Plant Corporation gave the manufacturer a future option to buy the plant, and the Reconstruction Finance Corporation offered him the option to sell the plant to the government. Subsequent to October 1940, investment in emergency facilities could be written off on a five year basis for tax purposes. As it turned out, however, the government financed and retained ownership to most of the facilities constructed during the war. Of the 1,955,613,000 pounds of airframe weight accepted from 1940 through 1944, a total of 1,019,980,000 pounds was produced by major plants in existence prior to 1940; 635,017,-000 pounds were produced by major new plants managed by aircraft companies; and 184,630,000 pounds were produced by major new plants not managed by aircraft companies.[32] New factory locations accounted for 38 percent of the pounds of airframes accepted. Of course, expansion was also great at the old sites. For example, the Martin plant in Baltimore increased in size from 1,100,000 to 5,650,000 square feet, Boeing in Wichita from 157,000 to 2,900,000, and Consolidated in San Diego from 541,000 to 4,510,000. Almost every airframe plant had grown to many times its pre-war size. Table 4 shows the extent to which plant floor space expanded during the

Table 4. Floor Space of Airframe, Engine, and Propeller
Facilities, 1940–1945
(Millions of Square Feet)

Date	Total	Airframe	Engine	Propeller
Jan. 1940	13.1	9.6	3.0	.5
Jan. 1941	25.5	17.6	6.5	1.1
Jan. 1943	117.1 [a]	77.5	31.8	5.2
Dec. 1943	175.0 [a]	110.4	54.2	6.8
Dec. 1944	167.4 [a]	103.0	54.9	7.9

[a] Includes glider facilities.
Source: Ben S. Lee, ed., Aviation Facts and Figures, 1957, p. 15.

war to provide for increased output. The cost of emergency facilities expansion in the aircraft industry from 1940 to 1945 was $3,894,-000,000; of this sum, $3,474,000,000 was financed by the government, and the remainder was privately financed. Of the total cost of expansion, $2,338,000,000 or about two-thirds was for equipment, while the remainder was for plant facilities.[33] The government investment was largely achieved through the Defense Plant Corporation, about 80 percent of it being for the Army Air Forces and the remainder for the Navy Bureau of Aeronautics.[34]

Besides the expansion carried on by the existing aircraft firms, they granted licenses to produce aircraft which they had designed and patented to non-aircraft producers. Major new plants were constructed for General Motors, which was licensed to build aircraft for Grumman; for Ford, which produced Consolidated's B-24; and for Goodyear Tire and Rubber Company, which manufactured the Chance Vought Corsair. Subcontractors produced approximately 30 percent of the total pounds of aircraft during the war compared with the less than 10 percent produced under license agreements.[35] Prime contractors generally did not prefer subcontracting to in-plant production. This was largely because of the loss of control over costs and quality and the difficulties of increased administration, but subcontracting was one way to attempt to meet production schedules.[36]

The impetus for output expansion became even greater after President Roosevelt's State of the Union Message on January 7, 1942. He disclosed to Congress that he had dispatched a directive to the appropriate government agencies instructing them to take the necessary steps for increasing production in 1942 to 60,000 planes, of which 45,000 were to be combat aircraft. In 1943 production was to be 125,000 planes, of which 100,000 were to be combat planes.[37] The industry, with a production of only 19,433 military planes in 1941, had not begun to fulfill his earlier request for 50,-000 planes. Output of aircraft, as did plant expansion, increased most rapidly between 1941 and 1943. Reflecting a growing emphasis on the production of medium and heavy transports and bombers was the increase in pounds of airframe production, which

TABLE 5. RATE OF INCREASE OF AIRCRAFT PRODUCTION,
1941–1945
(Number of Aircraft)

Year	Total	Percentage of Six Year Total	Percentage Increase Over Preceding Year
1940	12,804	4.0	. . .
1941	26,277	8.2	105
1942	47,836	15.0	82
1943	85,898	27.0	71
1944	96,318	30.2	12
1945	49,761	15.6	−48

Source: Ben S. Lee, ed., *Aviation Facts and Figures,* 1957, p. 9.

underwent an even greater percentage increase in 1941 and 1942 than did the production of aircraft.

Six of the top seven of the airframe producers during the war were represented among the top seven producers during the period of 1927–1933.[38] These were the firms which, along with several smaller producers, had been carrying on research and had been developing experimental models of aircraft in the period prior to the war. They got the bulk of the military orders because quantity production of aircraft could be realized sooner by mass producing already successful experimental models.[39] Fourteen companies produced about 95 percent of the airframe output during the period 1940–1944; the top seven produced 73.9 percent. See Table 6.

Profits in the industry were held down by wartime legislation.

TABLE 6. POUNDS OF AIRFRAME ACCEPTED FROM 14 COMPANIES, ENGAGED PRIMARILY IN PRODUCTION OF MAJOR WAR MODELS OF COMBAT AND LARGE TRANSPORT AIRCRAFT: 1940–1944
(Thousands of Pounds, Spares Excluded)

Company	Total 1940–1944	Percent of Five Year Grand Total
Douglas	306,573	15.3
Consolidated-Vultee	291,073	14.6
Boeing	226,477	11.3
North American	210,913	10.5
Lockheed	180,118	9.0
Curtiss	136,091	6.9
Martin	126,970	6.3
Ford	123,076	6.2
Republic	75,893	3.9
Grumman	73,767	3.7
Bell	53,037	2.7
Eastern (General Motors)	47,869	2.4
Chance-Vought	28,952	1.4
Goodyear	13,668	0.7
All Other Plants	101,136	5.1
Total, All Plants	1,995,613	100.0

Source: Tom Lilley, et al., Problems of Accelerating Aircraft Production During World War II (Boston: Division of Research, Harvard Business School, 1947), p. 90.

The Vinson-Trammell Act of 1934 had provided for profit limitations of 10 percent on contract prices, and Congress passed legislation in 1939 providing that profits in excess of 12 percent of contract
price on government aircraft procurement were refundable. The
Renegotiation Act of 1942 provided for returning profits judged
excessive on bases other than a fixed percent of production cost. In
the Renegotiation Act of 1944, several changes as to administration
and responsibility were made, among them the creation of the War
Contracts Price Adjustment Board. Its duty was to review defense
contracts to determine whether profits were too high even after
excess profits tax payments. In this manner the government made
special provisions to avoid any post-war scandal concerning excessive
profits received by defense industries such as had occurred after
World War I. Taxing and renegotiation appear to have brought
some measure of success in recapturing high profits. Although the
12 major airframe companies had net profits of $350,300,000 be-
tween 1940 and 1945 inclusive, they had paid $1,171,300,000 in
Federal taxes. Before renegotiation became operative, the 12 major
airframe companies had net profits after taxes of 12.9 percent of
sales in 1940 and 7.4 percent in 1941. For the duration of the war
after the Renegotiation Act of 1942 the rate was never more than
2.2 percent and it was as low as 1. percent in 1944. Federal taxes
as a percent of net income increased from 26.9 percent in 1940 to
a high of 72.6 percent in 1942 and remained around that rate until
1945.[40] The industry rate of profit as a percent of net worth was
understandably much higher than as a percent of sales because of
the relatively large proportion of government investment to that of
the producers. For example, Douglas had profits before taxes which
represented 112 percent of the company's net worth in 1941! Even
after income taxes its profits were 51 percent of net worth that year.
For 1944, the last complete year of the war, Douglas had profits
before taxes of 69 percent of net worth and profits after income
taxes representing a little over 15 percent of net worth.[41]

The high marginal efficiency of capital in aircraft production,
resulting from the increased demand by the government, was followed by an almost 1,200 percent expansion in plant floor space,
much of which was government financed, and a 3,300 percent expansion in aircraft output. Peak output of 96,318 aircraft was
reached in 1944. During the period 1941–1945 the total aircraft
produced was 306,090 of which 33,000 were given to the Allies on
lend-lease between March 11, 1941 and April 1, 1944. Employment

in the industry rose from 148,600 in 1940 to a peak of 2,100,000 in November 1943.[42] From a rank of forty-fourth in value of output in 1939, the United States aircraft industry rose to become the largest manufacturing industry in the world in 1944, with an output value of $16,745,000,000.[43]

VII

Expansion of aircraft production facilities had ceased long before the production quotas were realized and before the war was won. There was no notable expansion after December 1943. Production of airframes did not decrease, however, until after March 1944. The employment peak of 2,101,600 reached in November 1943 was subsequently reduced to 1,464,200 by VE Day, May 8, 1945.

Adjustments were needed to meet the post-war situation. The Aeronautical Chamber of Commerce immediately made recommendations to the Military Affairs Committee. It pointed out that the aircraft industry had only a small post-war market awaiting it, and for this reason cutbacks should first affect the temporary wartime manufacturers of aircraft, such as the automotive industry which would enjoy a substantial post-war demand. By the end of 1945 the Army and Navy had cancelled 18,267 contracts totalling $21,578,-462,000 in value. Industry sales had declined from the peak of $16,047,000,000 in 1944 to an estimated $1,200,000,000 in 1947. By December 1945 only 16 airframe plants remained of the 66 in the industry one year earlier.[44] In general, the firms making military deliveries in December of 1945, although in greatly reduced amounts, were the major pre-war producers.

In its report of October 11, 1945, the Air Coordinating Committee stated the conditions necessary if the industry were to survive sufficiently to provide a safe nucleus from which to expand in a national emergency.[45] It recommended that, taking into consideration prospective civilian aircraft production, 3,000 to 5,780 military aircraft would need to be purchased annually. Despite this recommendation, the industry received orders for a much smaller number; the production and sales for the following years are shown in Table 7. Although aircraft production for the civil market appeared high in 1946, it was insufficient to offset the extreme cutback in military purchases. Actually, only 38,400,000 pounds of airframe weight were produced that year against a range of 54,300,000 to 104,300,000 pounds recommended by the Air Coordinating Committee.

TABLE 7. AERONAUTICAL PRODUCTION AND SALES, 1946–1958

Year	Number of Aircraft			Sales of Aircraft and Parts Produced (Millions of Dollars)			Other Products and Services
	Total	Military	Civil	Total	Military	Civil	
1946	36,418	1,417	35,001	N.A.	N.A.	N.A.	N.A.
1947	17,739	2,122	15,617	$ 1,200ª	N.A.	N.A.	N.A.
1948	9,838	2,536	7,302	1,158ᵇ	$ 884	$ 177	$ 97
1949	6,137	2,592	3,545	1,781	1,438	230	113
1950	6,293	2,773	3,520	2,274	1,836	238	200
1951	7,923	5,446	2,477	3,456	2,525	347	584
1952	12,811	9,302	3,509	6,497	5,004	650	843
1953	14,760	10,626	4,134	8,511	7,026	734	751
1954	12,129	8,740	3,389	8,305	6,649	822	834
1955	12,852	8,032	4,820	8,470	6,445	786	1,239
1956	13,319	6,114	7,205	9,496	6,559	1,166	1,771
1957	12,346	5,619	6,745	11,765	7,884	1,598	2,283
1958	10,860ª	4,000ª	6,860	11,470	7,289	1,372	2,809

ª Estimate, Aerospace Industries Association.
ᵇ Sales total for last three quarters only.
N.A.—Not Available.

Source: Ben S. Lee, ed., *Aviation Facts and Figures, 1959* (Washington: American Aviation Publications, 1959), pp. 7, 9.

The appalling condition of the industry in 1947 led to further investigations by two Federal groups, the President's Air Policy Commission and the Congressional Air Policy Board. The crux of their recommendations was that immediate action should be taken to support the aircraft manufacturers.[46] The reports alerted the public to the collapsed state of the industry and spurred Congress to increase appropriations for aircraft procurement. Military aircraft sales rose subsequently.

Civil demand, however, had decreased significantly from its 1946 level. The growing interest in flying personal planes, especially on the part of former military pilots, didn't last. Production of light planes dropped off from 34,568 units in 1946 to only 3,391 in 1950. Also, the output of civil transports declined yearly from 433 in 1946 to 160 in 1949, and total civil airframe weight declined from 25,500,000 pounds to 6,700,000 pounds over the same period. The postwar demand for new transports was depressed by the sale of surplus military transports.

The period prior to 1950 was characterized by declining and generally low levels of output of civil aircraft and a rising though unimpressive, output of military aircraft after 1948.[47] Even with the increased military appropriations, most of the firms in the industry were struggling to avoid financial losses.

With the outbreak of the Korean War the necessity for maintaining strong peace-time defenses and the necessity for peace-time support of the aircraft industry became more generally accepted. As a representative of the Aircraft Industries Association noted: "The year 1950 will probably go down in aviation history as the one in which the industry, greatly aided by the Korean crisis, finally won its three-decade campaign for adequate peace-time air defenses." [48] Between 1949 and the end of 1953, the year the Korean War was terminated, annual output of military aircraft expanded. Although civil output didn't change appreciably over the period, the annual value of aeronautical production increased sharply from $1,781,000,-000 to $8,511,000,000. Employment in the industry rose from 281,-800 to 779,100 employees.

The government played an important role in financing the industry during the Korean War. At first the government was reluctant to finance new plant expansion because of the existence of 21,200,000 square feet of available floor space which the government owned. But these plants were dispersed and generally geographically removed from locations deemed desirable to the existing producers of military aircraft. As a consequence, the industry privately financed $805,000,000 of aircraft plant facilities from 1950 to 1953 in contrast to the $280,000,000 provided by the government. The latter, however, financed $2,044,000,000 of the equipment expansion in contrast to only $399,000,000 privately purchased. Therefore, it was responsible for roughly two-thirds of the total expenditure of $3,528,000,000 on plant and equipment expansion.[49]

The government also facilitated private expansion. By the passage of the Defense Production Act of 1950 it allowed, for tax purposes, a five year amortization of new facilities and through the Federal Reserve System it guaranteed defense production loans.

The reluctance of the government to finance new plant expansion in effect caused much subcontracting. Prime contractors, who were not willing to expand privately financed facilities, were faced with production orders larger than they could handle. Because the limited nature of the aerial warfare, relative to World War II, did not demand so large an increase in output, the industry was able to supply most of the market by itself. That part it could not supply it subcontracted, but much of the subcontracting remained within the industry, as did whatever licensing there was.

The contraction in the industry following the cessation of hostilities in Korea in August 1953 naturally was not as violent as that after World War II. As indicated in Table 7, military aircraft production declined, though dollar value of military aeronautical production increased subsequent to 1953. The value of civil aeronautical production also increased; the annual output of light planes rose from 3,788 units in 1953 to 6,414 units in 1958, while the average annual output of civil transport aircraft for this time period was 371 aircraft. There was an apparent growing demand for utility aircraft for the use by private business and farmers. Export demand was also on the increase. From a low of $115,300,000 in 1946, the value of aeronautical exports had climbed to $1,059,300,000 by 1956, the high for the post-war period. These exports rose from 1.2 percent of the value of total United States merchandise exports in 1946 to 5.4 percent in 1958.[50] Despite the continuation of the Renegotiation Act of 1951, the industry's profit after taxes was approximately 13 percent of net worth in 1958.[51]

Without a doubt the most significant development in the industry since the Korean War has been the manufacturing of guided missiles. Just as the all-metal airplane proved to be superior to the airplane of wooden construction, the monoplane superior to the biplane, the jet aircraft superior to those with reciprocating engines, so now the guided missile is demonstrating its superiority to the airplane as a weapon of war. Indeed, as the transition from combat aircraft to missiles becomes more rapid, the very existence of most firms in the airframe industry is threatened. Because of the importance of electronics to the successful operation of missiles, 16 of 40 missiles projects in 1958 had non-aircraft producers as prime contractors, most of which were electronics firms.[52] For one of the few times in its history the aircraft industry was experiencing outside competition in the end products it was producing. Expenditures for missile procurement have increased steadily from $21,000,000 in 1951 to $3,444,000,000 in 1958.[53] According to Undersecretary of the Air Force Malcolm A. MacIntyre, in 1961 the Air Force will spend on aircraft less than half of the amount it spent in 1956, whereas compared with the earlier date Air Force spending on missiles is anticipated to be more than five times greater in 1961, at which time it will surpass the annual rate of spending on manned aircraft.[54] With respect to this transition from manned aircraft to missiles, USAF policy states: "As readily as missiles become operationally suitable, they will be phased into units either to completely or partially substitute for manned aircraft according to military requirements." [55] In support of these observations, the 1957 reports of the Curtiss Committee pointed to a somewhat growing demand for civil aircraft but a significantly decreased demand for military aircraft as missiles production increased.[56]

In time the "Space Age" will undoubtedly provide new opportunities for the industry. It would appear, however, that, in view of the declining demand for military aircraft, the success of the aircraft companies in the near future depends largely on their ability to secure missile contracts. The demand for aircraft for commercial transport is growing as is the demand for utility aircraft, but these components of the total industry demand are small relative to the military demand. For the industry to maintain its position of eminence, the demand for its missiles and civil aircraft must increase sufficiently to offset the seemingly inevitable decline in demand for military aircraft.

NOTES

1. This is according to the industrial classifications used by the Department of Labor. In February 1959 there were 756,600 workers in the aircraft and parts industry compared to 724,100 workers employed in the second-ranking, that for motor vehicles and equipment. U.S. Department of Labor, *Monthly Labor Review*, LXXXII (May 1959), 596.

2. It appears that the Wrights were not motivated to invent their airplane by an economic incentive. Orville Wright is quoted as saying: "At the time we first flew our power plane we were not thinking of any practical uses at all. We just wanted to show that it was possible to fly." Orville Wright, *How We Invented the Airplane*, ed. by Fred C. Kelly (New York: David McKay Co., 1953), p. 78.

3. Note that when the Wrights were placed in a competitive situation, their asking price declined by 75 percent. The Army also signed contracts with two other bidders, A. M. Herring and J. F. Scott. Fred Hamlin and Eleanor Thayer Miller, eds. *The Aircraft Year Book*, 1955 (Washington: The Lincoln Press, 1956), p. 386.

4. Eaton Manufacturing Company, *A Chronicle of the Aviation Industry*, 1903–1947 (Cleveland: Eaton Manufacturing Co., 1948), p. 8.

5. *Ibid.*, pp. 13–15.

6. Civil Aeronautics Administration, *CAA Statistical Handbook of Civil Aviation*, 1957 (Washington: Government Printing Office, 1957), p. 65.

7. Howard Mingos, *Birth of an Industry* (New York: W. B. Conkey Co., 1930), p. 15.

8. G. W. Mixter and H. H. Emmons, *United States Army Aircraft Production Facts* (Washington: Government Printing Office, 1919), p. 7.

9. The principal patent holders, the Wright and Curtiss companies, were

members of the association. At the outset, the patent holders received $200 for each plane of their design produced by a licensee, but the licensee included this in the price charged the government. Public indignation led to a new agreement between the Manufacturers Aircraft Association and the government which cut the patent royalties in half. Mingos, *Birth of an Industry*, pp. 39–40.

10. Charles Evan Hughes, *Report of Aircraft Inquiry* (Washington: U.S. Justice Department, 1918), p. 137.

11. Eaton, *Chronicles*, p. 20.

12. *Ibid.*, and Mingos, *Birth of an Industry*, pp. 46–47. Whether military aviation and the aircraft industry of the United States made enough of a contribution to the winning of the war to justify their expense is a subject of some controversy. Elsbeth Freudenthal's position is that government war expenditures of $1,068,637,739 for military aviation were not justified when the end product was only 196 planes at the front at the time of the Armistice. Elsbeth Freudenthal, *The Aviation Business* (New York: The Vanguard Press, 1940), pp. 58–59. On the other hand, Howard Mingos, a former official of the industry, has pointed out that after considering what the government regained through post-war liquidation, the net cost of wartime aviation was less than $400,000. Mingos, *Birth of an Industry*, p. 44.

13. *U.S. Statutes at Large*, 43, Part 1 (1923–1935), pp. 805–06.

14. *U.S. Statutes at Large*, 44, Part 2 (1925–1927), pp. 368–76.

15. *Ibid.*, pp. 764–68.

16. *Ibid.*, pp. 784–90.

17. Freudenthal, *The Aviation Business*, pp. 117–18.

18. For detailed accounts concerning the numerous companies controlled by each of these organizations, see Eaton, *Chronicles*, pp. 45–46; Freudenthal, *The Aviation Business*, pp. 100–01; and William Glenn Cunningham, *The Aircraft Industry: A Study in Industrial Location* (Los Angeles: Lorrin L. Morrison, 1951), p. 37.

19. Boeing School of Aeronautics, *Air Transportation*, Part One (Oakland Airport, California: Boeing School of Aeronautics, 1938), p. 29.

20. Freudenthal, *The Aviation Business*, pp. 123–24. Profits as a percent of costs or sales is certainly a less meaningful measure than profits as a percent of net worth. Strangely enough, most of the literature on the industry, including government publications, considers profits on the base of costs or sales.

21. *Ibid.*, p. 143.

22. U.S. Congress, Committee on Post Offices and Post Roads, *House Report 2087*, 72d Cong., 2d Sess. (Washington: Government Printing Office, 1933), p. 20.

23. *U.S. Statutes at Large*, 48, Part 1, (1933–1934), pp. 933–39.

24. Special Committee on Army Air Corps, *Final Report* (Washington: U.S. War Department, July 18, 1934).

25. U.S. Congress, *Address of the President of the United States on National Defense*, House Miscellaneous Documents, II, No. 751, May 16, 1940, 76th Cong., 3d Sess., (Washington: Government Printing Office, 1940), p. 3.

26. Aircraft Industries Association, *Aviation Facts and Figures, 1945* (New York: McGraw-Hill Book Co., 1945), p. 73.

27. In 1932 Douglas had sales of $2,000,000; in 1937 its sales were almost $21,000,000, largely as a result of the increase in demand for its larger trans-

port aircraft. Frank Cunningham, *Sky Master, the Story of Donald Douglas* (Philadelphia: Dorrance and Co., 1943), pp. 213, 257.

28. Emergency facilities could be amortized over a five year period for tax purposes. Tom Lilley, *et al.*, *Problems of Accelerating Aircraft Production During World War II* (Boston: Division of Research, Harvard Business School, 1947), p. 27.

29. Harold B. Hinton, *Air Victory: The Men and Machines* (New York: Harper & Bros., 1948), p. 191.

30. The main reason why the government was so anxious to get the automotive industry engaged in aircraft manufacturing was to obtain mass production of aircraft by utilization of assembly line production techniques. See Westley W. Stout, *Great Engines and Great Planes* (Detroit: Chrysler Corporation, 1947), p. 103. Productivity increased markedly as assembly line techniques became more widely utilized. In 1941 the average monthly weight output per employee was 28 pounds; by 1944 it had risen to 125 pounds. See Reginald M. Cleveland and Frederick P. Graham, eds., *The Aviation Annual of 1945* (Garden City: Doubleday, Doran & Co., 1944), p. 78.

The conversion was not done without a great deal of difficulty. For example, when licensed to produce the Consolidated B-24, Ford was forced to break the task down and illustrate it in 20,000 drawings before an assembly line could be set up at Willow Run. Previously highly skilled workmen had made aircraft. Accurate details concerning standard parts, job processes, and manufacturing procedures had not been written out and the work broken down into specialized tasks which could be done by relatively unskilled personnel. Ford had to accomplish this before its assembly line became functional. Lilley, *et al.*, *Problems of Accelerating*, p. 49.

31. "Mass Production of Skilled Workers," *Automotive Industries*, LXXXIV (Apr. 1, 1941), 365.

32. Lilley, *et al.*, *Problems of Accelerating*, p. 35.

33. These figures are based on the cost of manufacturing facilities authorized between July 1940 and June 1945. Rudolph Modley and T. S. Cawley, eds., *Aviation Facts and Figures, 1953* (Washington: Lincoln Press, 1953), p. 11.

34. United States Surplus Property Administration, *Airplane Plants and Facilities* (Washington: Government Printing Office, 1946), p. 40.

35. Lilley, *et al.*, *Problems of Accelerating*, p. 67.

36. Administering subcontracting by the prime firms was an extremely complex operation. The 18 foot nose of the B-29, for example, had over 50,000 rivets and 8,000 kinds of parts. These parts were produced by over 1,500 major subcontractors and assembled in four different locations. Stout, *Great Engines*, pp. 113–14.

37. Lilley, *et al.*, *Problems of Accelerating*, p. 30.

38. Lockheed had achieved a new position of prominence, while North American had ceased being a holding company and had become an operating company in the latter period.

39. This procedure would cut down the time between the government's usual submission of general purpose requirements for an experimental model and the realization of quantity output; it would eliminate all the stages in the procurement process prior to the award of production contracts. By adopting for production aircraft which were already at least in an experimental stage of development, the government saved between one and two years. Actually only two models, the P-47 and the F-6-F, on which design work was begun after

1940, were used extensively during the war, although only 4 of the 19 major airframe models were in production by mid-1940. This meant that 17 of the 19 models used extensively during the war were being developed before the entry of the United States into it. Lilley, *et al., Problems of Accelerating,* pp. 16–18.

40. Ben S. Lee, ed., *Aviation Facts and Figures,* 1958 (Washington: American Aviation Publications, 1958), pp. 71, 73.

41. These percentages were derived from data contained in Moody's Investors Service, *Moody's Industrial Manual,* 1948 (New York: D. F. Shea, 1948), pp. 1114–15.

42. Leonard G. Levenson, "Wartime Development of the Aircraft Industry," *Monthly Labor Review,* LIX (Nov. 1944), 915.

43. This sum equals the total value of the combined output in 1939 of the nine leading United States industries: the auto industry, steel industry, meatpacking industry, petroleum industry, cigarette companies, bakeries, smelters of non-ferrous metals, paper mills, and printers and publishers of newspapers. Eaton, *Chronicles,* p. 85.

44. John S. Day, *Subcontracting Policy in the Airframe Industry* (Boston: Division of Research, Harvard Business School, 1956), p. 148. Coincident with the contraction were sharply declining profits in marked contrast with the almost guaranteed profits during the war. For example, Boeing, Bell, Consolidated Vultee, Piper, and Lockheed all reported losses for 1947, while Martin, Curtiss-Wright, Douglas, Ryan, and North American were reporting reduced net returns. Eaton, *Chronicles,* pp. 92–93.

45. Hinton, *Air Victory,* p. 48.

46. See President's Air Policy Commission, *Survival in the Air Age* (Washington: Government Printing Office, 1948) and Air Coordinating Committee, *Air Coordinating Committee Report,* 1947 (Washington: Government Printing Office, 1947).

47. Notable technological advance was made during the period. The conventional type fighters and bombers were being replaced with jet aircraft. There was improvement in the industry in 1949 because of increased government expenditures for research and development of jet aircraft, atomic energy, rockets, missiles, and supersonic airplanes. Fred Hamlin, *et al., Aircraft Year Book,* 1949 (Washington: The Lincoln Press, 1949), p. 69.

48. Fred Hamlin, *et al., Aircraft Year Book,* 1950 (Washington: The Lincoln Press, 1950), p. 70.

49. Modley and Cawley, *Aviation Facts and Figures,* 1953, p. 11.

50. Ben S. Lee, ed., *Aviation Facts and Figures,* 1959 (Washington: American Aviation Publications, 1959), p. 125.

51. Derived from data contained in *ibid.,* pp. 76, 79.

52. Lee, *Aviation Facts and Figures,* 1958, pp. 41–42.

53. *Ibid.,* p. 39.

54. *Los Angeles Times,* April 9, 1958.

55. U.S. Air Force, "The Guided Missile," *The Air Reservist,* IX (Dec. 1957), 4.

56. Edward P. Curtiss, *National Requirements for Aviation Facilities: 1956–1975,* I (Washington: Government Printing Office, 1957), p. 1.

17

Agriculture in an Industrial Age

SINCE World War I, American agriculture has been unstable during even its most prosperous periods and severely deranged during its worst. Throughout the 1920's, farm spokesmen pressed for an effective national solution to the agricultural problem. Interest centered chiefly upon the commodity-purchase and surplus-disposal program embodied in the McNary-Haugen bills, debated in Congress from 1924 to 1928. But the national discourse on farm questions went well beyond the McNary-Haugen approach. Many of the diverse proposals put forward in the twenties for strengthening of cooperatives, imposition of marketing controls by government or voluntary organizations, achievement of direct production controls, and expansion of federal farm-credit programs had a marked influence on the development of the New Deal's agricultural policy.* Some contemporary critics charged that the New Deal farm program went too far—interfering with the operation of the free market economy and spawning a massive bureaucracy to manage the farm sector. Critics of another persuasion argued that the Roosevelt policies were too conservative—that they favored farm owners at the expense of tenants and share-croppers, propped up the private marketing system without regard to consumer interests, and failed to rationalize farm production. Agricultural economists and histori-

* See Chester C. Davis, "The Development of Agricultural Policy Since the End of the World War," in *Farmers in a Changing World* (U.S. Department of Agriculture Yearbook, 1940).

ans are still divided today in their appraisal of the New Deal program. Some maintain that the Roosevelt administration devised the best program possible, given depression conditions and the political climate of the 1930's. Others assert that New Deal policies embodied hopelessly conflicting objectives, or they deplore the creation of a vested political interest in permanent subsidy and crop-control programs.

The following study of Georgia agriculture indicates the complexity of farm problems in the post-1920 period. It provides a basis, moreover, for assessment of the New Deal policies as they affected farmers on the land in one important agricultural region.

THE LANDED AND THE LANDLESS: GEORGIA AGRICULTURE, 1920–1940

Willard Range

The Georgia farmer's days of prosperity were numbered, coming to an abrupt end during the summer of 1920 when there began two decades during which the farmers experienced the same economic misery their fathers had known so well before the turn of the century.

During the years 1920–33 Georgia's farmers were hit triple blows, and before they were able to recover from one blow, the next one was upon them. In 1920 agricultural prices dropped precipitately throughout the nation, spreading consternation and havoc on farms and in small towns everywhere. The panic was only temporary for many farm areas, but before the farmers of Georgia could recover, the boll weevil was upon them, destroying acre upon acre of cotton, reducing literally thousands of rural families to hunger and destitution, and driving supply merchants and bankers into bankruptcy. Some recovery from this was achieved during the late twenties; but before it was completed, the Wall Street crash of 1929 and its subse-

Reprinted by permission of the University of Georgia Press from Willard Range: *A Century of Georgia Agriculture, 1850–1950* (Athens, Ga.: University of Georgia Press, 1954), pp. 267–79.

quent lean years hit the Georgia farmer a third blow; and from that he did not recover entirely until he reached the prosperous years of World War II.

The 1920 collapse of farm prices was in itself disastrous to many farmers. Although the cost of producing cotton in 1920 was as high as in 1919, they found themselves able to get only 16¢ a pound rather than the 35¢ a pound received for their crop the year before —a drop of more than 50 percent. Cottonseed dropped from $70 a ton in 1919 to $31 a ton in 1920; sweet potato prices declined from $1.06 a bushel to 76¢ a bushel; and corn dropped even more—from $1.07 to 66¢ a bushel. Farmers who had recently begun planting pea-nuts saw the price decline two years in a row—from 9.8¢ a pound in 1919 to 5.1¢ in 1920, and then to a record low of 2.8¢ in 1921. To-bacco waited a year to drop, but drop it did finally, from 25¢ a pound in 1920 to 16¢ in 1921. And so it went with virtually everything the Georgia farmer produced.

Yet his expenses stayed up and actually rose 11 points during 1920 over the fabulous high they had already reached in 1919.[1] The mule the Georgia farmer bought to make his 1920 crop, for example, cost him about $17 more than he had paid the year before.

These developments were a calamity in themselves, but the worst was yet to come. During the three ensuing years, 1921–23, the boll weevil plague was at its worst. The per-acre yield in those years was 30 percent to 45 percent below normal, the state's usual crop of 1,500,000 to 2,000,000 bales dropped by 1923 to 600,000 bales; by 1925 the farm population had declined by about 375,000 and nearly 3,400,000 acres of land had been taken out of farming.

Many writers have insisted that the boll weevil was "only the straw that broke the camel's back"; that the evils of soil erosion, the one-crop economy, the constant moving of tenants, and so on would have eventually punctured Georgia's bubble of prosperity even if the boll weevil had never come. But whatever the cause, the years of the plague and those immediately thereafter put an end to farm-ing as a way of life for thousands of people. By 1922 farm wages in Georgia were down again to pre-World War I levels of $15 to $17 per month (with board).[2] Landlords took whatever they could get as rent and some offered tenants free rent to keep them on the land. The Black Belt was particularly hard hit. By 1924, 35 counties there had reduced their harvested acreage by 40 percent and many a landlord was selling his timber to make ends meet.[3] Even a bumper crop of cotton in 1926 failed to restore "good times"; rather it depressed prices and the total price received was several million dollars less than was received for the much smaller crop of the year before.

The result was that thousands of landlords were forced to restrict operations; credit at banks and supply firms dried up; thousands of acres of land were abandoned to erosion or wild growth; hundreds of farms were forfeited to mortgage companies or sold for taxes; hundreds of unfortunate landowners who lost their land were forced to become tenants, and thousands of farm families, particularly Negro families, were pushed off the land entirely and driven into the labor market of the cities.

The exodus of the tenants from the farms of Georgia during the decade was a tragic drama. Fortunately for the migrants, a labor shortage prevailed in the cities when the boll weevil struck and farm hands going there were able to get jobs as common laborers at a wage of $5 a day. Northern agents appeared in the state promising farm hands an attractive life in Chicago, Pittsburgh, and elsewhere,

NUMBER OF FARMS IN GEORGIA, 1850–1950

1850	51,759	1910	291,027
1860	62,003	1920	310,732
1870	69,969	1930	255,598
1880	138,626	1940	216,033
1890	171,071	1950	198,141
1900	224,691		

Source: U. S. Census reports.

and Negroes left by the trainload for those Eldorados despite the efforts of local sheriffs to stop them.[4] President Soule of the State Agricultural College estimated that 100,000 farm people left Georgia in the first six months of 1922, and a survey by county agents showed that 11,000 farms had been abandoned.[5] By 1925 there were 61,000 fewer farms and 375,000 fewer farm people in the state.

After 1925 the exodus to the city slowed down considerably. By that time the labor shortage of the cities had become saturated and many a migrant found himself able to get only irregular work at low pay. Some migrants were cared for temporarily by welfare agencies, but many a sad tale was told also of fathers who had deserted and of children who had run away in the hope of finding life easier without the burden of family ties.[6] By 1925, moreover, the boll weevil scourge was subsiding and the need to leave the land declined with it. The exodus had not only slowed down but there was even a slight movement back to the land. By 1930 the farm population recovered by 100,000 persons. Nevertheless, the census of 1930 showed that 55,000 farms, 3,400,000 acres of farm land, and 266,000 people had disappeared permanently during the decade from Georgia's agricultural establishment.

Number of Workers in Georgia Agriculture, 1870–1950

Year	Number	Percentage of all workers in agriculture
1870	336,145	72.5
1880	432,204	64.6
1890	461,222	60.0
1900	522,848	60.0
1910	734,366	63.3
1920	601,827	53.3
1930	497,716	42.8
1940	375,543	33.9
1950	327,698	25.2

Source: U. S. Census reports.

However, the worst was yet to come. The Great Depression that began with the Wall Street crash in 1929 not only wiped out what slight recovery had been achieved during the late 'twenties but also it plunged the Georgia farmer into a poverty as bad as and perhaps worse than that caused by the boll weevil. Within three years the prices received for Georgia farm products dropped 60 percent. The price of cotton declined 64 percent—down to 5¢ a pound for the first time in the new century. The gross income for each farm person in the state dropped from $206 in 1929 to a meager $83 in 1932, and in the next spring many a farmer found himself too poor to buy a mule to make a crop. Thousands of impoverished small owners and tenants sank to the status of sharecroppers, and oxen began to appear in the fields in place of the more expensive mule.[7] On many a farm, production came to a complete standstill for lack of cash or credit to buy seed, fertilizer, work stock, and tools. In some places not even food was being raised and the Red Cross was called in to provide food and clothing to prevent starvation and nakedness—a development that land-

ords feared might influence their croppers to "never work again." [8]
ifty cents a day or $8 to $10 a month became the prevailing
wage for hired farm laborers—and thousands could get no work at
all. Cash almost disappeared from the state's agricultural economy
and barter became a common practice. In 1932 per capita cash
farm income in the state was down to $46 and thousands of families
saw far less than $100 cash during the entire year.

Meanwhile the spread between the prices of farm produce and
urban commodities got wider. During the years 1929–32, when
the prices received for Georgia's agricultural produce dropped 60
percent, the prices farmers paid for city-made goods dropped only
24 percent.

Land values sank with everything else after 1920. The value of
farm real estate in Georgia was already low because of the setback
suffered in the early 'twenties. During 1920–25 the value of the
state's farm real estate had declined 40 percent—a drop exceeded by
only three other states in the nation.[9] In areas hard hit by the boll
weevil land had become almost worthless. One plantation in Greene
County that had sold for $52,000 in 1919 was resold in 1928 for
slightly more than $8,000; land in the Black Belt that had sold in
1919 for $150 an acre was available after the boll-weevil plague at
$35 an acre; and farms that were located off the roads dropped in
value in some cases from $25 to $2 per acre.[10] During the late
'twenties values held steady at an average of about $26 per acre for
the state as a whole. But the year after the crash of 1929 saw land
values drop again—from $26 in 1930 to $17 per acre in 1935. Thus
in fifteen years the value of an acre of Georgia's farm real estate
declined nearly two-thirds, and many a happy speculator of 1918–20
became a long-faced, land-poor, impoverished investor. An epidemic
of foreclosures, sheriffs' sales, and bank and merchant failures spread
over the state. Here was a repetition of the financial disaster that
had accompanied the boll weevil a mere decade earlier and it occurred before any appreciable recovery had been achieved from the
first disaster.

THE NEW DEAL

Although the Democratic administration in the spring of 1933 acted
boldly to rescue the American farmer from his despair, the New
Deal Brain Trust did not come into office with any magic formula
to solve the problem. Until that time the prevailing American philosophy had been that it was not within the province of government

to render more than slight assistance to the economy and the whole idea of controlling production and marketing was, in the words of the Republican Secretary of Agriculture of 1932, "Repugnant to our Constitution and . . . our economic system." [11] Such a great demand for drastic federal action developed, however, that New Dealers were compelled to improvise something, even if it were no more than a temporary panacea.

The New Dealers plunged into the problem with zeal, developing one emergency solution after another; and then promoting for the "long haul" the greatest program of research into the problems of agriculture and rural life ever performed anywhere on the earth. Educational foundations, state extension services, colleges, experiment stations, and civic organizations joined the national government in these inquiries; and rural sociologists and agricultural economists probed into every conceivable aspect of rural life and labor.

In due time the New Dealers concluded that the depression in American agriculture was due to accumulated evils, many of which had become especially accentuated after the Civil War. They were (1) land speculation which had pushed the price of American land above the resources of many farmers and had produced tenancy and all its accompanying evils; (2) the closing of the frontier and the filling up of all plowable areas; (3) technological improvements in farming which reduced the need for farm labor and pushed thousands of people from the land; (4) a poor tenure system with insecure verbal leases, constant moving, high-cost credit, neglect of the soil, etc.; (5) under-employment on the land because of the fact that farming is a seasonal occupation and, therefore, only a part-time occupation; (6) over-population on the land because of the high rural birth rate; (7) single cropping for cash; (8) soil erosion; (9) low prices received for farm produce resulting in part from the world economic situation but resulting in part also from the inability of unorganized farmers to control prices as urban industry can do; and (10) natural catastrophes.[12]

In due time also, the improvised measures used by the New Dealers to overcome these forces evolved into a five-pronged program that was still operating at the end of this study in 1950. This included (1) a system of production and marketing controls accompanied by subsidies and price supports designed to guarantee the farmer a fair return for his production; (2) greatly expanded credit facilities; (3) a soil conservation program; (4) a rehabilitation program to put depressed farmers back on their feet, reduce tenancy, improve rural health, and restore dignity to the pursuit of agriculture; and (5) a program to make rural life easier and more attractive by bringing to the farm such urban facilities as electricity and modern appliances.

The programs concerned with production and marketing controls, credit facilities, and soil conservation have already been discussed elsewhere in this study. Suffice it to say here that while observers still debate the effectiveness of these programs in lifting agriculture out of the depression, there is no doubt that they began a revolution in Georgia agriculture that in 1950 showed no signs of being completed, nor any signs of slowing down.

It was soon discovered that these programs were, on the whole, more helpful to "the top third of the farmers" than they were to the "lower two-thirds" who made up the vast bulk of the agricultural population. The small landowners, tenants, sharecroppers, wage hands, and migrant workers who composed the majority of the farm population received only indirect benefits and, in some cases, were actually harmed by these programs. The AAA program, for example, that caused land to be withdrawn from such soil depleting crops as cotton, lessened the need for tenants and croppers and drove many of them off the land. The benefit payments program also sometimes made it advantageous for landowners to demote their croppers to wage hands.[13] Croppers and tenants were still either destitute or at the mercy of landlords and merchants for credit; rural housing for all but owners remained on a slum level; the small owner still lacked the funds to do many of the things the soil conservation experts suggested; and despite a rise in prices, the little one-horse farmer who produced only small quantities of produce was still poor. In other words, the three programs mentioned above largely helped the commercial farmers who produced substantial produce for market. These programs had been their "brain-children" and it was they also who dominated the county, state, and national committees which guided the programs. Whatever benefits the "lower two-thirds" received were indirect benefits of a relatively meager sort. Thus a supplementary program was needed to rehabilitate the "lower two-thirds."

During the first hectic months of the New Deal direct relief was the only aid made available directly to needy farmers. It was soon decided that a more constructive program was needed. Idle land was abundant and the farmers on the relief rolls were anxious to farm. In Georgia there were 35,000 stranded tenant farmers trying to find places, but neither landlords nor tenants had funds to begin operations.[14] Complaints that people on relief would not again be willing to work in the fields also led the federal government to agree that relief was not the answer to the problem.

During 1934, therefore, the Georgia Rehabilitation Corporation was created with funds from the Federal Emergency Relief Administration. This first rehabilitation program consisted of loans to farm families to enable them to buy livestock, feed, and supplies. The loans were for three to five years; they could be repaid in cash, in kind, or in work on public works projects; and the borrowers had to operate on a farm-and-home management plan approved and supervised by the Rehabilitation Corporation. A live-at-home program and a soil conservation program were requisites for each borrower. Within a year 14,000 Georgia families had received loans under this program.[15]

It was soon discovered, however, that the problem of rehabilitation was bigger and more complicated than anyone had anticipated, and that the program was too small. Some of the farmers who received help were on land too poor to produce an adequate living. More than 32,000 farmers in Georgia, three-fourths of them white, were still on relief and thousands of others were still being supported by work on WPA projects.

The result was that in 1935 the federal government created the Resettlement Administration and took complete charge of the problem. The Resettlement Administration bought up vast quantities of sub-marginal land and turned it into pastures, forests, game preserves, and parks. The people removed from the land were employed temporarily on WPA projects and then resettled on usable land. This agency also continued the development of community farming projects that had been begun by the WPA. In Georgia four such projects had been started in Putnam, Irwin, Grady, and Jasper counties, which eventually were to accommodate 300 farm families, each in possession of their own well-equipped, family-size farm. The new agency also continued and expanded the rehabilitation program already begun.

In addition to advancing credit and giving its borrowers training in sound farming and home management methods, the Resettlement Administration also made loans to groups of farmers for such community needs as a combine, a pure-bred sire, spraying equipment, etc. Since many borrowers were overburdened with debt which needed to be reduced before rehabilitation could take place, the agency also helped its borrowers get their old debts adjusted. Within a year 12,000 Georgia families were operating under this program with loans that averaged about $300 each, and several thousand others had received grants to help them over an emergency situation.[16]

But the new program was still inadequate. The result was that in 1936 President Roosevelt appointed a Committee on Tenancy, which in its report a year later dramatized the desperate plight of many American farmers. "The extreme poverty," said the report, "of one-fifth to one-fourth of the farm population reflected itself in a standard of living below any level of decency."

This report produced a third reorganization. In 1937 the Bankhead-Jones Tenant Purchase Act was passed, and the Farm Security Administration was created to replace the Resettlement Administration. The FSA was given the double task of continuing the rural rehabilitation program as well as handling the new program whereby tenants, sharecroppers, and farm laborers could borrow money for 40 years at 3 percent interest to buy farms of their own.

During its ten years of life (1937–46) the Farm Security Administration was a busy agency. It continued to make standard rehabilitation loans, emergency rehabilitation loans, community service loans, to assist with debt adjustment, and to make relief grants. It also continued operating the idealistic homestead projects started in the early days of the New Deal, and to maintain camps for migrant farm workers. By that time also loans had been inaugurated whereby FSA borrowers in a county could organize group insurance co-operatives to pay for medical care. FSA helped tenants who borrowed from it to develop and carry out sound farm-and-home management plans. It also helped its tenants secure written tenure contracts. The FSA also worked to develop low cost farm homes and buildings to fit low income farmers; and it endeavored to persuade farmers to screen their houses, build sanitary privies, protect their water supplies, and do other things conducive to good health and a more productive farm.[17] Like the AAA, it co-operated with the Soil Conservation Service and other agencies, and had a multitude of local and state committees to guide and advise its programs and agents.

Although these programs were never big enough to meet the demands made upon them, their record of achievement was significant. Most impressive of all the efforts was that of rehabilitation. During

1934-41, nearly 54,000 Georgia families received rehabilitation loans or grants totaling more than $28,000,000; and by 1946, when FSA was abolished, the rehabilitation loans made in Georgia amounted to $41,000,000—76 percent of which had been repaid.[18] By 1946, also, emergency crop and feed loans had been made in Georgia amounting to $40,000,000—and by 1950, 94 percent of this had been repaid. Impressive also is the fact that by 1941 more than 82,000 farm people were covered by the group medical insurance programs that had been organized in 121 Georgia counties. By then, also, more than 34,000 people were included in similar programs for dental care in 54 counties. But in a state which in 1940 had 216,000 farms, nearly 130,000 tenants, and over 1,300,000 farm people, much remained to be done.

The tenant purchase program got off to a slow start. During its first three years (1937-40), 30,000 tenant purchase applications were filed in the 99 Georgia counties approved for loans—but only 1,187 loans were actually granted; and while the nearly $17,000,000 loaned by 1946 sounds impressive, it was enough to cover the purchase of probably fewer than 4,000 farms.[19]

Not all observers agreed with the prevailing view of the 'thirties that tenancy was an inherently evil institution. As early as 1923 the United States Department of Agriculture pointed out that the alarm over the increase in tenancy in America was unwarranted. While tenancy was rare in pioneering countries, it was a natural development in mature nations where the land had been filled up, said the department—and the United States had simply filled up. Tenancy was not so undesirable as many people supposed, the department reported, noting that some of the most prosperous agricultural states in the nation had a high degree of tenancy. In both Iowa and Illinois, for example, more than 40 percent of all the farms were operated by tenants; and in the state of Washington 50 percent or more of the land was operated by tenants.[20] The department also argued that a man with limited capital could do better as a tenant than as an owner. Land had become so expensive and gave such a small return that it was better for a small operator to put his capital into equipment and operations rather than into land.[21] Studies made in Newton and Terrell counties in Georgia in 1936-37 verified these arguments. Those surveys showed that many of the "crimes" charged to tenancy (neglect of soil, buildings, fruit trees, etc.) were committed by owners as well as by tenants and that many tenants and sharecroppers had higher incomes than some of their neighbors who owned their own small farms.²² These factors contributed to the national government's unwillingness to make an all-out effort to abolish tenancy.

Meanwhile the community resettlement projects had more or less proved themselves to be failures, and as early as 1937 the FSA proceeded to liquidate them through sales of the individual farms to private owners—preferably to their current occupants who thereby were aided in the purchase of their own family-type farm.

The relative prosperity achieved by American farmers during World War II produced a decline in interest in the problems of rehabilitation and tenancy, with the result that in 1946 Congress reorganized the program. This time a Farmers Home Administration was created to take over the work of both the Farm Security Administration and the emergency feed and crop loan program. The FHA continued practically all the rehabilitation program— but without calling it rehabilitation. The old standard rehabilitation loans became operating loans or production and subsistence loans, and more than $12,000,000 was loaned in Georgia under this label during 1946–50. In 1947 FHA began making what it called adjustment loans to help farmers shift into an all-year farming program, reduce the need for seasonal borrowing, and—as usual—strengthen the family-type farm. The Bankhead tenant purchase program was continued, with veterans of World War II given preference— 531 of whom in Georgia had secured loans amounting to nearly $3,000,000 by 1950. Since federal funds had never been sufficient to meet the needs of all those who applied to buy farms, the 1946 act authorized the insuring of loans from private sources. The first such guaranteed farm purchase loan in the nation was made in Sumter County, Georgia, in 1947; and by 1950, 225 such loans totaling more than $1,000,000 had been made in the state. Throughout all these years and in all these programs, however, it was still the "lower two-thirds" of the farm population who were helped, loans being made only to those who were not able to borrow elsewhere and being limited to the development of the family-type farm.

Meanwhile the program to make rural life easier and more attractive by bringing to the farm electricity and modern appliances was being developed. In 1935 the Federal Rural Electrification Administration was created, and a year later Congressional authorization was given the REA to lend money to co-operatives and other agencies who were willing to construct and operate power lines and plants for rural consumers, and to finance the wiring of rural buildings and the purchase of appliances. Georgia, which at that time had electricity on only about 7,400 of its 250,000 farms, took to the new program quickly and by 1950 was able to show the best record of rural electrification in the South and one of the best in the nation. Within 15 years Georgia had established 43 REA co-operatives, built more than 52,000 miles of lines, and electrified practically all the farms in the state.[23] The 1950 census showed also that Georgia's farmers were putting this electricity to work. Nearly 53,000 of the state's 198,000 farms were reported to own electric water pumps, more than 62,000 had washing machines, more than 24,000 had water heaters, more than 14,000 had electric chicken brooders, and more than 11,000 had home freezers. While the majority of farmers still had apparently nothing more than electric lights, it was plain that labor saving devices and conveniences of modern civilization were changing the life and habits of a huge proportion of Georgia's farm people. In 1949, the Rural Electrification Administration was authorized to begin a similar program to put telephones into rural homes—and since only 18,600 of Georgia's farm homes had phones in 1950, the prospects for development looked excellent.

The effectiveness of the New Deal programs designed to lift agriculture out of depression is still being debated. Unquestionably there were many other forces at work besides those inaugurated by the Roosevelt administration, and the proportion of credit that should be given here or there for recovery can not as yet be settled accurately.

Nevertheless, from 1933 on, farmers' incomes and land values rose perceptibly. The per capita gross income of Georgia's farm people rose from its low of $83 in 1933 to $183 in 1941. The average value of an acre of farm real estate rose also from about $17 in 1935 to $20 in 1940. Even when allowances are made for price changes, the per capita gross income of the farmer rose 42 points during the first eight years of the New Deal. And for all this the Democratic administration naturally took credit.

Regarding the rehabilitation and tenant purchase program there is less room for argument. While all the experiments were not successful, there is little doubt but that the effort as a whole was constructive and sufficiently forward looking to become a permanent function of the federal government. And regarding REA there is practically no room for argument at all. Its beneficial effects are self evident.

NOTES

1. U. S. Dept. of Agriculture, *Yearbook* (1920), 818.
2. *Ibid.* (1923), 1148.
3. *Ibid.* (1935), 242.
4. Hal Steed, *Georgia: Unfinished State* (New York, 1942), 121.
5. Rupert B. Vance, *Human Factors in Cotton Culture* (Chapel Hill, 1929), 138.
6. Arthur F. Raper, *Preface to Peasantry: A Tale of Two Black Belt Counties* (Chapel Hill, 1936), 195–200.
7. *Ibid.*, 77–78.
8. *Ibid.*, 233, 256.
9. U. S. Dept. of Agriculture, *Yearbook* (1926), 474–476.
10. Raper, *Preface to Peasantry*, 210–211.
11. U. S. Dept. of Agriculture, *Yearbook* (1932), 16–17.
12. U. S. Dept. of Agriculture, *Toward Farm Security* (Washington, 1941), 10–27.
13. Max M. Tharp, "The Farm Tenure Situation in the Southeast," South Carolina Agric. Experiment Station, *Bulletin*, No. 370 (January 1948), 9–11.
14. *Atlanta Constitution*, November 22, 1934.
15. *Ibid.*, June 24, 1935.
16. U. S. Resettlement Administration, *First Annual Report* (1936), 161.
17. Greene County, Georgia, was selected as a demonstration area to show what a rehabilitation program could do in a depressed community. For an account of that, see Farm Security Administration, *Greene County, Georgia* (Washington, 1941).
18. For this and other data see the annual reports of the Resettlement Administration, Farm Security Administration, and Farmers Home Administration.
19. FSA's last annual report, for 1945–46, gives a figure of 3,513 active borrowers for Georgia in the tenant purchase program as of March 31, 1946. It is unlikely that more than a small percentage of them had paid off their loans by that date.
20. U. S. Dept. of Agriculture, *Yearbook* (1923), 73–74, 507–508.
21. *Ibid.* (1930), 349–350.
22. Georgia Experiment Station, *A Study of Farming by Tenure of Farms in Terrell County, Georgia*, Bulletin No. 234 (June 1944); Georgia Experiment Station, *Some Aspects of the Farm Tenure Situation in Newton County, Georgia*, Bulletin No. 237 (January 1945).
23. The Report of the Administrator of the Rural Electrification Administration for 1950 differs from the 1950 Census Report considerably. The REA report declares there were 216,000 farms electrified in 1950, but the Census Bureau found a total of only 198,000 farms in the state, 149,000 of which were electrified.

18

The House of Labor

THE position of organized labor in the American economy has undergone radical change in the last sixty years. Total union membership has increased impressively, militant industrial unions have organized the mass-production manufacturing industries, and labor has won a new legal status since 1933. Each of the following essays appraises an important part of labor's record in the twentieth century. In the first, David Saposs deals with the attitudes of union leaders toward political action. Concentrating upon the strategy of Samuel Gompers as president of the American Federation of Labor, Saposs contends that the gains of the post-1933 period could not have been won had labor continued to rely on the "pure and simple unionism" to which Gompers had dedicated himself in earlier years.

Since World War II, American unions have met with serious difficulty in achieving some of their basic objectives. Despite such achievements as merger of the A.F. of L. and C.I.O., the unions have encountered stiffened employer resistance to "inflationary" wage agreements; they have been subject to restrictive state legislation and increased federal control since passage of the 1948 Taft-Hartley Act; and they face a critical problem in adjusting to the impact of automation upon industrial organization and employment. In the second of the following essays, Benjamin Solomon identifies still another fundamental problem: the declining relative strength of unions that has accompanied the growth of the "white collar" labor force.

VOLUNTARISM IN THE AMERICAN
LABOR MOVEMENT

David J. Saposs

American labor unions have progressed spectacularly, in terms of membership and collective bargaining coverage, since the 1930's, when the Government became a party to labor relations procedures and sponsored social welfare programs. This advance, as well as that during the World War I period of Government intervention in the handling of industrial relations, contrasts sharply with labor's position during earlier periods when it followed a policy of voluntarism, relying chiefly on economic action to achieve objectives and shunning Government assistance. A concomitant of labor's progress in recent years has been a metamorphosis of its philosophy. While the unions have expanded and refined their primary function of collective bargaining, they have become adherents of the concept of Government intervention in economic and social affairs and have found it profitable to engage extensively in political action. Only in structure has the change not been drastic.

EARLY DAYS OF VOLUNTARISM

Voluntarism,[1] the labor version of the laissez-faire philosophy, was described by its founders as a policy under which workers were to be schooled to rely exclusively on their trade unions for promoting and protecting their interests as wage earners. The unions, in turn, were to accomplish their objectives chiefly through collective bargaining and its concomitants, such as the strike and boycott. Above all, no positive aid from the Government through legislative or administrative action was to be sought or accepted. Indeed, positive Government aid was to be resisted.

Reprinted from *The Monthly Labor Review* (published by the U.S. Department of Labor, Bureau of Labor Statistics), LXXVII, No. 9 (September, 1954), pp. 967–71.

Voluntarism came into its own with the fading away of the Knights of Labor and the practically simultaneous defeat of the Socialists' efforts to commit the American Federation of Labor to their broad program of independent political action, comprehensive social reform legislation, and basic social reorganization. These AFL victories over its two outstanding rivals occurred on the eve of the Spanish-American War. (However, as early as 1908, the AFL wavered from its course of voluntarism by expressing sympathy for William Jennings Bryan and supporting his presidential candidacy.[2])

In 1897, shortly after the AFL expounded the philosophy of voluntarism, it had a membership of 264,825. "Labor's Mass Offensive," launched in 1899, was countered by the "Employers' Mass Offensive" of 1903–08.[3] By the time of the 1907 depression, AFL unions, although gaining in membership, had lost out in most basic industries, which reduced their collective bargaining coverage considerably.

One of its important affiliates, the Amalgamated Association of Iron, Steel, and Tin Workers, had been violently eliminated from the basic steel industry in 1901.[4] "The expulsion of the union from the plants of the United States Steel Corp. was a natural sequel to the unsuccessful strike of 1901. . . . [Its elimination] from the steel industry was the major but not the sole blow struck . . . against unionism." [5] In meatpacking, as a result of a strike in 1904, "the union was destroyed until the Government, during the war, resurrected it with a Federal administrator. After the war, the companies converted it into an 'employee representation' system." [6] And in metalworking, in 1904 also, "the National Founders' Association transformed its policy of peaceful negotiation [with the International Molders' Union] into one of aggressive attack. . . . Industrial relations in the machinery industry duplicated the course of events in the machinery and job foundry industry, only with greater rapidity." [7]

Notwithstanding these and other significant early setbacks, the AFL continued to grow slowly, meantime reiterating its policy of voluntarism. For example, at its 1914 convention, the report of the Committee on Resolutions on a resolution favoring the enactment of legislation regulating hours of labor (which was rejected by the convention) stated:

We have tried in this country, as workingmen have endeavored to do in others, to secure through legislation a guarantee that our rights to organization and to trade union effort should not be interfered with. That has been one form of legislation which the trade union movement has most heartily and effectively applied. We have endeavored through legislative enactment to have our rights as free men guaranteed so that we could then apply our trade union method to regulate the terms of employment.[8]

In the debate which followed, Samuel Gompers said, "In the law to limit and regulate injunctions we propose to clip the power of the court insofar as labor is concerned, and in an 8-hour law for men it is [proposed] to give the courts still greater power." [9] And, further, "If we can get an 8-hour law for the working people, then you will find that the working people themselves will fail to have any interest in your economic organization, which even advocates declare is essential in order that such a law can be enforced." [10]

THE WORLD WAR I PERIOD

By 1916, the AFL had grown to 2,072,702 members, since industry was expanding.[11] However, outside of building and construction, coal mining, and railroads, its operations remained on the fringe of important industries.[12] It was strong only in highly competitive industries with relatively small industrial units. The so-called "trustified" industries with chain plants were practically closed to it. Only unions of highly skilled craftsmen like patternmakers and tool- and die-makers were able to maintain a foothold in these large and basic industrial establishments; and these unions usually had only verbal agreements. Thus, simultaneously with its considerable gain in membership, the AFL was actually losing out rapidly in the more important industries.

Then during World War I, the Government intervened in labor relations as it did in all other economic functions affecting the war effort. This "marked a turning point in collective bargaining. Before this country entered the war, Government had taken no part in union organization and negotiation of trade agreements except to mediate in disputes." [13] Administrative orders and legislation creating such agencies as the War Labor Board and providing for Government operation of railroads,[14] gave organized labor a tremendous stimulus so that it again became a power in all important industries except steel. AFL membership soared to new heights during and immediately following the war, as shown below.[15]

Year	Membership
1917	2,371,434
1918	2,726,478
1919	3,260,068
1920	4,078,740

THE PROSPEROUS '20'S AND THE EARLY '30'S

With the advent of peace and the withdrawal of Government regulation of the economy of the country, the AFL, as a whole, reverted to voluntarism,[16] to which it adhered consistently until the middle 1930's. Shortly after the war, the unions became involved in costly and bitterly contested strikes, practically all of which were unsuccessful. Management, taking advantage of the weakened condition of organized labor, introduced the "American Plan" and "Welfare Capitalism," with their company unions, labor spies, armed guards, accelerated implementation of the yellow dog contract, and black list.[17] A variety of welfare programs were introduced simultaneously in an attempt to "sugarcoat" management's forceful resistance.

The depression of 1920–21 contributed only incidentally in precipitating the disastrous reverses for organized labor. In 1921, when non-agricultural employment dropped by 3 million to 24 million, AFL membership declined only slightly, as did total union membership, which had doubled between 1915 and 1920, reaching 5,110,800 in the latter year. But, during the rest of the twenties, as employment climbed to 31 million, both total union membership and AFL membership first declined precipitously to 1924 (3,536,100 and 2,865,799, respectively) and stayed at about those levels. The great depression brought employment down to about 23,500,000 in 1933, when union membership declined even further, with the total skidding to 2,973,000 and the AFL to 2,126,796.[18] Thus, even during the unprecedented period of prosperity in the 1920's, union membership declined drastically, with collective bargaining coverage receding at even a faster pace.

So discouraging was the situation that many students of labor began to wonder and some even to despair about the future of trade unionism in the United States. As early as 1922, an outstanding scholar, the late Professor Henry R. Seager, regretfully declared that, particularly as regards "public service industries," a labor movement based on trade unions was hardly possible in the United States. He also commented on the marked increase in the number of company unions and the simultaneous decline in trade union membership. But, as a sympathizer of organized labor, he found some ground for optimism:

There is one aspect of the situation which this analysis seems to overlook. Consciousness of the opposition of interests between employers and employees has given vitality to the trade union, but an even stronger cohesive influence has been consciousness of common interests that is causing the workers of all countries to unite even across national boundaries. Is this growing sense of solidarity to be eclipsed by the increasing realization fostered by company unions that employers and employees have common interests as well as conflicting interests? Nothing is further from my own expectation. What I think rather is that the sense of common interests which holds wage earners together in trade unions will be in part transferred from the industrial to the political field. The principal circumstance that may render the trade union less indispensable is not any overnight conversion of employers, but the taking over of the regulation of working conditions in public service industries by the government. In the constitution of adjustment boards, in the formulation of legal standards as to working conditions, in the progressive development of social insurance and other protective legislation, wage earners will have an ever increasing motive for concerning themselves with politics. The United States has been relatively backward in this development but what has happened in other English-speaking countries, in the United Kingdom, in Australia, and in New Zealand, the growth of a labor party until it has become the principal opposition party, is prophetic of what is likely to happen here.[19]

However, as late as 1931, the AFL rejected at its convention a resolution endorsing unemployment insurance legislation. During its adherence to voluntarism, its only concession was to favor child labor legislation and government intervention in regulating the working conditions of women. On the other hand, such negative governmental assistance as restriction of immigration and judicial interference with trade union activity, mainly by anti-injunction legislation, was permissible and desirable. In fact, it was the devastating issuance of injunctions in labor disputes which led the AFL to embark seriously on its early nonpartisan political action, with its "Reward your friends, and punish your enemies," slogan, now more politely worded as "Reward your friends, and defeat your enemies." It was with great reluctance and only out of desperation that the AFL deviated from its original course. Only after its lobbyists were scorned and rebuffed, particularly with the taunting refrain to show a capacity to deliver votes, was the momentous decision made to embark on nonpartisan political action.

THE LAST TWO DECADES

In 1933 came Government assistance through Section 7A of the National Recovery Act, followed by the Wagner Act, and other sympathetic legislation and administrative orders, and the unions began to regain their vitality.

It now became Government policy not only to encourage labor organizations, but also to protect the right of the workers to organize into unions. Moreover, the Government also made it mandatory for management to bargain in good faith with the union selected by its employees, and to incorporate the agreed-upon conditions of employment into written and signed trade agreements.[20] By 1939, AFL membership practically doubled over 1933, rising to 4,006,354 from 2,126,796, notwithstanding the fact that a number of substantial unions withdrew to form the CIO; likewise, total trade union membership rose from 2,973,000 to 7,734,900.[21] It is significant that this membership increase occurred in years when unemployment never averaged less than 14 percent of the civilian labor force.

It is questionable whether the mass production industries would have been as readily and effectively organized, if thoroughly organized at all, without the aid, first, of Section 7A of NRA, and then of the Wagner Act and NLRB decisions. The new and sympathetic pro-labor sentiment of the Government also contributed materially to labor's success. Indeed, as industry became more integrated, organized labor would have found it more difficult without Government intervention to rise from its intermittent doldrums. Such obstacles as recessions, prolonged strikes, and management resistance may have hindered trade union organization and limited its advances, as in certain industries in the South, but have not reversed the steady progress of organized labor. By 1953, total union membership was estimated at slightly over 17 million.[22] This advance would have been impossible through sole reliance on "pure and simple" union action, as dictated by voluntarism.

CHANGING CHARACTERISTICS OF ORGANIZED LABOR

The conclusion that "To the American labor movement, the conquest of the right to exist was ever its paramount problem" [23] is no longer applicable. Government, management, and society as a whole now recognize organized labor as an indispensable and constructive functional group in our civilization. Organized labor is still concerned, of course, with increasing its membership and extending collective bargaining coverage. But it has expanded its activities into all fields affecting the social and economic interests of wage earners and society. It subscribes to the concept of Government intervention in these fields, so that political action is now regarded not only as necessary to securing preventive legislation, but as vital to obtaining positive legislation. Moreover, through its political power, labor aims to participate also in Government administrative procedures. Notwithstanding the fact that labor considered as political reverses the enactment of the Taft-Hartley Act and the outcome of the 1952 election, neither the AFL, the CIO, nor the oustanding unaffiliated unions have seriously considered returning to voluntarism. Rather, even a brief glance at the labor press and a superficial familiarity with developments at union conventions and other conferences reveals organized labor's determination to broaden its political activity. Contrary to predictions, Government intervention and the simultaneous broadening of organized labor's horizon did not lessen either labor's ardor or its militancy. Indeed, it has enjoyed unprecedented success, as measured by size of union membership and extent of collective bargaining coverage, as already indicated.

The metamorphosis of the labor movement left its salient structural characteristics essentially unaltered. The labor movements of the greater part of the world usually operate through two or three broad and equally autonomous divisions: the national trade union federation, the political party, and the cooperative association. In England, the three are linked by a national labor council which coordinates their activities. Invariably, the leadership in these three divisions of the labor movement is overlapping, so that they are truly governed by interlocking directorates. In the United States, since the advent of the AFL, the trade union organization has functioned as the sole, basic, and controlling institution in the labor movement. All other organized activities, such as political action, insurance, community services, banking, and education, emanate from it and are organically a part of the trade unions. Some activities are carried on by auxiliaries rather than subsidiaries but are nevertheless initiated and sanctioned by the union and are wholly dependent upon it.

In fact, the AFL and CIO have begun to resemble each other more closely in recent years—in structure, activity, and ideology. Most of the AFL affiliates are no longer operated as craft unions, having enlarged their jurisdiction to encompass several crafts or trades, one or more entire industries, or to become general unions. In action, affiliates of both groups, by and large, differ little in militancy with respect to labor-management relations; they are dynamic and aggressive, yet circumspect and farsighted, adapting their collective bargaining activities as occasion requires. Both federations, as well as some of the largest affiliates, now [1954] maintain specialized political arms (the CIO Political Action Committee and the AFL Labor's League for Political Education) manned by experienced staffs which function continuously on a professional basis, in contrast to their former practice of establishing temporary committees for each election. The official organs of both the AFL and the CIO and of international affiliates devote considerable space to domestic and international political issues and specific legislative acts. They likewise report and evaluate events in State legislatures and in the Congress, urge regional and local union bodies to participate in politics, and exhort members to register and to vote for the "right" candidate. For example—and without attempting to "gild the lily"—an article in *The American Federationist* [24] proposed that labor support legislation setting up a "minimum code of propriety and responsibility" in the handling of union welfare funds. The article, by David Dubinsky, president of the International Ladies' Garment Workers' Union and a vice president of the AFL, stated:

It appears to me that under these circumstances, where labor recognizes the existence of a real evil—no matter how limited—and where the internal union structure does not provide controls for the elimination of abuses, the pressure for legislative action to control union welfare funds will inevitably mount.

Further, union conventions and conferences of the federations and of affiliated internationals, as well as State conventions and conferences and local central labor union gatherings, devote as much time to the discussion of political and legislative matters as to union or collective bargaining issues.

Both their publications and their discussions indicate that practically all unions in the AFL and the CIO expect the Government to play an important role, not only in keeping our economy on an even keel, but also in stimulating its expansion. The Government is likewise expected to maintain and improve various social welfare services in the interest of the wage earners, such as social security. And the federations are not interested merely in influencing favorable legislation and Government policies; they are equally concerned in participating in Government administrative functions. . . .[25]

NOTES

1. David J. Saposs, *Readings in Trade Unionism* (New York, 1926), 40–44, 395–398.

2. George Meany, "Political Education is an AFL Tradition," *The American Federationist*, September 1953.

3. Selig Perlman and Philip Taft, *History of Labor in the United States, 1896–1932* (New York, 1935), IV, 489 ff.

4. Leo Wolman, *The Growth of American Trade Unions, 1880–1923* (New York, 1924), 89.

5. Perlman and Taft, *History of Labor*, IV, 143–144.

6. John R. Commons, *History of Labor in the United States, 1896–1932* (New York, 1935), III, p. xxv.

7. Perlman and Taft, *History of Labor*, 113–115.

8. American Federation of Labor, *Report of the Proceedings of the 34th Annual Convention* (1914), 424.

9. *Ibid.*, 440.

10. *Ibid.*, 442.

11. *Report of the Executive Council of the American Federation of Labor to the 72nd Convention* (1953), 17.

12. Wolman, *Growth of American Trade Unions*, 90.

13. Twentieth Century Fund, *Trends in Collective Bargaining* (New York, 1945), 6.

14. Alexander Bing, *Wartime Strikes and Their Adjustment* (New York, 1921).

15. AFL Executive Council, *Report, op. cit.*

16. Its affiliates in association with other unions operating in the railroad industry refused to follow. See the author's review of Keating's *The Story of "Labor"* in *Monthly Labor Review*, June 1954, pp. 675–676.

17. Perlman and Taft, *History of Labor*, 489 ff.

18. Wolman, *Growth of American Trade Unions*, 33, and *Ebb and Flow in Trade Unionism* (New York, 1936), 34; Irving Bernstein, "The Growth of American Unions," in *The American Economic Review*, June 1954, p. 303.

19. "Company Unions vs. Trade Unions," in *The American Economic Review*, March 1923, pp. 1 ff.

20. Joel Seidman, *American Labor from Defense to Reconversion* (Chicago, 1953), 1–19.

21. AFL Executive Council, *Report, op. cit.*; Bernstein, "Growth of American Unions."

22. Bernstein, "Growth of American Unions."

23. Perlman and Taft, *History of Labor*, 621.

24. "Safeguarding Union Welfare Funds," in *The American Federationist*, July 1954, pp. 10–13.

25. (EDITOR'S NOTE: This article was originally published prior to the merger of the AF of L and CIO. For the 1955 merger and the new federation's almost immediate involvement in the national election campaign in 1956, see Joseph G. Rayback, A *History of American Labor* [New York, 1961], 422 et seq.)

DIMENSIONS OF UNION GROWTH, 1900–1950 *

Benjamin Solomon

At this juncture in the history of the American labor movement the question arises as to its ability to go forward—to be a dynamic, expanding force in American society. In the past few years, many signs have appeared to support the persuasive thesis that an era of stabilization is naturally following upon the great, long surge of union growth which commenced with the depression years. In good measure, however, a challenge to this thesis is offered by an event that clearly is of great historical import—the recent merger of the two leading federations into a single trade union center. Will the giant federation provide the vehicle for a new surge in "organizing the unorganized," or will it merely furnish a different home for a labor movement with no place in particular to go?

This analysis does not presume to supply an answer to this broad question, but it does attempt to provide some statistical guides to past growth and some information on the current scene that will improve, it is hoped, our perspective with regard to the issue. The article first deals with measurements of the growth of the union movement. In this connection, there are set forth for a fifty-year period two parameters important in consideration of the development of the union movement—*real membership* and *union poten-*

Reprinted by permission from the *Industrial and Labor Relations Review*, IX, No. 4 (July, 1956), pp. 544–61.

* The author expresses indebtedness for helpful comments and criticisms to Professor Val R. Lorwin and to Bernard Goldstein.

tial. An important aspect of the union potential is in the changes that have occurred in its internal composition, the most significant among these being the rising importance of white-collar occupations. In large part, it is the exceptional development of the white-collar sector which explains organized labor's growing concern about the prospects for union expansion in this area. To help evaluate these prospects, the article surveys the entire white-collar field to ascertain the unions active here, the number of workers organized, and to examine other pertinent material relating to white-collar employment.

REAL MEMBERSHIP AND THE UNION POTENTIAL,
1900–1950

An important aspect of the study of trade unionism is analysis of the course of union power. The quantitative measure normally used to chart the trend of labor strength over the modern period is the annual membership figure. It is true that membership size is only one evidence of union power, but it is an important indication; and it must be added, it is the only available quantitative measure.

While membership is the basic datum, it is, when taken by itself, a deceptive figure by which to evaluate and compare the union achievement at different periods. The reason is that the *potential* available for organization at different times has varied greatly with two factors: (1) changes in the size of the work force; (2) changes in the numerical importance within the work force of those wage and salary groups which are the objectives of unionism. The significance of the membership figure is greatly heightened, therefore, if it is corrected for these variations, i.e., for changes in the *union potential.* This procedure has the additional advantage of bringing the union potential—that section of the work force which is the field for action of unionism—more fully into the picture as an important parameter in its own right.

To correct or "deflate" the membership figure, it is taken as a percentage of the union potential. Wolman investigated this relationship, which he called the "percentage organized," in his authoritative works on union membership.[1] In a recent article Irving Bernstein employed the term "real membership" for a corrected membership figure, although he used the total labor force for his correction, rather than the union potential.[2] Since the term is apt and has caught on as a description of the general procedure, I shall employ *real membership* here to denote actual union membership adjusted by the union potential (instead of by the work force).

The table sets forth relevant variables for describing the over-all growth of union membership for the census years 1900 to 1950. These are: civilian labor force, union potential, union potential as a percentage of the civilian labor force, actual union membership, and real union membership. A series based on union potential can be calculated only for the census years, since only for these years are detailed occupational data available. For a period of several decades, the over-all trend in real membership is nevertheless revealed in a reasonably adequate fashion.[3]

To obtain the union potential, the following groups were subtracted from the work force: farmers and farm workers; other proprietors, managers, and officials; family servants; the clergy and professions with a high proportion of fee practitioners; and a few minor groups. In 1940 and 1950, it was also possible to deduct significant numbers of self-employed and unpaid family workers. Further details on the make-up of the union potential are found in footnotes to the table. A discussion of some issues involved in the concept of union potential follows an examination of the data in the table.

MEMBERSHIP GROWTH BY DECADES

The figure for union membership in 1900 (868,500) given by Wolman is a near doubling of the number in 1897 (447,000), the year his series started. Real membership, 6 percent in 1900, must have grown almost as swiftly as actual membership, since the union potential probably only rose moderately over this brief period. In 1900, the union potential included almost half of the civilian work force.

The large work-force gain from 1900 to 1910 and the increase in union potential percentage to 55 percent resulted in a substantially larger union potential. Union membership in this decade grew by 133 percent, to total over two million. The large gain in the union potential offset the increase in actual membership sufficiently to hold the real membership figure to 10 percent. During the World War I decade, the rate of growth of actual membership was about at the same rate as in the previous decade. However, real membership, 18.8 percent in 1920, rose more sharply than in the previous ten years. This reflected the somewhat smaller percentage increase of the union potential, though it did rise substantially in absolute

TABLE. CIVILIAN LABOR FORCE, UNION POTENTIAL, ACTUAL AND
REAL UNION MEMBERSHIP, FOR CENSUS YEARS, 1900 TO 1950

(1)	(2)	(3)	(4)	(5)	(6)
			Union Potential as Percent of Civilian		Real Union Membership (Percentage Column 5 is
Year	Civilian Labor Force *	Union Potential †	Labor Force	Actual Union Membership ‡	of Column 3)
900	29,030,000	14,236,000	49.0	868,500	6.1
910	37,194,000	20,397,000	54.8	2,021,100	9.9
920	41,010,000	25,392,000	61.9	4,780,600	18.8
930	48,462,000	31,237,000	64.5	3,189,300	10.2
940	51,798,000	33,701,000	65.1	7,873,900	23.4
950	58,999,000	42,783,000	72.5	13,304,100	31.1

* 1900–1940, from Alba M. Edwards, *Sixteenth Census of the United States: 1940, Population, Comparative Occupation Statistics for the United States, 1870 to 1940,* U. S. Bureau of the Census (Washington: G. P. O., 1943). For 1900, Table 8; 1910, 1920, and 1930, Table 4; and 1940, Table 23. Armed forces were deducted from the totals. For 1950, from U. S. Bureau of the Census, *U. S. Census of Population: 1950,* Vol. II, *Characteristics of the Population,* Part 1, Chapter C (Washington: G. P. O., 1953), Table 124.

† For 1950, the following categories were subtracted from the experienced civilian labor force: farmers and farm managers; farm laborers and foremen; managers, officials, and proprietors, except farm (except railroad conductors and postmasters); private household workers; among professional, technical and kindred workers—physicians and surgeons, lawyers and judges, clergymen, dentists, funeral directors, therapists and healers (n.e.c.), optometrists, chiropractors, veterinarians, and osteopaths; among service workers, except private household—boarding and lodging housekeepers, housekeepers and stewards, policemen and detectives, sheriffs and bailiffs, marshals and constables, midwives; among sales workers—real estate agents and brokers, hucksters and peddlers, auctioneers. There were also deducted from the included occupations, the self-employed and unpaid family classes of workers (except for the self-employed male craftsmen and kindred workers and male barbers, beauticians, and manicurists). See *ibid.,* Tables 124, 128. For 1940 and earlier years, the list of occupations deducted was as close as possible to that given above. For the occupational distribution of the work force for these years, the major source was Edwards, *op. cit.* For 1940, the deductions for self-employed and unpaid family workers were obtained from the U. S. Bureau of the Census, *Sixteenth Census of the United States: 1940, Population. The Labor Force (Sample Statistics), Occupational Characteristics* (Washington: G. P. O., 1943), Table 6.

For 1930, 1920, and 1910, Table 4 (gainful workers 14 years old and over) and, for 1900, Table 8 (gainful workers 10 years old and over), of Edwards' work were used. (It was impossible to deduct self-employed and unpaid family workers from the included occupations, since these classifications first came into use by the Bureau of the Census in 1940.) For 1920 and 1910, the size of a few occupations had to be determined from Edwards' list by estimates based on 1930 relationships. Considerably more estimation was required for 1900, most of it based on 1910 relationships.

‡ For 1900–1930, from Leo Wolman, *Ebb and Flow in Trade Unionism* (New York: National Bureau of Economical Research, 1936), p. 16. For 1940 and 1950, from Irving Bernstein, "The Growth of American Trade Unions," *American Economic Review,* Vol. 44, June 1954, Table I, pp. 303–304. Totals for 1910 and succeeding years were reduced by Canadian membership of American international unions, obtained from Canadian Department of Labour, *Labour Organization in Canada,* annual issues. The 1910 total was reduced by the 1911 Canadian membership, since this was the first year this information became available.

numbers. Over the next decade, the 1920's, the decline of union membership by one third, while the union potential continued to rise, brought real membership in 1930 back to the 1910 level, 10 percent.

From 1930 to 1940, the union movement experienced a nearly 150 percent increase in size, as membership reached 7.9 million. Real membership, 23.4 percent in 1940, rose at almost the same rate, reflecting the rapid expansion of actual membership within a relatively stationary union potential. The relatively small change in the work force and in the union potential percentage, which in the immediate sense accounted for the small change in the union potential, was no doubt related to the slower pace of economic activity in the depression years. It should be noted, however, that the 1940 union potential was reduced by nearly 1.4 million self-employed or unpaid family workers (or 2.7 percentage points). This category could not be removed from the union potential in earlier years, since the census did not give this data until 1940.[4] Furthermore, more than the usual statistical difficulties may have obscured the picture. The change in the 1940 census from the "gainful-worker" to the "labor-force" concept and the large-scale unemployment in that year affect comparisons with previous censuses.

Over the World War II decade, union membership made great gains, reaching 13.3 million in 1950, an increase of 70 percent over 1940. The rise in the union potential percentage to 72.5 percent and the growth of the work force brought the union potential up to 42.8 million, an expansion of 27 percent. Real membership, reflecting the effect of this gain in the union potential on the increase in actual membership, rose by one third to 31 percent.

THE FIFTY-YEAR PERIOD

Taking this period as a whole, the civilian labor force rose from 1900 to 1950 by slightly over 100 percent, while its component, the union potential, grew by 200 percent, going from 14.2 to 42.8 million persons. The greater rate of gain of the union potential is explained, of course, by the fact that the union potential became a greater proportion within the work force, rising from 49 to 72.5 percent. If the union potential had increased at the same rate as the work force, i.e., if the proportion held by this sector had remained at 49 percent, the resulting union potential in 1950 would have been only 28.9 million persons.

Turning now to membership figures, union strength experienced more than a 1,400 percent growth, rising from 868,500 in 1900 to 13.3 million in 1950. Real membership, in contrast, rose from 6 percent at the turn of the century to 31 percent in 1950, an increase of but 400 percent. By the nature of the parameter, of course, real membership would grow at a lesser rate than actual membership, as long as there was an increase in the union potential. Furthermore, the condition for a positive rate of growth of real membership is that actual membership should expand at a faster rate than the union potential. These are the conditions which have existed for most of the period under study—the union potential has grown substantially, but not at as fast a rate as has actual union membership.

It is interesting to note the effect on the real membership figure if the union potential had grown at the same rate as the work force. As stated above, there would then be in 1950 only 28.9 million persons in the union potential. Real membership based on this figure would be 46 percent (as compared to the 31 percent it actually is). The increase within the work force of the scope for union operation has clearly been a significant factor in keeping the real membership figure at a lower level.

It may thus appear that a lesser rate of expansion of the union potential would have resulted in a correspondingly higher figure for real membership. While this may be true to some extent, it should also be recognized that a smaller union potential certainly would have had an adverse effect on the growth of union membership. Actually, the trend of the union potential has been a powerful factor in favor of labor organization, since it has meant a much larger arena for the operation of the union movement. From 1900 to 1950, the labor movement has multiplied its effectiveness (at least, with respect to membership size) by about five times—considering the much larger labor force and the greater proportion within it who are the union target.

The size of the real membership figure has somewhat of a dual significance with respect to future possibilities of union growth. On the one hand, a larger figure has a pessimistic connotation, since it calls attention to the fact that the union movement must tackle ever more difficult areas if it wishes to expand its membership. On the other hand, a high real membership connotes a more successful union movement, one which has established a base of power from which it can proceed to organize in areas which would have been unfeasible at an earlier and weaker stage.

THE UNION POTENTIAL

The proportion of the work force in the union potential rose from 49 percent in 1900 to 72.5 percent in 1950. As stated above, these proportions were obtained by deducting certain occupations from the work force but leaving in the bulk of the urban wage earners and white-collar employees.

The union potential includes that section of the work force which is the field for action of the union movement, although it does not constitute an area likely to be 100 percent organized (nor is there implied any specific lesser proportion which is likely to be organized). Some of the occupations included are marginal as possibilities for unionism. Also, unionism has special difficulties in certain spheres which cut across the occupational classification. For example, workers in small firms, in small towns, and in certain regions, notably the South, generally are more difficult to organize. Further, even occupations most receptive to unionism are usually less than completely organized. Finally, there are, of course, many other factors which influence the extent of union organization. Nevertheless, the union potential, insofar as it shows the changing proportion of the work force which is the field for action of unionism, is a significant dimension in the study of the labor movement. It also gives greater meaning to the notion of real membership.

The major occupations of employees excluded from the union potential set forth here are family servants and farm workers. There is little question about exclusion of the first group, but some observers may not agree to the omission of farm laborers. Small numbers of farm workers are unionized and there are periodic attempts to unionize more. Unionization in the agricultural field is restricted, however, to areas where the work units are relatively large. The greater part of the hired workers on farms are spread quite thinly over the rural areas of the country. Until some significant change occurs in this condition, the farm workers as a group should probably not be included in the union potential. (If farm workers, excluding unpaid family workers and the self-employed, were included in the union potential for 1950, it would rise to 75.2 percent of the work force. Real membership for 1950, based on this union potential, would then stand at 30 percent.)

The union potential during the earlier part of the period 1900–1950 considerably exceeded what the labor movement then viewed as the practicable area for its operations. For example, in 1900 the main section of the white-collar group was not seriously considered to be an objective of the union movement, although it has since come to be regarded as such. If the union potential for the earlier periods were measured by the shorter-term outlook then current—thus excluding, for example, most of the white-collar employees—the resulting union potential would be considerably smaller. However, a significant trend in the labor field has been its steady broadening. Over the period from 1900, many occupations entered for the first time within the scope of the labor movement's organizing operations. In consequence, the broadly feasible range of union organizing activities today more nearly coincides with the occupations included in the union potential. The outlook of the union movement has widened; its perspective encompasses the entire union potential, even though unionism as yet has made little headway in a number of the included occupations.

WHITE-COLLAR COMPONENT OF
UNION POTENTIAL

The focus of this analysis will now shift from statistics pertaining to the union movement as a whole to data about a highly dynamic component of the union potential—the white-collar occupations. The over-all picture is, of course, essential; at the same time, it is true that the history of unionism in particular periods has been dominated by developments in specific sectors of the union potential. Recently, speculation as to significant expansion in future years has centered on the white-collar field. To a large degree, this has resulted from an increasing awareness of its numerical importance and from the rise in union activity since the 1930's. The remainder of the article presents data on these two aspects of the white-collar question in order to assist in evaluation of what may be the key field for future union growth.

The present section will examine the influence of the white-collar vocations in the enlargement of the union potential over the 1900 to 1950 period. The following section will then turn to a second set of data bearing on white-collar unionism—an inclusive, if brief, breakdown of the current status of unionism in the various white-collar fields.

What proportion do the white-collar occupations (clerical, sales, and professional employees, and foremen) constitute of the union potential? The answer for the fifty-year period is as follows:

Year	Percent
1900	20.8
1910	25.2
1920	29.6
1930	33.7
1940	33.8
1950	35.5

In 1900, the white-collar sector comprised one fifth of the workers in the union potential. This proportion has risen to more than one third by 1950, an increase of about 75 percent. Accounting for the greater importance of the white-collar group was a growth rate of over 400 percent for the 1900–1950 period. In contrast, the remainder of the union potential, the manual sector, grew by but 150 percent over the same period. (As a proportion of the union potential, the manual occupations dropped from 79.2 percent in 1900 to 64.5 percent in 1950.)

Perhaps an even more revealing comparison of the white-collar and manual components of the union potential may be gained by considering their changing positions relative to the work force as a whole. As indicated in column 4 of the table, the union potential rose from 49.0 percent of the work force in 1900 to 72.5 percent in 1950, an increase over the period of 48 percent, or 23 percentage points. If the proportion is calculated with the white-collar occupations omitted, growth was at a much slower rate. The resulting all-manual potential constituted 38.8 percent of the work force in 1900 and 46.8 percent in 1950. The increase in relative position was only slightly over 20 percent, or 8 percentage points. But if only the white-collar portion of the union potential is considered, it rose from 10.2 percent of the work force in 1900 to 25.7 percent in 1950, an increase of 150 percent over the period, or 15.5 percentage points.

While the manual element of the union potential improved its position in the work force over the half-century period, its gain can at most be described as moderate, considering the dynamic nature of this period and the larger increase of the white-collar sector. The expansion of both groups was largely at the expense of agriculture. It is difficult to say what the future holds for the relative positions of these two components of the union potential. Past trends need not necessarily be good guides for future projections, particularly in view of the greater maturity of our industrial economy and the difficulty in estimating the effects of a number of recent technological developments.

But labor leaders must consider as a serious possibility that there may be no further increase and even a decrease in the importance of the manual sector of the work force. Indeed, without the existence of a large agricultural sector to encroach on, future gains of the white-collar occupations, if they take place, may be in part at the expense of the manual sector. This possibility, even if vaguely perceived, has served to heighten the interest of the labor movement in the white-collar force, over and above the concern arising from its present size.

In any case, even if present relationships hold, the white-collar group has become an extremely significant supplement to the potential influence and power of organized labor. The manual sector alone would tremendously increase in strength if organization were expanded to a point approaching the full numerical limit (in 1950, roughly two fifths of the manual part of the union potential was organized), but the union movement would still be restricted to less than half of the work force. In 1950, it is estimated that the white-collar sector was less than one sixth organized. If a substantial increase were obtained in this proportion, it might represent the decisive addition to labor's strength in the economy and in society generally. Labor's role would be significantly enhanced and broadened if unionism penetrated deeply into the white-collar areas.

In order to provide the factual foundation necessary for a perspective on union growth, the current status of unionism in white-collar fields will be surveyed briefly.[5] Where organization is weak, some indication will be given of the distribution of the potential—by establishment, firm, or geographically—since this is an important dimension in considering the feasibility of unionism.

Analysis of the white-collar field will be based primarily on the occupational and industrial distribution set forth in the 1950 census,[6] since this is the most recent source of detailed information. Union figures, however, may be for any one of the last few years. Further, they represent the white-collar strength of the union (often estimated), which in many cases is less than the full strength of the organization. Thus, a good deal less than absolute precision is claimed for the figures that are provided below. Among other reasons for this roughness are the following: some union claims must be viewed skeptically; many white-collar workers are scattered among unions completely outside of the white-collar field; to only a partial degree was it possible to obtain information on the scattered local independent unions; union membership did not always follow census categories; and finally, there is a varying inadequacy of information necessary for a complete picture of each field. Nevertheless, it is hoped that the result is somewhat close to the objective of giving an over-all view of union activity among white-collar people.

CLERICAL AND KINDRED WORKERS

The clerical occupations, embracing close to seven million wage and salaried employees in private and government employment, made up 12 percent of the work force in 1950. Included were groups as diverse as letter carriers, telephone operators, telegraphers, library attendants, office-machine operators, cashiers, typists, stenographers, secretaries, and general clerical workers, among others. Five eighths of the workers were women.

Railroads and telecommunications. A high proportion of the clerical workers in these fields are organized, and powerful unions are active. In railroads and railway express, the Brotherhood of Railroad Clerks has organized some 260,000 clerical employees, practically its entire jurisdiction. The Order of Railroad Telegraphers, with 62,000 members, accounts for most of the telegraphers. Strong unions are also found among the approximately 400,000 telephone operators, office workers, and telegraphers in the telecommunications sector. About 200,000 members of the Communications Workers of America are telephone operators or office workers. The Alliance Independent Telephone Unions, a group of independent locals in the East, has about 75,000 white-collar employees. Of less importance are a number of smaller local unions and the International Brotherhood of Electrical Workers. In the telegraphy field, the Commercial Telegrapher's Union has some 35,000 members and the American Communications Association about 7,000.

Federal, state, and local public administration. In 1950, about 1,100,000 clerical workers were employed in public service. On the federal level there is extensive unionism only in the postal service. Here a number of well-established AFL-CIO and independent unions have organized over 300,000 of the 370,000 persons in the various clerical occupations found in the post office. The membership of the National Federation of Federal Employees (90,000) and the American Federation of Government Employees (50,000) is mainly concentrated among the remaining 465,000 office workers in the federal establishment.[7] The Government and Civic Employees Organizing Committee also functions in this field but has only a few thousand federal white-collar workers.

A high proportion of federal clerical employees work in large offices or for large departments or agencies. Nearly 20 percent are in Washington, and many of the rest are in federal office buildings in the larger cities.

In the state and local field, with one quarter of a million clerical employees, the most powerful national union is the American Federation of State, County and Municipal Workers, with an estimated 30,000 office employees. The Government and Civic Employees Organizing Committee has about 15,000. Other local or state groups, such as the Federation of State, City, and Town Employees (Massachusetts), have an estimated total of 100,000 members. Some of these are relatively weak organizations. The two national unions in this field organize both manual and clerical employees. In the larger cities and the state capitals, where the greater part of such workers are to be found, there are sizable concentrations.

Nonprofit institutions and membership organizations. The jurisdiction of the Government and Civic Employees Organizing Committee also includes nonprofit civic, educational, and welfare organizations and membership institutions. There are about 275,000 clerical employees in these areas. Another 200,000 are in the medical and health services, but it is not known what part are in hospital and public health services and what part are employed by individual physicians. The GCEOC has made little headway as yet. Many of the institutions, such as state universities, are large and employ sizable clerical staffs.

Retail and wholesale trade. Most of the small amount of organization which has taken place among the 800,000 clerical workers in retailing has been accounted for by the retail unions, particularly in department stores. This will be considered in the discussion of sales employees below. (At this point, it may be noted that the one union with office employees in nongovernmental fields as its jurisdiction, the Office Employees International Union, is not a significant factor either among retail clerical employees or in other areas. It has only about 40,000 members.)

In wholesaling, unionism of the 400,000 clerical employees has been negligible. Probably the most significant effort has been that of the Distributive, Processing and Office Workers Union (now a part of the Retail, Wholesale, and Department Store Union) which organized a host of small firms in some New York wholesale districts. However, only a small dent in the wholesale industry—scattered over many cities and composed typically of small firms—has been made. Although firms are usually small, a large part of wholesaling is concentrated in crowded districts in the larger cities. The operations of several other unions, for example, the International Brotherhood of Teamsters, involve the wholesale field, and undoubtedly these unions have picked up small numbers of office workers.

Manufacturing. In recent years, a start of some significance has been made in unionization of the 1.6 million clerical employees (55 percent female) in manufacturing. Some industrial unions achieved considerable success when they turned their attention to the offices in or near the plants where they had organized wage earners. The United Auto Workers, for example, claims 100,000 white-collar employees and the United Steel Workers, about 70,000. Other unions which have smaller numbers of clerical employees are the International Union of Electrical Workers, the International Brotherhood of Electrical Workers, the Oil, Chemical and Atomic Workers International Union, and the United Rubber Workers. All told, including those in local independent unions, an estimated 275,000 office workers in manufacturing are union members.

The possibilities for industrial unions to organize the clerical staffs of manufacturing concerns diminish sharply, of course, in the case of headquarters offices located in the downtown sections of large cities. Information on the number of employees in these separate administrative offices is lacking, but there is considerable concentration of employment in manufacturing. In 1951, one half of total manufacturing employment was in 1,850 firms with 1,000 or more employees.[8] Assuming that one half of all clerical employees also worked for this group of firms (a conservative assumption), there is indicated an average of 435 per firm. The clerical staffs actually range from about 100 for the smallest firms in this group to several tens of thousands for the largest. The size of individual work units is, of course, smaller. Most of the presently organized office employees in manufacturing are with large firms.

Banking and other finance. Five eighths of the work force in this field is comprised of clerical employees. Organization among the lightly under 400,000 office workers (almost two thirds female), however, is negligible. The Office Employees International Union has been unsuccessful in most of its attempts, and the United Office and Professional Workers of America, a former CIO affiliate which also operated in this field, is now defunct. Probably less than a dozen banks (some of these union-owned) are under contract. An affiliate of the OEIU, the United Financial Employees, has a membership of about 1,500 among sections of the clerical staffs of the New York Stock, American Stock, and Cotton Exchanges. Brokerage and other financial houses, with perhaps isolated exceptions, are not organized. In banking (more than two thirds of the total field), much of the employment is in large units, as indicated by the fact that the 100 largest banks in 1951 held 46.4 percent of the country's deposits.[9] There are also many large offices in brokerage; these tend to be concentrated in the financial districts of large cities.

Insurance and real estate. The 400,000 office workers (84 percent female) in insurance and real estate make up almost one third of the work force in this field. Few are unionized. In insurance (where about two thirds of this total is located) there are unions concerned with industrial life insurance agents. Only one of the two national unions in the field, the Insurance Workers of America, has expressed an interest in the clerical force, but results have yet to be obtained. There is no activity in real estate.

Large companies dominate the insurance field, and home offices of the leading firms have clerical staffs running into the thousands. For instance, in life insurance (less than half of the total insurance field), the four leading companies in 1953 held 45 percent of all life insurance in force. The clerical force in life insurance is estimated to be 120,000, of whom two thirds are in home offices.

Downtown business areas. The major segments of clerical employment have been discussed. Most of the clerical employees in the smaller areas not covered are office employees of private firms and presumably fall under the jurisdiction of the Office Employees International Union. As already indicated, this union has made little progress in its vast jurisdiction.

Unionism in the clerical field has been surveyed according to the industry in which the employees are located. Another way of looking at the organizational problem is to consider the fact that very large numbers of office employees from the various industrial sectors are located in close physical proximity in the downtown areas of

large cities. While no exact figures are available, it is clear tha·
in these areas there are concentrated a multitude of large and smal·
offices, which give employment to thousands of clerical workers·
Further advances in unionization of clerical workers means, t·
a large extent, organization in these areas. As yet, there has bee·
little penetration. The concentration in these areas suggests som·
form of over-all attack, rather than individual, piecemeal campaign·
aimed at clerical workers in specific business categories. However·
the feasibility of such an approach has yet to be established.

It is probably even less feasible at present to organize the man·
clerical employees in small offices in the outlying sections of larg·
cities or in the smaller cities. Some may be picked up by othe·
unions incidentally to a campaign against an establishment—fo·
example, the cashier of a restaurant by the Hotel and Restaurant
Employees—but there seems little reward in a drive aimed specifically at these scattered clerical employees.

SALES EMPLOYEES

Over 3.4 million out of a total of more than 4 million sales workers
in 1950 may be included within the union potential. Nearly 65 percent are employed in the large retail trade sector. Other important
groups of sales employees are in wholesale trade, manufacturing,
and insurance. Women make up 35 percent of the total.

Retail sales employees.[10] Some 2.2 million sales employees,[11]
almost one-half female, are the dominant occupational group in the
complex network of stores which is spread over the country. Chief
union targets (mainly in large cities) have been department stores;
chain stores, particularly in the food field; and recently, mail-order
houses. Two unions consider the entire retail field as their jurisdiction: the Retail Clerks International Association and the Retail,
Wholesale and Department Store Union. These unions attempt to
organize both selling and nonselling employees, but they are limited,
especially the RCIA, by claims of other unions. These include the
various skilled crafts unions, the Building Service Employees International Union, the International Brotherhood of Teamsters, and
the OEIU. Since the OEIU lacks power, clerical employees as well
as sales employees are often the target of the retail unions, particularly in department stores. (Clerical employees may amount to as
much as 20 percent of the total force in a large department store.)
The RCIA has organized about 250,000 white-collar workers, most

of them sales workers but including clerical employees also. An estimated 60,000 retail selling (and clerical) employees are members of RWDSU. The International Brotherhood of Teamsters, already powerful in the retail field through its control of delivery services, has contracts for 15,000 Montgomery Ward employees, mainly in mail-order houses but also including store employees. Clerical workers are the predominant group in the mail-order operation. Of less importance with respect to retail white-collar employees are: the Amalgamated Meat Cutters, which has tried to organize food-store workers other than butchers in some areas; the Building Service Employees, which has several thousand selling employees in Chicago; and the Amalgamated Clothing Workers of America, which has a few thousand members in Detroit clothing stores.

More than half of the membership of the RCIA is in the food-store field, particularly chain supermarkets. About one fifth is estimated to be in department stores, and the remainder is in smaller stores, chiefly apparel shops but also drug stores and variety stores. About one half of the RWDSU's retail membership is in department stores. The rest is divided among the apparel, drug, variety, and food fields. Geographically, the RCIA has the main base of its strength in the West in the San Francisco and Seattle region; it also has strong centers in large Eastern cities, such as New York, Boston, Pittsburgh, and Philadelphia; while in the Midwest, its strength is more scattered. New York City is the main base of the RWDSU; most of the rest of its strength is spread among several other leading Eastern cities. There is very little retail unionism in the South. With a few exceptions (applying mainly to the RCIA), unionism among retail sales and clerical employees is confined to the larger cities.

In 1951, there were 350 retail firms with 1,000 or more employees each, a total of 1,669,000 employees.[12] It is estimated that sales and clerical personnel account for about 50 percent of this total. In the general merchandise field—which includes department stores, variety stores, and mail-order houses—there were 60 firms with 1,000 or more employees, a total of 949,000 workers. In the food field, 50 firms of this size had 324,000 employees.[13] Another measure of concentration in retailing is obtained from a compilation of the 100 largest retail corporations in 1950. These included firms with single stores, large chains in a variety of lines, and mail-order houses (including their store outlets). These companies operated 26,907 stores and furnished employment to 1,140,000 persons.[14] Concentration in the department store field is indicated by figures from the 1948 business census. In that year, there were 1,211 department stores with 100 or more employees, which employed 767,000 persons, or an average of 633 employees per store.[15]

Sales employees in wholesaling and manufacturing. There are some 385,000 sales employees in the wholesale trades and about 310,000 in manufacturing. Both of these sectors, by and large, are unorganized. There are some instances of organization in the wholesale field, e.g., wholesale liquor salesmen by the Distillery, Rectifying, and Wine Workers' International Union and salesmen in parts of the New York wholesale district by District 65 (now part of the RWDSU), which has organized many firms in this area. But the number is few, and there is even less to be said for the manufacturing field.

While no exact figures are available, this is a field in which there are relatively few large work units. Further, the sales staff is likely to be scattered over a large territory.

Insurance agents. There are about 250,000 insurance agents. Unionism so far has developed in one branch of this field—among industrial life insurance agents, who constitute over half (90,000–95,000) of the total force of 175,000 life insurance agents. The two major unions in this area are the Insurance Workers of America, with about 14,000 members, and the Insurance Agents International Union, with 20,000 members. The bulk of this membership is in the larger insurance companies. The International Union of Life Insurance Agents bargains for some 3,000 members in Minnesota, Wisconsin, and Ohio. Organization is centered mainly in cities of medium and large size, where big forces of agents are located.

PROFESSIONAL AND TECHNICAL EMPLOYEES

The 1950 census listed nearly 5 million professional and technical (or semiprofessional) persons. In this category some 3.9 million employees may be regarded as within the union potential. The largest professional group, totaling well over a million persons, is made up of schoolteachers. Engineers and nurses, each numbering about a half million, constitute the next largest groups. The professional field is marked, of course, by a considerable variety of distinct occupations.

Entertainment and musicians. Except for a fringe of the less desirable jobs, these occupations are close to 100 percent organized. The American Federation of Musicians has about 240,000 members. The Associated Actors and Artistes of America, a federation of entertainment unions, has 36,000 members.

Airline pilots. Most commercial airline pilots, of whom there are some 9,000, are members of the Air Line Pilots Association. The pilots have also organized the airline stewardesses in the affiliated Air Line Stewards and Stewardesses Association.

Teachers. In 1950, 82 percent of the 1,127,000 schoolteachers in the nation were employed by governments. About three quarters of the teaching force is female. The major union in this field is the American Federation of Teachers, which has 47,000 members. There are a few thousand teachers in independent local unions. The Government and Civic Employees Organizing Committee also operates among teachers, but so far has accomplished little.

Even if only the urban part of this jurisdiction is considered, it remains a large one. It is estimated that in 1955 there were upwards of 450,000 public schoolteachers in cities 10,000 and over in size. The number of teachers per school system runs from about sixty in the smaller communities in this group to several tens of thousands in New York City. Most of the presently organized teachers are in large cities.

Engineers, scientists, architects, draftsmen, and technicians. Of the approximately 850,000 salaried personnel in the technical fields —over 500,000 engineers, 150,000 draftsmen and designers, 100,000 technicians, more than 70,000 chemists, and 15,000 architects— only an estimated 50,000 are union members. The Engineers and Scientists of America, composed of groups of engineers or scientists who have obtained bargaining rights with their respective companies, numbers about 25,000 members. Eleven of the affiliated groups represent bargaining units in corporations (or in two cases, government agencies) which contain 1,000 to 5,000 technical personnel each. Several thousand more engineers, scientists, and technicians are in local, nonaffiliated groups.

The American Federation of Technical Engineers has close to 10,000 members. These are mainly concentrated in defense industries—airplane plants, shipyards, electrical equipment firms—and in federal, state, and local government units. The majority of members are technicians, subprofessionals, and lower-paid professionals. That part of the federation's strength which is located in the construction field (mainly government employees) is subject to a high rate of turnover, since the work force is scattered with the completion of a construction project.

About 5,000 in engineering and technical occupations are estimated to be scattered among industrial unions in the auto, steel, aircraft, electrical equipment, and other industries. Several thousand are also scattered among various craft unions, including the International Association of Machinists. Some engineers and scientists employed by the federal government are members of the National Federation of Federal Employees.

Over 90 percent of this occupational sector is male. About one sixth is in government employment. While no precise figures are available as to the distribution of these employees, staffs of several hundred to several thousand are common among the larger corporations in manufacturing, mining, transportation, communication, other utilities, and in the growing research firms, as well as in government agencies.

Newspaper reporters and editors. A strong union, the American Newspaper Guild, has established a firm basis of unionization in the journalism profession. The Guild, with 26,000 members, has bargaining units in many of the large and medium-sized newspapers across the country and with the major press services. It holds about 175 contracts. It has also started to organize among the other white-collar employees on newspapers—those in the advertising, circulation, and business departments. Of minor influence in newspapers are a few federal locals chartered by the AFL.

The 1950 census listed 91,000 editors and reporters, a little over two thirds of whom were male. It is impossible to determine how many of these are scattered among the many daily and weekly newspapers which cover the smaller communities of the country. In 1950, there were 1,785 daily newspapers. While the ANG is well established, it clearly still has a sizable part of its jurisdiction to organize, even if only medium and large cities are considered.

Social workers. The 1950 census listed 76,000 social workers, a little over two thirds of whom are female. Perhaps one out of eight are union members. These are scattered among several organizations. The Government and Civic Employees Organizing Committee has about 3,500, mainly in New York. The American Federation of State, County and Municipal Employees claims 3,500 members in its social-service locals. The American Federation of Government Employees and the National Federation of Federal Employees probably together account for another 1,000. Another 2,000 or 3,000 social workers, remnants of the large groups once organized by the United Office and Professional Workers of America and the United Public Workers—both now nonexistent—are in independent locals or have been picked up by other unions. At present, there is little organizing activity going on among social workers.

Sixty percent of the members of this profession are government employees. Although there are government and private agencies which employ more than 100 social workers in single cities, the majority work in small units. The organization which has taken place has been in the large urban centers, with New York accounting for the greatest number.

Other professions. The Authors League of America, Inc. has 7,000 members divided among five guilds: Authors, Dramatists, Screen Writers, Radio Writers, and Television Writers. Some 16,000 authors are listed in the 1950 census.

In a larger professional group, the pharmacists, almost half of the total of 89,000 are salaried employees. A number of these, but no more than a few thousand, have been organized by the retail unions (RCIA and RWDSU).

There are a number of other relatively small professional or technical occupations, e.g., librarians (56,000), medical or dental technicians (78,000), dietitians and nutritionists (23,000), etc., about whom little can be said. To some extent, members of these groups would be picked up by unions organizing in the firms or institutions where they were employed. A large proportion of the medical technicians and dietitians, for instance, are found in hospitals, part of the jurisdiction of the GCEOC. However, little organizing has been accomplished as yet in hospitals.

Professional nurses (400,000 graduates and 75,000 students) constitute a sizable group in which there appears to be no union activity. Hospitals and public health agencies (both public and private) are the largest employers in this field, and staffs per work unit are often sizable. Another large group of professional employees among whom there has been scarcely any union activity is the accountants. Some 340,000 (out of a total of about 380,000) accountants are salaried employees. A little more than one out of six is employed by government units. While there are some firms with large staffs of accountants, the group generally is widely distributed among private firms and government departments.

FOREMEN

Of the various white-collar groups, the first-line foremen or super-visors are undoubtedly the most remote from the union movement, although in Europe the unionization of lower levels of supervision is widespread. The census lists 853,000 foremen in manufacturing, construction, railroads and other transportation, and public utilities. Five hundred thousand of these foremen are in manufacturing. Foreman unionization is common in the crafts: for example, in the printing, building, and metal trades the pattern traditionally is to include foremen in the bargaining unit with the men they supervise. In manufacturing, however, unionism among foremen is a recent phenomenon. The Foreman's Association of America has 22,000 members, with its main strength in the Detroit region. In recent years, it has undertaken little organizing activity.

In large companies in manufacturing, mining, transportation, and public utilities, staffs of foremen run from several hundred to several thousand per company.

SUMMARY AND OBSERVATIONS

The early sections of this paper set forth data on the growth of the union movement which included as variables real membership and union potential in addition to actual membership. Real mem-bership rose about 400 percent over the 1900 to 1950 period, a much smaller increase than that of actual membership, 1,400 percent. The real membership figure, reflecting changes in the union po-tential, is in many respects a more realistic measure of the per-formance of organized labor over this period. The level of real membership in 1950, 31 percent, indicates the existence of a sub-stantial labor movement but one with a considerable challenge yet facing it.

The union potential, that section of the work force which is the field for action of unionism, comprised about one half of the 1900 work force; the proportion had risen to 72.5 percent fifty years later. The growth of this sector is a reflection of the secular trend toward greater wage and salary employment, a trend which itself is related to the continued industrialization and urbanization of the country. However, the union potential is already so large that it is not likely to grow much larger; or to look at it from the other side, the core of the nonunionizable group, managers and proprietors, is not likely to be a much smaller part of the work force than it is now. Over the next few decades then, the union potential probably will not reach higher than 80 percent of the work force. Four out of five persons in the labor force represents, of course, a tremendous field for the operation of the union movement. To what extent the union movement will be able to develop the unorganized parts of this field remains to be seen.

One of the major areas of the union potential—one in which organization has lagged—is white-collar employment. The rapid growth of this segment of the work force is an important aspect of the evolution of the American economy, in which a shift has occurred from a numerical preponderance of nonorganizable groups (particularly agrarian proprietors) to a preponderance of occupations involving a dependent employee status. Although until recently the growth of white-collar employment has been viewed dubiously by most trade unionists, the sheer weight exerted by increasing numbers has been one factor in reminding these union leaders that white-collar employees hold in common with wage earners the status of dependent employees. By 1950, over one third of the union potential, one quarter of the work force, was white-collar employees. If previous trends continued, the relative importance of the white-collar sector might be even greater in the not-too-distant future.

Another factor leading to increased interest by organized labor in the white-collar field has been the considerable advance of unionism in this field in the last two decades. A significant union base has been established among white-collar employees. It is estimated that in 1953 a total of 2.75 million white-collar employees were union members, representing about 17 percent of the estimated potential. The extent of unionism in white-collar occupations varies greatly, however. A few fields are almost completely organized or have well-established union organizations capable of carrying out whatever task remains. Other areas, large and small, have weak unions, which at present appear unable to make much headway. Still other sectors, including large numbers of workers, have no union apparatus at all. The last two groups include the greater part of the white-collar field.

Although a great number of occupations are lumped together under the term, "white collar," they obviously constitute an extremely heterogeneous lot. The lack of uniformity in unionization is, to a considerable extent, a reflection of this heterogeneity. The attempt to unionize is further confused by the fact that a large section, particularly general office employees (the bulk of the clerical force) and to a lesser extent some of the professional occupations, are cross-industry occupations. As a result, the union attack is weakened, since either principle of organization—by industry or by occupation—has serious disadvantages.

It is questionable whether the present union apparatus, impressive as it may be compared with twenty years ago, is capable of securing more than small gains. While the effects of steady, moderate gains should not be discounted, this process implies little change in the basic situation for a number of years.

The organizing job which remains in the white-collar field largely involves groups which are spread geographically over the nation, though concentrated to some extent in metropolitan areas. Competition in the labor market for these groups, and with respect to the products or services of the firms which employ them, is essentially local. Most of retailing, for example, has to be located close to the consuming public, and the labor market for retail sales and clerical employees is the metropolitan area. Thus the economic interests of retail employees are distinctly local. Organized retail employees in one city have little reason in terms of these interests to support union campaigns in another city. This element of localism and isolation also applies to teaching, though in ways specific to the occupation and with somewhat less strength, probably, than in retailing. It also is true with respect to most office workers, the bulk of the clerical group. Many of these are employed by industries in which, as in retailing, the product or service must be produced and distributed locally. As for firms whose products compete on the national market, the differences in clerical salaries among cities rarely is an important element in location. With few exceptions, the labor market for clerical employees is local.

The isolation (in terms of competitive economic pressures) of the local concentrations of these large white-collar groups makes it difficult for union leaders to arouse enthusiastic support for expensive organizing campaigns in other areas. Unless the unorganized communities embark on unionism through their own efforts, or large-scale resources for organizing appear from some outside source, the prospect for much of white-collar unionism would appear, at best, to be the slow, grinding work of organizing city by city.

Turning now to another aspect, it is worth noting some recent technological trends which affect the white-collar occupations. The development of electronic data-processing machines is likely to reduce the size of the office staffs attached to giant corporations. Electronic systems are being introduced in manufacturing, electric utilities, telephones, railroads, banks, insurance, and retailing. Clerical workers unionized by the UAW, USW, IUE, and other industrial unions, and by the Brotherhood of Railway Clerks and the Communications Workers of America are likely to be among those early affected by this trend. In the engineering and scientific fields, on the other hand, the advance of technology and the growth of research will mean greater employment and larger staffs of technical personnel. To some extent, these trends will also result in a greater volume of paper work, somewhat counteracting the anticipated effect of the electronic office systems. In retailing, the spread of self-service operation will tend to reduce the ratio of selling to nonselling employees.

The merger of the two trade union federations raises the possibility of more effective union organizing. The conflicts of dual unionism have been harmful to the growth of organization in a number of white-collar fields. Union leaders have also raised the possibility that one of the results of the merger may be a large-scale organizing campaign in the white-collar sector. Whether this will come about, what resources would be assigned, what tactics would be adopted, what white-collar areas would be targets, and what results might be expected are all questions whose answers at present lie in the realm of speculation.

NOTES

1. Compare the following by Leo Wolman: *Ebb and Flow in Trade Unionism* (New York: National Bureau of Economic Research, 1936), pp. 110–116; *The Growth of American Trade Unions, 1880–1923* (New York: National Bureau of Economic Research, 1924), pp. 82–86; and "The Extent of Labor Organization in the United States in 1910," *Quarterly Journal of Economics,* Vol. 30, May 1916, pp. 501–504.

2. Irving Bernstein, "The Growth of American Unions," *American Economic Review,* Vol. 44, June 1954, p. 302.

3. It may be asked to what extent the census years correspond with the highs and lows of the annual union membership series. Wolman's series begins in 1897 with 447,000 members. The years 1900 and 1910 fall within a period of union growth (with minor dips in only a few years) which culminated in a peak at 1920. There followed a sharp decline in the early twenties, which continued at a more moderate rate through 1930 to reach a low of 2,973,000 in 1933. From 1934 through 1940, there occurred the expansion of the New Deal and war periods. A small decline in 1950 was the first to inter-

rupt the continuous growth since 1934. For a series from 1897 to 1953, see *ibid.*, pp. 303–304.

4. In 1950, 1.65 million self-employed and unpaid family workers were deducted.

5. Most of the data on white-collar unionism in this section is drawn from the findings of the White-Collar Unionism Research Project of the Industrial Relations Center of the University of Chicago. The data on white-collar membership in unions were gathered as follows: questionnaires were sent to all unions in the Bureau of Labor Statistics *Directory* for which there was the slightest possibility of white-collar membership; there was additional correspondence with respondents when necessary; a number of personal investigations were undertaken by the staff; the usual sources, such as convention proceedings and union newspapers, were consulted; and data from the various sources were cross-checked and evaluated. For further material in this field, see forthcoming volumes by Robert K. Burns and Jay Tabb, "White-Collar Unionism," and "The Salaried Employee and Unionism," and by Robert K. Burns and Raulston G. Zundel, "Unionism in Retailing."

6. U. S. Bureau of the Census, *U. S. Census of Population:* 1950, Vol. 2, *Characteristics of the Population,* Part I, Chapter C (Washington: G.P.O., 1953), Tables 124, 128, and 134.

7. This is the census figure for 1950. Since then clerical employment has risen by well over 100,000. See U. S. Civil Service Commission, *Pay Structure of the Federal Civil Service* (annual).

8. Betty C. Churchill, "Size Characteristics of the Business Population," *Survey of Current Business,* Vol. 34, May 1954, p. 23.

9. U. S. Congress, House, A Staff Report to Subcommittee No. 5 of the Committee on the Judiciary, *Bank Mergers and Concentration of Banking Facilities,* 82nd Cong., 2nd Sess., Sept. 17, 1952 (Washington: G.P.O., 1952), p. 29.

10. Recent articles on retail unionism include: Marten S. Estey, "Patterns of Union Membership in the Retail Trades," *Industrial and Labor Relations Review,* Vol. 8, No. 4 (July 1955), pp. 557–564, and "The Strategic Alliance as a Factor in Union Growth," *ibid.,* Vol. 9, No. 1 (October 1955), pp. 41–53; and Raulston G. Zundel, "Conflict and Cooperation among Retail Unions," *Journal of Business,* Vol. 27, October 1954, pp. 301–311.

11. Not including self-employed or unpaid family workers.

12. Churchill, *loc. cit.,* p. 23.

13. *Ibid.*

14. National City Bank of New York, *Monthly Letter on Economic Conditions, Government Finance,* October 1951, p. 115.

15. U. S. Bureau of the Census, *U. S. Census of Business: 1948, Trade Series—Department Stores,* Bulletin No. 3–2 (Washington: G.P.O., 1952), Table 8.

19

The New Deal and After

COMING to power in 1933, after three years of disastrous economic dislocation and human distress, Franklin D. Roosevelt offered the American people a "New Deal." Even today, it is difficult to characterize accurately the New Deal program. Some scholars assert that the early Roosevelt policies, especially those of the storied Hundred Days, foretold the basic purpose of all the major domestic legislation of his presidency. Others argue that the early objectives of Roosevelt's administration were centered upon providing relief and restoring prosperity whereas after 1935, during what these students term the "Second New Deal," reform characterized the most important measures that were adopted. Arthur M. Schlesinger, Jr., has argued more recently, in *The Age of Roosevelt*, that the early New Deal was marked by an optimistic commitment to the philosophy of planning, while a new emphasis on restoration of competition, linked with a policy of deficit spending, characterized the program after 1935.

Another major area of interpretive controversy relates to the long-range impact of the Roosevelt policies. Scholars have reached no consensus as to how fully one may attribute changes in the structure of the American economy since 1933 to New Deal legislation, and to what extent such changes have flowed from other causes. The following selections will help to provide a basis for consideration of these issues.

Probably no area of New Deal policy was marked by so dramatic an admixture of expediency, improvisation, and theory as was fiscal policy. During the last two years of his Presidential administration, Herbert Hoover advocated emergency legislation which, despite its limited scope, involved deficit spending. But during the 1932 campaign, Hoover gradually retreated toward an inflexible orthodox position on the question of government spending. In his last budget message, Hoover implored Congress to "limit expenditures and avoid additional obligations, not only in the interest of the already heavily burdened taxpayer but in the interest of the very integrity of the finances of the Federal Government." * When Roosevelt first took office, he expressed a view on spending similar to Hoover's, but Roosevelt proved ready to set orthodoxy aside in the face of urgent human needs. The continued depression forced Roosevelt's administration to plan large budgetary deficits; and meanwhile, in government and academic circles, there developed a new interest in planned "pump-priming" as a temporary measure designed to stimulate private spending. There was renewed interest as well in a more sweeping doctrine, that of "compensatory spending," according to which government should stimulate the economy by deficit expenditures during depressions, while cutbacks of public spending in expansionary periods would restore budgetary stability and slow excessively rapid economic growth. However, not until John Maynard Keynes published his classic *General Theory of Employment, Interest and Money* in 1936 did the doctrine begin to gain wide currency as part of a highly developed economic theory. In the first selection below, Lewis Kimmel assesses the effects on fiscal policy of the New Deal's simultaneous pursuit of recovery and reform objectives, against a background of widely held popular views of budgetary deficits.

In the second selection, Thomas Cochran takes a broad view of the long-range impact of the New Deal, considering the relations of business and the public. There is little question that business spokesmen greeted many of the New Deal measures, particularly after 1935, with adamant hostility. But how accurate is Cochran's view that Roosevelt's rhetoric was more radical than his programs? And if, as Cochran avers, the New Deal created a new partnership between government and business, is he correct in his assertion that by the late 1940's the public and even business itself had come to accept this new relationship?

* Quoted in Arthur E. Burns and Donald S. Watson: *Government Spending and Economic Expansion* (Washington, 1940), pp. 36–37.

KEYNESIAN THEORY, PUBLIC OPINION, AND THE NEW DEAL

Lewis H. Kimmel

Keynes' theory had an immediate impact on economic thought. To numerous economists—especially members of the younger generation —who found important elements of traditional doctrine unacceptable, it provided both a rallying ground and a basing point for the analysis of economic problems. The reasons for the great appeal of Keynesian economics have been well stated by J. M. Clark. It "takes hold of the problem which the interwar experience drove home deep in the feelings of mankind as the major sickness of Western economic society, and it does so with an analysis that commands standing as objectively scientific, centering in a formula of the way in which the economic mechanism operates, the analysis being translatable into statistically observable quantities." [1]

Acceptance of Keynes' theory was by no means instantaneous. Some economists found the exposition confusing. Others regarded Keynes' theory with skepticism because they felt that the suggested policy tended to establish too strong a presumption in favor of governmental spending. Some economists and numerous other people believed any marked increase in public expenditures would result in a qualitative deterioration of the national income or would be undesirable on social grounds. [2]

Nevertheless, by 1940 there were few economists whose thinking was not influenced in some degree by Keynes' theory of how the economy functions. Literally "hundreds of economists and government policy planners had come . . . to accept the Keynesian analysis as the new orthodoxy." [3] Even those economists who had held that economic theory, at least in its broad outlines, was virtually complete were compelled to re-examine received doctrine and the underlying premises. Though the reactions to Keynes' theory covered the widest

Reprinted from Lewis H. Kimmel: *Federal Budget and Fiscal Policy, 1789–1958* (Washington: The Brookings Institution, 1959), pp. 213–28. By permission of The Brookings Institution. The above title supplied by the editor.

possible range, *The General Theory* had not been available for many months before one fact was quite evident. Economics would never be the same again.

THE THEORIES AND BUDGET POLICY OF THE 1930'S

At no time during the period 1933–1937 was the compensatory fiscal theory officially accepted as a basis for public policy. Relief and other emergency needs . . . were the dominant influence during these years. It was the urgency of these needs that compelled the temporary abandonment of the annually balanced budget as a policy goal. They did not lead to the immediate adoption of an alternative theory as a guide for policy. If for no other reason, the reluctance of the administration to accept an alternative theory could be justified on the basis of the maxim that public policy should not run too far ahead of, or diverge too greatly from, public opinion.[4] But there was a more compelling reason. Up to 1937 President Roosevelt himself believed in a balanced budget.[5]

When in 1933–1934 the President and other officials took the position that large-scale loan-financed federal expenditures were required to restore the economy to a sound condition, they were in effect advocating the pump-priming approach to recovery. For the longer run no departure from traditional budget policy was contemplated. It was merely planned to use the federal credit as the cornerstone in laying the foundation for recovery; a "definitely balanced budget for the third year of recovery" was part of the plan. From the standpoint of the pump-priming theory, a period of something like three years was perhaps unduly long for the priming operation. In official circles, however, the emergency program was viewed as a continuing or composite operation and, to this extent, it met the requirements of the theory.

The basic assumption underlying pump priming is that private investment can be stimulated to a point where deficit financing can be discontinued. Bridging the gap between deficit spending and private investment assumes the existence of a resilient economy capable of response to a priming operation. To many thoughtful students it seemed that a basic need was to see that any operational or structural barriers impeding an independent revival of private investment were removed or minimized. Little was done in this direction. In the opinion of some observers, the pursuit of conflicting recovery and reform objectives lessened the possibility that the transition from deficit spending to adequate private investment would be achieved.[6]

Two examples will suffice. First, the investigations of investment methods and practices, together with the legislation enacted in 1933 and 1934, unsettled the investment climate.[7] That reforms were necessary is recognized, but it was not so much the reforms as the zeal of the reformers that had an unsettling influence.[8] Second, in formulating tax policy, little or no consideration was given to the impact of the tax structure on investment. Taxes on investment income became heavier than at any time after World War I. Sight was lost of the fact that high income taxes may act as a deterrent to investment—that "taxation, especially taxation of income, shifts the odds against the risk taker." [9]

A certain amount of working at cross purposes was doubtless inevitable, as long as the administration held to the view that recovery and reform could be pursued simultaneously.[10] That these two goals required radically different approaches was emphasized by J. M. Keynes, among others. "For the first, speed and quick results are essential. The second may be urgent too, but haste will be injurious, and the wisdom of long-range purpose is more necessary than immediate achievement. It will be through raising high the prestige of your administration by success in short-range recovery that you will have the driving force to accomplish long-range reform." [11] This advice was not heeded.

It would be easy to overemphasize the role played by the pump-priming philosophy during Roosevelt's first term. Pump priming "was not one of the principal methods relied on to bring about recovery. Monetary experiments and the controls of production and competition in the NRA and AAA were the major recovery programs." [12] In this sense, pump priming was not even a secondary "method" of bringing about recovery. Realistically viewed, the pump-priming doctrine merely provided theoretical justification for federal expenditures in excess of revenues under adverse economic conditions. The deficits incurred were "more the unintentional results of policies designed to give direct relief to farmers, home owners, business, and unemployed workers, than the conscious aim of a recovery policy through deficit spending." [13]

Prior to the recession of 1937–1938 whatever influence the pump-priming and compensatory fiscal theories may have had on policy was indirect. Though these ideas were advanced in informal discussions, at no time was any group or committee assigned the task of ascertaining how the newer budget theories might be implemented. The most that can be said is that the relief and recovery programs had pump-priming overtones, and that officially a balanced budget remained the goal of fiscal policy—though a deferred one.

It was not until after the recession of 1937–1938 set in that a comprehensive recovery program was formulated and discussed by a top government committee on monetary and fiscal policy. Referring to the work of this committee, Colm states that its program "was, broadly speaking, in line with Keynes' recommendations for a national investment policy." [14] Members of the committee were well grounded in Keynes' theory and regarded his policy recommendations favorably. In turn, the efforts of the committee strongly influenced the President's message of April 14, 1938. [15]

For the first time, there was a clear affirmation that the federal government should do whatever is necessary to bring the national income to a tolerable level of about $80 billion. It was pointed out that "today's purchasing power—the citizens' income of today—is not sufficient to drive the economic system at higher speed." The President then stated: "Responsibility of government requires us at this time to supplement the normal processes and in so supplementing them to make sure that the addition is adequate." [16]

The idea that the federal government should endeavor to bring the national income to a high level and then do whatever was necessary to maintain a suitable growth trend was not accepted by the Congress. Though the appropriations requested in April 1938 were approved, there is no evidence that the Congress had any real interest in any theory of deficit finance or the new concept of public investment. The combined executive and congressional effort was predicated on the assumption that the unemployment problem was essentially a cyclical problem. It was hoped that in time the economy would go forward without the aid of deficit spending. In a sense, this was equivalent to a denial of the validity of the stagnation thesis, which assumed that the problem was primarily a secular one and that deficit finance would be necessary on a continuing basis, except in unusual circumstances.

Only in retrospect is it possible to say that the federal program of 1938–1940 conformed with any theory. Thus viewed, the entire effort might appropriately be classified under pump priming. In taking this position, one author emphasizes both the size of the program and the phraseology of the special message of April 14, 1938. [17] Perhaps the best way of putting the matter is that the program, as proposed in April 1938, was a work relief program with pump-priming and compensatory fiscal overtones. The program in its entirety was justified by the President in the budget messages of January 1939 and January 1940 on the basis of what we have called the optimistic version of the compensatory fiscal theory. It was appraised by some economists who accepted the stagnation thesis and recommended permanent deficit financing (public investment) as a solution.[18] But no one took the position that it represented a full-fledged commitment to incur more or less continuous deficits if they should appear necessary in order to keep the economy operating at or near full employment.

In the period 1938–1940 there was a fairly pronounced upward trend in business activity and income payments. However, the large volume of unemployment at the middle of 1940, when the defense program was instituted, indicated that the economic problem was far from solved. To the advocates of compensatory fiscal policy the reason was obvious. As a nation, we had not adopted a real expansionist program.[19] It was because of inadequate public spending that employment and national income remained at unsatisfactory levels. In brief, neither the new aim of fiscal policy—ensuring the full employment of the factors of production—nor Keynesian theory with which it is closely allied had been fully accepted.[20]

The foregoing discussion does not imply that the federal spending programs of the 1930's were not justified. Under the conditions of 1933–1934 and 1937–1938 large-scale relief and recovery expenditures were inevitable.[21] Programs such as those of the Civil Works Administration not only mitigated the worst consequences of unemployment; they also had a stimulative effect on the economy. A marked rise in employment occurred during Roosevelt's first term, and again in 1938–1939.[22] Perhaps the only important basis for criticism was that recovery and reform objectives were pursued at the same time. Though they were a response to the challenge of popular discontent, the reform measures "were not dictated by the emergency and might have been imposed later and in more leisurely fashion." [23]

THE PUBLIC VIEW ON DEFICITS AND FISCAL POLICY

In the early 1930's the balanced budget idea remained firmly embedded in the social fabric. For almost a century and a half an annually balanced federal budget had been equated with fiscal solvency and sound finance. In the depth of the depression a majority of citizens who had any interest in governmental finance continued to have an "almost instinctive and intuitive belief in the sanctity of balanced budgets." [24] Whatever direction budget and fiscal policy might take, it was apparent that the balanced budget philosophy would not soon disappear as a social force.

When in the summer and autumn of 1933 it became clear that for a few years no attempt would be made to balance the budget, the reaction was immediate. Senator Dickinson was reflecting an influential segment of public opinion when he said that the government "is overwhelmed with debt." Spending for relief and recovery that resulted in substantial deficits was not an appropriate policy for the times. "Instead of putting our financial house in order, we are facing the other way by adding billions of debt to the already crushing load." The debt outstanding plus present commitments and authorizations would mean a debt of "approximately $30 billion, a peak of all time, and a load that would break the back of the nation." The proper course is to return to "sane living as a government as well as a people." [25]

A return to normalcy in public finance was urgently required, according to one publicist who endeavored to influence public opinion. The "fantastic spending of the money of the people" by the Democratic Congress was one of the "powerful issues for the opponents of the New Deal." We are not "a normal country." The abnormality arose because of attempts at planning and the prevailing levels of spending and taxes. The real issue was said to be taxes, which the people understand more readily than public spending. "Taxes are a necessary and inevitable concomitant of government, and the people are educated to pay them, grudgingly, perhaps; or pay them, if possible, to escape penalties the laws have set for nonpayers. Taxes are the bane of every country and every people, but there they are, and there is no escaping them." [26]

The fear of unbalanced budgets was based in part on the belief that they would lead to inflation. According to the traditional view, a balanced budget was both a weapon against depression and a guarantee against inflation. It is a powerful anti-depression weapon because "it gives absolute security to the currency. Thus it develops an atmosphere of confidence in which capital, with a pent-up demand for improvements and expansion, can reasonably seek investment." [27] Unbalanced budgets inevitably lead to inflation. "History demonstrates without exception that whenever a government continuously spends more than it takes in the social consequences are tragic." The American colonies, it was pointed out, had destroyed their currency and impoverished their people, and France had experienced an extreme inflation about the same time. The Civil War inflation in the United States and the post-World War I inflation in France were other outstanding examples. The reason for the universal experience resides in two powers of government. "The first is the power to appropriate and to expend money. The second is the power to manufacture money." [28]

The fate of the Roosevelt administration, it was said, would be determined in large part by whether federal expenditures could be met without an excessive rise in prices. The other major consideration was whether the taxes required to bring the budget into balance could be held within bearable limits. The relief question was "the crux of the federal financial problem." Concrete plans were necessary in order "to deal with the relief problem within the limits of the people's capacity." No one denies "the obligation to protect the unemployed. But more economical methods must plainly be pursued through the return of responsibility to local communities, through tightened administration, and through less expensive methods of relief." [29]

The federal finances, it was asserted, were not being handled in a manner conforming with the traditional virtues of thrift, prudence, and common sense. One author believed that "those traits which are traditionally feminine should be given a chance in our national housekeeping. . . ." These traits are "thrift, carefulness, simple common sense, the ability to face things as they are." Their exercise "would mean that we would get more for our money. . . . The Nation . . . can, if it will, draw upon women for the strength and shrewdness that life has developed in them." [30] These observations are suggestive of the household analogy that had long been used to support the annually balanced budget formula.

The attitudes of the public toward deficit finance thus far considered reflect what was generally regarded as a conservative outlook on federal finance. Though there is no reason to believe that the alleged deficiencies of budget policy weighed heavily on the public at large, any suggestion that these attitudes were found only among an ultra-conservative minority would be unwarranted. For example, in March 1933, Alvin Johnson, a moderate or liberal economist, discussed the perils of excessive debt. "If one re-reads with modern eyes Cicero's and Sallust's analyses of Cataline's following, or the diatribes of the orators preceding the French Revolution, he will agree that the way of excessive debt is, for a state, the way to the Devil." [31]

The apparent inability of the Roosevelt administration to develop a well-rounded budget policy was criticized by people of widely divergent views. Thus, the editors of *The Nation* observed that the failure to formulate a consistent policy was dangerous because it presented an invitation to pressure groups to launch "new raids" on the Treasury. "Billions of the taxpayers' dollars have been handed out to organized groups merely because the Administration was unable to present Congress with a carefully worked-out program." The silver interests were mentioned as an example. "The tragedy is that once the money has been distributed to these pressure groups there is none left for such socially necessary projects as slum clearance, social security, or adequate public-health activities." [32]

The record for the period 1933–1936 supports the charge of inadequate fiscal planning. Yet curiously a major charge against the Roosevelt administration was that the intention was to establish a planned economy. For example, Frank Knox believed that federal deficits would lead to a regimented economy.[33] According to a leading authority on banking, by 1936 we had "already gone beyond the limit, both of taxation and borrowing, that is safe and wise for the nation as a whole." If this limit is to be extended, "we must make up our minds to great changes, both in average consumption or in cost of living and in conditions of employment." [34] These observations were typical of the comments made before and during the election campaign of 1936. They did not go unchallenged.

The opposite tack was taken by Robert H. Jackson, then Assistant Attorney-General in charge of the Tax Division of the Department of Justice. As a nation, we had only begun to draw on our resources. The campaign opens with the cry of "Wolf," and the candidate for Vice President talks of "a rendezvous with a receiver for the Treasury." In pungent language Jackson continued: "Opposition leaders who promise a tight financial policy in loose language and seek to impress the country with their patriotism by slandering the nation's credit are trying to capitalize an honest anxiety which Mr. Willis expresses and many share." [35]

The sharp difference of opinion evidenced by the debate between Willis and Jackson may seem to suggest that there was little unanimity of opinion concerning the consequences of deficit finance and the increase in debt. But Jackson was closely identified with the Roosevelt administration, and his views were far from typical. In 1936 the sheer bulk of the $30 billion debt, together with the fact that it was "the epic obligation of human history," had considerable emotional impact. Yet deficits and the rising public debt were not particularly effective as campaign issues. Those who believed that the federal debt was the greatest of all evils, basing their case on the canons of fiscal orthodoxy, were in the minority.

The opinion most commonly held during the mid-1930's was that continued deficits were undesirable, but large-scale unemployment was intolerable. An increasing number of people, particularly in the middle- and low-income groups, regarded the deficits and the rising federal debt in a spirit of tolerance. This was true of the unemployed and W.P.A. workers in particular. Farmers and others who had been saved from economic disaster by federal programs reacted similarly. There is also reason to believe that the younger generation took a more optimistic view of federal finances than did their elders. To them the large and increasing federal debt did not appear prohibitive if the economy could be set aright.[36] The deficits incurred had not resulted in disaster. If the administration had not succeeded in effecting a full-scale recovery, it had at least faced up to the relief problem and attempted to "shore up" the economy.

Yet to even a casual observer it was apparent that the balanced-budget rationale and the belief that in time of peace a rising public debt was an evil remained firmly embedded in our financial folklore. To numerous persons in all strata of society the balanced budget idea remained a basic tenet of what is perhaps the best described as dogmatic financial orthodoxy.[37] At no time during the 1930's could it be said that deficit finance had attained popularity in itself. The popularity of the Roosevelt administration, as shown by the 1936 election, did not mean that unbalanced budgets were both acceptable and popular among the people generally. To the extent that deficit finance was accepted by the public, it was for the most part regarded with misgivings. The consequences, it was believed, were less objectionable than those that might follow a hastily balanced budget and the adjustment of other policies in conformity with this objective.

The evidence that deficit finance was accepted with reluctance is quite definite, especially with respect to the late 1930's. Early in 1939 a survey conducted by Elmo Roper for *Fortune* included this question: "If you were a member of the incoming Congress, would you vote yes or no on a bill to reduce federal spending to a point where the national budget is balanced?" The distribution of replies is shown in the following table.

	Yes	No	Don't Know
Total	61.3%	17.4%	21.3%
Prosperous	76.3	11.1	12.6
Upper middle class	67.1	17.8	15.1
Lower middle class	62.2	17.8	20.0
Poor	54.8	18.3	26.9

Only 17.4 percent of those polled would not attempt to balance the budget. At the same time *Fortune* reported that 63.5 percent regarded the President—and presumably his administration—favorably. Among those classified as "poor" the figures are even more remarkable—18 percent would not attempt to balance the budget through reduced spending and 74 percent regarded the President favorably.[38]

In their interpretation of the answers to the question about balancing the budget, the editors of *Fortune* suggested that "at the very moment that President Roosevelt was defending deficit spending and reiterating the theory that balancing the budget is the least of our problems, a wave of deflationary sentiment suddenly swept across his path." [39] To one who has followed federal fiscal developments continuously from 1929, "a wave of deflationary sentiment" seems an exaggeration. That there were changes in popular attitudes goes without saying. But they were at best gradual and influenced by changes in the economic tide. Numerous persons who in 1933–1934 and again in 1937–1938 were willing to accept an unbalanced budget did so with a feeling of uncertainty. In some instances no more than a change in personal fortunes was required to place them in the opposite camp. It was not a case of apostates coming back to the ancient faith, but a return of those who had not strayed very far away.

NOTES

1. J. M. Clark, *Economic Institutions and Human Welfare* (1957), p. 14.
2. At the time *The General Theory* appeared the idea that the private or market sector of the economy supports all public activities financed from revenues other than fees and charges still enjoyed a wide vogue. See, for example, Paul F. Cadman, *National Income and Deficit Financing* (1939), p. 11.
3. Stephen K. Bailey, *Congress Makes a Law* (1950), p. 20.

4. Full and unqualified acceptance of compensatory fiscal theory would have been construed as a revolutionary break with tradition. The public . . . had long been accustomed to a purely financial approach to the federal budget. During the 1920's the virtues of the annually balanced budget had been extolled to a greater extent than ever before.

5. Roy Blough, *The Federal Taxing Process* (1952), pp. 240–242.

6. "If prosperity is to flourish, people must have confidence in their own future and that of their country. This basic truth was temporarily lost sight of during the 1930's in the process of grafting new economic ideas and practices onto the old." Arthur F. Burns, *Prosperity Without Inflation* (1957), p. 27. "After the collapse of 1932–1933 a New Deal of some sort was imperative. But not everything that has been dealt out was imperative. That has depended upon the temperament, the prejudices, the quick judgments of the dealers." Walter Lippmann, *The Method of Freedom* (1934), p. 25.

7. The reference here is to the Securities Act of 1933 and the Securities Exchange Act of 1934 (48 Stat. 74, 881) and the investigations that preceded their enactment.

8. For an overseas view, see T. Balogh, "Chaos or Recovery?" *Nineteenth Century and After*, Vol. 114 (1933), pp. 540 ff.

9. Carl Shoup, Milton Friedman, and Ruth P. Mack, *Taxing to Prevent Inflation* (1943), p. 76. According to one school of thought, taxes were not the major reason private investment remained sluggish during the 1930's. Nearly all sectors of the economy were operating far below capacity. Under these conditions, it was held, little more investment in additional productive capacity than occurred could have been expected without a revival of consumption—irrespective of tax rates and reform measures.

10. The President did not accept the view that reform should be subordinated to recovery. See, for example, the introduction to *Public Papers and Addresses of Franklin D. Roosevelt, 1938* (1941), pp. 3–10.

11. An Open Letter to the President, *New York Times* (Dec. 31, 1933), sec. 8, p. 2.

12. Blough, *The Federal Taxing Process*, p. 241.

13. Gerhard Colm, "Fiscal Policy," in *The New Economics*, Seymour Harris, ed. (1947), p. 451. In Colm's opinion, it "is likely that, without a line written by economists on deficit spending, we would have had the same policy."

14. *Ibid.*

15. (EDITOR'S NOTE: Roosevelt's message of April 14 called for increased appropriations for the Works Progress Administration and other agencies, easing of credit by reduction of Federal Reserve member-bank reserve requirements, and appropriations to put unemployed back to work on federal projects. See Roosevelt, *Public Papers and Addresses, 1938*, pp. 226–230.)

16. *Ibid.*, 230.

17. Sherwood M. Fine, *Public Spending and Postwar Economic Policy* (1944), pp. 118–119.

18. These economists believed there was little hope that private investment could be stimulated and deficit spending discontinued. A "new conception of the problem" was said to be needed. "The government should announce its intention to spend as long and as fast as necessary to get the national income to a satisfactory level, let us say $100 billion as an immediate goal. Then it should announce its intention to keep it there." ("Public Spending, Its Tasks and Limits," discussion by Paul Sweezy in *Social Research*, Vol. 6 [1939],

pp. 230–231.) Though the goal of a $100 billion national income is here described as "an immediate goal," the next sentence suggests a lack of perception of the growth factor. Observations that seemed to assume the economy had lost all capacity for future growth were fairly common during the 1930's.

19. "It is, it seems, politically impossible for a capitalistic democracy to organize expenditures on the scale necessary to make the grand experiment which would prove my case—except in war conditions." J. M. Keynes, "The United States and the Keynes Plan," *New Republic*, Vol. 103 (1940), p. 158.

20. Those who criticized federal spending on the ground that it was inadequate perhaps did not give suitable recognition to three factors: (1) the compensatory fiscal theory and Keynes' theory of how the economy operates were comparatively new developments; (2) it requires considerable time for any theory—no matter how convincing—to attain acceptance at the policy-making level; and (3) any theory that becomes the basis for public policy must be implemented in a political environment.

21. "Regardless of the candidate elected to the Presidency in 1932, an expansionist budgetary policy was inevitable." Fine, *Public Spending and Postwar Economic Policy*, p. 88.

22. A factor frequently overlooked in discussions of employment and unemployment in the 1930's is the increase in the labor force. Reduction in unemployment to a tolerable level required not only re-employment of those who had lost their jobs, but also finding employment for the annual addition to the labor force.

23. Walter Lippmann, "The Permanent New Deal," *Yale Review*, new series, Vol. 24 (1935), p. 661. In Lippmann's opinion the distinction between recovery and reform should not be too sharply drawn. "In one sense, the most radical of all the reforms are these very recovery measures themselves." The "acceptance by the government of responsibility for recovery, and the corollaries," such as the resort to monetary management, the use of government credit, and the expansion of government enterprise "mark great changes in a political system which until 1929 was committed to the general doctrine of *laissez faire*."

24. Dan T. Smith, *Deficits and Depressions* (1936), p. 170.

25. L. J. Dickinson, "The Drift in Federal Finance," *Review of Reviews and World's Work*, Vol. 88 (December 1933), pp. 17, 58.

26. Samuel G. Blythe, "The Real Issue," *Saturday Evening Post*, Vol. 208 (Nov. 30, 1935), pp. 5–6. The program of the Roosevelt administration had been previously referred to in the same journal as the third great spending spree. "The first of these sprees began when we tried to make the world safe for Democracy; the second when we tried to make it safe for speculators. In the third . . . Government is trying to make it safe for everyone except those who have saved." ("Our Three Great Spending Sprees," an editorial, *ibid.*, Vol. 206, Jan. 20, 1934, p. 22.)

27. Lewis W. Douglas, "Recovery by Balanced Budget," *Review of Reviews*, Vol. 91 (January 1935), pp. 25, 69.

28. Douglas, "Over the Hill to the Poorhouse," *ibid.*, Vol. 91 (June 1935), p. 23.

29. Grenville Clark, "Federal Finances and the New Deal," *Atlantic Monthly*, Vol. 154 (1934), pp. 755 ff. The belief that the federal budget must be balanced to avoid inflation was held by numerous persons well versed in finance. See, for example, the statement by Russell C. Leffingwell, *New York Times* (March 22, 1934), p. 16.

30. Henrietta Ripperger, "What This Country Needs is a Woman," *Harper's Magazine*, Vol. 172 (1936), pp. 373, 376. The same idea had been advanced at the time of the 1932 campaign. The "right kind of woman" could govern the country effectively. The "dominant trait of the best women is realism—an educated insight into values, a cool remorseless discrimination between what you want and what you can get." Elmer Davis, "The Collapse of Politics," *Harper's Magazine*, Vol. 165 (1932), p. 393.

31. Johnson, "Debt and the Devil," *Yale Review*, new series, Vol. 22 (1933), pp. 450 ff.

32. "The Budget in Chaos," *The Nation*, Vol. 142 (Feb. 19, 1936), p. 209.

33. The "one sure way to bring Fascism to this country is through prolonged government spending of large sums of borrowed money." Frank Knox, *We Planned It That Way* (1938), p. 41.

34. H. Parker Willis, "Up to Our Neck in Debt," *The Forum*, Vol. 96 (1936), p. 108.

35. Jackson, "America Has Only Scratched Her Resources," *The Forum*, Vol. 96 (1936), p. 108. The candidate for Vice President here referred to was Frank Knox.

36. Duncan Aikman, "America Talks Debt," *Harper's Magazine*, Vol. 174 (December 1936), pp. 92–96.

37. The moral connotation of indebtedness did not vanish during the depression. At best the influence of so-called "moral precepts" receded gradually. See, for example, Duncan Aikman's account of his visit with a lady living in the Ozark Mountains just before the 1936 election. *Ibid.*, p. 97.

38. "The Fortune Survey: XIX," *Fortune*, Vol. 19 (March 1939), pp. 66, 135.

39. *Ibid.*, p. 135. The references to public expenditures and debts in the message of January 4, 1939, on the State of the Union were interpreted by the editors of *Fortune* as indicating a continuance of "the free-spending philosophy."

BUSINESS AND THE PUBLIC

Thomas C. Cochran

In 1929 business, particularly big business, enjoyed a degree of public approval unique in American history. The "robber barons" of the last century and the "malefactors of great wealth" of the Progressive Era were now the leaders of the nation. Brief biographies of

Reprinted by permission of the publishers from Thomas C. Cochran: *The American Business System: A Historical Perspective*, 1900–1955 (Cambridge, Mass.: Harvard University Press, Copyright, 1957, by The President and Fellows of Harvard College), pp. 140–63.

successful businessmen helped to sell the ubiquitous *Saturday Evening Post* and *American* magazines. In 1928, when the Democratic National Chairman was also Chairman of General Motors, both major party candidates pledged their faith to Wall Street and the self-regulating economy. Bruce Barton, a leading advertising agent, took the final step when he pictured Christ in the image of the businessman.

LOSS OF BUSINESS PRESTIGE AND MORALE

The transition from this high point of public belief in the American business system to an attitude of greater distrust of both business honesty and ability than had characterized any previous period was cataclysmic. As late as June 1930 the panic of November 1929 was being written off as past history, and in the words of the President, prosperity seemed "just around the corner." But instead there came mass unemployment, bank failures, and the exposé of spectacular business scandals. Within less than two years the results of a generation of public-relations work lay in ruins, and the "puff" stories and planted news by which good will had been built were being ridiculed by journalists and other public leaders. The well-educated members of the public, acutely conscious of the pitfalls of propaganda, were now determined to view things realistically.

Voluntary efforts by business groups to halt the depression were futile. To cushion the shock of European bank failures in the fall of 1931, for example, American bankers had formed a National Credit Association. But in the words of President Hoover, "After a few weeks of enterprising courage the bankers' National Credit Association became ultraconservative, then fearful, and finally died. It had not exerted anything like its full possible strength. Its members—and the business world—threw up their hands and asked for governmental action." [1]

In January 1932 Hoover, for the moment working in harmony with a Democratic House of Representatives, gave business the Reconstruction Finance Corporation. This government lending agency, with potential resources up to three and a half billion dollars, marks a turning point in the relations of business and government. Never before had either a presidential administration or business leaders thought it necessary for the government to intervene on a large scale to prevent economic collapse. The RFC symbolizes not only the end of adherence, in practice, to the concept of the self-regulating economy, but also the assumption of a new measure of economic power and direction by government. Over the next fifteen years the RFC was to overshadow the largest banks as a lending agency.

No one was more sensitive to these changes in prestige and leadership than the businessmen themselves. Bankers were particularly shaken by failures and investigations that revealed loose practices by some of the leaders of Wall Street. In the late twenties the words of a Morgan partner were often given more publicity than those of the President or Secretary of State. In the early months of 1933 the term "bankster" classed these erstwhile paragons of respectability with the underworld, and President Roosevelt in his inaugural address promised to drive the money-changers from the temple. Whether or not they had acted carelessly in the boom enthusiasm, all leaders of finance were forced to share a collective guilt.

Furthermore, by the summer of 1932 many businessmen themselves had frustrating inner doubts about the self-regulating nature of the economy and its continued expansion. Labor and materials were obtainable at bargain rates, perhaps never to be reached again, yet few entrepreneurs decided to buy and build. The most advanced business thinking ran more along the line of coöperative arrangements to raise prices and stabilize production at low levels than toward free competitive efforts to seize new opportunities.[2] Some conservative journalists talked in terms of Hoover's assuming dictatorial powers or transferring authority to twelve dictators of the nation commissioned to revive the economy.

Politicians seemed equally at a loss as to what to do. Aside from Democratic advocacy of federal rather than local relief payments and of the repeal of prohibition, there was no important difference in the views of the two major parties or their candidates. In the presidential election of 1932 both Hoover and Franklin D. Roosevelt talked economy and a balanced budget, both professed belief in the ability of the economy to right itself with the aid of minor government action, although it was thought that Roosevelt might define such action more broadly than Hoover. Immediately after the election both men stood aloof from the deteriorating situation. They were unable to agree on joint action, and neither would take important steps separately, Hoover because he no longer had the popular mandate, and Roosevelt because he felt he could not act without power.

Meanwhile, the lack of confidence in the future of the economy produced continual withdrawal of bank deposits and hoarding of currency and gold. Banks already teetering on the brink of insolvency as a result of uncollectable loans and devalued securities found it impossible to withstand the drain on their resources. During 1931 and 1932 nearly four thousand banks suspended payment. By October of the later year, the Governor of Nevada declared a bank "holiday," to relieve banks of the necessity of making payments. By the beginning of 1933 failures were approaching a thousand a month, and industrial states such as Michigan and Ohio were following the lead of Nevada.

GOVERNMENT TAKES THE INITIATIVE

The final stage of the crisis came with dramatic timing. On March 3, 1933, old and new treasury officials urged all governors to suspend banking operations. Late in the evening of that day Governor Herbert Lehman of New York gave way and by closing the banks of New York State and, as a result, of New York City, virtually stopped the nation's financial machinery. After his inauguration the following day President Roosevelt, using emergency powers granted in World War I, made the closing nation-wide and complete.

Although finance had undergone the most spectacular collapse, other segments of the economy were scarcely better off. About one third of the normal labor force was unemployed, and national income in current dollars was only half that of 1929. In spite of the fact that taxes were consuming a third of the meager national income, state and local relief and public services were breaking down. For lack of money to pay jurors Atlantic City had not opened its courts to civil actions in the fall of 1932; Chicago was paying its school teachers in scrip; and Cleveland lacked money to feed the unemployed on a subsistence level.

Obviously Roosevelt was right when he said in his inaugural address: "The People of the United States . . . have registered a mandate that they want direct, vigorous action." [3] It appeared that this applied equally to the business interests. The acts of the first hundred days of the New Deal, the "honeymoon" period, had a large measure of bipartisan support, and appear to have followed the thinking of such businessmen as Owen D. Young, Bernard Baruch, and the leaders of the United States Chamber of Commerce. Opposition came largely from either local or special interests, or those to the left of the administration who would have nationalized banks and railroads.

President Roosevelt's view of the situation was not only strictly capitalistic, but also rather narrowly financial. He saw charges such as taxes, interest on indebtedness, and other overhead expenses as rocks on which business had foundered in an ebbing tide of purchasing power. The solution was to restore purchasing power and raise prices. In doing this he also desired to improve the income of farmers relative to that in industry, and to raise the real wages of labor.

Federal unemployment relief, by now a necessity, an expanded public-works program, and provisions for reopening the banks with the federal guarantee of small deposits may all be seen as a part of the economic program for increasing purchasing power. Even repeal of the prohibition amendment may be regarded in this light.

Two acts, primarily designed to raise prices and readjust the distribution of national income, also passed with bipartisan majorities. The first, the Agricultural Adjustment Act of May 1933, contained provisions to pay farmers for restricting the acreage planted to certain staple crops, with the money to come from a tax on agricultural processors. Just as the RFC inaugurated the peacetime practice of government advances of credit to private enterprise, the AAA marked the beginning of a long-run policy of government support for agriculture.

The second major bill to revive and readjust national income was the National Industry Recovery Act, passed in June 1933. This law followed the general philosophy of the United States Chamber of Commerce and many leading businessmen, that prices should be raised by coöperative effort on the part of producers, but the administration added the feature that real wages of labor should also be raised. General Hugh S. Johnson, who headed the new agency, said: "We are going to ask something in the nature of an armistice on increased producing capacity, until we see if we can get this upward spiral started . . . We are going to plead very earnestly . . . not to use any further labor-saving devices or anything further to increase production at present." [4] Few professional economists subscribed to this view that recovery could be brought about by limiting new investment.

While the act gave legal sanction to a "just" price adhered to by all competitors—an idea that had been gaining ground since the early years of the century—it ran directly counter to the concepts of free competition embodied in the antitrust laws. Now competitors were urged by law to get together, usually under the aegis of their trade association, and draw up a code for price control or "fair" competition. Except for the inability to place quotas on production, these codes resembled the cartel arrangements of Europe. In return for suspending the antitrust laws and allowing what would formerly have been collusive arrangements respecting terms of sale, the business representatives had to agree to a thirty-hour week for manual labor, forty hours for clerical workers, and increased minimum wages. Finally, the code had to be accepted by the National Recovery Administration.

The sudden effort to draw up codes for every activity produced endless confusion. Afraid that compliance would be so slow that the beneficial effects of the act would be dissipated, the government issued a blanket code to which all were urged to subscribe. Those who agreed to a code were allowed to display a blue eagle on their labels or advertising; those who then violated the code's provisions might lose their eagle as well as be brought into court.

If one regards the NRA as primarily an effort to stimulate recovery by raising prices, it appeared to be successful. The expectation that prices were going up produced a wave of buying, increased production, and brought a moderate gain in employment. Looked at as an effort to increase consumer purchasing by raising real wages, NRA was less successful. Wage increases were equalled by the upswing in prices. The great power presumably given to labor by Section 7a, which called for collective bargaining, was neutralized by the rapid spread of company unions and General Johnson's weak administration of this part of the act.

Probably no hasty experiment of this magnitude that tried to adhere to democratic processes and protect the rights of all parties, including the consumer, could have been an immediate success. And NRA did not last long enough to overcome the initial problems. In May 1935 the Supreme Court declared that Congress could not constitutionally use its power over interstate commerce to dictate conditions of manufacture and sale, and that it could not delegate loosely defined powers to code authorities.[5] By this time all groups seemed content to see the end of so complex and hybrid a system of government and private controls.

THE NEW DEAL IN FINANCE

Although there was little initial opposition either in or out of Congress to federal relief, rehabilitation of the banking system, AAA, or NRA, the President's effort to raise prices by monetary inflation revived the traditional struggle over the gold standard. Having behind him a sweeping Democratic majority, and supported by a group of economists who believed essentially in the quantity theory of money, Roosevelt obtained cancellation of gold payment clauses in federal bonds and other loan contracts, the power to devaluate the dollar up to 50 percent in relation to gold, and ultimately a silver purchase program. He aimed to provide "the kind of dollar which, a generation hence, will have the same purchasing and debt paying power as the dollar value we hope to attain in the near future." [6]

Because of the belief of his advisers in the stimulating effects of inflation on the domestic economy, the President refused to enter into any fixed exchange relations at an International Monetary Conference held in June 1933. In January 1934 he fixed the gold content of the dollar at 59.06 percent of the previous amount. This marked the end of his experiments with the dollar. In spite of later changes in price no revaluation was attempted. The country never returned to free and unlicensed exchange of paper money for gold. Since no foreign country did either, the United States could be said to have returned to the modern version of the gold standard, that is, gold issued by special application to pay international trade balances.

Some critics have blamed the inflation of World War II on the expanded gold base for American currency provided by devaluation. Yet the price changes in the North during the Civil War and in the World War I period were of about the same magnitude as in World War II and its aftermath. More immediate effects of the monetary policies were to hinder international agreements regarding convertibility of currencies, and hence to discourage international trade, and to drive silver standard countries, such as China and Mexico, off a metallic base by raising the market price of silver.

Offsetting the reduction in trade due to monetary readjustments was the government's policy of reciprocal trade pacts. By the Act of 1934 Congress allowed the executive to negotiate with individual nations special agreements that might lower tariffs by as much as 50 percent. Before World War II such agreements, affecting about a third of American trade, had been negotiated. Since many coun-

tries had treaties specifying "most-favored-nation" treatment fo
their goods, the tariff reductions spread beyond the new trade pact:
In spite of the efforts of tariff lobbyists, these policies were still i·
effect in 1955.

Early business opposition to the New Deal centered on th·
abandonment of the gold standard, but it is probable that mos
businessmen were opposed to all of the reform, as distinct fron
relief, measures. Herbert Hoover spoke for conservative businessmer
when he said in 1934 that the New Deal represented "a vast shif·
from the American concept of human rights which even the govern
ment may not infringe to those social philosophies where men ar·
wholly subject to the state." [7] But faith in a self-regulating econom·
led inevitably to a negative position. Business leaders had no posi
tive program of their own to oppose the Roosevelt formulas fo·
curing the abuses of the twenties.

The banking reforms, carried out chiefly under an emergency ac·
of 1933 and a subsequent act of 1935, had as their two main feature:
an increase in government control of the Federal Reserve System
and deposit insurance. The seven-member control board, now called
the Board of Governors of the Reserve System, was given power ove·
rediscount rates and over open market operations previously exercised by the Reserve Banks, and the ability to increase reserves,
which had formerly required presidential approval. Bank deposits
up to $5,000 were guaranteed in each account, and state banks with
average deposits of over $1,000,000 had to join the Federal Reserve
System by July 1, 1942, or forfeit their right to insurance.

These measures fell considerably short of the ideas of liberal
Democrats who stood for government ownership of the Federal
Reserve Banks and compulsory membership in the System for all
banks. But neither did the Act of 1935 please the big metropolitan
bankers who had previously dominated the Reserve policies in their
areas and who felt that because they had many very large accounts
a premium for insurance based on total deposits might make them
pay more than their share.

By 1935 mergers and failures had halved the 1920 total of 30,000
banks, and the downward trend in state banks continued. Nevertheless, in 1942, when the larger state banks had been forced into the
Reserve System, there were still 7,600 banks on the outside and only
6,600 members, although the members had 85 percent of the total
deposits.

Opposition to the banking act was confined to criticism of specific terms, but the financial community objected to the Securities Act of 1933 and the Securities Exchange Act of 1934 in both detail and principle. By these laws elaborate information had to be provided about companies offering new security issues, and the conditions of trading were regulated by a Securities Exchange Commission. In general, the requirements were similar to those that had been enforced by leading nations of Europe since the late nineteenth century, but at first they seemed an intolerable burden to previously unregulated Americans. "Evidence accumulates," wrote the President of the New York Stock Exchange, "that the quality of the market has been seriously affected . . . to the extent that excessive regulation stifles individual initiative, intimidates and confuses honest men . . . such regulation is not in the public interest." [8]

Through subsequent laws, the SEC was given power to break up pyramided public-utility holding companies, to supervise bankruptcies and reorganizations, and to regulate the issuing of trust certificates, the operation of investment trusts, and investment advisors. In short, the Commission could police the security operations of the United States.

Like many people in the new administrations or commissions, the original members of the SEC brought a missionary spirit to their tasks; they saw themselves as protectors of the public against the machinations of the "money-changers." But as time went on the commissions mellowed, and legitimate business, in turn, came to recognize certain benefits from strict policing. After further experience in World War II, it appeared doubtful that the businessmen affected would eliminate such boards as the Federal Communications Commission, those regulating transportation, or the SEC if they could.

Pursuing the policies of relief for debtors and recovery through stimulating construction, the New Deal made changes of fundamental importance in the finance of American housing. Farm and nonfarm mortgages on small properties were refinanced and guaranteed by federal agencies. Important relief measures as these were, the Federal Housing Administration, created in 1934, was in the long run even more important. It not only initiated the government-guaranteed mortgage for small-home construction, but also popularized the idea of uniform monthly payments that included both principal and interest—the packaged mortgage.[9] Without these two devices the great expansion in the building of small houses from 1948 on would have probably been impossible.

For slum clearance the government offered direct subsidies. Private enterprise could not erect a new building in which apartments could be rented for the same low rates as for the run-down, vermin-infested tenements that housed much of the urban working class. "Model tenements" built without government aid invariably turned out to be middle class in their rents and clientele. In 1937 Congress, impelled by Senator Robert F. Wagner of New York, set up a United States Housing Authority to assist local governments in slum clearance and low-income housing. Local real-estate interests feared the competition of the new buildings, and in the beginning progress was slow. But for the first time America's slums stopped growing, and the government after World War II continued legislation to support new construction.

BUSINESS ATTACKS THE NEW DEAL

By early 1935 President Roosevelt was only beginning what came to be called the second phase of the New Deal. But to the majority of businessmen he had already gone much too far. Their opposition took two forms, better organized lobbying in Congress and a drive to win public opinion to their side.

The National Association of Manufacturers had had little support from big business in its earlier years, and in the late twenties its income and activities dropped off.[10] But Roosevelt alarmed some of its members, "a few advance thinking souls who realized that only top-leadership could serve the purposes of business salvation." [11] Gradually the big money came in, and the NAM became a central agency for business defense against the New Deal. The American Farm Bureau became a similar central agency, carrying on work in Washington for a number of trade associations, including the National Automobile Chamber of Commerce.

On the public-opinion front the Liberty League was established in August 1934 to protect the Constitution and American liberties from the assaults of New Deal legislation. Two former Democratic presidential candidates, John W. Davis and Alfred E. Smith, joined with leading businessmen and lawyers in the work of the League. Anti-Roosevelt publicity was easy to secure, since by 1935 most of the nation's newspapers had turned against him. Roosevelt was attacked for extravagance and consequent increase in the national debt, as well as for infringement of personal liberties.

These charges had a basis in reality. The President was a loose administrator and Americans were relatively inexperienced in creating bureaucracy. Deficits were mounting, and there was a widely held fear of public debt even among those who supported the New Deal. Businessmen, unaccustomed to government forms and regulations, bitterly resented the new burdens of paper work, legal advice, and federal supervision.

To the ordinary citizen, however, who never came in direct contact with business regulations, who saw in public finance an unsolved mystery, and who felt his savings, his home, and his income were all better protected than ever before, the appeals of the Liberty League had little force. Furthermore, the businessmen's informal campaign of vituperation against the President went to lengths that appeared ridiculous to the wage or salary earner. In upper-class circles he was referred to as "that man," and a steady stream of malicious jokes about the President emanated from clubs and offices.

Correctly diagnosing the popular desires, Roosevelt by the beginning of 1935 was emphasizing greater security for the common citizen rather than more regulation of business. In his annual message to Congress on January 4, the President said: "We find our population suffering from old inequalities, little changed by past sporadic remedies . . . we have not effectively lifted up the underprivileged." Further aid to farmers, unemployment insurance, old-age pensions, and more government projects were the President's solution. These measures were disliked in principle by businessmen because of the expense involved, and the threat that too much security would weaken in individuals the drive to save money or get ahead, but except for the Works Progress Administration, whose wage rates were in some instances so high as to exert an upward pressure on those paid by private industry, none of the early acts of 1935 directly affected the conduct of business.

The armistice, however, was brief. Soon the most serious conflict of all between business and the New Deal arose indirectly from the action of the Supreme Court. In May 1935 the Court declared the National Industrial Recovery Act unconstitutional. Liberals in Congress were now determined to assert in a stronger form the principles of collective bargaining in the repudiated law. The reassertion in Senator Wagner's National Labor Relations Act of July 1935 went further than the provisions of Section 7a of the NIRA, further even than previous plans of the President, who had not played an active part in the initial framing of the measure.

In the new law specific clauses were inserted to prevent a company from influencing its workers or supporting a company union. The union that could win a majority at an election was given the power to speak for all wage-roll employees. A new three-man National Labor Relations Board could make rules and regulations, and in case of legal dispute, the Board's findings of fact were binding. In a chapter of his memoirs entitled "Fascism Comes to Labor— with Consequences," Herbert Hoover wrote, "In violation of the whole spirit of American justice, the Board was judge, jury, and prosecutor. There was no effective appeal from its decisions . . . The Board appointed by Roosevelt presents a prime exhibit of the collectivist character of his officials and also of the collectivist character of the regime." [12] A more objective historian writing nearly a generation later has called the Wagner Act "probably the most bluntly anti-corporation legislation the United States has ever known." [13] The long arm of government touched the plant at two of its most sensitive areas, cost and authority. For the employer this was by far the most intolerable act of the New Deal.

In the same session of Congress a steeply graduated personal income-tax bill, popularly referred to as a "soak the rich" measure, was put through by the same leftist-liberal leadership. As in the case of the Wagner Act, the terms of the final bill were probably in advance of the President's thinking, but in both instances business leaders blamed him.

The election of 1936 demonstrated once more the strength of President Roosevelt and the lack of popular support for business leadership. The Republican party polled less than 40 percent of the popular vote and elected only about 20 percent of the members of Congress. For the next four years business appeared to lack political defense. But the Supreme Court and the southern Democrats might still be relied on for last-ditch protection. During 1935 and 1936 the Court had declared seven major New Deal acts unconstitutional, and the National Labor Relations Act might well be headed for the same fate.

At this juncture the President sought to use his sweeping majority to change the complexion of the Supreme Court. Taking an initial stand that the justices were overworked, he proposed that Congress pass a law allowing him to appoint one additional justice for each member over 70 years of age until the Court reached a total of 15. Previous Congresses had altered the composition of the Court, but never by more than two justices. The President's plan met a conservative attack of increasing strength from both Democrats and Republicans, and passed Congress only in a drastically revised form. No additions were to be made to the Court, but justices were to be tempted to retire by high pensions.

But meanwhile, the Court had reversed its attitude through the changed thinking of Justice Owen D. Roberts. Much of the New Deal legislation had been invalidated by 5 to 4 decisions; now, on April 12th, 1937, the National Labor Relations Act was declared constitutional by a 5 to 4 margin.[14] The retirement of Justice Willis Van Devanter at the end of the 1937 term confirmed the breakdown of the judicial barrier to the extension of federal power.

Had the prosperity of 1937 continued there might have been no more major legislation affecting business. The depression of 1938, however, led Congress to use its power over interstate commerce in the passage of a Fair Labor Standards Act setting a maximum of 40 hours a week, a minimum wage of 25 to 40 cents an hour, depending on the section, and prohibiting the labor of children under sixteen in industries producing goods for interstate shipment. This law, objectionable to business in principle, did not greatly affect conditions of employment outside the South. With its passage the New Deal, except for antitrust investigations and prosecutions, virtually came to an end.

THE NEW DEAL IN PERSPECTIVE

Early in 1951 the editors of *Fortune* collaborated with Russel W. Davenport in an issue of the magazine, published later the same year as a book entitled *U.S.A.: The Permanent Revolution*, in which they compared the bad old days with the happy, prosperous United States of mid-century. The factors that they saw as responsible for the better society, such as higher real wages, fairer labor relations, greater security, more honest financial dealings, greater social responsibility by corporation executives, stem largely from the days of the New Deal. One cannot help but conclude that unpleasant as this period may have been, many big-business executives, at least, came to see the reforms as inevitable adjustments to changing economic conditions.

Except for the Wagner Act, which was subsequently replaced by the Taft-Hartley Act more favorable to employers, the enlightened executive of mid-century might conclude that his objection was more to the way Roosevelt talked than the things he did. The propaganda of the New Deal against "economic royalists" and the "greedy" was highly offensive to most businessmen; the legislation, in retrospect, appeared more moderate.

Although many of the principles necessary for a better society were put into law by the New Deal, the wide-spread entry of government into economic activity during World War II brought perhaps more change in American business life. Out of the war came greatly increased real wages, stronger unions, and the dependence of wide areas of business upon government policy. Furthermore, Congresses from 1943 on, which were dominated by conservatives, either through Southern-Democrat-Republican coalitions or Republican control, did very little to alter the New Deal legislation, except for the Wagner Act, and generally proceeded on the assumption that business recessions should be met by government remedies. Whether or not this represented a "permanent revolution," it appeared by the fifties to represent the majority policy of both parties.

PUBLIC RELATIONS

One element in what the late Frederick Lewis Allen called "the big change" rather than the "permanent revolution" was less reliance on the older slanted news story or advertising type of public relations and the use of new, positive, and practical approaches to the position of large companies in their communities. Public relations in the 1920's were based on spreading favorable stories and facts in widely read media. Inspired press releases were often forced on editors by their fear of loss of advertising if they refused to publish; pressure was brought on textbook publishers to see that public ownership was condemned and private enterprise extolled; and emphasis was placed on such institutional or protective advertising as Packard's billboard slogan of 1932, "a dollar for a job or a dollar for a dole."

During the depression these exhoratory forms were labeled as propaganda and became relatively ineffective or in some cases were likely to produce the opposite results from that intended. There ensued seven or eight years of relative bankruptcy in public relations. Business performance was poor, and public-relations offices learned that it was action rather than fine talk that counted. As A. H. Batten, president of an advertising agency, said in 1937, "Any public relations worthy of the name must start with the business itself. Unless . . . it can meet at every point the test of good citizenship and usefulness to the community, no amount of public relations will avail." [15]

The rise of the new public relations must be seen against the background of fifteen years of prosperity, of performance by business that exceeded most citizens' expectations. Although statements by top executives may often have done their company harm by making it appear that the economic and social ideas of businessmen had not changed in the last fifty years, the old forms of public relations, such as speeches, news stories, and advertisements, were not abandoned. They were basic to communication. Public relations came to be seen as a "two-way street" which the company officials as well as the public had to explore. It was increasingly recognized by public-relations advisers that unless the company lived up to the image they were trying to create, their effort would fail. As a result the more advanced multiplant companies began to conduct a realistic type of public relations among their workers and in the local communities.

In the DuPont Company, for example, the new public relations was called the precinct system. Each of nearly one hundred separate plants was charged with creating a friendly attitude toward the company among its employees and in its area. The means to this end were wages as high but no higher than those paid by the best employers in the area; "fringe benefits" in excess of those generally incorporated in union contracts, although a few plants had outside unions; a strong emphasis on safety and health; contributions to community activities and active participation in them by the local executives. A General Electric *Employee Relations News Letter* of January 7, 1953, urged: "First, let our employees' families and their neighbors know what we are *trying* to do (and are doing) to be good employers, good buyers of local products and services; good tax payers, good contributors to charity and other worthwhile projects, and good corporate and individual citizens." [16] "When we put a manager in a town," said President McHugh of the New York Telephone Company, "we say to him in effect, 'This is your town . . . you are going to be loyal to this community.'" [17] Some men who were rising rapidly in big companies moved on to other areas, but many middle-level executives spent their lives in one plant and became an integral part of the community.

Another public-relations development of the thirties was the creation of foundations or institutes by which companies invested tax-free money in furthering public understanding through research or free services. The Brewers Foundation, cited by Bernays as a good example of his accomplishment in this connection, carried on statistical work and research for the benefit of the public and the industry.[18]

In assessing these new corporate attitudes based on good relations from positive performance, two factors should be noted. First, the liberal policies of pay and contribution and the new assumption of social responsibility had grown up during a period of unprecedented prosperity. A real test of the strength of such elements in business behavior would come when the nation faced a period of depression. Second, these policies perhaps had continuing strength because of their suitability to the managerial role. . . . The managers of most big companies were not large owners of company securities and to many of them, at least, good employee and public relations gave more personal satisfaction than their relations with the stockholders.

Consumer democracy was more emphasized than in the earlier part of the century. The consumer by his choices was held to decide what products would continue on the market, and which companies would succeed. Like municipal democracy, this is true in a broad sense. If lack of enterprise by existing producers limits choices for too long a period, some outside company will probably enter that market with a more desirable product, just as a long period of corrupt machine control usually leads to a municipal reform movement; but the adjustment is far from automatic.

Two contrary trends may be noted in providing the goods the consumer wanted most at the lowest possible price. On the one hand the cost of starting complicated mass-production processes increased greatly in the years after 1941. In the 1950's a hundred million dollars was probably too little with which to establish a successful automobile company. On the other hand, the great corporations increasingly became all-purpose companies with large capital resources that could be invested in anything promising a good continuing profit. Their specialists were constantly surveying the industrial field for soft spots in the production of other companies where competition would pay, or for new products that could find a market. The search on the part of both manufacturers and distributors to find new uses for old products was also a response to "consumer sovereignty."

While a large part of advertising, as distinct from public relations, was aimed at sustaining the demand for old products or preserving market positions, some of it performed the social function of acquainting the public with new utilities. Advertising expenditures for all media in 1953 were about one-third higher in real dollars per capita than in 1929.

THE REVIVAL OF ANTITRUST PROSECUTION

In the late thirties the federal government attempted to aid the consumer by a new antitrust policy. During the twelve years of Republican control that ended in 1933, the Sherman and Clayton antitrust acts had been used sparingly. The philosophy of the National Industrial Recovery Administration was to set these laws aside. In 1937, however, with NRA an unpleasant memory and a new administrator, Thurman W. Arnold, in charge of the antitrust division of the Department of Justice, antitrust policy was revived.

The Arnold philosophy, endorsed by the administration, was to prosecute collusive agreements rather than to try to break up big companies. By introducing more competition into semi-monopolistic markets, Arnold hoped to lower prices and increase production. In 1940 prosecutions had reached eighty-seven a year, more than were brought during the entire "trust-busting" administration of Theodore Roosevelt. From 1940 to 1948, the Sherman Act was invoked by the Department of Justice more times than in the preceding fifty years.[19]

In spite of the great energy of government prosecutors, the results were not striking. The Sherman and Clayton Acts had been warped and twisted by generations of judicial decisions until their legal applications were far from clear. The chief effects of the many court actions were to make companies more careful in the creation of records that would indicate collusion in pricing, and less anxious to drive out the medium-sized competitors who constituted proof that competition still existed.

In the export market the Webb-Pomerene Act of 1918 allowed American firms to join international cartels without risking antitrust prosecution. International trade in raw materials, such as rubber, coffee, nitrates, potash, copper, and tin, fell under the control of cartels in which American companies participated. Use of patents and erection of branch plants in foreign nations also led to cartel arrangements. For the firms on the inside the agreements spelled security and price maintenance, for those on the outside they appeared to be barriers to progress. At the end of World War II, President J. Howard Pew of Sun Oil Company denounced cartels as "the primary reason for the backwardness of European industry . . .

Their effect has been to destroy initiative; close the door of opportunity for new individual entrepreneurs and small business units; encourage inefficiency; raise prices and thus lower the standard of living." [20] In spite of their unpopularity with many American businessmen, international cartels continued to thrive in the forties and fifties.

BUSINESS AND GOVERNMENT IN
PARTNERSHIP

In spite of loud protests and mutual distrust, the New Deal forced business and government to work more closely together, to form a kind of partnership which grew in importance in later years. Business firms had to assign special employees to the tasks of understanding new federal regulations and of dealing with new agencies. One company framed a set of extracts from relevant statutes and hung it in the front office as a reminder of how much it had come to be regulated. In most big companies someone at about the level of vice-president had to spend much time in Washington learning to know the operations and personnel of important bureaus and commissions. Small businesses that could not afford to have specialists in federal relations dealt with these matters through trade or other associations. Soon Washington was the home of large numbers of legislative counselors, or lobbyists, representing all varieties of business activity.

Federal agencies such as the Federal Trade or Securities Exchange Commissions soon found it valuable to seek the advice of business. For this purpose conferences were held and advisory committees of businessmen appointed. If business and government were both to be held socially responsible for the general welfare, there had to be considerable communication between them.

The new personal income and corporation taxes led to changes in business structure and procedures. High taxes on earnings encouraged prosperous companies to merge with money-losing firms that could be built up, rather than pay what were regarded as unwarranted returns to the government. Wartime excess-profits taxes worked in the same direction. Companies that currently showed losses but might expect good earnings in the future, when it was hoped that taxes would be lower, were valuable investments for firms with large profits. Since a maximum tax of only 25 percent was paid on capital gains, it was better for the receivers of large incomes to make additional money from property manipulation rather than from salaries or dividends. The tax laws, therefore, were an incentive toward the business concentration that the government was trying to prevent.

War contracting also tended to make big business bigger. Of eighteen billion dollars' worth of war plants built by private companies betwen 1940 and 1943, three quarters were units exceeding ten million dollars and nearly a third were units exceeding fifty million. Of plants built directly by the government, about half, over seven billion dollars' worth, were constructed and operated under contracts with only thirty-one corporations.[21]

Government contracts continued to provide a large part of the income of big manufacturing companies. In the fiscal year 1950–1951, during the Korean war, 100 corporations received over eighteen billion dollars in defense contracts. General Motors led with 2.4 billion followed by United Aircraft with 1.2 billion.[22] The Korean war brought a resumption of the excess-profits tax, so effectively employed in World War II, but fast write-offs of depreciation drew much of the sting for those companies that needed to expand. During the period of the Korean war seventeen billion dollars of new plant expenditures were rapidly written off, allowing the companies involved to acquire large tax-free reserves.

The foreign-aid program initiated by President Truman and continued by President Eisenhower was another government support for business. Nations that could not have otherwise bought in the American market were given the ability, and were often compelled, to enter large contracts with American firms.

The development of atomic power, which would be a major field of capital investment for the late fifties and sixties, depended upon progressive release of the results of government research. In 1954 certain companies such as General Electric were being given approval for experimentation with atomic equipment, and in 1955 public-utility companies were starting to build atomic plants.

At the close of his book, *Laissez-Faire and the General Welfare State,* Sidney Fine chooses the Employment Act of 1946 to symbolize the final blow to the idea of a government of closely restricted powers, separated from the activities of business. This law established the President's Council of Economic Advisers with responsibility for reporting the measures necessary to preserve economic stability and full employment. In the words of President Truman, the act specifically rejected *laissez faire* and asserted that "our economy within reasonable limits will be what we make it, and intelligent human action will shape our future." [23] President Eisenhower continued to make active use of the recommendations of the advisers, but a generally booming economy prevented serious issues between the Council and business leaders.

Taxes, contracts, and legislation made business dependent on the advice of specialized lawyers and men who knew their way around Washington. Ex-government officials were valuable in the latter capacity. A man who had just left a government agency not only knew how to deal with it from the business side but also had friends among its personnel. Defense contracts made retired military or naval men valuable corporate officials. Big companies were also glad to have one or two of their executives take leave to work in government departments where a sympathetic understanding of the business side would be of use. "Time and again," wrote E. Pendleton Herring, "our commissions have been run by officials who are merely the pale reflections of the very interests they are supposed to regulate." [24]

So, without either partner desiring it in principle, business and government grew closer together. Major business decisions came to depend on government spending, contracting, and tax policies to an extent not dreamed of in 1929, while some of the traditional bargaining points between business and government such as the tariff sank into the background.

POLITICS AND PUBLIC OPINION

Congresses steadily friendly to business smoothed the operation of the partnership of business and government. Part of the harmony came from virtually continuous prosperity after 1941, which weakened the force of reform or regulatory movements. President Truman in 1948 framed an advanced liberal program, but Congress was not interested. The legislative and executive record of his two administrations seemed on most issues about all that conservatives could reasonably ask.

Aside from the perennial battles over antitrust prosecutions, the problem of hydroelectric power was the major business issue between the two political parties. President Truman had continued the policy of regional public-power development begun with the Tennessee Valley Authority in 1933. The Columbia River was the great area of dispute at the end of the Truman regime. Secretary of Interior Douglas McKay in the Eisenhower administration did not propose to withdraw federal aid entirely but advocated local development and a chance for private enterprise to share in the process.

How the close relations of business, particularly big business, and government would work under the pressure of hard times no one could tell. Coöperation depended upon the recognition by men like Secretary of Defense Charles Wilson, former president of General Motors, that there could be times when what was best for the company was not best for the country. Coöperation also depended on popular acceptance of the wisdom of business leadership.

In May 1949 *Fortune* pointed out that according to a Roper poll "a majority of the people . . . believe that very few businessmen have the good of the nation in mind when they make their important decisions." [25] In February 1955 *Look* in a differently worded poll found 80 percent approval. But when the reasons for approval were scrutinized, it was seen that they all hinged on material benefits rather than on responsibility for leadership. Three respondents out of four "thought that regulation in the present form was necessary and proper." [26] When one considers that "present" regulation included practically all the acts of the New and Fair Deals, except the National Labor Relations Act, the public attitude appeared ambiguous.

Granting that polls correctly reflected opinion, the mixed views were not surprising. The public in the early fifties as in the twenties appeared to be generally complacent regarding domestic affairs. Reform movements aroused little enthusiasm. The system worked well and the public was content to let it alone. On the surface, at least, business in the mid-fifties seemed to have as little to fear in the way of adverse action by either government or the public as at any previous time in the twentieth century.

NOTES

1. Herbert Hoover, *Memoirs of Herbert Hoover: The Great Depression, 1929–1941* (New York, 1952), 97.

2. Hermann Krooss, "Business Opinion Between Two Wars: An Analysis of Statements of Business Leaders on Economic Issues" (Ph.D. thesis, New York University, 1948), 119 ff.

3. Franklin D. Roosevelt, *Public Papers and Addresses*, II, 11 ff.

4. Quoted in Richard Hofstadter, *The American Political Tradition* (New York, 1948), 329 n.

5. Schecter Corporation v. United States, 295 U. S. 495 (1935).

6. Franklin D. Roosevelt, Message to World Economic Conference, London, 1933.

7. Herbert Hoover, *The Challenge to Liberty*, quoted in E. C. Rozwenc, editor, *The New Deal* (Amherst College Series: Problems in American Civilization, Boston, 1949), 70.

8. Report of the President, New York Stock Exchange, August 11, 1937, quoted in Humphrey B. Neill, *The Inside Story of the Stock Exchange* (New York, 1950), 257–258.

9. Miles L. Colean, *The Impact of Government on Real Estate Finance in the United States* (New York, 1950), 94–99.

10. U. S., 76th Cong., 1st Session, Senate Report No. 6, part vi, Report of the Committee on Education and Labor, pp. 42–43.

11. Testimony of Robert B. Henderson, Vice-President, National Association of Manufacturers, *ibid.*, p. 44.

12. Hoover, *The Great Depression*, 433–434.

13. Eric F. Goldman, *Rendezvous with Destiny* (New York, 1952), 365.

14. The N. L. R. B. v. Jones and Laughlin Corp., 301 U.S. 1 (1937).

15. Quoted in Edward L. Bernays, *Public Relations* (Norman, Okla., 1952), 104.

16. General Electric Company, *Employee Relations News Letter*, Jan. 7, 1953.

17. Quoted in Eugene Staley, ed., *Creating and Industrial Civilization: A Report of the Corning Conference* (New York, 1952), 143.

18. Bernays, *Public Relations*, 108.

19. Joe S. Bain, "Industrial Concentration and Anti-Trust Policy," in Harold F. Williamson, ed., *Growth of the American Economy* (New York, 1951), 879.

20. Quoted in Charles R. Whittlesey, *National Interest and International Cartels* (New York, 1946), 6.

21. A. D. H. Kaplan, *Big Enterprise in a Competitive System* (Washington, 1954), 31.

22. *Time*, December 10, 1951, p. 91.

23. Sidney Fine, *Laissez-Faire and the General Welfare State* (Ann Arbor, Mich., 1956), 399.

24. E. Pendleton Herring, *Public Administration and Public Interest* (New York, 1936), 173.

25. *Fortune*, May 1949, p. 67.

26. *Look*, February 8, 1955, pp. 19–20.

20

Symbols and Rituals

RICHARD Hofstadter has asserted that little political writing of
enduring significance came out of the Roosevelt years, despite the
turmoil and heated controversy that marked New Deal politics. He
admits one major exception, however: the works of Thurman Arnold.* In *Symbols of Government* (1935) and *The Folklore of Capitalism* (1937), Arnold scornfully attacked the "rituals," "symbols,"
"myths," and "folklore" that comprised common American pre-
conceptions about government and the economy. According to the
traditional, commonly held view, "anything which could be called
government interference in business necessarily created bureaucracy,
regimentation, inflation and put burdens on posterity." † What he
hoped to achieve with his books, Arnold declared, was to discredit
stereotyped conceptions that had paralyzed "modern realists" in
their efforts to achieve reform of the economic system. Once Americans had renounced their uncritical reverence for myths that they
confused with principles, Arnold wrote, then they might get down
to such basic tasks as "day-to-day distribution of food, housing, and
clothing to those who needed them." ‡

Thurman Arnold's books now stand as basic documents of the
thirties, evincing the spirit of the new pragmatism which he sought
to make respectable and which the New Deal represents to many
students of the period. They remain important as well for their
analyses of American economic thought and of the economic order

* Richard Hofstadter: *The Age of Reform, From Bryan to F. D. R.* (New
York, 1955), p. 317.
† *The Folklore of Capitalism* (New Haven, 1937), p. 50.
‡ *Ibid.*, p. 47.

of the time. In the following essay, Arnold attempts the difficult
tasks of identifying the major changes that have occurred since 1937
and assessing the relevance of *The Folklore of Capitalism* today.

THE FOLKLORE OF CAPITALISM
REVISITED

Thurman W. Arnold

The Folklore of Capitalism, as I originally saw it in 1937, was written to describe the frustrating effects, in times of revolutionary
change, of ideals and symbols inherited from a different past. It
therefore may be useful to describe what has happened to our folklore in the quarter of a century since that book was published.

Since that time the greatest war in history has been fought. That
war pulled us out of the stagnation of the depression. It forced us
to utilize our industrial resources to the utmost and to expand them
at a rate which would have been considered impossible twenty-five
years ago. We came out of the war far richer in terms of real wealth,
by which I mean productive capacity, than when we went in. We
became the richest nation the world has ever known.

For a short time after that war we were a confident nation, sure
of our destiny. We believed that we were at the beginning of a
new age of world order based on fundamental principles acceptable to all civilized nations. The symbol of that belief was the United
Nations, which represented world unity under a new kind of international law. The first step we took to dramatize the ideal of
international law and order was the Nuremberg trials. The purpose
of those trials was to establish a great legal precedent which would
outlaw forever the kind of aggressive war Germany had forced
on the Western world. And so the United States, England, and
Russia set up a joint international tribunal to clothe the ideal of
international order with a judicial opinion which would be a guide

Reprinted by permission of the publisher from *The Folklore of Capitalism*
(New Haven: Yale University Press, 1962). This article is the preface to the
new edition and originally appeared in *The Yale Review*, LII, No. 2 (Winter,
1963), pp. 188–204. Copyright 1962, Yale University Press.

for the indefinite future. The Nuremberg verdict was designed to teach Germany a lesson it would never forget and to be a permanent warning to all future Hitlers that the new world would no longer put up with military aggression.

With the twin symbols—the United Nations, where international disputes were to be resolved, and the Nuremberg trials, establishing a new principle of international morality—we believed we had achieved an enduring foreign policy. The age-old dream of all utopians—that if we can get men to agree on a principle, institutions and social organizations will arise which will adhere to and carry out that principle—was the basis of short-lived optimism and confidence which followed the destruction of the German empire.

In saying this I do not mean to imply that the United Nations has not made a tremendous contribution to world order. It was the first formal recognition in our history that the industrial revolution of the twentieth century had created a world in which even a nation as large as the United States could no longer exist as an isolated economic or political unit. It would have been indeed a tragedy had the United States rejected the ideal of which the United Nations was a symbol. The significance of the United Nations was the fact that it marked the end of a century of isolationist thinking.

Nevertheless we expected too much of it. The apparent agreement between the Soviets and the Western democracies expressed in the Nuremberg trials, that international aggression was abolished as a matter of international law, coupled with a new organization designed to unite every nation in the world in a common humanitarian purpose, lulled us into a sense of false security. And so we cheerfully dismembered Germany into four zones, French, British, Russian, and American, so that all could be partners in eliminating the menace of another Hitler. To have established a corridor giving access to Berlin would have shown distrust of our Russian partner and disturbed that atmosphere of confidence and cooperation which was to remove the threat of future wars.

The disillusionment that followed the collapse of these shining symbols of peace and international morality gave rise to fears and anxieties about the stability of our own institutions at home which grew to a national neurosis. Somebody had to be blamed for our short period of amity with Russia. The idealistic attempt to establish in cooperation with Russia some sort of world order could only have been caused by the infiltration of local Communists into our own government. The idea spread over the entire nation that the American Communist Party, through devious and secret ways, had the potential power to overthrow the government of the United States. The real danger to our institutions was not Russian power abroad but Communist infiltration at home.

We became more afraid of ideas than realities. This fear increased in intensity as the cold war proceeded. It wasn't enough to discharge suspected persons from government service. A public badge of infamy had to be pinned on them. We had to celebrate our achievements in ridding the country of its internal dangers by a public ceremony. And so President Truman established a hierarchy of quasi-judicial institutions clothing the hunt for subversives with the sanctity of judicial process. It was in this atmosphere that Senator McCarthy rose to power and was able to dictate to the President who should be discharged and who should be retained. Any idea which did not conform to the McCarthy pattern was sufficient to destroy the career of a liberal in government if by some accident his name got into the files of a congressional committee.

It soon became apparent that there weren't enough Communists to keep the costly and rapidly expanding bureaucracy of security officers, hearing boards, and congressional committees supplied with victims. Most of the material they had to work on was hearsay and secret reports by professional informers. To use such material as evidence was contrary to every American ideal of a fair trial. Indeed, an American tribunal in Germany had convicted German judges on the ground that the use of secret evidence was an international crime.

But this ideal of a fair trial had to give way in order to keep the vast bureaucracy in business. And so it was determined that accused individuals could be convicted on secret evidence given by faceless informers whose identity was unknown to the accused. Nor was the accused permitted to see and rebut the secret evidence given against him. This process tremendously enlarged the supply of game which the security system could track down and shoot. The Supreme Court of the United States gave its tacit approval to the use of this sort of evidence by affirming the conviction of Dorothy Bailey on secret evidence in a four-to-four decision. And from then on, for years, the most publicized policy of government was the rooting out of subversives in government and industry.

Our cold war with Russia assumed all of the aspects of the religious wars of the Reformation. Both the Soviets and the United

States engaged in worldwide propaganda appealing to the hearts and souls of men to adopt the only true religion. The preaching of each side was as violent as any delivered during the Reformation. The only difference was that in the Reformation hell was in the next world. In the religious war of the twentieth century the respective hells of communism and capitalistic imperialism were in this world, just around the corner. Millions were spent by the United States on the Voice of America, and counter-millions were spent by Russia in jamming its broadcasts. And so for years we believed that our national salvation depended on preaching the glories of capitalism abroad and the rooting out of subversives at home. This is the kind of phenomenon which always occurs when a religious war is being fought.

Today we have fixed our attention on Russian power instead of internal subversion. Yet the essentially religious character of the cold war still continues. Neither Russia nor the United States is pursuing materialistic objectives. It is indeed a battle for the minds and hearts of men in which symbols are still more important than realities. For example, we have planted our flag in Berlin and are prepared to defend it even at the risk of an atomic war. Berlin is a symbol of the reunification of Germany. The ideological conflict could be resolved, at least with respect to that city, if the United States would recognize the legality of the East German government. Few intelligent men believe that as a practical matter reunification of Germany is even a remote possibility. Yet concessions by either side would be a moral victory for the other with far-reaching psychological consequences in Germany and Western Europe. When wars are fought over markets or for trade advantages they can be ended when they appear too costly. When they are fought for the minds and hearts of men, when it is a struggle between the Catholic and the Protestant churches, or between Communism and Capitalism, neither side can risk defeat on the issue of any symbol which dramatizes its faith. This is true even though defense of that symbol might possibly mean the extinction of half the human race. From a rational point of view this may seem like nonsense. From an anthropological point of view, however, we must recognize that such symbols as Berlin are the cement that holds Western society together, that holds the promise of unity, both political and economic, for Western nations. To abandon such a symbol might utterly defeat the brightest promise of the future. The risk must therefore be taken.

Out of this risk there is emerging a new ideal, and a new set of symbols. The European Common Market, which seemed completely utopian only a few years ago, has become a reality. An international court has been set up to adjudicate the trade practices of the citizens of independent sovereignties. An international code of antitrust laws after the American model has been enacted and is being enforced by the European international court. The United States and England are seeking to join that international economic union.

And here in the Western Hemisphere we have accepted the ideal of the economic unity of the United States and Latin America. That ideal has been embodied in an organization called the Alliance for Progress. The basic concept of that organization is expressed in a treaty by which the United States and Latin American nations committed themselves to an acceleration of economic growth, a more equitable distribution of the fruits of economic development, and recognized the need for tax, land, and institutional reform and new investment capital. In the language of the treaty of Punta del Este these nations and the United States agreed "to unite in a common effort to bring our people accelerated economic progress and broader social justice within the framework of personal dignity and political liberty."

These words could not have been written without a storm of outraged protest when *The Folklore of Capitalism* was published in 1937. No such treaty could possibly have been approved by the Senate of the United States at that time.

In those times Henry Wallace was being denounced as a man who wanted to give a bottle of milk to every Hottentot because of ideas which were insignificant in scope compared with the Alliance for Progress. And yet the Alliance for Progress, which goes further in assuming responsibility for the poverty and economic chaos of Latin American nations than anything Henry Wallace ever dreamed of, has become a political reality supported by liberals and conservatives alike.

Another tremendous change in our ideals and symbols that has taken place since that book was written is in our personification of great corporations as individuals. We no longer feel that government control of industry is something that will end in the destruction of individual liberty. My chapters on "The Personification of Corporations" and "The Ritual of Corporate Reorganization" are largely obsolete today. The amount of regulatory interference with business today which is represented by our vast government bureaus would have been unthinkable to a conservative in 1937. Now these tremendous bureaucratic hierarchies have lost their radical tinge. They have obtained an almost invulnerable place in the hierarchy of our institutions. Our courts, which before the great depression were accustomed to review decisions of administrative tribunals with meticulous care, now affirm them if there is the slightest supporting evidence.

The ideological doctrine which supports the immunity of our present administrative tribunals from judicial review is the theory that they are composed of experts in their particular narrow lines. Under the cloak of this doctrine many of the evils and oppressive bureaucratic practices which were protected by conservatives in 1937 have become a part of our administrative machinery. Yet so securely has our system of administrative tribunals become entrenched that there is no effective protest made today against bureaucratic aggression. This is indeed a revolutionary change since 1937 in our ideas of the proper function of government.

The chapter entitled "The Effect of the Antitrust Laws in Encouraging Large Combinations" needs comment in the light of what has happened since the book was published. That chapter was written after ten years of nonenforcement of the Sherman Act when the total appropriation for the Antitrust Division was less than $250,000. Today it is over $5 million. The decisions of the Supreme Court of the United States since 1937 have tremendously broadened the enforcement of antitrust policy. As Milton Handler said in a recent article: "In few areas of the law is a mature jurisprudence reinforced by so powerful an arsenal of investigative powers and remedies."

And even more astonishing from the point of view of one writing in 1937, when the ideal of the antitrust laws was recognized in no other country in the world except the United States, is the fact that the antitrust ideal has spread to Europe. The Treaty of Rome, which was the foundation of the present European Common Market, contains a set of antitrust rules which is now embodied in regulations and enforced by a supernational European court. The system of domestic and international cartels which in 1937 was legitimate in Europe is under heavy attack, though not completely abolished, in the European Common Market—a development no one would have dreamed of in 1937 before the Second World War.

In the field of monetary and fiscal policy, however, nineteenth-century economic symbols still cloud the realities of the twentieth-

century industrial revolution and frustrate American economi
progress. Just as during the depression we were unable to utiliz·
our full productive capacity because of a lack of consumer purchas
ing power, so today we are still unable to utilize it for the same
reason. Since 1953 our annual economic growth has not been enough
to keep up with our tremendously increasing labor force. The top
of every curve in the roller coaster of booms and depressions on
which we have been riding since 1953 has shown greater unemploy·
ment than the top of the last curve. During this period of nearly
ten years our economy has been stagnant and sluggish in growth.
During the same period France, Germany, and Italy have been
advancing, in terms of goods and services produced, more than twice
as fast as we have. We are accumulating an increasing number of
unemployed. During the same period France, Germany, and Italy
have had an actual shortage of labor.

The actual cost in terms of goods and services resulting from
our failure to utilize our full industrial capacity has been estimated
by Leon Keyserling to amount to the stupendous sum of $387
billion from 1953 to the middle of 1962. This enormous wealth was
available to us but we could not use it because there was not enough
purchasing power in the United States economy to absorb the
products which our industrial plant was able to produce.

And thus under the same economic symbols and rituals that we
had during the great depression we are developing today the same
symptoms that prolonged that depression. The only time we were
free from the tyranny of these nineteenth-century economic images
was during the Second World War. Then, for the first time since
the depression began, we were able to use and to expand our
production to the full limit of our industrial ability. As a result we
came out of that war richer in our productive capacity than at any
time before. But after the Second World War the old religion took
over. Since 1953 we have been progressively slowing down and increasingly unable to sustain the economic growth necessary for full
employment.

Today we write about ourselves as an affluent society. But in
1960 there were almost 10½ million families (households of two
or more persons) with annual incomes of under $4,000 before taxes.
This means that one family in every four was living in poverty in
the United States in 1960. Out of this group of families with under
$4,000 a year, over 3,000,000 were living in actual deprivation with
incomes of under $2,000 a year, and as for the unattached individ-

als almost 4,000,000 had annual incomes of under $2,000. These figures are taken from Leon Keyserling's pamphlet *Poverty and Deprivation in the United States,* written for the Conference on Economic Progress. To sum up, Leon Keyserling concludes that there were living in poverty 34,000,000 people in families and 4,000,-000 unattached persons. There were living in deprivation 37,000,000 people in families and 2,000,000 unattached persons. This makes a total of 77,000,000 people who are unable to attain what we like to think of as an American standard of living. They are unable to buy the products of our industrial economy. As a result the nation has lost in goods and services a staggering total of $387 billion from 1953 to the middle of 1962.

Yet the *Wall Street Journal,* in a typical editorial (July 26, 1962) attacking government spending in a period when our industrial plant is [25] percent idle, says with absolute religious conviction: "There is no visible lack of purchasing power today."

Our failure to realize our economic potential has occurred during a period when Western Europe has no problem of unemployment and has been operating its industrial plant, in many ways superior to ours in efficiency, at full capacity. This is today a constant source of bewilderment to Europeans. After a recent visit to the United States, Gunnar Myrdal said that the stagnant condition of the American economy was a menace to the prosperity of the Western world. He regarded it as inexcusable for so rich a country as ours to have so many slums, obsolete houses, inadequate schools, and inadequate social services. He attributed it to the illiteracy of our economic thinking. When asked to comment on Myrdal's observations all President Kennedy could say was this: "Well, I think it is regretable that we have not been able to develop an economic formula which maintains the growth of our economy. If we were moving ahead at full blast today, of course, you would have full employment."

In July, when the President made that comment, the rosy January predictions of his economic advisers had collapsed. The Gross National Product, though it was the highest in our country's history, was billions of dollars short of the January prediction. There had been no change whatever in the problem of unemployment.

The reason why no acceptable formula has been developed to achieve full utilization of the tremendously increased capacity of the twentieth-century industrial revolution is that the majority of our respectable and conservative citizens are still obsessed with the economic folklore of the nineteenth century.

That folklore consisted of a series of very simple mental pictures. The government was pictured as the thrifty head of the family who balances his budget and saves money for the future. If he does not do so he goes bankrupt and his children suffer. The national debt which had been constantly increasing since the First World War was a mortgage on the property of every citizen, which sooner or later would have to be paid by the next generation. Prosperity and full employment could only be forthcoming by balancing the national budget and taking the burden of taxation from the backs of our taxpayers. The money and credit necessary to operate our economy and full employment would then be produced by private industry and our economy would begin to grow and expand, as it did in the nineteenth century. The idea that government credit or government debt could be used to create the purchasing power necessary to distribute the products of the twentieth-century industrial revolution was unsound, radical, crackpot, dangerous, and subversive. It was leading us straight to socialism. Such was the economic folklore of 1962.

When the President said that we had been unable to develop an economic formula which would maintain the growth of our economy he meant that we had no such formula which was consistent with our theology of balancing the fiscal budget. It was an admission that there was no way under the folklore of capitalism existing in 1962 in which we could maintain full employment and full utilization of our resources. We had to go on losing about $10 billion in goods and services every year, which wealth we might have had had our folklore allowed us to distribute it. The principle of balancing the fiscal budget was so sacred that any other course was economic sin and would inevitably lead to some sort of unspecified economic or social hell.

It was not true that no formula had been developed to maintain economic growth. It was only true that no *respectable* formula had been developed. For years a group of economists led by Leon Keyserling had advocated balancing the economic budget rather than the fiscal budget. By this they meant that on one side of the balance sheet the President should estimate the productive capacities of our national industrial plants. On the other side there should be listed the demands on that productive capacity for necessities such as schools, public works, water conservation, health, and so on through a long list. Congress could then formulate programs which would not put an inflationary burden upon our productive capacity but at the same time would utilize it to its fullest extent. France has such a plan. Germany, though without a formal plan, has for years thought in terms of production rather than money. In other words, balancing the economic budget consists in the establishment of economic goals and the implementation of those goals by practical methods.

But the trouble with this practical approach to the problem of maintaining economic growth is that there is no automatic fiscal principle by which it can be carried out. Of course the practical ad hoc approach is the one we use in time of war. In the last war we were able to allocate production between the war effort and consumers' goods. We not only maintained our economic growth but expanded it tremendously. Indeed, it was only the enormous spending of the World War which pulled us out of the depression. We also have no difficulty in applying the concept of balancing the economic rather than the fiscal budget in our program for the Alliance for Progress among Latin American nations. Here economic goals are set. Economic planning is the key to the solution; the economic budget rather than the fiscal budget is the center of the program.

But the approach to the problem of economic growth which is possible in time of war, or is freely used in the Alliance for Progress, is as yet impossible in the domestic economy of the United States in time of peace. We are obsessed with the dream of an automatic economy which operates without planning, and the center of the whole thing is the balanced fiscal budget. Given a balanced fiscal budget the private economy is supposed, through credit mechanisms which it creates without government interference, to supply the purchasing power to operate the industrial plant of the twentieth century at full capacity. The fact that it has not been able to do so since 1929 is in conflict with this theory and, therefore, is ignored because it is inconsistent with our folklore.

The central idea of the economic folklore which frustrates our ability to use the capacity of the modern industrial revolution may be expressed as follows: Private enterprise with its tremendous variety of credit devices is able to supply the purchasing power which will not only utilize our full productive capacity but enable it to expand. It is the duty of the government to prevent that expansion from proceeding too rapidly. The government performs that duty by balancing the budget.

This was true before the First World War. But since the end of the First World War it has become increasingly apparent that private credit mechanisms are not by themselves sufficient to distribute the tremendously increased industrial capacity created by the twentieth-century scientific revolution.

The persistence of the idea that through the expansion of private credit alone the economy of the twentieth-century revolution can grow and be utilized to its fullest capacity is illustrated by a recital of our popular economic thinking during the boom of the 'twenties and through the depression. Before the First World War sound economic opinion estimated that a national debt of $500 million was all that our economy could safely absorb. But during the war our national debt grew from less than one billion dollars to the incredible sum of $26 billion in 1919. We followed our accepted theory. The sole function of government was to balance the budget. The Republican Administration reduced the national debt in ten years by $9 billion, saving about a billion dollars a year.

Then came the crash of 1929 and the depression which followed. There was not enough purchasing power to begin to take up the productive capacity we had achieved. But our economic folklore prevented us from seeing this outstanding fact. Roosevelt ran for office on the tried and true principle of balancing the budget. It was not lack of purchasing power but rather lack of business confidence that was supposed to be the cause of prolonging the great depression.

Roosevelt was forced to abandon his devotion to the principle of a balanced fiscal budget in favor of measures which were absolutely required to keep people from starving. He was bitterly attacked on the ground that these measures were leading to inflation and would inevitably result in the destruction of the capitalistic system. The fear of inflation haunted the business community throughout the entire depression in spite of the fact that a realistic appraisal clearly showed that the only thing we had to fear was continued deflation and a sluggish, nonexpanding economy.

In 1937 Roosevelt did succeed in balancing his cash budget, that is, in taking out of the economy more money than the government was putting in. There followed the recession of 1938. But that recession was still not attributed to lack of purchasing power. Conservative economists and bankers pointed out that it was due to lack of business confidence as a result of Roosevelt's attack on the Supreme Court.

The war pulled us out of the depression. It gave us the greatest industrial plant the world has ever known. In spite of gloomy predictions to the contrary which were made by conservatives at the end of the Second World War the country enjoyed an unprecedented boom. Then in 1953 the conservative Republican Party took over, determined to combat inflation and to balance the national budget, and finally to stop inflation by stopping the money supply.

But it soon appeared that the program was impossible. The failure of the conservatives in power has been described by Edwin Dale, Jr., financial editor of the *New York Times*, in a brilliant book, *Conservatives in Power: A Study in Frustration* (Doubleday, 1960):

After five years of trying, the regime had produced (or found itself with), in fiscal 1959, the biggest budget deficit in peacetime history and the first really serious wave of "inflationary psychology" in modern times.

The only answer seemed to be more conservative than ever. Squeeze the budget—Russian challenge and depressing slums and dirty streams to the contrary notwithstanding. Stretch out the national debt at every opportunity—at the risk of even more uncertainty in the bond markets. Keep money tight and interest rates high—even with nearly five million people out of work in the winter of 1958–59. Keep trying to return functions to the states to relieve federal finance—even with the State of Michigan so tightly pinched for money that it had to appeal to large corporate taxpayers to pay in advance.

And given their view of the world and the dollar, the conservatives were right. The only cure for the disease was a stronger dose of the familiar medicine.

And so Eisenhower achieved through his budget-balancing policies the greatest peacetime deficit in our history and the greatest peacetime inflation.

The real difficulty is that we have failed to realize the tremendous productive capacity of the twentieth-century scientific revolution. That capacity is so great that the credit mechanisms invented by the private sector of the economy cannot fully employ it. Those credit mechanisms, which we will call the private printing of money, have never before in our history pumped as much money into the nation's purchasing power. The automobile companies print the money for even the lowest income groups to buy cars. FHA prints the money for private organizations to build houses. Never before in our history has the down payment on houses been so little or the mortgages so long that they outlast the houses themselves. Almost anyone can get an unlimited letter of credit for travel by joining something like the Diners' Club. Department stores are printing the money their customers use to buy goods through revolving credit accounts and whatnot. No one has to pay cash for anything but food. In fact, anything which can be capitalized and on which a dollar income may be attributed can be financed. And this financing, though fantastically unsound according to nineteenth-century standards, is actually working. It is a new type of currency based on faith that the consumer will have a job and pay the installments on his debt. And by and large that faith has been justified.

But this new reservoir of credit, vast as it is, has only kept our industrial plant running since 1953 at about 75 percent of its capacity and $10 billion a year in goods and services has been lost. We are as yet unable to think of our national wealth in terms of productive capacity. We are unable to utilize that productive capacity for pressing national needs such as schools, health, and education because it would unbalance the fiscal budget.

The Potomac River is a good illustration of this folklore. It is an open sewer. A vast recreation area badly needed has gone to waste. The more the sludge accumulates the greater will be the burden on posterity. We have the productive capacity to clean up this river and all the other rivers. But we cannot do so because it would be an intolerable burden on our taxpayers. According to our folklore there is only one economic situation which would justify cleaning up the Potomac, and that is if Washington, D. C., became a depressed area. In that case, perhaps, we might clean it up, not because the job itself was worthwhile doing but because the expenditures might prime the pump and get Washington on its economic feet again. But until Washington becomes a depressed area it is better to let the Potomac fill up with sludge so that it will remain a handy way of priming the pump in the future.

There seems no way, according to our present folklore of capitalism, to utilize our productive capacity to clean up the Potomac because it is a very necessary thing to do with respect to the health and recreation of our nation's capital.

In the nineteenth century our productive capacity was not enough for such public projects. To have engaged in them might have been inflationary. Today, when our productive capacity is so great that only 75 percent of it can be absorbed by the purchasing power created by private credit, we still consider it inflationary to utilize that capacity. We cannot accept as a rational plan for ourselves the basic formula which even the conservatives have been willing to accept for Latin America.

And thus the old folklore of capitalism which I attempted to describe in my book of a quarter-century ago still frustrates our economic growth. The fact that Western European economics are not so frustrated is a continuing source of bewilderment to us. We are at present sending economists to Western Europe to find out why those countries have no unemployment and are moving ahead at more than double our speed. I suggest that nothing will come of such economic inquiries. Each inquiring economist will look at Western Europe through the spectacles of a preconceived theory. He will then disregard all the facts which do not fit in with that theory. Finally he will come back with the report that the lesson we must learn from the booming economies of Western Europe is to balance our fiscal budget at home. Many reports of this character are already being published in our conservative journals. To paraphrase Karl Marx, "Economic theology is the opiate of the middle classes."

Each year more and more goods can be produced with less and less labor. For the past ten years we have been able to use only about 75 percent of what we can produce. As a practical matter it would not be difficult to avail ourselves of that unused production. As an ideological matter it is a present impossibility to carry on the public works and services which our economy could so easily afford. This is because private money and credit are not available for such things as conservation of our water supply, our health, our recreational facilities, and so on through a long list of public necessities. Things which cannot be bought and sold for dollars on the marketplace cannot be financed by private credit. Therefore, we must do without them even though this means a colossal waste of our real productive resources.

If it were just a matter of wasting resources perhaps we could live with it. The nineteenth century was an era of colossal waste. But the present industrial revolution is gradually destroying the purchasing power necessary to distribute its productive ability. This is in spite of fantastic credit schemes which provide private credit that a nineteenth-century banker would consider insane. And so the backlog of unemployment grows as our labor force increases. A new phrase has become part of our economic vocabulary, "structural unemployment." It means that an incredibly rich country can find no ideological way of providing its citizens with the standard of living which it is physically capable of giving them.

The problem is a psychological one, not to be solved by either preaching or learning. It involves a recognition that things without a dollar value on the marketplace are nevertheless national assets of incalculable value. A trained scientist, engineer, or physician is an asset. The university that trains him is as valuable to our economy as a General Motors plant. An unskilled laborer, or an unemployed person, is a liability. A public debt owed by a nation to its own citizens is not a mortgage which their children must pay off. The building of necessary public works is an asset both for the present and the future.

It is this central idea that gives the Russian economy such strength as it has. It is the rigid and inflexible philosophy that such assets cannot be built or maintained by private enterprise that is the principal weakness of Russia. Budgets of course have to be balanced. But the budget of the twentieth century is a balance between productive capacity and the effective demands which are made on that capacity. When those notions become part of our folklore of capitalism the only limit on American progress will be the extent to which modern science can expand productive capacity.

How will this change come about? I expect that the process of the adjustment of inherited economic images to the reality of the vast potential productive capacity of the twentieth century may turn out to be as painful as it was during the great depression when we finally became acclimated to social security, unemployment relief, guarantee of bank deposits, the TVA, control of security markets, and so on through a long list of changes for which Roosevelt was so bitterly denounced. Basic economic beliefs are religious in character. We are struggling today through a period more like the period of the Reformation than any other period in history, but the frustrating effects of religious economic beliefs can be overcome, and in a period of revolutionary change they must be.

BIBLIOGRAPHY

EDITOR'S NOTE: The bibliographies provided for each selection are by no means complete, but will, it is hoped, aid the student who wishes to do further reading on the subjects of these essays. The footnotes to many of the individual selections in this volume provide an excellent source of bibliographic information as well. Basic reference works that offer useful bibliographies include Oscar Handlin et al.: *The Harvard Guide to American History* (Cambridge, 1955); and American Economic Association: *Index of Economic Journals, 1886–1959* (Homewood, Ill., 1961–62). The March 1959 issue of *The Journal of Economic History*, XIX, no. 1, is devoted to review articles on writings in economic history since 1945. Harry Stevens summarizes regional studies in "Recent Writings on Midwestern Economic History," *Ohio Historical Quarterly*, LXIX (1960). On land policy, see U. S. Department of the Interior: *Public Lands Bibliography* (Washington, 1962); on business history, Lorna M. Daniells: *Studies in Enterprise* (Boston, 1957), and her annual list of articles and books in the field, since then, in *The Business History Review;* on labor history, G. S. Stroud and G. E. Donahue: *Labor History in the United States*, and Fred D. Rose: *American Labor in Journals of History*, both published by the Institute of Labor and Industrial Relations of the University of Illinois. A valuable guide to articles in collections is Hedwig Schleiffer's *Index to Economic History Essays in Festschriften, 1900–1950* (Cambridge, 1953). Full bibliographies are appended to the volumes in *The Economic History of the United States*, edited by Henry David et al., 8 volumes to date, (New York, 1947–); these are cited by author and title of each individual volume in the bibliographies below. Since 1902 The American Historical Association has annually published its comprehensive *Writings in American History*. It has a cumulative index to 1940 and the latest volume to date lists publications in 1955; writings that have appeared since 1955 can often be traced through reviews and listings of articles in *The American Historical Review* and *The Missis-*

sippi Valley Historical Review. In addition to these two journals, others important in the field of economic history are: *The Journal of Economic History, The Economic History Review* (British), *Agricultural History, The Business History Review, Labor History, The Pacific Historical Review, Technology and Culture,* and the various state historical quarterlies. *The William and Mary Quarterly* covers early America.

Statistical material is available in convenient form in U. S. Bureau of the Census: *Historical Statistics of the United States, Colonial Times to 1957* (Washington, 1960); and the various publications of the National Bureau of Economic Research, especially its *Trends in the American Economy in the 19th Century* (Princeton, 1960). Studies of agricultural price data are listed in D. A. Brown: "Historical Prices of Farm Products by States, A Bibliography," *Agricultural History,* XXXVI (1962).

1. FARMERS ON THE LAND

A pioneer effort to identify cultural factors in colonial agriculture was made by Richard Shryock, in his study of the Virginia agricultural region, "British versus German Traditions in Colonial Agriculture," *Mississippi Valley Historical Review,* XXVI (1939). Compare with Rodney Leohr: "The Influence of English Agriculture on American Agriculture, 1775–1825," *Agricultural History,* II (1937). The best general surveys of colonial agriculture remain Percy W. Bidwell and J. I. Falconer: *History of Agriculture in the Northern United States, 1620–1860* (Washington, 1925); Lewis C. Gray: *History of Agriculture in the Southern United States to 1860,* 2 vols. (Washington, 1933); and relevant chapters of Curtis P. Nettels: *The Roots of American Civilization* (New York, 1938). Detailed regional studies that offer a basis for comparison with eastern Pennsylvania include Willard Range: "The Agricultural Revolution in Royal Georgia, 1752–1775," *Agricultural History,* XXI (1947); Solon J. Buck: "Frontier Economy in Southwestern Pennsylvania," *Agricultural History,* X (1936); and Avery Craven: *Soil Exhaustion as a Factor in the Agricultural History of Virginia and Maryland, 1606–1860* (Urbana, Ill., 1926). See also Wesley Frank Craven: *The Southern Colonies in the Seventeenth Century* (Baton Rouge, 1949). Special studies include Theodore Saloutos: "Efforts at Crop Control in Seventeenth Century America," *Journal of Southern History,* XII (1946); William S. Sack: "Agricultural Conditions in the Northern Colonies before the Revolution," *Journal of Economic History,* XIII (1953), which rests on price data for the most part; Warren C. Scoville: "Did Colonial Farmers 'Waste' Our Land?" *Southern Economic Journal,* XX (1953); and Rodney C. Loehr: "Self-

Sufficiency on the Farm," *Agricultural History*, XXVI (1952). The Revolutionary and early national periods are surveyed in Curtis P. Nettels: *Emergence of a National Economy, 1775–1815* (New York, 1962), which includes an extensive bibliography on agriculture.

2. COMMERCE AND URBAN GROWTH

An article close to Bailyn's in interpretation, although it deals with a later period, is Robert A. East's "The Business Entrepreneur in a Changing Colonial Economy, 1763–1795," *Journal of Economic History*, VI (1946); see also East: *Business Enterprise in the American Revolutionary Era* (New York, 1938). On the trade of the seventeenth century, see Bailyn's full-length study of *The New England Merchants in the Seventeenth Century* (Cambridge, 1955). Urban rivalry for trade with the colonial hinterland and factors underlying urban growth comprise the themes of Curtis P. Nettels: "The Economic Relations of Boston, Philadelphia and New York, 1680–1715," *Journal of Economic and Business History*, III (1931). Carl Bridenbaugh is author of two classic studies of urban growth in the early period: *Cities in the Wilderness* (New York, 1955) and *Cities in Revolt* (New York, 1955). See also James Soltow: "The Role of Williamsburg in the Virginia Economy, 1750–1775," *William and Mary Quarterly*, 3rd ser., XV (1958).

Studies of individual merchants and firms include James B. Hedges: *The Browns of Providence Plantations, Colonial Years* (Cambridge, 1952); W. T. Baxter: *The House of Hancock* (Cambridge, 1945); Glenn Weaver: *Jonathan Trumbull, Connecticut's Merchant Magistrate* (Hartford, 1956); and Byron Fairchild: *Messrs. William Pepperell* (Ithaca, 1954). Frederick B. Tolles: *Meeting House and Counting House: The Quaker Merchants of Colonial Philadelphia, 1682–1763* (Chapel Hill, 1948), is a penetrating study of one mercantile center.

3. BRITISH MERCANTILISM AND THE
AMERICAN ECONOMY

The standard sources on British mercantilism include L. A. Harper: *The English Navigation Laws* (New York, 1939); L. H. Gipson's monumental treatise on *The British Empire Before the American Revolution*, 10 vols., (New York, 1936–1962); Oliver M. Dickerson: *The Navigation Acts and the American Revolution* (Philadelphia, 1951); and Robert L. Schuyler: *The Fall of the Old Colonial System . . . 1770–1870* (New York, 1945). Curtis P. Nettels: "British Mercantilism and the Economic Development of the Thirteen Colonies," *Journal of Economic History*, XII (1952), argues that the mercantilist system was restrictive in purpose and operation and that the colonists had developed a rival mercantilist policy by 1776. A similar view is argued in Louis M. Hacker: *Triumph of American Capitalism* (New York, 1940); and William A. Williams: *The Contours of American History* (Cleveland, 1961). J. B. Brebner portrays a colonial economy which never outgrew its status under mercantilism, in *The Neutral Yankees of Nova Scotia* (New York, 1937). Richard Pares, in *Yankees and Creoles* (Cambridge, 1956), discusses the trade between the West Indies and the American mainland. An invaluable case study of mercantilist policy in practice is provided by Gilman M. Ostrander in "The Colonial Molasses Trade," *Agricultural History*, XXX (1956). Richard B. Sheridan provides a useful complement to the Ostrander study in his article, "The Molasses Act and the Market Strategy of the British Sugar Planters," *Journal of Economic History*, XVII (1957). In this analysis of the planters' economic situation in 1733, Sheridan emphasizes the importance of Molasses Act provisions that affected the English and European markets for products of the Indies. See also Albert B. Southwick: "The Molasses Act, Source of Precedents," *William & Mary Quarterly*, 3rd ser. VIII (1951). Allan S. Johnson: "The Passage of the Sugar Act," ibid., 3rd ser., XVI (1959), traces formulation of the revised customs law by Crown officials in 1763-64. On the related problem of the Stamp Act, see Edmund S. Morgan and Helen Morgan: *The Stamp Act Crisis* (Chapel Hill, 1953); and Charles S. Ritcheson: "The Preparation of the Stamp Act," *William and Mary Quarterly*, 3rd ser., X (1953). For a summary of the crisis precipitated by revision of British policies after 1763, see Gipson's *The Coming of the Revolution, 1763–1775* (New York, 1954).

4. THE REVOLUTIONARY ERA

Edmund S. Morgan has analyzed the interpretative controversies relating to the Revolutionary period in *The American Revolution: A Review of Changing Interpretations* (Washington, 1958). Two recent studies that have aroused much controversy are Robert E. Brown's *Middle-class Democracy and the Revolution in Massachusetts* (Ithaca, 1955); and Forrest McDonald's *We, the People* (Chicago, 1958). Jackson Turner Main and McDonald debate the issues in an exchange, in *William and Mary Quarterly*, 3rd ser., XVII (1960). See also Main's book, *The Antifederalists* (Chapel Hill, 1961); and Elisha P. Douglass: *Rebels and Democrats* (Chapel Hill, 1955). Essays that review the interpretative issues include Merrill Jensen: "Democracy and the American Rev-

olution," *Huntington Library Quarterly*, XX (1956–57); and Richard
B. Morris: "The Confederation Period and the American Historian,"
William and Mary Quarterly, 3rd ser., XIII (1956), and "Class Struggle and the American Revolution," ibid., 3rd ser., XIX (1962). J.
Franklin Jameson: *The American Revolution Considered as a Social
Movement* (Princeton, 1926), and Allan Nevins: *The American States
during and after the Revolution* (New York, 1924), were pioneering
studies. Jameson's work is reconsidered in the light of recent scholarship by Frederick Tolles, in "The American Revolution Considered as
a Social Movement: A Re-evaluation," *American Historical Review*,
LX (1954). More recent studies that bear on the problems that concern Lynd include E. James Ferguson: *The Power of the Purse: A History of American Public Finance, 1776–1790* (Chapel Hill, 1961);
George Billias: *The Massachusetts Land Bankers of 1740* (University
of Maine Studies, 2nd ser., No. 74, Orono, 1959); Robert S. Lambert:
"Confiscation of Loyalist Property in Georgia, 1782–1786," *William
and Mary Quarterly*, 3rd ser., XX (1963); and Curtis P. Nettels: *Emer-
gence of a National Economy, 1775–1815* (New York, 1962). Robert
E. Brown's hostile critique of the Beard thesis may be found in *Charles
Beard and the Constitution* (Princeton, 1956); Brown debates his al-
ternative hypothesis with John Cary in "Statistical Method and the
Brown Thesis," *William and Mary Quarterly*, 3rd ser., XX (1963).
Consult also Lynd's book, *Anti-Federalism in Dutchess County, New
York* (Chicago, 1962).

5. PUBLIC POLICY

On the role of state and local governments in promotion of transport,
consult Carter Goodrich: *Government Promotion of American Canals
and Railroads, 1800–1890* (New York, 1960). For a list of recent
studies of state and local policy, see Broude's footnote 19. An appraisal
of the impact of canal construction on cyclical fluctuations may be
found in Carter Goodrich, editor: *Canals and American Economic
Development* (New York, 1962). Nathan Miller provides a suggestive
analysis of state activism as revealed in control of state canal-fund surpluses, in *Enterprise of a Free People: Aspects of Economic Development in New York State* (Ithaca, 1962). The role of state and local
government in western transport is surveyed in H. N. Scheiber: "Urban
Rivalry and Internal Improvements in the Old Northwest, 1820–1860,"
Ohio History, LXXI (1962). Edward C. Kirkland: *Men, Cities and
Transportation, A Study in New England History, 1820–1900* (2 vols.,
Cambridge, 1948), is a basic work.

On state banking and transport policy, see George R. Taylor: *The*

Transportation Revolution, 1815–1860 (New York, 1951). Curtis P. Nettels' survey of the economy from 1775 to 1815 emphasizes government policy: *Emergence of a National Economy* (New York, 1962). Bray Hammond portrays banking policy on a broad canvas of economic, social and political history in *Banks and Politics in America* (Princeton, 1958); while Treasury Department relations with private banks comprise the theme of H. N. Scheiber: "The Pet Banks in Jacksonian Politics and Finance, 1833–1841," *Journal of Economic History*, XXIII (1963). On state policy toward corporations, in the context of colonial origins, see Oscar Handlin and Mary F. Handlin: "Origins of the American Business Corporation," ibid., V (1945).

Broude's article probably gives too little weight to the effects of federal land policy on development. On this subject, see Paul W. Gates: *The Farmer's Age* (New York, 1960). Important studies of public policy that have appeared since Broude's essay was published include Wiley E. Hodges: "Pro-Governmentalism in Virginia, 1789–1836," *Journal of Politics*, XXV (1963); M. E. Reed: "Government Investment and Economic Growth: Louisiana's Ante-Bellum Railroads," *Journal of Southern History*, XXVIII (1962); and Julius Rubin: "Canal or Railroad?" in American Philosophical Society *Transactions*, new ser., LI, Part 7 (1961). Robert Hunter: "Turnpike Construction in Antebellum Virginia," *Technology and Culture*, IV (1963), is one of the few studies that give close attention to technology in its relationship to public enterprise and its administration.

6. AGRICULTURE AND REGIONALISM

The best introduction to pre-Civil War agriculture is Paul W. Gates: *The Farmer's Age* (New York, 1960), which includes a full bibliography. A recent study by Allan G. Bogue: "Farming in the Prairie Peninsula, 1830–1890," *Journal of Economic History*, XXIII (1963) deals with the grasslands area of Illinois and Iowa and farmers' adaptation to the prairie environment. Earl D. Ross: *Iowa Agriculture, An Historical Survey* (Iowa City, 1951) may be consulted for further data relating to Iowa. A classic study by James C. Malin: *Winter Wheat in the Golden Belt of Kansas* (Lawrence, Kansas, 1944) will suggest the complexity of the problems of the subhumid environment. The Throne essay may be used as a starting point for comparative study of the influence of soil and climate, transport, and other factors in regional development. A model regional study is Neil A. McNall: *An Agricultural History of the Genesee Valley, 1790–1860* (Philadelphia, 1952).

Among recent studies of the profitability of slavery are Robert Evans, Jr.: "Some Economic Aspects of the Domestic Slave Trade,

1830–1860," *Southern Economic Journal*, XXVII (1961); Evans, "The Economics of American Slavery," with comment by Thomas P. Govan, in National Bureau of Economic Research: *Aspects of Labor Economics* (Princeton, 1962); Alfred H. Conrad and J. R. Meyer: "The Economics of Slavery in the Ante Bellum South," *Journal of Political Economy*, LXVI (1958), and comment by Douglas F. Dowd, ibid., LXVI (1958). A thesis that conflicts with Genovese's is presented by William L. Miller in "Slavery and the Population of the South," *Southern Economic Journal*, XXVIII (1961). A suggestive study of agriculture and industry in one southern state is Alfred G. Smith's *Economic Readjustment of an Old Cotton State: South Carolina, 1820–1860* (Chapel Hill, 1958). John Hebron Moore: *Agriculture in Ante-Bellum Mississippi* (New York, 1958) documents the pathetic readiness with which southern planters abandoned attempts at diversification when cash markets for cotton reopened after depression periods. Two of Genovese's own articles: "Cotton, Slavery and Soil Exhaustion in the Old South," *Cotton History Review*, II (1961), and "Livestock in the Slave Economy of the Old South," *Agricultural History*, XXXVI (1962) are relevant to the theme of the essay reprinted above.

7. FOREIGN TRADE AND DOMESTIC GROWTH

The essay reprinted here summarizes a central part of the thesis of Douglass North's important study of *The Economic Growth of the United States, 1790–1860* (Englewood Cliffs, N. J., 1961). Other valuable studies of the Anglo-American connection include J. Potter: "Atlantic Economy, 1815–60," *Studies in the Industrial Revolution*, ed. L. S. Presnell (London, 1960); Jeffrey G. Williamson: "The Long Swing: Comparison and Interactions Between British and American Balance of Payments, 1820–1913," *Journal of Economic History*, XXII (1962); and R. C. O. Matthews: *A Study in Trade Cycle History* (Cambridge, England, 1954). See also the broad-ranging article by Simon Kuznets: "Foreign Economic Relations of the United States and their Impact upon the Domestic Economy," *Proceedings of the American Philosophical Society*, October 1948.

Ralph W. Hidy and Muriel E. Hidy: "Anglo-American Merchant Bankers and the Railroads of the Old Northwest, 1848–1860," *Business History Review*, XXXIV (1960) examines provision of long- and short-term British credit to American railways; and Bernard M. Olsen: "A Representative Study of Capital Origins," *Economic Development and Cultural Change*, VI (1958) deals with movement of capital into Indiana manufacturing. Other studies of capital movements include Ralph W. Hidy: *The House of Baring in American Trade and Finance*

(Cambridge, 1949), which is valuable for footnote citation of older works; and Nathan Miller: *Enterprise of a Free People* (Ithaca, 1962), which examines sources of Erie Canal investment.

Among North's other writings, consult his study of "The United States Balance of Payments, 1790–1860," in National Bureau of Economic Research: *Trends in the American Economy in the 19th Century* (Princeton, 1960); and "The United States in the International Economy," *American Economic History*, ed. Seymour E. Harris (New York, 1961). On emergent regional specialization, see Paul W. Gates: *The Farmer's Age* (New York, 1960); and George R. Taylor: *The Transportation Revolution* (New York, 1951). Recent interpretations of business fluctuations are reviewed and an alternative hypothesis is offered in J. R. T. Hughes and Nathan Rosenberg: "The United States Business Cycle before 1860: Some Problems of Interpretation," *Economic History Review*, 2nd ser., XV (1963).

8. THE RISE OF INDUSTRY

Some of the social factors that shaped American industrialization are discussed in John E. Sawyer: "The Social Basis of the American System of Manufacturing," *Journal of Economic History*, XIV (1954); Charles L. Sanford: "The Intellectual Origins and New-Worldliness of American Industry," ibid., XVIII (1958); Samuel Rezneck: "Rise and Early Development of Industrial Consciousness in the United States, 1760–1830," *Journal of Economic and Business History*, IV (1932); and Robert S. Woodbury: "The Legend of Eli Whitney and Interchangeable Parts," *Technology and Culture*, I (1960). Local as well as national chauvinism marked early efforts to promote industrialization; on this subject see Herbert Collins: "The Southern Industrial Gospel before 1860," *Journal of Southern History*, XII (1946).

Caroline F. Ware: *The Early New England Cotton Manufacture* (Boston, 1931) is a classic study. Lance E. Davis considers the use of long-term and short-term credit by early textile manufacturers in "The New England Textile Mills and the Capital Markets," *Journal of Economic History*, XX (1960). See also Evelyn H. Knowlton: *Pepperell's Progress, History of a Cotton Textile Company, 1844–1945* (Cambridge, 1948), Chapter 6. George R. Taylor: *The Transportation Revolution* (New York, 1951) has full treatments of both labor and industry, 1815–60, and includes a valuable bibliography. Douglass C. North: *Economic Growth of the United States, 1790–1860* (Englewood Cliffs, N. J., 1961) includes a terse, analytic treatment of industrial growth.

On special topics, see G. H. Evans, Jr.: *Business Incorporations in* the United States (Princeton, 1948); Martha Van Hoesen Taber: A History of the Cutlery Industry in the Connecticut Valley (Northampton, Mass., 1955), which documents the early origins of price-fixing by American manufacturers; Vera Shlakman: Economic History of a Factory Town (Northampton, Mass., 1934), on Boston investment and promotion of Chicopee; articles in Growth of the American Economy, edited by Harold F. Williamson (Englewood Cliffs, N. J., 1954); and Hugo Meier's suggestive study of "Technology and Democracy, 1800–1860," Mississippi Valley Historical Review, XLIII (1956–57).

For a full account of the Pennsylvania laborer, see William A. Sullivan: The Industrial Worker in Pennsylvania, 1800–1840 (Harrisburg, 1955). John G. Rayback: History of American Labor (New York, 1959) is the best one-volume survey of labor. On labor in New England, see Oscar Handlin: Boston's Immigrants (Cambridge, 1941); Donald B. Cole: "Lawrence, Massachusetts," Historical Collections of the Essex Institute, XCII (1956); Ray Ginger: "Labor in a Massachusetts Cotton Mill, 1853–1860," Business History Society Bulletin, XXVIII (1954); and Roy P. Fairfield: "Labor Conditions at the Old York, 1831–1900," New England Quarterly, XXX (1957). There is material on western labor in Richard C. Wade: The Urban Frontier (Cambridge, 1959), and R. M. Nolen: "The Labor Movement in St. Louis Prior to the Civil War," Missouri Historical Review, XXXIV (1939); while river labor is discussed in Louis C. Hunter: Steamboats on the Western Rivers (Cambridge, 1949). Clifton K. Yearley, Jr.: Britons in American Labor (Baltimore, 1957); and Rowland T. Berthoff: British Immigrants in Industrial America (Cambridge, 1953), are complementary studies of the British worker. Although it deals with an earlier period, Carl Bridenbaugh's study of The Colonial Craftsman (New York, 1950) is the best source for an understanding of artisanship in the pre-factory era. Norman J. Ware: The Industrial Worker, 1840–1860 (Boston, 1924) is still valuable. On Negro labor, slave and free, see John Hope Franklin: From Slavery to Freedom (2nd edition, New York, 1956).

9. THE CIVIL WAR AND INDUSTRIAL GROWTH

A critique of Cochran's thesis on the Civil War and industrialization appears in The Economic Impact of the American Civil War (Cambridge, 1962), a valuable collection of articles and statistics edited by Ralph Andreano. In War for the Union, 2 vols. (New York, 1959–60), Allan Nevins gives attention to the economic impact of mobilization. Older economic surveys still valuable include Charles W. Ramsdell: Behind the Lines in the Southern Confederacy (Baton Rouge,

La., 1944); John C. Schwab: *The Confederate States of America* (New York, 1901); and Emerson D. Fite: *Social and Industrial Conditions in the North during the Civil War* (New York, 1910). Newer works that give considerable attention to the wartime economy include Clement Eaton: *A History of the Southern Confederacy* (New York, 1954); E. Merton Coulter: *The Confederate States of America* (Baton Rouge, La., 1950); and J. G. Randall and David Donald: *The Civil War and Reconstruction* (2nd edition, Boston, 1961), which has a full critical bibliography.

On Southern industry and the central government's role in fostering manufacturing, see works by Ramsdell and Eaton, already cited; and Paul P. Van Riper and H. N. Scheiber: "The Confederate Civil Service," *Journal of Southern History*, XXV (1959). On railways refer to Robert C. Black, III: *The Railroads of the Confederacy* (Chapel Hill, 1952), and Thomas Weber: *The Northern Railroads in the Civil War* (New York, 1952). See also the special issue on railroads of the journal *Civil War History*, VII (September, 1961). Frederick Merk's classic study, *The Economic History of Wisconsin during the Civil War Decade* (Madison, 1916), deals with the effects of war on northern agriculture. Robert L. Jones: *Ohio Agriculture during the Civil War* (Columbus, 1962); and Richard Sewell: "Michigan Farmers and the Civil War," *Michigan History*, XLIV (1960) are comparable studies in briefer compass. The politics of economic policy in Congress are treated by Wallace D. Farnham in two articles on the 1862 railroad land grants: "The Pacific Railroad Act of 1862," *Nebraska History*, XLIII (1962), and " 'The Weakened Spring of Government,' A Study in Nineteenth-Century American History," *American Historical Review*, LXVIII (1963); see also Bray Hammond's appraisal of greenback legislation in "The North's Empty Purse, 1861–1862," ibid., LXVII (1961); and Richard Hofstadter: "The Tariff Issue on the Eve of the Civil War," ibid., XLIV (1938) and Reinhard H. Luthin: "Abraham Lincoln and the Tariff," ibid., XLIX (1944). The agrarian reaction to eastern domination of Congress is treated by Frank Klement in "Middle Western Copperheadism and the Genesis of the Granger Movement," *Mississippi Valley Historical Review*, XXXVII (1952). Eugene M. Lerner: "Southern Output and Agricultural Income, 1860–1880," *Agricultural History*, XXXIII (1959) is a careful study of the effects of the war on industry and agriculture in the South.

Economic issues in post-Civil War politics are treated in Stanley Coben: "Northeastern Business and Radical Reconstruction, A Reexamination," *Mississippi Valley Historical Review*, XLVI (1959), a study which reveals the diversity of interests within the business community; Irwin Unger: "Business Men and Specie Resumption," *Politi-*

cal Science Quarterly, LXXIV (1959); C. Vann Woodward: *Reunion and Reaction* (Boston, 1951), a classic analysis of the 1877 compromise; and Robert P. Sharkey: *Money, Class and Party* (Baltimore, 1959), which includes a critical bibliography. Edward C. Kirkland's study of the period 1860–1897, *Industry Comes of Age* (New York, 1961) and Rendigs Fel's account of *American Business Cycles, 1865–1897* (Chapel Hill, 1959) are both of prime importance to an understanding of the post-war period.

10. DETERMINANTS OF REGIONAL DEVELOPMENT

The literature on land policy and western development has been much influenced, as one would expect, by the work of Frederick Jackson Turner. Turner's theory, in *The Frontier in American History* (New York, 1920) and other works, that "free land" served to relieve social pressures in the East by inducing westward migration has been widely studied. The "safety-valve thesis," as Turner's view has been termed, has now inspired a series of historiographical articles that review the varying interpretations since Turner. Of these the most useful are Fred Shannon: "A Post Mortem on the Labor-Safety-Valve Theory," *Agricultural History*, XIX (1945); Norm Simler: "The Safety-Valve Doctrine Reevaluated," ibid., XXXII (1958); and Ellen von Nardroff: "The American Frontier as a Safety Valve," ibid., XXXVI (1962). The place of the land speculator is considered in Paul W. Gates: "The Role of the Land Speculator in Western Development," *Pennsylvania Magazine of History and Biography*, LXVI (1942); Ray A. Billington: "The Origin of the Land Speculator as a Frontier Type," *Agricultural History*, XIX (1945); and Allan G. Bogue and Margaret Bogue: " 'Profits' and the Frontier Land Speculator," *Journal of Economic History*, XVII (1957). *The Public Lands*, edited by Vernon Carstensen (Madison, Wisc., 1963) reprints some of the most important writings on land policy and its effects. Chapters on land disposal are central to two surveys of agriculture that cover the nineteenth century, Paul W. Gates: *The Farmer's Age* (New York, 1960); and Fred Shannon: *The Farmer's Last Frontier* (New York, 1945). For a comparison of land policy in the West and South, Paul W. Gates's article, "Federal Land Policy in the South, 1866–1888," *Journal of Southern History*, VI (1940), is a useful starting point. Margaret Beattie Bogue: *Patterns from the Sod; Land Use and Tenure in the Grand Prairie, 1856–1900* (Springfield, Ill., 1959), an intensive study of this region, concentrates on the impact of land policy. Lawrence B. Lee: "The Homestead Act: Vision and Reality," *Utah Historical Quarterly*, XXX (1962) examines the law in operation in Kansas, Utah and California.

On the special nature of southern development before 1860, see Eugene Genovese's article, reprinted in this volume. On the postwar period, the most complete source is C. Vann Woodward: *Origins of the New South, 1877–1913* (Baton Rouge, 1951). C. S. Belissary reviews the "New South" campaign for industrialization in "Industry and Industrial Philosophy in Tennessee, 1865–1885," *Journal of Southern History*, XIX (1953). Dominance of southern railroads by northern investors and railway corporations is a major theme of John F. Stover: *The Railroads of the South, 1865–1900* (Chapel Hill, 1955). In addition to works cited by Dowd, see Rupert B. Vance: *Human Geography of the South* (Chapel Hill, 1932); and Gunnar Myrdal: *An American Dilemma: The Negro Problem and Modern Democracy*, 2 vols. (New York, 1944), both basic studies.

11. THE AGRARIAN PROBLEM: ITS WORLD CONTEXT

The standard work on agriculture in the late nineteenth century is Fred A. Shannon: *The Farmer's Last Frontier* (New York, 1945). Statistical data are available in works cited by Rothstein in his footnote 2; and in Frederick Strauss and Louis H. Bean: *Gross Farm Income and Indices of Farm Production and Prices in the United States, 1869–1937* (U. S. Dept. of Agriculture, *Technical Bulletin*, No. 703, Washington, 1940). For the role of agriculture in business cycles, see Rendigs Fels: *American Business Cycles, 1865–1897* (Chapel Hill, 1959). The traditional view of farm protest movements derives from Solon J. Buck: *The Granger Movement* (Cambridge, 1913); and John D. Hicks: *The Populist Revolt* (Minneapolis, 1931). But see also Theodore Saloutos: "The Agricultural Problem and Nineteenth Century Industrialism," *Agricultural History*, XXII (1948). A recent reappraisal of the Populists is provided by Norman Pollack, in *The Populist Response to Industrial America* (Cambridge, 1962). Theodore Saloutos: *Farmer Movements in the South, 1865–1933* (Berkeley and Los Angeles, 1960) is a valuable regional study. See also Roy V. Scott: *The Agrarian Movement in Illinois, 1880–1896* (Urbana, Ill., 1962). Allan G. Bogue: *Money at Interest: The Farm Mortgage on the Middle Border* (Ithaca, 1955) is a revisionist work on mortgage lending. The December 1962 issue of *The Journal of Economic History*, XXII, No. 4, is devoted to American agricultural history; several of the articles therein pertain to the late nineteenth century. The best introduction to the international economy is William Ashworth's superb study, *A Short History of the International Economy, 1850–1950* (London, 1952). For references to other recent works on the agrarian problem, see Saloutos: *Farmer Movements in the South*, already cited; and

Harry R. Stevens: "Recent Writings on Midwestern Economic History," *Ohio Historical Quarterly*, LXIX (1960).

Special studies of value on related aspects of agricultural development in this period include Fred Kohlmeyer and Floyd H. Herum: "Science and Engineering in Agriculture," *Technology and Culture*, II (1961); Clark C. Spence: "Early Uses of Electricity in American Agriculture," ibid., III (1962); Walter P. Webb: "The Story of Some Prairie Inventions," *Nebraska History*, XXXIV (1953); Gilbert C. Fite: "Republican Strategy and the Farm Vote . . . 1896," *American Historical Review*, LXV (1960); and monographs in the Stanford University series, *Food Research Institute Studies*.

12. STATE INTERVENTION: THE GRANGER LAWS

Works dealing with early regulatory activities of the state include Frederick Merk: "Eastern Antecedents of the Grangers," *Agricultural History*, XXIII (1949); David M. Ellis: "Rivalry between the New York Central and the Erie Canal," *New York History*, XXIX (1948); and H. N. Scheiber: "The Rate-Making Power of the State in the Canal Era," *Political Science Quarterly*, LXXVII (1962). Lee Benson: *Merchants, Farmers, and Railroads: Railroad Regulation and New York Politics, 1850–1887* (Cambridge, 1955), is a full-length study of policy in New York state. State promotional activities are treated in Carter Goodrich: *Government Promotion of American Canals and Railroads, 1800–1880* (New York, 1960). Solon J. Buck: *The Granger Movement* (Cambridge, 1913), provided what soon became the standard interpretation of the Grangers. The Illinois Granger law is re-examined, in terms of its political origins, by Harold D. Woodman in "Chicago Businessmen and the 'Granger' Laws," *Agricultural History*, XXXVI (1962). For later Illinois development, see Roy V. Scott: *The Agrarian Movement in Illinois, 1880–1896* (Urbana, Ill., 1962). On the movement for railroad regulation in Wisconsin, see R. T. Daland: "Enactment of the Potter Law," *Wisconsin Magazine of History*, XXXIII (1949); and Robert S. Hunt: *Law and Locomotion: The Impact of the Railroad on Wisconsin Law in the 19th Century* (Madison, 1958). See also Graham A. Cosmas: "The Democracy in Search of Issues: The Wisconsin Reform Party, 1873–1877," *Wisconson Magazine of History*, XLVI (1963). On the later history of the Iowa law, see Mildred Throne: "The Repeal of the Iowa Granger Law, 1878," *Iowa Journal of History*, LI (1953). Edward C. Kirkland reviews railroad regulation in *Industry Comes of Age* (New York, 1961). Regulatory legislation in the southern states is summarized in Arthur S. Link: "The Progressive Movement in the South, 1870–1914," *North*

Carolina Historical Review, XXIII (1946); see also James F. Doster: *Railroads in Alabama Politics, 1875–1914* (University, Ala., 1957).

13. THE RISE OF BIG BUSINESS

The combination movement is analyzed in Edward C. Kirkland: *Industry Comes of Age* (New York, 1961). See also Alfred D. Chandler, Jr.: *Strategy and Structure: Chapters in the History of the Industrial Enterprise* (Cambridge, 1962), which carries the subject of Chandler's article into the twentieth century; and Thomas C. Cochran and William Miller: *The Age of Enterprise,* revised edition (New York, 1961). Harold F. Williamson and Arnold Daum: *The American Petroleum Industry: The Age of Illumination* (Evanston, Ill., 1959), discusses the emergent dominance of Standard Oil. For the oil industry, see also Harvard Graduate School of Business: *Oil's First Century* (Cambridge, 1960), a valuable collection of essays; and works cited in Chandler's article.

The student of industrial consolidation will want to consult the multi-volume *Report of the Industrial Commission* (Washington, 1900–2); and the valuable summary in Harold U. Faulkner: *The Decline of Laissez Faire, 1898–1917* (New York: 1951). William B. Gates, Jr., studies integration and combination in *Michigan Copper and Boston Dollars* (Cambridge, 1951). Considerable attention has been lavished upon the question of social origins of business leaders: see essays in William Miller, ed.: *Men in Business,* revised edition, (New York, 1962); and Seymour M. Lipset and Reinhard Bendix: *Social Mobility in Industrial Society* (Berkeley and Los Angeles, 1959). Scholarship in the field of business history is reviewed by John E. Sawyer in "Entrepreneurial Studies," *Business History Review,* XXXII (1958); and by John G. B. Hutchins in "Recent Contributions to Business History," *Journal of Economic History,* XIV (1959). On the movement of financiers into industry, see Thomas Navin and Marian V. Sears: "The Rise of the Market for Industrial Securities," *Business History Review,* XIX (1955); and on the stock market, George Garvy: "Interlopers in the History of the New York Security Market," *Journal of Political Economy,* LII (1944). Marian V. Sears: "The American Businessman at the Turn of the Century," *Business History Review,* XXX (1956), is valuable on business thought. Early efforts at regulation of "trusts" are treated by Hans B. Thorelli in *The Federal Antitrust Policy* (Baltimore, 1955); and by Arthur M. Johnson in "Antitrust Policy in Transition, 1908," *Mississippi Valley Historical Review,* XLVIII (1961), and "Theodore Roosevelt and the Bureau of Corporations," *ibid.,* XLV (1959). One aspect of tariff history, which has been rather neglected in recent years, is considered by Carroll W. Pursell, Jr., in "Tariff and Technology: The Foundation and Development of the American Tin-Plate Industry, 1872–1900," *Technology and Culture*, III (1962).

Two topics related to the central theme of Chandler's article are discussed in Blake McKelvey: *Urbanization of America* (New Brunswick, N. J., 1963); and Robert W. Fogel: "A Quantitative Approach to the Study of Railroads in American Economic Growth," *Journal of Economic History*, XXII (1962). The impact of technology is treated in H. J. Habakkuk: *American and British Technology in the Nineteenth Century* (Cambridge, England, 1962); and W. Paul Strassmann: *Risk and Technological Innovation* (Ithaca, N. Y., 1959).

14. BUSINESS EXPANSIONISM IN THE NINETIES

For the early-nineteenth century background of American expansionism, see Norman A. Graebner: *Empire on the Pacific* (New York: 1955); Charles Vevier: "American Continentalism: An Idea of Expansion, 1845–1910," *American Historical Review*, LXV (1960); and Ray Allen Billington: *The Far Western Frontier, 1830–1860* (New York, 1956). Especially valuable is R. W. Van Alstyne's perceptive overview of the nineteenth century, *The Rising American Empire* (New York, 1960). Several important studies of interrelated economic, missionary and strategic interests in Asia have appeared recently, among them Charles S. Campbell, Jr.: *Special Business Interests and the Open Door Policy* (New Haven, 1951); Fred H. Harrington: *God, Mammon and the Japanese* (Madison, Wisc., 1944); S. K. Stevens: *American Expansion in Hawaii, 1842–1898* (Harrisburg, 1945); Paul A. Varg: *Missionaries, Chinese and Diplomats* (Princeton, 1958); Charles Vevier: *The United States and China, 1906–1913* (New Brunswick, N. J., 1955); and William A. Williams: *American-Russian Relations, 1781–1917* (New York, 1952). Julius Pratt underplays the role of business expansionists in *America's Colonial Experiment* (New York, 1950) and *Expansionists of 1898* (Baltimore, 1936). Diplomacy of the Taft period is reviewed in George E. Mowry: *The Era of Theodore Roosevelt* (New York: 1958), which has an up-to-date bibliography; while Harold U. Faulkner treats business interest in imperialism in *The Decline of Laissez Faire, 1897–1917* (New York, 1951). For American interest in Latin America, Benjamin H. Williams: *Economic Foreign Policy of the United States* (New York, 1929) is still useful. The story of business in its relationship to foreign policy is carried forward into the World War I period by Paul Birdsall, in "Neutrality and Economic Pressures, 1914-1917," *Science and Society,* III (1939). Arthur S. Link treats another aspect of economic interests in foreign-policy formulation in "The Cotton Crisis, the South, and Anglo-American Diplomacy, 1914–15," in *Studies in Southern History* (Chapel Hill, 1957). Charles C. Tansill: *America Goes to War* (Boston, 1938) is marked by an anti-British bias, but has much of value on the business community and American involvement in World War I.

15. IMMIGRATION

Among the most valuable studies of immigration in American economic development are Brinley Thomas: *Migration and Economic Growth* (Cambridge, Eng., 1954); UNESCO: *The Positive Contribution by Immigrants* (Paris, 1955), esp. Chapter 1, on the United States, by Oscar Handlin and Mary F. Handlin; Oscar Handlin: "International Migration and the Acquisition of New Skills," in *Progress of Underdeveloped Areas,* edited by Bert F. Hoselitz (Chicago, 1952); and Maldwyn A. Jones: *American Immigration* (Chicago, 1960). See also the older works by I. A. Hourwich: *Immigration and Labor* (New York, 1912); and Harry Jerome: *Migration and Business Cycles* (New York, 1926). The United Nations publication *The Determinants and Consequences of Population Trends* (New York, 1953), discusses the theoretical basis of migration studies. Brinley Thomas analyzes the recent literature in *International Migration and Economic Development: A Trend Report and Bibliography* (Turin, Italy: UNESCO, 1961). Elizabeth W. Gilboy and Edgar M. Hoover: "Population and Immigration," in *American Economic History,* edited by Seymour Harris (New York, 1961), is also useful, although it does not go much beyond the Handlin and Thomas studies.

Edward C. Kirkland: *Industry Comes of Age* (New York, 1961) treats the labor force, including immigrants, in the period 1860–97. Special studies of value include Charlotte Erickson: *American Industry and the European Immigrant, 1860–1885* (Cambridge, 1957), a study of contract labor; Folke Dovring: "European Reactions to the Homestead Act," *Journal of Economic History,* XXII (1962); Morrell Heald: "Business Attitudes Toward European Immigration, 1880–1900," ibid., XIII (1953); Oscar Handlin: *Race and Nationality in American Life* (New York, 1957), Chapter 5; Rowland T. Berthoff: *British Immigrants in Industrial America* (Cambridge, 1953); and Marcus Lee Hansen and J. B. Brebner: *Mingling of the Canadian and American Peoples* (New Haven, 1940).

Labor attitudes toward the immigrant are discussed by Gerald Grob in his study of the post-Civil War labor movement, *Workers and*

Utopia (Evanston, Ill., 1960); see also Henry Pelling: *American Labor* (Chicago, 1960), and Philip Taft: *The AF of L in the Time of Gompers* (New York, 1957). The nativist impulse that conjoined with labor hostility to the immigrant is the subject of John Higham's *Strangers in the Land* (New Brunswick, N. J., 1955); see also Rowland T. Berthoff: "Southern Attitudes toward Immigration, 1865–1914," *Journal of Southern History*, XVII (1951), and Melvin Dubofsky: "Organized Labor and the Immigrant in New York City, 1900–18," *Labor History*, II (1961). The related issue of the Negro in the American work force is treated in Gunnar Myrdal: *An American Dilemma* (New York, 1944); Gerald N. Grob: "Organized Labor and the Negro Worker," *Labor History*, I (1960); and the still-useful volume by S. D. Spero and A. L. Harris: *The Black Worker* (New York, 1931). See also Oscar Handlin: *The Newcomers: Negroes and Puerto Ricans in a Changing Metropolis* (New York, 1962).

16. THE NEW INDUSTRIAL ERA

The economic history of the World War I period and the twenties is surveyed in George Soule's superb study, *Prosperity Decade* (New York, 1947). Eugene Rotwein treats prices and the ineffective efforts to develop a federal policy, in "Post-World War I Price Movements and Price Policy," *Journal of Political Economy*, LIII (1945). See also Paul A. Samuelson and Everett E. Hagen: *After the War, 1918–1920: Military and Economic Demobilization* . . . (Washington, National Resources Planning Board, 1943); and G. A. Lincoln and others: "Mobilization and War," in *American Economic History*, edited by Seymour Harris (New York, 1961). Solomon Fabricant: *The Output of Manufacturing Industries, 1899–1937* (New York, 1940); Joseph Schumpeter: "The American Economy in the Interwar Period," *American Economic Review*, XXXVI (1946); William E. Leuchtenberg: *The Perils of Prosperity, 1914–32* (Chicago, 1958); and relevant articles in *Growth of the American Economy*, edited by Harold F. Williamson (revised edition, Englewood Cliffs, N. J., 1951), are also valuable. John D. Hicks makes federal economic policy a major theme of his *Republican Ascendency, 1921–1933* (New York, 1960), which has an extensive bibliography. G. Cullom Davis: "The Transformation of the Federal Trade Commission, 1914–1929," *Mississippi Valley Historical Review*, XLIX (1962) treats one agency in detail. On finance, consult Raymond W. Goldsmith: *Financial Intermediaries in the American Economy Since 1900* (Princeton, 1958). John Kenneth Galbraith has written a lively yet learned account of *The Great Crash, 1929* (Boston, 1955). Trends in industry are the subject of M. A. Adelman: "The Measurement of Industrial Concentration," *Review of Economics and Statistics*, XXXII (1951); F. J. Kottke: "Mergers of Large Manufacturing Companies, 1951 to 1959," ibid., XLI (1959); and Saul S. Sands: "Changes in Scale of Production in United States Manufacturing Industry, 1904–1947," ibid., XLIII (1961). Yale Brozen: "Trends in Industrial Research and Development," *Journal of Business*, XXXII (1960), and Leonard S. Silk: *The Research Revolution* (New York: 1960) treat a topic of major importance for the recent period.

Space permits listing of only a few studies of particular industries or firms, among them Allan Nevins and Frank E. Hill: *Ford, Expansion and Challenge, 1915–1933* (New York, 1957); John B. Rae: *American Automobile Manufacturers, The First Forty Years* (Philadelphia, 1959); Jack Blicksilver: *Cotton Manufacturing in the Southeast: An Historical Analysis* (Georgia State College of Business Administration, *Studies in Business and Economics*, Bulletin 5, Atlanta, 1959); Mannie Kupinsky: "Growth of Aircraft and Parts Industry, 1939 to 1954," *Monthly Labor Review*, LXXVII, 12 (1954); Forrest McDonald: *Insull* (Chicago, 1962), on Samuel Insull's utilities empire; Paul H. Giddens: *Standard Oil Company (Indiana)* (New York, 1955); and John G. B. Hutchins: "The American Shipping Industry Since 1914," *Business History Review*, XXVIII (1954). Harold G. Vatter: *The U. S. Economy in the 1950's* (New York, 1963), includes a survey of industry in the recent period. Arthur R. Taylor: "Losses to the Public in the Insull Collapse," *Business History Review*, XXXVI (1962) is closely related to the Pontecorvo essay; and Richard E. Caves: *Air Transport and Its Regulators* (Cambridge, 1962), contains historical material related to Simonson's article.

17. AGRICULTURE IN AN INDUSTRIAL AGE

James H. Shideler: *Farm Crisis, 1919–23* (Berkeley and Los Angeles, 1957), introduces the farm problems of the immediate post-war years; see also John D. Hicks and Theodore Saloutos: *Agricultural Discontent in the Middle West, 1900–1939* (Madison, Wisc., 1951), an important regional study, and Murray R. Benedict: *Farm Policies of the United States, 1790–1950* (New York, 1953). In *Can We Solve the Farm Problem?* (New York, 1955), Benedict deals suggestively with the full breadth of objectives in federal farm policy. In *The Agricultural Commodity Program, Two Decades of Experience* (New York, 1956), Benedict and co-author Oscar Stine provide a more intensive analysis of specific programs. The standard account of the McNary-Haugen program is Gilbert C. Fite: *George N. Peek and the*

Fight for Farm Parity (Norman, Okla., 1952). A special study dealing with the labyrinth of overlapping controls over the dairy industry is Leland Spencer and S. K. Christensen: *Milk Control Programs of the Northeastern States* (Cornell University Agricultural Experiment Station, *Bulletin*, 908, November 1954).

The October 1959 issue of the journal *Agricultural History* contains a symposium on New Deal farm policy. On special subjects relating to the New Deal period, see H. C. M. Case: "Farm Debt Adjustment During the Early 1930's," *Agricultural History*, XXXIV (1960); S. Person, "The R.E.A. in Perspective," ibid., XXIV (1950); M. S. Venkataramani: "Norman Thomas, Arkansas Sharecroppers, and the Roosevelt Agricultural Policies, 1933–1937," *Mississippi Valley Historical Review*, XLVII (1960); Richard S. Kirkendall: "A Professor in Farm Politics," *Mid-America*, XLI (1959); and Christiana McF. Campbell: *The Farm Bureau and the New Deal* (Urbana, Ill., 1962). Arthur M. Schlesinger, Jr.: *The Age of Roosevelt*, Vol. 2: *The Coming of the New Deal* (Boston, 1959), deals at length with evolution of the Roosevelt farm program. R. M. Christenson: *The Brannan Plan* (Ann Arbor, 1959) treats the recent period, as does Asher Byrnes in a brief article, "Economics of the Farm Problem," *Commentary*, XXX (1960).

Special studies of the South include William H. Nicholls: *Southern Tradition and Regional Progress* (Chapel Hill, 1960); Anthony M. Tang: *Economic Development in the Southern Piedmont, 1860–1950* (Chapel Hill, 1958); John L. Fulmer: *Agricultural Progress in the Cotton Belt Since 1920* (Chapel Hill, 1950); and Gunnar Myrdal: *An American Dilemma* (New York, 1944). For comparative purposes, consult John D. Black's classic study of *The Rural Economy of New England* (Cambridge, 1950). On cooperatives, see Joseph G. Knapp's history of the Grange League Federation, *Seeds that Grew* (Hinsdale, N. Y., 1960); and the penetrating article by Clarke A. Chambers, "The Cooperative League of the United States of America, 1916–1961," *Agricultural History*, XXXVI (1962).

18. THE HOUSE OF LABOR

General studies of American labor in the twentieth century include Joseph G. Rayback: *A History of American Labor* (New York, 1961); two articles by Lloyd Ulman in *American Economic History*, edited by Seymour Harris (New York, 1961); and two volumes on the American Federation of Labor by Philip Taft: *The AF of L in the Time of Gompers* (New York, 1957) and *The AF of L from the Death of Gompers to the Merger* (New York, 1959). Irving Bernstein provides the best history of labor in the period 1920-33, in *The Lean Years* (Boston, 1960); see also James O. Morris: "The AF of L in the Twenties," *Industrial and Labor Relations Review*, XI (1958). The story is continued in *Labor and the New Deal*, edited by Milton Derber and Edwin Young (Madison, Wisc., 1957); Harry A. Millis and Emily C. Brown: *From the Wagner Act to Taft-Hartley* (Chicago, 1950); and James O. Morris's more specialized study of the thirties, *Conflicts within the AFL* (Ithaca, 1958). Marc Carson: *American Labor Unions and Politics, 1900–1918* (Carbondale, Ill., 1958) treats in full detail, and with a different interpretative emphasis, some of the issues raised in the Saposs article. See also Robert D. Leiter: "Organized Labor and the Tariff," *Southern Economic Journal*, XXVIII (1961), which analyzes labor's position on an important political issue. Recent legislation is treated in Clyde Summers: "A Summary Evaluation of the Taft-Hartley Act," *Industrial and Labor Relations Review*, XI (1958); and in a symposium on Taft-Hartley in *Annals*, 274 (March 1951). An older, but still valuable, study of the legal status of unions is Calvert Magruder: "A Half Century of Legal Influence upon the Development of Collective Bargaining," *Harvard Law Review*, L (1937).

Important quantitative studies include three books on labor-force composition, John D. Durand: *The Labor Force in the United States* (New York, 1946); Gertrude Bancroft: *The American Labor Force* (New York, 1948); and Clarence Long: *The Labor Force under Changing Income and Employment* (Princeton, 1958). On salaried and professional workers, see C. Wright Mills: *White Collar* (New York, 1951); and four provocative articles by Vera Shlakman: "Business and the Salaried Worker," "Status and Ideology of Office Workers," "White Collar Unionism and Professional Organizations," and "Unionism and Professional Organization among Engineers," in *Science and Society*, XIV-XVI (1950–52). The Autumn 1959 issue of *Dissent*, VI, 4, contains a valuable symposium on "Workers and their Unions." On wage differentials, see Martin Segal: "Regional Wage Differentials in Manufacturing in the Postwar Period," *Review of Economics and Statistics*, XLIII (1961); H. Gregg Lewis: "The Effects of Unions on Industrial Wage Differentials," in National Bureau of Economic Research: *Aspects of Labor Economics* (Princeton, 1962); W. H. Cook: "Recent Developments in the North-South Wage Differential," *Industrial and Labor Relations Review*, VI (1952); and M. W. Reder: "Trends in Wages, Earnings and Per Capita Income," *Monthly Labor Review*, LXXXII, 5 (May 1959), a study of the western states. The broader issue of regional development is treated in Richard A. Easterlin: "Regional Income Trends," in *American Economic History*, edited by Seymour Harris (New York, 1961); see also Frank A. Hannah: *State Income Differentials, 1919–1954* (Durham, N. C., 1959), and Stephen L. McDonald: "On the South's Recent Economic Development," *Southern Economic Journal*, XXVIII (1961).

Anne Ratner Miller: "Components of Labor Force Growth," *Journal of Economic History*, XXII (1962); and Benjamin Solomon and Robert K. Burns: "Unionization of White-Collar Employees," *Journal of Business*, XXXVI (1963), complement the Solomon study reprinted in this volume.

19. THE NEW DEAL AND AFTER

Lewis Kimmel's thesis is argued fully in the volume from which the above selection is drawn, *Federal Budget and Fiscal Policy, 1789–1958* (Washington, 1959); Cochran's, in *The American Business System: A Historical Perspective, 1900–1955* (Cambridge, 1957). Critiques of the Cochran study by Kenneth Boulding and J. K. Galbraith appear in *Business History Review*, XXXII (1958). Basic to any study of the New Deal period is Arthur M. Schlesinger, Jr.'s *The Age of Roosevelt* (3 volumes published to date), especially Vol. III: *The Politics of Upheaval* (Boston, 1960), in which Schlesinger traces what he terms a shift in New Deal ideology beginning in 1935. Broadus Mitchell: *Depression Decade* (New York, 1947) is the best economic study of the thirties, but marked by a distinct bias against the New Deal for attempting too little. Clay J. Anderson traces precedents in the literature of economic theory and public policy of two New Deal doctrines, in "The Compensatory Theory of Public Works Expenditure," *Journal of Political Economy*, LIII (1945), and "The Development of the Pump-Priming Theory," ibid., LII (1944). See also Harold G. Moulton: *The New Philosophy of Public Debt* (Washington, 1943); J. V. Garland: *Government Spending and Economic Recovery* (New York, 1938); and Arthur E. Burns and Donald S. Watson: *Government Spending and Economic Expansion* (Washington, 1940). The related issue of tax policy is covered in Sidney Ratner: *American Taxation* (New York, 1942). General works of value on the New Deal and its impact include Mario Einaudi: *The Roosevelt Revolution* (New York, 1959); and Calvin B. Hoover: *The Economy, Liberty and the State* (New York, 1959). On business in the recent period, see Arthur H. Cole: "Twentieth Century Entrepreneurship and Economic Growth," *American Economic Review*, XLIV (1954); David Lilienthal: *Big Business, A New Era* (New York, 1953); and Adolph A. Berle: *The Twentieth Century Capitalist Revolution* (New York, 1954). See also J. K. Galbraith's widely-read study of *American Capitalism: The Concept of Countervailing Power* (Boston, 1952). The early writing of an important New Deal-period writer on the corporation is analyzed in Richard S. Kirkendall: "A. A. Berle, Student of the Corporation, 1917–1932," *Business History Review,* XXXV (1961). For further references, see bibliography for Section 20, below.

20. SYMBOLS AND RITUALS

Richard Hofstadter provides a lucid analysis of Thurman Arnold's writings, in *The Age of Reform, From Bryan to F. D. R.* (New York, 1955), pp. 316 ff. In addition to *The Folklore of Capitalism,* see Arnold's *The Symbols of Government* (reprinted with a new preface, New York, 1962). *Postwar Economic Trends in the United States,* edited by Ralph E. Freeman (New York, 1960), includes valuable essays on recent economic change. Arthur F. Burns takes an optimistic view of recent business cycles in "Progress Toward Stability," *American Economic Review,* L (1960); while a contrasting view, that stagnation rather than stability characterizes the recent economy, is the theme of "Lunacy in the Midst of Plenty," an editorial article in *Monthly Review, An Independent Socialist Magazine,* XI (1959). Among writings on income distribution, especially valuable are Gabriel Kolko: "The American 'Income Revolution,' " *Dissent,* IV (1957); and I. B. Kravis: "Relative Income Shares in Fact and Theory," *American Economic Review,* XLIX (1959). Calvin B. Hoover: *The Economy, Liberty and the State* (New York, 1959), and Kenneth E. Boulding: *The Organizational Revolution* (New York, 1953) assess long-term economic changes of the recent period. John Kenneth Galbraith's survey of current problems, *The Affluent Society* (Boston, 1958), stirred considerable controversy; see, for example, Ernest Van den Haag: "Affluence, Galbraith, the Democrats," *Commentary,* XXX (1960). Special studies of value in appraising Arnold's essay include Simon Kuznets: *Capital in the American Economy* (Princeton, 1961); John W. Kendrick: *Productivity Trends in the United States* (Princeton, 1961); American Assembly of Columbia University: *Automation and Technological Change* (Englewood Cliffs, N. J., 1962); and Bert G. Hickman: *Growth and Stability of the Postwar Economy* (Washington, 1960). A valuable survey of recent economic development is provided by Harold G. Vatter, in *The U. S. Economy in the 1950's* (New York, 1963). *The American Economic System,* edited by Massimo Salvadori (Indianapolis, 1963), includes documents and essays pertaining to the recent period. Arthur F. Burns reappraises economic policy and planning since 1946 in "Some Reflections on the Employment Act," *Political Science Quarterly*, LXXVII (1962). Current problems are examined in historical perspective by Alvin H. Hansen in *The Postwar American Economy* (New York, 1964).

A NOTE ON THE TYPE

This book is set in Electra, a Linotype face designed by W. A. Dwiggins. This face cannot be classified as either modern or old-style. It is not based on any historical model, nor does it echo any particular period or style. It avoids the extreme contrasts between thick and thin elements that mark most modern faces, and attempts to give a feeling of fluidity, power, and speed.

Composed, printed and bound by
American Book–Stratford Press, Inc., New York
Typography by Vincent Torre